CRITICAL COMPANION TO

# James Joyce

## A Literary Reference to His Life and Work



A. NICHOLAS FARGNOLI

MICHAEL PATRICK GILLESPIE

*An imprint of Infobase Publishing*

**Critical Companion to James Joyce: A Literary Reference to His Life and Work**



This is a revised edition of *James Joyce A to Z: The Essential Reference to His Life and Work.*


Checkmark Books
An imprint of Infobase Publishing
132 West 31st Street
New York NY 10001

**Library of Congress Cataloging-in-Publication Data**

Fargnoli, A. Nicholas.
Critical companion to James Joyce : a literary reference to his life and work / A. Nicholas Fargnoli and Michael Patrick Gillespie.—[Rev. ed.].
p. cm.
Rev. ed. of: James Joyce A to Z : The essential reference to his life and work. 1995.
Includes bibliographical references and index.
ISBN 0-8160-6232-3 (hc : alk. paper)—ISBN 0-8160-6689-2 (pb : alk. paper)
1. Joyce, James, 1882–1941—Handbook, manuals, etc. 2. Novelists, Irish—20th century—Biography—Handbooks, manuals, etc. 3. Ireland—In literature—Handbooks, manuals, etc. I. Gillespie, Michael Patrick. II. Fargnoli, A. Nicholas. James Joyce A to Z. III. Title.
PR6019.O9Z533376 2006
823'.912—dc22 2005015721

Checkmark Books are available at special discounts when purchased in bulk quantities for businesses, associations, institutions, or sales promotions. Please call our Special Sales Department in New York at (212) 967-8800 or (800) 322-8755.

You can find Facts On File on the World Wide Web at http://www.factsonfile.com

Text design by Erika K. Arroyo
Cover design by Cathy Rincon
Charts by Dale Williams

Printed in the United States of America

VB Hermitage 10 9 8 7 6 5 4 3 2 1

This book is printed on acid-free paper.

*In Memory of*
*Nick Fargnoli, Sr.,*
*and*
*Vince Gillespie*

# CONTENTS

# ACKNOWLEDGMENTS

We must acknowledge a deep gratitude to our many colleagues and friends who aided us during the writing of *Critical Companion to James Joyce,* and we do so without deleting the names of those individuals who aided us during the writing of its predecessor, *James Joyce A to Z:* Anne Aicher, Megan Barnard, Morris Beja, John Boly, Zack Bowen, Linda Costa, Luca Crispi, Robert Adams Day, Elizabeth Doran, Roger Dupré, Diane Eckes, Jean Eylers, Charles Fanning, Ronan Fanning, Alessandro Fargnoli, Giuliana Fargnoli, Sidney Feshbach, Paula Gillespie, Warwick Gould, Al Gravano, Joel Greenberg, Michael Groden, Ciceil Gross, Murray Gross, Silvia Happ, Ok-Sook Hong, Lorraine Jackson, Li Ju, Carol Kealiher, Robert Kinpoitner, Sean Latham, James LeBlanc, Philip Lyman, Sister Maria Genevieve Lynch, O.P., Lucretia Lyons, Robert Martin, Sister Grace Florian McInerney, O.P., Elizabeth Murnane, Valerie Murrenus, Roger Norburn, Anne O'Gorman, Christine O'Neil, Michael O'Shea, Strother B. Purdy, Ruth F. Quattlebaum, Jean-Michel Rabaté, Katharine Reagan, Thomas Dillon Redshaw, Margaret Reiber, Bernice Relkin, Albert Rivero, Joseph Roughan, Myra T. Russel, Fritz Senn, Ruth Sherry, Sam Sloate, Robert Spoo, Thomas Staley, Faith Steinberg, Patricia Sullivan, Tim Szeliga, Jack Wayne Weaver, Norman A. Weil, and Rosemary Wildeman.

We are grateful also to the University of Washington Press for permission to use Bernard Benstock's "A Working Outline of *Finnegans Wake,*" reprinted from *Joyce-Again's Wake: An Analysis of Finnegans Wake* (1965), pp. xv–xxiv; to Indiana University Press and Aitken, Stone & Wylie, London, for permission to use "The Plan of Ulysses," reprinted from Hugh Kenner, *Dublin's Joyce* (1956), chapter 14; and to Indiana University Press for permission to use the list of *Chamber Music* composers, reprinted from Myra T. Russel's *James Joyce's Chamber Music: The Lost Settings,* pp. 113–114.

Special thanks to Ruth Moran of the Irish Tourist Board, 345 Park Avenue, New York, New York 10154, for graciously providing so many of the illustrations, and to the reference departments of the Rockville Centre Public Library, Rockville Centre, New York, and the Great Neck Library, Great Neck, New York.

A special acknowledgment of gratitude must be given to Jeff Soloway, our editor at Facts On File, who facilitated the revision of this book with professional ease and poise; to John Wright, our literary agent; and to Lincoln P. Paine and Drew Silver, our former editors, who were instrumental in publishing the first edition.

# ABBREVIATIONS

To simplify citations, we have at times used the following abbreviations for Joyce's works. For complete publishing information, see the Joyce bibliography at the end of this volume.

CM *Chamber Music*
CP *Collected Poems*
CW *The Critical Writings of James Joyce*
D *Dubliners*
E *Exiles*
FW *Finnegans Wake*
GJ *Giacomo Joyce*
Letters *Letters of James Joyce, vols. I, II, and III*
P *A Portrait of the Artist as a Young Man*
SH *Stephen Hero*
SL *Selected Letters of James Joyce*
U *Ulysses*

We identify references to most of Joyce's works simply through page numbers. For *Ulysses* we use the chapter/line format of the Gabler edition (for example, 2.377 identifies a passage from chapter 2, line 377). For *Finnegans Wake* we have used the page/line format commonly followed by *Wake* scholars (for instance, 169.5 indicates line five on page 169). We cite the *Letters of James Joyce* by volume/page (for example, I.185 stands for volume I, page 185).

# INTRODUCTION AND GUIDE TO USE

The change in title of the original version of this volume from *James Joyce A to Z: The Essential Reference to His Life and Work* to its new title *Critical Companion to James Joyce* is meant to signal an extensively revised edition, with more than 40 percent additional and updated material. The arrangement of the material has also been reorganized to expedite the retrieval of information. This new organization focuses on each of Joyce's works supplemented by annotations. *Critical Companion to James Joyce* has the same ambitions and scope as the earlier volume. We still intend our book to be a kind of scholarly primer or reference tool that can both provide timely reminders to those familiar with Joyce's oeuvre but whose immediate recollections of the canon need some refreshing and, at the same time, offer a useful introduction to those who wish to develop a more comprehensive understanding of Joyce's work and the wider world within which he wrote and lived.

*Critical Companion to James Joyce,* like its predecessor, is geared to the nonspecialist. It is our aim to provide a clear and comprehensive companion to Joyce's work, offering information primarily to new readers. Over the course of the book, our entries encompass explanations of expressions that occur in the works as well as terms whose elucidation can provide an indirect but significant understanding of particular works. Ultimately, we hope that our efforts contribute to an enrichment of the reader's experience of Joyce, but we specifically reject the notion that this, or any other guide for that matter, can serve as anything but a supplement to that reading.

The emphasis in *Critical Companion to James Joyce* is on providing contextual and critical information of an introductory, wide-ranging, but not exhaustive, nature. We wish to offer in a single volume an overview of Joyce's work, and of material related to it, that will both give satisfaction to the casual reader and provide encouragement for those approaching Joyce's work with a more ambitious study in mind. This guide provides enough background in its entries on a variety of specific topics to enhance the immediate enjoyment of Joyce's works without burdening the reader with the superabundance of detailed information necessary for highly focused critical readings. We have, however, included detailed bibliographies to direct readers to biographical and critical studies offering more specific accounts of aspects of Joyce's life and work.

Joyce scholars, or Joyceans as they commonly designate themselves, will find much of the information in this book quite familiar. That familiarity comes in part from the generosity of a number of critics—whom we name in the acknowledgments—who have reviewed our work, corrected some errors, and greatly supplemented our comments with their own insights. It also comes from our avid mining of the scholarly studies that have preceded and in many cases inspired this volume for information that will enhance the reader's understanding of Joyce's work. We have also profited from comments made by reviewers of *James Joyce A to Z* and from the observations offered by our Joycean colleagues and students.

Like any writer in any age, Joyce wrote for his time. Joyce, born in Dublin, became an expatriate at the age of 22 and lived from the Victorian era to the beginning of World War II. His vision was shaped by his particular experience and his unusually broad and acute cultural sensitivity. His writings embody an enormous range of reference, and he seldom felt compelled to explain or elaborate. Even in his lifetime his work was considered difficult; in a greatly changed world, his much more numerous readers perhaps need a little assistance to find their way to the enjoyment that awaits them.

To increase this enjoyment, we have presented an extensive range of critical and biographical material. Hundreds of books, thousands of articles, and innumerable notes about Joyce and his work have been published, and there is simply too much material for most Joyceans—let alone non-Joyceans—to digest. At the same time, these interpretive works offer tremendously informative insights on Joyce that will greatly enhance anyone's reading, and they should not be ignored.

Thus, our work draws the conclusions of these scholars into a form more accessible to the ordinary reader. We offer this volume fully cognizant and deeply appreciative of the work of generations of scholars who have created a wealth of important secondary material on Joyce and his work.

Critical writing on the work of James Joyce falls into at least three major categories. The first of these includes a number of fine general interpretive responses, either to individual works or to the canon as a whole. William York Tindall's *A Reader's Guide to James Joyce* is an early example of this type, but such broad explication is so general that it gives readers little direction for developing their own interpretive responses.

Then there are topical studies designed to provide detailed annotations of particular works or to illuminate a particular class of references in the canon, such as Zack Bowen's examination of musical allusions in Joyce, Weldon Thornton's *Allusions in Ulysses,* Don Gifford's *Ulysses Annotated,* or any of the various guides to *Finnegans Wake.* Such studies have an immense and widely acknowledged scholarly value. But these books provide more specialized information than most general readers would want. They address themselves to scholars and students in need of specific glosses that they can apply to their own interpretive projects.

Such projects in turn produce a third category of critical material, very finely delineated analyses of virtually every imaginable aspect of Joyce's life and work. To accommodate this scholarly interest, since the mid-1950s a half-dozen periodicals devoted to Joyce studies have been established. At the same time the study of Joyce has flourished not only in the college and even high school curricula, but in independent reading groups and scholarly organizations that hold regular national and international conferences and symposia. With this ever-increasing body of work in mind, we attempt to offer sophisticated and enlightening material that does not blunt the interest of the general reader through overspecialization.

*Critical Companion to James Joyce* is designed to clarify aspects of Joyce's writings on two levels. It identifies major intratextual literary influences, glossing allusions to significant characters, locations, ideas, and events that abound in his work. The book also focuses attention upon the extratextual material that shaped Joyce's fiction, relating persons, places, concepts, and events in his life to corresponding features in his work.

As is true of any reference work, the usefulness of our guide rests on the clarity of its format and the breadth and depth of the information it presents. We therefore outline for the reader our criteria for inclusion of material in this book.

In *Critical Companion to James Joyce,* we attempt to provide, in concise form, the basic information needed to understand and enjoy reading each of Joyce's works. Part I of the book contains a brief outline of Joyce's life. In Part II, we offer detailed examinations of Joyce's works. Entries on the major works of fiction include subentries on characters. Those characters who appear several times in a single work and who function to advance the plot or who are referred to in several works are included as subentries; however, characters to whom there is only passing reference are not. (For example, Denis Breen, who spends the day of 16 June walking around Dublin, and Martin Cunningham, who appears in both "Grace" and *Ulysses,* are included, but Pisser Burke in *Ulysses* is not.) When appropriate, we have also included references to characters, places, and related ideas pertinent to that work under consideration.

In Part III, we include entries on related persons, places, ideas, and more, covering culture, history, biography, and criticism. Hence, our entry in Part III on the Wild Geese attempts to clarify the status of Kevin Egan, a character alluded to in the Proteus episode of *Ulysses.* Our discussion of the Pigeon House seeks to explain its significance to the boys who skip school in the *Dubliners* story, "An Encounter." Our sketch of St. Thomas Aquinas, supplemented by remarks on Scholasticism, endeavors to present a clearer picture of the intellectual and philosophical ethos that informed Joyce's education and that, in consequence, shaped the way that he saw and wrote about the world.

The particular categories of entries covered in Part III are as follows:

*Ideas:* concepts directly introduced in the texts themselves, such as the term "parallax" that troubles Bloom all through *Ulysses,* or such related terms as "Scholasticism," the philosophical approach that plays a critical part in Stephen Dedalus's Jesuit education.

*Events:* both those that occur in the works, such as the Gold Cup race that occupies so much attention in *Ulysses,* and those that have shaped Irish consciousness over the centuries, such as the Battle of the Boyne, which while not specifically mentioned informs a number of scenes throughout Joyce's work.

*Geography:* places mentioned in Joyce's work or locations that played an important part in his life. For example, Eccles Street is identified not only as the location of the home of the fictional Leopold Bloom but also as the address of Joyce's actual university friend J. F. Byrne.

*Historical characters:* real people who were significant in Joyce's life are included, as are those who are either incorporated in the work or were models for fictional characters. There are, for example, entries on Charles Stewart Parnell, the Irish politician mentioned so often in Joyce's fiction, and an entry on Oliver St. John Gogarty, the real-life model for Buck Mulligan. There are entries on Paul Léon, a good friend of Joyce's later life, and on Stanislaus Joyce, the author's brother, who served as, among other things, the model for Stephen Dedalus's brother Maurice in *Stephen Hero* and *A Portrait of the Artist as a Young Man.* There is no entry on Stanislaus's wife Nellie or their son James.

Throughout the book, reference to any name or term that appears as an entry in Part III is printed on first appearance in an entry entirely or partly in SMALL CAPITAL LETTERS.

We realize, of course, that few readers will wish to read this book from cover to cover, and indeed we could hardly in good conscience recommend such a practice. Rather, we hope that readers of Joyce will consult the book as needed, for illumination of particular topics. Of course we also encourage browsing. Because we envision readers sampling various portions of the text, a certain amount of repetition will occur from entry to entry. We have, however, endeavored to keep this to a minimum, employing it only for the sake of clarifying a specific entry.

This new volume also contains revised and expanded appendices and additional illustrations. The index helps readers identify more quickly the location of the information they desire and in particular information that does not warrant a separate entry. Another new feature of this edition consists of quotations from selected contemporary reviews of Joyce's major works; these quotations come immediately after the annotations.

James Joyce was arguably the greatest of the modernist writers, and one of the most musical writers of any time. A comic genius, a formal innovator, and an unsentimental poet of Irish life and language, Joyce explored in his work such characteristically modern themes as the nature of art, the social responsibility of the artist, the character of social institutions and public life (and the relation of the individual to them), and the ultimate nature and significance of human culture itself. In his fiction Joyce pioneered the interior monologue and stream-of-consciousness techniques, and brilliantly employed such modern fictional devices as parody and pastiche, through them transforming the mundane business of life into a comic work of cultural commentary. Joyce's most famous work, *Ulysses,* is an account of a single day in the life of Dublin, and an exploration of the meaning of ordinary lives. His last, *Finnegans Wake,* is its dreamlike nighttime counterpart; in it Joyce attempted to represent through myth, music, symbol, and metaphor a universal and comic synthesis of all human culture—a book about, literally, everything. Possibly no one but Joyce could have realized such a project; he was unsurpassed in his ability to manipulate language for effect. In every respect, James Joyce is probably the most influential writer of the 20th century—and not only on those who read and write in English. Though acknowledged as a "difficult" writer, Joyce is now very likely the most widely read, studied, and taught of all modern writers.

To read the work of James Joyce is to commit oneself to a world of brilliant artifice, a "chaosmos" (*FW* 118.21) of poetic mystery, that few writers have achieved. Not to read at least some of his work is to deprive oneself of the life-enhancing (to use an old-fashioned phrase) richness of a body of work that has radically altered the character of literature. Joyce's writings place demands upon the reader that can be difficult and even upsetting at times, but the rewards are well worth the effort.

# PART I

# *Biography*

# *James Joyce*

(1882–1941)

James Joyce was born on February 2, 1882, into a comfortable middle-class Catholic home. Joyce was the oldest surviving child of John Stanislaus JOYCE and Mary Jane (May) JOYCE (née Murray), then living at 41 Brighton Square West in what was then the south-side DUBLIN suburb of Rathgar. (A son, John, had been born on November 23, 1880, and had died eight days later.) Joyce's father came from a prosperous Cork family, a condition that contributed to a lifelong sense of entitlement. Joyce's mother was the daughter of a Dublin wine and spirits agent, and there was little in her sheltered upbringing to prepare her for life with a spoiled man-child like John Joyce.

Over the next 11 years, May Joyce would have nine more children. (See the appendix on page 402 for the Joyce family tree.) However, James, as the oldest, would always be the favored child. As the family began to grow, the Joyce family moved from Rathgar to a succession of houses on the south side of the city: 23 Castlewood Avenue, Rathmines; 1 Martello Terrace, Bray; and 23 Carysfort Avenue, Blackrock. In the meantime, young James was sent to CLONGOWES WOOD COLLEGE, a prestigious Jesuit boarding school in County Kildare, which he attended from September 1888 to July 1891. In 1891, when his family could no longer afford the cost of his tuition, James left the school. (There is some disagreement among scholars as to whether Joyce left the school in the summer or returned briefly in the fall to leave in October.)

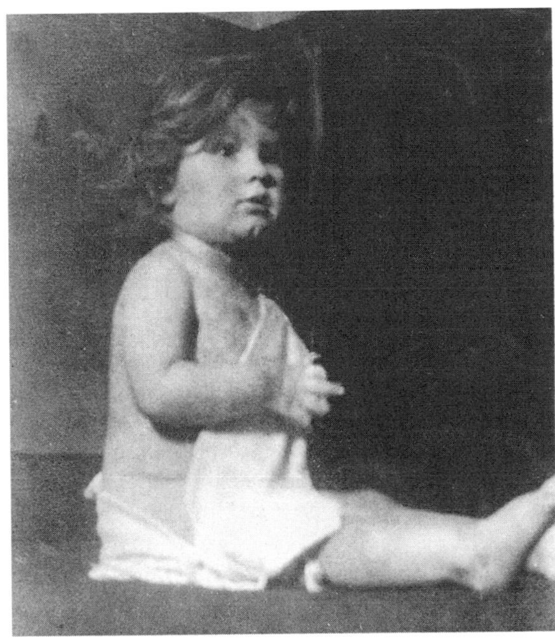

James Joyce as a baby *(James Joyce Collection, Beinecke Rare Book and Manuscript Library, Yale University)*

Birthplace of James Joyce, 41 Brighton Square West *(Irish Tourist Board)*

Their son's withdrawal from Clongowes Wood did not represent a temporary setback but rather provided a graphic illustration of the diminution of the family's finances. John Joyce saw the erosion of his fortunes as tied directly to the fall of the Irish statesman Charles Stewart PARNELL and the consequent loss of Joyce's patronage appointment as a tax collector in the Rates Office. While Parnell's expulsion as head of the Irish Home Rule Party may have accelerated the family's financial decline, in fact John Joyce had never quite acquired the habit of industry necessary to ensure the support of a family that continued to grow in size over the first decade of his marriage. He steadily consumed the income inherited from his father and maternal grandfather, and after losing his job in the Rates Office never again held steady employment. In consequence, the family experienced a steady decline into poverty, punctuated by frequent changes of address and deteriorating domestic conditions.

Early in 1893 the Joyce family moved north of the river, a symbolic as well as literal displacement, for the house that they occupied at 14 Fitzgibbon Street, in the city of Dublin, proved to be the last of their good addresses. For a few months, James, who was being educated at home, and his brother Stanislaus JOYCE were sent to the Christian Brothers' school in North Richmond Street. This was later to become the setting of the opening of the *Dubliners* story "Araby," and that signaled a characteristic that would mark all of Joyce's writing. From *Dubliners* and *A Portrait of the Artist as a Young Man* through *Ulysses* and *Finnegans Wake,* Joyce's narratives are filled with references that mark his experiences while growing to manhood on the streets of the city.

James Joyce at two years old *(Croessman Collection of James Joyce, Special Collections/Morris Library, Southern Illinois University)*

Joyce's contact with the Christian Brothers, which he rarely mentioned later in life, quickly came to an end. On April 6, 1893, he and his brother Stanislaus were enrolled as day students at another esteemed Jesuit school, BELVEDERE COLLEGE, on North Great George Street. They probably attended on scholarship assistance obtained through the efforts of the former rector of Clongowes Wood College, the Rev. John CONMEE, SJ. (Joyce would later memorialize Conmee with a fictionalized version of his character appearing in both *A Portrait of the Artist as a Young Man* and *Ulysses;* see characters under those titles.)

Stanislaus, two years younger than James, was very much in his brother's shadow. Though more plodding and careful than James, Stannie (as he was known in the family) had a deep affection for his older brother. James responded by making him a confidant, and would refer to Stannie as his sounding board. Though this relationship became less intimate and more strained as the two grew into adulthood, Stanislaus had a lifelong effect upon James's personal and creative development.

Joyce had a successful academic career as a student at Belvedere. He won several prizes for scholarship in national exams and was elected president of the Sodality of the Blessed Virgin Mary. In his last year at school he had one of the leading roles in the comic play *Vice-Versa.* He was both a popular student and a class leader, respected by his fellow students and the men who taught him. At the same time, he remained guided by the intellectual and spiritual independence that would characterize his life. By all accounts, in his mid-teens he also underwent a religious crisis, and abandoned his Catholic faith. Pinpointing an event like this, of course, is a difficult matter. Later in life when a friend asked Joyce when he left the church, Joyce replied: "That's for the Church to say."

No matter what alienation he felt from the Catholic Church, Joyce always valued the training that he received from the Jesuits. It was only logical then that, when Joyce graduated from Belvedere in 1898, he would continue his Jesuit education by entering UNIVERSITY COLLEGE, Dublin. As a result, no matter what his spiritual disposition, SCHOLASTICISM exercised a profound impact on his thinking for the rest of his life. (Although Joyce's experiences growing up and attending Clongowes Wood, Belvedere, and University College seem to parallel those of his fictional character Stephen Dedalus (see characters under *Ulysses*), it would be a serious mistake to attempt to read either *A Portrait of the Artist as a Young Man* or *Ulysses* as autobiographical accounts.)

At the university, at that time a magnet for upwardly mobile Catholics, Joyce quickly distinguished himself through his keen intelligence, aloof air, and iconoclastic views. Many of his classmates embraced conformity, seeking to use their university education as a stepping-stone to secure positions in the social, economic, and political institutions of their country. Others, while not dominated by career ambitions, nonetheless took a more conservative approach to their education. Joyce's friend George CLANCY (the model for Davin in *A Portrait of the Artist as a Young Man*) was an ardent nationalist who, as mayor of Limerick, would later be murdered by Black and Tans during the Irish War of Independence. Francis SHEEHY-SKEFFINGTON (the model for MacCann in *A Portrait of the Artist as a Young Man*), whom, after himself, Joyce considered the cleverest man at the university, shared Joyce's iconoclastic impulses, but resisted his reckless defiance of authority. The ever earnest Skeffington demanded equal rights for women, practiced vegetarianism, and did not smoke or drink. Like Clancy, he became a victim of the English. Skeffington was summarily executed by a British officer while trying to restrain looters during the Easter Rising. Joyce's closest friend at the university was John Francis BYRNE (the model for Cranly in *A Portrait of the Artist as a Young Man*). He became a close confidant of Joyce, to some extent replacing Stanislaus in the role as a sounding board for many of Joyce's ideas. Though there was a cooling in this friendship at some point, Byrne remained someone with whom Joyce could speak frankly—see below—and they kept in contact with each other until the former emigrated to the United States in 1910.

While even the outspoken friends whom Joyce cultivated exercised a degree of restraint with regard to critiquing the powerful institutions that shaped their world, Joyce, on the other hand, was articulating powerful criticisms of that Catholicism, Nationalism, Celtic revival, and Irish family life that would later become dominant themes in his fiction. In a world as homogeneous as that of University College, such individuality could have easily resulted in ostracism. Joyce, however, mitigated the effect of his nonconforming attitudes with a ready wit and a pleasing tenor voice. Although he did not seem to exert himself in his studies, Joyce had a ready grasp of the subject matter he studied that many classmates admired. Further, he had a great facility with languages and a remarkable understanding of contemporary literature, both English and Continental. This sophisticated knowledge, extending well beyond the ordinary curriculum of the college, overawed many of his more provincial classmates.

Joyce, however, was not content with the esteem of his contemporaries. Midway through his time at University College, he began to demonstrate the scope of his intellectual capabilities and his creative potential in a very public manner designed to achieve recognition beyond the precincts of the university. At a meeting of the college's LITERARY AND HISTORICAL SOCIETY on January 20, 1900, he read a paper entitled "Drama and Life," an essay on the relation of aesthetics to other aspects of human existence. Although Joyce had not yet turned 18 when he wrote the paper, it represented a clear break with conventional aesthetic attitudes, and it outlined views on art that would shape Joyce's own writings for the remainder of his life. (For more information on this and other papers and articles mentioned below, see Miscellaneous Works in Part II of this book.)

An even greater public triumph came fewer than three months later, when his essay "Ibsen's New Drama" (see Critical Writings in Part II) appeared in the prestigious English journal FORTNIGHTLY REVIEW. The article, a laudatory assessment of Ibsen's last play, *When We Dead Awaken*, was seen by William ARCHER, Ibsen's English translator, who brought it to the attention of the playwright. Ibsen, in turn, wrote to Joyce expressing his gratitude. Both Joyce's publication in the *Fortnightly Review* and Ibsen's recognition caused a sensation at the university and confirmed Joyce's belief in his artistic abilities.

Despite these achievements, ST STEPHEN'S, the unofficial college magazine, refused in 1901 to publish his next work, "The Day of the Rabblement" (see Critical Writings), Joyce's indignant attack on what he saw as the chauvinistic trend of the IRISH LITERARY THEATRE, influenced by nationalistic and provincial attitudes. The title reflects Joyce's outrage at what he perceives as the theater's pandering to the lowest common denominator. Although, after the article was rejected, Joyce appealed the decision to the university's president, he got no satisfaction. In response, Joyce and Francis Skeffington, who had an essay on women's rights rejected by the same journal, had their work printed privately and distributed around the school.

Not all of Joyce's work, however, met with official opposition. On February 1, 1902, Joyce delivered his second address to the Literary and Historical Society, a paper entitled "James Clarence Mangan." It purports to reintroduce an Irish audience to the works of the 19th-century Irish poet James Clarence Mangan, though a decade earlier both W. B. YEATS and Lionel Johnson had devoted considerable attention to Mangan's work. Nonetheless, this essay was well received, and fared somewhat better than "The Day of the Rabblement" when submitted to the university magazine, appearing in the May 1902 issue of St Stephen's.

During the summer of 1902 Joyce made a concerted effort to gain the acquaintance of Dublin's major literary figures. He first introduced himself to the writer, editor, and mystic George RUSSELL. Joyce called on Russell at midnight and talked for two hours about his work, ambitions, and his assessment of Dublin writers, including Russell. Nonetheless the older man proved gracious and open to further discussion. He went on to write to George Russell, Lady Augusta GREGORY, and W. B. Yeats about the young Joyce, and even arranged for Joyce to meet with Yeats. Yeats later wrote an account of the meeting in which Joyce is reputed to have told Yeats, "We have met too late. You are too old for me to have any effect upon you." Whether or not the story is true (Joyce denied it), Joyce very clearly was determined to assert his independence from the men who were at that time the most prominent figures among the Dublin literati.

He would later do the same to Lady Gregory, the well-known patroness of Irish writers. On March 26, 1903, Joyce's review of Lady Gregory's *Poets and Dreamers* appeared in the DAILY EXPRESS. It was a patronizing dismissal of Gregory for doing the best she could with the material available. The fact that his opportunity to review for the *Daily Express* came about because Lady Gregory had earlier introduced Joyce to its editor, E. V. LONGWORTH, had no effect on his approach to her writings. (In the Sirens chapter of *Ulysses*, Buck Mulligan chides Stephen Dedalus for doing the same thing: "Longworth is awfully sick, he said, after what you wrote about that old hake Gregory. O you inquisitional drunken jewjesuit! She gets you a job on the paper and then you go and slate her drivel to Jaysus. Couldn't you do the Yeats touch?" [*U* 9.1158–1161].)

In the fall Joyce began a course at the Royal University Medical School in Celia Street but did not complete it. On October 31, 1902, Joyce was awarded his university degree in modern languages, and decided to pursue his studies elsewhere. According to his lifelong friend Mary Colum: "he had already taken his B.A., I was told, and in modern languages as if he were a girl student, for the girls at this time were supposed to be specialists in modern language and literature, while the boys' domain was classics, mathematics, and similar masculine pursuits" (*Our Friend James Joyce,* 12). In early December Joyce left for PARIS, ostensibly to enroll in medical school. In fact, he saw the move as an opportunity to escape what he regarded as the intellectual and artistic claustrophobia that inhibited creative efforts in Ireland. After a stopover in London, during which Yeats bought breakfast, spent the day with him, and introduced the young man to Arthur SYMONS, Joyce took the night train to Dover and then crossed the channel. Paris, however, provided no immediate answer. This first, brief period abroad was characterized by loneliness and penury. After scarcely three weeks in that city, he returned to Dublin for Christmas and stayed nearly a month.

Joyce returned to Paris in late January 1903. In March John Millington SYNGE came to Paris, and he and Joyce spent a week of cautious familiarity. Joyce also befriended Joseph Casey, an exiled Fenian who became the model for Kevin Egan, who appears in Stephen's thoughts in the Proteus chapter of *Ulysses*. Joyce subsisted on loans, money from home, and occasional English lessons. By and large, however, isolation and poverty dogged him throughout the winter and early spring.

By April he was back in Ireland, summoned home by his father because of his mother's illness. Joyce spent a good deal of time with his ailing mother, resumed his friendship with J. F. Byrne, and renewed his acquaintance of the previous year with Oliver St. John GOGARTY, a well-to-do medical student with a wit as keen as Joyce's and a taste for wild living that Byrne did not share. Joyce and Gogarty continued an uneasy, competitive friendship throughout the time Joyce remained in Dublin. Meanwhile, May Joyce's condition continued to deteriorate, and she died of cancer in August of that year.

Joyce remained in Dublin, though he had no immediate prospects for employment. Nonetheless, he was not completely idle during this time. He began writing both the stories that would form *Dubliners* and, after a false start with a long prose meditation entitled "A Portrait of the Artist," he began his initial effort at composing a novel, *Stephen Hero*. Additionally, Joyce began writing many of the poems that he would publish in *Chamber Music*. Perhaps with an eye to another career, Joyce also took voice lessons, and in May won a bronze medal in the Feis Ceoil, Ireland's largest traditional music festival.

Despite the desultory nature of his life in Dublin at this time, Joyce was gathering creative material

The first edition of *Ulysses,* published in 1922 by the Paris-based publisher Shakespeare and Company *(Philip Lyman/Gotham Book Mart)*

that he would put to good use later. In the late spring he briefly taught at the Clifton House School in Dalkey and, for a week in September, lived with Gogarty in the MARTELLO TOWER in SANDYCOVE. The tower served as the setting for the opening scene of *Ulysses* (see the Telemachus episode [chapter 1]), and his teaching experience provided the background for the novel's Nestor episode (chapter 2). During this time, at the invitation of George Russell, Joyce published early versions of three of the stories that would later appear in *Dubliners*—"The Sisters," "Eveline," and "After the Race"—in the agricultural journal, the *IRISH HOMESTEAD*. Nonetheless, he was far from content in Dublin.

The real inspiration, however, came on June 10, 1904. On that day, Joyce met a 20-year-old girl from Galway, Nora BARNACLE, the woman with whom he would live for the rest of his life. Nora was working as a maid at Finn's Hotel in Leinster Street. He went out walking with her six days later on June 16, the day he would memorialize in *Ulysses*, and, over the next few months, they carried on a passionate courtship, albeit one circumscribed by the mores of Dublin life. As the fall approached, Joyce began making plans to leave

Ireland with Nora, trying to arrange employment on the Continent as a language teacher.

In October 1904, with a vague promise of a job for Joyce teaching English in a Berlitz school, Nora and James eloped from Dublin. They left in part because Joyce did not believe in the institution of marriage and because he and Nora could not live openly together in Ireland. More significant was the fact that the intellectual and artistic atmosphere of Dublin was simply too stifling. Joyce felt that he could never succeed there without conforming to the narrow conventions of a parochial aesthetic. After arriving in ZURICH to discover that the promised job did not exist, the couple traveled to TRIESTE, which proved to be another false hope. Then finally they went on to POLA (now Pula in Croatia but at that time part of Austria-Hungary), an Adriatic seaport about 150 miles south of Trieste on the Istria peninsula. There Joyce obtained a position as an English-language teacher at the local Berlitz School. Despite the good luck of Joyce's finding a teaching position, Joyce and Nora were not able to acclimate themselves to life in Pola. Nora, by now pregnant, could speak only English and felt completely isolated. Joyce was struggling to adapt to his new domestic situation. By early 1905 Joyce had become thoroughly dissatisfied with living in a place that he described scornfully as "a naval Siberia." Hoping for better conditions, he secured a job at the Berlitz School in Trieste (now in Italy but then, like Pola, part of Austria-Hungary), where he and Nora moved in March 1905.

Trieste provided a much more congenial atmosphere for both Joyce and Nora. The city was much more active than Pola. Work at the Berlitz language school proved relatively easy, and Joyce was a popular teacher with a number of the more affluent students. Perhaps more important, the couple soon made a number of friends, and Nora came to feel less alone than she had in Pola. At the same time, neither James nor Nora would ever acquire habits of frugality, and financial concerns dogged them for much of this period.

While living in Trieste, Joyce continued to work on the stories that would later constitute *Dubliners* and to expand the *Stephen Hero* manuscript. On July 27, 1905, his son, George JOYCE, was born, much to the delight of Joyce. In October of the same year Joyce's brother Stanislaus joined the family in Trieste, escaping from Dublin and coming to offer some help in the sustenance of his brother's family. Stanislaus also became an English-language teacher, but despite the addition of his income, Joyce's economic troubles continued.

In the autumn of 1905 Joyce approached Grant RICHARDS, who had in May of that year declined to publish *Chamber Music,* hoping that the latter would agree to publish *Dubliners.* On February 17, 1906, Richards accepted the manuscript, but, when his printer objected to passages in "Two Gallants," Richards became uneasy about the language in some of the other stories as well. In a series of letters discussing possible changes, Joyce tried to accommodate these concerns without compromising his narratives. These negotiations continued over the next few months, but finally at the end of September Richards withdrew his offer to publish the collection.

In the meantime, in July 1906, again in the hope of achieving greater fiscal stability, Joyce, Nora, and George moved to Rome. There, Joyce found employment as a clerk in the Nast-Kolb and Schumacher Bank. Life in Rome, however, proved both expensive and unpleasant for the family. He wrote to his brother Stannie that "Rome reminds me of a man who lives by exhibiting to travelers his grandmother's corpse." After a frustrating nine months in the city, Joyce, Nora, and George went back to Trieste in March 1907.

There they settled into a regular routine. Joyce resumed giving language lessons while he continued to write. As he and his family became more integrated into the life of Trieste, Joyce formed close friendships with the industrialist Ettore SCHMITZ, who had already published two novels—*Una Vita* (1892) and *Senilità* (1898)—under the pen name Italo Svevo, and with Silvio Benco, who eventually became the editor of the Trieste newspaper *Il PICCOLO DELLA SERA.*

The return to Trieste marked a creative burst for Joyce. In March he completed work on "The Dead," the final story in *Dubliners.* In April he gave the first of a series of three lectures on Ireland at the Università Popolare. He also published a series of three articles—"Fenianism," "Home Rule Comes of Age," and "Ireland at the Bar"—between March 22 and September 16, 1907, in *Il Piccolo della Sera.* And in May his suite of poems, *Chamber Music,* appeared.

Meanwhile, domestic life became more complicated. On July 26, 1907, Nora Joyce gave birth to the couple's second child, Lucia JOYCE, in the pauper's ward of the Municipal Hospital. Although Ellmann claims that at the same time, Joyce convalesced in the same hospital, recovering from a bout of rheumatic fever that he had contracted in mid-July, John McCourt, referencing Stanislaus, asserts that the convalescing took place at home.

Sometime in the autumn Joyce returned to the idea of writing an autobiographical novel, this time on a pattern very different from his original plan. He committed himself to recasting the conventionally realistic *Stephen Hero* into an original modernist form, and by the spring of 1908 he had completed the first three chapters. However, other concerns intruded, and seven years would elapse before the completion of *A Portrait of the Artist as a Young Man.*

Joyce had returned to Ireland for the first time since 1904 seeking to meet both personal and business obligations. In addition to wanting to introduce his son George to his Dublin and Galway relatives, he was again seeking a publisher for *Dubliners.* After Grant Richards abruptly retracted his acceptance of the collection, Joyce turned to Elkin MATHEWS, who had earlier brought out *Chamber Music.* That publisher also turned him down. However, while he was in Dublin, Joyce was able to secure a contract for the collection from MAUNSEL & CO. publishers. For a time, it seemed as if his personal and professional lives were stabilizing.

While Joyce was in Dublin, an old acquaintance, Vincent COSGRAVE, claimed that he and Nora had enjoyed an intimate physical relationship during the time she and Joyce were courting. The news was devastating for Joyce, and he wrote Nora a bitter, accusatory letter. Fortunately both J. F. Byrne and Stanislaus were able to persuade Joyce of Cosgrave's duplicity, and the breech was healed. (At that time Byrne was living at 7 Eccles Street, the address Joyce appropriated for the home of Leopold and Molly Bloom.) In early September Joyce and his son returned to Trieste, accompanied by his sister Eva.

In just over a month, however, a business opportunity brought him back to his native city. Noting the absence of a permanent cinema in Dublin, Joyce had interested four Trieste businessmen in a venture to establish a motion picture theater there. He returned to the city in October, and managed to have the VOLTA CINEMA, on Mary Street in the city center, open on December 20, 1909. Joyce felt comfortable leaving the city to return to Trieste in early January with another sister, Eileen. However, after an initial flurry of interest, the motion picture theater soon began to lose money. The partners sold the business at a loss in the summer of 1910.

Back in Trieste, Joyce resumed language instruction, fended off creditors, and continued work on

James Joyce as a young man in 1904 *(C. P. Curran/ James Joyce Collection, Beinecke Rare Book and Manuscript Library, Yale University)*

his novel. In 1912 he gave two more lectures, on Defoe and Blake, at the Università Popolare, and published three more articles in *Il Piccolo della Sera*—"The Shade of Parnell," "The City of the Tribes," and "The Mirage of the Fisherman of Aran." However, his central concern remained getting his short stories into print.

For several years Maunsel had been negotiating changes in the manuscript, but little progress was evident. In 1912 Joyce went to Dublin in what would prove to be a futile effort to get the publisher to live up to its agreement. Negotiations with Maunsel became extremely acrimonious, and finally George ROBERTS, one of the founders of the publishing house, proposed that Joyce purchase the printed sheets and publish *Dubliners* himself. However, before Joyce could do this, John FALCONER, the printer, destroyed the edition. On learning of this Joyce immediately left the city. En route home to Trieste in September, Joyce wrote the bitterly satirical poem "Gas from a Burner," chronicling what he saw as the perfidy of the publisher's behavior.

During this period Joyce continued to struggle to complete *A Portrait of the Artist as a Young Man.* He was, however, more successful in other writing projects. Perhaps as a relief from writing fiction, Joyce composed a number of the verses that would eventually appear in *Pomes Pennyeach.* He also was gathering impressions of life in Trieste in a notebook that would be posthumously published as *Giacomo Joyce.* It would be several more years, however, before he would bring his novel to a conclusion.

Late in 1913, a series of events began to unfold that would do much to alleviate Joyce's struggle for recognition and stimulate his writing. In December the American expatriate poet Ezra POUND wrote to Joyce seeking permission to reprint a poem from *Chamber Music,* "I Hear an Army," in an anthology of Imagist poets. Encouraged by Pound's interest, Joyce sent a copy of *Dubliners* and the first chapter of *A Portrait of the Artist as a Young Man* to Pound in mid-January 1914.

This correspondence marked the beginning of a decade of intense professional involvement between the two men. Pound became a tireless, enthusiastic backer of Joyce's work, and in a relatively short time, with insight and determination, succeeded in putting Joyce's work before the literary public. In 1914 Pound arranged to have a serialized version of *A Portrait of the Artist as a Young Man* published in the *EGOIST,* a prominent London journal, between February 1914 and September 1915. All the while Joyce continued his revisions on that novel, finishing shortly before the last serialized chapters appeared. Also in 1914, Grant Richards, dropping his objections to various passages in Joyce's short stories, finally agreed to publish *Dubliners.* It appeared in June of that year.

With his immediate publishing concerns alleviated, Joyce turned his energy back to writing. During 1914 and 1915, Joyce wrote his play, *Exiles.* It represents his final efforts as a playwright. (Two previous compositions, *A Brilliant Career* and *Dream Stuff,* written when he was a young man in Dublin, no longer exist.) *Exiles* presents an imaginative, and possibly cathartic, account of what life might have held for an artist like Joyce who chose to remain in Dublin. It reveals a structure that remains strongly influenced by the work of IBSEN. *Exiles* enjoyed at best limited success. Grant Richards, possibly hoping to capitalize on Joyce's growing popularity, published it in 1918, and the play was first performed in Munich in August 1919 under the German title *Verbannte.* However, *Exiles* never achieved the acclaim afforded to Joyce's novels or short stories, and it is now only rarely staged.

While finishing work on *Exiles,* Joyce turned his attention back to fiction. Early composition of *Ulysses* began in late 1914 or early 1915, though the idea for its story goes back to 1906, when he thought of including in *Dubliners* a story about Alfred H. Hunter, whom many believed to be Jewish and whose wife was rumored to be unfaithful. (In his biography of Joyce, Richard Ellmann also reports that Hunter reputedly assisted Joyce, as Bloom would Stephen Dedalus, after Joyce was knocked down during an altercation on ST STEPHEN'S GREEN.) Joyce decided to expand considerably upon the original notion, and by June 1915, Joyce had drafted the outline of the novel and had written several chapters. However, before he had gotten much further with his writing, international events intruded upon the process of composition.

Joyce sought to remain in Trieste after the outbreak of World War I. He had no sympathy for the English or for their involvement in the conflict. However, his brother Stanislaus had been interned because of irredentist sympathies for ceding Trieste to Italy. After Italy entered the war in May 1915 on the side of the Allies, because Joyce held a British passport, local Austro-Hungarian authorities compelled him and his family to leave. On June 28 the Joyces departed for neutral Switzerland, with their furniture and Joyce's library remaining behind in their Trieste apartment. Although they arrived in Zurich with few resources, Nora's Galway uncle, Michael Healy, immediately sent them more, and after a week in a hotel they were able to find a flat and settle into a fairly regular routine in the city in which they would remain until 1919.

Settling into life in Zurich proved easier than it had in Trieste or Pola. Joyce had a letter of introduction from one of his well-to-do Triestine students, and he quickly made friends within the expatriate community. Despite the conservative, bourgeois makeup of the city, the influx of refugees from all over Europe—including at one time Vladimir Lenin and the founder of Dadaism, Tristan Tzara, a coincidence made much of by Tom Stoppard in his play *Travesties*—made the intellectual climate of the city electrifying.

Although in August 1917, after an attack of glaucoma, Joyce underwent the first of what would be a series of eye operations, he seemed by and large to enjoy living in the city. Indeed, during his time in Zurich Joyce worked steadily on *Ulysses*, completing drafts of the first 12 chapters (Telemachus through Cyclops). He managed to support himself and his family while in Zurich by offering private language lessons, through grants from the British government—secured through the efforts of Pound and Yeats—and by a subsidy from Mrs. Edith Rockefeller McCormick and Harriet Shaw WEAVER. He also established long-lasting friendships with a number of individuals, most notably Frank BUDGEN and Claud SYKES, who exerted a marked impact on his work. Through Sykes, beginning in the spring of 1918, Joyce and Nora participated in a theatrical group, The ENGLISH PLAYERS, which gave performances of a range of plays from Wilde's *The Importance of Being Earnest* to Shaw's *The Dark Lady of the Sonnets*.

In the meantime, more of Joyce's writing began to appear in print. Although Duckworth, the English firm, had turned it down, in 1916 in the United States the publisher B. W. HUEBSCH brought out *A Portrait of the Artist as a Young Man*. Two years later in March 1918, at the urging of Ezra Pound, the American journal the *LITTLE REVIEW* began to serialize *Ulysses* with the publication of the Telemachus episode. It would continue to bring out chapters of the novel until the September–December 1920 issue of the magazine was suppressed by the U.S. Post Office on charges that it was publishing obscenity. Also that year, as noted above, Grant Richards published Joyce's play, *Exiles*, and in 1919 the *Egoist*, the English literary magazine, published several chapters of *Ulysses*. However, despite all of this attention and steady progress in writing, Joyce still was struggling with the monumental task of completing his novel.

In October 1919 the high cost of living in Zurich, with a climate that seemed hostile to his troubled eyesight, and the loss of many friends as other refugees returned home led Joyce to decide to leave as well. Thus, nearly a year after cessation of hostilities in Europe, Joyce and his family returned to Trieste, which the Austrians had ceded to Italy as part of the peace negotiations. However, crowded postwar living conditions had made the city a very different place from the one they had left four years before. For a time, Joyce, Nora, and their children lived in a flat with his brother-in-law, Frantisek Schaurek, his sister Eileen, and his brother Stanislaus, recently returned to the city from his four-year internment by the Austrians for his political views.

Not surprisingly, continuing work on his novel under these cramped living conditions proved to be extremely difficult for Joyce. Nonetheless, in November, he began work on the Nausikaa chapter, and by early 1920 he had gone on to Oxen of the Sun. Although this represented a genuine achievement, overall conditions remained unsatisfactory. Joyce resumed giving language lessons at the Scuola Superiore di Commercio Revoltella, but he remained restless and felt isolated. In June Joyce visited Ezra Pound in the Italian town of Sirmione.

Joyce expressed his desire to find a quiet, restful place to complete *Ulysses.* At the urging of Pound, the Joyce family left Trieste in July 1920 and went to Paris, where they planned to spend a brief period. They remained there for the next 20 years.

As he had seven years earlier with Joyce's literary career, Ezra Pound set about doing what he could to organize the family's domestic life. Pound made the rounds among Paris intellectuals who could promote Joyce's work. More important in the short term, Pound contacted people who could help the family settle into life in the city. Nonetheless the Joyces found themselves scrambling to make ends meet during their first few months in Paris.

Gradually the family grew accustomed to Paris life, and the prospect of returning to Trieste faded relatively quickly. Joyce continued writing. By now he was facing the monumental task of completing the Circe chapter. He labored on it through 1920, and it was not until late December that he finally felt satisfied with the draft.

Around the same time, Joyce learned that the serialization of *Ulysses* in the *Little Review* had been interrupted after the Society for the Suppression of Vice brought charges in the state of New York against the magazine, and in February 1921 Margaret ANDERSON and Jane HEAP, its editors, were convicted of publishing obscenity. All this had little effect upon Joyce's continued work. In March 1921 Ettore Schmitz brought notes for the novel that Joyce had left behind in Trieste, and Joyce turned to completing Ithaca and Penelope.

Although the *Little Review* decision seemed to make it less likely that anyone would take the risk of publishing *Ulysses,* in April Sylvia BEACH, the American owner of the English-language Paris bookshop SHAKESPEARE AND COMPANY, ensured its appearance by agreeing to publish it through her bookstore. Once committed to the project, Beach proved to be a tireless organizer, finding typists, soliciting subscribers, and in general seeing that Joyce was free to concentrate on composition. She also facilitated its reception, by introducing Joyce to the well-known French novelist, critic and translator, Valery LARBAUD, in December 1920. In December 1921, as Joyce was making the final emendations to *Ulysses,* Larbaud gave a public lecture at Shakespeare and Company to launch the book.

In the meantime Beach had found a printer in Dijon, Maurice DARANTIERE, and he proved to be a rare discovery. In June, Joyce began receiving proofs of the novel. Rather than simply correct any errors that he found in the narrative, Joyce used the occasion to continue the process of composition, eventually increasing the length of *Ulysses* by one-third. Although Darantiere showed remarkable patience with the process, the ongoing changes produced unintentional editorial problems that remain cruxes to this day. Finally, after months of proofreading and revision, the first two copies of the novel were sent to Paris on Joyce's 40th birthday, February 2, 1922.

The appearance of the full text of *Ulysses,* however, did little to resolve the intra- and extra-textual controversies that had erupted before its completion. In 1922 the U.S. Post Office destroyed all copies of the book mailed to America. Twelve years would pass before Bennett CERF and Random House publishers would win the right to publish the book in the United States and 14 years would elapse before it appeared in Great Britain.

Even after copies of *Ulysses* became more or less generally available, many of the issues raised while Joyce was still writing the book—centering on everything from interpretive approaches to editorial integrity—remained unresolved. Given the complexity of the work and the sometimes chaotic conditions surrounding Joyce as he composed it, one can hardly be surprised by this. At the same time, the creative achievement of the novel and its impact on subsequent writers has never been in question. Ezra Pound and T. S. ELIOT were quick to publish articles praising the work, and other prominent writers quickly joined the chorus, though Yeats seemed to vacillate before coming out with praise for it. At the same time, a number were at the very least ambivalent. George Bernard Shaw declined to join the list of subscribers. Virginia Woolf, whose Hogarth Press had toyed with the idea of publishing the book, dismissed the work with a deprecating reference to class differences. And George Moore simply judged Joyce's work as inferior to his own.

Despite the attention that *Ulysses* received in literary circles, it remained for many a curiosity. However, Joyce did not allow the public's response to *Ulysses* to interfere with his creative efforts. On March 10, 1923, a little over a year after the book's publication, Joyce began a project that would occupy the next 16 years of his life and provoke even more debate and disagreement than his previous work: the composition of *Finnegans Wake*. It was a book like no other before it, and even before its full publication in 1939, it became the symbol for artistic efforts that refused to accept the limits of the Cartesian world already challenged by Albert Einstein and other theoretical physicists.

In April 1924 Joyce began the practice of publishing fragments in various journals and as individual books with the appearance of a draft of the Mamaluju section in *TRANSITION*. During the next 14 years, drafts of much of the work appeared in various venues. Thus, by the time of its publication in May 1939, *Finnegans Wake*'s structure, at least, held few surprises for its readers.

Because he did not wish to reveal the true title of the work until it was completed, selections from it appeared simply under the title *Work in Progress*. Characterized by a dreamlike night language, a complex referentiality, and a nonlinear narrative evolution, these passages delineated a revolutionary approach to prose fiction. They highlighted a process of composition and of comprehension that privileged multilayered associations and that trusted the ability of readers to find interpretive unity in a work that refused to provide the standard literary markers for cohesion.

At the same time that he began this new project, nagging health concerns returned. In 1924 and 1925 Joyce went through a series of eye operations seeking to halt the degeneration of his sight. While the process proved extremely debilitating, he pressed on with his writing.

As one would expect, the avant-garde style of the published fragments of *Finnegans Wake* attracted a great deal of attention. However, it also drew sharp attacks from individuals who previously had been some of Joyce's strongest admirers. In particular, Ezra Pound and Joyce's brother Stanislaus felt that Joyce was wasting his talent with what they considered stylistically complex but substantially meaningless exercises. Despite this often harsh criticism, Joyce persisted in his writing, and did whatever he could to promote interest in and understanding of what he was attempting to do in *Work in Progress*. However, it did affect him, particularly when the usually unconditionally supportive Harriet Shaw Weaver expressed reservations in letters, written in January and February 1927. Indeed, in May Joyce told Sylvia Beach that he was thinking of asking the Irish writer James STEPHENS to complete the work for him. He soon dropped that plan, but criticism of his work did not abate. Although Weaver, in a September 17, 1927, letter, attempted to withdraw her criticism, during that same month Wyndham LEWIS, whom Joyce had previously befriended, published a fierce attack on Joyce's writing in *Time and Western Man*.

While generally confident in the correctness of his artistic vision, as was the case with *Ulysses*, mounting criticism made Joyce acknowledge the need to take steps to counter the impression that his work was unreadable. Along these lines, in May 1929, with Joyce's encouragement, a group of his friends—including Samuel BECKETT, Eugene JOLAS, Frank BUDGEN, and Stuart GILBERT—compiled a collection of essays entitled *Our Exagmination round His Factification for Incamination of Work in Progress*. This study endeavored to address many of the criticisms of *Finnegans Wake* that had already arisen, and it set the pattern for arguments for the value of the work for years to come.

In addition to the disagreements among his former supporters that grew up around *Work in Progress*, Joyce was forced to confront unforeseen difficulties relating to unauthorized publications of his writings. In 1926 an American, Samuel ROTH, began serialization of a pirated version of *Ulysses* in his journal *Two Worlds Monthly*. (Roth had previously published unauthorized versions of fragments from *Work in Progress*.) Two of Joyce's American friends, Ludwig Lewisohn and Archibald MacLeish, drew up a letter of international protest—eventually signed by 167 writers including such diverse figures as Robert Bridges, E. M. Forster, André Gide, D. H. Lawrence, Wyndham Lewis, Luigi Pirandello, George Moore, Havelock Ellis, Virgina

Woolfe, and W. B. Yeats—condemning this enterprise. Roth finally ceased serialization in the fall of 1927, but it was not until the very end of the next year that New York State Supreme Court Justice Richard H. Mitchell issued an injunction prohibiting Roth from using Joyce's name and from publishing any material without Joyce's consent.

Other projects also occupied Joyce's attention over this period. Earlier, in July 1927, Joyce published his second collection of verse, entitled *Pomes Penyeach.* A French translation of *Ulysses,* supervised by Valery Larbaud, appeared in 1929. (Portions of the French version of the novel had appeared as early as 1924.) Then in 1930, with Joyce's guidance, Stuart Gilbert published *James Joyce's Ulysses,* a work that offered a chapter-by-chapter analysis of the novel, and one that Joyce hoped would dispel the esoteric aura attached to it. While not completely successful in that regard, the Gilbert book did open up the text to many readers previously intimidated by its complexity.

In 1931 the peripatetic Joyces briefly settled in London. There, on July 4, James and Nora were married at the registry office. Although Joyce had been keenly opposed to marriage and the entire episode was extremely embarrassing for both him and Nora, they undertook it in an effort to protect the inheritance rights of their children. The visit also had another aim. Joyce had toyed with the idea of moving to England permanently. However, once there he found conditions less attractive than he had anticipated, and, after a seaside holiday in August, the family returned to Paris in the autumn. In December 1931 John Stanislaus Joyce, for whom Joyce had always retained a strong affection, died. The loss greatly affected Joyce, and, in memory of his father and to celebrate the birth of his own grandson Stephen JOYCE on February 15, 1932, Joyce wrote the poem "Ecce Puer."

In the midst of these personal disruptions, Joyce's literary fortunes achieved a measure of stability. In the United States and Europe, court rulings and public pressure began to resolve the heretofore ambiguous legal status of *Ulysses.* In 1933 in southern New York's federal district courts, Judge John M. WOOLSEY overturned the 12-year ban against importation of *Ulysses* into the United States. In his landmark decision, Judge Woolsey ruled unambiguously that the work was not pornographic (see the appendix on page 392). This decision cleared the way for Random House to publish the novel in the United States in 1934, and the first English edition followed two years later.

During the 1930s the composition of *Work in Progress* became even more challenging. The poor state of Joyce's eyes often interrupted the writing process, and he had to undergo numerous operations and prolonged treatments in the hope of arresting his deteriorating condition. Joyce's eye problems made the acts of reading and writing extremely difficult. He ultimately became quite dependent upon friends and family to research information for his book and to take dictation as he struggled to complete the work.

Additionally, domestic difficulties stemming from the behavior of Lucia Joyce, manifest in relatively mild disorders in the 1920s, could no longer be ignored. After casting about in the early 1920s for a career, from 1926 to 1929 Lucia trained rigorously as a dancer. In October 1929 she rather abruptly abandoned dance, and turned to drawing but still remained restless. In 1931, she caused a breach between Joyce and Samuel Beckett when she realized that the latter spent time at the family flat because of her father and not from an attraction for her. Then, on the afternoon of February 2, 1932, Joyce's 50th birthday, Lucia had such a violent fight with her mother that her brother George took her by taxi to a mental hospital where she spent the next few days. Later that year, after a failed engagement to Paul LÉON's brother-in-law, Lucia saw her condition worsen. The family spent much of their time traveling around the continent consulting various specialists, including Carl JUNG. None was able to effect a cure, and finally in March 1936 she was institutionalized. All this made Joyce more reclusive, and he became increasingly reliant upon friends like Eugene and Maria JOLAS and Lucie and Paul Léon.

This dependence no doubt was increased by the isolation he felt from others. His brother Stanislaus, still living in Trieste, was quite blunt in his view that *Work in Progress* was a waste of Joyce's talent. Ezra Pound, caught up in Italian fascism and arcane economic theories, now had few interests coinciding with Joyce. Perhaps most significantly, in the early 1930s Joyce's friendship with Sylvia Beach cooled progressively, due in part to Joyce's misunderstanding of the financial arrangements regarding the publication of *Ulysses.* As a result, in 1932 Paul Léon had begun to assume the unofficial role of manager-adviser-advocate previously held by Beach. It was a role that Léon continued to fulfill throughout the decade and even after Joyce's death. Though Léon bristled at the idea that he acted as Joyce's secretary, he certainly helped Joyce cope with the practical economic, literary, and social demands that regularly assailed an author of Joyce's stature. Undoubtedly, without Léon's devoted friendship, Joyce's often chaotic life would have been in much greater turmoil.

All the while, Joyce continued work on the final version of *Finnegans Wake.* By publishing fragments of it throughout the decade, Joyce had achieved a fairly good sense of how the public would receive the completed work, and these fragments also served to condition readers gradually to the radical change in prose fiction represented in his writing. Perhaps because so much of the work had already appeared in journals like *transition, Two Worlds,* and *Criterion,* the final printing attracted less attention than did the publication of *Ulysses.* Nonetheless, on May 4, 1939, *Finnegans Wake* appeared in Britain under the imprint of FABER AND FABER and in the United States under that of the VIKING PRESS.

Despite the decade of controversy over its structure and intent, Joyce had great hopes for the success of his last work. Unfortunately, its formidable reputation dissuaded readers, and the outbreak of World War II cast a pall over its promotion. (Even among literary critics today, *Finnegans Wake* is widely owned but rarely read.) In December 1939 the Joyces left Paris for SAINT-GÉRAND-LE-PUY, a village near Vichy in central France where they stayed for most of the next year as political events unfolded. Paul Léon, who with his wife had also traveled to Saint-Gérand-le-Puy, returned to Paris in the fall. He subsequently recovered a great deal of Joyce's books and personal papers from the Joyces' apartment in Paris. Unfortunately, Léon remained in the city into 1941, and was arrested by the Nazis and put to death as a Jew.

James Joyce in his graduation picture from University College, 1902 *(Croessman Collection of James Joyce, Special Collections/Morris Library, Southern Illinois University)*

Meanwhile, the Joyces struggled to find asylum from world war for the second time in their lives. Although they tried desperately to obtain permission to move Lucia to neutral Switzerland, in the end they had to leave her in a French sanitarium, hoping that they would later be able to move her. On December 14 they left Saint-Gérand-le-Puy and traveled, with their son George and grandson Stephen, to Zurich, the same city that had given the family shelter 25 years earlier.

The Joyces arrived in Zurich on December 17, 1940, and began the process of settling in. On January 10, 1941, however, Joyce was taken ill and rushed to a Zurich hospital. Doctors there diagnosed his problem as a perforated duodenal ulcer, and recommended surgery. Joyce underwent an operation the following day. Initially it seemed to have been a success, but early in the morning of the 13th, less than three weeks before his 59th birthday, Joyce died. He was buried in Zurich at Fluntern cemetery. When Nora died in Zurich on April

10, 1951, she was initially buried elsewhere in the cemetery, but in 1966 they were reburied next to each other.

With a body of work that embodies the evolution of 20th-century literature from symbolism (*Chamber Music;* see SYMBOLIST MOVEMENT) to REALISM and NATURALISM (*Dubliners*) through MODERNISM (*A Portrait of the Artist as a Young Man* and *Ulysses*) to POSTMODERNISM (*Ulysses* again and *Finnegans Wake*), Joyce is one of the most influential artists of the century. However a contemporary author chooses to write, he or she will be making use of techniques pioneered by Joyce. In a sense, all subsequent literature derives from his work and must be evaluated by the standard that he set.

See Appendix on page 381 for a chronology of Joyce's writings and publications, and Appendix on page 402 for Joyce's family tree.

For further information, see Richard Ellmann, *James Joyce;* Herbert Gorman, *James Joyce;* Chester Anderson, *James Joyce and His World;* Morris Beja, *James Joyce: A Literary Life;* Peter Costello, *James Joyce: The Years of Growth 1882–1915;* John McCourt, *The Years of Bloom: James Joyce in Trieste, 1904–1920;* E. H. Mikhail, ed., *James Joyce: Interviews and Recollections;* and Willard Potts, ed., *Portraits of the Artist in Exile: Recollections of James Joyce by Europeans.* Also see Joyce's June 24, 1921, letter to Harriet Shaw Weaver where he sardonically reviews the various rumors circulating about him and his family (*Letters,* I.165–167).

For further information on other members of the Joyce family, see individual entries in the A to Z section.

## OBITUARIES

From the obituary in the *New York Times* (January 13, 1941):

> The status of James Joyce as a writer never could be determined in his lifetime. In the opinion of some critics, notably Edmund Wilson, he deserved to rank with the great innovators of literature as one whose influence upon other writers of his time was incalculable. On the other hand, there were critics like Max Eastman who gave him a place with Gertrude Stein and T. S. Eliot among the "Unintelligibles" and there was Professor Irving Babbitt of Harvard who dismissed his most widely read novel, "Ulysses," as one which only could have been written "in an advanced stage of psychic disintegration."

From the obituary in the *New York Herald Tribune* (January 13, 1941):

> Not since the appearance in book form in the middle of the nineteenth century of Gustave Flaubert's "Madame Bovary" had a literary work provoked such a storm of controversy, of praise and pillorying, as did the "Ulysses" of James Joyce. Where Flaubert sought a scrupulously truthful portrayal of life, Joyce attempted what his admirers and interpreters called a stream of consciousness portrayal of what went on in the human mind, consciously and unconsciously—and in the human body, too. . . .

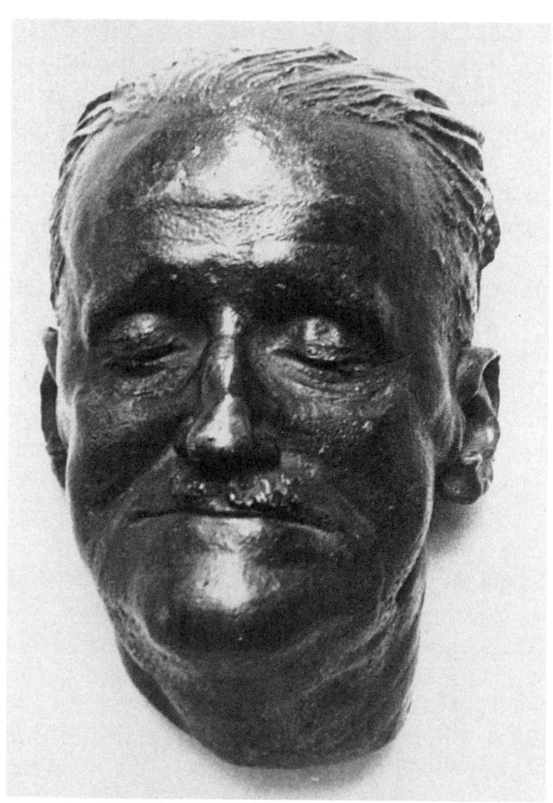

Joyce's death mask *(Marquette University)*

Through the post-war 1920's, an experimental decade in literature, Joyce was the idol of many a modern writer and reader. To hear them sing his praises, his "Ulysses" had created a new art form, revolutionized literature.

From a tribute by Thornton Wilder published in *Poetry*, 57 (1940–1941): 370–374:

Like Cervantes, he groped confusedly for his subject and his form. The history of a writer is his search for his own subject, his myth-theme, hidden from him, but prepared for him in every hour of his life, his *Gulliver's Travels*, his *Robinson Crusoe*. Like Cervantes, unsuccessful, Joyce tried poetry and drama. Knowing the incomparable resources of his prose rhythms one is astonished at these verses,—a watery musicality, a pinched ventriloqual voice. Knowing the vital dialogues in *Dubliners* and that electrifying scene, the quarrel at the Christmas dinnertable, in *A Portrait of the Artist as a Young Man*, one is astonished at the woodenness of his play *Exiles*.

Like Cervantes, he turned with greater success to short narratives, and like him found in the dimensions of the long book, his form and his theme.

# PART II

# *Works*

## *Chamber Music* (1907)

This volume consists of a suite of 36 lyrical poems reflecting the sentiments and moods of a youthful poet who experiences the rise and fall of an idealized love. With a recommendation from the literary critic and poet Arthur SYMONS, *Chamber Music,* Joyce's first book, was published by Elkin MATHEWS in London, May 1907. Composed between 1901 and 1904, the collection reflects Joyce's own emotional state during this period and contains many of the significant themes that appear in his later writings: companionship, the allure and frustrations of love, betrayal, rejection, loneliness and social censure, the role of the poet, and the function of art. Earlier collections of poems titled *Moods* and *Shine and Dark* may have anticipated the verses of *Chamber Music;* however, *Moods* is no longer extant, and only a few fragments of *Shine and Dark* exist. (Fragments from *Shine and Dark* and possibly from *Moods* have been published in *James Joyce: Poems and Exiles,* edited by J. C. C. Mays.)

Evidence from Joyce's letters indicates that he originally intended a two-part arrangement of the poems, portraying the rise and fall of a consummated but brief love affair. Joyce also intended that the poems be set to music. Soon after *Chamber Music* was published in 1907, the Anglo-Irish composer G. Molyneux PALMER wrote to Joyce asking permission to set the poems to music; by July 1909 Palmer completed musical settings for several of the poems. Shortly after Joyce received these settings, he wrote to Palmer, saying, "I hope you may set all of *Chamber Music* in time. This was indeed partly my idea in writing it. The book is in fact a suite of songs and if I were a musician I suppose I should have set them to music myself. The central song is XIV after which the movement is all downwards until XXXIV which is vitally the end of the book. XXXV and XXXVI are tailpieces just as I and III are preludes" (*Letters,* I.67). Palmer was one of the first three composers to write music for the poems; however, it was Adolf Mann's setting of "O, it was out by Donnycarney" (XXXI) that first reached a public audience in 1910. According to Myra T. Russel, who has done extensive research on the musical settings of *Chamber Music* and particularly on Palmer's, W. B. Reynolds, a music critic for *The Belfast Telegraph,* was the first composer to send Joyce settings of the poems, and Herbert Hughes, a collector of folk songs who later became Joyce's friend, was the second; their settings, unfortunately, have been lost (see *James Joyce's Chamber Music: The Lost Song Settings,* edited by Myra T. Russel, 20). Joyce, too, even composed a melody for CM XI, "Bid adieu to girlish days," with the musical setting by the American composer and conductor Edmund Pendleton, who was living in Paris when Joyce was there. Since then, *Chamber Music* poems have been set to music by many composers, including Samuel Barber, Luciano Berio, and Anthony Burgess. Ross Lee Finney and recently Alfred Heller, both American composers, have set all 36 to music. Palmer set 32 of the 36 poems, and his settings, as Russel points out, "were Joyce's lifetime favorites" (xvi). (See the appendix on page 381 for a more detailed list of *Chamber Music* composers.)

These Elizabethan-style lyrics or songs express a varying emotional tone, and like his Elizabethan predecessors, especially John Dowland, Thomas Campion, and Ben Jonson, Joyce achieves a graceful and delicate style difficult for readers, without a full appreciation of Joyce's musical intent behind the poems, to comprehend. In "*Chamber Music:* Words and Music Lovingly Coupled," Russel addresses this point directly. "Many who have read, or even better, have recited the *Chamber Music* poems," she observes, "enjoy their delicacy and gracefulness, finding them not only pleasurable but delightful. Critics, however, with few exceptions, have been far less accepting, judging the book as unworthy of a genius; their disapproval has ranged from embarrassment to outright ridicule or contempt. While the musical quality of Joyce's language is generally acknowledged, rarely has the vital importance of music to the poems been recognized" (*Bronze by Gold: The Music of Joyce,* edited by Sebastian D. G. Knowles, 58–59).

The musical effects and emotional tone of *Chamber Music* relate not only to its style but also to its themes, structure, diction, and imagery. The allure and disenchantment of love, the change of seasons, the passing of day into night, the presence of a portentous moon, the flight of a bat, the imagery of water and birds, the combinations of color, sound, time and place, among many other vivid, sensuous images and symbols, all contribute to the atmosphere and shifting moods Joyce creates in this suite of songs. The verses in *Chamber Music,* however, are more than mere Elizabethan imitations, as many readers recognize. Herbert Howarth, for example, observes: "Although they are not purely 'Shakespearean' or 'Jonsonian' or 'lutanist' (since other influences from Homer to the Victorian drawing room ballads, from the Irish come-all-yous to Verlaine, converge in them), yet their singer takes shape, if a blurred shape, as a grave-mannered gentleman of a pre-industrial world, a courtier" ("*Chamber Music* and Its Place in the Joyce Canon" in *James Joyce Today: Essays on the Major Works,* ed. Thomas F. Staley, 11–12).

## THE TITLE OF *CHAMBER MUSIC*

The title *Chamber Music* was not chosen by Joyce; indeed, he voiced his dissatisfaction in a letter to his brother Stanislaus JOYCE in the autumn of 1906: "The reason I dislike *Chamber Music* as a title is that it is too complacent. I should prefer a title which to a certain extent repudiated the book, without altogether disparaging it" (*Letters,* II.182). What he meant by this is not altogether certain, but his intention seems clearer in a letter to his brother in March 1907, when Joyce had just received the proofs of the book: "I don't like the book but wish it were published and be damned to it. However, it is a young man's book. I felt like that. It is not a book of love-verses at all, I perceive" (*Letters,* II.219). Although there are varying accounts of the title's origin, it most likely came from Stanislaus: "I had already suggested," he writes in *My Brother's Keeper,* "and Jim had accepted the title *Chamber Music* for the collection. Another version of the origin of the title is given in Herbert Gorman's biography of my brother, but the story there told . . . is false, whatever its source" (p. 209). In Gorman's version, Joyce and a friend one evening visited a widow, who after hearing Joyce's poems and drinking beer, withdrew behind a screen to use a chamber pot. Although out of sight, she could be heard as she urinated. " 'By God!' [Joyce's friend] cried, 'she's a critic! You hear how she appreciates your poems?' 'Critic or no,' replied Joyce gravely, 'she has given me a title for my book. I shall call it *Chamber Music*' " (*James Joyce,* p. 116). A reference to the "music" of a chamber pot appears in the Sirens episode of *Ulysses* when Leopold Bloom thinks, "Chamber music. Could make a kind of pun on that" (*U* 11.979–980).

In 1909 when Joyce was in Dublin while Nora Barnacle remained in Trieste, he sent her as a Christmas gift a bound handwritten parchment copy of *Chamber Music* with their initials interlaced on the cover. In September of that same year, Joyce had the last line of *Chamber Music* IX engraved on a necklace of ivory cubes that he designed for her. Expressing his sentiment at the time, the line simply reads: "Love is unhappy when love is away."

## THE ARRANGEMENT OF THE POEMS

The following numerical sequences of *Chamber Music* represent two different arrangements of the poems. The order of settings in Arabic numerals represents Joyce's intentions as found in the 1905 manuscript now at the Beinecke Rare Book and Manuscript Library, Yale University, and reflects the thematic and musical development of the suite. The last two poems of *Chamber Music,* XXXV and XXXVI, were later added by Joyce in 1906 just before he sent the manuscript to the publisher. This 1905 ordering helps the reader, or listener, to understand Joyce's original dramatic intent, which is obscured by the final published arrangement. The second sequence, in Roman numerals (including XXXV and XXXVI), is Stanislaus's 1906 arrangement, which Joyce himself had trouble grasping, as he admits in a letter to his brother dated October 18, 1906: "I do not understand your arrangement: write it out clearly again" (*Letters,* II.181). However, it is Stanislaus's ordering, which organizes the suite according to similarity of mood, that has become the standard published version. Joyce at this time, as he indicates in the same letter to Stanislaus, also appears to have lost interest in the poems with ambivalent feelings toward them: "I went through my entire book of verses . . . and they nearly all seemed to me poor and trivial: some phrases and lines pleased me and no more. A page of *A Little Cloud* gives me more pleasure than all my verses. I am glad the verses are to be published because they are a record of my past. . . ." (*Letters,* II.182). (For information regarding the manuscripts and various sequences of the poems, see A. Walton Litz, Preface, vol. 1, *The James Joyce Archive,* xxix–xlii.)

*Upward movement in the suite of songs*

*Preludial poems (the poet alone):*

1 (XXI) He who hath glory lost

2 (I) Strings in the earth and air

3 (III) At that hour when all things have repose

*The suite itself (poems portraying the relationship of the lovers)*

4 (II) The twilight turns from amethyst

5 (IV) When the shy star goes forth in heaven

6 (V) Lean out of the window

7 (VIII) Who goes amid the green wood?

8 (VII) My love is in a light attire

9 (IX) Winds of May, that dance on the sea

10 (XVII) Because your voice was at my side

11 (XVIII) O Sweetheart, hear you

12 (VI) I would in that sweet bosom be

13 (X) Bright cap and streamers

14 (XX) In the dark pine-wood

15 (XIII) Go seek her out all courteously

16 (XI) Bid adieu to girlish days

*The central poem of the suite*

17 (XIV) My dove, my beautiful one

*Downward movement in the suite of songs*

18 (XIX) Be not sad because all men

19 (XV) From dewy dreams, my soul, arise

20 (XXIII) This heart that flutters near my heart

21 (XXIV) Silently she's combing

22 (XVI) O cool is the valley now

23 (XXXI) O, it was out by Donnycarney

24 (XXII) Of that so sweet imprisonment

25 (XXVI) Thou leanest to the shell of night

26 (XII) What counsel has the hooded moon

27 (XXVII) Though I thy Mithridates were

28 (XXVIII) Gentle lady, do not sing

29 (XXV) Lightly come or lightly go

30 (XXIX) Dear heart, why will you use me so?

31 (XXXII) Rain has fallen all the day

32 (XXX) Love came to us in time gone by

33 (XXXIII) Now, O now, in this brown land

*Original end of the suite*

34 (XXXIV) Sleep now, O sleep now

*Tailpieces (not found in Joyce's 1905 arrangement and not initially intended by Joyce to be part of this work):*

(XXXV) All day I hear the noise of waters

(XXXVI) I hear an army charging upon the Land

These last two poems were written before 1905, around 1902 and 1903, respectively, and added to the suite of songs after Joyce's 1905 sequence.

## THE POEMS OF *CHAMBER MUSIC*

The order below follows Joyce's 1905 arrangement. The Arabic numerals correspond to this version; the Roman numerals correspond to the order of the published version. See above.

Throughout *Chamber Music,* Joyce mostly employs a rhyme scheme, cadence, and meter similar to popular Elizabethan prosody with the obvious exception of the central poem of the suite, number XIV. These and other recognizable poetic (and musical) devices—assonance, consonance, and alliteration, etc.—will not be included in the following discussions.

**"He who hath glory lost"** Poem 1 (XXI); this is the shortest poem in the suite, only six lines. The poem was originally entitled "To Nora," but Joyce decided to omit the title probably sometime in early June 1905 when he added the poem to *Chamber Music* (see *Letters,* II.92). According to Joyce's original arrangement, this opening poem forms part of the prelude to the suite of songs.

The speaker in the poem describes himself as alienated from his friends, who are now his foes. (In the 1905 manuscript at Yale the word *friend* instead of the word *foes* appears in line 3.) Nonetheless, he is still able to comport himself with dignity because of the support that his love, his new companion, gives to him. (For additional information see *Letters,* II.92 and 97n. 2.)

**"Strings in the earth and air"** Poem 2 (I); the second poem in Joyce's ordering introduces the reader to the stylistic features that characterize the whole suite and that echo the Elizabethan verse form. This poem also introduces the themes of love, music, and art that appear later in the suite, although it is not meant to be representative of the whole suite. In a July 1909 letter to G. Molyneux Palmer, Joyce labeled the poem a prelude (*Letters,* I.67). First published in *Chamber Music,* it also appeared separately (with its author identified only as a past Belvederian) in the summer 1907 issue of the *Belvederian,* the annual magazine of BELVEDERE COLLEGE, and in *The Dublin Book of Irish Verse: 1728–1909,* published in 1909. It was also reprinted in another poetry anthology, *The Wild Harp: A Selection of Irish Poetry,* edited by Katharine Tynan and published in 1913. (For additional details, see *Letters,* II.207, 323, and 330–331.)

**"At that hour when all things have repose"** Poem 3 (III); this poem expresses the mood of a lonely poet awakening to the "sweet music" of love. The first two of the poem's three stanzas rhetorically present the question of the poet's readiness for love. The image of dawn following night intensifies the natural emergence of love and an awakening emotional anticipation in the speaker. In the third stanza, the soft light of dawn has come, and the poet hears the music of love fill the heavens and the earth.

In a December 1920 letter to G. Molyneux Palmer, Joyce asked that a copy of his musical setting of "At That Hour" along with "Gentle lady, do not sing" (CM XXVIII) and "O, it was out by Donnycarney" (CM XXXI) be sent to the Irish singer JOHN MCCORMACK.

The poem was subsequently published separately in *The Wild Harp, A Selection of Irish Poetry* (1913). (For additional information see *Letters,* II.323 and 330–331, and III.35.)

**"The twilight turns from amethyst"** Poem 4 (II) opens with a lyrical emphasis as it describes darkening hues appearing at evening. The poem introduces the presence of the girl, whose piano-playing captures the speaker's attention and affections. Both the speaker and the girl are longing for love. In the opening two lines of the poem, the imagery of twilight turning to a deeper blue anticipates the last two lines of the poem when the twilight turns to an even darker blue, and together these lines ironically foreshadow the unanticipated eclipse of love.

In his memoir, *My Brother's Keeper,* Stanislaus Joyce recalls that this poem was originally entitled "Commonplace" and that it was part of either *Moods* or *Shine and Dark,* Joyce's youthful poems. "Commonplace" was also one of several poems that Joyce sent to William ARCHER in 1901. Stanislaus quotes a letter from Archer to Joyce offering guarded praise for these works and advice for future compositions. (For further information see *Letters,* II.10.)

**"When the shy star goes forth in heaven"** Poem 5 (IV); here the speaker in a roundabout way entreats his beloved to listen for him at night as he sings by her gate. According to Richard ELLMANN, the poem, in imitation of the style of the Elizabethan playwright Ben Jonson, was written while Joyce was in Paris in early 1903 (*James Joyce,* 121). (For further information see *Letters,* II.27–29.)

**"Lean out of the window"** Poem 6 (V); this poem presents a charming variation on the dichotomy of desire and intellect. The speaker has heard Goldenhair singing "[a] merry air," which has led him outdoors and away from his book. He now calls upon her to "[l]ean out of the window" to show herself to him.

**"Who goes amid the green wood?"** Poem 7 (VIII); this poem contains four stanzas. The first three rhetorically ask who so beautifully complements the green wood and for whom does the wood adorn itself. The last stanza identifies the speaker's "true love" as the one for whom "[t]he woods their rich apparel wear."

The idyllic description of the speaker's beloved as she walks through the woods evokes immediate (and unfavorable) comparison to the poem "Who Goes with Fergus?" by W. B. YEATS, a work that Joyce later integrated with telling effect into the final scene of the Circe episode (chapter 15) of *Ulysses,* where the semiconscious Stephen Dedalus quotes Yeats's opening lines to an incredulous Leopold Bloom.

**"My love is in a light attire"** Poem 8 (VII); this three-stanza poem describes the speaker's beloved as she moves "Among the apple-trees." The last lines of the poem, however, may also suggest that she is urinating: "My love goes lightly, holding up / Her dress with dainty hand." This twist adds a humorous touch to the poem and balances the solemnity in the poet's treatment of love. It also suggests a variant reading of the title of the suite of songs. Prior to its appearance in *Chamber Music,* it was published under the title "Song" in the August 1904 issue of the Dublin journal DANA.

**"Winds of May, that dance on the sea"** Poem 9 (IX); here the poet longs to find his love and addresses the dancing winds of May with a simple and direct question: "Saw you my true love anywhere?" The promise of spring awakens in the lonely speaker the hope of the union of love. In the final line of the second and last stanza of the poem, the speaker lyrically confesses that "Love is unhappy when love is away!"

Although this poem was composed sometime around 1902, before Joyce met Nora Barnacle, and published in 1907, Joyce had the last line engraved on the tablet of a necklace that he designed and sent to Nora in September 1909, when he was in Dublin without her; Nora had stayed behind in Trieste. Explaining to her his gift and purpose, Joyce wrote: "On the face [of the necklace's tablet] the words are *Love is unhappy* and the words on the back are *When Love is away.* The five dice mean the five years of trial and misunderstanding, and the tablet which unites the chain tells of the strange sadness we felt and our suffering when we were divided" (*Letters,* II.245–246).

**"Because your voice was at my side"** Poem 10 (XVII); this poem focuses on the conflict that can arise between the competing demands of romantic love and Platonic friendship. The speaker's growing affection for a young woman causes estrangement between him and a friend. The cooling of this friendship presages the estrangement of the lovers themselves that comes toward the end of the suite of songs. Richard Ellmann speculates that the origin of this poem arose from an actual occurrence in Joyce's life. (For additional information see *Letters,* II.46 and 126.)

**"O Sweetheart, hear you"** Poem 11 (XVIII); the speaker tells his beloved the sorrow he feels at the betrayal of his friends. But at the same time he gratefully acknowledges the emotional consolation he derives from the physical satisfaction of their love. The poem was first published in the July 1904 issue of the British periodical the SPEAKER. (For further information see *Letters,* II.70.)

**"I would in that sweet bosom be"** Poem 12 (VI); the poet-speaker desires to escape from the harshness of the world and find shelter within the heart of his beloved. In a September 1909 letter to Nora, Joyce quoted this poem in full when she was in Trieste and he in Dublin without her (see *Letters,* II.248–250). This poem was first published under the title "A Wish" in the October 8, 1904, issue of the London journal the *Speaker* (with the second and third lines transposed). (For further details relating to the poem, see *Letters,* II.69–70.)

**"Bright cap and streamers"** Poem 13 (X); this poem is constructed in two stanzas of eight lines each. The first stanza introduces the lively image of a minstrel, or jester, singing songs of love. In the second stanza the singer on a more serious note invites his sweetheart to step from dreaming about love to love itself.

**"In the dark pine-wood"** Poem 14 (XX); the speaker thinks of the "deep cool shadow" of the pine wood, and imagines how pleasurable it would be to lie there at noon with the woman he loves. The poem ends with the speaker calling out to his beloved to come away with him to the woods. In 1905 Joyce sent this poem to the *Saturday Review,* but the editors declined to publish it. (See *Letters,* II.100.)

**"Go seek her out all courteously"** Poem 15 (XIII); here the speaker invokes the wind to bid his sweetheart the bridal blessings soon to come. As in other poems of the suite but especially here, the speaker uses vental imagery to convey the unobtrusive softness of his love.

**"Bid adieu to girlish days"** Poem 16 (XI); the mood of this poem is seductive. The young poet, happy that love "is come to woo," urges the girl to welcome the moment and "undo the snood / That is the sign of maidenhood." The sexual overtones of the poem become even more vivid in the light of Joyce's original 1905 arrangement of the complete suite of songs (see above, "The Arrangement of the Poems"), in which it immediately precedes poem XIV, "My dove, my beautiful one," the suite's climax and central poem. Joyce had earlier labeled this poem "my obscene song" (see *Letters,* II.73).

In 1904 Joyce had tried unsuccessfully to publish the poem in the Dublin magazine *Dana.* He also submitted it to *Harper's* in January 1905, but again it was rejected. With two other poems from *Chamber Music* (I and XII), "Bid adieu to girlish days" was anthologized in *The Dublin Book of Irish Verse* (1909), edited by John Cooke. (This is the first time a work by Joyce was anthologized.)

Joyce's partiality toward this poem can also be seen in his efforts to have it set to music. In 1909 he tried actively to interest G. Molyneux Palmer in setting the poem musically: "It seems to me a pity you did not do the song 'Bid adieu' which I tried to music myself and hope you may turn to it some day" (*Letters,* II.227). (For more information see *Letters,* II.73, 77, 80, 117, and 227. Palmer eventually did set the poem to music.)

**"My dove, my beautiful one"** Poem 17 (XIV); in this four-stanza poem, the speaker calls to his love to awaken and rise from her bed, for he wishes her to come to him by the cedar tree where he awaits her. The poem celebrates the imminent consummation of love and its sensuous imagery directly alludes to the Song of Songs (*cf.* 5:1–16). The biblical image of the cedar, for instance, evokes the regal beauty of a majestic tree known for its fragrance and durability. In a letter to G. Molyneux Palmer of July 19, 1909, Joyce characterizes "My dove, my beautiful one" as "[t]he central song" of the collection (*Letters,* I.67). The movement of the suite shifts downward after this poem. (See above, "The Arrangement of the Poems.")

**"Be not sad because all men"** Poem 18 (XIX); in this poem the speaker comforts his sweetheart after the consummation of their love, described in "My dove, my beautiful one" (poem XIV), and consolingly urges her to be at peace with herself again. The effect Joyce intended is more poignant in his 1905 arrangement of *Chamber Music,* in which "Be not sad because all men" is the 18th poem and "My dove, my beautiful one" is 17th. This juxtaposition of the poems gives the reader a fuller sense of the complementary feelings of sensuality and sentimentality that comprise the concept of mature love.

**"From dewy dreams, my soul, arise"** Poem 19 (XV); this poem is made up of three four-line stanzas. In the first, the speaker addresses his soul, bidding it to rise from sleep and dreams, and to awaken to the new day. The next stanza alludes to the waking world that is now displacing sleep, while the final stanza offers a lyrical picture of the spirits of day rousing themselves.

**"This heart that flutters near my heart"** Poem 20 (XXIII); the first stanza proclaims the speaker's happiness at being close to the fluttering heart of his beloved. The apt use of the adjective *flutter* in the poem suggests the fleeting nature of love and anticipates the avian imagery in the second stanza where wrens store up treasures in their nests. The bird's nest is a metaphor for the heart as the repository in which the poet has placed so much of himself. The speaker urges his beloved to be at least as wise as the wrens and treasure the happiness of their love, though it may live but a day.

**"Silently she's combing"** Poem 21 (XXIV); in the first two stanzas, a narrative voice creates a languorous atmosphere and describes a woman in front of a mirror combing her hair. In the last two stanzas the speaker entreats the woman to stop her combing, in which he detects a narcissism that will exclude him (and others) from her love. According to Richard Ellmann, Arthur Symons helped secure the publication of this poem in the May 14, 1904, issue of the *Saturday Review.*

**"O cool is the valley now"** Poem 22 (XVI); this poem combines efforts at seduction with a lyrical description of the cool and pleasant valley where the speaker wishes to take his beloved.

**"O, it was out by Donnycarney"** Poem 23 (XXXI); this poem recollects a pleasant summer evening's walk in Donnycarney with the speaker's beloved. Both Adolph Mann and G. Molyneux Palmer set this poem to music. Palmer sent a transcription of the song to Joyce, who was in Trieste. The manuscript is presently in Joyce's Trieste library, now at the University of Texas. (For further details see *Letters,* II.287 and III.35.)

**"Of that so sweet imprisonment"** Poem 24 (XXII); the speaker addresses his beloved through metaphors of confinement. He calls her arms a prison but declares his compliance with detention in her embrace.

**"Thou leanest to the shell of night"** Poem 25 (XXVI); in the poem's first stanza, the speaker, discerning that his beloved is leaning "a divining ear" to "the shell of night," rhetorically inquires of her the sound that causes her heart to fear. In the second stanza, the speaker attempts to answer his own question by identifying her fearful mood with that of Coleridge or Shakespeare reading "some strange name" in Purchas or Holinshed, and creating "a mad tale," ghostly and terrifying. Joyce's allusions are obvious. Coleridge was inspired to write his visionary poem "Kubla Khan or, a Vision in a Dream" by reading Purchas. Holinshed was the major source behind Shakespeare's *Macbeth* and *King Lear.*

This poem was also published separately, along with "What counsel has the hooded moon" (XII), in the November 1904 issue of the London journal *Venture.* (For additional details see *Letters,* II.236–237.)

**"What counsel has the hooded moon"** Poem 26 (XII); this poem appeared with "Thou leanest to the shell of night" in the November 1904 issue of the London journal *Venture.* According to Stanislaus Joyce, his brother composed this poem one evening after walking with Mary Sheehy; Joyce wrote down the verses on the inside of a cigarette box that he had torn open. Stephen Dedalus follows the same procedure when composing the "Villanelle of the Temptress" in chapter V of *A Portrait of the Artist as a Young Man.* The reference that the poem makes to "the hooded moon" evokes what Joyce, or at least the speaker of the poem, had seen on his walk, and it touches upon the conflicting impulses of desire and self-restraint. (For further details see *Letters,* II.72 and 238n. 4.)

**"Though I thy Mithridates were"** Poem 27 (XXVII); in this poem, the speaker—who likens himself to Mithridates, king of Pontus (120–63 B.C.E.), a man so immune to poison that when his country was conquered by the Romans he was unable to commit suicide and had to be slain by a Gaul at his own order—admits his vulnerability, for he fears a poison in the "malice" of his beloved's "tenderness." A comment by Joyce in a November 1906 letter to his brother Stanislaus may shed some light on the poem's meaning: "a lot of this talk about love is nonsense. A woman's love is always maternal and egoistic. A man, on the contrary, . . . possesses a fund of genuine affection for the 'beloved' or 'once beloved' object" (*Letters,* II.192). The last lines of the poem elaborate upon the falseness of love. Joyce wrote the first version of this poem in mid-1904 but subsequently revised it. (For additional details see *Letters,* II.92, 148, and 220.)

**"Gentle lady, do not sing"** Poem 28 (XXVIII); this poem has two brief stanzas of four lines each. The speaker urges his "gentle lady" to "lay aside sadness" and not lament the end of love, since "in the grave all love shall sleep" and be forgotten.

While visiting in Dublin with his son George in 1909, Joyce wrote to his Nora: "You were not in a sense the girl for whom I had dreamed and written . . . poems like 'Gentle lady' or 'Thou leanest to the shell of night.' But then I saw that the beauty of your soul outshone that of my verses" (*Letters,* II.237). (For more information see *Letters,* II.96 and III.35.)

**"Lightly come or lightly go"** Poem 29 (XXV); this poem combines a straightforward articulation of the carpe diem theme with the speaker's determination not to let sorrow overcome the spirit. It recommends going lightly through life despite one's undeniable awareness of signs presaging sorrow, and indeed it calls for lighthearted sentiments even "[w]hen the heart is heaviest." (According to

Joyce's brother Stanislaus, this poem was—as was XII—inspired by Mary Sheehy; see *The Complete Dublin Diary of Stanislaus Joyce,* 24. Also see *Letters,* II.238n. 4.)

**"Dear heart, why will you use me so?"** Poem 30 (XXIX); in this three-stanza poem, the speaker's feelings express his realization of the dissolution of love, which he attributes to his beloved, and his fears of being made love's fool, "But you, dear love, too dear to me, / Alas! why will you use me so?"

**"Rain has fallen all the day"** Poem 31 (XXXII); this poem, with its autumnal imagery of rain and fallen leaves, reflects the somber mood of the speaker. The poet is resigned to express to his beloved the sentiments of his heart, though he sees their inevitable separation.

**"Love came to us in time gone by"** Poem 32 (XXX); in the opening lines of the poem, the speaker recalls—perhaps with a hint of nostalgia—the beginning of love, when one (the speaker) was fearful and the other (the girl) shy, and remembers that he and his beloved "were grave lovers." The tone shifts perceptibly, and in a voice more stoic than nostalgic the speaker acknowledges that love is gone, and he welcomes "the ways that we shall go upon."

**"Now, O now, in this brown land"** Poem 33 (XXXIII); in sharp contrast to the opening song of the suite, where "Strings in the earth and air / Make music sweet" (I), the speaker now realizes that he and his beloved will no longer together hear their songs of love. They must part "at close of day," but without grieving.

**"Sleep now, O sleep now"** Poem 34 (XXXIV); throughout the poem's three stanzas, the speaker urges sleep as a means of finding peace and soothing an "unquiet heart," for winter counters with " 'Sleep no more.' " (The reference to *Macbeth* 2.3.39 is obvious.) Joyce told the composer C. Molyneux Palmer in a letter of July 19, 1909, that this verse is "vitally the end of the book. XXXV and XXXVI are tailpieces just as I and III are preludes" (*Letters,* I.67). In a letter of February 23, 1921, Joyce told Palmer that " 'Sleep now' is in its place at the end of the diminuendo movement and the last two songs are intended to represent the awakening of the mind" (*Letters,* I.158). (For additional details see *Letters,* II.181 and 236.)

**"All day I hear the noise of waters"** Poem 35 (XXXV); this poem Joyce added in 1906. In the poem, the lonely speaker, like a solitary seabird, hears only the noise of waters and the sound of crying winds, foreshadowing a bleak and cold future.

This poem and poem XXXVI were not originally part of Joyce's 1905 arrangement of *Chamber Music,* but were added to the sequence by Stanislaus Joyce (see *Letters,* II.181; Joyce questions Stanislaus's placement of this poem and others in the suite).

Joyce composed "All day I hear the noise of waters" around December 1902, when he wrote out a copy of the poem on a postcard with his photograph and sent it to J. F. BYRNE (see *Letters,* II.20–21, and Richard Ellmann's *James Joyce,* illustration VII). In a letter to Joyce in December 1902, Yeats commented: "I think the poem that you have sent me has a charming rhythm in the second stanza, but I think it is not one of the best of your lyrics as a whole. I think that the thought is a little thin" (*Letters,* II.23). (For further information see *Letters,* I.67 and II.20–21, 23–24, and 181.)

**"I hear an army charging upon the land"** Poem 36 (XXXVI); like the previous poem, Joyce added this one to the suite in 1906; it serves as the final poem in *Chamber Music.* Its sweeping description of powerful forces jars against the highly individual evocation of the lover in the final two lines. This in turn sets the poem in sharp contrast to the more lyrical verses that make up the bulk of the suite.

On February 8, 1903, Joyce sent an early version of this work to his brother Stanislaus (see *Letters,* II.28). Katharine Tynan included this poem in her 1913 anthology *The Wild Harp, A Selection of Irish Poetry* and in January 1914 Ezra POUND sought permission from Joyce to include "I hear an army" in a collection of verse entitled *Des Imagistes,* which was published later in that year (see *Letters,* II.328). The contact marked the beginning of Pound's fervent efforts—carried on for nearly a decade—to bring Joyce's work to general public attention. (For further information see *Letters,* I.67, in which Joyce describes this poem as the "tailpiece" of the suite, and *Letters,* II.10n.5, 181, 328, 331, 351, 356, 381, and 405.)

For additional comments on *Chamber Music,* see *Letters,* I.39, 54, 56, 59, 65–70, 73, 98, 110, 116, 121, 127, 158–159, and 287; II.3, 70, 88, 110–112, 124, 128, 172, 176, 178–182, 184, 192, 216–217, 219–221, 223–224, 227–228, 233, 237, 244, 248, 258, 269–270, 277–278, 280, 284–285, 296, 304–305, 320–322, 332–334, 352, 354, 394, 399, 418, 427, 434, and 462; and III.35, 47, 55, 83, 167, and 365–366.

## CONTEMPORARY REVIEWS OF *CHAMBER MUSIC*

Joyce's university classmate and friend Thomas Kettle wrote one of the first reviews of *Chamber Music;* it appeared in the *Freeman's Journal* on June 1, 1907:

> Those who remember University College life of five years back will have many memories of Mr. Joyce. Wilful, fastidious, a lover of elfish paradoxes, he was to the men of his time the very voice and embodiment of the literary spirit. His work, never very voluminous, had from the first a rare and exquisite accent. One still goes back to the files of St Stephen's, to the *Saturday Review,* the *Homestead,* to various occasional magazines to find these lyrics and stories which, although at first reading so slight and frail, still hold one curiously by their integrity of form. *Chamber Music* is a collection of the best of these delicate verses, which have, each of them, the bright beauty of a crystal. The title of the book evokes that atmosphere of remoteness, restraint, accomplished execution characteristic of its whole contents.
>
> There is but one theme behind the music, a love, gracious, and, in its way, strangely intense, but fashioned by temperamental and literary moulds, too strict to permit it to pass over into the great tumult of passion. The inspiration of the book is almost entirely literary. There is no trace of the folklore, folk dialect, or even the national feeling that have coloured the work of practically every writer in contemporary Ireland. Neither is there any sense of that modern point of view which consumes all life in the language of problems. It is clear, delicate, distinguished playing with harps, with wood birds, with Paul Verlaine.
>
> But the only possible criticism of poetry is quotation.
>
> I
> Strings in the earth and air
> Make music sweet;
> Strings by the river where
> The willows meet.
>
> There's music along the river
> For Love wanders there,
> Pale flowers on his mantle,
> Dark leaves on his hair.
>
> All softly playing,
> With head to the music bent,
> And fingers straying
> Upon an instrument.
>
> XXVIII
> Gentle lady, do not sing
> Sad songs about the end of love;
> Lay aside sadness and sing,
> How love that passes is enough
>
> Sing about the long deep sleep
> Of lovers that are dead and how
> In the grave all love shall sleep.
> Love is aweary now.
>
> Mr. Joyce's book is one that all his old friends will, with a curious pleasure, add to their shelves, and that will earn him many new friends.

The following unsigned review appeared in the June 1907 issue of *Bookman* (xxxii): 113:

> A little book of poetry which charms, provokes criticism, and charms again. Mr. Joyce has a touch reminiscent of the sixteenth century poets, with here and there a break in his lines'

smoothness which can only be smoothed by an old-time stress on the syllable, such as Vaughan and Herbert demanded. At times there are bold liberties taken with rhyme and rhythm; but there is so much of music and quaintness in the little volume that we give praise instead of censure.

The literary journalist and editor of *Savoy* Arthur Symons wrote a review of *Chamber Music* that appeared in the *Nation,* 1 (June 22, 1907): 639. Symons was also a strong supporter of the French symbolist movement and his book, *The Symbolist Movement in Literature,* was widely influential. Joyce himself read it while a student at University College, Dublin, and its influence on him was significant.

> *Chamber Music,* by James Joyce, an Irishman, who was in no Irish movement, literary or national, has not anything obviously Celtic in its manner. The book is tiny, there are 37 pages, with a poem on each page. And they are all so singularly good, so firm and delicate, and yet so full of music and suggestion, that I can hardly choose between them; they are almost all of an equal merit. Here is one of the finest:
>
> Gentle lady, do not sing
> Sad songs about the end of love;
> Lay aside sadness and sing
> How love that passes is enough.
>
> Sing about the long deep sleep
> Of lovers that are dead and how
> In the grave all love shall sleep.
> Love is aweary now.
>
> No one who has not tried can realize how difficult it is to do such tiny evanescent things as that; for it is to evoke, not only roses in mid-winter, but the very dew of the roses. Sometimes I am reminded of Elizabethan, but more often Jacobean, lyrics; there is more than sweetness, there is now and then the sharp prose touch, as in *Rochester,* which gives a kind of malice to sentiment:
>
> For elegant and antique phrase,
> Dearest, my lips wax all too wise;
> Nor have I known a love whose praise
> Our piping poets solemnize,
> Neither is love where may not be
> Ever so little falsity.
>
> There is a rare kind of poetry to be made out of the kind or unkind insinuation of lovers, who are always in a state of rapture, even when the mood comes for singing, and it may, like this love-poet, be turned to a new harmony.
>
> And all for some strange name he read,
> In Purchase or in Holinshed.
>
> There is no substance at all in these songs, which hardly hint at a story; but they are like a whispering clavichord that someone plays in the evening, when it is getting dark. They are full of ghostly old tunes, that were never young, and will never be old, played on an old instrument. If poetry is to be a thing overheard, these songs, certainly, will justify the definition. They are so slight, as a drawing of Whistler is slight, that their entire beauty will not be discovered by those who go to poetry for anything but its perfume. But to those who care only for what is essentially poetry in a poem, they will seem to have so much the more value by all they omit. There is only just enough, but these instants are, in Browning's phrase, "made eternity."
>
> Perhaps the rare quality of these songs might captivate certain readers. Such a song as *Bright Cap and Streamers* or *Silently She's Combing* ought to catch every fancy, and the graver poems ought to awaken every imagination. But if anything in art is small, and merely good, without anything but that fact to recommend it, it has usually to wait a long time for recognition. People are so afraid of following even an impulse, fearing that they may be mistaken. How unlikely it seems, does it not, that any new thing should come suddenly into the world and be beautiful?

In 1914, when Joyce was reading the proofs for *Dubliners,* he sent his publisher, Grant Richards, excerpts of reviews of *Chamber Music* that he had a printer reproduce. Joyce intended that they be used as inserts in the press copies of the book. The following are a few quotations. (See *Letters,* II.332–333.)

*Daily News:* Light and evanescent, pretty and fragile. . . . His poems are attempts at music: he has tried to express one art in terms of another. His aim has been to catch in his great lyrical masters. . . . His poems have at once the music and the want of music of a harpstring played on by the winds in some forest of broceliande.

*Evening Standard:* Pretty lyrics with a delusive title.

*Manchester Guardian:* A welcome contribution to contemporary poetry. Here are thirty-six lyrics of quite notable beauty. . . . Something of the spirit of Waller and Herrick . . . grace and simplicity . . . an elegance and delicacy that are as uncommon as they are perilous. At their best they reveal a rare musical quality. His muse is a gently tender spirit that knows smiles and tears, the rain, the dew and the morning sun.

*Nottingham Guardian:* Lovers of verse will delight in many of the pieces for their simple unaffected merit. 'Chamber Music' has a tuneful ring befitting the title and both the rhythm and the smoothness of his lines are excellent.

*Irish Daily Independent:* . . . Music in verse, poems, sweet, reposeful and sublime; poems that lying in the shade amid the scent of new-mown hay one would read and dream on, forgetful of the workaday world.

*Scotsman:* A volume of graceful verse: it contains some little gems of real beauty.

*Country Life:* A very promising little volume.

## *The Critical Writings of James Joyce* (1959)

Edited by Ellsworth Mason and Richard Ellmann, this volume, published in 1959, is a collection of 57 pieces written by Joyce over a 40-year period, from about 1896 to 1937. The volume contains essays, book reviews, lectures, newspaper articles, broadsides in verse, letters to editors, and program notes. The following chronologically ordered list is from the book's table of contents: "Trust Not Appearances" (1896?); "Force" (1898); "The Study of Languages" (1898/99?); "Royal Hibernian Academy 'Ecce Homo' " (1899); "Drama and Life" (1900); "Ibsen's New Drama" (1900); "The Day of the Rabblement" (1901); "James Clarence Mangan" (first of two essays, 1902); "An Irish Poet" (1902); "George Meredith" (1902); "Today and Tomorrow in Ireland" (1903); "A Suave Philosophy" (1903); "An Effort at Precision in Thinking" (1903); "Colonial Verses" (1903); "Catilina" (1903); "The Soul of Ireland" (1903); "The Motor Derby" (1903); "Aristotle on Education" (1903); "A Ne'er-Do-Well" (1903); "Empire Building" (1903); "New Fiction" (1903); "The Mettle of the Pasture" (1903); "A Peep into History" (1903); "A French Religious Novel" (1903); "Unequal Verse" (1903); "Mr. Arnold Graves' New York" (1903); "A Neglected Poet" (1903); "Mr. Mason's Novels" (1903); "The Bruno Philosophy" (1903); "Humanism" (1903); "Shakespeare Explained" (1903); "Borlase and Son" (1903); "Aesthetics: I. The Paris Notebook, II. The Pola Notebook" (1903/04); "The Holy Office" (1904); "Ireland, Island of Saints and Sages" (1907); "James Clarence Mangan" (second of two essays, 1907); "Fenianism" (1907); "Home Rule Comes of Age" (1907); "Ireland at the Bar" (1907); "Oscar Wilde: The Poet of 'Salomé' " (1909); "Bernard Shaw's Battle with the Censor" (1909); "The Home Rule Comet" (1910); "William Blake" (1912); "The Shade of Parnell" (1912); "The City of the Tribes" (1912); "The Mirage of the Fisherman of Aran" (1912); "Politics and Cattle Disease" (1912); "Gas from a Burner" (1912); "Dooleysprudence" (1916); "Programme Notes for the English Players" (1918/19; includes Joyce's notes for *The Twelve Pound Look* by J. M. Barrie, *Riders to the Sea* by John Synge, *The Dark Lady of the Sonnets* by G. B. Shaw and *The Heather Field* by Edward Martyn); "Letter on Pound" (1925); "Letter on Hardy" (1928); "Letter on Svevo" (1929); "From a Banned Writer to a Banned Singer" (1932); "Ad-Writer" (1932); "Epilogue to Ibsen's *Ghosts*" (1934); and "Communication de M. James Joyce sur le Droit Moral des Écrivains" (1937).

Since the publication of *The Critical Writings of James Joyce* in 1959, a new edition, edited with an introduction and notes by Kevin Barry and with the Italian pieces translated by Conor Deane, was published by Oxford University Press, in 2000, under the title *James Joyce: Occasional, Critical, and Political Writing.*

## THE CONTENTS OF *THE CRITICAL WRITINGS*

The pieces in the volume are covered below in alphabetical order.

**"Ad-Writer"** This is the title given to Joyce's May 22, 1932, letter to Constant Huntington at G. Putnam's Sons Ltd., publisher of the English translation of a novel by Italo SVEVO (Ettore SCHMITZ), *As a Man Grows Older* (1932), for which Joyce had been asked to write the preface. Despite his longtime friendship with Schmitz, who had once been his language student in TRIESTE, Joyce followed his long-standing practice of refusing to write such commentaries for anyone. Stanislaus JOYCE eventually wrote the preface, but the publisher pressed James Joyce for some sort of comment. Joyce composed "Ad-Writer" as a witty response, explaining that he could add nothing to what had already been said by his "learned friend" and "professor of English at the University of Trieste" (*CW* 269).

"Ad-Writer" was first published in *A James Joyce Yearbook* (1949), edited by Maria Jolas. In addition to being reprinted in *The Critical Writings of James Joyce* (1959), it also appears in *Letters,* III.245–246.

**"Aesthetics"** This title was given by Ellsworth MASON and Richard ELLMANN to chapter 33 of *The Critical Writings of James Joyce.* That section contains "The Paris Notebook" and "The Pola Notebook," statements on aesthetic theory written by Joyce when he was in his early 20s and formulating the aesthetic and artistic values that would guide his writing over the following years.

"The Paris Notebook" consists of a series of short observations written in February and March 1903 following Joyce's return to Paris after spending the Christmas holidays in Ireland. In both form and content its entries retain the habits (and some of the pedantry) of academic composition that Joyce developed while a student at University College, Dublin. He begins, in Aristotelian fashion, by offering fairly conventional distinctions between tragedy and comedy. He then takes up the "three conditions of art: the lyrical, the epical and the dramatic." He goes on to explore the characterizing elements of a piece of art, and moves toward a definition of art itself. Finally, through a dialectically constituted series of questions and answers, he seeks to refine that concept of art.

The "Pola Notebook" contains just three entries, written on the 7th, 15th, and 16th of November 1904, shortly after Joyce and Nora Barnacle had first settled in the city where Joyce had found a job as an English-language teacher at the local Berlitz school. In this writing, Joyce moves from an Aristotelian investigation of aesthetics to one grounded in the SCHOLASTICISM of St. THOMAS AQUINAS. In an approach that anticipates the ontological efforts of Stephen Dedalus in *A Portrait of the Artist as a Young Man,* Joyce in three short paragraphs offers in truncated form his impressions of the nature of the good, the nature of beauty, and, finally, the act of apprehension.

Although these remarks on aesthetics are quite brief, they serve two important functions for students of Joyce. They provide a useful glimpse into Joyce's emerging creative consciousness, and they give us a clear sense of the extra-textual elements that influenced all his work. Additionally, these comments so clearly anticipate the views on art and aesthetics put forward in *Stephen Hero* and *A Portrait of the Artist as a Young Man* that, in effect, they provide a view of the early stages of the composition of these works.

**"Aristotle on Education"** This is the title given by the editors to Joyce's untitled review of John Burnet's *Aristotle on Education,* which first appeared in the September 3, 1903, issue of the *DAILY EXPRESS.* Joyce's review dismisses Burnet's work as a random and incomplete compilation of Aristotle's views, and judges the book as making no "valuable addition to philosophical literature." However, Joyce grudgingly accepts Burnet's claim that the book offers a useful corrective to the efforts of Émile Combes to use the ideas of Aristotle to justify the movement to secularize the French educational system.

**"Bernard Shaw's Battle with the Censor: *The Shewing-Up of Blanco Posnet*"** This was an article written by Joyce on Shaw's censored one-act play, *The Shewing-Up of Blanco Posnet.* Joyce composed the piece in Italian for the Trieste newspaper, *Il* PICCOLO DELLA SERA, in which it appeared under the title "La Battaglia Fra Bernard Shaw e la Censura. 'Blanco Posnet Smascherato' " on September 5, 1909.

Shaw's play concerns the trial of a thief, Blanco Posnet, who has been arrested for giving a stolen horse to a woman who was trying to reach a distant town in order to save the life of her sick child. The trial focuses on Posnet's denunciation of the lack of morality in the judicial system. The Lord Chamberlain of England had banned productions of the play in the United Kingdom because of its apparently blasphemous language. Although the Lord Chamberlain's jurisdiction did not extend to Dublin, he tried, unsuccessfully, to prevent its performance there. The play had its premiere on August 25, 1909, at the ABBEY THEATRE, whose codirectors, William Butler YEATS and Lady Augusta GREGORY, had been instrumental in securing its production.

Joyce, with his son, was in Ireland visiting his family, and he had arranged beforehand to cover the opening performance of the play for *Il Piccolo della Sera.* In the article that he wrote afterward, Joyce applauds the Abbey's victory over censorship, a problem that had begun to plague his own writings. (By this time Joyce had already endured the efforts of Grant RICHARDS to bowdlerize *Dubliners.*) Nonetheless, Joyce's review is not wholly uncritical. He accuses Shaw of sermonizing—calling him "a born preacher"—and of failing to make art "convincing as drama."

**"Borlase and Son"** This is Joyce's review of T. Baron Russell's novel *Borlase and Son,* which appeared in the *DAILY EXPRESS* on November 19, 1903, in untitled form. MASON and ELLMANN gave it a title when they reprinted the review. In his critique, Joyce stresses the realism of the work and the "unsentimental vigour" (*CW* 139) with which Russell depicts the suburban mind and the Armenian exiles living in Peckham Rye. In general, Joyce finds merit in Russell's novel.

**"Bruno Philosophy, The"** This is the title given to Joyce's review of J. Lewis McIntyre's *Giordano Bruno,* which was published in the *DAILY EXPRESS* on October 30, 1903. Joyce's review, sympathetic in tone toward the Italian Renaissance philosopher Giordano BRUNO, reveals at once a knowledge of his life and thought and an enthusiasm for his ideas. Throughout his short review, Joyce highlights McIntyre's assessment of Bruno's contribution to Western philosophy. By noting in the first sentence the paucity of books written in English on Bruno's life and thought, Joyce imparts a sense of importance to him as well as to McIntyre's critical study.

**"Catilina"** This is Joyce's review of a French translation of *Catilina* (1848), an early play by Henrik IBSEN. The review first appeared in the English literary journal *SPEAKER* on March 21, 1903. Joyce begins by briefly surveying the translators' preface, which contains biographical information on the history of the play, written when the playwright was a 20-year-old student. Although the Ibsen of *Catilina,* Joyce remarks, is not the Ibsen of his later social dramas, this play does contain the sort of naturalistic and social elements found in his later works. Joyce does not refrain from judging the failure of Ibsen's critics to assess accurately his works, and he notes that if *Catilina* has little merit as a work of art, it nonetheless comprises an example of Ibsen's early dramatic propensities and demonstrates what directors and publishers overlooked: "an original and capable writer struggling with a form that is not his own" (*CW* 101).

**"City of the Tribes, The"** This is an English translation of the title of a short travel piece written by Joyce for the Trieste newspaper *Il* PICCOLO DELLA SERA while he was visiting Galway in August 1912. One of several articles Joyce wrote in Italian for this newspaper over a five-year period, it was published that same month under the title "*La Città delle Tribù; Ricordi Italiani in un Porto Irlandese*" (The city of tribes: Italian echoes in an Irish port).

In this article, Joyce identifies a few broad connections among social, cultural, and historical conditions in Italy and those in Galway, and offers a brief account of Galway's social history, highlighting the story of the city's chief magistrate, James Lynch Fitz-Stephen, who presided over the hanging of his own son, Walter Lynch, in 1493. Most likely with this story resonating in his mind, Joyce used the name Lynch in *A Portrait of the Artist as a Young Man* and *Ulysses* as the fictional surname of the character based upon his erstwhile friend and sometime betrayer, Vincent COSGRAVE. See "Mirage of the Fisherman of Aran, the, England's Safety Valve in Case of War," below.

**"Colonial Verses"** Joyce's review of Clive Phillips-Wolley's *Songs of an English Esau,* a pithy assessment at little more than 100 words, appeared with two other reviews by Joyce (see their entries below)—one, entitled "A Suave Philosophy," of *The Soul of a People* by H. Fielding-Hall and the other, "An Effort at Precision in Thinking," of *Colloquies of Common People* by James Anstie—in the February 6, 1903, issue of the *DAILY EXPRESS.* Joyce's brief but sardonic evaluation focuses on the tone and subject matter of Phillips-Wolley's verses: "His verse is for the most part loyal, and where it is not, it describes Canadian scenery."

**"Communication de M. James Joyce sur le Droit Moral des Écrivains"** This is the title of Joyce's address to the 15th International P.E.N. Congress held in Paris June 20–27, 1937. (P.E.N. is the abbreviation of the International Association of Poets, Playwrights, Editors, Essayists and Novelists.) Joyce delivered the address in French and spoke of the decision by the United States District Court in New York prohibiting the pirated publication of *Ulysses* in the United States by Samuel ROTH (*Joyce* v. *Two Worlds Monthly and Samuel Roth*). Joyce asserted that the law must always reinforce and protect what he believed is the natural right authors have over their works.

**"Day of the Rabblement, The"** This was an essay written in 1901 expressing Joyce's disillusionment with the IRISH LITERARY THEATRE for succumbing to the demands of Irish nationalism and provincial attitudes. The title is an indictment of the theater's failure to make good on its claim to wage "war against commercialism and vulgarity" and reflects Joyce's cynicism toward a theater movement that comes to "terms with the rabblement." Joyce wrote the article in October and submitted it to the editor of ST STEPHEN's magazine, a newly founded undergraduate journal at University College, Dublin. The article was rejected by the Rev. Henry BROWNE, SJ, the magazine's faculty adviser. Joyce appealed the decision to the president of the college but got no satisfaction. He then joined with a classmate, Francis Skeffington, whose essay on women's rights, "A Forgotten Aspect of the University Question," had also been rejected by Father Browne (see Francis SHEEHY-SKEFFINGTON). Together Joyce and Skeffington had their essays printed privately and, with the help of Stanislaus JOYCE, they distributed about 85 copies.

**"Dooleysprudence"** This is the title of Joyce's short, satiric piece mocking the nations that had become combatants in World War I. It was written in 1916 while Joyce was living in neutral Switzerland, and depicts the uninvolved Mr. Dooley, whose tranquil life is juxtaposed with the war. The character of Mr. Dooley is derived from the philosophical tavern keeper created by the Irish-American humorist Finley Peter Dunne, who was also the subject of a popular song with which Joyce was familiar, "Mr. Dooley," by Billy Jerome (1901). "Dooleysprudence" was first published in *The Critical Writings of James Joyce.*

**"Drama and Life"** This is the title of a paper on the nature of drama and its relation to life that Joyce delivered before the Literary and Historical Society at UNIVERSITY COLLEGE, DUBLIN, on January 20, 1900, shortly before his 18th birthday.

The essay questions the conventional relationship between what occurs on stage and what passes in our daily existence. Joyce notes that in the new drama "the interplay of passions to portray truth" now dominates the consciousnesses of the playwright and the audience, and that this new form "will be for the future at war with convention." In this changing relationship, he notes the way that one looks at drama also has shifted: "It is hardly possible to criticize *The Wild Duck,* for instance; one can only brood upon it as upon a personal woe." In this respect, Joyce rejects approaches to drama that suppress aesthetic response in favor of descriptive explication. Despite the immaturity of some elements of this essay, with slight modification the notions Joyce puts forward in the paper are evident in his later work, particularly in the character of Stephen in *Stephen Hero* and *A Portrait of the Artist as a Young Man,* and they serve as a useful gloss to the aesthetic and artistic views that animated all of his writing from a young age.

**"Effort at Precision in Thinking, An"** This was the title given to Joyce's review of James Anstie's *Colloquies of Common People,* which appeared with two other reviews, "Colonial Verses" (see above) and "A Suave Philosophy" (see below), in the February 6, 1903, issue of the DAILY EXPRESS; it is reprinted in *The Critical Writings of James Joyce* (1959). In the review, Joyce dismisses Anstie's collection of formal conversations or colloquies, as a work actually filled with the discourse of uncommon people, for in Joyce's view no common person could sustain the level of tedium and fascination with minute and seemingly irrelevant detail that the speakers in this work evince.

**"Empire Building"** This is the title used to identify a letter Joyce wrote in 1903, apparently intended for publication in a newspaper but only published posthumously in 1959 in *The Critical Writings of James Joyce.* (The title is taken from the first two words of the essay, and was presumably given to the piece by Ellsworth MASON and Richard ELLMANN, the volume's editors.) Joyce addresses the mistreatment of sailors by the French adventurer and self-proclaimed empire builder Jacques Lebaudy. Acting privately, Lebaudy had sailed around the coast of northern Africa in the summer of 1903 with a force of mercenaries with whom he intended to carve out a personal fiefdom. According to Joyce, as a result of this voyage, Lebaudy was being sued by two sailors for "damages on account of the hardships and diseases" that they suffered through his neglect, and their subsequent capture by inhabitants of the land that Lebaudy wished to seize. (Ultimately the French government intervened to secure their release.) Joyce's letter expresses his disgust that the entire affair was being taken so lightly by the French government and by the general public.

**"Epilogue to Ibsen's *Ghosts*"** This is a poem written in April 1934 after Joyce had seen a performance of Ibsen's play the month before at the Théâtre des Champs-Élysées in Paris. Ibsen's recurring themes of the conflict of love and duty and the clash of guilt and responsibility are ironically presented by Joyce through the ghost of Ibsen's Captain Alving. In the play, the consequences of Alving's earlier promiscuity presumably include the illness of his legitimate son, Oswald. Joyce's Alving, however, sardonically sidesteps responsibility by suggesting that Parson Manders, who once was in love with Alving's wife, is the actual father of Oswald. The poem suggests that while Joyce in middle age retained his youthful interest in Ibsen, his enthusiasm had been replaced by a more detached and critical assessment of the playwright's work.

**"Fenianism: The Last Fenian"** This is the title of an article written by Joyce in Italian that appeared in the March 22, 1907, issue of the Triestine newspaper *Il* PICCOLO DELLA SERA under the title "Il Fenianismo. L'Ultimo Feniano." The article, a translation of which is reprinted in *The Critical Writings of James Joyce,* begins with an explanation of the term "Fenian" and then mentions other Irish nationalist and separatist groups, such as the WHITEBOYS and the INVINCIBLES, advocating physical force as a response to British imperialism. He touches on the specific policies of the new Fenians, Sinn Féin (We Ourselves), which included boycotting British goods and preserving the Irish language. He then gives a brief survey of the Irish revolutionary movement during the 19th century. Although he is often critical of the methods employed, Joyce is basically sympathetic to the drive for independence.

The essay also contains Joyce's self-referential observation that conditions in Ireland force its people into self-imposed exile. He notes that there "is the spectacle of a population which diminishes year by year with mathematical regularity, of the uninterrupted emigration to the United States or Europe of Irishmen for whom the economic and intellectual conditions of their native land are unbearable" (*CW* 190). The comment reveals a preoccupation in Joyce, particularly at this time, with the problematics of exile. In other essays such as "Home Rule Comes of Age" (1907) and "The Home Rule Comet" (1910) (see both below), Joyce incorporates similar ideas that are eventually assimilated into the thematic underpinnings of portions of *A Portrait of the Artist as a Young Man, Exiles, Ulysses,* and *Finnegans Wake.*

**"Force"** This is the title of an essay written by Joyce in September 1898 for a class assignment while he was a student at UNIVERSITY COLLEGE, DUBLIN. It analyzes the nature and effects of subjugation by physical force. Joyce touches upon several general types of subjugation, such as the subjugation of the elements, of animals, and of human populations. The first part of the title page and several other pages are missing, and its present title was affixed by the editors of *The Critical Writings of James Joyce,* Ellsworth MASON and Richard ELLMANN.

**"French Religious Novel, A"** This is the title of Joyce's review of *The House of Sin,* a novel by the French author Marcelle Tinayre. In it, Joyce offers a fairly conventional survey of the novel's plot—the conflict between physical love and spiritual aspirations in the life of the central character, Augustine Chanteprie. Perhaps because of the plotline, Joyce gives the narrative high praise, and also commends Tinayre's stylistic achievements. The review was first published in the *DAILY EXPRESS* on October 1, 1903.

**"From a Banned Writer to a Banned Singer"** This was the title of an "open letter" written by Joyce to help promote the career of the Irish-French tenor John SULLIVAN. It was first published in the *New Statesman and Nation* in 1932. The title reflects Joyce's hyperbolic tendencies in matters relating to artistic recognition. Despite his sense, justified or not, that Sullivan did not receive the roles that he deserved, Sullivan's career never earned him the designation "banned singer." The letter, peppered throughout with *Wake*anesque puns, allusions, operatic quotes, and foreign phrases, surveys the achievements of Sullivan's career, praises his abilities, and rates him above other tenors of the day, including Enrico Caruso and Giacomo Lauri Volpi.

Joyce's obsession with championing Sullivan's career could produce uncharacteristic public exuberance. For instance, one night in Paris in 1936, according to Lucie Noel (Paul LÉON's wife), Joyce—after hearing Sullivan's famous solo in *Wilhelm Tell*—jumped up and shouted "Bravo Sullivan et merde pour Lauri Volpi!" (*James Joyce and Paul L. Léon: The Story of a Friendship,* p. 20).

**"Gas from a Burner"** This is the title of an invective poem written by Joyce in 1912 bitterly satirizing the publisher George Roberts of MAUNSEL & CO. for reneging on his contract to publish *Dubliners,* and the printer John FALCONER for destroying the already printed sheets (though Joyce was somehow able to obtain a complete copy of the sheets before leaving Ireland for good in September 1912). Three years earlier Roberts had agreed to publish the stories, but at the last minute, on legal advice, insisted on changes unacceptable to Joyce. The poem, composed en route to Trieste, is written mostly in a voice that mimics that of Roberts. "Gas from a Burner" was originally printed as a broadside in Trieste, and then sent by Joyce to his brother Charles in Dublin for distribution there. See "A Curious History" in Miscellaneous Writings.

**"George Meredith"** This is the title of Joyce's review of Walter Jerrold's *George Meredith,* a critical biography of the novelist. The review first appeared in the December 11, 1902, issue of the *DAILY EXPRESS.* It is reprinted in *The Critical Writings of James Joyce* (1959). Joyce, who had read Meredith's novels with pleasure (although he was also critical of him), would have preferred a better assessment of Meredith's art than Jerrold's "superficial analysis" but concludes that the book is "worth reading" (*CW* 89).

**"Giacomo Clarenzio Mangan"** This is Joyce's lecture on the 19th-century Irish poet James

Clarence MANGAN, the second of three lectures on Irish topics that Joyce was to have delivered (in Italian) at the Università del Popolo in Trieste in 1907. However, he delivered only the first, entitled "Ireland, Island of Saints and Sages," and never even wrote the third, "The Irish Literary Renaissance." An English translation of "Giacomo Clarenzio Mangan" is collected in *The Critical Writings of James Joyce*, and both the original Italian and a translation are published in *James Joyce: Occasional, Critical, and Political Writings*.

In "Giacomo Clarenzio Mangan," Joyce returns to a poet whom he discussed in a previous lecture, "James Clarence Mangan," which he gave at UNIVERSITY COLLEGE, DUBLIN, in 1902, more than two years before Joyce's own experience of literary exile. Although this provided a basis for his Italian lecture, Joyce's critical assessment of Mangan had changed. Although he still regarded Mangan as a worthy figure who voiced for Ireland "the sacred indignation of his soul" (*CW* 186), the more experienced Joyce viewed Mangan in a more critical light. He criticized technical flaws and thematic limitations that he had earlier overlooked. "The poet's central effort," Joyce wrote, "is to free himself from the unfortunate influence of these idols [of the market place] that corrupt him from without and within, and certainly it would be false to assert that Mangan has always made this effort" (*CW* 185).

**"Holy Office, The"** This is the title of a satirical broadside poem that Joyce wrote some time around August 1904 attacking the Dublin literati, especially the poet and playwright William Butler YEATS and the mystic and poet AE (George RUSSELL). Although Joyce had it printed in August 1904, shortly after the poem's composition, he could not afford to pay the printer. It was not until early 1905, in Pola, that Joyce had it printed again and sent to Dublin to be distributed by his brother Stanislaus. In the broadside, Joyce gives himself the name Katharsis-Purgative, suggesting the cleansing role of the uninhibited artist whose straightforward honesty cannot be compromised (and anticipating the renewing waters of Anna Livia Plurabelle in Joyce's last work, *Finnegans Wake*).

Joyce's title specifically alludes to an official body of the church, the Congregation of the Holy Office, established in the 16th century as part of the Counter-Reformation. Its members were appointed to uphold doctrinal teachings and suppress heresy. The title is ambiguous, perhaps intentionally so. Joyce may be seen as righteously denouncing the false art of the Dublin literati or as a heretic protesting the imposition of doctrinal conformity by the provincial defenders of Irish art and culture.

**"Home Rule Comes of Age"** This is the English title of one of several articles Joyce wrote in Italian for the Trieste newspaper *Il* PICCOLO DELLA SERA. It appeared under the title "Home Rule Maggiorenne" on May 19, 1907, and was, among other things, intended by the paper's editor, Roberto PREZIOSO, to reinforce irredentist feelings in Trieste. (An English translation of the essay appears in *Critical Writings* and in *James Joyce: Occasional, Critical, and Political Writings*.) The term "home rule" had been coined around 1870 by the Irish political economist and politician Isaac Butt (1813–79) for the goal of the Irish campaign to achieve political self-determination.

The title conceals a deliberate irony. Joyce wrote the article 21 years after British prime minister William Gladstone introduced his first Home Rule Bill on April 8, 1886. (Joyce mistakenly dates it April 9 in the article's first sentence. Gladstone introduced another Home Rule measure on February 13, 1893, but it too was rejected.) As Joyce observes in the article, according to English custom one comes of age at 21, but such was not the case for Home Rule.

Joyce briefly outlines the history of this ill-fated measure, including an indictment of Gladstone and the Irish Catholic bishops for their complicity in what the author describes as the "moral assassination of Parnell." Joyce arrives at two conclusions concerning Home Rule: that the Irish parliamentary party is bankrupt, and that the British Liberal Party, the Irish parliamentary party, and the Catholic Church hierarchy are the forces the British government can use to frustrate efforts for Irish independence. Despite the differing positions these institutions take on the Home Rule question, they share the same determination to dominate the Irish without undertaking to offer serious responses to the political turmoil.

**"Home Rule Comet, The"** Like the work mentioned in the previous entry, this was an article written by Joyce in Italian; it originally appeared under the title "La Cometa dell' 'Home Rule' " in the December 22, 1910, issue of the Trieste newspaper *Il* PICCOLO DELLA SERA. (An English translation appears in *The Critical Writings of James Joyce* and in *James Joyce: Occasional, Critical, and Political Writings.*) In the article, Joyce uses the image of a comet as a metaphor for the introduction of an Irish Home Rule measure in the British parliament; it periodically appears on the political horizon, and then passes out of sight.

Joyce's disapproval of Ireland's failure to achieve autonomy is directed as much toward the Irish as toward the English. At one point in the penultimate paragraph, Joyce accuses Ireland of betraying itself, a theme prevalent throughout his work:

She has abandoned her own language almost entirely and accepted the language of the conqueror without being able to assimilate the culture or adapt herself to the mentality of which this language is the vehicle. She has betrayed her heroes, always in the hour of need and always without gaining recompense. She has hounded her spiritual creators into exile only to boast about them.

These sentiments anticipate the views expressed by Robert Hand in his newspaper article about Richard Rowan described in the last act of Joyce's play, *Exiles.* These views appear again in chapter V of *A Portrait of the Artist as a Young Man* when Stephen Dedalus explains bitterly to his friend Davin why he will not become involved in the Irish nationalist movement.

**"Humanism"** This is the title of Joyce's review of F. C. S. Schiller's *Humanism: Philosophical Essays.* It first appeared in the DAILY EXPRESS on November 12, 1903. According to Joyce, Schiller, the leading European proponent of the views of William James, professes a hybrid philosophy that radically redefines conventional humanism by forming it into a system of belief closer to pragmatism. Unsurprisingly, Schiller's aggressive pragmatism went against the grain of Joyce, who (as he noted in "The Holy Office," see above) was "steeled in the school of old Aquinas."

**"Ibsen's New Drama"** This was Joyce's first published work, a straightforward and laudatory essay on the last of Henrik IBSEN's plays, *When We Dead Awaken.* The piece appeared in the April 1, 1900, issue of the FORTNIGHTLY REVIEW. The article came to Ibsen's attention, and through his English translator, William ARCHER, he expressed his gratitude to Joyce. Publishing a work in such a prestigious English literary journal gained Joyce great renown at UNIVERSITY COLLEGE, DUBLIN, but more important, it served as a validation of his confidence in his own genius. In addition to appearing in *The Critical Writings of James Joyce* and in *James Joyce: Occasional, Critical, and Political Writings,* the essay was reprinted by Ulysses Bookshop, London, in March 1930.

**"Ireland at the Bar"** This is the English version of an article that Joyce wrote in Italian entitled "L'Irlanda alla Sbarra," for the September 16, 1907, issue of the Trieste newspaper *Il* PICCOLO DELLA SERA. The essay focuses on a murder trial that took place in Galway in 1882. Although Joyce considers broad questions of justice, the nub of his argument is a very specific cultural and linguistic separation between the English legal system and the Irish defendant. The trial itself was conducted in English, but one of the defendants, Myles Joyce (no relation), spoke no English and the proceedings had to be translated into Irish for him. Despite the fact that Myles Joyce was generally considered to be innocent and lacked a genuine grasp of the proceedings, he was found guilty and hanged with his codefendants. Joyce uses the incident to focus attention upon the unfeeling, imperial attitude of the English in Ireland.

*Ireland at the Bar* was also the tentative title of a book relating to Ireland and the Home Rule issue that Joyce hoped to have published in 1914 and for which he proposed gathering the articles that he had written for *Il Piccolo della Sera.* Although he contacted a publisher in Rome, Angelo Fortunato Formiggini, nothing came of the project. Nonetheless, this ambitious scheme and the essay on Myles Joyce that served as its genesis offer an insight into Joyce's complex attitude toward Ireland that would become increasingly evident in *A Portrait of the Artist as a Young Man* and *Ulysses*.

Although as a very young boy Joyce shared his father's Parnellite sympathies, going so far as to compose the lament "Et Tu, Healy" (see Miscellaneous Works) on the betrayal and death of Parnell, from his adolescence onward Joyce held an ambivalent view of Irish nationalism. When he left Ireland in 1904, Joyce felt a marked antipathy toward conventional Irish patriotism. Further, he could never bring himself to support the terrorist violence advocated in the 19th century by groups like the WHITEBOYS, the MOLLY MAGUIRES, and the RIBBONMEN, and in the early 20th century by the Irish Revolutionary Brotherhood and the Irish Republican Army. At the same time, as indicated by the series of articles that Joyce wrote in Trieste, his attitude underwent a marked evolution during his years on the Continent. Just as Stephen Dedalus (see characters under *Ulysses*) shows in *Ulysses* that he has come to see Irish nationalism as a concept far broader than simple confrontation with the British, over the years Joyce demonstrated an increasingly pronounced concern for Irish cultural and social institutions even as he dismissed, with ever greater contempt, the machinations of Irish politics.

**"Ireland, Island of Saints and Sages"** This is the English title of a lecture that Joyce gave in Italian, entitled "Irlanda, Isola dei Santi e dei Savi," in Trieste on April 27, 1907. It was the first of three proposed talks that Joyce was to present at the Università Popolare. Joyce used this lecture to introduce his audience to central (the literary, intellectual, and spiritual) features of Irish culture and history and to underscore Ireland's troubled relations with England. The tone of the lecture alternates between an ironic sense of the Irish cultural foibles and of the missed political opportunities that have punctuated Irish history, and an affectionate account of the characteristic elements of Irish society. Joyce does not hesitate to praise specific individuals and take note of important events, in particular, the GAELIC LEAGUE's revival of the Irish language and the many Irish contributors to English literature and culture, such as Jonathan Swift, William Congreve, and George Bernard Shaw.

**"Irish Poet, An"** This is the title of Joyce's review of William Rooney's posthumously published *Poems and Ballads* in the DAILY EXPRESS on December 11, 1902. Rooney strongly supported the founding of the Sinn Féin (We Ourselves) movement and frequently contributed to its newspaper, the *United Irishman*. In his review Joyce criticizes the pedestrian nature of Rooney's verse and rebukes those who had praised it because of its nationalistic themes.

**"James Clarence Mangan"** This was an essay written by Joyce as a university student and first delivered as a lecture at the February 1, 1902, meeting of the Literary and Historical Society of UNIVERSITY COLLEGE, DUBLIN. It was subsequently published in the unofficial university magazine, St Stephen's, in May of the same year.

The essay purports to introduce the work of the 19th-century Irish poet James Clarence MANGAN to the Irish people, although in fact Mangan had been the object of considerable intellectual and artistic interest throughout the 1890s, especially from W. B. YEATS and Lionel Johnson, a well-known English poet and essayist. At the same time, Joyce took care in this essay to avoid the role of a devoted acolyte. Even as he singles out Mangan for praise because of the imaginative power of his verse, Joyce takes care to qualify his assessment of the poet; he is particularly critical of the fatalistic acceptance of Irish melancholy that he finds in Mangan's work. For Joyce, Mangan's life as a minor poet living on the fringes of literary success, plagued by addiction to opium and alcohol, illustrates his sense of the frustration caused by Irish society's equivocal attitude to the needs of its artists. (See also "Giacomo Clarenzio Mangan" above.)

**"Letter on Hardy"** This letter, dated February 10, 1928, was written by Joyce in French and published in the January–February 1928 issue of the

French journal *Revue Nouvelle,* a special number devoted to the English novelist and poet Thomas Hardy (1840–1928). Composed in response to the editor's request for Joyce's views of Hardy, the letter, in fact, says very little about Hardy as an author, for Joyce pleads a lack of familiarity with his work. Instead, he offers a few innocuous remarks about the man. The letter is also collected in *Critical Writings,* and both English and French versions appear in *Letters,* III.169–170.

**"Letter on Pound"** This was a letter written by Joyce on March 13, 1925, and published in the inaugural issue (Spring 1925) of the literary journal *This Quarter,* which was dedicated to Ezra POUND. The magazine's editor, Ernest Walsh, had solicited a number of testimonials from well-known individuals who were at one time or another close friends of Pound. Although the period of intense association between Joyce and Pound had passed and the two men regarded each other with a certain coolness, Joyce made a concerted effort to pay tribute to what he sincerely felt were Pound's considerable contributions to modern literature and studiously avoided areas of disagreement. Although the letter says little about Pound's work, Joyce freely acknowledged the debt he owed Pound for "his friendly help, encouragement and generous interest in everything that I have written." The letter also appears in *Letters,* III.117.

**"Letter on Svevo"** This was a letter written in Italian by Joyce on May 31, 1929, and published in the March–April issue of the Italian journal SOLARIA, a section of which was devoted to memorializing Ettore SCHMITZ, who wrote under the name Italo SVEVO. Schmitz had died in an automobile accident the previous year. He was Joyce's former Trieste English-language student and his close friend, and it was with Joyce's strong encouragement that Schmitz, as Svevo, resumed his efforts to write and to have his work published. Joyce somewhat surprisingly avoids discussing his friend's literary achievements and focuses instead upon personal recollections, mentioning the fond memories that he has of his friend. A translation of this letter is published in *The Critical Writings of James Joyce* and the original version and English translation appear in *Letters,* III.189–190.

**"Mettle of the Pasture, The"** This was the title of a review by Joyce of James Lane Allen's book of the same name. The book deals in a melodramatic fashion with a young man whose fiancée deserts him after learning of his previous immoral behavior and who returns to him only when he is on the brink of death. Joyce's review was published in the DAILY EXPRESS of September 17, 1903, along with his review of Aquila Kempster's *The Adventures of Prince Aga Mirza,* a "collection of stories dealing chiefly with Indian life."

**"Mirage of the Fisherman of Aran, The. England's Safety Valve in Case of War"** This is one of two essays written by Joyce in 1912. It is based upon his experiences during an excursion with Nora BARNACLE to the Aran Islands, located off the coast of Galway in the west of Ireland. Originally written in Italian, it appeared in the September 5, 1912, issue of *Il* PICCOLO DELLA SERA under the title "Il Miraggio del Pescatore di Aran. La Valvola dell'Inghilterra in Caso di Guerra."

The essay describes in great detail the passage by ship across Galway Bay to the island of Aranmor, and it offers a highly flattering view both of the Galway countryside and of the Aran Islands. Joyce recounts having tea in the home of one of the Aran villagers with a sensitivity that presages the complex yet sympathetic allusions to the west of Ireland that appear at the close of *A Portrait of the Artist as a Young Man.* He also seems fascinated by pampooties, the local footwear. He uses the term again in the Scylla and Charybdis episode (chapter 9) of *Ulysses,* when Buck Mulligan invokes it to lampoon John Millington SYNGE's efforts to immerse himself in rural Irish culture.

The rather cryptic subtitle of the essay refers to a proposal that it makes for developing a new deepwater port on Aranmor. Using a line of argument that is unexpected from someone who considered himself a pacifist, Joyce contends that the port would be useful because it would provide a strategic naval advantage to England during a war, for it would allow Canadian grain to come to Great

Britain via Ireland, thereby avoiding "the dangers of navigation in St. George's Channel between Britain and Ireland and the enemy fleets" (CW 235). (See also the entry on Joyce's companion essay, "The City of the Tribes" above.)

**"Motor Derby, The"** This is the title of an article by Joyce, published in the April 7, 1903, issue of the *IRISH TIMES.* It consisted of the transcript of an interview that Joyce conducted with French race car driver Henri Fournier, who was scheduled to compete in the second James Gordon Bennett cup race scheduled for Dublin in July of that year. Joyce drew upon his recollections of this interview for background for the *Dubliners* short story "After the Race."

**"Mr. Arnold Graves' New Work"** This is the title given to Joyce's review of Arnold F. Graves's play *Clytaemnestra: A Tragedy.* Joyce describes this work as "a Greek story treated from the standpoint of a modern dramatist." The review appeared in the October 1, 1903, issue of the *DAILY EXPRESS,* and in it Joyce, in his own somewhat disjointed fashion, anatomizes the inherent drawback of constructing a play along the lines of an ethical argument.

**"Mr. Mason's Novels"** This title identifies Joyce's review of three popular novels written by A. E. W. Mason: *The Courtship of Morrice Buckler, The Philanderers,* and *Miranda of the Balcony.* Joyce's review appeared in the October 15, 1903, issue of the *DAILY EXPRESS,* and it patronizingly (though doubtless with justification) dismisses Mason for reusing in each of the novels essentially the same plot animated by the same characters with only slight variations.

Mason was perhaps best known for his 1902 novel of contemporary life, *The Four Feathers* (made into a movie in 1939 and remade in 2002), and a series of detective novels featuring Inspector Hanaud of the French police.

**"Ne'er-do-Well, A"** This is the title of a review by Joyce of a book of that title by Valentine Carl (Valentine Hawtrey). Joyce's review was published in the September 3, 1903, issue of the *DAILY EXPRESS,* and consists simply of three acerbic sentences. The first one attacks the author for using a pseudonym (something Joyce himself would do a year later when he published his first short story, "The Sisters," in the IRISH HOMESTEAD). The second dismisses the contents of the book. And the third excoriates the publisher for bringing the book into print.

**"Neglected Poet, A"** This is a review written by Joyce of Alfred Ainger's edition of the English poet George Crabbe (1754–1832). It was published in the October 15, 1903, issue of the *DAILY EXPRESS.* Despite the admission that "much of Crabbe's work is dull and undistinguished," Joyce offers the opinion that Crabbe is nonetheless superior to the better-known Anglo-Irish writer Oliver Goldsmith (1730–74); he goes on to express the hope that Ainger's edition will "succeed in securing a place [of renown] for one like Crabbe."

**"New Fiction"** This is the title of a review by Joyce of Aquila Kempster's book *The Adventures of Prince Aga Mirza* published in the September 17, 1903, issue of the *DAILY EXPRESS.* In it, Joyce freely admitted to finding little satisfaction in this "collection of stories dealing chiefly with Indian life." Although his own reading suggests that the topic itself may have interested him, he states quite bluntly that the book's literary merit is seriously hampered by a coarseness and brutality that panders to the lowest appetites of the reading public.

**"Oscar Wilde: The Poet of 'Salomé' "** This is the English title of an essay composed by Joyce in Italian and published in the March 24, 1909, edition of *Il PICCOLO DELLA SERA* under the title "Oscar Wilde: Il Poeta di 'Salomé'." It was written on the occasion of the first production in Trieste of Richard Strauss's opera *Salomé,* a work based upon the play by the same name written (originally in French) by Oscar WILDE in 1892. Joyce's article provides a thumbnail sketch of Wilde's life and career, with a conscious emphasis on Wilde's Irish ties. Joyce draws attention to the self-righteous, hypocritical persecution of Wilde by the British authorities, and indeed by the British public, after his arrest and conviction on charges of sodomy. Wilde had been imprisoned from 1895 to 1897, and died bankrupt and deserted by his friends in 1900.

**"Peep into History, A"** In this article Joyce reviews John Pollock's history *The Popish Plot,* published in the September 17, 1903, issue of the *DAILY EXPRESS.* In their edition of Joyce's critical writings, Ellsworth MASON and Richard ELLMANN note a number of factual errors which indicate that Joyce gave little more than cursory attention to the volume and which suggest the generally perfunctory nature of his reviews at this time.

**"Politics and Cattle Disease"** This is the title of an unsigned essay that Joyce wrote as an editorial in the September 10, 1912, issue of the Dublin newspaper the *FREEMAN'S JOURNAL.* In a letter to Stanislaus JOYCE, Charles Joyce identified their brother James as the author of the piece. In the article Joyce considers seriously a recent outbreak of hoof-and-mouth disease among cattle in several locations in Ireland, and he discusses the resulting English efforts to keep Irish beef out of British markets.

This letter and one written by a Trieste friend, Henry N. Blackwood Price (originally from Ulster) for the *EVENING TELEGRAPH,* provide the basis for the fictional letter on the same subject written by Garrett Deasy in the Nestor episode (chapter 2) of *Ulysses.* Although Stephen Dedalus views Deasy's letter with contempt, he does agree to help Deasy get it into print, and in the Aeolus episode (chapter 7), Stephen secures a promise from the newspaper's editor Myles Crawford to print it, and it does appear in his paper, the *Telegraph* (see the Eumaeus episode, chapter 16 [*U* 16.1244–1245]). In the Scylla and Charybdis episode (chapter 9), George Russell is less positive, but he agrees to consider it for the *IRISH HOMESTEAD.* Anticipating the response of Buck Mulligan to these efforts, Stephen gives himself the name "the bullock-befriending bard" (*U* 2.431).

**"Programme Notes for the English Players"** This is the title of a collection of playbill notes gathered together in *The Critical Writings of James Joyce.* They were written by Joyce during the 1918–19 theater season of the ENGLISH PLAYERS, a Zurich acting troupe formed by Joyce and Claud SYKES. Joyce wrote introductions for J. M. Barrie's *The Twelve Pound Look* (see below), John M. SYNGE's *RIDERS TO THE SEA,* George Bernard Shaw's *The DARK LADY OF THE SONNETS,* and Edward Martyn's *The HEATHER FIELD.*

**"Royal Hibernian Academy 'Ecce Homo' "** This is the title of an essay written by Joyce in September 1899 as part of a regular course of studies at UNIVERSITY COLLEGE, DUBLIN. The paper offers an analysis of the painting *Ecce Homo* (Latin, Behold the Man, the words of Pilate referring to Jesus, crowned with thorns, in John 19:5) by the Hungarian artist Michael Munkacsy (1844–1900), which was then on exhibit at the Royal Hibernian Academy in DUBLIN. In headnotes provided by Ellsworth Mason and Richard Ellmann when they reprinted the piece in *The Critical Writing of James Joyce,* the volume's editors praise Joyce's comments on the dramatic elements of the composition. For most readers, however, the essay, which incorporates some of Joyce's earliest ideas of drama, is juvenilia, and in consequence of little interest beyond its biographic value.

**"Shade of Parnell, The"** This is the English translation of the title of one of a series of articles by Joyce commissioned by Roberto PREZIOSO, editor of the Trieste paper *Il PICCOLO DELLA SERA.* "The Shade of Parnell" was published in Italian under the title "L'Ombra di Parnell" in the May 16, 1912, issue. In the essay, Joyce addresses the passage of the third Home Rule Bill by the British House of Commons on May 9, 1912, which at the time seemed, in Joyce's words, to have "resolved the Irish question." Joyce reflects on Irish and English political efforts over the past century to settle upon a mutually satisfactory solution to the question of the status of Ireland, and contrasts the current machinations of various political figures and parties with the efforts of Charles Stewart PARNELL to secure home rule for his country a generation earlier. He predictably offers a favorable summary of the life and career of Parnell, whom he compares, to Parnell's advantage, to the British Liberal Party leader and four-time prime minister, William Ewart Gladstone.

**"Shakespeare Explained"** This is the title of a review by Joyce of A. S. Canning's book *Shakespeare Studied in Eight Plays,* published in the November 12, 1903, issue of the Dublin DAILY EXPRESS. The title is clearly ironic, for, in a tone that at times borders on pedantry, Joyce sharply criticizes what he sees as Canning's flippant approach to Shakespeare and his lack of regard for rudimentary scholarship. He concludes: "It is not easy to discover in the book any matter for praise."

**"Soul of Ireland, The"** This is the title of Joyce's review of the book *Poets and Dreamers* written by Lady Augusta GREGORY. The review appeared in the March 26, 1903, issue of the Dublin DAILY EXPRESS. Lady Gregory's book includes stories collected from peasants in the west of Ireland, translations of Irish-language poetry, and translations of four one-act Irish-language plays by Douglas Hyde. Nonetheless, despite the work's wide range, Joyce dismisses Lady Gregory's efforts in a tone that makes clear his antipathy toward the enthusiasms of the Celtic Revival.

According to Richard ELLMANN, Lady Gregory had persuaded E. V. LONGWORTH, the editor of the *Daily Express,* to give Joyce the opportunity to review for the paper, and she was deeply offended by Joyce's treatment of her book. In the Scylla and Charybdis episode (chapter 9) of *Ulysses,* Joyce recalls the incident. As they leave the NATIONAL LIBRARY OF IRELAND, Buck Mulligan accuses Joyce's fictional counterpart, Stephen Dedalus, not so much of poor criticism as of a failure of tact: "Longworth is awfully sick . . . after what you wrote about that old hake Gregory. O you inquisitional drunken jewjesuit! She gets you a job on the paper and then you go and slate her drivel to Jaysus. Couldn't you do the Yeats touch?" (*U* 9.1158–1161). Mulligan is asking Dedalus to compromise his critical integrity to placate a supporter, as W. B. YEATS was thought to have done, having praised Lady Gregory's work.

**"Study of Languages, The"** This is the title of an essay that Joyce wrote probably in 1898 or 1899 while at UNIVERSITY COLLEGE, DUBLIN. A portion of the manuscript survives in the Joyce collection at Cornell University, and the essay was first published in *The Critical Writings of James Joyce.* Exhibiting an unformed style, relying upon topical generalities, and showing a tendency towards garrulousness and digression, it nonetheless has some critical value as an early sample of Joyce's rhetorical arguments and process of composition. As one might expect, the essay itself presents no particularly startling insight into the study of linguistics, but it does show Joyce's growing erudition and intellectual confidence.

**"Suave Philosophy, A"** This is the title of Joyce's review of H. Fielding-Hall's *The Soul of a People.* The review appeared in the February 6, 1903, issue of the Dublin newspaper the DAILY EXPRESS, together with "An Effort at Precision in Thinking" and "Colonial Verses" (see both above). The book examines the fundamental tenets of Buddhism, and Joyce's review is punctuated by a thinly veiled skepticism toward Fielding-Hall's grasp of his topic. Nonetheless, Joyce's enthusiastic response to the book's subject matter shows the essential strength of his sympathies for the pacifistic approach informing the Buddhist philosophy.

**"Today and Tomorrow in Ireland"** This is the title given to Joyce's review of Stephen Gwynn's book of the same name, which appeared in the January 29, 1903, issue of the DAILY EXPRESS. The book consists of 10 essays on topics related to Ireland and Irish life from the Nationalist perspective. Joyce shows an appreciation of Gwynn's accounts of the fishing industry in the west of Ireland, of Irish dairies, and of Irish carpet making. But he takes a less sanguine view of Gwynn's expansive, laudatory comments on the state of Irish literature, calling Gwynn's criticism "in no way remarkable."

**"Trust Not Appearances"** This essay represents the only surviving example of the kind of weekly themes that Joyce had to write when he was a student at BELVEDERE COLLEGE. Evidence suggests that it was composed around 1896, when Joyce was 14. In dealing with the topic of this assignment, Joyce relies upon a self-consciously literary style that shows both the extent of his reading at the time and the still undeveloped condition of his creative ability. The essay moves from images of nature to those of humanity to demonstrate, through the reiteration of clichés, the foolishness of basing any judgment upon external forms. The holograph manuscript of this essay is now in the collection of the Cornell University Library.

**"Twelve Pound Look, The"** This was a play by J. M. Barrie, and it served as the title of Joyce's program notes for a production of the play staged by the ENGLISH PLAYERS in ZURICH in 1918. Joyce's commentary consists basically of a plot summary that ends on a humorous but subtly sarcastic note. "She had saved twelve pounds and bought a typewriter. The twelve pound look, she says, is that look of independence in a wife's eye which every husband should beware of. The new knight's new wife, 'noted for her wit'—chary of it, too—seems likely to acquire the look if given time. Typewriters, however, are rather scarce at present" (*CW* 250).

**"Unequal Verse"** This is the title of Joyce's review of *Ballads and Legends* by Frederick Langbridge (1849–1922), rector of St. John's Church in Limerick. The review appeared in the October 1, 1903, issue of the *DAILY EXPRESS*. Joyce dismisses most of Langbridge's verse and describes it as "this farrago of banal epics," although he does single out one poem for praise, "To Maurice Maeterlinck."

**"William Blake"** This is the English title given by translators to one of two lectures (the other being "Daniel Defoe") that Joyce presented in March 1912 at the Università Popolare Triestina. About two-thirds of the original lecture survives in a holograph manuscript of 20 pages in the Slocum Collection at Yale's Beinecke Library. Joyce devotes the bulk of the essay to a detailed examination of the mystical and artistic influences on Blake's art. The talk traces the features of Blake's artistic nature, emphasizing his independence and integrity, and situating him in the social context of his time. In a digression, inspired perhaps by the parallel Joyce perceived between Blake's wife and his own, Nora Barnacle, the lecture takes note of the intellectual and cultural disparity between Blake and his wife and comments on Blake's efforts to educate her. Recent biographical criticism, however, has strongly questioned the accuracy of such a characterization of Nora.

# *Collected Poems* (1936)

This is the title of a collection of Joyce's poetry published by the Black Sun Press in 1936. The edition contains two previously published works, *Chamber Music* (1907) and *Pomes Penyeach* (1927), as well as the poem "Ecce Puer," published for the first time in the November 30, 1932, issue of the *New Republic*. (For information on the other poems, in this volume, see the separate entries on *Chamber Music* and *Pomes Penyeach*.)

**"Ecce Puer"** Combining emotions of joy and sorrow, this poem celebrates the birth of Joyce's grandson, Stephen James Joyce (February 15, 1932), even as it mourns the death of the writer's father, John Stanislaus JOYCE (December 29, 1931). The poem is made up of four stanzas of four lines in paired rhymes (abcb). In each of the first three stanzas the first two lines examine the joy that the birth of his grandson has brought Joyce, while the last two explore his pain over the death of his father. The final stanza foregrounds a cri de coeur as the speaker exclaims "O, father forsaken, / Forgive your son!"

"Ecce Puer" was later published in the January 1933 issue of the CRITERION and then in *Collected Poems* (1936).

# *Dubliners* (1914)

This is the title that Joyce gave to his collection of 15 short stories written over a three-year period (1904–07). Though he finished the final story, "The Dead," in spring of 1907, difficulties in finding a publisher and Joyce's initial refusal to alter any passage thought to be objectionable kept it from being published by Grant RICHARDS until 1914. The first American edition was published by HUEBSCH sometime between December 15, 1916, and January 1, 1917. (According to John J. SLOCUM and Herbert CAHOON, the New York publishers Albert and Charles Boni would have been the first to bring out the American edition, but the sheets that Grant Richards sold to the Boni brothers without Joyce's consent were lost at sea when the SS *Arabic* was torpedoed on its way to the United States in August 1915.)

From their inception, Joyce intended the stories to be part of a thematically unified and chronologically ordered series. It was a searing analysis of Irish middle- and lower-middle-class life, with DUBLIN not simply as its geographical setting but as the emotional and psychological locus as well. Originally he had 10 stories in mind: "The Sisters," "An Encounter," "The Boarding House," "After the Race," "Eveline," "Clay," "Counterparts," "A Painful Case," "Ivy Day in the Committee Room," and "A Mother." Toward the end of 1905, before he sent the collection to the London publisher Grant Richards, Joyce added two more stories—"Araby" and, what was then the final story, "Grace." During 1906, he wrote "Two Gallants" and "A Little Cloud," which he submitted to Richards along with a revision of "The Sisters," thus expanding the number of stories to 14.

Almost immediately after agreeing to bring out the stories, however, Richards began to voice objections to portions of Joyce's writing. In a letter to Joyce dated April 23, 1906, Richards singled out for criticism certain passages in "Two Gallants," "Counterparts" and "Grace" that he thought offensive to public taste. This began a series of challenges to the integrity of the collection which Joyce strove to address without compromising his work. These impediments to the publication of *Dubliners*, repeatedly invoked by several different potential publishers, would delay the appearance of the volume for another eight years. Joyce offers an account of his publishing problems in an essay entitled "A Curious History" (see Miscellaneous Works). He also wrote a satiric broadside entitled "Gas from a Burner" (see *Critical Writings*) that presents a more sardonic account of his difficulties.

Statue of James Joyce on Earl Street N., Dublin *(Faith Steinberg)*

While in Rome, where he and his family lived between July 1906 and March 1907, Joyce conceived yet another story, "The Dead," which he wrote after returning to Trieste in early 1907. This raised the number of stories in *Dubliners* to 15, and served as a conclusion to the collection. Joyce had continued negotiations with Richards over proposed changes, but by the fall of 1907 they had come to an impasse and Richards canceled his contract. Joyce found himself without a publisher, and it would be the spring of 1914, after many unsuccessful attempts to have the work published, before Joyce was again offered a contract by Richards, who finally brought out *Dubliners* in June of that year.

## COMMENTARY

The delays that Joyce encountered were not simply the result of an author's inflexibility in the face of criticism. Joyce had a clear idea what he hoped to accomplish with the collection, and feared extensive changes would damage those aims. In a letter to Grant Richards written in May 1906, Joyce, attempting to justify his work, clearly stated his overall purpose and design in writing the stories:

> My intention was to write a chapter of the moral history of my country and I chose Dublin for the scene because that city seemed to me the centre of paralysis. I have tried to present it to the indifferent public under four of its aspects: childhood, adolescence, maturity and public life. The stories are arranged in this order. I have written it for the most part in a style of scrupulous meanness and with the conviction that he is a very bold man who dares to alter in the presentment, still more to deform, whatever he has seen and heard. (*Letters,* I.134)

A number of times Joyce made clear his intention of presenting "Dublin to the world" (see *Letters,* II.122) at least as he conceived the city and its inhabitants. He did so in a direct, unadorned, realistic style that included unvarnished descriptive elements and commonplace diction. However, these elements that he saw as essential to conveying the gritty essence of his narrative vision proved to be obstacles to publication, as publishers feared that the realistic evocation of the city would give offense to the merchants whose businesses were named and the readers whose coarse everyday language was captured on the page. At the same time, as Joyce well knew, it is this attention to detail, the ordering of the stories according to the stages of human maturation, the pervasive theme of paralysis, manifest in multiple variations like entrapment, disillusionment, and death, and the stories' common setting that give the collection coherence and provide a comprehensive and lifelike portrait of Dublin and its citizens. It would be a mistake, however, to read the collection as a vindictive assault upon the city in which Joyce grew to manhood. His significant use of the word *moral* also throws light on what he meant by "a style of scrupulous meanness." It does not primarily signify ethical judgment or valuation; rather, derived from the Latin *moralis,* the word means the custom or behavior of a people, and Joyce is portraying the customs, behavior, and thoughts of the citizens of Dublin. In effect, he feels that by conveying a realistic impression of his city, readers of *Dubliners* will come to their own conclusions regarding its citizens.

That is not to say that the narratives shy away from harsh representations. Rather, Joyce endeavors to capture as accurately as possible the atmosphere that he felt made life in the city so difficult for its inhabitants. The oppressive effects of religious, political, cultural, and economic forces on the lives of lower-middle-class Dubliners provided Joyce the raw material for a piercingly objective, psychologically realistic picture of Dubliners as an afflicted people. The arrangement of the stories and the use of imagery and symbolism peculiar to each and to its place within the whole sharpen the variations on Joyce's central theme of a stultified city. "I call the series *Dubliners,*" Joyce wrote in August 1904 to his former classmate Constantine Curran, "to betray the soul of that hemiplegia or paralysis which many consider a city" (*Letters,* I.55). In the opening lines of "The Sisters," paralysis confronts the reader as the collection's initial and dominant theme. It emerges as more complex than simple inertia, evoking both stasis and an underlying sense of despair, a combination of resignation and loss that emerges throughout the collection.

The psychological, spiritual, and emotional ambiances of the collection evolve slowly, along carefully delineated lines paralleling human growth and development. As early as 1905, Joyce had established a fourfold division of three stories each for *Dubliners.* Although this structure changed somewhat as the number of stories grew, its basic design remained intact. In the first maturational division of *Dubliners,* childhood, there are three stories: "The Sisters" (written in 1904 and first published that same year in the *IRISH HOMESTEAD* under Joyce's pseudonym, Stephen DAEDALUS), "An Encounter," and "Araby" (both written in 1905). The second division, adolescence, includes four stories: "Eveline" and "After the Race" (both composed in 1904 and first published in that year in the *Irish Homestead* under the name of Stephen Daedelus), "Two Gallants" (written in 1905–06), and "The Boarding House" (written in 1905). The third group, adulthood, consists of four stories: "A Little Cloud" (composed in 1906), "Counterparts" (written at the same time as "The Boarding House" in 1905), "Clay" (composed in 1905–06), and "A Painful Case" (written in 1905). The fourth and last division, public life, consists of "Ivy Day in the Committee Room," "A Mother," "Grace" (all written in 1905), and "The Dead" (written in 1906–07).

In her essay "The Life Chronology of *Dubliners*," Florence L. Walzl has examined the reasoning that motivated Joyce to order the stories in progressive stages corresponding to the stages of human life. According to Walzl, Joyce employed the terms *childhood, adolescence,* and *maturity* in ways that parallel the Roman division of life rather than the division commonly identified with these concepts. "Joyce had a strong awareness," Walzl argues, "of the Roman divisions of the life span. His statements and practices indicate that he adopted the view that childhood (*pueritia*) extended to age seventeen; adolescence (*adulescentia*) from seventeen through the thirtieth year; young manhood (*juventus*) from thirty-one to forty-five, and old age (*senectus*) from forty-five on." Joyce's concern for chronology and age distinction reveals the general importance for him of order in his art, and it also touches on his sense of the fluctuating forms of identity through which we pass as we slowly mature.

Despite the significance of context for the cohesion of the collection, stylistic expression is as important to Joyce as thematic development. His concern with and careful attention to word order and overall structure began with *Chamber Music,* a work completed prior to *Dubliners,* and it remains a central element in his compositional strategy throughout his oeuvre. Indeed, as his thematic endeavors became more complex and diffuse, stylistics functions as the primary means by which Joyce achieves coherence in and among all of his writings. Although some of Joyce's methods in the short stories may seem understated when compared with the formal experimentation that he undertook in subsequent prose fiction—*A Portrait of the Artist as a Young Man, Ulysses,* and *Finnegans Wake*—time and again passages in *Dubliners* wonderfully adumbrate fully developed techniques that characterize the later work. Indeed, realizing the stylistic and thematic virtuosity of the short stories stands as the first step to full comprehension of their significance.

In "Araby," for example, religious iconography counterpoints the basic narrative thread, making both ironic and straightforward commentary on the quest of the young narrator. In "An Encounter," "Two Gallants," and "Counterparts," detailed representations of Dublin geography enforce the claustrophobic atmosphere of each story. In "A Mother," "Ivy Day in the Committee Room," and "The Dead," Dublin's social mores reflect not only universal human concerns but the very precise ways in which they are played out in Joyce's city. Perhaps most significantly, throughout the collection a series of rich literary, theological, philosophical, and cultural allusions bring a variety of perspectives and possible meanings to the text, and they test a reader's ability to comprehend and unify the diverse associations.

While readers rightly see *Dubliners* as marking an early stage in Joyce's creative development, one needs to avoid a simplistic sense of what that means. One can certainly trace a growing artistic sophistication over the course of Joyce's fiction writing. *A Portrait of the Artist as a Young Man, Ulysses,* and *Finnegans Wake* each manifests abilities not evident in the works that preceded it. Nonetheless, as early as *Dubliners* one can find the fundamental artistic elements that will characterize Joyce's writing over the course of his career as an author. Furthermore, it is important to remember that these stories were created during a time of economic trial, emotional upheaval, and cultural disorientation. Joyce, Nora, and his growing family were struggling to adjust to a radically different environment from life in Dublin, and evidence of those trials, while not explicit, is certainly embedded in his short stories.

## HELPFUL ANNOTATIONS

Don Gifford and Robert J. Seidman, *Notes For Joyce: Dubliners and A Portrait of the Artist as a*

*Young Man* and John Wyse Jackson and Bernard McGinley, *James Joyce's Dubliners: An Illustrated Edition with Annotations*. See the appendix on page 405 for other helpful titles. For additional details relating to Joyce's views on the composition in *Dubliners*, see Joyce's correspondence to Grant Richards in *Letters*, I.55 and 60–64; and in *Letters*, II.122–123, 132–144, 324–325, 327–329, 332, and 340–341. For more on the controversies surrounding publication of the collection, see Grant Richards's correspondence, published in *Studies in Bibliography*, edited by Fredson Bowers, Vol. XVI, pp. 139–160.

## INDIVIDUAL STORIES

### "The Sisters"

"The Sisters," which opens the *Dubliners* collection, introduces the book's "childhood" division, and was the first story in the collection to be written. The original version of this story appeared in the August 13, 1904, issue of the IRISH HOMESTEAD under the pseudonym Stephen DAEDALUS, which Joyce briefly used. (He later claimed to regret the decision not to publish from the start under his own name.) Joyce greatly revised "The Sisters" before it appeared in the 1914 publication of the book. (For a reprint of the *Irish Homestead* version, see *Dubliners: Text, Criticism and Notes*, edited by Robert Scholes and A. Walton Litz, pp. 243–252.)

"The Sisters" introduces many of the themes that define the descriptive trajectory of the collection: narrow, though often unstated, cultural norms; ambiguity regarding the consequences of events; and an inability to take definitive action. It focuses the reader's attention on the psyche of the narrator, a young boy, as he struggles to come to grips with the world that he inhabits. One sees his frustrations as he strives to engage change in a narrow and restrictive society. In the process, the discourse underscores the early and presumably lifelong influence of the claustrophobic environment described throughout the collection. As "The Sisters" traces the reactions of the unnamed young narrator as he endeavors to cope with his feelings about the death of an old priest, Father James Flynn, who had befriended him, it also outlines a pattern of conflict and frustration common to most of the major characters in *Dubliners*.

The story opens somewhat deceptively, with a seemingly straightforward phrase that captures the complexity of the story without prescribing a way to resolve the issues that will arise from it: "There was no hope for him this time." With graceful but arresting brevity the narrative sums up the physical troubles of Father Flynn as he struggles to overcome the debilitating effects of his third stroke. More significantly, however, Joyce also obliquely introduces the notion of the utter hopelessness that seems to surround Father Flynn's life. Finally, through the momentary ambiguity over to whom the word "him" refers and what has precipitated this lack of hope, the phrase also suggests the danger of spiritual desolation with which the boy must contend over the course of the story. The words *paralysis*, *gnomon*, and *simony*, all occurring in the opening paragraph, underscore the physical, spiritual, and religious decay found in the story.

In the opening lines, the young narrator quickly reveals that he is attempting to keep watch over Father Flynn's house in anticipation of the priest's death, setting for himself the goal of being the first outside the immediate family to know of the old man's passing. However, the boy is frustrated in this desire, for when he comes down to supper one evening in the home of his aunt and uncle, with whom he lives, a neighbor, Mr. Cotter, has already brought the news. In this scene, the boy must deal not only with his own immediate disappointment and grief but also with his uncle's and Mr. Cotter's ambivalence toward Father Flynn.

As the reality of Father Flynn's death begins to sink in, the boy undertakes a closer scrutiny of the priest's life than what he had previously allowed himself. Although Father Flynn was diligent in his religious instruction of the boy, the child's recollections suggest that his teacher's own response to Catholic dogma had become highly idiosyncratic, to say the least. Indeed, the most striking elements of the priest's behavior recollected by the boy go well beyond what one might explain as the eccentricities of a man of advancing age and in fact seem to reflect a corrosive bitterness and a profound disillusionment linked to a fundamental loss of belief.

The next evening, the boy and his aunt go to pay their respects at the house in Great Britain

Street in which, during the final days of his life, Father Flynn had lived with his sisters. The tawdriness of the home adds to the aura of shameful gloom that has permeated the narrative. In the story's closing pages, as Father Flynn's sister Eliza describes what she chooses to see as her brother's eccentric behavior, the priest's profound alienation from society becomes all too evident to readers. Eliza tries to overcome her own chagrin over her brother's actions with a simple bromide meant to explain it all away, "[H]e was too scrupulous always" (*D* 17). Nonetheless, when she recounts how two other priests had discovered her brother one night sitting "in his confession-box, wide-awake and laughing-like softly to himself" (*D* 18), the tremendous strain that his erratic conduct has produced in his sisters becomes all too apparent to readers.

In Father Flynn's seeming inability to counteract the despair and lethargy that blighted his last years, in his probable loss of faith, and in his certain mental breakdown, Joyce introduces multiple manifestations of the spiritual paralysis that underlies all of *Dubliners*. At the same time, he deftly avoids allowing despair to impose a single unambiguous approach to the story or to the rest of the work. Too much uncertainty surrounds Father Flynn's behavior and its impact on the boy to allow a simple interpretation. Further, although the poignancy not only of Father Flynn's life but of the lives of all the characters invites the reader's empathy, even this feeling is not unmixed. A willful smallness circumscribes all their lives, making unalloyed sympathy impossible.

Even the story's title resists easy explanation. Foregrounding the women who will not appear until late in the narrative and who will function only at the margins of the narrative leaves us unsure of the degree of irony Joyce means to convey. In the end, "The Sisters" offers a keen sense of what Joyce himself described as "the odour of ash-pits and old weeds and offal [that] hangs round my stories" (*Letters*, I.64) without forcing upon the reader a particular meaning for that impression.

Despite its chronicle of frustration and despair, "The Sisters" stops short of leaving the reader with the feeling of desolation. The tragedy inherent in the daily lives of Joyce's characters need not, and indeed should not, be seen as justifying nihilism. Indeed, in the very action of recounting the story, the unnamed narrator attests to its complexity and to his own determination to resist, even if only instinctively, the deadening effect of the world that overwhelmed Father Flynn.

For additional information regarding Joyce's attitudes toward this story, see *Letters*, II.86, 91, II.4, 134, 143, and 305–306.

## CHARACTERS IN "THE SISTERS"

**Flynn, Eliza** She is one of the two sisters who provide the title of the story and who cared for their retired brother, the Rev. James Flynn. Together with Nannie Flynn, Eliza runs a shop "under the vague name of *Drapery*" that sells umbrellas and children's booties (*D* 11). At the end of the story, when the unnamed narrator and his aunt attend Father Flynn's wake at Eliza and Nannie's home above their shop, Eliza attempts to rationalize a reason for her brother's nervous breakdown. Her conversation shows a propensity for denial even as her tendency toward employing malapropism lends an unintended humor to what she says.

**Flynn, Rev. James** He is the dead priest whose inability in this story to cope with the world sets a tone for the entire collection. Although he never actually appears as a character, his erratic behavior, spiritual paralysis, and eventual death dominate the narrative and are the central focus of the story. Father Flynn, in his relationship with the unnamed boy who narrates the story, serves to illuminate the young man's own nature and to clarify the forces of the claustrophobic Dublin world against which the boy will have to contend, in much the same fashion as Father Flynn did. Over the course of the story, one hears of various incidents from Father Flynn's life from characters as diverse as old Cotter (a neighbor), the unnamed boy, and the dead priest's two sisters. No single perspective gives a full view of the man, and no two accounts offer the same picture. It remains for the reader to reconcile the diverse accounts to form an idea of Father Flynn's life.

**Flynn, Nannie** She is one of the two sisters who give the story its title and who cared for their retired brother, the Rev. James Flynn, during his paralytic illness. Nannie and Eliza Flynn hold Father Flynn's wake in their home, above their dry goods shop where they sell umbrellas and children's booties. When the unnamed narrator of the story and his aunt attend the wake, Nannie, at her sister's bidding, offers them a glass of sherry. Although Nannie's actions are narrated, she has no dialogue, and is thus an example of the voiceless characters found throughout Joyce's writings.

### *"An Encounter"*

This is the second story in *Dubliners* placed in the first division of the collection, childhood. It was written in September 1905, and was the ninth in order of composition.

Although its sexual overtones and oblique references to pederasty may seem innocuous in comparison to descriptions appearing in contemporary fiction, "An Encounter" caused Joyce considerable problems with his publishers. Grant RICHARDS, who in 1906 had agreed to publish *Dubliners,* was uneasy over the depiction of the old man at the center of the story and wanted to omit it from the collection. Joyce's refusal to make this and other changes caused Richards to withdraw his offer to publish the collection. In August 1912, Joyce reluctantly agreed to delete the story if certain conditions were met by another potential publisher, George ROBERTS (see letter dated August 21, 1912, in *Letters,* II.309–310). Nonetheless, this concession proved insufficient to persuade Roberts to continue with the project. When Grant Richards finally published the collection in 1914, however, he dropped all objections and the story appeared as Joyce had originally written it.

The plot of "An Encounter" revolves around the escapades of two young boys who spend a day "mitching," skipping school classes to wander about the city. The opening paragraphs set the emotional tone of the story with themes of freedom, adventure, and conflict introduced through allusions to America's Wild West and the mock Indian battles the boys would arrange after school. There is also a sense of restlessness and boredom. "The summer holidays were near at hand," says the unnamed narrator, "when I made up my mind to break out of the weariness of school-life for one day at least" (*D* 21).

The scheme is soon put into action when the unnamed narrator and his friend Mahony, on "a mild sunny morning in the first week of June," meet near the Royal Canal, and wander along the North Circular Road toward the dock area of Dublin. They marvel at the sights along the quays, and then take a ferry across the River LIFFEY to Ringsend, an area on the south side of the city. After a lunch of biscuits and chocolate washed down by raspberry lemonade, they abandon their planned trip to the PIGEON HOUSE and laze about on a field near the Dodder River.

As they sit in the field unsure of what to do next, they are approached by a "queer old josser" who shows an obvious, if unspecified, interest in them. While the reader will quickly pick up on the man's pederastic inclinations, Mahony and the narrator do not have such a clear sense of him. Nonetheless, they remain uneasy in his presence. When Mahony runs off to chase a cat, the man is left alone with the narrator and begins to talk of whippings and of young girls. This proves too much for the boy to take, and he abruptly leaves and calls to Mahony to join him.

The story ends with no apparent harm having been done, but with a great deal left unsaid. Although clearly upset by the old man, the narrator does not seem either able or willing to articulate the specific source of his discomfort. When the boy rejoins Mahony, he feels both relieved to be in the relative safety of his friend's company and "penitent; for in my heart I had always despised [Mahony] a little" (*D* 28). The story ends there, leaving the reader with a vague sense of dissatisfaction, if not a sense of the spiritual paralysis the boys unwittingly encounter in the old man. We read as much into the scene as we wish, giving the situation whatever degree of gravity seems appropriate to our interpretation.

For more information relating to Joyce's views on the composition of "An Encounter," see *Letters,* II.108, 115, 134, 137–138, 141–142, 177, 298, 306, 309–310, 314, 325, and 327.

## CHARACTERS IN "AN ENCOUNTER"

**Mahony** The young schoolboy who skips classes with the unnamed narrator of the story. He pretends to be named Murphy to hide his identity from the Queer Old Josser.

**Queer Old Josser** The man who accosts the young boys as they lie in a field near the River Dodder.

**Smith** The name that the unnamed narrator of the story assumes to hide his identity from the Queer Old Josser.

### *"Araby"*

This is the third story in the *Dubliners* collection, and the final one in the initial group of stories dedicated to childhood. Written in October 1905, "Araby" is the 11th story that Joyce composed for the collection.

Like the first two stories, "Araby" relies upon an introspective, unnamed narrator who is recollecting his adolescent infatuation with the sister of a neighborhood friend, Mangan. More than a simple account of childhood love, however, the story lays out the larger question of the proper use of the imagination. In asking what differences, if any, exist between the images that an active mind produces as a source of aesthetic pleasure and those created as a form of escapism, the story challenges readers to articulate the interpretive values that allow one to distinguish a powerful narrative from idle speculation.

In the opening paragraphs the narrator vividly depicts the confining environment of North Richmond Street where he lived as a boy. (Although the time of the narrative remains indeterminate for most of the story, as will be noted later, the final lines give a strong indication of a retrospective analysis of events.) The narrator immediately highlights a central concern of the story by contrasting the physically circumscribed limits of this dead-end street with the imaginative potential offered by the books found in "the waste room behind the kitchen" (*D* 29). At the same time, the narrator does not restrict his search for imaginative stimulus to books. With no apparent concern for the implications of voyeurism, he recounts how on school mornings he would peer through a lowered blind in a front parlor window to watch Mangan's sister—herself unnamed—leave her house. He describes how he would then shyly follow her and pass her with a few perfunctory words when she reached the point where their paths separated. He was never able to engage her in an extended conversation, and so he was nonplussed when one evening she addressed him and asked whether he was going to the Araby bazaar (*D* 31). When he learns that Mangan's sister is much taken by the bazaar but cannot go to it, the narrator volunteers to attend and to bring her a present.

Although they remained events that attracted a good deal of attention, in Joyce's time such bazaars were fairly common in Dublin. In fact, a "Grand Oriental Fête" was actually held in May 1894, which corresponds with the approximate time of the story. Postcolonial interpretive theory has given readers a sophisticated sense of Orientalism, but nonetheless one needs to avoid making an overdetermined response to the setting. When Joyce wrote the story, the word *Araby* would be read as a variation of the term Arabia; applied to the bazaar, it would immediately evoke the exotic overtones of a distant and mysterious land. At the same time, the commercial banality of the fair would be apparent to all but the most determinedly idealistic Dubliner.

The narrator, however, has no interest in exposing the tawdry shabbiness of Araby. Rather, the bazaar becomes for him a symbol of the evocative power of his own awakening imagination. During the days preceding the fair, images of its splendor dominate his thoughts. Conflating Araby and Mangan's sister into an idealized alternative to the mundane existence around him, the boy fixes all his attention on the time that must pass until he is able to go to the bazaar.

Tension mounts on the Saturday of the bazaar, as the boy waits expectantly for his uncle to return home to give him the money needed to travel to the fair. In predictable dramatic fashion, as the hour grows later, his uncle's delayed return compounds the boy's anxiety. His uncle finally appears at a time that seems too late for a trip to Araby. He is slightly drunk and has forgotten the boy's plans. The consequent juxtaposition of the boy's frustration and his uncle's lack of concern neatly highlight the relative importance and unimportance of Araby.

The narrator then tells how he set out on what he sees at the moment as a romantic quest to purchase the gift for Mangan's sister. On the rail journey across town narrative details underscore the urban squalor through which the boy must pass, and it prepares the reader for the disappointment he will feel when he finally arrives at the bazaar just as it is closing. The boy finds the exhibition area nearly empty, the bazaar's attendants uninterested in his desire to make a purchase, and Araby's tawdry wares unacceptable for the portentous mission that he has undertaken.

The story ends on a note of frustration and bitterness. As he describes himself leaving the fairground, the now seemingly more mature narrator offers a brief but bitter insight into his youthful consciousness: "Gazing up into the darkness I saw myself as a creature driven and derided by vanity; and my eyes burned with anguish and anger" (*D* 35). While the shift in perspective may seem a jolt at first reading, the sardonic tone that has recurred throughout the story both substantiates the more mature view and leaves to readers the task of interpreting the significance of the boy's disappointment. Is he crestfallen because he realizes how foolish he had been to inflate the significance of his trip to Araby, or does he feel a deeper, more lasting disappointment over the deceptive power of an incautious imagination? The story avoids prescriptive interpretation by ending too abruptly to resolve the question, but it has deftly advanced the issue of the role of the imagination for the reader to consider.

The thematic organization neatly sustains this aura of ambiguity. Like many of the stories in *Dubliners*, "Araby" contains an abundance of religious and folk imagery. It makes allusions to Catholic litanies and to mythological symbols evoking the Grail quest, blending the two to give a sense of the boy's efforts to impose meaning on the world as dominated by a mixture of faith and fantasy. More specifically, his conflation of dogma and romanticism foregrounds the impulse for escape that anyone with imaginative powers living on North Richmond Street would feel. The imagery associated with these attitudes heightens the reader's sense of the struggle and painful awareness of the narrator's spiritual journey through the pleasures of the flesh without pointing to a clear interpretive response that one should make. Whether the "confused adoration" (*D* 31) of the young boy's childhood has in fact been resolved by insights gained at a more mature age remains an open question, but the complexity and intensity of the forces precipitating that struggle stand out clearly.

For references to Joyce's attitude about the composition of "Araby," see *Letters,* II.123–124, 128, and 437.n.3. See also the appendix on page 381.

## CHARACTERS IN "ARABY"

**Mangan** He is a friend of the unnamed narrator in the story and the only major figure identified by name. It is Mangan's sister, identified only by her relationship to her brother, who inspires the narrator with the desire to visit the bazaar that gives the story its title.

### *"Eveline"*

This is the fourth story in *Dubliners*. "Eveline" introduces the beginning of the volume's second division, accounts of adolescence. It also marks the shift in narrative point of view from the first person, which characterized the first three stories, to the third person, which will inform the discourse for the remainder of the collection. It was the second story of the collection that Joyce wrote, and it was first published under Joyce's nom de plume, Stephen DAEDALUS, in the September 10, 1904, issue of the *IRISH HOMESTEAD.*

With ample use of the FREE INDIRECT DISCOURSE narrative technique, the story unfolds both within and at a distance from the consciousness of its protagonist, Eveline Hill, a young woman whose life has become circumscribed by her job as a store clerk and by her responsibilities as a housekeeper for her father and a surrogate mother for her siblings. Straining against these stifling conditions, she has planned to elope with Frank, a sailor who is her presumptive "fiancé," to "Buenos Ayres" [*sic*]. Eveline imagines that away from the petty and demanding world of Victorian Dublin she will find the stable home life and experience the tender love currently absent from her life, and, perhaps most important, where, as a married woman, she will be treated with a respect that she does not now enjoy.

The story opens with Eveline sitting by a window in her home. She watches the evening descend upon the lonely neighborhood, mulling over events from her childhood, considering life with her family, and decrying the tedium of her own drab existence. Eveline feels trapped and conflicted. She had promised her dying mother to do what was necessary to keep the family together, but she now feels a restiveness that comes from realizing the limited options open to her in Dublin. She has met a young sailor, Frank, who has enthralled her. Her father, whether from selfishness or shrewd sense of human nature, disapproves of the young man, but that has only made their courtship more furtive than it would otherwise have been. Frank wishes her to elope with him, and promises her a life completely unlike anything she has ever known. However, Eveline's timidity causes her to agonize over her decision to renounce the promise she made to her mother and leave the family forever. Paradoxically, only after she recollects the scene of her mother's death do her feelings crystallize. Eveline is seized by "a sudden impulse of terror" (*D* 40) and she feels an urgent need to escape with Frank, who alone, she believes, "would save her" and "give her life" (*D* 40). Nonetheless, the inertial force of Dublin life proves extremely powerful. When Eveline arrives at the North Wall to board the boat with Frank, she is suddenly immobilized—paralyzed—by fear of the unknown, and she remains transfixed, unable to move. As Frank frantically pleads with her to join him on board the ship, "[h]er eyes gave him no sign of love or farewell or recognition" (*D* 41). The paralysis of death reaches beyond her mother's grave.

Although the meaning of the story may seem obvious at first, as with all of Joyce's works an inherent ambiguity, heightened by the oscillating views of free indirect discourse, disrupts easy interpretations. Because a good portion of the reader's information comes from Eveline's point of view, nothing from her sense of the world has the assurance of an objective account. At the same time that she tells us about the trials of her life, the narrative pulls back to show the flaws that inhibit her observations. Critics have played upon this duality to offer a wide range of interpretations of the story, particularly relating to Eveline's refusal to leave Dublin and to the options opened or foreclosed by her decision. No single interpretation is completely convincing. (Perhaps the most striking is Hugh KENNER's speculation that Frank had never intended to take Eveline to Buenos Aires but rather meant to turn her into a prostitute in Great Britain.) Cumulatively, however, these various readings underscore the ambivalence that runs through Eveline's narrative. Despite its implicit criticism of the limited provincial perspective of the story's title character, the narrative's willingness to evoke her feelings leaves one wondering what realistic options Eveline has. The reader must decide whether to center the pessimism of the story in its ending, or whether to take the broader and darker view that her patriarchal upbringing has so traumatized her as to negate the possibility of any alternative.

For further information on Joyce's attitude toward this story, see *Letters,* II.43 and 91.

## CHARACTERS IN "EVELINE"

**Frank** In the *Dubliners* story "Eveline," he is the young man with whom Eveline Hill plans to elope to Buenos Aires. In fact, the narrative does relatively little to flesh out his nature. Consequently, at the end of the story, even though their passage has been booked, when Frank is forced to leave without Eveline because of her incapacitating fear of change, it remains difficult to tell what effect this has upon him.

**Hill, Eveline** She appears as the listless title character in the *Dubliners* story "Eveline." To escape from a life of domestic oppression, she plans to elope with her fiancé, a sailor named Frank, to Buenos Aires. She plans to start a new life there as a married woman, and hopes to achieve the respect she believes she deserves. Before leaving her home, Eveline reminisces about her family, dwelling upon the abusiveness of her father and the entrapment she feels because of the death of her mother. However, when she arrives at the North Wall to meet Frank and board the ship, she is seized with an overwhelming terror that paralyzes her and saps her will to leave.

### *"After the Race"*

This is the fifth story in the *Dubliners* collection, and it is the second of the four stories in the second division of the collection, adolescence. In order of composition, it was third. An earlier version appeared in the December 17, 1904, issue of the IRISH HOMESTEAD.

The background for the story comes from an April 1903 interview with the French racing-car driver Henri Fournier, entitled "The Motor Derby" (see *Critical Writings*), which Joyce published in the IRISH TIMES. The information that came from Fournier would allow Joyce to contrast the international perspectives of the men who participated in this emerging sport with the insistent provincialism of the citizens of Dublin, an idea that implicitly informs the thematic organization of all of *Dubliners*. Joyce gained additional material for developing this concept when, on July 2, 1903, Ireland held the fourth annual Gordon Bennett Cup Race, won by a Belgian driver in a Mercedes.

Despite these obvious thematic and stylistic signatures that distinguish all of Joyce's work, the narrative shifts its emphasis from the central issues that characterize the other pieces in the collection—alienation and frustration within the middle and lower-middle classes—to focus attention on the nouveaux riches. Joyce himself was keenly aware of this dichotomy, for, almost two years after its composition, in an August 19, 1906, letter to his brother Stanislaus, he commented that he would have liked to rewrite the story (see *Letters*, II.151), although he was more concerned with getting the volume into print than with polishing this piece. His unease over the story remained, however, and on November 13 of the same year, Joyce wrote to Stanislaus that in his opinion "After the Race" was one of "the two worst stories" in the collection, the other being "A Painful Case" (*Letters*, II.189).

Whatever its quality, as one begins to read "After the Race" striking differences between it and the other stories in *Dubliners* emerge almost immediately. While most of the pieces in the volume offer detailed views of the lives of Dubliners desperately struggling to survive in a hostile economic and social environment, "After the Race" highlights the mindless prodigality of Jimmy Doyle, a popular young man from a well-to-do Dublin family. The story also introduces, as an intrinsic feature of the plot, other characters whose wealth and foreign citizenship distance them from the few poor Irish figures who appear in "After the Race" and throughout the collection. In this fashion, Joyce makes telling points about the environment from which Jimmy and the rest of the Doyle family seek to escape, but, unlike the other accounts in the collection, the differences highlighted here are drawn sharply, almost didactically, without the subtlety that characterizes the other stories.

In the opening paragraph of "After the Race," the narrative offers ironic commentary on the tempo of life in Ireland and on the Continent and adds to that a heavy-handed comment that contrasts the prosperousness of the racers with the penury of their audience: "At the crest of the hill at Inchicore sightseers had gathered in clumps to watch the cars careering homeward and through this channel of poverty and inaction the Continent sped its wealth and industry" (*D* 42). Though none of the characters has been introduced, readers can see retrospectively that the tone of this opening, employing free indirect discourse, mimics the nonchalance of Jimmy and his friends and their patronizing disdain for the provincial curiosity of the Irish spectators. Although the narrative moves quickly beyond the scene to develop the action of the story, these opening images form an emblematic impression of the unarticulated struggle for identity that takes place within Jimmy's consciousness.

Despite the relentless emphasis on materiality in the opening pages, in short order the narrative of "After the Race" foregrounds personal spiritual alienation and communal privation as insistently as any of the other stories. Presaging the dilemma that James Duffy will face in "A Painful Case," "After the Race" portrays Jimmy's emotional entrapment, or paralysis, in a tone of chilling finality that belies his material security. Although these themes are embodied by most of the major characters throughout the collection, "After the Race" represents its central figures in a fashion closer to that of the Russian writers Dostoyevsky or Lermontov than to anything else in *Dubliners*.

Throughout the hectic day Jimmy moves from one location and situation to another as a passive observer rather than an active participant. In many ways this is the most suitable role for him to adopt, for despite his 26 years and lifelong familiarity with Dublin, the places and incidents featured or alluded to in the story—life at Cambridge University, a drunken, private dinner in a Dublin restaurant, a late-night card party on a yacht—even when he appears as a participant are all outside his field of comprehension. When he does endeavor to inject himself into the midst of the action, it is always with an unvoiced sense of being on the brink of a social misstep.

Thus, if the wealthy Jimmy Doyle embodies the hopes for social acceptance of an affluent Irish Catholic upper-middle class, the success of that prospect remains uncertain. With the encouragement of his father, Jimmy plans to invest a substantial amount of his inheritance "in the motor business" (*D* 45), a plan he takes seriously, but which—given his behavior throughout the story—the reader may view with skepticism. By the end of "After the Race," Jimmy is exhausted and in debt after heavy losses in an all-night card game, an apt symbol for his future. The new day breaks "in a shaft of grey light" (*D* 48) that brings Jimmy personal remorse and prefigures what is to come: "He knew that he would regret in the morning but at present he was glad of the rest, glad of the dark stupor that would cover up his folly" (*D* 48).

Despite the significant difference between Jimmy's social position and that of other characters in *Dubliners*, these final lines situate him in the same moral landscape they all inhabit. In his ambivalence between guilt and denial, Jimmy reflects the same lack of assurance that countless other characters express in Joyce's stories. It is not simply that he is unable or unwilling to judge his behavior dispassionately. Rather, he reflects a stark lack of faith in the ability of any standard of values to provide an accurate assessment of his life. Further, the ambiguity of the situation makes it difficult to discern the real consequences of Jimmy's folly. Has he lost so much that his future is genuinely in jeopardy, or has he simply incurred more debt than his father will be willing to pass off with a tolerant laugh?

For additional information on Joyce's views on the story and on his process of composing it, see *Letters*, II.39 n.4, 109, 151, and 189.

## CHARACTERS IN "AFTER THE RACE"

**Doyle, Jimmy** He is the protagonist of the story. Though relatively nondescript, it is noteworthy that he and Gabriel Conroy in "The Dead" are the only principal characters in the collection who are not clearly members of Dublin's middle or lower-middle class. The son of an aspiring Dublin family, Jimmy Doyle first appears as one of the passengers in the racing car of Charles Ségouin. He afterward entertains and socializes with the young men—French, Hungarian, Canadian, American, and English—who have participated in the race. In his efforts to emulate the wild life he imagines these fellows must lead, Jimmy in fact embodies the insecurities and the gaucheries of the nouveaux riches.

**Farley** He is the American on whose yacht Jimmy and the others play cards.

**Ségouin, Charles** He is the owner of the French automobile in the race that opens the story, and one of the winners in the card game that ends it. Ségouin's character is most likely based upon the French racing car driver Henri Fournier, whom Joyce interviewed before the 1903 running of the James Gordon Bennett Cup Race. The interview appeared in the April 7, 1903, issue of the *Irish Times* under the title "The Motor Derby" and is reprinted in *The Critical Writings of James Joyce*.

### *"Two Gallants"*

This is the sixth story in *Dubliners*, and, according to Joyce's own division of the book, it is the third tale of adolescence. Overall, "Two Gallants" is the 13th *Dubliners* story in order of composition. Joyce wrote it over the course of the winter of 1905–06.

"Two Gallants" details the dubious activities of two venal, self-absorbed, and worthless young men, John Corley and T. Lenehan, over the course of one hollow evening in DUBLIN. The story ironically parallels the exploitive amorous adventures of Corley, represented indirectly through speculation and insinuation, with the forlorn and sullen peregrinations around the city center of his friend Lenehan, depicted graphically in the text. (Both characters reappear in *Ulysses,* each in significantly reduced circumstances that provide a material commentary on their spiritually degraded natures.) Although the narrative focuses upon Lenehan and his misfortune, his self-pity and pettiness deprive him of any claim to our sympathies. Further, his venal complicity with Corley's exploitation of the servant girl ("a slavey" in Dublin slang) at the close of the story forcefully brings home to the reader the degraded nature of his behavior.

In its opening lines, "Two Gallants" first foregrounds images of smug materiality, and then quickly undercuts them with descriptions introducing the themes of futility, insensitivity, hypocrisy, and bitterness that emerge over the course of the narrative. As Lenehan and Corley near the end of a desultory walk around the city, Corley, with an aura of vapid self-satisfaction, is discussing his crass affairs with various young women, and Lenehan is encouraging him with fawning responses to make further disclosures.

Bust sculpture of James Joyce in St Stephen's Green, Dublin *(Faith Steinberg)*

Abruptly, but with the promise of meeting later, Corley leaves Lenehan near St Stephen's Green and goes off for his assignation with a young slavey who works and lives nearby in a well-to-do household. In a scene that combines frank vulgarity with an even coarser strain of voyeurism, Corley by prearrangement allows Lenehan to walk past the couple to get a clearer look at the young woman. After Corley and the girl have gone off to catch the Donnybrook tram that will take them out to the suburbs, Lenehan moves listlessly through the streets, seeking diversions that will help him pass the time until 10:30, when the two men have arranged to get together again.

Lenehan's solitary walk covers roughly the same area that he and Corley had traversed a bit earlier in the evening, and the retracing of their route and the desultory thoughts that occupy Lenehan's mind as he walks underscore for readers not simply the aimlessness of his wandering but the greater pointlessness of his life. Despite his bravado, Lenehan seems quite aware that he is in a degraded state, both morally and materially. While impatiently awaiting the return of Corley and the young woman, Lenehan spends his time resenting his marginalized social status and dreaming of living a comfortable middle-class life. As he moves through the fashionable crowd walking along Grafton Street, he feels acutely his alienation from the men and women who pass him by. Indeed, Lenehan is estranged not merely from his fellow Dubliners but also from his own nature. Although he appears to be a man who can make himself pleasant in certain company, displaying a chameleon-like ability to adapt his demeanor to any circumstance and a seemingly limitless capacity for toadying, a clear sense of self-loathing lurks beneath the surface of his consciousness. Indeed, when alone Lenehan is so completely alienated and without even minimal resources for amusement that the mere task of occupying himself for the few hours until his companion returns baffles him: "The problem of how he could pass the hours till he met Corley again troubled him a little. He could think of no way of passing them but to keep on walking" (*D* 56).

When Lenehan breaks off his restless wanderings around the city to eat in a cheap restaurant situated off Rutland Square, his real circumstances become clear. He grumbles because he has not eaten since breakfast, and now he can afford nothing more than a two-pence-halfpenny meal consisting of a plate of peas and a bottle of ginger beer. The narration vividly delineates Lenehan's condition in terms of class awareness. Prohibited by his finances from patronizing a more expensive restaurant in a more respectable part of town, he feels embarrassed to be seen entering a rundown eating house that caters to a working-class trade. Lenehan attempts to compensate for the apparent inappropriateness of his choice and his own sense of social awkwardness by speaking to the waitress "roughly in order to belie his air of gentility for his entry had been followed by a pause of talk" (*D* 57). Clearly uncomfortable in this proletarian café, Lenehan, at age 31, is caught between his middle-class expectations and the reality of his diminished prospects, which he is reluctant to acknowledge. Although his future looks bleak, he deludes himself with dreams of finding a good job and a pleasant home.

After his awkward meal north of the river, Lenehan turns south, crosses the Liffey, and heads toward the area near the city hall. There he meets several acquaintances, and the lethargic conversation of these men, summarized in a terse paragraph of indirect discourse, underscores the superficial, perfunctory nature of most of Lenehan's social relationships. Neither he nor his peers have any interest in conversation beyond an exchange of brief pleasantries and banal observations.

The tempo of the narrative and coincidentally of Lenehan's movements picks up as the time approaches for Corley to return to town with the young servant girl. While Corley walks the woman home, Lenehan follows the pair at a distance to the door of her employer's home. In keeping with the theme of voyeurism introduced earlier in the story, he watches as the woman enters the house, quickly returns to give something to Corley, and then goes back inside. Lenehan eagerly joins Corley, and after a dramatic pause Corley opens his hand to reveal the small gold coin that the woman had given to him.

A general feeling of exploitation and manipulation dominates the narrative of "Two Gallants." It deftly suggests that Lenehan, Corley, and even the young woman who seems to be their victim approach each other with self-serving ends in mind. No character shares anything with another without an instrumental motive. Further, the voyeuristic emphasis in the narrative on gazing, looking, and observing does not suggest that these Dubliners feel empathy for one another. Rather, an ongoing, low-grade envy impels each to keep a close account of the material gains of everyone else.

Characterization reinforces these ideas. In his paralyzing listlessness, Lenehan is the type of an embittered, self-pitying Dubliner, and his venality overrides any pity the reader might initially feel for him, or for any of the other characters similarly affected. As will be graphically illustrated in *Ulysses*, Corley exudes a smug, self-congratulatory air, based on nothing more than momentary good fortune insufficient to sustain him when real trouble arrives. The nature of the unnamed slavey proves less easily analyzed, but the smirk she displays when she first meets Corley suggests a vapid self-satisfaction similar to his. Certainly, in its relentless examination of the brutal, ugly conditions of the lives of lower-middle-class Dubliners, and those falling out of the middle class, and in its compelling representation of the rhythms of Dublin street life, "Two Gallants" assumes a paradigmatic status among the *Dubliners* stories.

In a letter of May 20, 1906, Joyce told Grant RICHARDS, that "Two Gallants" "is the story (after 'Ivy Day in the Committee Room') which pleases me most" (*Letters*, I.62). Readers, however, have not always shared Joyce's affection for the story. Two prospective publishers, Grant Richards in 1906 and George ROBERTS in 1912, raised strenuous objections to the blunt exposition of various passages, and both said that it needed revisions and excisions before it could appear in print. Although in each instance Joyce showed a willingness to modify the narrative to the extent of deleting certain terms deemed objectionable (like the word "bloody"), he vigorously resisted all efforts to exclude the story completely from *Dubliners*. The disagreement over "Two Gallants" contributed to the decisions by Richards in 1906 and Roberts in 1912 not to publish the collection. (Roberts's decision was partly instigated by his printer, John FALCONER, who refused to complete the typesetting because he objected to certain passages.) Nonetheless, when Richards finally did agree to bring out *Dubliners* in 1914, "Two Gallants" retained the form that Joyce had originally given it.

For a more detailed view of this controversy and of the stages of the story's development, see *Letters*, II.130–138, 141–144, 166, 176, 181, 184–185, 199, 212, and 315. See especially "A Curious History" in *Letters*, II.291–293 and 324–325, reprinted in *Dubliners*, pp. 289–292.

## CHARACTERS IN "TWO GALLANTS"

**Corley, John** He is one of the two principal characters in the story. As the son of a police inspector, Corley comes from a solid middle-class background, though his coarse sensuality belies it. He casually seduces a servant girl as a means of getting money from her. See also characters under *Ulysses*.

**Lenehan, T.** He is the hanger-on who is Corley's companion in the story, and he reappears in a similar role throughout *Ulysses*. Despite his affected nonchalance when he is with others, Lenehan spends most of his time desperately trying to ingratiate himself with various people. He draws upon a store of coarse humor, ribald gossip, and horse racing tips to gain the approbation of others. Joyce consistently portrays him as a shameless sponger. Lenehan relentlessly plays the buffoon in anticipation of drinks and with the hope of gaining small favors from anyone willing to oblige him.

The pathetic quality of his life emerges in graphic, concentrated form in "Two Gallants." In the middle portion of the narrative, as Lenehan walks aimlessly around the center of town waiting for the return of John Corley and the young servant girl Corley had taken out, the reader gets a palpable sense of the profound alienation he feels. Alternating between Lenehan's thoughts and a description of the tawdry world through which he moves, the narrative underscores the emotional and spiritual toll exacted from Lenehan by the necessity of toadying to men like Corley.

Joyce modeled Lenehan on Michael Hart, a Dublin friend of his father. See also characters in *Ulysses*.

### *"The Boarding House"*

This is the seventh story of *Dubliners*, and it is the last of the four stories that make up the second division of the work devoted to adolescence. "The Boarding House" was the fifth story in Joyce's order of composition. He finished on July 1, 1905, and it was first published in 1914 when the complete *Dubliners* appeared. It subsequently appeared, along with "A Little Cloud," in the May 1915 issue of the American magazine *Smart Set*, edited by H. L. Mencken.

The story focuses on the efforts of Mrs. Mooney, the landlady of a north-side Dublin boardinghouse, to compel one of her roomers, Bob Doran, to marry her daughter Polly (see Polly Mooney). The story's events reflect in miniature a critique of the broader sexual and marital tensions of Irish life. The recurring conflict of the story stands out not regarding the proper moral choice for a character to make but rather as an inquiry into whether the option of choice in fact exists. As the reader glimpses details of the lives of Mrs. Mooney, Polly, and Bob Doran, it becomes evident that none of the characters has any real options to exercise. Rather, the weight of social convention immediately overwhelms the opportunity for choice, ensuring that every decision made by every character is a foregone conclusion from the opening lines to the end.

Chronologically, the narrative unfolds during the brief period between Sunday breakfast and the noon mass at the Pro-Cathedral (the seat of the Catholic Church in Dublin, used as a substitute for a cathedral because the English had appropriated that term for two Church of Ireland places of worship, St. Patrick's and Christ Church Cathedral) on Marlborough Street in the city center. However, through a series of flashbacks, the story traces the increasingly intimate relationship between Polly and Bob Doran. Despite initial appearances, the narrative is not a straightforward account of seduction and its consequences. Instead, the events that ultimately cause the confrontation between Mrs. Mooney and Doran are shown to the readers alternately from the points of view of a determined Mrs. Mooney, a frightened and angry Bob Doran, and a self-confident, though in this instance an uncharacteristically subdued, Polly.

While their interpretation of events varies, the facts as seen by all three characters are consistent: Doran has had sexual intercourse with Polly on at least one occasion. Polly does not appear to have become pregnant as a consequence, but her status has nonetheless changed radically in the eyes of the Dublin moral world in which all of the characters live. The reader, from a position of detachment, might speculate on questions of responsibility, and indeed the narrator has provided ample grounds for seeing Bob Doran as a man as much the seduced as the seducer. Indeed, the calculated response of Polly and her family can be read in the ironic overtones used by the narrator who states that the pragmatic Mrs. Mooney "knew he had a good screw [wages] . . . and . . . suspected he had a bit of stuff put by" (*D* 65). In the rapidly unfolding confrontation between Doran and Mrs. Mooney, the choice, if one could call it that, is made clear. Doran and Polly must marry or both will be disgraced. (The threat of physical violence from Polly's brother Jack if Doran did not agree to this also hovers in the air. Additionally, Doran has already been told in confession that his actions were sinful and that he must make reparation.) In the end Doran's assent appears more a recognition of the fait accompli than an actual choice.

As one takes a closer look at the story, however, any consideration of guilt and responsibility quickly recedes into the background, for the narrative raises more fundamental questions regarding the nature of free will and human behavior. It shows the actions of all of the characters who play a prominent role in the story—mother, daughter, and lodger—circumscribed by the conventions of society, which impose complex and rigidly prescriptive roles on each. They are all equally victims and predators.

While the narrative makes the decisions of these characters based on their actions foregone conclusions, a complex social interdependence informs what transpires. Mrs. Mooney, Polly, and Doran have all based their behavior upon fundamental needs—material, cultural, or sexual. At the same time, each has come to realize that only accepted societal conventions can legitimize the gratification of those needs. Each has acted without first securing the approval of others, and now, whatever the long-term cost, each wrongdoer must make reparation to bring his or her behavior into conformity with social norms.

In the end, one cannot understand "The Boarding House" without remaining clearly attentive to the influence of social strictures and the consequent expectations placed upon the characters. Joyce's story carefully avoids the clichéd, melodramatic view of lower-middle-class seduction. Instead, it highlights not the behavior of individuals but the moral context of that behavior—the most active and powerful "character" in the story.

For additional information about Joyce's views on the composition of "The Boarding House," see *Letters*, II.92, 98, 115, 130, 131, 134, 136–138, 177, 179, 212, 315, and 325.

## CHARACTERS IN "THE BOARDING HOUSE"

**Doran, Bob** He is the figure around whom the action of the story turns. Doran, one of the roomers at Mrs. Mooney's boardinghouse in Hardwicke Street, is identified throughout the narrative with ironic formality as *Mr. Doran*. The narrative gradually makes it clear that Doran has become sexually involved with Mrs. Mooney's daughter, Polly Mooney, and that his landlady is determined to force him to marry her daughter as reparation for the supposed loss of the girl's honor (*D* 65). Although Doran is not guiltless, the narrative makes him out to be as much the victim as the offender in this situation. See also characters under *Ulysses*.

**Mooney, Jack** Jack is the brother of Polly Mooney and the son of the landlady. He works as a "clerk to a commission agent in Fleet Street [and] had the reputation of being a hard case" (*D* 62). Although he is a relatively minor character in the story, his propensity for violent behavior puts added pressure on Bob Doran, who thinks of Jack when struggling to decide how to respond to the demands of Mrs. Mooney regarding Polly.

**Mooney, Mrs.** She is one of the characters who control much of the action in the story. She is the mother of Polly Mooney and Jack Mooney, and is also the formidable proprietress of the boardinghouse where Bob Doran lives. As the narrative quickly makes clear, Mrs. Mooney, who "dealt with moral problems as a cleaver deals with meat" (*D* 63), is a calculating woman with a harsh, pragmatic view of the world that blends cynicism and animal cunning in roughly equal measures. She has a clear sense of what she wants and feels absolutely no qualms about manipulating others to achieve her ends. At the same time, the narrative clearly represents her as rather shortsighted, with no real grasp of, or concern for, the long-term consequences of her actions. Thus after learning of sexual relations between her daughter and Doran, she follows the most expeditious course of action and bullies Doran into marriage by threatening to provoke a scandal. The unhappy consequences of this precipitous act become obvious in *Ulysses,* in the course of which various characters, mixing pity and contempt, comment upon the Dorans' disorderly married life.

**Mooney, Polly** She is one of the more ambiguous characters in the story. Polly is the spoiled and self-absorbed daughter of Mrs. Mooney, the proprietress of the boardinghouse. Polly's sexual intimacy with one of her mother's roomers, Bob Doran, leads to the crisis at the center of the story and to Mrs. Mooney's forcing Doran to marry Polly. Although at first she seems to be little more than a stock seduction figure, the narrative draws her character in such a way as to suggest that her engagement in the events of the story is more ambiguous than the basic plot would indicate. Polly clearly initiates intimacy with Bob Doran, and she certainly wishes to be married. However, by the end of the story it is quite apparent that at this stage in her life at least, Polly's inclinations are more sentimental and less calculating than those of her overbearing mother, who forces her into the marriage as well.

### *"A Little Cloud"*

This is the eighth story in the *Dubliners* collection. It marks the beginning of the third section of stories, those concerned with maturity. Written in early 1906, "A Little Cloud" was the 14th story in Joyce's order of composition. Along with "The Boarding House," it was published in the May 1915 issue of the American magazine *Smart Set,* edited by H. L. Mencken.

Joyce took the story's title from a biblical verse, 1 Kings 18.44: "And it came to pass at the seventh time, that he said, Behold, there ariseth a little cloud out of the sea, like a man's hand." The passage punctuates an account of the defeat of the prophets of Baal by God's prophet Elijah. By ending a long drought that had plagued the people of Israel, Elijah manifested to them the power of God, and brought the people of Ahab back to the worship of the Lord. The line from which Joyce draws his title marks the turning point in Elijah's struggle to overcome the prophets of Baal. Joyce depicts a similar contest, arguably based on this struggle, in his account of the confrontation of St. Patrick and the Druid in *Finnegans Wake.*

"A Little Cloud" centers on a series of frustrations, disappointments, and insecurities that mar the seemingly contented bourgeois existence of a law clerk, Thomas Malone Chandler. He is known to his friends and to the story's narrator by the diminutive, "Little Chandler," and that provides an eponymous identification of the source of his trouble: a progressively shrinking sense of possibilities. The narrative describes in detail Chandler's meeting with Ignatius Gallaher, a man whose life stands as the antithesis of Chandler's. Gallaher is an old acquaintance, though calling him a friend would exaggerate their relationship, who now, after a number of years' absence, is revisiting Dublin as a successful London journalist. After being patronized by Gallaher when they meet for a drink, Little Chandler goes home to a domestic scene that makes clear that the dissatisfaction with his life that he has felt throughout the day will more than likely continue and even grow for the remainder of his life.

Stylistically, the story unfolds using the free indirect discourse technique that is by now becoming familiar to readers of the collection. As the narrator describes events in the third person, while punctuating the discourse with poignant observations drawn from Chandler's point of view, the reader has exposure to both a detached and a highly subjective sense of events. The effect of this bifurcated technique is to play off any sympathy one might feel for the main character's growing dissatisfaction against an awareness of the banal, conventional nature of his life. These divergent points of view combine to emphasize Little Chandler's frustration with his own inability as a man to develop the artistic aspirations that he felt as a youth.

Predictably, the return of Ignatius Gallaher to Dublin for a brief visit brings Little Chandler's feelings of dissatisfaction to a head. Gallaher's achievements as a journalist remind Chandler of his own frustrated efforts to gain recognition as a poet. Further, Gallaher's material success and open way of living underscore for Chandler the circumscribed physical, emotional, and psychological conditions of his own household.

From the perspective of the reader, the character of Ignatius Gallaher may seem less than meets the eye. One can hardly fail to notice the bluff and bluster that overlay the accounts of his otherwise pedestrian professional and personal successes. At their meeting in the bar of the Burlington Hotel (known to locals in Joyce's day as Corless's, the surname of its manager, Thomas Corless), Gallaher's conversation takes on the nature of a performance, undertaken perhaps as much for his own benefit as for Chandler's. (Gallaher's journalistic exploits are recounted, inaccurately, in laudatory fashion by the drunken editor of the *FREEMAN'S JOURNAL*, Myles Crawford, in the Aeolus episode, chapter 7, of *Ulysses*.)

While the reader may find Gallaher's achievements suspect, the opportunities that he has had, and taken, nonetheless sharply underscore for Chandler the timidity of his own life. When Gallaher speaks of living in London and Paris, the mere mention of the cities confers for Chandler an aura of glamour upon the stories. This is not to say that Chandler naively accepts everything that Gallaher says at face value, but he does stand in awe of Gallaher's willingness to seize the opportunities that were presented to him.

In the final scene, which plays off the story's hopeful title with painful irony, the domestic tranquility that readers might have assumed stood in contrast to Gallaher's hectic bachelor life is now represented as smothering. Whatever euphoria Chandler may have taken away from his meeting with Gallaher quickly dissipates as his wife, Annie, criticizes him for coming home late and for neglecting to buy coffee at Bewley's. When she rushes out to purchase tea, Chandler is left to watch their infant son and to brood.

While waiting for his wife to return, he expresses his feelings in a series of desperate rhetorical questions: "Could he not escape from his little house? Was it too late for him to try to live bravely like Gallaher? Could he go to London?" (In the Ithaca episode, chapter 17, of *Ulysses*, Leopold Bloom—contemplating his options after the adultery of his wife—will ask himself these same basic questions, and come no closer to answering them than does Chandler.) During this reverie, the baby awakens and begins to cry. Chandler's attempts to soothe him only increase the child's unhappiness. When Annie returns, she berates him for his ineffectual efforts, shunts him aside, and, while he watches in shame and chagrin, proceeds to comfort the baby and seemingly call into question Chandler's role in the family by cooing to the infant: "My little man! My little mannie!" (*D* 85). Joyce has prepared this final scene that underscores both for Chandler and for the reader his sense of entrapment and emasculation in the materially comfortable middle-class life that he has created for himself. At the same time, Joyce refuses to allow a single point of view to dictate the full meaning of the story.

Chandler's feelings show that he lacks the courage to turn his back on the material and psychological ties that sustain his domestic life. When the baby begins to cry uncontrollably, Chandler is angered by its outburst, but he also feels measurable concern: "He counted seven sobs without a break between them and caught the child to his breast in fright. If it died!" (*D* 84). As Annie comforts the baby while he stands by helplessly, genuine contrition replaces his resentment and anger. "He listened while the paroxysm of the child's sobbing grew less and less; and tears of remorse started to his eyes" (*D* 85). This last line of the story cannot redeem the harsh critique of bourgeois Irish domestic attitudes so carefully built up over the course of the narrative, nor is it meant to. Nonetheless, it underscores for readers the complexity and even the contradictory nature of Chandler's attitudes. If he inhabits a sort of domestic hell antithetical to a supposedly carefree life like the one that Gallaher lives, it is one that Chandler has carefully constructed and conscientiously maintains for himself.

Joyce was fully aware of the aesthetic complexity inherent in the structure of the story. In a letter of October 18, 1906, to his brother Stanislaus, he underscores his sense of satisfaction at the story's achievements when he asserts that "a page of A Little Cloud gives me more pleasure than all my verses" (*Letters,* II.182). For a more detailed account of his attitude toward the story, see *Letters,* II.178–181, 184, and 199.

## CHARACTERS IN "A LITTLE CLOUD"

**Chandler, Little (Thomas Malone)** He is a law clerk and a self-pitying would-be poet who serves as the central figure in the story. After an eagerly awaited meeting with his expatriate friend, Ignatius Gallaher, who is visiting from London, Little Chandler begins to feel dissatisfied with his own drab and circumscribed life. Gallaher's seemingly successful life and sophisticated ways—his speech, his manner, his dress—are in sharp contrast to his own circumstances, which Little Chandler comes to see as impediments to happiness that he has imposed on himself, out of timidity. The story ends with Little Chandler humiliated at losing his temper after being unable to comfort his crying infant son as he is reprimanded by his wife, whose love and concern are directed only to the baby.

**Gallaher, Ignatius (Fred)** He is a character whose success as a reporter plays a prominent role in highlighting the dissatisfaction of Little Chandler. Gallaher is now a self-assured reporter working in the London press, but at one time he was with the *FREEMAN'S JOURNAL* in Dublin. In "A Little Cloud," Gallaher's carefree, affected continental ways are sharply contrasted to the monotony and entrapment of Little Chandler's daily life. Gallaher displays a generally condescending attitude toward life in Ireland. He is also mentioned in passing in the Aeolus episode of *Ulysses*—under the headline The Great Gallaher (*U* 7.626–656)—Myles Crawford, the editor of the *EVENING TELEGRAPH,* recounts Gallaher's unique journalistic coverage of the PHOENIX PARK MURDERS.

### *"Counterparts"*

This is the ninth story in *Dubliners.* "Counterparts" is the second story in the third division, maturity, and it was the sixth story in order of composition. Joyce had finished it by July 12, 1905.

The story follows the movements of Farrington, a nondescript solicitor's clerk, through an unsatisfying afternoon at work and into a series of evasions and humiliations that occur over the course of an evening's debauch. The compelling element of the description of Farrington's behavior is not so much the self-indulgence with which he drinks away the money he has gotten from pawning his watch or his categorical disregard for the welfare of his family but rather the joylessness that characterizes his actions. He does not regard drinking as a means to pleasure or satisfaction. On the contrary, he seems to drink merely to dull the ache of existence.

"Counterparts" opens with a tone that combines anger and frustration—with Mr. Alleyne, one of the firm's partners issuing the harsh peremptory command to "Send Farrington here" (*D* 86)—that alerts the reader to Farrington's tenuous grip on employment. This presages the first of a series of humiliations that Farrington will endure, and in some cases precipitate, over the course of the afternoon in his job at the firm of Crosbie & Alleyne. While the narrative carefully points to Farrington's complicity in bringing this abuse upon himself, it also makes clear the insensitivity and boorishness of the martinet who employs him.

After Mr. Alleyne confronts a plodding and lazy Farrington several times with his shortcomings, the matter comes to a head when Farrington is publicly rebuked and made to apologize for an inadvertent witticism made at the expense of his employer. The exchange puts Farrington in a towering rage. It forces him to confront his impotent position at the firm, and whets his appetite for alcohol. He pawns his watch to finance an evening of drinking, and sets off to use alcohol as a means of forgetting the day's humiliations.

As he makes the rounds of a series of pubs located in the center of the city, Farrington recounts the story of his exchanges with Mr. Alleyne altering the details and omitting the embarrassing portions to show himself in a better light. As the evening wears on, however, he finds himself getting increasingly less satisfaction from the rounds of drinks that he has been buying. Finally, his night of carousing comes to a bitter end when he finds himself teased by a young actress at Mulligan's pub and then beaten at arm wrestling by a young man whom he had treated to drinks.

Not surprisingly, Farrington returns home in a sullen, angry state. He rages that with all the money he has spent he still cannot feel properly drunk. Seeking some way to vent his fury, Farrington threatens and then beats his son Tom, on the grounds that the boy has let the hearth fire go out, though in fact his violence strikingly reflects frustration over his own inadequacies.

The harsh realistic theme of the story underscores a complex portrait of the psychological frustrations that punctuate the lives of many of the lower-middle-class Dublin men. In a November 13, 1906, letter to his brother Stanislaus, Joyce made the following comment on the story: "I am no friend of tyranny, as you know, but if many husbands are brutal the atmosphere in which they live (vide Counterparts) is brutal and few wives and homes can satisfy the desire for happiness" (*Letters*, II.192).

This was one of the stories that the printer for publisher Grant RICHARDS refused to set in 1906, because of Joyce's description of the young woman in Mulligan's pub whom Farrington fancies (see *Letters*, II.132). Joyce, in fact, did modify the description, but Richards still resisted publishing the collection. For additional information about this controversy and the composition of "Counterparts," see *Letters*, II.92, 98, 106, 115, 131–134, 136–142, 144, 176–177, 179, 181, 184, 312, and 314.

## CHARACTERS IN "COUNTERPARTS"

**Alleyne, Mr.** He is a minor but pivotal character. Alleyne, as one of the partners at the firm of solicitors Crosbie & Alleyne, is the direct supervisor of the clerk Farrington, and the one particularly irritated with the performance of the central figure of the story.

**Farrington** He emerges as the main character in the story. Farrington works as a scrivener (copyist) for the legal firm of Crosbie & Alleyne. Throughout the story, Farrington is subjected to humiliations and defeats, first at his place of employment and then later in a pub, where he loses an armwrestling match to an Englishman. At the end of "Counterparts," the humiliated Farrington vents his rage and frustration on his little son Tom. As Joyce explained in a November 1906 letter to his brother Stanislaus, the savagery of Farrington's actions at the end of the story reflects the viciousness Farrington himself experiences in the world in which he lives (see *Letters*, II.192). That explains the significance of the title. Farrington and his son Tom are counterparts. They both suffer unjustly from the casual brutality of an unfeeling world. The irony that Farrington not only has no sympathy for his son but also that the father's acts of violence will likely make the son evolve into a brutal husband is borne out by the story's title.

**Flynn, Nosey** He appears as a minor character in the story, standing Farrington a drink (see *D* 93) after hearing a rather distorted account of Farrington's exchange with Mr. Alleyne. See also characters under *Ulysses*.

**Tom** He is Farrington's young son. He is bullied by his father when the latter returns home drunk and humiliated by his arm-wrestling loss.

### *"Clay"*

This is the 10th story of *Dubliners* and the third in the third division of the collection, maturity. In order of composition, it was the fourth story written by Joyce, composed early in 1905, shortly after he had abandoned work on a story called "Christmas Eve." It was originally entitled "Hallow Eve" (see Miscellaneous Works). Joyce tried several times, unsuccessfully, to have "Clay" (and the earlier version, "Hallow Eve") published before it finally appeared as part of the *Dubliners* collection in June 1914.

"Clay" focuses on the impressions of an aging, unmarried woman, Maria, who works as a scullery maid in the Dublin by Lamplight laundry, a Protestant institution for reformed prostitutes in Ballsbridge. (The Catholic Church had similar establishments called Magdalene Homes. Dubliners at the time would have had some sense of the austere conditions faced by women who lived in these places, though perhaps not have been aware of the possibilities for abuse highlighted in the 2002 motion picture *Magdalene Sisters*.) On the day on which the story takes place—Hallow Eve—Maria has been given permission to take the evening off after serving tea and cake to the women at the laundry, and she has planned to visit the home of Joe Donnelly, his wife, and their children in Drumcondra to attend a Hallow Eve party. Maria's ambiguous position with the family comes out gradually, over the course of the narration. She had worked for the Donnelly family when Joe and his brother Alphy were children, and, as adults, they had gotten her a position at the laundry.

The visit to the Donnelly home obviously means a great deal to Maria, and she makes a special effort to see that all will go well. She stops first at Downes's pastry shop—at the time a well-known store on what is now O'Connell Street—to buy penny cakes, and then at a store around the corner on Henry Street to buy a plumcake because "Downes's plumcake had not enough almond icing on top of it" (*D* 102). Despite her careful plans, however, Maria remains easily flustered by strangers, and, when she finds herself sitting next to a drunken man on the tram to Drumcondra, she becomes so rattled that she forgets her plumcake.

When she arrives at the Donnellys' house, the family makes a great fuss over Maria, but her response suggests that the conviviality has an inauthentic quality. As the party progresses, it seems quite clear that Maria is very much on edge, carefully scrutinizing every gesture and hoping that nothing signals a change in the festive mood of the gathering. One source of concern for Maria is the estrangement between Joe Donnelly and his brother. While the cause of their falling out remains unclear, Joe's refusal to see his brother ever again attests to its gravity. The strength of Joe's resolution becomes quite clear when Maria attempts to mediate the quarrel between the two men and succeeds only in increasing Joe's sense of outrage.

Nonetheless, all wish the party to proceed pleasantly, so as a diversion they begin a round of games. Maria joins a game of saucers (a game of divination of the future based on which object the blindfolded person selects) and is tricked by one of the neighborhood girls into choosing clay, which symbolizes death. This brings a sharp rebuke from Mrs. Donnelly. Although the matter seems to be forgotten, afterwards, when singing "I Dreamt That I Dwelt" (a song from Michael BALFE's opera, *The Bohemian Girl*), Maria mistakenly repeats the first verse of the song. Whether the lapse comes from her faulty memory or from a desire to avoid unpleasant reminders of her mortality, it brings the story to an ambiguous and uncomfortable conclusion.

Despite the ostensibly mundane features of urban domesticity surrounding the story, "Clay" in fact presents a rather ominous view of the life of lower-middle-class Dublin women. Superficially, Maria's existence seems ordered and secure. However, the lapses in memory, awkward public exchanges, and mild social embarrassments she suffers over the course of the evening suggest at best a tenuous control over her environment. The events that unfold in the story attest that as a woman without the support of a family or the security of sound financial resources, she is acutely vulnerable, continuously if subtly under threat. Although she seems to enjoy the goodwill of the Donnelly family, Joe's moodiness and the spitefulness of the neighborhood girl show how much her position rests upon the sufferance of others. Like those of characters in other stories in *Dubliners,* Maria's life is circumscribed by a lack of options and opportunities. The deft maneuvers that she employs to avoid acknowledging the precariousness of her situation leaves it unclear how conscious she may be, but the reader cannot deny the bleakness of her existence.

For additional information regarding the composition of "Clay" and Joyce's attitude toward the story, see *Letters,* II.77, 83, 87–88, 91, 109, 147, 186, and 192.

## CHARACTERS IN "CLAY"

**Donnelly, Alphy** This is the name shared by two characters, uncle and nephew, in the story. The elder Alphy Donnelly, an offstage character, is the estranged brother of Joe Donnelly. When Maria mentions Alphy's name while visiting the Donnellys on Halloween, Joe responds indignantly and denies any possibility of ever seeing him again. The younger Alphy Donnelly is Joe Donnelly's son, apparently named after the uncle in happier times. Maria gives him a bag of cakes to divide among the children when she visits the Donnelly family on Halloween.

**Donnelly, Joe** He appears as the head of the Donnelly household, the family that Maria visits on Halloween. Maria had worried that he would be drunk (*D* 100) and spoil the evening, but Joe proves to be a pleasant host, although he does become irritated momentarily when Maria brings up the name of his estranged brother, Alphy. However, his anger is quickly dispelled and when Maria sings "I Dreamt That I Dwelt," from Michael William Balfe's opera *The Bohemian Girl,* Joe's eyes tear up. At the same time, the narrator ironically undercuts the sincerity of his emotion by linking his sentimentality with drink: "his eyes filled up so much with tears that he could not find what he was looking for and in the end he had to ask his wife to tell him where the corkscrew was" (*D* 106).

**Donnelly, Mrs.** She is the wife of Joe Donnelly. The narrative never does reveal her given name. During Maria's visit to the Donnelly family on Halloween, Mrs. Donnelly provides entertainment for her guests by playing the piano and by accompanying Maria when she sings "I Dreamt that I Dwelt," from Michael William Balfe's *The Bohemian Girl.* She attempts to provide the moderating influence between the children's high spirits and her husband's emotionality.

**Maria** She is the central character in the story. The narrative identifies her as a woman well into middle age who works as a cook's assistant in a Protestant institution dedicated to the reformation of prostitutes. As is made clear early on, Maria seems almost willfully unaware of the more brutal aspects of day-to-day life. Early in the story, she is described by the matron as "a veritable peace-maker!" (*D* 99), a description that yields ironic overtones as the story unfolds. In fact, this imperative for tranquility emerges from Maria's aversion to unpleasant behavior, like the public drunkenness of the man on the Drumcondra tram, a subtle reminder to the reader of her detachment from the troubled lives around her.

The action of "Clay" revolves around Maria's movements from the time that she leaves work at the Dublin by Lamplight laundry in Ballsbridge to her performance of "I Dreamt That I Dwelt" at the close of a Hallow Eve party at the Donnelly house in Drumcondra. Her journey across the city highlights Maria's fastidious determination to follow her plans, come what may; but her flightiness proves too much for her and through inattention she leaves behind the expensive cake that she had purchased for the Donnelly family.

Once at the party, she feels great discomfort over the quarrel that had alienated Joe Donnelly from his brother, Alfy. Later, the embarrassment and even pain she feels after choosing a piece of clay (a sign of death) during a parlor game underscores the vulnerability that lies beneath her veneer of charming eccentricity. Her mistake in repeating the first verse of the song that she sings rather than going on to the second brings the story to the point of bathos. (In a contrasting way, it also presages the performance of Julia Morkan in the last story of the collection, "The Dead.")

### *"A Painful Case"*

This is the 11th story in *Dubliners,* and it is the final work in the book's third division, accounts of maturity. "A Painful Case" was seventh in order of composition, written in July 1905 (originally composed under the title "A Painful Incident") and then repeatedly revised, indicating Joyce's dissatisfaction with the story. (See *Letters,* II.189.) Eight years after publication of *Dubliners,* "A Painful Case" was translated into French by Yva Fernandez, and it appeared in the March 1922 issue of the Swiss journal *Revue de Genève.* An Italian translation of the story, done by Giacomo Prampolini, was published in the June 3, 1928, issue of the journal *Fiera Letteraria.*

"A Painful Case" gives an account of the events that characterize the ultimately frustrated and sterile relationship between James Duffy and Mrs. Emily Sinico. What begins as a normal, healthy acquaintance takes a nasty turn when Mrs. Sinico makes a tentative gesture toward blending affection with friendship. Duffy peremptorily rebuffs her overtures, and immediately severs the relationship. Four years later, Duffy comes across a newspaper article, with the subheading "A Painful Case," that details the inquest into Mrs. Sinico's death. She had been struck by a railroad train while trying to cross the tracks at the Sydney Parade Station. The story touches on problems with alcohol, and Duffy cannot resist feeling a measure of self-justification over his actions four years previously. Joyce's brother Stanislaus JOYCE claimed that Joyce got his inspiration for this story from Stanislaus's own experience with an older woman, an account of which he recorded in his diary.

The story opens with a bit of geographical irony. It locates the residence of the misanthropic James Duffy in the Dublin suburb of Chapelizod, a locale near PHOENIX PARK long associated with the mythical lovers TRISTAN AND ISOLDE. In implicit contrast to their sensuous world, the narrative's description of Duffy's rooms emphasizes their ascetic quality without bringing forward a corresponding spiritual foundation. By highlighting Duffy's attraction to discipline and self-denial for their own sake, the opening description establishes him as an isolated man living a life without direction or convictions: "He had neither companions nor friends, church nor creed" (*D* 109).

Despite his aloofness, Mr. Duffy's reserve is not impenetrable. One evening during a concert given at the ROTUNDA, a woman seated next to him, Mrs. Emily Sinico, strikes up a casual conversation. The two meet again by chance at another concert, given at the National Concert Hall in Earlsfort Terrace, which leads to an opportunity "to become intimate" (*D* 110). Today's readers might interpret such a phrase as an indication of an established sexual relationship, but the narrative quickly disabuses us of such an idea, indicating that Duffy and Mrs. Sinico have begun to establish emotional ties. The potential for such a misreading, however, points out one of the strengths of the story. Sexual tension runs throughout the narrative, and Duffy's ignorance of its presence, at least until he is forcefully confronted with it, is nicely summarized by the term alluded to above.

Indeed, more than any other condition, the tendency to misperceive situations and characters—on the part of both Duffy and Mrs. Sinico—drives the action. While a sexual liaison, or at least some form of physical tenderness, may be precisely what Mrs. Sinico seeks, for Mr. Duffy the very existence of such a desire stands as an impediment to establishing a deep, personal relationship. He says as much in a journal entry (in words that are an almost exact quote of a phrase found in the diary of Stanislaus Joyce [*My Brother's Keeper,* pp. 165–166]) two months after breaking off his relationship with Mrs. Sinico because of her growing demands for greater intimacy: "Love between man and man is impossible because there must not be sexual intercourse and friendship between man and woman is impossible because there must be sexual intercourse" (*D* 112). The chilling brittleness of Duffy's assessment of human relations provides an unambiguous representation of his circumscribed nature, and it allows readers to understand how he could absolve himself from any culpability when he learns of the death of Mrs. Sinico four years later. However, Joyce does not leave matters there to impose a single possible interpretation upon the story.

Rather than close the narrative with Duffy's reaction to the newspaper's announcement of Mrs. Sinico's apparent suicide (allusions to her melancholy and drinking problem make the cause of death ambiguous), Joyce places this event just past the midpoint in the story, the second half of which gives an account of Mr. Duffy's faltering efforts to absorb the full impact of the news. After reassuring himself that this tragedy underscores the correctness of his decision, Mr. Duffy experiences a growing unease as he moves from the restaurant in the city where he read of the news, to a pub at the Chapelizod Bridge near his home where, uncharacteristically, he drinks several hot whiskey punches. After Mr. Duffy leaves the pub, he wanders into Phoenix Park. There, standing on top of Magazine Hill, he looks into the city. "He could hear nothing: the night was perfectly silent. He listened again: perfectly silent. He felt that he was alone" (*D* 117).

In these closing lines the sense of alienation that Mr. Duffy has experienced from the beginning of the story reasserts itself in the reader's imagination. Duffy's tone has changed dramatically. While previously Duffy had gloried in his aloofness from the rest of humanity, the certitude that enabled such a view now seems missing. The narrative does not elaborate upon what Mr. Duffy does feel, but it does ambiguously seem to acknowledge his new sense of the complexity of human relations and the profound desolation that permeates his own psyche.

As noted above, Joyce's frequent revisions indicate that he was not fully satisfied with the story. Nonetheless, one can see that "A Painful Case" easily fits into the overall pattern and themes of *Dubliners*. The forced confinement of Mrs. Sinico's life and the cultivated barrenness of Mr. Duffy's exemplify the sterile atmosphere that permeates all the stories in the collection. At the same time, the conscious ambiguity of the narrative's final lines frustrates the type of closure that Mr. Duffy's own reductive nihilism invites. Whether or not Mr. Duffy's experiences and insights into his life will lead to any change in his nature or behavior are questions not appropriate to the structure of the story. What is clear is that the modernist ideas that were emerging in Joyce's work at this time ensure that the story resists the easy resolution of the issues raised in the narrative through some conventional form of literary closure.

For further information relating to Joyce's attitudes toward this story and regarding its process of composition, see *Letters*, II.81n.3, 105, 115, 148, 151–153, 182, 189, 314–315, and 325.

## CHARACTERS IN "A PAINFUL CASE"

**Duffy, James** He is a cashier at a private bank and the main character in the story. Throughout the narrative one sees Mr. Duffy as a very private person set in his mundane ways. He is a man who "had neither companions nor friends, church nor creed" (*D* 109). He is given the chance at a romantic relationship with a woman, Mrs. Emily Sinico, whom he first meets at a concert and begins to see frequently. However, he rejects it as antipathetic to his nature. When Mr. Duffy later records the following summary of his thoughts on the incompatibility of humans, it clearly delineates his own abhorrence of human contact: "Love between man and man is impossible because there must not be sexual intercourse and friendship between man and woman is impossible because there must be sexual intercourse" (*D* 112). Joyce drew these sentiments from the journal of his brother, Stanislaus JOYCE, and he most certainly used his brother as a source for a number of Duffy's idiosyncrasies. It would, however, be a mistake to assume a strict parallel between Stanislaus and this fictional partial counterpart.

**Sinico, Captain** He is a character alluded to, but never seen, in the story. His title comes from his occupation as the captain of a merchant ship that regularly sails between DUBLIN and Holland. He is the husband of one of the story's central characters, Mrs. Emily Sinico. The incompatible temperaments of the captain and Mrs. Sinico, his frequent and extended absences, and his general indifference to his wife's needs contribute to Mrs. Sinico's restlessness and to her eventual decline. (Joyce borrowed the name Sinico from the composer Giuseppe Sinico, whom he knew in Trieste.)

**Sinico, Mrs. Emily** With Duffy, she is one of the central characters in the story. Mrs. Sinico is the alienated and isolated wife of Captain Sinico. After what seems to be a chance encounter with Mr. James Duffy at a music concert at the ROTUNDA, a friendship springs up between the two. Although for a time they seem to be progressing toward a greater intimacy, Mr. Duffy's temperamental aloofness prevents their relations from developing into real affection. After he rebuffs Mrs. Sinico's efforts to force the issue, the two drift apart, and Mrs. Sinico takes to drink. A few years later, while crossing some railroad tracks at a Sydney Parade Station, she is struck and killed by a train. With revulsion and possibly a degree of guilt, Mr. Duffy reads of her death in a newspaper article that hints that Mrs. Sinico was drunk and suicidal at the time.

**Sinico, Mary** She appears as the daughter of Mrs. Emily Sinico. Mary accompanies her mother to a concert where they first meet Mr. James Duffy. When Duffy subsequently visits Mrs. Sinico at her home, Mary's inattentive father wrongly assumes it is in pursuit of Mary's hand. In a newspaper article describing the inquest into her mother's death, Mr. Duffy reads Mary Sinico's account of the desultory nature of her mother's final years.

### *"Ivy Day in the Committee Room"*

This is the 12th story in *Dubliners*, and the first of the fourth and final division of the book, stories relating to public life. (The final story "The Dead," serves as a coda to the collection.) It was the eighth story in order of composition. Joyce completed it in the late summer of 1905.

"Ivy Day in the Committee Room" takes place on a cold, bleak, rainy October 6 in an unspecified year—either 1901 or 1902. (It is clear from the narrative that the action takes place some time after the death of Queen Victoria in January 1901 and before the visit of King Edward VII to Ireland in July 1903.) It derives its title in part from the day set aside to commemorate the death of Charles Stewart PARNELL (IVY DAY). Further Parnell associations come from the committee room mentioned in the title. It not only designates a political headquarters in Dublin's Royal Exchange Ward. It also alludes to Committee Room No. 15 in the Houses of Parliament in London, where on December 6, 1890, Parnell lost control of the Irish Home Rule Party.

The story centers on a number of professional campaign workers of various political loyalties who have, for reasons of expediency, accepted employment from "Tricky Dicky" Tierney (a candidate for local office). They are canvassing various parts of the ward to solicit votes for him. At the end of the day, these men gather in Wicklow Street at the Royal Exchange Ward office of the Nationalist ticket. There, they drink stout and express cynical opinions relating to the current municipal elections, the political process, and the various politicians whom they have encountered. Despite their critical attitude, their sentimental affections for the memory of Parnell come to the fore at the end of the story after the recitation by Joe Hynes of his poem, "The Death of Parnell." Indeed, their uncritical acceptance of this maudlin work indicates to the reader their distorted sense of a political past and calls into question their abilities to assess the present state of affairs.

Like Simon Dedalus in *A Portrait of the Artist as a Young Man*, where he is called "praiser of his own past," the men in "Ivy Day in the Committee Room" fill the narrative with nostalgic recollections, which are often compared by various speakers with what they see as the deteriorating condition of contemporary Irish society; however, the narrative undercuts such a perspective. For example, Old Jack is the caretaker of the building in which the men have gathered. However, his job is as ironic as so many other elements in the story. The description of the feeble old man in the opening paragraph makes it seem as if Old Jack himself needs looking after. When he goes on to fulminate against his worthless son to the other man in the room, the party hack Mat O'Connor, impotence is laid over fragility. As the narrative progresses and various political workers pass in and out of the Committee Room, they reinforce this impression of human failure, weakness, and self-delusion as the dominant features in their lives.

A group of these men—O'Connor, Joe Hynes, John Henchy, J. T. A. Crofton, and a man identified only as Lyons (possibly Frederick M. "Bantam" Lyons, a character who later appears in *Ulysses*)—have been hired to go through the Royal Exchange Ward seeking votes for Tierney, the Nationalist candidate. They all freely admit that their personal political views cover a broad spectrum, that they are motivated by little more than the promise of financial gain, and that their actual efforts to secure votes often consist of little more than sitting by the fire all day.

This combination of personal apathy and dependence upon political patronage leads them to numerous denunciations of the electoral process in general and of a wide range of political figures, from Edward VII to their employer Tierney, in particular. For all of their bluster, however, each man has achieved little in his own life. In consequence, an undertone of cynicism and bitterness pervades all of their remarks.

While this representation may seem a familiar modernist concern, Joyce nonetheless does not allow the narrative to slip into a predictable linear discourse. Just as the men have reached the height of their self-serving criticism of the world, Joe Hynes, fueled by alcohol and sentimentality, steps forward and recites his poem on Parnell. The tone of the poem echoes the same trite and maudlin sentiments that others in the room have expressed throughout the story, but it also conveys a measure of respect that no other figure or institution has been able to evoke. (Indeed, some critics have speculated that Hynes's verse may be a variation of the now lost poem "Et Tu, Healy" that a nine-year-old James Joyce wrote to commemorate the death of Parnell.) By putting the poem at the end of the story, Joyce reinforces the reader's experience of the twin modes of ambivalence and ambiguity that play such important roles in his work. The pedestrian quality of the verses points toward the simplistic nostalgic view of Parnell that sustains Hynes and the others. At the same time the undeniable sincerity of Hynes's recitation and of the verses themselves are in stark contrast to the apathy and the hypocrisy of the present day.

The poem genuinely seems to move the men in the room, who offer unreserved praise. At the same time, as Hynes sits mutely after his recitation, a cork from a Guinness bottle laid on the fire loudly pops. It reminds the reader that alcohol invariably plays a role in much of this sentiment expressed by the men and leaves one ambivalent about how sustained these feelings will be.

In a letter to his publisher Grant RICHARDS dated May 20, 1906, Joyce identified this story as his favorite (see *Letters*, I.62). "Ivy Day in the Committee Room" also proved to be one of his most troublesome, for it was among the stories that the publishers Grant Richards and later George ROBERTS urged Joyce to alter. They objected particularly to references to the adulterous habits of the Prince of Wales and to the appearance of the expletive "bloody" at several points in the narrative. Although Joyce offered to address some of their criticisms, his refusal to make all the changes they demanded contributed to the decisions by Richards in 1907 and by Roberts in 1912 not to publish *Dubliners*. When Grant Richards finally agreed to publish *Dubliners* in 1914, he withdrew his previous objections, and this story and all the others appeared in the form that Joyce intended.

For further details on Joyce's exchanges with his publishers, see "A Curious History" (see Miscellaneous Works). For more on this matter and for Joyce's attitude toward the story see also *Letters*, II.105, 109, 114–115, 134–136, 144, 177, 179, 288, 292–293, 306, 309, 314–315, and 329.

## CHARACTERS IN "IVY DAY IN THE COMMITTEE ROOM"

**Henchy, Mr. (John)** He is one of the canvassers for the Nationalist politician Richard J. Tierney, the politician running for office in the story. In the conversations that run through the narrative, Mr. Henchy expresses the moderate, accommodating sentiments of a political pragmatist, and his tolerant attitude toward King Edward VII provides a neat contrast to the ideologically hard-line positions of the Parnellite, Joe Hynes, and the Unionist, Crofton.

**Hynes, Joe** He is a newspaper reporter and a staunch admirer of Charles Stewart Parnell. The end of the story focuses attention on Hynes when he recites the sentimental poem that he has composed entitled "The Death of Parnell." For comments on his appearance in *Ulysses*, see characters under *Ulysses*.

**Old Jack** He is the caretaker of the offices where the men gather awaiting their pay for their canvassing efforts.

**Tierney, Richard J.** He is the politician and pub keeper, nicknamed "Tricky Dicky Tierney," for whom the men in the story are canvassing. Though he never appears with their pay, he does send up bottles of stout to placate them.

### *"A Mother"*

This is the 13th story in the *Dubliners* collection, it is the second in the fourth and final division of the volume, public life. (The final story, "The Dead," serves as a coda.) "A Mother" was the 10th story in order of composition. Joyce finished working on it sometime in late September 1905.

The narrative of "A Mother" focuses on the efforts of the snobbish, social-climbing Mrs. Kearney, the mother to which the title refers, to forward the musical career of her daughter, Kathleen Kearney. The story details the backstage machinations that surrounded the promotion and staging of concerts in turn-of-the-century Dublin, and through these representations Joyce is able to make a subtle, ironic commentary on the effect of the IRISH LITERARY REVIVAL on the popular culture of the time.

As the story opens, Mrs. Kearney's disposition hints at the way her obstinacy will shape subsequent events. "Miss Devlin had become Mrs. Kearney out of spite" (*D* 136). The reader soon sees that her malice is not directed at her husband, for she has a fierce loyalty to her family, but at "her friends [when they] began to loosen their tongues about her [remaining single for so long]" (*D* 137). Public opinion obviously has meant a great deal to Mrs. Kearney all her life, but her deeply ingrained pride also pushes her to seek ways of gaining esteem on her own terms rather than according to the dictates of others. It is these opposing forces that shape her behavior over the course of the story.

After her marriage, Mrs. Kearney concentrates her desire for attaining esteem within the community on her daughter Kathleen, whom she is ambitious to establish socially. The increasing popularity of the Celtic Revival provides her with a handy vehicle for her efforts, and Mrs. Kearney sees to it that Kathleen's musical talents are cultivated in a manner that will enable her to exploit the growing popular interest in Irish culture.

To further these ends, Mrs. Kearney agrees to allow her daughter to be the piano accompanist for a series of four concerts planned by the Eire Abu Society. (*Eire Abu,* "Ireland to Victory," is a very common slogan that appears on flags from the time of the Williamite Wars on through to the Irish Volunteers at the height of the Ascendancy during Grattan's Parliament and thence on into the 19th century. Joyce probably intended his readers to associate this fictitious society with any of the many similar groups springing up at that time as offshoots of the Celtic Revival.)

The importance of this event to Mrs. Kearney becomes clear to the reader through the tremendous effort she puts into preparing her daughter for the concert. She even goes so far as to give a hand to the desultory efforts of Mr. "Hoppy" Holohan, assistant secretary of the society, to promote it. As a result, she quickly comes to realize that much of the concert's success—and by extension, her daughter's—depends upon ticket sales and that in turn relates to the energies of the nebulous group of men who are responsible for the organizing and the staging of the performances. Mrs. Kearney becomes concerned when, after two evenings of disappointing attendance, the Friday concert is canceled, in order "to secure a bumper house on Saturday night" (*D* 140).

In keeping with this underlying concern, on the evening of the final performance, the narrative begins with great subtlety to shift its emphasis away from music and toward more mundane social concerns. This in turn highlights the smallness of Mrs. Kearney's ambitions. Although the narrative pays ample attention to Mrs. Kearney's point of view, it reveals that she gives little or no thought to the actual quality of the performance. Rather, she is fixated upon the question of how successful the concert will be perceived to be.

By this point, she has understood that she has no control over the number of people who will attend, and perhaps as compensation she turns her attention to the money that Kathleen is to be paid for her performance. This becomes for Mrs. Kearney the definitive index of her own success. Consequently, in the moments before the Saturday night performance is to begin she pursues Holohan with dogged determination throughout the backstage area, seeking assurances that Kathleen will receive the full eight guineas agreed upon by contract.

When the organizers are not forthcoming with the payment, she threatens to hold up the performance by refusing to let her daughter go on stage. As a compromise, Mrs. Kearney is given four pounds, and the first half of the concert gets under way. At the interval, however, the organizers decline to pay any more money until "after the Committee meeting on the following Tuesday" (*D* 148). Mrs. Kearney again refuses to allow her daughter to perform, but by now the organizers have found a replacement for Kathleen and the second half of the concert begins without her. The story concludes with Mrs. Kearney stalking out of the hall and threatening further action.

In its representation of the character of Mrs. Kearney, "A Mother" deftly portrays a domineering, social-climbing woman who exercises complete and unquestioned authority within the matriarchal realm of her family. However, her lack of real control over the people and events outside her home clearly delineates the limited scope of her authority. At the same time, this is not simply an account of a snobbish woman whose ambition causes her to overreach. Like the other stories of the *Dubliners* collection, "A Mother" critiques not simply the foibles of one person or even a particular type of individual. Rather, it holds up for scrutiny the petit-bourgeois mentality that permeates so much of Dublin life. The irony that runs through the narrative is that the strength of character that impels Mrs. Kearney rests upon a profound insecurity and reveals an intense dependence for validation from a rather tenuous social structure. As a result, Mrs. Kearney is compelled to fawn upon and ultimately importune men like "Hoppy" Holohan (a man with whom she would refuse to consort in any other circumstance), and as a result she ultimately leaves herself vulnerable to their oafish behavior.

The reader can easily and with obvious justification condemn her behavior throughout the story, but to stop at that point blunts the force of "A Mother." At the same time, one can find ample evidence to support the view that Mrs. Kearney turns out to be as much a victim as an oppressor. While she bullies her husband and her daughter whenever she feels the necessity to do so, the men who have organized the concerts prove less susceptible to her demands. In the end, she falls victim to the tyranny of a set of values associated with a social class to which she can only vainly aspire. If one cannot feel pity for her, one must at least acknowledge the moral complexity of her situation.

In a December 27, 1934, letter to his son George JOYCE, Joyce revealed the origins of "A Mother" in an experience of his own. "In my first public concert I too was left in the lurch. The pianist, that is the lady pianist, had gone away right in the middle of the concert" (*Letters*, III.340). Other instances of Joyce's attitude toward "A Mother" and of his process of composing it can be found in *Letters*, 11.111, 113, 114, and 117.

## CHARACTERS IN "A MOTHER"

**Holohan, Hoppy** He is the assistant secretary of the *Eire Abu* Society and the man responsible for arranging the concert at the center of the story.

**Kearney, Kathleen** She is a supporting character in the story, and also is mentioned in Molly Bloom's soliloquy in the Penelope episode (chapter 18) of *Ulysses*. Kathleen Kearney is a pianist, a singer, and an enthusiastic supporter of the IRISH LITERARY REVIVAL. Although Kathleen is portrayed as the docile child who becomes the victim of her mother's bullying in "A Mother," Molly Bloom resents her as a figure who is representative of a group of younger singers who receive preferment over herself. Despite her aura of sweetness through most of the story, Kathleen's callous dismissal of Madam Glynn, the soprano performing at the concert in "A Mother"—"I wonder where did they dig her up. . . . I'm sure I never heard of her" (*D* 143)—seems to justify Molly's animosity.

**Kearney, Mr.** He is a minor character in the story, a shoemaker by trade, the father of Kathleen Kearney, and the meek "much older husband" of the title character. The absence of dialogue for him in the story underscores his principal function in the household—namely, to provide a comfortable living for the family and to serve as his wife's factotum. His reticence allows Mrs. Kearney to assume the role of the head of the family.

**Kearney, Mrs.** She is the title character in the story. From the opening lines, she displays a pronounced and willful aggressiveness and a calculating, if relatively modest, drive for social recognition. From the first lines that identify her—"Miss Devlin had become Mrs. Kearney out of spite"—to her final words in the story—"I'm not done with you yet"—her behavior combines equal measures of determination and ruthlessness, coarseness and pretension, cunning and foolishness all marshaled to advance her banal aspirations. Mrs. Kearney's tenacity in promoting her daughter's musical career is the motivating force of the story, and her alternating concern and disdain for the opinions of society animates her efforts. The key feature of her character, however, hinted at throughout and made evident in the final pages of the story, is her temperamental inflexibility, which repeatedly undermines her own best efforts to succeed.

### *"Grace"*

This is the 14th story in *Dubliners.* It is the third story in the fourth and final division of the collection, scenes of public life. (The final story, "The Dead," serves as a coda to the collection.) "Grace" was the 12th in the order of composition, written in late 1905. It did not appear in print until *Dubliners* was published in 1914.

The narrative traces the efforts of a group of friends of Tom Kernan, an alcoholic commercial traveler for a tea company, to make him reform his drinking habits. The story begins with an account of Kernan's fall down a flight of stairs into the basement of a pub during a drinking bout and of his subsequent extrication from this extremely embarrassing situation by Jack Power. The central portion of the narrative focuses on the visit paid by Martin Cunningham, Jack Power, C. P. M'Coy, and Mr. Fogarty, the grocer, to the recuperating Kernan, with the intention of setting in motion the process of reforming him.

The men gather around Kernan's bedside, and Martin Cunningham turns the discussion toward religious subjects. Gradually the men reveal their intention to make an evening's retreat. (A retreat in Roman Catholic practice is a period of group withdrawal for prayer, meditation, or study.) Kernan, a convert to Catholicism, shows an initial skepticism toward the project, but despite this early reluctance, he eventually agrees to accompany the others to the evening service at St. Francis Xavier, a Jesuit church in Gardiner Street. The story ends with the opening words of the sermon by Father Purdon, who emphasizes a commercial view of the spiritual life as he exhorts his congregation to set right their accounts (see *D* 174).

Stanislaus JOYCE has noted that in its broad structural design "Grace" can be read as a parody of DANTE's *DIVINE COMEDY.* Mr. Kernan's fall represents the descent into the *inferno.* His convalescence is analogous to the *purgatorio.* And St. Francis Xavier Church becomes a kind of *paradiso.* While that may well be true, given the scope of the story, this point has a rather limited interpretive significance. (Allusions to the *Divine Comedy* can be found, however; see Mary Reynolds, *Joyce and Dante,* 160, 245–246.)

More tellingly, and in keeping with the general tone of the collection, the narrative offers a sharp commentary on the relationship between commerce and religion. In the easy way that the men convince Kernan of the relative harmlessness of the evening's exercise—using the homey, domestic image of a time to "wash the pot" to signify their intention to purge themselves of sin—there emerges a sense of the whole matter moving forward on a mercantile footing. Further, Joyce develops the character of the retreat master, Father Purdon, as a figure who makes conscious efforts in his sermon to link the act of spiritual renewal to sound business practices by using commercial metaphors for spiritual transactions. Thus, Joyce introduces another Dantean theme, simony (a concept that is also present in "The Sisters," the opening story of *Dubliners*).

One can see in the discourse of "Grace" an unvoiced cynicism toward the middle-class Dublin Catholic milieu that figures prominently in so many of the preceding stories in the collection. Here, however, the narrative does not single out some easily identifiable spiritual or psychological flaw, as is the case in earlier stories. Rather it is the complacency of the central characters, their inability to look critically at the way that they live their lives—here Martin Cunningham and the others seem to come under even greater criticism than Kernan, who is merely a heavy drinker—that makes their behavior so profoundly disturbing.

## CHARACTERS IN "GRACE"

**Cunningham, Martin** He is a supporting character in the story. In the context of Joyce's narratives, people express sympathy for him because of his wife's alcoholism. Because of his sensitivity and persuasive manner, Cunningham is given the responsibility of convincing the convalescing Tom Kernan to attend a retreat and to remain sober (*D* 157). See also characters under *Ulysses.*

**Kernan, Tom** His behavior drives the action in the story. It begins when he injures himself in a pub by falling drunk down the stairs leading to the toilets. Shortly thereafter, a group of Kernan's friends led by Martin Cunningham scheme to reform him by bringing him to a men's retreat conducted by Father Purdon at the Jesuit Church of St. Francis Xavier on Gardiner Street. Several ironies inform the action of the story. Kernan, a tea taster and salesman, has nearly bitten off his tongue as a result of his drunken accident. He is brought to the Catholic retreat to "wash the pot," although, as one who converted in order to marry, his opinion of the efficacy of Catholic rituals is rather low. Finally, Father Purdon's sermon seems so tailored to a business mentality that its spiritual intentions all but disappear. See also characters under *Ulysses.*

**M'Coy, C. P. "Charlie"** Like Simon Dedalus, M'Coy is sometimes down on his luck, a fact highlighted in "Grace." M'Coy, who plays the buffoon for the company, is treated coolly by Jack Power, who remembers that M'Coy had borrowed luggage from him "to enable Mrs. M'Coy to fulfill imaginary engagements in the country" (*D* 160) and had then pawned the luggage. Also see characters under *Ulysses.*

**Power, Jack** He is a minor character who appears in "Grace" and again, at various points, in the narrative of *Ulysses.* Power is a member of a unit of the Royal Irish Constabulary based in Dublin Castle. Early in "Grace," he fortuitously encounters the drunken and injured Tom Kernan. He uses his influence to prevent Kernan's arrest for public drunkenness, and then sees the man home. Subsequently Power, in the company of Martin Cunningham, C. P. M'Coy, and several other men, visits Kernan at home with a scheme to get Kernan to rehabilitate himself. Together, the men convince Kernan to accompany them to a men's retreat being conducted a few days later by Father Purdon at St. Francis Xavier's, the Jesuit church in Gardiner Street. See also characters under *Ulysses.*

**Purdon, Father** He is a Jesuit priest who appears at the end of the story, conducting an evening of recollection, or spiritual reflection, for businessmen at the Jesuit St. Francis Xavier's Church. Father Purdon's surname would have had a peculiar resonance for Dubliners of Joyce's generation, for Purdon Street was a main thoroughfare in the red-light district of Dublin during Joyce's youth. Rev. Bernard Vaughan, SJ, according to Richard Ellmann, was Joyce's model for Father Purdon; see *Letters,* II.182, n1.

### *"The Dead"*

This is the last and longest story in *Dubliners.* In fact, its length and density make it in effect a novella. Because of its thematic complexity and wide-ranging characterization, readers often view "The Dead" as a coda to the collection. Joyce wrote "The Dead" in the spring of 1907 in Trieste, soon after he and his family had returned from Rome, where they resided between July 1906 and March 1907.

A number of factors make "The Dead" a fitting conclusion to the *Dubliners* collection. Most obviously, it recapitulates and elaborates upon the major theme of paralysis that permeates the narratives of all the stories, but it does so with a measure of sympathy that makes its application far more open to interpretation than had been the case in the preceding stories. In particular, one sees the bitterness over the protagonist's apparent inability to affect the status quo—so obvious in such stories as "Counterparts" and "A Painful Case"—balanced by a sense of possibility, an awareness of options not present in the other pieces in the collection. While "The Dead" hardly exudes optimism, it moves beyond the fatalistic vision that seems to crush many of the characters of the other *Dubliners* stories.

From the start, oscillating perspectives, in the sense developed by John Paul Riquelme's study of Joyce's canon, balance a sense of exuberance and energy against the muted feelings and truncated responses of Gabriel Conroy that make up so much of the narrative. Indeed, the narrative opens by presenting a view of exaggerated motion: "Lily, the caretaker's daughter, was literally run off her feet" (*D* 175). The fussiness, the hyperbole, the aura of intimacy created by the use of her first name only—all these pull the reader willy-nilly into the flow of the narrative. The first few paragraphs continue this tone and convey the excited bustle of guests arriving at the annual Christmas dinner-dance given by the Misses Morkan, sometime between New Year's Day and January 6, the Feast of the Epiphany (Twelfth Night). With a mixture of good nature and pomposity, their favorite nephew, Gabriel Conroy, comes to the door grumbling over the length of time his wife, Gretta Conroy, spends dressing and clumsily tries to compliment Lily. In both instances, Conroy manages to make himself look and feel slightly foolish without becoming a caricature. (Here more than in any other story in the collection Joyce captures the complex and even contradictory elements of the identities of his central figures.)

Counterpointing Gabriel's behavior and that of the other guests at the party is a narrative voice that unfolds the story with an intimate sense of the various characters' perspectives, even as it maintains an ironic distance from them. The narrative thus leads the reader to sharp insights into the natures of these individuals without categorizing them or alienating them from our sympathy. Joyce subsequently used a similar narrative technique in *A Portrait of the Artist as a Young Man.*

As the evening progresses, the detailed representations of the hostesses and their guests illustrate the complex dynamics of Dublin society. The Misses Morkan and their niece Mary Jane stand for a kind of sentiment and hospitality that evokes both sentimentality and feelings of loss. Freddy Malins's inebriated good nature reflects both a stereotype of an Irish alcoholic and a sharply delineated individual with a very real human failing. Bartell D'Arcy and Mervyn Browne are variants of sententious pomposity, while Molly Ivors stands as both a parody of nationalism and a poignant representation of genuine longing for community and personal relationship. Through all this Gabriel functions as the presiding spirit who animates events at the party, carving the goose, giving an after-dinner speech, and offering a running, if unvoiced, critical commentary on all that transpires.

Up to the end of the party, Gabriel's sometimes caustic views delineate the familiar parameters of a typical *Dubliners* story. However, in the final pages the narrative introduces a series of events that suggest that Joyce has begun to modify this harsh perspective. As guests are leaving the house Gretta has an EPIPHANY of sorts, in the form of memories of the now dead Michael Furey—memories sparked by D'Arcy's singing of the forlorn love ballad "The LASS OF AUGHRIM." The implications of Gretta's recollections are not immediately apparent to the reader or to her husband; but from this point, there is a marked shift in the tone of the narrative.

After the party, Gabriel and Gretta return to the GRESHAM HOTEL, where they plan to spend the night before journeying back to their home in Monkstown. As they cross the city in a cab, Gabriel's increasing sexual desire for his wife becomes evident to the reader. At the same time, the preoccupied Gretta remains detached and unaware of Gabriel's feelings. She has focused her attention on the memory of Michael Furey, a young man who was in love with her when she was a girl in Galway.

When they reach their hotel room, Gabriel is finally confronted with Gretta's fixation. The details of Michael Furey's adolescent devotion to Gretta force Gabriel to consider the depth of the other man's love and the contrasting shallowness of his own. Gabriel also must deal with the hold the dead man has over Gretta and with his powerlessness to loosen it. These insights prove to be both humbling and illuminating, for it serves not simply as a critique of his feelings but as a revelation of the possible depth of human emotion. At this point, the story takes on a kind of ambiguity not found in the other pieces in the collection. While it may seem relatively easy to dismiss Gabriel's feelings as shallow in comparison with those of Michael Furey, it remains unclear whether he possesses the ability to change.

In the final moments of his self-examination the major themes in *Dubliners*—death, paralysis, sexual frustration, hopelessness, and futility—run through

Gabriel's thoughts and shape his feelings. Recollections of Michael Furey, a sense of doubt regarding the value of his own life, his unsatisfied desire for Gretta and a growing feeling of aimlessness threaten to overwhelm Gabriel's consciousness. In this moment of desolation, he is drawn to the window by the sound of falling snow. "His soul swooned slowly as he heard the snow falling faintly through the universe and faintly falling, like the descent of their last end, upon all the living and the dead" (*D* 224). For Gabriel—in contrast to characters in other *Dubliners* stories—this moment of crisis also contains the potential for illumination. The empathy reflected in those lines shows a break in Gabriel's solipsism. Whether this is a momentary or a lasting change remains unclear, for the reader sees Gabriel at the instant of recognition with no indication in the narrative as to its effect on him. The reader is left to consider Gabriel's possible moral future and, by extension, that of the Irish society that is the real subject of the entire work.

For additional information on Joyce's views on the process of composition of "The Dead," on events surrounding the story, and on other details, see *Letters*, II.51, 56, 63–64, 72, 86, 166, 186, 209, 212, 239, 300, 306, and 380; and III.348. See also the appendix on page 381.

## CHARACTERS IN "THE DEAD"

**Browne, Mervyn Archdale** He appears as a minor character in the story, acting as a fatuous nemesis to Freddy Malins. According to Richard ELLMANN, a first cousin of Joyce's mother married a Protestant by that name who was a music teacher and insurance agent, and he probably provided Joyce, at the very least, with the name of this fictional figure. There is also a reference to Mervyn Browne in the Hades episode (chapter 6) of *Ulysses*, in which Leopold Bloom recalls an anecdote that Browne told him about the burning off of gas that accumulates in coffins.

**Conroy, Gabriel** He stands as the central character in the story. He and his wife, Gretta Conroy, are among the guests at the annual dinner party given by his aunts, Kate and Julia Morkan, sometime between New Year's Day and January 6 (Twelfth Night). Much of the narrative reflects, through FREE INDIRECT DISCOURSE, Gabriel's perception of events.

In many ways Gabriel represents a better educated, more sophisticated version of the average man—*l'homme moyen sensuel*—who will be personified by Leopold Bloom in *Ulysses*. Though much more at ease with his fellow Dubliners than is Bloom, Gabriel nonetheless sees himself as set apart from the society that he inhabits. He is neither belligerent nor accommodating, but rather asserts his independence from Ireland without severing the material ties that bind him to his country.

Conroy is a teacher and book reviewer upon whom his aunts rely to serve both as paterfamilias and as a toastmaster who can provide an intellectual cast to their annual celebration. While to all appearances he is eminently suited to fulfill these roles, it is evident from the narrative's description of his nature that Gabriel occupies a position psychologically far removed from local customs and from the celebration over which he presides. From his Continental affectations to his hostility toward the renewed interest in Irish culture—evident in his responses both to Molly Ivors and to his wife—he clearly inhabits a world markedly different from that of those around him.

These broad differences between Gabriel and his fellow Dubliners become increasingly evident over the course of "The Dead." As the story moves to its conclusion, however, a shift in emphasis in Gabriel's identity emerges. Sexuality and sexual appetites come to dominate his consciousness, and they sharply underscore his isolation from other characters in the story. The degree to which his own responses to love and desire have set Gabriel apart becomes painfully obvious in the final scene at the Gresham Hotel. There, unaware of the sexual desire that has been building in her husband during their ride from the Morkans' to the hotel, his wife abruptly quashes his cravings by her offhand recollections of her innocent love affair long ago in Galway with young Michael Furey. It quickly becomes clear that not only did Gabriel know nothing of this attachment, but he comes to feel that he had never experienced a love as profound as that which Gretta describes.

The story ends without a definitive resolution of Gabriel's final condition. He obviously feels a sense of rejection and isolation, and his relations with his wife certainly cannot go back to their former condition. This does not irrevocably mean that the experience was disastrous. Clearly, the final pages of the story underscore the fact that Gabriel has gained a great insight into his life. Its significance, however, is left to the reader to decide. Joyce's technique makes it impossible to say with certitude whether Gabriel's new knowledge will lead to a greater sensitivity and a fuller life or simply to a keener awareness of what he has lost. Indeed, the power of the story comes from its willingness to allow the reader to witness Gabriel's spiritual crisis and then to interpret the impact that it has upon his consciousness.

**Conroy, Gretta** After Gabriel Conroy, her husband, she is the character in the story upon whom the action hinges. While she lacks her husband's education and his sophistication, Gretta is clearly the erotic and emotional center of his life. The story does not elaborate upon her nature, but it does offer insights, especially in the final pages, into the features that so dominate Gabriel's interest. His feeling for her, however, remains muted until near the end of the story. As they return from the party to the hotel where they will spend the night, Gabriel's sexual desire for his wife becomes increasingly strong. Before he can act upon his desire, however, Gretta unwittingly precipitates a spiritual crisis for him when she speaks about the long-dead Michael Furey, a young man who had loved her deeply years before in Galway. In Gretta's romantic vision, Furey died for her, having gotten up from his sickbed on a rainy night to visit her before she left for Dublin. Joyce modeled aspects of Gretta on Nora BARNACLE, and the character of Michael Furey on a figure from Nora's past, Michael BODKIN.

**D'Arcy, Bartell** He is a minor but recurring character in Joyce's fiction who first appears in "The Dead." At the Morkans' Christmas party he emerges as a fussy and insecure man, an operatic tenor still seeking to establish his reputation in music-mad Dublin. Because he is suffering from a cold, D'Arcy is reluctant to perform before the assembled guests at the dinner, and it is only at the end of the evening that he is prevailed upon to sing "The LASS OF AUGHRIM," the song that brings to Gretta Conroy's mind the memory of Michael Furey. D'Arcy appears through allusion in the Lestrygonians episode (chapter 8) of *Ulysses*, where Bloom dismisses him as a "conceited fellow with his waxedup moustache" (*U*, 8.182). He is also mentioned in passing in Molly's soliloquy in the Penelope episode (chapter 18). According to Richard ELLMANN, Joyce's biographer, the character of D'Arcy was based on a singer of Joyce's father's day, Barton M'Guckin (see *James Joyce*, p. 246).

**Furey, Michael** He is the now deceased adolescent boy whom the young Gretta Conroy knew in Galway and whose spectral presence dominates the story's last pages. Gretta fondly recalls his memory when she hears Bartell D'Arcy singing "The LASS OF AUGHRIM," a song that Furey often sang for her. When she tells Gabriel about her recollections of Michael Furey and of his untimely death, it causes a major shift in the mood of the story. Gabriel broods upon the circumstances of Michael Furey's death, and a profound sadness overwhelms him. The biblical echoes in the names Michael (the archangel of God's judgment and fury) and Gabriel (God's messenger) are analyzed by Florence Walzl in an essay reprinted in the A. Walton Litz & Robert Scholes edition of *Dubliners*. Joyce modeled Michael Furey on Nora Joyce's adolescent friend Michael BODKIN.

**Ivors, Miss Molly** She is a minor but significant character in the story. Miss Ivors is an ardent Irish nationalist. While dancing with Gabriel Conroy at the Misses Morkans' annual Christmas party, she chastises him as a "West Briton" (that is, any Irish person more inclined to identify with the English point of view than the Irish) because of his emphatic lack of interest in anything relating to Irish culture. Miss Ivors goes on to tease Gabriel because he has written a book review that appeared in the pro-British *DAILY EXPRESS*, and she urges him to spend his summer holiday on the Aran Islands in order to regain a sense of his Celtic culture. Though good-natured, her mockery strikes a sensitive spot and greatly offends Gabriel. Perhaps because she too has been affected by their exchange, Miss Ivors leaves the party before dinner and Gabriel's speech.

**Lily** She is a minor character who appears in the opening pages. Identified simply as "the caretaker's daughter," Lily, in fact, acts as a housemaid to Kate and Julia Morkan. As the story opens, Lily is meeting guests and taking their coats as they arrive for the Morkans' annual Christmas party. The clumsy efforts at gallantry made by Gabriel Conroy, and Lily's unexpectedly sharp retort about the nature of men—"The men that is now is only all palaver and what they can get out of you" (*D* 178)—marks the first in a series of assaults by women of all ages and backgrounds upon Gabriel's complacency regarding Irish history, culture, society, and relations between men and women.

**Malins, Freddy** He appears in the story as a guest at the annual Christmas party given by the sisters Julia and Kate Morkan and their niece Mary Jane. Freddy's inebriation both causes concern and provides a source of amusement for others at the party. Over the course of the narration, however, Malins comes to serve a more important function than that of a minor disruption in the otherwise tranquil proceedings. His inability to control his drinking, his profound respect for popular custom, and his gushing sentimentality set him in sharp contrast to the aloof, abstemious, and somewhat disdainful Gabriel Conroy. In his lack of self-control, Freddy comes across as the weaker individual, and he reflects many of the same flaws that hamper such characters as Farrington, Bob Doran, and Joe Hynes in other *Dubliners* stories. At the same time, Freddy's kindhearted empathy and his uninhibited openness stand in sharp contrast to Gabriel's brittle nature.

**Mary Jane** She is one of the figures at the center of the action in the story because of her role in setting its atmosphere. As the unmarried niece of the sisters Kate and Julia Morkan, she is a very popular music teacher who every year organizes a concert given by her pupils in the ANTIENT CONCERT ROOMS. Mary Jane's earnings have become the major source of support for the three women, and the story gently hints at the frustration she sometimes endures because of her contrasting roles as breadwinner and as niece. Mary Jane has assumed the role of one of the hosts of the annual Christmas party that dominates the action of the story. Both by her profession and by her demeanor, Mary Jane reflects the continuity of the tradition of culture and gentility embodied by her aunts and patronizingly alluded to by her cousin Gabriel Conroy in his after-dinner speech. Mary Jane affirms the determined, if guardedly optimistic, view of the world that these three women hold.

**Morkan, Julia** She is an aunt of both Mary Jane and Gabriel Conroy. Despite her advanced age, she is "still the leading soprano in Adam and Eve's" Catholic Church (*D* 176). As a reflection of the importance that she gives to custom and hospitality, Julia Morkan (with her sister Kate) still hosts the annual Christmas party that dominates the action of the story. She sings "Arrayed for the Bridal" as part of the entertainment at the party, in a scene that—both in her choice of the song and in her delivery—ironically echoes similar entertainment by Maria in the *Dubliners* short story "Clay." In both cases the songs these women select are clearly more suitable to young girls whose prospects and talents are as yet unaffected by age. Nonetheless, in both cases, a measure of poignancy in the representation mitigates the final effect.

**Morkan, Kate** She is an aunt of both Mary Jane and Gabriel Conroy. Although younger than her sister, Julia, she is clearly a woman of advanced years. Nonetheless, Kate, with Julia, still hosts the annual Christmas party that is the setting for most of the story. She also gives piano lessons for beginners to supplement the household's income. Kate Morkan is alluded to in *Ulysses* as the godmother of Stephen Dedalus (*U* 17.139–140).

**O'Callaghan, Miss** She is a minor character in the story. As a guest at the Christmas party given by the Morkan sisters, she unsuccessfully urges the tenor Bartell D'Arcy to sing.

## CONTEMPORARY REVIEWS OF *DUBLINERS*

Excerpt from an unsigned review published in the *Times Literary Supplement,* June 18, 1914, p. 298:

> *Dubliners* may be recommended to the large class of readers to whom the drab makes an appeal, for it is admirably written. Mr. Joyce avoids exaggeration. He leaves the conviction that his people are as he describes them. Shunning the emphatic, Mr. Joyce is less concerned with the episode than with the mood which it suggests. Perhaps for this reason he is more successful with his shorter stories. When he writes at greater length the issue seems trivial, and the connecting thread becomes so tenuous as to be scarcely perceptible. The reader's difficulty will be enhanced if he is ignorant of Dublin customs; if he does not know, for instance, that 'a curate' is a man who brings strong waters.

Excerpt from an unsigned review published in the *Athenæum,* June 20, 1914, p. 875:

> Mr. George Moore says in his *Confessions,* if our memory does not deceive us, that when he and a certain French writer are dead no more 'naturalistic' novels will be written. Whether this is one of his characteristic outbursts of candour as to his and his friend's abilities, or merely a statement to the effect that novelists as a whole have no taste for such writing, we need not discuss. But we can frankly say that Mr. Joyce's work affords a distinct contradiction of the saying.
>
> The fifteen short stories here given under the collective title of *Dubliners* are nothing if not naturalistic. In some ways, indeed, they are unduly so: at least three would have been better buried in oblivion. Life has so much that is beautiful, interesting, educative, amusing that we do not readily pardon those who insist upon its more sordid and baser aspects. The condemnation is the greater if their skill is of any high degree, since in that case they might use it to better purpose.
>
> Mr. Joyce undoubtedly possesses great skill both of observation and of technique. He has humour, as is shown by the sketch of Mrs. Kearney and her views on religion, her faith 'bounded by her kitchen, but if she was put to it, she could believe also in the banshee and in the Holy Ghost.' He has also knowledge of the beauty of words, of mental landscapes (if we may use such a phrase): the last page of the final story is full evidence thereto. His characterization is exact: speaking with reserve as to the conditions of certain sides of the social life of Dublin, we should say that it is beyond criticism. All the personages are living realities.
>
> But Mr. Joyce has his own specialized outlook on life—on that life in particular; and here we may, perhaps, find the explanation of much that displeases and that puzzles us. That outlook is evidently sombre: he is struck by certain types, certain scenes, by the dark shadows of a low street or the lurid flare of an ignoble tavern, and he reproduces these in crude, strong sketches scarcely relieved by the least touch of joy or repose. Again, his outlook is self-centred, absorbed in itself rather; he ends his sketch abruptly time after time, satisfied with what he has done, brushing aside any intention of explaining what is set down or supplementing what is omitted.
>
> All the stories are worth reading for the work that is in them, for the pictures they present; the best are undoubtedly the last four, especially 'Ivy Day in the Committee Room.' The last of all, 'The Dead,' far longer than the rest, and tinged with a softer tone of pathos and sympathy, leads us to hope that Mr. Joyce may attempt larger and broader work, in which the necessity of asserting the proportions of life may compel him to enlarge his outlook and eliminate such scenes and details as can only shock, without in any useful way impressing or elevating, the reader.

Gerald Gould's review of *Dubliners, New Statesman,* iii (June 27, 1914), pp. 374–375:

> It is easy to say of [the Russian writer Maxim] Gorky that he is a man of genius. To say the same of Mr. James Joyce requires more courage, since his name is little known; but a man of genius is precisely what he is. He has an original outlook, a special method, a complete reliance on his own

powers of delineation and presentment. Whether his powers will develop, his scope widen, his sympathies deepen, or not—whether, in short, his genius is a large one or only a little one, I cannot pretend to say. Maturity and self-confidence in a first book (and I believe that, in prose, this is Mr. Joyce's first book) contain a threat as well as a promise. They hint at a set mode of thought rather than a developing capacity. Certainly the maturity, the individual poise and force of these stories are astonishing. The only recent work with which they suggest comparison is *The House with the Green Shutters* [by the Scottish writer George Douglas Brown], and even that was very different, for one heard in it the undertone of human complaint—its horrors were partly by way of expressing a personal unhappiness; while Mr. Joyce seems to regard this objective and dirty and crawling world with the cold detachment of an unamiable god.

He has plenty of humour, but it is always the humour of the fact not of the comment. He dares to let people speak for themselves with the awkward meticulousness, the persistent incompetent repetition, of actual human intercourse. If you have never realized before how direly our daily conversation needs editing, you will realise it from Mr. Joyce's pages. One very powerful story, called 'Grace', consists chiefly of lengthy talk so banal, so true to life, that one can scarcely endure it—though one can still less leave off reading it. Here is one of the liveliest passages:

> "Pope Leo XIII," said Mr. Cunningham, "was one of the lights of the age. His great idea, you know, was the union of the Latin and Greek churches. That was the aim of his life."
>
> "I often heard he was one of the most intellectual men in Europe," said Mr. Power. "I mean apart from his being Pope."
>
> "So he was," said Mr. Cunningham, "if not the most so. His motto, you know, as Pope was *Lux upon Lux—Light upon Light.*"
>
> "No, no," said Mr. Fogarty eagerly. "I think you're wrong there. It was *Lux in Tenebris*, I think—*Light in Darkness.*"
>
> "O yes," said Mr. M'Coy, "Tenebre."
>
> "Allow me," said Mr. Cunningham positively, "it was *Lux upon Lux*. And Plus IX his predecessor's motto was *Cruz upon Cruz*—that is, *Cross upon Cross*—to show the difference between their two pontificates."
>
> The inference was allowed. Mr. Cunningham continued.
>
> "Pope Leo, you know, was a great scholar and a poet."
>
> "He had a strong face," said Mr. Kernan.
>
> "Yes," said Mr. Cunningham. "He wrote Latin poetry."
>
> "Is that so?" said Mr. Fogarty.

You see the method? It is not employed only in conversation. The description of mood, of atmosphere, is just as detailed and just as relentless. Horrible sordid realities, of which you are not spared one single pang, close in upon you like the four walls of a torture-chamber. It is all done quite calmly, quite dispassionately, quite competently. It never bores. You sometimes rather wish it did, as a relief.

The best things in the book are *Araby*, a wonderful magical study of boyish affection and wounded pride, and 'The Dead', a long story (placed at the end) in which we begin with a queer old-fashioned dance where the principal anxiety is whether a certain guest will arrive 'screwed,' and are led on through all the queer breathless banalities of supper and conversation and leave-taking till we find ourselves back with a husband and wife in their hotel bedroom, the husband's emotion stirred, the wife queerly remote and sad, remembering the boy, Michael Furey, whom she had loved and who had died because of her. To quote the end without the innumerable preparatory touches that prepare for it seems unfair; yet it must be quoted for its mere melancholy beauty:

> A few light taps upon the pane made him turn to the window. It had begun to snow again. He watched sleepily the flakes, silver and dark, falling obliquely against the lamplight. The time had come for him to set out on his journey westward. Yes, the

> newspapers were right: snow was general all over Ireland. It was falling softly upon the Bog of Allen and, farther westward, softly falling into the dark mutinous Shannon waves. It was falling, too, upon every part of the lonely churchyard on the hill where Michael Furey lay buried. It lay thickly drifted on the crooked crosses and head-stones, on the spears of the little gate, on the barren thorns. His soul swooned slowly as he heard the snow falling faintly through the universe and faintly falling. Like the descent of their last end, upon all the living and the dead.

Frankly, we think it is a pity (perhaps we betray a narrow puritanism in so thinking) that a man who can write like this should insist as constantly as Mr. Joyce insists upon aspects of life which are ordinarily not mentioned. To do him justice, we do not think it is a pose with him: He simply includes the "unmentionable" in his persistent regard.

Review: Unsigned, *Everyman,* July 3, 1914, xc, p. 380:

> Mr. James Joyce writes with a sense of style that makes his work distinctive. *Dubliners* is a collection of short stories dealing with undercurrents of Irish character. The author understands the technique of his craft to perfection, and uses words as a sculptor uses clay. Every phrase is pregnant with suggestion, but the suggestion for the most part is unpleasantly and curiously tinged with a pessimism that finds virility and purpose only in the power of evil. 'A Painful Case,' one of the best-written sketches in the volume, strips life of all hope of consolation and leaves the reader faced by a cold, cruel egotism that finds expression in perpetual self-exultation. 'Two Gallants' reveals the shuddering depths of human meanness. The men, villainous of soul and repugnant of aspect, trade on the affections of young servant-girls, and the story reproduces the hopes of the one who waits the results of the wiles of the other. Even for these outcasts some hope might remain. But the author, with a ruthless callousness, decides they shall be doomed and damned. The book may be styled the records of an inferno in which neither pity nor remorse can enter. Wonderfully written, the power of genius is in every line, but it is a genius that, blind to the blue of the heavens, seeks inspiration in the hell of despair.

Excerpt from an unsigned review published in *Academy,* July 11, 1914, lxxxvii, p. 49:

> In the matter of literary expression these sketches—of which the book contains fifteen in all—are akin to the work of Mr. Cunningham Graham and of Mr. George Moore; there is a clarity of phrasing and a restraint such as characterises the work of these two authors, and in every sketch atmosphere is so subtly conveyed that, without mention of a street or of a jaunting car, we feel Dublin about us as we read. In one, 'Counterparts,' is power enough to make us wish for a novel from Mr. Joyce's pen, and in the earlier, schoolboy stories are all the dreaming and mystery of an imaginative boy's life. The book is morbid, to a certain extent, in its tone, but it is of such literary quality that we forgive the defect for the sake of the artistic value. The work is not all morbid however, for here and there are flashes of humour, rendered more forceful by their settings. Altogether, this is a book to recommend evidently written by a man of broad sympathies and much human understanding.

Ezra Pound's review " 'Dubliners' and Mr. James Joyce" in *The Egoist,* i, no. 14 (July 15, 1914), p. 267. (This essay was republished in Pound's *Pavannes and Divisions* [1918] and *The Literary Essays of Ezra Pound* [1954], edited by T. S. Eliot.)

> Freedom from sloppiness is so rare in contemporary English prose that one might well say simply, 'Mr. Joyce's book of short stories is prose free from sloppiness,' and leave the intelligent reader ready to run from his study, immediately to spend three and sixpence on the volume. . . .
>
> Unfortunately one's credit as a critic is insufficient to produce this result. . . .

The readers of *The Egoist,* having had Mr. Joyce under their eyes for some months, will scarcely need to have his qualities pointed out to them. Both they and the paper have been very fortunate in his collaboration. . . .

Mr. Joyce writes a clear hard prose. He deals with subjective things, but he presents them with such clarity of outline that he might be dealing with locomotives or with builders' specifications. For that reason one can read Mr. Joyce without feeling that one is conferring a favour. I must put this thing my own way. I know about 168 authors. About once a year I read something contemporary without feeling that I am softening the path for poor Jones or poor Fulano de Tal.

I can lay down a good piece of French writing and pick up a piece of writing by Mr. Joyce without feeling as if my head were being stuffed through a cushion. There are still impressionist writers. English prose writers who haven't got as far as impressionism (that is to say, 95 percent of English writers of prose and verse) are a bore.

Impressionism has, however, two meanings, or perhaps I had better say, the word 'impressionism' gives two different 'impressions'. . . .

There is a school of prose writers, and of verse writers for that matter, whose forerunner was Stendhal and whose founder was Flaubert. The followers of Flaubert deal in exact presentation. They are often so intent on exact presentation that they neglect intensity, selection, and concentration. They are perhaps the most clarifying and they have been perhaps the most beneficial force in modern writing.

There is another set, mostly of verse writers, who founded themselves not upon anybody's writing but upon the pictures of Monet. Every movement in painting picks up a few writers who try to imitate in words what someone has done in paint. Thus one writer saw a picture by Monet and talked of 'pink pigs blossoming on a hillside', and a later writer talked of 'slate-blue' hair and 'raspberry-coloured flanks'.

'These impressionists' who write in imitation of Monet's softness, instead of writing in imitation of Flaubert's definiteness, are a bore, a grimy, or perhaps I should say, a rosy, floribund bore. . . .

The spirit of a decade strikes properly upon all of the arts. There are 'parallel movements'. Their causes and their effects may not seem, superficially, similar.

This mimicking of painting ten or twenty years late is not in the least the same as the 'literary movement' parallel to the painting movement imitated. . . .

The force that leads a poet to leave out a moral reflection may lead a painter to leave out representation. The resultant poem may not suggest the resultant painting. . . .

Mr. Joyce's merit, I will not say his chief merit but his most engaging merit, is that he carefully avoids telling you a lot that you don't want to know. He presents his people swiftly and vividly, he does not sentimentalise over them, he does not weave convolutions. He is a realist. He does not believe 'life' would be all right if we stopped vivisection or if we instituted a new sort of 'economics.' He gives the thing as it is. He is not bound by the tiresome convention that any part of life, to be interesting, must be shaped into the conventional form of a 'story.' Since De Maupassant we have had so many people trying to write 'stories' and so few people presenting life. Life for the most part does not happen in neat little diagrams and nothing is more tiresome than the continual pretence that it does.

Mr. Joyce's 'Araby,' for instance, is much better than a 'story,' it is a vivid writing. . . .

It is surprising that Mr. Joyce is Irish. One is so tired of the Irish or 'Celtic' imagination (or 'phantasy' as I think they now call it) flopping about. Mr. Joyce does not flop about. He defines. He is not an institution for the promotion of Irish peasant industries. He accepts an international standard of prose writing and lives up to it.

He gives us Dublin as it presumably is. He does not descend to farce. He does not rely upon Dickensian caricature. He gives us things as they are, not only for Dublin, but for every city. Erase the local names and a few specifically local allusions, and a few historic events of the past, and substitute a few different local names, allusions and events, and these stories could be retold of any town.

That is to say, the author is quite capable of dealing with things about him, and dealing directly, yet these details do not engross him, he is capable of getting at the universal element beneath them.

The main situations of 'Madame Bovary' or of 'Dona Perfecta' do not depend on local colour or upon local detail, that is their strength. Good writing, good presentation can be specifically local, but it must not depend on locality. Mr. Joyce does not present 'types' but individuals. I mean he deals with common emotions which run through all races. He does not bank on 'Irish character.' Roughly speaking, Irish literature has gone through three phases in our time, the shamrock period, the dove-grey period, and the Kiltartan period. I think there is a new phase in the works of Mr. Joyce. He writes as a contemporary of continental writers. I do not mean that he writes as a faddist, mad for the last note, he does not imitate Strindberg, for instance, or Bang. He is not ploughing the underworld for horror. He is not presenting a macabre subjectivity. He is classic in that he deals with normal things and with normal people. A committee room, Little Chandler, a nonentity, a boarding house full of clerks—these are his subjects and he treats them all in such a manner that they are worthy subjects of art.

Francis Jammes, Charles Vildrac and D. H. Lawrence have written short narratives in verse, trying, it would seem, to present situations as clearly as prose writers have done, yet more briefly. Mr. Joyce is engaged in a similar condensation. He has kept to prose not needing the privilege supposedly accorded to verse to justify his method.

I think that he excels most of the impressionist writers because of his more rigorous selection, because of his exclusion of all unnecessary detail.

There is a very clear demarcation between unnecessary detail and irrelevant detail. An impressionist friend of mine talks to me a good deal about 'preparing effects,' and on that score he justifies much unnecessary detail, which is not 'irrelevant,' but which ends by being wearisome and by putting one out of conceit with his narrative.

Mr. Joyce's more rigorous selection of the presented detail marks him, I think, as belonging to my own generation, that is, to the 'nineteen-tens,' not to the decade between 'the 'nineties' and today. . . .

At any rate these stories and the novel [*A Portrait of the Artist as a Young Man*] now appearing in serial form are such as to win for Mr. Joyce a very definite place among English contemporary prose writers, not merely a place in the 'Novels of the Week' column, and our writers of good clear prose are so few that we cannot afford to confuse or to overlook them.

Excerpt from an unsigned review published in the *Irish Book Lover*, November 1914, vi, no. 4, pp. 60–61:

> Dublin, like other large cities, shelters many peculiar types of men and women, good, bad and indifferent; in fact some, whose knowledge of it is extensive and peculiar, would say more than its fair share. Of some of these Mr. Joyce here gives us pen portraits of great power, and although one naturally shrinks from such characters as are depicted in 'An Encounter' or 'Two Gallants,' and find their descriptions not quite suited 'virginibus puerisque,' one cannot deny the existence of their prototypes, whilst wishing that the author had directed his undoubted talents in other and pleasanter directions. . . .

# *Exiles* (1918)

This is Joyce's only extant play. It was written in Trieste during 1914 and 1915, and first published by Grant RICHARDS in London and by B. W. Huebsch in New York on May 25, 1918. Joyce purposely waited to publish the play until after *A Portrait of the Artist as a Young Man* appeared in book form in

1916. In many ways the structure of *Exiles* resembles those in the plays of IBSEN that Joyce had so admired a decade earlier. The play also reflects an autobiographical projection of what life might have been like for Joyce and his family had they returned to Ireland around this time. Overall, however, it sums up Joyce's sense of the precarious position of any artist who tries to practice his craft in Ireland. Two previous dramatic attempts written by Joyce while he was still a young man in Dublin, *A Brilliant Career* (1900) and *Dream Stuff* (c. 1900), no longer exist (see Miscellaneous Works). However, given his enthusiasm for Ibsen and concern at the time for his development as an artist, it seems likely that their themes and structures resembled those of *Exiles*.

## SYNOPSIS

The action opens in a suburban Dublin sitting room in Merrion (a fictitious location that seems to correspond with the Sandymount area) with an encounter between Beatrice Justice and Richard Rowan, the play's protagonist. Their conversation touches upon a series of increasingly personal topics: his writing, their eight-year correspondence while Richard was living in Rome with Bertha (his common-law wife) and Archie (Richard and Bertha's child), Beatrice's love for Robert Hand (Richard's long-time friend and Beatrice's cousin), and the attitude of Richard's mother—who had died three months earlier—toward Richard's relationship with Bertha.

Richard breaks off the conversation and leaves the room to avoid meeting Robert, who subsequently enters with a large bunch of red roses for Bertha. The awkward exchange that follows between Beatrice and Robert lasts only a few minutes before she goes off to give Archie a piano lesson, but the feeling of distance and the tone of embarrassment that dominates their conversation clearly signal their changed relationship. Robert and Bertha on the other hand seem to enjoy a much more intimate bond. When the others have left them alone, they talk of their affection for one another, hold hands, embrace, and kiss. The scene is intentionally ambiguous. Robert appears consumed by his passion for Bertha. She, on the other hand, neither encourages nor discourages his advances. This ambivalent attitude will emerge as the central issue of the play. Robert also mentions that he will encourage Richard to take a position at the university in order to ensure Bertha's stay at Merrion. Just before Richard returns, Bertha consents to go later to Robert's home at Ranelagh.

In the scene that unfolds after Robert has left, the conflicted sexual relationships of the central characters come to the foreground. It becomes clear that Richard is fully aware of Robert's attempts at seduction. Bertha and Richard discuss her conversation with Robert in detail. Bertha's own feelings are by no means clear, and she accuses Richard of doing the work of the devil by trying to turn Robert against her, as, she claims, he had tried to turn Archie against her. In addition, Bertha, who knew of the correspondence between Richard and Beatrice, accuses Richard of being in love with Beatrice and also of trying to manipulate Robert's relationship with Bertha. By the end of the act, when Bertha asks Richard to forbid her to go to Robert's home, the inability or unwillingness of the characters to act independently has become a dominant and oppressive condition. Although Richard says that she must decide for herself, it remains clear to the audience that he has manipulated the situation by, at the very least, allowing it to progress without his intervention.

Act 2 opens with Robert in his cottage in Ranelagh (at that time a suburb south of Dublin), waiting for Bertha. However, Richard arrives first, and declares that Bertha has told him everything. The conversation that follows raises, but does nothing to resolve, the questions of fidelity, friendship, and freedom central to the play. When Bertha finally arrives, Robert leaves to wait in the garden. Richard and Bertha then discuss trust and their own relationship before Richard departs. Bertha calls Robert in from the garden. They too talk about freedom, love, and choice, and the act ends ambiguously, giving the audience no clear sense of what, if anything, will transpire between Bertha and Robert.

The third act begins early on the morning of the following day at Richard Rowan's home, with Bertha seated alone in the drawing room. Beatrice

Justice enters, ostensibly to bring a copy of the morning newspaper which contains a leading article (i.e., an editorial) on Richard's life written by Robert. In fact, however, Bertha and Beatrice quickly confront one another on the issues of Richard's return to Ireland and his writing. Although the central concerns remain unresolved, before Beatrice leaves Bertha offers her friendship.

At this point Richard comes into the drawing room, and he and Bertha begin a conversation in which they attempt to resolve the conflict in their attitudes toward freedom and fidelity. Robert Hand enters the room but not before Richard leaves for his study. Bertha chides Robert for planning to leave the country without a word to her. She also seeks to bring about a reconciliation between Richard and Robert. She calls Richard back from his study, and Robert confesses his failure to him. After Robert has left, however, it becomes apparent that he has given Richard little consolation. Richard speaks of the "wound of doubt" in his soul, and the play ends with Bertha, speaking softly, asking him to return as a lover to her once again.

## COMMENTARY

While critics continue to debate whether *Exiles* stands as a substantial work in its own right, few would disagree with the view that it remains an important transitional piece between *A Portrait of the Artist as a Young Man* and *Ulysses*. Whatever one thinks of its dramaturgy, the play clearly highlights themes crucial throughout Joyce's creative process: exile, friendship, love, freedom, betrayal, and doubt. Of all his other works, *Chamber Music*, with its similar themes, comes closest to such concentration. (And, one might argue, labors under the same flaws that beset the play.) In *Dubliners*, *Stephen Hero*, and *A Portrait* (written prior to *Exiles*) and in *Ulysses* and *Finnegans Wake* (written after *Exiles*), these themes compete with others and, to that extent, become marginalized. Throughout *Exiles*, however, they remain at center stage.

As one would expect from the title, the theme of exile operates both literally and figuratively throughout the play. On the literal level, one sees the slipperiness of the term. Richard's self-imposed banishment of nine years, though absolute, is also temporary, ending with his return to Ireland. On the other hand, at the figurative level, the exile recurs through the estrangements between the main characters. It is a spiritual separation that alienates one from the other and that, by the end of the play, has the literal effect upon Robert that Richard experienced before the play began, forcing him to leave his country. Joyce makes us aware of the way that estrangement, though not bound by place, can produce the same effect as literal exile. Paradoxically, it results not from the failure of a country to sustain its people but from the failure of unrestrained freedom to sustain friendship and love. This deeper, more primal form of expulsion acts as the major concern and provides the central metaphor of Joyce's play.

Joyce recognizes that just as unlimited freedom can nourish, it can burden the soul and paralyze the mind. (This of course stands as the opposite of the restrictions in *Dubliners* that produce this condition.) Bertha, feeling abandoned in the freedom given her by Richard, suffers "mental paralysis," a phrase used by Joyce about her in his notes for the play, which follow the version published by the VIKING PRESS. Bertha's paralysis comes to the foreground at the end of the first act. She asks Richard to decide whether she should or should not visit Robert, and he refuses, leaving the choice to her.

As the second act demonstrates, such putative freedom, however, can easily prove less substantial and more tyrannical than overt repression. When Bertha does go to Robert's cottage, she finds Richard waiting there, unwilling to exert his own will but unable to relinquish engagement with what transpires. Whether or not it is intentional, this move intimidates Robert, who is unable to face Bertha and Richard together, and absents himself until Richard leaves. Betrayal seems inevitable in Richard's world of unrelenting freedom, because he proves to be as incapable as a conventional husband of surrendering control. At the end of the play, which Joyce referred to as "three cat-and-mouse acts," Richard admits to Bertha: "I have wounded my soul for you—a deep wound of doubt which can never be healed." However, even here a note of ambiguity remains. Given Richard's behavior during the course of the drama it remains an open question whether he masochistically luxuriates in that wound.

When explaining the play's title in his notes, Joyce declared that "[a] nation exacts a penance from those who dared to leave her payable on their return." The same penalty might be said to apply to those who test the limits of friendship and love. The action of the play repeatedly explores not simply the price one must pay for leaving one's country but also the emotional consequences that one must face as a result of segregating oneself from others. Richard Hand stands as much more than a geographic exile. He demonstrates the consequences of imposing emotional and spiritual independence upon every aspect of his life.

This complex exploration of the theme of exile recurs throughout Joyce's writing. In his Italian lecture "Ireland, Island of Saints and Sages" (in *Critical Writings*), for example, he touches upon ideas that also resonate in Robert's newspaper article on Richard, such as the effects that emigration has upon those who must stay at home. In his fiction, from *Dubliners* to *Finnegans Wake*, the consequences of spiritual and emotional exile dog the central characters. Nowhere, however, is the topic presented more overtly than in this play.

Despite suggestions that *Exiles* does not match the creative achievements of his fiction, the dramatic structure of the work reflects how deeply committed to it Joyce was. For *Exiles*, Joyce wrote precise and extensive stage directions, detailed the scenery, specified the year, and identified the season. The play takes place during the summer of 1912. (As it happens, this was an important period in Joyce's life as an exile. He was in Ireland from mid-July to mid-September of that year in an unsuccessful effort to get *Dubliners* into print, and left bitterly disappointed, never to return again.) Autobiographical material and (to some degree) personal longings were assimilated into the play. The death of a mother, the return of an exiled writer with a common-law wife and their child, the publication of a book, and the desire for financial security seem to parallel Joyce's life and aspirations. One cannot say whether this use of autobiographical material actually liberated Joyce from any lingering thought that he need ever return to Ireland, but once he had completed *Exiles* he was able to forge ahead with his most innovative works, *Ulysses* and *Finnegans Wake*.

Although the dramatic mode figures significantly in Joyce's aesthetics and writings, *Exiles* did not enjoy the theatrical success for which Joyce had hoped, perhaps in part because of difficulties imposed by the play itself. In a 1915 letter to Joyce, Ezra POUND bluntly commented that the play "won't do for the stage" and that "even [to] read it takes very close concentration of attention. I don't believe an audience could follow it or take it in" (*Letters*, II.365). Pound, however, did suggest that Joyce send the play to the Stage Society in London. Pound suspected that *Exiles* would not be suitable for the ABBEY THEATRE, and, in fact, the play was rejected in August 1917 by W. B. Yeats, on the grounds that it was not Irish folk drama, and therefore was not the type of play he believed his actors could perform well. As of the date of this publication, *Exiles* has not been performed at the Abbey, although the company participated in a joint television production that aired on Telefis Eireann on October 2, 1974, and proposed to stage it in 2004 until the James Joyce estate raised objections. (The estate threatened to sue on the grounds of copyright infringement. Although in 1991, 50 years after Joyce's death, *Exiles* went out of copyright, it went back into copyright in 1995 when in the European Union a new law went into effect extending the time period to 70 years after the death of the author.)

The first stage production of *Exiles* was not in English but in German at the Münchener Theater in Munich, in August 1919. (The German title of the play is *Verbannte*.) In February 1925, the Neighborhood Playhouse in New York City staged the first English-language production; it ran for 41 performances, the longest-ever run for the play. The Stage Society produced *Exiles* at the Regent Theatre in London in February 1926, almost 10 years after Joyce's initial request. The second American production of the play was by the Boston Stage Society and took place at The Barn in Boston in April 1926. In 1930, *Exiles* was again produced in German, this time at the Deutsches Volkstheater in Berlin, and in Italian at the Convegno Theater in Milan.

In September 1945, the Torch Theatre in London performed *Exiles*. The Equity Library Theatre at the Hudson Park Branch of the New York Public Library produced the play in January 1947. *Exiles* was not performed in Dublin until the Gaiety Theatre presented it on January 18, 1948, seven years after Joyce's death. The Q Theatre in London staged it in May 1950. Harold Pinter, the British playwright, also staged *Exiles* in that city in 1970. Other productions, many for one or two performances only, have been staged occasionally in Europe and the United States; a few of the most recent productions have been at the Calo Theatre in Chicago in 1991, the Milagro Theatre in New York in 1995 (produced by the Daedalus Theatre Company), and the Ontological Theatre in New York in 1996.

In fact, *Exiles* is rarely performed, and infrequently read and studied. Nonetheless, the play remains an important document for anyone interested in the evolution of Joyce's canon and in the development of his art. As a dramatic work, it embodies, albeit imperfectly, a vital principle in Joyce's aesthetics, one that he formulated years earlier in his *Paris Notebook* (March 6, 1903). In Aristotelian style, Joyce characterized the differences among the lyrical, the epical, and the dramatic forms of art, the dramatic being the least personal and thus the purest: "that art is dramatic whereby the artist sets forth the image in immediate relation to others." Particular concern for the dramatic mode can be found in Joyce's early essays as well as in the thoughts of Stephen Dedalus in *A Portrait of the Artist as a Young Man*.

## CHARACTERS

**Bertha** She is one of the principal characters in *Exiles*. Bertha, whose surname is not given in the play, is the unmarried companion of the writer Richard Rowan and the mother of their son, Archie Rowan. Although much is made of the fact that her social class is beneath Richard's, she emerges as a formidable figure in the complex and tense relationship that they share. Bertha's direct and tenacious approach to life stands in sharp contrast to the opaque and often passive positions adopted by Richard.

With Richard's knowledge and tacit consent, she develops a relationship with Richard's friend Robert Hand. Although this seems on the point of becoming an affair, it is not clear whether the sexual relationship is ever consummated. Although, as the play reveals, Richard was himself unfaithful to Bertha many times, he announces that her assignation with Robert wounds him spiritually, and it convinces him of the inevitability of betrayal if freedom is permitted. Joyce's notes to the play indicate that certain aspects of Bertha's character—the most obvious being her status as a common-law wife of an Irish writer and her sexual attractiveness—were modeled on his wife, Nora BARNACLE. (See also PREZIOSO, ROBERTO.)

**Brigid** She is an old servant of the Rowan family who continues to work for Richard Rowan after he inherits the family residence from his mother.

**Hand, Robert** He is one of the principal characters, a journalist, neighbor, and longtime friend of Richard Rowan and cousin and former fiancé of Beatrice Justice. Robert is an example of the archetypal betrayer or Judas figure who recurs throughout Joyce's writings. In his notes to the play, Joyce described Robert variously as "an automobile" and "the elder brother in the fable of the Prodigal Son" (*E* 113, 114). While the significance of the automobile reference remains obscure, the analogue between Robert and the elder brother from Jesus' parable is clear. Both remained in their native country while others left and returned to a measure of acclaim. As does Buck Mulligan in relation to Stephen Dedalus in *Ulysses*, Robert represents what Richard Rowan might become were he to submit to the demands of Irish society. Throughout *Exiles*—a play Joyce characterized as "three cat and mouse acts" (*E* 123) in which each character assumes the role of one or the other animal—Robert tries to seduce Bertha and win her away from Richard by flaunting the benefits of normalcy. Although it appears that by the end of the play he fails, the outcome is not certain. (See also PREZIOSO, ROBERTO.)

**Justice, Beatrice** She is one of the principal characters in Joyce's play. She gives piano lessons to Archie Rowan, the son of Bertha and of her common-law husband, Richard Rowan. More significantly, she maintains a complex spiritual and intellectual bond with Richard that complements the equally multifaceted physical and emotional relationship that Richard shares with Bertha. Beatrice's already unconventional ties to Richard are further complicated by the fact that she had at one time been secretly engaged to her first cousin, Robert Hand, a man who at the time of the play is deeply infatuated with Bertha.

Although Joyce modeled the other main characters in *Exiles* on recognizable Dublin friends and acquaintances, no critic has suggested an analogue for Beatrice. This absence in itself may account for the woodenness of her actions and attitudes. Joyce does, however, outline attributes of her character in his notes for *Exiles:* "Beatrice's mind is an abandoned cold temple in which hymns have risen heavenward in a distant past but where now a doddering priest offers alone and hopelessly prayers to the Most High" (*Exiles,* "Notes by the Author," p. 119). Joyce goes on to articulate the need to keep the image of Beatrice in the minds of the audience during the second act, despite the fact that she does not appear on stage then.

**Rowan, Archie** He is a minor character in the play, more a symbol than an individual. Archie is the young son of Richard Rowan and of his common-law wife, Bertha. His status as a child born out of wedlock is of more significance than his actual presence as the play unfolds. Many of the attributes of Archie's nature correspond to traits of Joyce's own son, George JOYCE, and in fact Joyce incorporated the experiences of his son while in Rome into the play, as Archie's. By and large, Archie's dialogue serves to do little more than to advance the action. At the same time, his very appearance on stage emphasizes the physical relationship between Bertha and Richard. This in turn complicates the interlocking system of emotional relations among Richard, Bertha, Beatrice, and Robert, and enhances the audience's understanding of the major characters' motivations.

**Rowan, Bertha** See Bertha.

**Rowan, Richard** He is one of the central characters in Joyce's play. Richard is a Joycelike artist figure, returned to Ireland after a self-imposed exile on the Continent. In his notes for the play, Joyce says that "Richard has fallen from a higher world and is indignant when he discovers baseness in men and women." In any number of ways Richard Rowan embodies the type of writer that Joyce felt he had become, and Rowan's response to Irish society reflects many of Joyce's assumptions about the conditions he would encounter and the way he would be received were he to return to his native land.

At the same time, while there are similarities between the author and his character, there are significant differences as well. For example, in the play Richard seems to encourage the potential for a sexual liaison between Bertha and Robert Hand, and ultimately refuses to intervene to avert its possible consummation. When a similar possibility appeared to arise between Nora BARNACLE and Roberto PREZIOSO, however, Joyce acted quickly to prevent it (although at one point Nora felt that Joyce was pushing her toward such an affair so he could write about it).

Throughout the dialogue, in a series of highly charged encounters, the play explores the diverse elements of Richard's nature elaborated in several expository speeches (sometimes unfortunately stiff and stilted) on his relations with Beatrice Justice, Bertha, and Robert Hand. Although Bertha seems to come very close to comprehending his nature, none of these characters has a full sense of Richard's intellectual, artistic, emotional, and sexual temperaments. Only the audience, having seen his interactions with all of the other characters, has an adequate sense of Richard's value.

In his notes for the play, Joyce characterizes Richard as "an automystic," and says of Richard's relations with Bertha, "Richard's jealousy . . . must reveal itself as the very immolation of the pleasure of possession on the altar of love. He . . . knows his own dishonour."

## CONTEMPORARY REVIEWS OF *EXILES*

Review: Desmond MacCarthy, "Exiles," *The New Statesman,* xi (September 21, 1918), pp. 492–493:

> *Exiles* is a remarkable play. I am more sure of this than of having understood it. I could never

undertake to produce it unless the author were at my elbow; and when a critic feels like that about a play which has excited him it means he has not quite understood it. What I can do is to give an account of the play and show where I was puzzled. But first I must come to terms with a misgiving. It is a treat to be puzzled by a play, so perhaps I overrate this one because it has puzzled me? I do not think that is the case, but that possibility is the grain of salt with which what follows must be taken. To be made to wonder and to think about characters in a play is a rare experience—outside the drama of Ibsen. It is a pleasure far excelling the simple pleasure of delighted recognition which is all that the character drawing in the ordinary respect-worthy play provides. On the stage temptations to superficiality and exaggeration are so many, and the drama is a form which requires so much condensation of subject-matter and imposes so many limitations that, within those limits, all except duffers and men of genius are, alas! more or less on a level. Once a certain knack is learnt the happy proficient in play-writing finds he can produce a play with an expenditure of a fifth of the intellectual energy and emotion necessary to produce a novel of the same calibre. If he has more to give it, it does not show; if he has not, it does not matter, for what he may still be able to produce may be on a par with the work of a far better intellect. Hence it is that there is so much truth in sayings like: "In the art of play-writing construction is everything"; "The idea of a good play should be capable of being written on half a sheet of notepaper," etc., etc. They are certainly true of the common run of respect-worthy plays, but only true of them. . . .

Review: Francis Hackett, *New Republic,* October 12, 1918, xvi, no. 206, pp. 318–319:

So good are the fine qualities of *Exiles* that the defects seem to be an illusion, but the more the play is examined the more fundamental and inexplicable seem its defects. It is part of Mr. Joyce's gift that he appears intuitive and occult. It does not seem possible that all his intuition and penetration could go astray. But *Exiles* neither creates a perfect conviction of being like human experience nor quite recalls experience in terms anything like its own. On the contrary, Mr. Joyce seems definitely to force human beings to do and say unlikely things, and to jumble up the true perspective of their lives. He is exceedingly keen in making people talk like people. He has a genius for idiom and idiosyncrasy and no one could be better than he in the way he dovetails his conversations. His ear is sharp, also, for the click of one personality against another, and for the corroborative phrase. But when it comes to comprehending men and women in their skins and under them, he can hardly be said to be reliable. There is an unreality around certain passages in *Exiles* that suggests the literary alchemist vaguely striving to transmute pretty theories into honest flesh and blood. The flesh and blood of *Exiles,* so far as it is honest, does not fit the theories. They are imposed by their author on subjects unwilling and rebellious. The result is a disharmony that almost defies literary analysis. It condemns *Exiles* to a limbo outside the normal hell and heaven of appraisal. . . .

Symposium: "*Exiles,* A Discussion of James Joyce's Play," *Little Review* v, no. 9 (January 1919), pp. 20–27:

John Rodker—Again in this play Mr. Joyce exploits that part of mind merging on the subconscious. The drama is one of will versus instinct, the protagonist Richard Rowan, a writer. This particular psychological triangle is one of barely comprehended instincts, desires for freedom (equally undefined), emotions that hardly crystallise before fading out. Inter-action of thought and will is carried so close to this borderline that the reader fears continually lest he miss any implication. Analysis digs continually deeper. At a certain moment it is lost. Mind will go no further. . . .

Israel Solon—Let me say at once I was most painfully disappointed with James Joyce's *Exiles.* My disappointment was so keen because of what he might have achieved and came near achieving but failed to achieve. His merely good is not good enough where the great was so nearly within his reach. With that theme, the author of the *Portrait* and *Ulysses* should have achieved nothing short of the sublime. No poet since Sophocles has had so dramatic a vehicle. Indeed, I think Joyce's the more dramatic. . . .

Samuel A. Tannenbaum, M.D.—*Exiles* will in all probability prove to be caviar to the general, not only because it is open to the obvious criticism that it is not true to life, but because its subject-mater is one that unconsciously stirs up the most passionate resistances of a reader unaccustomed to the most honest and deep-searching self-analysis. To the psychologist trained in psychoanalysis, on the contrary, the book will be agreeably welcome as an inspired contribution from the depths of an artist's soul to one of the most tabooed and falsified motives of human conduct,—we mean homosexuality. It is true that the reader unlearned in such matters, and perhaps the author too, may not be aware that this is the theme of the play and may look for it in vain. Of course, this is not all there is to the play; just as in a dream the main motive is overladen and disguised with other subsidiary motives and rationalizations, so is it in the drama before us. . . .

j h—I find it difficult to put any of my thoughts on *Exiles* into words. They are not used to words: they die. I feel that Joyce's play had died in words. I do not mean because of the words literally,—all art linguistic. But even Art must fail many times before it conquers those things whose nature it is to keep themselves a secret from us forever.

On the surface the play gives itself up to many interpretations. Propagandists declare it is a play on the freedom of the individual. Other reviewers talk of triangles and Ibsen and neurotics. All these things are easy and semi-intelligent things to say. But when it is unanimously agreed that Joyce hasn't 'put over his idea clearly' or that he hasn't known just what he was trying to put over, I grow a bit nervous and wonder why it doesn't appear to them that perhaps Joyce couldn't reach their darkness. I also wonder why not read *Exiles* with Joyce in mind. The man who wrote *A Portrait of the Artist* and *Ulysses,* a highly-conscious, over-sensitized artist living at the vortex of modern psychology, would scarcely go back to dealing with material in a pre-Nietzsche manner. Joyce is not Galsworthy; on the other hand he is not D. H. Lawrence. And to discuss courage in connection with Joyce is ridiculous. Joyce outlived courage in some other incarnation. . . .

Review: Bernard Bandler, "Joyce's Exiles," *Hound & Horn* vi., no. 2 (January–March 1933), pp. 266–285:

> If *Exiles* were presented in its relative truth, as a play that distilled the sorrow of human isolation, the office of the critic would be limited to understanding and enjoyment. But *Exiles* goes further; the vision claims to be universal and as final and as irrevocable as the Last Judgment. From such a sentence there is no appeal; mercy has no lien on truth; and *Exiles* is held up as the Medusa head of truth. Hence it is the truth itself of *Exiles* that one must question, its absolute truth about human destiny. . . .

Review: Padraic Colum, "James Joyce as Dramatist," *Nation* cvii, no. 2780 (October 12, 1918), pp. 430–431:

> James Joyce's *Portrait of the Artist as a Young Man* is dated "Dublin 1904, Trieste 1914." The action of *Exiles* is indicated as passing in 1912. The play, therefore, succeeds the novel in time. But if *Exiles* be more recent than *Portrait of the Artist,* it is far less modern. In the novel James Joyce created a form that was individual and distinctively modern, that suggested new horizons. The play is in Ibsen's form, without the symbolism that haunted Ibsen's plays and without his conclusiveness and his climaxes. Mr. Joyce may return to the drama and bring into it some of the discoveries that make his narrative so startling. Meanwhile, *Exiles* would make it appear that narrative is his peculiar domain. . . .
>
> Bertha is the first notable woman character that James Joyce has created. She is a subtle character. We get the suggestion that she has

had little education, yet she carries herself with real simplicity and dignity. For all her contact with the super-subtle Richard she remains unspoiled, alluring, unconventional, faithful. She has her outbreaks and she knows where to strike at Richard. Her simplicity and her good sense are shown in her last dialogue with Beatrice Justice, the woman who is able to understand her husband's mind and work. . . .

## *Finnegans Wake* (1939)

This is Joyce's last and most innovative prose work, a linguistic tour de force written in a revolutionary narrative style. Portions appeared serialized from 1924, and the entire text was published in 1939. The most common interpretative assumption of the work's narrative technique is that it approximates the protean nocturnal dream world. Joyce alluded to this oneiric style when, in a November 1926 letter to Harriet Shaw WEAVER, he commented that a "great part of every human experience is passed in a state which cannot be rendered sensible by the use of wideawake language, cut and dry grammar and goahead plot" (*Letters*, III.146). The *Wake*'s central characters are Humphrey Chimpden Earwicker and his family: Anna Livia Plurabelle; Shem and Shaun, their twin sons; and Issy, their daughter (see Characters, below). Throughout *Finnegans Wake*, these figures appear in many guises and undergo numerous transmutations that range from the mythological to the geographical. The *Wake*'s nonlinear and often humorous universe includes, among other things, historical, political, cultural, philosophical, theological, mythical, geographical, literary, and linguistic themes and references. The challenge for readers remains how to form a unified impression of these elements.

James Joyce *(Irish Tourist Board)*

These transformations and Joyce's unconventional discourse may well mimic the dynamics of a dream world. They certainly announce a radical shift in narration that transcends the boundaries of realistic fiction anticipated by Joyce in the later chapters of *Ulysses* (particularly chapter 14, The Oxen of the Sun episode, and chapter 15, the Circe episode). The reader, nonetheless, is confronted with a multilayered text of extraordinary richness and fluidity.

Many readers take Joyce's remark to Weaver at face value and approach the narrative framework of *Finnegans Wake* as an artistic expression of a dream. Nonetheless, the exact identity of the dreamer (or dreamers) remains open to speculation. Possibilities include H C E, or one of his family members, or his mythic avatar, Finn MacCool. Some believe that Joyce himself has taken the role of the dreamer, or that the reader or even Joyce and the reader together fill that function. Any and all combinations may be possible. The critic Clive Hart offers a plausible commentary concerning the identity of the dreamer:

> "Like the anonymous narrator of more conventional 'third-person' novels, the Dreamer is omniscient; we are involved in his dream as we are involved in any narrative; in each case the

narrator's identity is almost entirely irrelevant. Like Stephen's Artist-God, Joyce's Dreamer has been 'refined out of existence' " (*Structure and Motif in Finnegans Wake*, pp. 82–83).

An overemphasis on the role and identity of the dreaming agent(s), however, can skew the dynamics of the *Wake*'s narrative. As another critic, John Bishop, observes, "people have customarily treated the book, at Joyce's invitation, as the 'representation of a dream,' " and he cautions that the *Wake* is "not about a dream in any pedestrian sense of that word" (*Joyce's Book of the Dark*, p. 6). If we accept this view, Bishop challenges us to refine our notion of that dream.

Resolving this issue requires a clear sense of its origin. The *Wake*'s "mechanics," as Joseph CAMPBELL and Henry Morton ROBINSON said early on in 1944, "resemble those of a dream" (*A Skeleton Key to Finnegans Wake*, p. 3). These two coauthors, the first to publish a book on *Finnegans Wake*, may have taken a cue, as others may have done, from Edmund Wilson's influential essay titled "The Dream of H. C. Earwicker" that appeared in *The New Republic*, 91 (July 12, 1939): 270–274. The dream technique as a narrative strategy, these and other critics hold, gave Joyce the freedom he needed to weave together archetypal and historical themes that embrace motifs exploring the creation, the fall, and the resurrection of humanity. By using the dream technique in combination with Giambattista VICO's cyclical theory of history, which postulates three ages—the divine, the heroic, and the human, followed by a *ricorso* or a period of transition and renewal (marked in *Finnegans Wake* by the thunderclap)—Joyce was able to create a structure broad and open enough to allow an inclusive nonlinear narrative for his book. This, as readers come to recognize immediately, incorporates an abundance of highly original linguistic and stylistic devices.

The opening and closing lines of *Finnegans Wake* merge into the circularity of a single sentence that at once ends and begins the work, a fitting metaphor for the book's cyclical patterns that transcend the verisimilitude of linear representation. Although varied and diverse, the typologies of human experience Joyce identifies are indeed essentially cyclical. They are patterned and recurrent. In particular, the experiences of birth, guilt, judgment, sexuality, family, social ritual, and death recur throughout the *Wake*, as they do in human lives, in societies, and throughout history.

These concepts, however, have not met with universal acceptance. Patrick Parrinder and Bernard BENSTOCK, along with others, have questioned the claim that the narrative technique of *Finnegans Wake* exploits a dream language. In *James Joyce*, Benstock cautions against this perspective and observes that when in *Finnegans Wake* a dream is recounted—see, for instance, page 404 of the *Wake*—the language is noticeably conventional. "The easy conclusion that '*Finnegans Wake* is a Dream,' " Benstock writes, "does not account for the multiple discontinuities that not only disrupt but give coherence to the narrative structures of the text—dreams are invariably overdetermined in their continuities, quite unlike the *Wake*" (152). The interpretative framework of a dream, as Derek Attridge concludes in his assessment of the question in "Finnegans Awake: The Dream of Interpretation," may be "one among a number of such [interpretative] contexts which, though incompatible with one another, all have some potential value" (*James Joyce Quarterly* 27, 1989, p. 26). As with so much of Joyce's writing, in the end the narrative leaves to the individual reader the task of finding a consistent perspective that reconciles his or her impressions of *Finnegans Wake*.

## CITING *FINNEGANS WAKE*

In its overall arrangement, *Finnegans Wake* contains 17 chapters divided into four books. Book I consists of eight chapters; Book II, four; Book III, four; and Book IV, one. Almost all editions of the *Wake* have the same pagination and line spacing. Following the customary practice, *Critical Companion to James Joyce* uses Arabic numerals to designate page and line references and to indicate chapter numbers. Roman numerals are used to designate the books (and in some instances, in lowercase form, the chapters). For example, *FW* 482.34–36 refers to page 482, lines 34 to 36; this passage is found in *FW* III.3 (Book III, chapter 3). Book II, chapter 2 is the only chapter in the *Wake* to contain marginalia and footnotes. References to this chapter are made in the following manner: *FW* 276.L3 refers to the third set of notes in the left margin of the text on page 276; *FW* 260.R1 refers to the first set of notes in the right margin of the text on page 260; *FW* 299.F4 refers to footnote 4 on page 299. References to the main body of the text are made in the manner explained above, by the use of page and line numbers.

## COMPOSITION AND PUBLICATION HISTORY

Joyce began writing *Finnegans Wake* in March 1923, a little more than a year after the publication of *Ulysses*. For the next 16 years, the *Wake* commanded Joyce's full attention, until its publication on May 4, 1939. Joyce's initial method of composing *Finnegans Wake* was piecemeal. In a comment he made to the sculptor August Suter, recorded by Frank BUDGEN in *James Joyce and the Making of Ulysses*, Joyce said: "I feel like an engineer boring through a mountain from two sides. If my calculations are correct we shall meet in the middle. If not . . ." (p. 320). Joyce used engineering imagery again in a November 1924 letter to Harriet Shaw Weaver: "I think that at last I have solved one—the first—of the problems presented by my book. In other words one of the partitions between two of the tunneling parties seems to have given way" (*Letters*, III.110). Until the *Wake* formed the linguistic, thematic, and structural unity that Joyce intended, he continued to rework, revise, and reorganize portions of it even after they first appeared in various journals between 1924 and 1938.

While composing the *Wake*, Joyce would often use sigla, or signs, to designate the main characters and aspects of their identity. In a March 1924 letter to Weaver, Joyce identified his sigla:

ᗰ (Earwicker, H C E by moving letter round)
Δ Anna Livia
[ Shem-Cain
∧ Shaun
≤ Snake
P S. Patrick
T Tristan
⊥ Isolde
X Mamalujo
□ This stands for the title but I do not wish to say it yet until the book has written more of itself
(*Letters*, I.213)

Joyce incorporates some of these sigla throughout the *Wake*. At one point, he includes seven of them together (see *FW* 299.F4), and changes ⊥ (Isolde) to ⊣ (Issy). Although the shapes remain constant for each siglum, Joyce could at times vary the position of one or another siglum, rotating it in increments of 90 degrees, on its side or its back, to indicate a particular emotion or condition that the character was then experiencing and to emphasize a particular thematic motif. As Joyce worked on *Finnegans Wake*, the role of the sigla enlarged, becoming more complex as traits of individual characters developed. If at first the sigla were a form of shorthand to distinguish one character from another, they eventually came to indicate character motifs as well. In another letter to Harriet Shaw Weaver, dated May 31, 1927, Joyce explains that the sign for Earwicker as Ш "means H C E interred in the landscape" (*Letters*, 1.254; also see *FW* 6.32). In a footnote in the Lessons chapter of *Finnegans Wake*, several sigla (respectively representing H C E, A L P, Issy, the Four Old Men, the title of the book, Shaun, and Shem) appear together: "The Doodles family ᗰ, Δ, ⊣, X, □, ∧, [ Hoodle doodle, fam.?" (*FW* 299.F4). (A structural and thematic analysis of Joyce's use of the sigla can be found in Roland McHugh's *The Sigla of Finnegans Wake* [1976].)

Joyce's first drafts were small sections that are now altered and scattered throughout the final version of the *Wake*: "King Roderick O'Conor" (see Roderick O'Conor below) (in II.3, 380–382), "TRISTAN AND ISOLDE" (in II.4, 383–399), "St. Patrick and the Druid" (in IV, 611–612), "St. KEVIN" (in IV, 604–606), "Mamalujo" (in II.4, 383–399, interpolated into "Tristan and Isolde"), and "Here Comes Everybody" (I.2, 30–34). Joyce began sketching these mock-heroic pieces in March 1923 and continued through October, during which time his ideas concerning the direction of this groundbreaking work took more definite shape in his imagination. On October 9, 1923,

Joyce wrote to Harriet Shaw Weaver explaining to her that these short pieces would eventually cohere as the work matured: "I work as much as I can because these are not fragments but active elements and when they are more and a little older they will begin to fuse of themselves" (*Letters,* I.205). The *Wake,* which began as pastiche and burlesque, was intended from its inception to be humorous and universal.

While *Finnegans Wake* was being composed, it was called WORK IN PROGRESS, a title suggested by the British novelist and editor Ford Madox FORD in 1924, according to Joyce (*Letters,* I.405). This provisional title Joyce readily accepted when the first excerpt of his new work (what eventually became Book II, chapter 4—*FW* 383.1–399.36) appeared in the April 1924 issue of the TRANSATLANTIC REVIEW, the Paris-based journal Ford edited. Joyce continued to use this title to identify his work for the next 14 years while other excerpts and chapters were being published in different journals or as separate booklet-editions. This approach also added a sense of mystery about the final designation, a mystery Joyce fostered. He enjoyed challenging people to guess the book's title.

After the initial excerpt entitled "From Work in Progress" appeared in the *transatlantic review,* other fragments soon followed in different journals: "Fragment of an Unpublished Work" in the CRITERION, London III.12 (July 1925): 498–510 [*FW* 104.1–125.23]. Five fragments were pirated—reprinted without permission—from *Criterion* (July 1925), *Contact Collection of Contemporary Writers* (1925) [*FW* 30.1–34.29], *Navire d'Argent* (October 1925): [*FW* 196.1–216.5], *This Quarter* (Autumn–Winter, 1925–26): 108–123 [*FW* 169.1–195.6], and *transition* (April 1927): 9–30 [*FW* 3.1–29.36]. They were published between September 1925 and September 1926 in *Two Worlds Monthly,* a New York–based journal edited by Samuel ROTH.

The Paris journal *transition* published 17 installments of *Work in Progress* between April 1927 and April–May 1938. These serialized fragments include: "Opening Pages of A Work in Progress," 1 (April 1927) 9–30 [*FW* 3–29] and "Continuation of A Work in Progress" in the following issues: 2 (May 1927) 94–107 [*FW* 30–47]; 3 (June 1927) 32–50 [*FW* 48–74]); 4 (July 1927) 46–65 [*FW* 75–103]; 5 (August 1927) 15–31 [*FW* 104–125]; 6 (September 1927) 87–106f [*FW* 126–168]; 7 (October 1927) 34–56 [*FW* 169–195]; 8 (November 1927) 17–35 [*FW* 196–216]; 11 (February 1928) 7–18 [*FW* 282–304]; 12 (March 1928) 7–27 [*FW* 403–428]; 13 (Summer 1928) 5–32 [*FW* 429–473]; 15 (February 1929) 195–238 [*FW* 474–554]; 18 (November 1929) 211–236 [*FW* 555–590]; and 22 (February 1933) 49–76 [*FW* 219–259]. The title "Work in Progress" again appeared in *transition,* 23 (July 1935) 109–129 [*FW* 260–275, 304–308], and 26 (February 1937) 35–52 [*FW* 309–331]; finally, "Fragment from Work in Progress" in 27 (April–May 1938) 59–78 [*FW* 338–355].

By 1938, virtually all of *Finnegans Wake* was in print, either serialized in *transition* or in the form of individual booklets, which included *Anna Livia Plurabelle* (New York: Crosby Gaige, 1928; and London: Faber and Faber, 1930 [*FW* 196–216]); *Tales Told of Shem and Shaun* (Paris: The Black Sun Press, 1929 ["The Mookse and the Gripes," *FW* 152–159; "The Muddest Thick That Was Ever Heard Dump," *FW* 282–304; "The Ondt and the Gracehoper," *FW* 414–419]); *Two Tales of Shem and Shaun* (London: Faber and Faber, 1932 ["The Mookse and the Gripes" and "The Ondt and the Gracehoper"]); *Haveth Childers Everywhere* (Paris: Henry Babou and Jack Kahane; New York: Fountain Press, 1930; London: Faber and Faber, 1931 [*FW* 532–554]); *The Mime of Mick, Nick and the Maggies* (The Hague: Servire Press, 1934 [*FW* 219–259]); and *Storiella as She Is Syung* (London: Corvinus Press, 1937 [*FW* 260–275, 304–308]). Even after the excerpts and booklets were in print, Joyce continued to make revisions in his text until it was published as *Finnegans Wake* in 1939.

## THE TITLE OF *FINNEGANS WAKE*

When Joyce decided on the title *Finnegans Wake* is not certain. He revealed it to Nora BARNACLE, but to no one else. His correspondence with Harriet Shaw Weaver indicates that Joyce encouraged her, as he did others, to guess the book's name. In May 1927, Joyce wrote to her, "I shall use some of your suggestions about □, [Joyce's siglum for the title of the book] . . . The title is very simple and as commonplace as can be" (*Letters,* I.252). In 1938, to Joyce's astonishment, his friend Eugene Jolas correctly guessed the title of the book and won a wager Joyce had made on the possibility of such a feat (see Joyce's letter to Maurice James Craig in *Letters,* III.427 and Richard Ellmann's account of the story in *James Joyce,* 708). Modern critics, such as Danis Rose and John O'Hanlon, have argued that the original title Joyce had in mind, but later abandoned, was *Finn's Hotel,* a possibility suggested by the context of the passage: "—. i . .' . . o . . l" (*FW* 514.18). Finn's Hotel was the establishment where Nora worked when Joyce first met her in 1904.

Joyce decided on *Finnegans Wake* and intended a pun on the name of the Irish ballad "Finegan's Wake," which humorously recounts the fall and resurrection of Tim Finegan, a hod carrier born with the love of the liquor. In the ballad, Tim falls from a ladder and is thought to be dead. The mourners at his wake become rowdy and spill whiskey on his face, causing Tim to rise and join in the fun. (*Whiskey* comes from the Gaelic word *usquebaugh,* meaning "water of life," an image foreshadowing Anna Livia's role in the book.) Without the apostrophe in the title, Joyce presents Tim as the comic prototype of all who fall and rise again: Finnegans wake. The possessive case, however, is also suggested even without the apostrophe. Thus, the word *wake* in the book's title is, at once, a noun and a verb, signifying both the period of mourning and the moment of rising/resurrection. *Finnegans Wake* as a title, then, implies the plurality of identity and the polarity of opposites. The title also anticipates the structural and thematic design of a work distinguished by its multiple voices, multiple identities of character, place, and events, and by its interplay of opposites typified by the Shem/Shaun and ALP/Issy dualisms and the typology of the fall/resurrection, sin/acquittal, decay/renewal.

The title is also evocative of another Irish hero, Finn MacCool, the legendary warrior and giant who lies sleeping beneath the city of Dublin. Joyce continued to exploit the title's play on words even in the work's last lines spoken through the voice of Anna Livia (the book's maternal archetype whose

An Irish 10-pound note, the back of which has the first line of *Finnegans Wake* as part of the design

life-giving waters symbolize promise and renewal): "Finn, again! Take" (*FW* 628.14). All in all, Joyce weaves allusions to the title in and out of the pages of *Finnegans Wake* and, keeping in mind the critical analogy often made between *Finnegans Wake* and the arabesque ornamentation characteristic of the illustrations and lettering illuminating the *Book of Kells,* these allusions take on different forms, in the cadence and rhyme of a sentence or phrase: "to Finnegan, to sin again and to make grim grandma grunt and grin again" (*FW* 580.19–20) or "Timm Finn again's weak" (*FW* 93.35–36).

## BOOKS AND CHAPTERS OF THE *WAKE*

With a few exceptions, Joyce did not specify book or chapter titles for the *Wake,* but on occasion he did identify by name sections or chapters published separately. Book and chapter titles, however, have been designated by others, starting with Joseph Campbell and Henry Morton Robinson in *A Skeleton Key to Finnegans Wake* (1944). In some cases, critics have suggested working outlines specifying divisions within the chapters themselves, as in

Bernard BENSTOCK's *Joyce-Again's Wake: An Analysis of Finnegans Wake* (see the appendix on page 397). Although chapter and book titles are effective (or, at least, practical) ways of focusing attention on the narrative episodes of the work, we do not use them in this discussion.

The following lists of book and chapter titles are taken from Campbell and Robinson's *A Skeleton Key* and from William York TINDALL's *A Reader's Guide to James Joyce.* Tindall used divisions derived from the philosophical system of Giambattista VICO. Adaline GLASHEEN's *Third Census of Finnegans Wake* designates titles for the *Wake*'s chapters but not for its books. "One of the minor irritations of *Wake* scholarship," Benstock observes, "results from chapter-title confusion" (Joyce-Again's *Wake,* p. 4), but because these designations have become part of that scholarship, they are included here:

*Campbell and Robinson*

- Book I THE BOOK OF THE PARENTS
  - chp 1: Finnegan's Fall
  - chp 2: HCE—His Agnomen and Reputation
  - chp 3: HCE—His Trial and Incarceration
  - chp 4: HCE—His Demise and Resurrection
  - chp 5: The Manifesto of ALP
  - chp 6: Riddles—The Personages of the Manifesto
  - chp 7: Shem the Penman
  - chp 8: The Washers at the Ford
- Book II THE BOOK OF THE SONS
  - chp 1: The Children's Hour
  - chp 2: The Study Period—Triv and Quad
  - chp 3: Tavernry in Feast
  - chp 4: Bride-Ship and Gulls
- Book III THE BOOK OF THE PEOPLE
  - chp 1: Shaun before the People
  - chp 2: Jaun before St. Bride's
  - chp 3: Yawn under Inquest
  - chp 4: H C E and A L P—Their Bed of Trial
- Book IV *RECORSO* [*sic*]

*Tindall*

- Part I THE FALL OF MAN (Vico's divine age)
  - chp I The Fall of Man (Vico's divine age)
  - chp II The Cad (Vico's heroic age)
  - chp III Gossip and the Knocking at the Gate (Vico's human age)
  - chp IV The Trial (Vico's *ricorso*)
  - chp V The Letter (Vico's divine age)
  - chp VI The Quiz (Vico's heroic age)
  - chp VII Shem (Vico's human age)
  - chp VIII A. L. P. (Vico's *ricorso*)
- Part II CONFLICT (Vico's heroic age)
  - chp IX Children at Play (Vico's divine age)
  - chp X Homework (Vico's heroic age)
  - chp XI The Tale of a Pub (Vico's human age)
  - chp XII Tristan (Vico's *ricorso*)
- Part III HUMANITY (Vico's human age)
  - chp XIII Shaun the Post (Vico's divine age)
  - chp XIV Jaun's Sermon (Vico's heroic age)
  - chp XV Yawn (Vico's human age)
  - chp XVI The Bedroom (Vico's *ricorso*)
- Part IV RENEWAL (Vico's *ricorso*)
  - chp XVII New Day (Vico's *ricorso*)

*Glasheen*

- Book I
  - chp i: The Wake or The Giant's Howe
  - chp ii: Ballad
  - chp iii: Goat
  - chp iv: Lion
  - chp v: Hen
  - chp vi: Questions and Answers
  - chp vii: Shem
  - chp viii: Anna Livia Plurabelle
- Book II
  - chp i: The Mime of Mick, Nick and the Maggies
  - chp ii: Night Lessons
  - chp iii: Scene in the Pub
  - chp iv: Mamalujo
- Book III
  - chp i: First Watch of Shaun
  - chp ii: Second Watch of Shaun
  - chp iii: Third Watch of Shaun
  - chp iv: Fourth Watch of Shaun
- Book IV
  - chp i: Dawn [in Glasheen's first *Census of Finnegans Wake;* in the *Third Census of Finnegans Wake,* Glasheen leaves Book IV untitled]

## SYNOPSIS

A definitive synopsis or plot summary of *Finnegans Wake* is a virtual impossibility. The *Wake*'s linguistic complexity and multidimensional narrative strategies produce a work so rich in meaning on so many levels that it cannot be adequately summarized or reduced to a simple plot. A synopsis of any work is necessarily selective and reductive, and a synopsis of *Finnegans Wake* must be even more so because of its multilayered complexity. (For a brief review of selected resources, other than Joyce's *Letters,* which help facilitate the reading of *Finnegans Wake,* see *Finnegans Wake* Criticism at the end of this entry.)

### *FW* I.1 (*FW* 3.1–29.36)

The first chapter is an overture. It introduces major themes and concerns of the book: Finnegan's fall, the promise of his resurrection, the cyclical structure of time and history (dissolution and renewal), tragic love as embodied in the story of Tristan and Iseult, the motif of the warring brothers, the personification of the landscape, and the question of Earwicker's crime in the park, the precise nature of which is left uncertain throughout the *Wake.* Other motifs recurring throughout the *Wake,* such as a mysterious letter from Boston, Massachusetts, scratched up from a midden heap by a hen (*FW* 10.25–12.17), are also presented in the chapter. Although particular attention is given to Earwicker, all the characters of the book are introduced.

By opening in the middle of a sentence whose origin is the last line of the work, *Finnegans Wake* begins with renewal. "The book really has no beginning or end," Joyce wrote in a November 8, 1926, letter to Harriet Shaw WEAVER. "It ends in the middle of a sentence and begins in the middle of the same sentence" (*Letters,* I.246). The moment between end and beginning is suspended as in a Viconian *ricorso,* the time before a new cycle of events occurs and before anything yet happens: "riverrun, past Eve and Adam's, from swerve of shore to bend of bay, brings us by a commodius vicus of recirculation back to Howth Castle and Environs" (*FW* 3.1–3). In another letter to Weaver a week later (see *Letters,* I.247–248), Joyce glosses an early draft of the passage that would become the opening 14 lines of *Finnegans Wake* (*FW* 3.01–14).

To mark the initial cycle of Vico's three periods of history, the divine age, the first 100-letter thunderclap appears (*FW* 3.15–17). There are 10 altogether in the *Wake* (for the other nine, see *FW* 23.5–7, 44.2–21, 90.31–33, 113.9–11, 257.27–28, 314.8–9, 332.5–7, 414.19–20, 424.20–22), the last of which contains 101 letters, 101 being a numerical palindrome symbolizing completion and cyclic return. This first thunderclap announces the presence and fall of Finnegan, and in the guise of Finnegan, H C E, the "Bygmester Finnegan" (*FW* 4.18). By extension, all falls are suggested, including those of Adam and Humpty Dumpty.

After the wake itself is described (*FW* 6.13–7.19), H C E's sleeping body lying alongside the River LIFFEY (A L P) is identified as part of the landscape where the Willingdone Museyroom is located. During the tour of the museyroom (*FW* 8.9–10.23), the voyeuristic, sexual, or scatological nature of Earwicker's alleged crime in the park is revealed through the description of the museyroom's contents. The narrative then turns to the letter that the hen finds (*FW* 10.25–11.28), followed by a brief account of Humphrey Chimpden Earwicker and his family given within the context of a short history of Ireland.

In this section, the dates 1132 (a number repeated throughout the *Wake* and prominent in II.4) and 566 (half of 1132) occur as sets twice. The number 1132 in the *Wake* is associated with the fall and also anticipates renewal. (Elsewhere, Joyce associates 32 with falling. Leopold Bloom in *Ulysses* calls to mind the rate of falling bodies: "Thirtytwo feet per second per second. Law of falling bodies: per second per second" [*U* 5.44–45]. The sentence rendered numerically, however, would be 3211 [32 feet per 1 second per 1 second = 3211], a transposition of 1132, underscoring the importance of reversal throughout Joyce's oeuvre and especially in *Finnegans Wake.* Eleven stands out as the number of renewal, the beginning of a new decade and the end of another. In *Ulysses* Bloom's son Rudy lived for 11 days and would have been 11 in December 1904 had he lived [see *U* 4.420, 14.267, 17.2280–2282].)

The Mutt and Jute (Shem and Shaun) dialogue continues the narrative with a snippet of Dublin history as the invader and the native "swop hats" (*FW* 16.8) and exchange views on the Battle of Clontarf. (That engagement, fought near Dublin on Good Friday, April 23, 1014, ended in the defeat of Viking forces by the native Irish, a defining moment in Irish history.) After a diversion into the formation of an alphabet (*FW* 18.17–20.18), the episode of Jarl van Hoother and the Prankquean is narrated (*FW* 21.5–23.15), a story based on an incident from the life of Grace O'Malley ("grace o'malice," *FW* 21.20–21), who purportedly was refused entrance at the Earl of Howth's castle when he was at dinner. In Joyce's account the angry Prankquean presents the Earl with a riddle (*FW* 21.18–19) that he is unable to solve and kidnaps Tristopher, one of his twin sons. The Prankquean arrives a second time, asks another riddle (*FW* 22.5–6) that the Earl cannot answer, returns Tristopher, and takes Hilary, the other twin. After another interval, the Prankquean returns Hilary and asks a third riddle (*FW* 22.29–30) that is also left unanswered. Just before she leaves holding "her dummyship" (*FW* 23.13), Jarl van Hoother's daughter, a second thunderclap is heard (*FW* 23.6–7) anticipating re-creation after the fall: "O foenix culprit! Ex nickylow malo comes mickelmassed bonum" (*FW* 23.16–17).

The narrative returns to the now waking Finnegan, who is told not to get up just yet: "Now be aisy, good Mr. Finnimore, sir. And take your laysure like a god on pension and don't be walking abroad" (*FW* 24.16–17). Again when he attempts to rise, he is reminded to "lie quiet" (*FW* 27.22) as he must acclimate himself to the new world of "Edenborough," where his replacement, H C E, "will be ultimendly respunchable for the hubbub caused" there (*FW* 29.34–35). "Repose you now! Finn no more!" (*FW* 28.33–34).

### *FW I.2 (FW 30.1–47.32)*

Now that Earwicker has officially arrived on the scene, chapter 2 gives the reader some background. The important opening episode (*FW* 30.1–34.29), which Joyce composed in 1923, is often called "Here Comes Everybody." Earwicker's person is described in mock-heroic terms, and his offense in the park, which was first brought up in the Willingdone Museyroom section of the previous chapter (*FW* 8), is again alluded to here (*FW* 34). The episode begins by humorously reviewing the origin of Earwicker's surname, "the genesis of Harold or Humphrey Chimpden's occupational agnomen" (*FW* 30.2–3), and by asking the reader to dismiss those sources that wrongly link him with certain notable families of the past. Out of his initials, H. C. E., the populace gave him "the nickname Here Comes Everybody" (*FW* 32.18–19), but "certain wisecrackers" have suggested that they stand for something "baser" and that "he suffered from a vile disease" (*FW* 33.14–18). Earwicker is accused of being a nuisance to Welsh soldiers in the park (*FW* 33.26–27), and the question of his alleged offense there, indecent exposure or at least "a partial exposure" resurfaces (*FW* 34.25–29). The "Here Comes Everybody," episode, intended to open the work, was one of five seminal sketches marking a significant moment in Joyce's artistic development, in which it played a particularly important part, and marks an early stage in the creation of *Finnegans Wake*. The *Wake* is essentially plotless, so episodes like this do a great deal to impose narrative unity upon it, for they provide entry into the work through a structure of motifs, an alternative to conventional linear narrative.

Earwicker denies the accusation when he meets "a cad with a pipe" (*FW* 35.11). (The story of meeting a cad with a pipe is based on an incident that occurred to Joyce's father and, like so many other details from his father's life, Joyce incorporates it into *Finnegans Wake* [see *Letters,* I.396].) Earwicker's denial, however, forms the germ of a rumor that the Cad quickly begins to spread. Different versions of Earwicker's crime circulate until one is uttered by Treacle Tom in his sleep. Peter Cloran (Shaun), Mildew Lisa (Issy), and Hosty (Shem) overhear him, and Hosty is inspired to compose "The Ballad of Persse O'Reilly" (see "Separately Published Fragments," below), which charges Earwicker with public crimes and mockingly identifies him with Humpty Dumpty (*FW* 44.24–47.32). A third thunderclap is heard immediately preceding the ballad. Putting the shredded pieces of his reputation together again becomes impossible for Earwicker.

### *FW I.3 (FW 48.1–74.19)*

The alleged criminal episode in the park is investigated, but to no avail because the individuals involved and the facts surrounding the case cannot clearly be determined. Visibility is obscured "in a freakfog" (*FW* 48.2), communication is uncertain, and so, too, are the precise facts, but scandals still abound regarding Earwicker's crime. Hoping that "Television" will kill "telephony," for "eyes demand their turn" (*FW* 52.18–19), Earwicker presents a televised version of the encounter in the park (*FW* 52.18–55.2), which commences a review of the episode—"The scene, refreshed, reroused, was never to be forgotten . . ." (*FW* 55.10–11). (Television as a means of communication was introduced in England by John L. Baird in 1926, a fact of which Joyce was well aware.)

Several interviews are conducted and opinions gathered as to Earwicker's offense, but all is hearsay and nothing conclusive (*FW* 58.23–61.27). After the interlude of a short film, a variant of the episode in the park (*FW* 64.22–65.33), inquiries are resumed as to when a letter by "A Laughable Party" (A L P) to "Hyde and Cheek, Edenberry" (H C E) might arrive (*FW* 66.10–27) and as to the removal of a coffin "from the hardware premises of Oetzmann and Nephew" (*FW* 66.31–32). Accusations continue against Earwicker (*FW* 67.7–27), and an "unsolicited visitor" (*FW* 70.13), locked out and unable to get into the pub for a drink (*FW* 70.13–30), utters "a long list . . . of all abusive names" (*FW* 71.5–6) that Earwicker has been called (*FW* 71.10–72.16). Earwicker, "respectsful of the liberties of the noninvasive individual" (*FW* 72.17), is unresponsive to him even after this traveler "from the middle west" (*FW* 70.14) "pegged a few glatt stones" (*FW* 72.27) at the pub before leaving. At the end of the chapter, H C E falls asleep and, like Finn, "skall wake" (*FW* 74.1) again.

### *FW* I.4 (*FW* 75.1–103.11)

Earwicker is asleep, dreaming of death and burial places. The missing coffin appears, here described as "teak" and "Pughglasspanelfitted" (*FW* 76.11). The allusions to various battles, including some from the American Revolution and the American Civil War, that occur at the beginning of this chapter (*FW* 78.15–79.26) suggest an apocalyptic dissolution at the end and an anticipation of a new beginning: "abide Zeit's [time's] sumonserving, rise afterfall" (*FW* 78.7). In *A Skeleton Key to Finnegans Wake,* Joseph Campbell and Henry Morton Robinson comment: "The great wars which follow the death of H C E correspond to the noisy brawl at the wake of Finnegan and the brother battles of the sons. With the death of the Master, chaos supervenes" (*FW* 82. n 4). The supervening chaos is a Viconian *ricorso* that foreshadows a new age. But this new age is still in the making, for the widow Kate Strong (*FW* 79.27), who appeared without the surname as the museyroom tour guide in chapter 1, directs the reader's attention back in time to the "filthdump near the Serpentine in Phornix Park" (*FW* 80.6) and recounts her view of the way things were. A variation of H C E's encounter with the Cad follows (*FW* 81.12–84.27). This account of the confrontation, told in the guise of "the attackler" (*FW* 81.18) and the adversary, is a significant modification of the Cad story, which, like the Jute and Mutt encounter in I.1, adumbrates the Shem/Shaun opposition and struggle central to the book's thematic development.

The trial of the accused Festy King (H C E) and a review by the four judges of confusing and contradictory evidence occupy the next several pages of the chapter (*FW* 85.20–96.24). The witnesses, including Festy King himself in disguise (*FW* 86.7–11), testify against him. During his trial, the fourth thunderclap sounds (*FW* 90.31–33), the letter resurfaces (*FW* 93.24), and the witnesses fuse with one another, making identification uncertain. The four judges, "fourbottle men . . . [and] . . . analists" (*FW* 95.27), argue the case, but settle nothing. After his indeterminate trial, H C E flees like a fox pursued by dogs, but sightings of him are reported (*FW* 96.26–100.36) before the chapter concludes by focusing attention on A L P and her arrival: "So tellus tellas allabouter" (*FW* 101.2–3).

### *FW* I.5 (*FW* 104.1–125.23)

In the rhythm of the prayer the *Our Father,* the fifth chapter opens with an invocation to Anna Livia, followed by the various names (*FW* 104.5–107.7) of her "untitled mamafesta memorialising the Most-highest" (*FW* 104.4). This chapter concentrates on the letter from Boston, to which references were made in I.1 and in the passage immediately following the trial scene of Festy King in the previous chapter (*FW* 93.22–94.22). The chapter also contains the fifth thunderclap (*FW* 113.9–11).

An investigation into the letter's authorship, content, envelope, origin, and retriever constitutes the chapter's basic subject matter. Patience will be needed, however, before one can find out "who in hallhagal wrote the durn thing" (*FW* 107.36), and surely before one can interpret its meaning. In mock seriousness, various theories and approaches to the interpretation of the letter, which can, and indeed does, stand as an analogy of the *Wake* itself, are advanced. Included are textual, historical, and Freudian analyses followed by a discussion of the intricacy and beauty of the letter (*FW* 119.10–123.10). In order to illustrate the elaborate complexity of the letter, Joyce mimics Sir Edward Sullivan's commentary on the BOOK OF KELLS and highlights the Tunc page of this work. This chapter is about the letter, its arrangement of words, and the deciphering of its meaning, but, analogously, the chapter is also about reading and understanding *Finnegans Wake:* "here keen again and begin again to make soundsense and sensesound kin again" (*FW* 121.14–16).

### *FW* I.6 (*FW* 126.1–168.14)

Chapter 6 contains 12 questions, the first 11 asked by Shem and the 12th by Shaun. The questions and answers, among other things, relate to the Earwicker family, to other characters, and to Ireland and its capital cities. The structure of the chapter intensifies the ongoing polarity between Shem and Shaun, one of the major themes of conflict throughout the *Wake.*

The interrogation opens by focusing on the two main characters. The first question (*FW* 126.10–139.13) is the longest and deals with Earwicker, the master builder of myths. Shaun easily identifies the person and answers: "Finn MacCool!" (*FW* 139.14). Shem's second question, one of the briefest, relates to their mother, Anna Livia: "Does your mutter know your mike?" (*FW* 139.15). Shaun's answer (*FW* 139.16–28) reveals his unbounded pride in her.

Next, the interrogation takes up the subtle influence of the city on the narrative. In the third question (*FW* 139.29–140.5), Shem asks Shaun to come up with a motto for Earwicker's pub. Shaun gives a variation, one of many throughout the *Wake,* of Dublin's motto: *obedientia civium urbis felicitas,* obedience of the citizens is the happiness of the city (*FW* 140.6–7). Shem's fourth question seems simple enough. It asks for the name of the Irish capital city that has "two syllables and six letters," beginning with *D* and ending with *n,* and that contains the largest park, the most expensive brewery, the widest street, and most horse-loving, "theobibbous" (God-drinking/God-consuming) population in the world (*FW* 140.8–14). The obvious answer is Dublin, but Shaun's reply (*FW* 140.15–141.7) lists Ireland's four major divisions (Ulster, Munster, Leinster, Connaught) and includes *a*) Delfas (Belfast), *b*) Dorhqk (Cork), *c*) Nublid (Dublin), and *d*) Dalway (Galway). At one point the cities, like Mamalujo (the four evangelists combined), merge, "*abcd*" (*FW* 141.4).

The next group of queries highlights the supporting figures in the narrative. The fifth question deals with the identity of the person who performs the menial tasks at Earwicker's pub (*FW* 141.8–26). The answer given is "Pore ole Joe!" (*FW* 141.27). Question six concerns the Earwicker family's housekeeper (*FW* 141.28–29), whose griping is echoed in the answer (*FW* 141.30–142.7). The seventh question focuses on the 12 "partners" at Earwicker's pub (*FW* 142.8–28), and the answer suggests that they are sleeping dreamers: "The Morphios!" (*FW* 142.29). Question eight asks about the "maggies" (*FW* 142.30), the multiple personalities of Issy, to which Shaun responds by listing their traits (*FW* 142.31–143.2).

The closing inquiries take up thematic issues. Shem's ninth question concentrates on what a tired dreamer may see (*FW* 143.3–27): "then *what* would that fargazer seem to seemself to seem seeming of, dimm it all?" (143.26–27)—the answer, "A collideorscape!" (*FW* 143.28). The 10th question deals with love (*FW* 143.29–30). An extended answer, the second-longest in the chapter, offers a facile response to a serious question (*FW* 143.31–148.32). Question 11 asks Jones (Shaun) whether he would help his brother in a time of dire need (*FW* 148.33–149.10).

An immediate "No" begins the longest answer in the chapter (*FW* 149.11–168.12). The answer is broken into three main segments starting with a discussion by Professor Jones on the dime-cash problem (*FW* 149.11–152.14) and followed by two illustrations. The first is *The Mookse and the Gripes* (*FW* 152.15–159.5; see Separately Published Fragments, below), a table of unresolved conflict between two parties told within the theological framework of the FILIOQUE dispute (see *Letters,* III.284–285). This dispute was the cause of separation between the Latin church in the West, identified here as the Mookse, and the Greek church in the East, identified as the Gripes. An interlude relating to Nuvoletta (*FW* 157.8), a passing cloud dropping rain into the Liffey, precedes the second illustration (*FW* 161.15–168.12), which, alluding to Brutus and Cassius, the Romans who assassinated Julius Caesar, tells of Burrus (Brutus/Shaun) and Caseous (Cassius/Shem). The last and shortest question and answer (*FW* 168.13–14), asked by Shaun (and perhaps answered by him in the voice of Shem), marks Shem as the accursed brother and prepares the reader for Shaun's execrations against him in the next chapter.

### *FW I.7 (FW 169.1–195.6)*

This chapter, also known as "Shem the Penman" (see Separately Published Fragments, below), is about Shem and a portrait of the artist, but indirectly it is also a portrait of Shaun. Except for a short passage at the end (*FW* 193.31–195.6), chapter 7 is narrated from Shaun's point of view, prejudiced as that may be: "Putting truth and untruth together a shot may be made at what this hybrid actually was like to look at" (*FW* 169.8–10). Shem's physical appearance is pointedly described (*FW* 169.11–20). When seeing himself as an infant for the first time (*FW* 169.20–22), he asked his siblings the first riddle of the universe: "When is a man not a man?" (*FW* 170.5).

Unable to answer and win "the prize of a bittersweet crab" (*FW* 170.7), they gave up, and Shem "took the cake" (*FW* 170.22) and gave the solution: when he is a "Sham" (*FW* 170.24), that is, a fraud. He is a creature whose character is contemptuously attacked starting with his eating habits: "Shem was a sham and a low sham and his lowness creeped out first via foodstuffs" (*FW* 170.25–26). The lowness of this "farsoonerite" (*FW* 171.4), who abandoned Ireland for Europe, is delineated throughout the following pages (170.25–175.4).

In some obvious ways, Shem is a self-parody of Joyce. Shem's favorite wine (as described in *FW* 171.15–28) was, according to Richard Ellmann, also preferred by Joyce. It was a white Swiss wine known as *Fendant de Sion,* which Joyce labeled the archduchess's urine. See *James Joyce,* p. 455, and also *Letters,* I.131 where Joyce in a 1919 letter to Frank Budgen quips: "Her Most Excellent Excellency's the Archduchess's most excellent piss (Pardon! Fendant de Valais)." (Valais is the region in Switzerland where *Fendant de Sion* is produced, and *Valais* is also a name for a white Fendant wine.) In the *Wake,* the name appears as "Fanny Urinia" (*FW* 171.28). A game song redolent of "The Ballad of Persse O'Reilly" appears on *FW* 175 as a segue into Shem's cowardly nature. He would rather find "himself up tight in his inkbattle house" (*FW* 176.30–31) than outside fighting. His artistic endeavors are ridiculed, culminating in the Latin passage on *FW* 185 and continuing in the paragraph (in English) that follows. (For a translation of the Latin, see the appendix III). In the scatological process of making ink, Shem "through the bowels of his misery" (*FW* 185.33) is the "alshemist" (*FW* 185.35) who becomes "transaccidentated" (*FW* 186.3–4) into his art. Although marked by self-ridicule, this passage in the *Wake* reflects a profound and highly original artistic principle expounded by Joyce. (See TRANSACCIDENTATION.) Shem as MERCIUS is accused by Shaun as JUSTIUS of numerous sins and faults (*FW* 187.24–193.28). Shem will need a thorough purging (*FW* 188.5–7). At the end of the chapter, MERCIUS attempts to vindicate himself through his art. (Scattered throughout the chapter, from page 182 through page 190, the reader can find distorted titles of Joyce's works, adding to Joyce's self-parody.)

### *FW I.8 (FW 196.1–216.5)*

In a March 1924 letter to Harriet Shaw Weaver, Joyce commented that the Anna Livia chapter "is a chattering dialogue across the river by two washerwomen who as night falls become a tree and a stone. The river is named Anna Liffey" (*Letters,*

I.213). Joyce was very pleased with this chapter, and had it published separately several times and made a recording of its last four pages (*FW* 213–216). The Irish writer James STEPHENS praised the chapter as "the greatest prose ever written by a man" (*Letters,* I.282), and Joyce himself signaled his satisfaction when, in Cambridge in 1929, he made a recording reading the opening lines of the chapter.

The chapter opens with a double symbol. The first word is the capital letter *O,* representing circularity, and the first three lines are in the shape of a triangle, forming the siglum for Anna Livia, the chapter's abiding presence. (The opening letter of the chapter can also symbolize completion and perfection and signify renewal, since Anna Livia, associated with the flow of the River Liffey, is the dominant voice in the closing lines of the work, a passage that simultaneously anticipates completion and renewal.)

As the two washerwomen clean dirty laundry belonging to Earwicker and others, they gossip about him and about Anna Livia and her role in his fall (*FW* 196.1–204.20). The image of Anna Livia as a cleansing river is a sign of change and renewal, but she too is implicated in Earwicker's guilt. If Mrs. Magrath (*FW* 204.34) and Laura Keown (*FW* 205.9–10) are "variant incarnations" of Anna Livia, as Campbell and Robinson claim (*A Skeleton Key,* p. 136n.14), then her dirty drawers are being washed also, drawers that should have been aired first (*FW* 204.34–35).

The gossip continues about how Anna Livia, upset by all the rumors circulating about Earwicker and herself, planned to get even (205.16–212.19). After she had gotten ready (206.29–207.20), she distributed presents from "a shammy mailsack" (*FW* 206.10). In the same letter to Harriet Shaw Weaver referred to above (*Letters,* I.213), Joyce wrote: "Her Pandora's box contains the ills flesh is heir to." As night begins to fall, the river gets noisier and the washerwomen find it difficult to hear one another. Interest begins to shift to the tales of Shem and Shaun before Book I ends: "Beside the rivering waters of, hitherandthithering waters of. Night!" (*FW* 216.4–5).

### *FW* II.1 (*FW* 219.1–259.10)

In the first chapter of Book II, the children play a game called the "Mime of Mick, Nick and the Maggies" (*FW* 219.18–19; see Separately Published Fragments, below). Joyce explained his intent in a November 1930 correspondence with Harriet Shaw Weaver: "The scheme of the piece I sent you is the game we used to call Angels and Devils or colours. The Angels, girls, are grouped behind the Angel, Shawn, and the Devil has to come over three times and ask for a colour. If the colour he asks for has been chosen by any girl she has to run and he tries to catch her" (*Letters,* I.295). Joyce also pointed out in this letter that he filled the chapter with "rhythms taken from English singing games."

The characters in the play are Glugg (Shem as Devil), The Floras (28 maidens as variant aspects of Issy), Izod (Issy as a bewitching blonde), Chuff (Shaun as Angel), Ann (A L P as mother-in-law and woman of the house), Hump (H C E as innkeeper and cause of all grievances), The Customers (a dozen citizens), Saunderson (a spoiled bartender and butt of Kate), and Kate (a cook and charwoman). The Mime ends with the *Wake*'s sixth thunderclap (257.27–28).

After each time Glugg fails to answer a riddle, three in all (*FW* 225.22–27, 233.21–27, 250.3–9), the rainbow girls dance, sing, or praise Chuff. The answer is "heliotrope," as Joyce pointed out in a July 1939 letter to Frank Budgen (*Letters,* I.406). Between the questions, Glugg's various failures of one form or another—as exile, writer, and defender of self—are brought up. Included in the rainbow girls' singing (*FW* 236.19–32), after Glugg's second failed attempt to answer a riddle, is Joyce's favorite passage from the French poet and historian Edgar QUINET.

In the letter to Harriet Shaw Weaver cited above (*Letters,* I.295), Joyce explained: "When he [Glugg/Shem] is baffled a second time the girl angels sing a hymn of liberation around Shawn [Chuff]. The page enclosed is still another version of a beautiful sentence from Edgar Quinet which I have already refashioned in *Transition* [*sic*] part one beginning since the days of Hiber and Hairyman etc'. E.Q. says that the wild flowers on the ruins of Carthage, Numancia etc have survived the political rises and falls of Empires. In this case the wild flowers are the lilts of children." (Joyce's parody of the Quinet passage occurs in three other sections in the *Wake: FW* 14.35–15.11, 281.4–15, 615.2–5.) Interwoven into the mime are the themes of Earwicker's resurrection and A L P's willingness to forgive him (*FW* 240.5–243.36). "The curtain drops" (*FW* 257.31–32) as the mime comes to an end, and the chapter closes with the children praying before going to sleep (*FW* 258.25–259.10).

### *FW II.2 (FW 260.1–308.36)*

About two months after *Finnegans Wake* was published, Joyce explained the organization of this chapter in a July 1939 letter to Frank Budgen: "[T]he technique here is a reproduction of a schoolboy's (and schoolgirl's) old classbook complete with marginalia by the twins, who change sides at half time, footnotes by the girl (who doesn't), a Euclid diagram, funny drawings etc." (*Letters,* I.406). This chapter (often called the Lessons chapter) represents a day in the life of schoolchildren at "triv and quad" (*FW* 306.12–13), that is, the trivium and quadrivium (the lower and upper divisions, respectively, of the seven liberal arts in medieval universities; the trivium comprises grammar, rhetoric, and logic; the quadrivium, arithmetic, geometry, astronomy, and music). The opening and closing of the chapter (*FW* 260.1–275.2 and 304.5–308.32) was published as *Storiella as She Is Syung* (see Separately Published Fragments, below).

The chapter covers a variety of topics that include grammar, history, letter writing, and geometry. It also includes a range of interests that stretch across cosmological, theological, religious, political, and sexual subjects. Throughout the episode the boys comment in marginal remarks while their sister puts in her views in footnotes. When the lesson turns to sexuality and to portions of A L P's anatomical geometry, it is not immediately understood by Kev (Shaun). As a graphic aid for the visually oriented Shaun, Dolph (Shem) draws and labels intersecting circles as a way to demonstrate his point (*FW* 293). On the same page, Dolph shifts from the left to the right margin and Kev from the right to the left. Dolph's explanation goes on for several more pages before Kev finally understands. Essay topics comprise the last part of their lessons (*FW* 306.15–308.2), but the children avoid them and instead write a letter to their parents, entitled "NIGHTLETTER" as the chapter ends.

### *FW II.3 (FW 309.1–382.30)*

This chapter is the longest of the *Wake.* Its setting is Earwicker's pub, and its main divisions include the story of the Norwegian captain and the tailor Kersse (*FW* 311.5–332.9; see "Norwegian Captain" under Separately Published Fragments, below); Buckley's shooting the Russian General, a tale from the Crimean War humorously rendered by Butt and Taff (*FW* 337.32–355.7) and generally referred to as Buckley and the Russian General (see Separately Published Fragments below); Earwicker's self-defense and the judgment of the four old men against him (*FW* 361.35–369.17); and the closing of the pub, after which H C E, alone, drinks the dregs, passes out, and begins to dream as the ship the *Nansy Hans* sails off (*FW* 369.18–382.30). There is eating in the chapter as well, an activity that occurs throughout the *Wake,* but here the god of drink, Buccas (*FW* 378.3)—Bacchus-Earwicker—is to be consumed (*FW* 378.3–4), as in the ancient Greek religious ritual of theophagy, the eating of the god Dionysus (Bacchus). Campbell and Robinson have pointed out: "This chapter . . . will show the denizens of HCE's tavern consuming the life substance of their host—and not only eating and drinking him out of house and home, but tearing apart with their talk the garment of his reputation" (*A Skeleton Key,* p. 196). Further suggestive both of the eucharistic associations that run through the narrative and of a link to the god Dionysus, the tearing apart can be likened to *sparagmos,* the ritual rending of the sacrificial victim.

The chapter opens with a radio broadcast interspersed within the talk of the customers. Earwicker is tending bar when the story of the Norwegian captain and the tailor begins. According to Richard Ellmann, the source of this story was Joyce's godfather, Philip McCann, who told Joyce's father "of a hunchbacked Norwegian captain who ordered a suit from a Dublin tailor, J. H. Kerse of 24 Upper Sackville Street. The finished suit did not fit him, and the captain berated the tailor for being unable to sew, whereupon the irate tailor denounced him for being impossible to fit" (*James Joyce,* p. 23). In the setting of the *Wake,* however, the story is much more complex. Its details become an obscure and extended variation on H C E's past, including his alleged crime in the park and his marriage; The seventh thunderclap occurs at the beginning of the story (*FW* 314.8–9) and the eighth at the very end of the story (*FW* 332.5–7). These incidents signify the motif of the fall of Finn MacCool/Finnegan/ Persse O'Reilly "Fine, again. Cuoholson! Peace, O wiley" (*FW* 332.08–9).

Butt and Taff (a variation of the Mutt/Jute, Shem/Shaun typology) broadcast a television version of the tale "Buckley and the Russian General," a story Joyce first heard from his father (see Ellmann, *James Joyce,* p. 398). Butt takes the role of an Irish soldier, Buckley, about to shoot a Russian general. Buckley, however, momentarily spares the Russian when he sees him defecating, but when the general wipes himself with a clod of turf, the insulted Irishman shoots: "For when meseemim, and tolfoklokken rolland allover ourloud's lande, beheaving up that sob of tunf for to claimhis, for to wollpimsolff, puddywhuck. Ay, and untuoning his culothone in an exitous erseroyal *Deo Jupto.* At that instullt to Igorladns! Prronto! I gave one dobblenotch and I ups with my crozzier. Mirrdo! With my how on armer and hits leg an arrow cockshock rockrogn. Sparro!" (*FW* 353.15–21).

By the end of the television program, Butt and Taff merge together and become one (*FW* 354.8). Attention shifts to Earwicker's self-defense and the judgment of the four old men against him (*FW* 355.8–369.5). It is time for the pub to close and the customers to leave. H C E, alone, drinks the customers' leftovers, passes out (another type of fall), and begins to dream. Joyce likens this scene to a ship leaving port. The "King Roderick O'Conor" portion at the end of this chapter (*FW* 380.7–382.30) can be traced back to one of Joyce's earliest sketches for *Finnegans Wake* (see Composition and Publication History, above). Earwicker is here identified with Ireland's last king, buried in 1198.

### *FW II.4 (FW 383.1–399.36)*

The last chapter of Book II is one of the shortest episodes in *Finnegans Wake.* In it, Joyce combines material from two of his early sketches for the book, "Tristan and Isolde" and "Mamalujo," both of which he began in March 1923. Mamalujo, a shortened form of the evangelists Matthew, Mark, Luke, and John, was the first fragment of *Finnegans Wake* to be published (see below), appearing in the April 1924 issue of the *TRANSATLANTIC REVIEW.* Mamalujo, the four old men, identified here as Matt Gregory, Marcus Lyons, Luke Tarpey, and Johnny MacDougall, are four reflections of H C E. The poem at the beginning of the chapter is sung by "seaswans" (*FW* 383.15) and mockingly recounts Tristy's (Tristan's) imminent triumph over a defenseless Muster Mark (King Mark/Earwicker).

Joyce's chief source for the Tristan and Isolde story was Joseph Bédier's French version of the romance. Like the four jealous barons at the court of King Mark in Bédier's version, the four old men, "all sighing and sobbing" (*FW* 384.4–5), listen in on Tristan and Isolde and reflect upon the past (*FW* 386.12–395.25). The four also spy on Tristan and Isolde's sexual union (*FW* 395.26–396.33) after which they fashion a four-quatrain hymn for Iseult la belle at the end of the chapter (*FW* 398–399). See TRISTAN AND ISOLDE.

This chapter also reintroduces the motif of the date 1132, which first appears in I.1. Although the number is found throughout the *Wake,* it recurs most often within II.4. Such references as "in the year of the flood 1132" (*FW* 387.23) and others indicate a connection between this number and the theme of dissolution/renewal. The flood, as in the biblical prototype, symbolizes both dissolution/ destruction (a fall from grace) and renewal/re-creation (a rebirth and promise of new life). For Joyce, the numbers 32 1 1 (a slightly different arrangement of 1132) are directly related to the notion of a fall. (As noted above, in *Ulysses,* Leopold Bloom thinks of the law of falling bodies: "Thirtytwo feet per second . . ." [*U* 5.44–45]; see *FW* I.1 above.) Here the narrative directly links the number 11, a sign of renewal (the beginning—one—repeating itself) with Anna Livia, the archetype of renewal in the *Wake*—intensifying the connection by making her number 111, a numerical palindrome.

### *FW III.1 (FW 403.1–428.27)*

Joyce's working name for Book III (*FW* 403.1–590.30) was "Shaun the Post" (see Separately Published Fragments, below). Book III opens with the sound of bells tolling at midnight. In the repose of the "heartbeats of sleep" (*FW* 403.5), the speaker "dropping asleep somepart in nonland"

(*FW* 403.18) pictures the public acclaim achieved by Shaun the Post, the central figure of this and the next two chapters. In a letter to Harriet Shaw Weaver, dated May 24, 1924, Joyce comments on his description of Shaun as "a postman traveling backwards in the night through the events already narrated. It is written in the form of a *via crucis* of 14 stations but in reality it is only a barrel rolling down the river Liffey" (*Letters,* I.214). Since Shaun is at center stage in chapters 1, 2, and 3 of Book III, Joyce's comment may cover all three chapters and not only III.1. Throughout the chapter, the recurring theme of the Shem/Shaun conflict resurfaces in many different ways that become obvious in Shaun's responses to the questions.

Like Nick Bottom in William Shakespeare's *A Midsummer Night's Dream,* a play that the narrative of *Finnegans Wake* frequently invokes, the speaker/narrator expounds upon his dream, but in the voice of an ass (*FW* 405.6). The episode also includes a graphic depiction of Shaun's eating practices. The bulk of the chapter, however, consists of an extended interview with Shaun (*FW* 409.8–426.4)—14 questions in all—conducted by the public. The first of a series of increasingly probing inquiries asks Shaun who gave him the permit to speak (*FW* 409.8–10). The second question continues along these lines; the third touches upon the hearsay that Shaun will be the bearer of the letter (*FW* 410.20–23). The fourth question asks where he works (*FW* 410.29–30). The fifth accuses him of painting the town green, to which he responds by saying it was a "freudful mistake" (*FW* 411.35–36). The sixth question starts by commending Shaun's song, but asks of him what he is really after (*FW* 412.9–12). The seventh question asks Shaun to explain the (Swiftian) references in his letter (*FW* 413.27, 29). (Cadenus was the pseudonym Swift used in his correspondence with Vanessa, the name he gave to Esther Vanhomrigh.) In this seventh, the people also seek more biographical information from Shaun.

In Shaun's response to the eighth question—what happened to your money?—he includes the fable of the "Ondt and the Gracehoper" (*FW* 414.16–419.106; see Separately Published Fragments, below), a story of the practical-minded Ondt (Shaun) and the prodigal Gracehoper (Shem). This fable is also Joyce's defense of *Finnegans Wake* against his critics, in particular Wyndham LEWIS. The ninth thunderclap word occurs at the beginning of the fable when Shaun clears his throat (*FW* 414.19–20).

The people begin the ninth question with praise for Shaun's vocabulary and ability to express himself and then ask would he "read the strangewrote anaglyptics of those shemLetters, patent for His Christian's Em?" (*FW* 419.18–19), a letter about H C E. In their 10th question, the people impute that Shaun has written 10 times worse than his "cerebrated brother," Shem (*FW* 421.19).

The audience now, in the 11th question, petitions Shaun "to unravel" the letter in his "own sweet way" (*FW* 422.20–21) and to offer another "esiop's foible" (*FW* 422.22). In his answer, Shaun, bitter and defensive, accuses Shem of modifying his (Shaun's) words: "As often as I think of that unbloody housewarmer, Shem Skrivenitch, always cutting my prhose to please his phrase, bogorror, I declare I get the jawache!" (*FW* 423.14–17). Shaun concludes his response by ridiculing events in Shem's life.

In the 12th question, the people ask Shaun why he is so hostile to Shem. Shaun answers that it is because of "his root language" (*FW* 424.17). The 10th and last thunderclap, this time with 101 letters, follows Shaun's 12th response (*FW* 424.20–22) and alludes directly to Thor, the Norse god of thunder: "Thor's for yo!" (*FW* 424.22). They next ask, in question 13, how Shaun "could come near" (*FW* 424.24) the letter, to which Shaun says that everything in it is a forgery: "Every dimmed letter in it is a copy and not a few of the silbils and wholly words I can show you in my Kingdom of Heaven" (*FW* 424.32–34). The final challenge is for him to write a letter better than Shem's. Without doubt Shaun retorts that he can, but will not take the trouble: "I would never for anything take so much trouble of such doing" (*FW* 425.33). After Shaun's last response (*FW* 425.9–426.4), he falls into a barrel that rolls backward into the river: "he spoorlessly disappaled and vanesshed, like a popo down a papa, from circular circulatio" (*FW* 427.6–8). His sister Issy mourns his loss.

### *FW III.2 (FW 429.1–473.25)*

Shaun reappears as Jaun. After stopping "to fetch a breath" and "loosen . . . both of his bruised brogues" (*FW* 429.2–5), Jaun meets 29 girls from "Benent Saint Berched's national nightschool" (*FW* 430.2), St. Bride's school, to whom he sermonizes. He begins cordially by addressing Issy and then the others. When the topic turns to sex, however, Jaun concentrates attention only on his sister. He warns her about Shem, whom he scorns, and advises self-control: "The pleasures of love lasts but a fleeting but the pledges of life outlusts a lifetime" (*FW* 444.24–25).

Before ending his sermon, Jaun encourages civic-minded social responsibility: "We'll circumcivicise all Dublin country" (*FW* 446.35). He then focuses on one of his favorite topics, food. (Concern for food is characteristic of Shaun, see III.1, above, and the opening of the previous chapter where his attitude toward food and drink is vividly depicted by the ass [*FW* 405.30–407.9].) Toward the end of the chapter, Issy begins to speak for the first time (*FW* 457.25–461.32) and disingenuously comforts the departing Jaun, who in her words becomes Juan (*FW* 461.31). After Jaun leaves his "darling proxy behind" (*FW* 462.16), he attempts, like the departing god Osiris, to ascend to heaven (*FW* 469.29–470.21) as the girls wail good-bye (*FW* 470.12). But he is unsuccessful, and his spirit lingers as "rural Haun" (*FW* 471.35) before departing as a litany is recited (*FW* 471.35–473.11).

Joyce summarized this chapter in a June 1924 letter to Harriet Shaw Weaver: "after a long absurd and rather incestuous Lenten lecture to Izzy, his sister, [Shaun] takes leave of her 'with a half a glance of Irish frisky from under the shag of his parallel brows'. These are the words the reader will see but not those he will hear" (*Letters*, I.216). (It should be noted that four years later in another letter to Weaver, dated August 8, 1928, Joyce detailed his intentions concerning the use of the Maronite liturgy and the chorus of girls elsewhere in *Finnegans Wake*, 470.13–471.34 [see *Letters*, I.263–264].)

### *FW III.3 (FW 474.1–554.10)*

Here Shaun becomes Yawn, exhausted, wailing, and collapsed over a hill (*FW* 474.1–15). Four old men pass by: "Those four claymen clomb together to hold their sworn starchamber quiry on him" (*FW* 475.18–19). They spot the reposing Yawn and wonder whether he is "boosed" or "rehearsing somewan's funeral" (*FW* 477.5, 9). They then begin an extensive cross-examination of Yawn (*FW* 477.31–483.14), after which the provoked Yawn responds defensively and, at one point, in French.

The four inquire about his place of origin, his language, the letter, and his family, including his dealings with his brother, Shem, and his father, H C E. Different accounts of the fall are presented by Treacle Tom (introduced in I.2) and others, but before Earwicker gets a chance to defend himself (beginning at *FW* 532.6 and running to the end of the chapter), other witnesses (Issy, Sackerson, and Kate) speak (*FW* 527.3–531.26). During his defense, Earwicker gives a survey of his accomplishments, but he begins with a caveat: "Things are not as they were" (*FW* 540.13).

Earwicker surveys his achievements. He includes in his accomplishments his marriage to Anna Livia: "I pudd a name and wedlock boltoned round her" (*FW* 548.5) and the many feats and good deeds he has performed. The success of his self-defense, however, is uncertain. (*FW* 532–554 was published as Haveth Childers Everywhere [see under Characters, below], a separate booklet, in 1930 and then again in 1931.)

### *FW III.4 (FW 555.1–590.30)*

The opening pages of this last chapter of Book III repeat that it is night. The reader quickly becomes aware that it is very late in the night at the Porter household (another avatar of the Earwickers). Mr. and Mrs. Porter, aroused from their sleep by a cry from Jerry (Shem), go upstairs to comfort him, after which they return to their bed where they endeavor to engage in sexual intercourse before falling asleep again. During all of this time, a dumbshow (starting on *FW* 559.18) presents four views of the parents, each by one of the four bedposts (variants of the four old men and the four evangelists). "First position of harmony" (*FW* 559.21) is Matt's, which describes the parents and their concern for the children.

Mark's "second position of discordance" (*FW* 564.1–2) covers, among other things, the park episode and adjudicates as in a trial the present activities of the parents. "Third position of concord!" (*FW* 582.29–30) belongs to the unnamed Luke, a view that beholds the parents' sexual encounter interrupted by a cock crowing at dawn. "Fourth position of solution" (*FW* 590.22–23) is, with a lowercase *j*, johnny's, the shortest view and the end of the chapter. The fourth view ends the Viconian cycles and initiates a *ricorso* that continues into the next and final book of the *Wake*.

### *FW IV (FW 593.1–628.16)*

The last book of *Finnegans Wake* consists of only one chapter. Starting with the triple repetition of the Sanskrit word *Sandhyas* (which refers to the twilight before dawn), the chapter marks a period of promise and renewal that inaugurates the coming of a new day and a new age: "it is our hour or risings" (*FW* 598.13). The earth itself sings out in praise through the voices of 29 girls celebrating the appearance of Saint Kevin (Shaun), who, among other actions, consecrates the waters of regeneration (*FW* 604.27–606.12).

Embedded within the chapter's main themes of change and rejuvenation, however, is the issue of the perception of truth. This issue is of central importance in the encounter between Balkelly, the Archdruid (see both under Characters, below) and St. Patrick (*FW* 611.4–612.36), an episode anticipated by the meeting between Muta and Juva that occurs immediately before the encounter (*FW* 609.24–610.32). (Muta and Juva are variants of the Jute/Mutt–Shem/Shaun conflict throughout the *Wake*.)

The issue of the perception of truth also relates to *Finnegans Wake* and to the mystery of artistic expression. In a letter to Frank Budgen, dated August 20, 1939 (three and a half months after the *Wake*'s publication), Joyce explained his meaning behind the references to St. Patrick and the archdruid Balkelly (George BERKELEY) when he wrote: "Much more is intended in the colloquy between Berkeley the arch druid and his pidgin speech and Patrick the arch priest and his Nippon English. It is also the defence and indictment of the book itself, B's theory of colours and Patrick's practical solution of the problem. Hence the phrase in the preceding Mutt and Jeff banter 'Dies is Dorminus master' = Deus est Dominus noster plus the day is Lord over sleep, i.e. when it days" (*Letters,* I.406).

The episode informally titled "St. Patrick and the Druid" (*FW* 611.4–612.36) is based upon accounts of St. Patrick's return to Ireland as a missionary, his lighting a fire at Slane on Holy Saturday in defiance of the Irish king Leary, and his confrontation with Leary's archdruid. "St. Patrick and the Druid" is one of the earliest passages Joyce composed for *Finnegans Wake* (see *Letters,* III.79).

In Joyce's version of events, Paddrock (St. Patrick) and Balkelly (representing the archdruid, but also evoking associations with the 18th-century philosopher George Berkeley) argue over theological and philosophical beliefs. Their dispute centers upon differing conceptions of space and time, and both the shamrock and the rainbow serve as material illustrations at key points in the argument. The shamrock recalls the story of St. Patrick's use of it to explain the central mystery of the Christian faith, the Holy Trinity (three persons in one God); the rainbow has obvious Old Testament associations with Noah and the Flood. These parallels are central to the theme of rebirth that runs through *Finnegans Wake*. Paddrock seems to triumph over the Archdruid Balkelly, although, as is the case with most episodes in *Finnegans Wake,* the language of the narrative so obscures the event that the results remain inconclusive.

After the debate between Balkelly and St. Patrick, the focus turns to Anna Livia Plurabelle, to renewal, and to a new day. Anna Livia speaks, first through her letter (*FW* 615.12–619.16), which she signs "Alma Luvia, Pollabella" (*FW* 619.16), and then in her monologue (*FW* 619.20–628.16). Anna Livia Plurabelle's signature resonates with meaning and contains imagery expressing the character and role she plays throughout the *Wake*. *Alma* (in Latin) means "nourisher"; *Luvia,* a play on words—*Livia,* life/Liffey, and *alluvial,* material deposited by a river, as is her letter in the post (Anna is "seasilt" [*FW* 628.4]); *polla* (in Italian) means "spring" or "source" (and *pollo* means "chicken," implying an allusion to the hen motif); and *bella,* a beautiful woman. Anna is the nourishing spring flowing into the sea, depositing her silt and her leaves (her pages) and her memory: "My leaves have drifted from me. All. But one clings still. I'll bear it on me. To remind me of. Lff!" (*FW* 628.6–7). Alone, and as the River Liffey, she speaks her final words and flows into the sea.

## *FINNEGANS WAKE* CRITICISM

Reading *Finnegans Wake* takes patience, but, as Harry Levin notes, "the prerequisite is not omniscience. It is no more than a curiosity about Joyce's unique methods and some awareness of his particular preoccupations. His work is enriched by such large resources of invention and allusion that its total effect is infinite variety" (*James Joyce: A Critical Introduction*). Consequently, reference works, annotations, dictionaries, and studies of *Finnegans Wake* are tools that can greatly aid the reader in deciphering not only specific portions of the *Wake* but also in interpreting its thematic and narrative elements. Listening to a recording of the *Wake* or reading it aloud by oneself or with others can also facilitate understanding and enjoyment. In several instances, as Joyce seemed to intend, the import of certain passages is clearer when the auditory and visual are linked, as in *FW* III.3: "What can't be coded can be decorded if an ear aye sieze what no eye ere grieved for" (*FW* 482.33–36). The ear seizes upon that which the eye cannot hear and the eye sees (sieze) that which the ear cannot. (The sentence is also an allusion to Shakespeare's *A Midsummer Night's Dream* (4.1.209–210) where Bottom upon awakening from his dream confuses St. Paul's statement in 1 Corinthians 2:9.)

Attempting to understand *Finnegans Wake* is a collective endeavor that Joyce himself initiated with the authors of *Our Exagmination round His Factification for Incamination of Work in Progress,* first published in 1929 by Shakespeare and Company and reprinted in 1974. (The title is taken from *FW* 497.2–3.) Several of the 12 essays in the collection had been previously published in *transition,* the Paris journal in which fragments of *Work in Progress* also appeared. The authors and titles include Samuel BECKETT's "Dante . . . Bruno. Vico . . . Joyce," Frank Budgen's "James Joyce's Work in Progress and Old Norse Poetry," Stuart Gilbert's "Prolegomena to Work in Progress," Robert MCALMON's "Mr. Joyce Directs an Irish Word Ballet," and William Carlos WILLIAMS's "A Point for American Criticism." The essays in the collection center mostly on Joyce's poetics and use of language. The volume also includes two letters of protest, one written in the style of *Finnegans Wake* by Vladimir Dixon. (Recent scholarship, notably by Robert Spoo, has shown that Stuart Gilbert, Sylvia BEACH, and others incorrectly assumed that Dixon was Joyce parodying himself.)

In 1929, Cyril Connolly's "The Position of Joyce" appeared in *Life and Letters,* but it was not until after *Finnegans Wake* was published in 1939 that essays and books gradually began to appear. In *James Joyce: A Critical Interpretation,* Harry Levin devotes three chapters in the section entitled "The Fabulous Artificer" (pp. 139–222) to a discussion of Joyce's language and technique in *Finnegans Wake.* The chapters are an insightful introduction to the *Wake,* and the book ranks among the finest studies on Joyce. One of the first attempts at unraveling the identity of Earwicker and at explaining the language, myth, and psychology of the work was Edmund WILSON's "The Dream of H. C. Earwicker" in *The Wound and the Bow* (1947). The essay is a revision of Wilson's reviews of the *Wake* that had appeared in the June 28 and July 12, 1939, issues of the *New Republic;* the revision is also reprinted in *James Joyce: Two Decades of Criticism* (1948), edited by Seon Givens. Regarding Wilson's observations, Joyce, however, in a July 1939 letter to Frank Budgen, commented: "Wilson makes some curious blunders, e.g. that the 4th old man is Ulster" (*Letters,* I.405). Other essays by Leon Edel, John Crowe Ransom, Dorothy Richardson, and William Troy had also appeared in 1939. This early criticism focused particularly on language, rhetorical techniques, the dream motif, and the mythological patterns of the *Wake;* one of the greatest challenges facing any reader of *Finnegans Wake* is establishing an interpretative framework.

The first book-length study of the *Wake,* Joseph Campbell and Henry Morton Robinson's *A Skeleton Key to Finnegans Wake* (1944), concentrates almost exclusively on the mythological elements in the work. It also gives a "translation" of the *Wake* interspersed with commentary. Although *A Skeleton Key* contains inaccuracies, it was a very influential study and still cannot be casually disregarded. The authors provided pioneering forays into *Finnegans Wake,* and they did so without the aid of the manuscripts and letters that are available to scholars and readers today.

Just a few years before Campbell and Robinson's study, Harry Levin had published his work cited above in 1941; a revised, augmented edition appeared in 1960. In 1956, Adaline Glasheen published *A Census of Finnegans Wake: An Index of the Characters and Their Roles.* In 1963, *A Second Census* appeared, and in 1977 *A Third Census* was published. Her work is invaluable for its clear presentation of the characters and the many names occurring throughout *Finnegans Wake.* Before the entries on the characters and names, a brief synopsis of the *Wake* is provided followed by a comprehensive chart, titled "Who is Who when Everybody is Somebody Else," that identifies the multifaceted personalities of the *Wake*'s characters. Clive Hart's *A Concordance to Finnegans Wake* (1974) is also a useful tool for the reader.

Detailed analyses explicating the themes, allusions, foreign words, and structure of *Finnegans Wake* followed Glasheen's initial study. James S. Atherton's *The Books at the Wake: A Study of Literary Allusions in James Joyce's Finnegans Wake* (1959), Clive Hart's *Structure and Motif in Finnegans Wake* (1962), Bernard Benstock's *Joyce-Again's Wake: An Analysis of Finnegans Wake* (1965), Dounia Bunis Christiani's *Scandinavian Elements of Finnegans Wake* (1965), a collection of essays edited by Jack P. Dalton and Clive Hart, *Twelve and a Tilly: Essays on the Occasion of the 25th Anniversary of Finnegans Wake* (1965), Helmut Bonheim's *A Lexicon of the German in Finnegans Wake* (1967), Brendan O Hehir's *A Gaelic Lexicon for Finnegans Wake* (1967), Brendan O Hehir and John Dillon's *A Classical Lexicon for Finnegans Wake* (1977), Louis O. Mink's *A Finnegans Wake Gazatteer* (1978), and Roland McHugh's *Annotations to Finnegans Wake* (1980, revised 1991) all appeared within two generations or so after the publication of the *Wake.*

Joyce's manuscript and his compositional techniques also began to be scrutinized during this early period of *Finnegans Wake* criticism, particularly by Walton Litz in *The Art of James Joyce: Method and Design in Ulysses and Finnegans Wake* (1961), Thomas Connolly's *James Joyce's Scribbledehobble: The Ur-Workbook for Finnegans Wake* (1961) (see "Scribbledehobble" below), and David Hayman in "Dramatic Motion in *Finnegans Wake,*" "From *Finnegans Wake:* A Sentence in Progress," and in his full-length study, *A First-Draft Version of Finnegans Wake* (1963). (This critical approach, known as genetic criticism, focuses on the *avant-texte*—the writer's notes, drafts, manuscripts, typescripts, and so forth—and provides a very useful perspective to the reader grappling with Joyce's intentions in writing *Finnegans Wake.* Interest in genetic criticism continues with, among other works, Hayman's *The "Wake" in Transit* [1990], Danis Rose's *The Textual Diaries of James Joyce* [1995], and, with the first volume published in 2001, *The Finnegans Wake Notebooks at Buffalo,* edited by Vincent Deane, Daniel Ferrer, and Geert Lernout.) *A Wake Newslitter* that appeared between 1962 and 1980 published notes and brief essays on aspects of the *Wake.* (A CD-ROM version of *A Wake Newslitter* with the *Occasional Papers* and *A Wake Digest* is available through Split Pea Press.) General introductory studies also appeared with William York Tindall's *A Reader's Guide to James Joyce* (1959) and later with his *A Reader's Guide to Finnegans Wake* (1969). *Understanding Finnegans Wake: A Guide to the Narrative of James Joyce's Masterpiece* (1982), by Danis Rose and John O'Hanlon, provides a comprehensive paraphrase of the *Wake* with explanatory notes. Patrick A. McCarthy in "The Structures and Meanings of *Finnegans Wake*" (published in *A Companion to Joyce Studies,* edited by Zack Bowen and James F. Carens, pp. 559–632 [1984]) and John Gordon in *Finnegans Wake: A Plot Summary* (1986) both provide helpful summaries of the *Wake.*

Since 1965 *Finnegans Wake* criticism has been greatly enhanced with the publication of lexicons, glossaries, annotations, topographical identifications, and narratological studies. *The James Joyce Quarterly* has had three special issues on *Finnegans Wake* (Spring 1965, Winter 1972, and Summer 1974). A brief but very helpful introduction to the *Wake* for first-time readers can be found in Bernard Benstock's *James Joyce* (1985); a more technical introduction is Roland McHugh's *The Finnegans Wake Experience* (1981).

Book-length discussions on specific components of the *Wake* and on methods of interpreting it have also appeared. Margaret C. Solomon's *Eternal Geomater: The Sexual Universe of Finnegans Wake* (1969) details sexual themes in relation to geometric forms, and Margot Norris's *The Decentered Universe of Finnegans Wake: A Structuralist Analysis* (1974) provides a structuralist approach to reading *Finnegans Wake*. Patrick A. McCarthy's *The Riddles of Finnegans Wake* (1980) examines the strategy and thematic importance of Joyce's use of riddles, and Barbara DiBernard's *Alchemy and Finnegans Wake* (1980) uncovers the role of alchemical imagery and its metaphorical significance in the *Wake*. Using the dream motif as an interpretative framework, John Bishop's *Joyce's Book of the Dark: Finnegans Wake* (1986) is a thorough discussion of the *Wake*'s integral dream-state language.

For a more extensive list of books and articles and for Web sites on *Finnegans Wake*, see the bibliography under *Finnegans Wake* in the appendix on page 405.

For an online text of *Finnegans Wake*, see http://www.trentu.ca/jjoyce/. Readings of *Finnegans Wake* have been recorded by Patrick Horgan (produced by AFB and intended for the Royal Blind Society; unabridged), Patrick Healy (published by Lilliput Press; abridged and unabridged), Jim Norton and Marcella Riordan (Naxos Audiobooks; abridged), Patrick Ball (Celestial Harmonies; abridged), and Cyril Cusack (Caedmon; abridged). See also the appendix on page 381 (Musical, Theatrical, and Cinematic Adaptations of Joyce's Works Other Than *Chamber Music* and *Exiles*).

For additional information surrounding the composition and interpretation of *Finnegans Wake*, see *Letters* I.26, 29–30, 202–203, 205–210, 212–214, 216, 220, 222, 224, 226–227, 230, 232, 234–237, 240, 243, 245–254, 257–259, 263–264, 275, 280–281, 285–286, 288 –291, 295, 300–302, 311–312, 329, 340, 345, 405, and 412; II.87 and 97; and III.4–6, 73, 79, 108, 110, 114, 117, 118, 144–149, 161, 163, 165–166, 168, 170–172, 193, 205, 209, 211, 216, 228, 232, 233, 235, 239, 259, 271, 284–286, 296, 300, 303, 306, 309, 311, 345, 351–352, 354, 364, 370, 393–394, 397, 399, 401–404, 408–410, 415, 418, 421–423, 425, 427–429, 433, 435–438, 440, 442, 455–456, 461, 463, 464–466, 470–472, 483, 503, and 506.

## CHARACTERS

**A L P** These initials designate the mature female principal of *Finnegans Wake*, Anna Livia Plurabelle. (The male counterpart is H C E, Humphrey Chimpden Earwicker.) Throughout *Finnegans Wake*, the letters *A L P* occur in different order and in various combinations in words and phrases that allude to or identify Anna Livia or that evoke or signify her presence. For example, in the lessons episode of *Finnegans Wake*, Book II, chapter 2, the initials appear, among other ways, as "A.L.P.," "Pla!," and "apl lpa!" The letters are also used to begin each word of a phrase, such as "appia lippia pluvaville" (*FW* 297.25) and "Alma Luvia, Pollabella" (*FW* 619.16), or they can be found concentrated within a single word, as in "allaph" (*FW* 297.32). (See H C E below.)

**Ann** This is a variant of Anna Livia Plurabelle's name in *Finnegans Wake*. It occurs, for example, in the "Mime of Mick, Nick and the Maggies" episode in Book II, chapter 1. Among other variants are Anne, Anna, A. N., and Nann.

**Anna Livia Plurabelle (A L P)** She is the matriarchal figure and one of the main characters of *Finnegans Wake*. Anna Livia is the wife of H. C. Earwicker and the mother of Shem, Shaun, and Issy. In *FW* 215.24, her name appears in full in a line that reads: "Anna was, Livia is, Plurabelle's to be." She is perpetual presence and the mystery of renewal. Anna Livia is also a representation of the River LIFFEY, as well as all rivers that appear in *Finnegans Wake*. She also stands as the symbol of life and renewal. *Anna* is formed from an Irish word meaning "river" and *Livia* from *Liphe* (Liffey), the provenance of the river's source. *Plurabelle* is a neologism rooted in Latin, with Italian and French overtones, that suggests multiple beauty or most beautiful and loveliest. Joyce used the siglum Δ to signify Anna Livia's name when he was composing *Finnegans Wake* (see *Letters*, I.213). Her sign can be found in *FW* 299.F4 and in the deltaic design opening the chapter named for her (*FW* 196.1–216.5):

O
tell me all about
Anna Livia! I want to hear all
about Anna Livia. Well, you know Anna Livia?

(*FW* 196.1–4)

The siglum also appears in the drawing that pertains to Anna Livia on page 293 of the *Wake* together with her initials in the Roman (A L P) and Greek (α λ π) alphabets.

Standing as the mature female archetype throughout *Finnegans Wake,* Anna Livia conjures up a range of maternal, sexual, and communal associations through her various figurations and identities, the most important one of which is perhaps the biblical Eve, the mother of all. Anna Livia's presence is dominant throughout *Finnegans Wake.* By evoking her image and voice in the initial and final pages of the work, Joyce underscores the significance of this all-embracing female figure of rebirth and renewal.

Joyce based much of Anna Livia's physical description on Livia Schmitz, the wife of his TRIESTE friend Ettore SCHMITZ, and he intentionally played upon the close association between her first name and that of the River Liffey, which flows through the heart of Dublin. In a letter to Schmitz dated February 20, 1924, Joyce wrote: "A propos of names: I have given the name of Signora Schmitz to the protagonist of the book I am writing. Ask her, however, not to take up arms, either of steel or fire, since the person involved is the Pyrrha of Ireland (or rather of Dublin) whose hair is the river beside which (her name is Anna Liffey) the seventh city of Christianity springs up. . . ." (*Letters,* I.211–212; *cf. Letters,* III.132–133). (Deucalion and his wife Pyrrha were the survivors of the flood in Greek myth, and subsequently the parents of Hellen, eponymous ancestor of the Hellenes, that is, the Greeks.)

Joyce also derived many of Anna Livia's traits from his wife, Nora, as he had done with Molly Bloom in *Ulysses.* "Yet in many ways," Brenda Maddox, Nora's biographer, remarks, "she is more Nora than Molly could ever be. Anna Livia has lived through all the stages of womanhood, reaching disillusioned old age, and has worn herself out looking after her family. Some of the physical correlations with Nora are close. Anna Livia is both beautiful and ugly. She has or had red hair; she has it marcel waved" (*Nora,* p. 253). Even Noah's wife, Elizabeth, the literary figure in medieval mystery plays (and Christian equivalent of Pyrrha), served as a model for Anna Livia (see Joyce's January 1925 letter to Harriet Shaw WEAVER in *Letters,* I.224, and his July 1925 letter to Sylvia BEACH in *Letters,* I.230).

Some of the most lyrical and poetic passages in the *Wake* relate to Anna Livia, particularly those found in the Anna Livia Plurabelle chapter. It was a section from this chapter (*FW* 213.11–216.5) that Joyce, in the summer of 1929, chose to record at the Orthological Institute in London. In 1935 the composer Hazel Felman published a musical score using Joyce's text of the Anna Livia chapter. In 1962 the director and choreographer Jean ERDMAN produced *The Coach with the Six Insides,* a three-act play based on the life cycle of Anna Livia Plurabelle as the River Liffey and heroine of *Finnegans Wake.* By integrating dance and music into the play, Erdman centers attention on A L P as the personification of life's energy as well as the feminine half of humanity.

For additional information about the creation of this character, see *Letters,* I.212–213.

**Archdruid, The** He is the opponent of St. Patrick in St. Patrick and the Druid, a short vignette that appears in Book IV of *Finnegans Wake* (*FW* 611.4–613.16). In *FW* 611.5, the character is identified as the archdruid Balkelly (analogous to George BERKELEY), wearing a "heptachromatic sevenhued septicoloured roranyellgreenlindigan mantle" (*FW* 611.6–7) and arguing a philosophy of colors based on Berkeley's ideas concerning perception and reality. According to this philosophy, objects have no knowable existence outside of the mind that perceives them, and the color white, containing all colors, creates the illusion of the different colors perceived.

Despite the calculated comedy of the piece, Joyce sought in it to consider sophisticated philosophical ideas relating to aesthetics and pragmatism. In a letter to Frank BUDGEN dated August 20, 1939, Joyce expressed his concern that readers might not see beyond the slapstick tone of the farcical exchange. He wrote: "Much more is intended in the colloquy between Berkeley the arch druid and his pidgin speech and Patrick the arch priest and his Nippon English. It is also the defence and indictment of the book itself, B's theory of colours and Patrick's practical solution of the problem" (*Letters,* 1.406). Joyce's comments relate to two distinct classes of interpretation of *Finnegans Wake* itself, one embodied by the rationalist St. Patrick (and those antagonistic critics temperamentally allied to him) and the other by the idealist Balkelly, culminating in the Shem/Shaun dichotomy found throughout the book.

**Ass** This is the "fourpart tinckler's dunkey" (*FW* 405.6–7) who serves as a traveling companion to the Four Old Men who appear throughout *Finnegans Wake.* At the beginning of Book III, chapter 1, of the *Wake,* Earwicker, who falls asleep and begins to dream, starts expounding on Shaun through the ass's voice. As a literary motif, the ass is associated with dreams, prophecy, and transformation, as, for example, in the story of Balaam's ass found in the Bible and the transformation of Bottom into an ass in Shakespeare's *Midsummer Night's Dream.*

**Balkelly** He is the Archdruid in the "St. Patrick and the Druid" passage of *Finnegans Wake* (Book IV, pages 611.4–613.4). In the debate with St. Patrick, Balkelly represents the position of the 18th-century idealist thinker George BERKELEY, who professed a philosophical immaterialism which holds that perception is the basis of all reality. Balkelly also expounds Berkeley's theory that white is the basis of all color and that any other color is an illusion.

**Doran, Biddy** This is the name of the Hen and avatar of Anna Livia Plurabelle in *Finnegans Wake,* who is observed unearthing a letter from the midden heap (*FW* 110.22–31). The letter, "originating by transhipt from Boston (Mass.)" (*FW* 111.9–10), becomes a recurring motif in the work. In the first chapter of the *Wake,* she appears as the "gnarlybird" (*FW* 10.32, 34) rummaging through a battlefield. This action of hers in Book I, chapter 1, anticipates the discovery of the letter in Book I, chapter 5, where she appears as "Belinda of the Dorans" (*FW* 111.5). At one point, a conflation of Anna Livia's voice with Biddy's embodies the textually diverse presence of the feminine principle retrieving "lost histereve" (*FW* 214.1).

**Druid, The** See Archdruid, The.

**Earwicker, Humphrey Chimpden** He is the main figure of *Finnegans Wake.* For those whose interpretative framework of *Finnegans Wake* is a dream, Earwicker is most often identified as the sleeping hero whose dreaming mind is the central consciousness of the *Wake* and the psychological space in which the action of the work takes place. Whether he is the *Wake*'s dreamer or not, his presence, identity, occupation, and history (as well as those of his wife, Anna Livia Plurabelle, and their three children—twin sons Shem and Shaun, and daughter Issy) are subject to multiple changes and mutations that occur within the narrative dynamics of the work. Throughout the *Wake,* Earwicker and his wife appear as polar opposites, forces that are distinct yet dependent on each other for their identities and very existence—Earwicker as the principle of space and time, Anna Livia as the source of rebirth and life. Shem and Shaun frequently emerge as conflicting aspects of Earwicker's own troubled self, and the split embodiment of his fear of aging. His relationship with his daughter, who reminds him of a younger Anna Livia, has incestuous overtones, for she appears to arouse sexual desire in him.

Like Anna Livia Plurabelle's initials, A L P, Earwicker's—H C E—recur in various combinations in words and phrases throughout *Finnegans Wake* that allude to or evoke his presence. His initials can also stand for a variety of names, ideas, and places; for example: Haroun Childeric Eggeberth, Here Comes Everybody, Howth Castle and Environs, and—in reverse order—ech. Among his various roles, Earwicker is at different times an innkeeper, a

Norwegian captain, a master builder (like the title character of IBSEN's play), and a Russian general. The narrative also identifies Earwicker with other recurring figures: King Roderick O'Conor, the last king of Ireland; Tim Finnegan, the hod carrier whose fall and resurrection is the subject of the comic Irish ballad "FINEGAN'S WAKE"; and Humpty Dumpty.

These punning references to individuals who have fallen allude to the major crux of the *Wake*—the precise nature of Earwicker's alleged fall or crime in the park. Although the exact identity of his crime never emerges, it is clear that Earwicker remains deeply troubled by its consequences. Indeed, it seems to evoke in him a profound sense of shame and causes almost immediate disorientation in him whenever a reference to it occurs.

Through his mythical avatar FINN MACCOOL, Earwicker is identified with the Dublin landscape. Joyce equates Earwicker with the legendary giant who lies sleeping beneath Dublin, his head the BEN OF HOWTH and his feet the two mounts near PHOENIX PARK (*FW* 3:18–24). Earwicker also appears as Persse O'Reilly, the subject of the satirical poem "The Ballad of Persse O'Reilly" (*FW* 44.24–47.32). In this fashion the narrative invites the reader—without presenting a prescriptive course of action—to extend the meaning of Earwicker's name even further. Persse O'Reilly emerges as an anglicized form of the French *perceoreille* (earwig or ear-worm), and this association invites the reader to discern another pun—insect/incest—which ties into the *Wake*'s multiple themes. On an August 1940 postcard to his friend Nino Frank, the Italian writer and collaborator in translating into Italian "Anna Livia Plurabelle," Joyce inquired about an author who wrote an article on the "earwig" and mentioned to Frank that the hero of *Finnegans Wake* is "Persse-Oreilly Earwigger" (*Letters*, III.483). For further information on Joyce's view of Earwicker, see also *Letters*, III.5 and 96n.3. See the appendix on page 402 for the Earwicker family tree.

**Four, the** This identifies a foursome with various avatars, such as the Four Masters, the Four Old Men, the Four Waves, Mamalujo (see Separately Published Fragments, below), or the four evangelists (Matthew, Mark, Luke, and John): Matt Gregory, Marcus Lyons, Luke Tarpey, and Johnny MacDougall (see *FW* 384–399).

**Four Masters, the** This is the epithet for the authors or compilers (actually six) of *THE ANNALS OF THE FOUR MASTERS*. Although the spelling of their names varies, they occur in *Finnegans Wake* (*FW* 398.15) as "Peregrine and Michael and Farfassa and Peregrine" (also see *Letters*, III.81). Their anglicized names are Michael O'Clery, Peregrine O'Clery, Peregrine O'Duigenan, and Fearfesa O'Mulconry. In *Finnegans Wake*, the identity of the Four Masters is fluid and ambiguous, for Joyce identifies them with any foursome throughout the *Wake*: the Four Old Men, the Four Waves, and Ireland's four provinces, Ulster, Munster, Leinster, and Connacht. (For further information, see *Selected Letters*, pp. 296–297.)

**Four Old Men, the** This is the collective name in *Finnegans Wake* given to the four evangelists (Matthew, Mark, Luke, and John), also known in their abbreviated form as Mamalujo (see Separately Published Fragments, below). Accompanied by an Ass, they appear as Matt Gregory, Marcus Lyons, Luke Tarpey, and Johnny MacDougall throughout *FW* II.4 and III.3. In book 2, chapter 4, the Four Old Men, like the four barons in the court of King Mark in *The Romance of Tristan and Isolde*, spy on the lovemaking of Tristan and Isolde (an action underlining a voyeuristic theme in the *Wake*). This passage (*FW* 383–399) was the first part of *Finnegans Wake* to be published, appearing under the title "From Work in Progress" in Ford Madox Ford's *TRANSATLANTIC REVIEW* (April 1924).

**Four Waves, the** This is an avatar of the Four, closely allied to the Four Masters. These "four maaster waves of Erin" (*FW* 384.6) are also closely allied to Mamalujo (see Separately Published Fragments, below), the four evangelists (Matthew, Mark, Luke, and John): Matt Gregory, Marcus Lyons, Luke Tarpey, and Johnny MacDougall.

**Gregory, Matt** He is one of the avatars of the Four (the Four Masters, the Four Old Men, the

Four Waves) and the first figure in the Mamalujo (see Separately Published Fragments, below) group (the collective name for the four evangelists, Matthew, Mark, Luke, and John). Throughout *Finnegans Wake* II.4 and III.3, Matt Gregory appears with Marcus Lyons, Luke Tarpey, and Johnny MacDougall, who are often accompanied by an Ass. With his "Belfast accent," Matt Gregory corresponds to, among other things, the province of Ulster and to Peregrine O'Clery, one of the Four Masters of the Irish *Annals*. See *Selected Letters*, pp. 296–297.

**Haveth Childers Everywhere** This is one of many variations of Humphrey Chimpden Earwicker's name in *Finnegans Wake*, appearing in this form only once (*FW* 535.34–35). It was also used by Joyce as the title of a section of Book III, chapter 3 of the *Wake*. (Also see H C E.)

**H C E** These are the initials of the central character, Humphrey Chimpden Earwicker, and his nickname, Here Comes Everybody. Throughout the *Wake*, these initials often occur as the beginning letters, in phrases, such as "Howth Castle and Environs" in the opening line of the book and "elegant central highway" (*FW* 321.13–14), but they also occur within words and phrases, such as "Mr. Whicker whacked a great fall" (*FW* 434.11) and "uhrweckers" (*FW* 615.16), and in numerous combinations, such as "his hes *hec*itency *Hec*" (*FW* 119.18) and "Mista *Ch*imepiece" (*FW* 590.11). The initials and their multiple variations all allude to Earwicker. (See A L P.)

**Hen, The** She is a representation of Anna Livia Plurabelle in her role as Biddy Doran, the discoverer of the letter "from Boston (Mass.)" (*FW* 111.9–10). In association with the letter, the hen appears in several places throughout the *Wake*, and together they dominate Book I, chapter 5 (*FW* 104.1–125.23), a chapter designated "The Hen" by Adaline GLASHEEN (see above Books and Chapters of the *Wake*). The multiple versions of the letter that she unearths from the midden heap are too vague to be adequately interpreted, and its contents remain a mystery. At one point, Anna Livia uses the letter to exonerate her husband, but she only complicates matters (*FW* 113.11–18) and strengthens the accusations against him. The character of the hen throughout *Finnegans Wake* reinforces the image of Anna Livia as the archetypal maternal figure, who forages for traces of universal human history.

**Here Comes Everybody** This is a nickname given by the common people to Humphrey Chimpden Earwicker in the opening part of Book I, chapter 2 (appropriately called "Here Comes Everybody"): "it was equally certainly a pleasant turn of the populace which gave him as sense of those normative Letters, the nickname Here Comes Everybody" (*FW* 32.16–19). Variations of the name appear as "Howe cools Eavybrolly" (*FW* 315.20) and "hulm culms evurdyburdy" (*FW* 378.4–5), and as the initials H C E. Here Comes Everybody is an all-inclusive and universal name, an archetypal image, and one of the clearest expressions throughout *Finnegans Wake* of Earwicker as a universal figure.

**Hosty** He is the author of "The Ballad of Persse O'Reilly," a satirical piece that concludes Book I, chapter 2 (*FW* 44–47). Hosty's name suggests both the host as master of ceremonies and the host (the wafer) as ritual gift in the Eucharist. He is associated with Shem the Penman; his ballad mocks Humphrey Chimpden Earwicker, accusing him of wrongdoing and comparing his fall to that of Humpty Dumpty.

**Hump** This is a truncated variation of Humphrey Chimpden Earwicker's name. Resonating with literary and geographical overtones, Earwicker as Hump can be identified with Humpty Dumpty (*FW* 45.1–6) and with Dublin landscape (*FW* 3.20). Sexual overtones can also be heard in the name (*FW* 584.1–8).

**Isabel** This is a variant of Issy (Isabella and Isabelle), the daughter of Humphrey Chimpden Earwicker and Anna Livia Plurabelle and the young principal female character in *Finnegans Wake*. See Iseult and Isolde. (Isabel is also the name of Stephen Daedalus's sister who dies in *Stephen*

*Hero;* see Daedalus, Isabel in Characters under *Stephen Hero.*)

**Isolde** This is a variant of Iseult, the Irish princess who becomes enamored of Tristan. The name is also an alternative rendering of Issy, one of the principal characters of *Finnegans Wake.*

**Issy** She is the young principal female character in *Finnegans Wake.* Issy is the daughter of Humphrey Chimpden Earwicker (H C E) and Anna Livia Plurabelle (A L P) and the sister of Shem and Shaun. Isolde, or Issy as she is known throughout the *Wake,* is the archetypal young woman. She combines innocence and sensuality, license and prohibition, promise and denial.

In her relations with the men in *Finnegans Wake,* Issy has an evocative role. She responds to the incestuous urges of her father and brothers, alternately promising satisfaction and spurning such attention as shameful. She additionally demonstrates a range of precocious attitudes toward sense and sensibility, and evokes such prominent women as Cleopatra, Salome, Joan of Arc, and Mata Hari. As both temptress and paragon of innocence, Issy acts as a commentator on the diverse attitudes of men toward young women. She also stands in self-conscious contrast to her mother, A L P, and in this role she underscores typical mother-daughter rivalries.

As with the other central characters of *Finnegans Wake,* however, no single personality trait dominates the reader's perceptions of Issy. In her multiple roles as daughter, sister, rival, and seductress, she appears in a number of guises and embodies diverse characteristics and attitudes, to which the variant spellings of her name (Isolde, Izzy, and Isabel) also attest. In the Lessons chapter (*FW* 260–308), the footnotes, as Joyce explained in a July 1939 letter to Frank BUDGEN (*Letters,* I.406), are written by her, giving the reader a concentrated focus on her independent personality and humor, both of which are clearly juxtaposed to those of her brothers. While Joyce doubtless drew upon the character of his own daughter, Lucia JOYCE, and perhaps as well upon youthful recollections of his sisters, to assist in his creation of Issy, it would be an oversimplification to identify Issy with them in a literal fashion.

**Lyons, Marcus** This is the second archetypal figure in the Mamalujo quartet (see Separately Published Fragments, below) and one of the Four Old Men who appear in different guises as H C E's avatars throughout *Finnegans Wake.* His name derives from St. Mark the Evangelist, whose symbol is the lion. He is also associated with the province of Munster in the south of Ireland. With Matt Gregory, Luke Tarpey, and Johnny MacDougall, he spies on the lovemaking of Tristan and Iseult (see *FW* II.4.395–396). For Joyce's initial ideas behind Marcus Lyons (and Mamalujo, an abbreviated form of the names of the four evangelists, Matthew, Mark, Luke, and John), see his October 1923 letter to Harriet Shaw WEAVER in *Selected Letters,* pp. 296–297.

**MacDougall, Johnny** This is the fourth archetypal figure in the Mamalujo group (an abbreviated form of the names of the four evangelists, Matthew, Mark, Luke, and John—see Separately Published Fragments, below) and one of the Four Old Men who appear in different guises as possible extensions of the Humphrey Chimpden Earwicker personality throughout *Finnegans Wake.* His name derives from St. John the Evangelist, whose symbol is the eagle. MacDougall is also associated with the province of Connaught in the west of Ireland. With Matt Gregory, Marcus Lyons, and Luke Tarpey, he spies on the lovemaking of Tristan and Iseult in Book II, chapter 4 (*FW* 395–396). In an October 1923 letter to Harriet Shaw WEAVER, Joyce outlined his initial plan regarding Johnny MacDougall in relation to the other three members of this foursome. For additional details, see *Selected Letters,* pp. 296–297.

**Nuvoletta** She is an avatar of Issy as a little cloud (in Italian *nuvoletta*) appearing toward the end of the Mookse and the Gripes episode (*FW* 152–159). She intervenes in the dispute between the Mookse and the Gripes, but her attempts at reconciling them fail. As her tears become raindrops, she disappears "into the river that had been a stream" (*FW* 159.10).

At one point in the episode, she is referred to as "Nuvoluccia" (*FW* 157.24), an obvious allusion to Joyce's own daughter, Lucia JOYCE. "Una Nuvoletta" was also the title given to the Italian translation of the *Dubliners* story "A Little Cloud."

**O'Reilly, Persse** This is an alternative name for Humphrey Chimpden Earwicker and the central figure of "The Ballad of Persse O'Reilly" (see Separately Published Fragments, below) (Book I, chapter 2). Composed and sung by the enigmatic Hosty (Shem), this satirical poem ridicules Hosty's hapless father and accuses him of unspecified public crimes committed in PHOENIX PARK. Derived from the French term *perce-oreille* (earwig or earworm, that is, an insect), *Persse O'Reilly* is a pun on the name "Earwicker." On a postcard to a friend, the Italian writer Nino Frank, in August 1940, Joyce explained that the hero of *Finnegans Wake* is "Persse-Oreilly Earwigger" (*Letters*, III.483).

**Prankquean, The** She is a character in *Finnegans Wake* (*FW* 21–23) who appears as an exaggerated version of the 16th-century Irish pirate-queen Grace O'Malley (in Irish, Gráinne Ní Mháille). According to tradition, in 1575 Grace O'Malley was returning to her home in the west of Ireland after paying a visit to Queen Elizabeth I of England, when she stopped at HOWTH CASTLE on Christmas Day. She sought lodging for the night and demanded to see the earl of Howth. The earl was at dinner and refused to admit her. In response to this insult, Grace O'Malley kidnapped the earl's young son and held him captive in Connaught until the earl gave his solemn promise that the doors of Howth Castle would always be kept open during the dinner hour. When the Prankquean is refused entrance to Jarl van Hoother's castle, she returns to pose riddles that Jarl van Hoother cannot answer (*FW* 21.18–19; 22.5–6, 29.30); each time he fails to answer, she kidnaps one of his three children.

**Shaun** He is one of the young male principals of *Finnegans Wake,* a son of Humphrey Chimpden Earwicker and Anna Livia Plurabelle, the twin of Shem, and brother of Issy. *Finnegans Wake* represents Shaun as the pragmatic, middle-class, materially successful male. He is the practical-minded figure, in opposition to the artistic Shem, and he is a constant critic of the imaginative but undisciplined and irresponsible character of his brother.

The archetypal pragmatist, Shaun is represented in various literary and historical guises: the Ondt (in "The Ondt and the Gracehoper"), the Archdruid, Stanislaus JOYCE, Wyndham LEWIS, ST. KEVIN, Chuff, Mick (in "the Mime of Mick, Nick, and the Maggies"), the biblical Esau, Butt, and Burrus. Despite these patterns, however, the easy distinctions between Shaun and Shem, which initially seem all too evident, at times become blurred, as in representations of the characters that appear in the marginalia of the Lessons chapter. In this and numerous other instances, the self-conscious oscillations in the narrative's descriptions lead the reader to realize the striking similarities between the twin brothers.

**Shaun the Post** This is one of the narrative's variations on Shaun's name; see Shaun, above.

**Shem** He is one of the young male principals in *Finnegans Wake,* son of Humphrey Chimpden Earwicker (H C E) and Anna Livia Pleurabelle (A L P) and twin brother of Shaun and brother of Issy. Shem is depicted as a dreamy, bohemian artistic failure. He represents the imaginative type, in contrast to the pragmatic Shaun, and is a constant, if often timid, critic of the rigidity, lack of imaginative freedom, and intolerance that characterizes his brother.

Shem is the archetypal artist figure, one of various literary and historical representations of this personality that appear throughout *Finnegans Wake:* the Gracehoper (in "The Ondt and the Gracehoper"), St. Patrick, Jeremiah, Joyce himself, Cain, Chuff, Nick (in "The Mime of Mick, Nick, and the Maggies"), Jacob, Jute, and Caseous. The rivalry between Shem and Shaun, and what they stand for, is one of the major themes in *Finnegans Wake.*

**Shem the Penman** This is one of the narrative's variations on Shem's name; see Shem, above.

**Tarpey, Luke** This is the third figure in the Mamalujo quaternity (see Separately Published

Fragments, below) that appears in *Finnegans Wake.* (Mamalujo is an abbreviation for the four evangelists, Matthew, Mark, Luke, and John.) Among other things such as "a Dublin accent" and the province of Leinster in the east of Ireland, he represents St. Luke the Evangelist, whose symbol is the ox or the calf. He also stands for one of the Four Masters of the *Annals* of Ireland, namely, Farfassa O'Mulconry. Joyce's initial plan for Luke Tarpey and the foursome was included in an October 1923 letter to Harriet Shaw WEAVER (see *Selected Letters,* pp. 296–297).

## SEPARATELY PUBLISHED FRAGMENTS OF *FINNEGANS WAKE* AND RELATED ITEMS

***Anna Livia Plurabelle*** The title of Book I, chapter 8, of *Finnegans Wake* (*FW* 196.1–216.5), first published in *TRANSITION* in November 1927 and later as a separate booklet by Crosby Gaige in New York in 1928. The first English edition of this fragment of *WORK IN PROGRESS* was published by FABER AND FABER in 1930. The chapter is named after its heroine, Anna Livia Plurabelle (see Characters, above), and contains some of the most lyrical passages Joyce ever wrote. It may well be the most famous chapter of the work. In *Anna Livia Plurabelle: The Making of a Chapter,* Fred H. Higginson traces the chapter's development from its initial stages to its final form in *Finnegans Wake.*

For additional information on this section of *Finnegans Wake,* see *Letters,* III.6, 90–91, 97, 121–122, 125, 128, 132–133, 142, 163–165, 169, 183, 191, 209, 212, 464, 468–471, and 476–477.

**"Ballad of Persse O'Reilly, The"** A ballad in *Finnegans Wake* (*FW* 44.24–47.32) that identifies H. C. Earwicker with Humpty Dumpty and his fall. Composed and sung by Hosty, the ballad mocks Earwicker and charges him with public crimes. In selecting the name of the balladeer, Joyce also invokes the presence of H C E by punning on the French word for earwig, *perce-oreille.* (Also see Earwicker, Humphrey Chimpden and O'Reilly, Persse (under Characters, above); and Book I, chapter 2 of *Finnegans Wake.*)

**"Buckley and the Russian General"** This is the title of a humorous story that Joyce heard from his father and retold through Butt and Taff in *Finnegans Wake* Book II, chapter 3 (*FW* 346–353). (Other allusions to the story occur in the *Wake.*) During the Crimean War (1853–56), Buckley, an Irish soldier in the British army, gallantly declines to fire at a Russian general whom he spies defecating. But when the general rips up a clod of turf (in the soldier's mind a symbol of Ireland) to wipe himself, Buckley interprets the act as an "insult against Ireland" and shoots him (*FW* 353.15–21).

**"Buy a book in brown paper"** A six-line poem by Joyce (in the rhyme scheme aaa b cc) written as a blurb and printed on the dust jacket of the 1930 two-shilling FABER AND FABER edition of the *Anna Livia Plurabelle* chapter of *Finnegans Wake,* Book I, chapter 8 (*FW* 196.1–216.5). This humorous verse in mock *Finnegans Wake* style entreats the reader to buy a copy and read about Anna Livia, who "ebb[s] music wayriver she flows." (See also Anna Livia Plurabelle under Characters.)

***Haveth Childers Everywhere*** This is the title of a fragment of *WORK IN PROGRESS* first published in June 1930 by Henry Babou and Jack Kahane in Paris and by the Fountain Press in New York. It comprises the last part of chapter 3 in Book III of *Finnegans Wake* (*FW* 532.1–554.10). According to Richard ELLMANN, Joyce composed an advertisement for the first British edition, published by Faber and Faber in 1931:

> Humptydump Dublin squeaks through his norse,
> Humptydump Dublin hath a horrible vorse
> And with all his kinks english
> Plus his irismanx brogues
> Humptydump Dublin's grandada of all rogues.
>
> (*James Joyce,* p. 617)

As the initial letters of the title *Haveth Childers Everywhere* indicate, this fragment is concerned with H C E, who, at this point in the *Wake,* is given the chance to attempt some defense of himself against the ambiguous charges that have been brought against him. But the stuttering Earwicker only makes matters worse. He attempts to explain his guiltlessness, prove his innocence of any crime in Phoenix Park, and clear any libel against him: "I contango can take off my dudud dirtynine articles of quoting here in Pynix Park before those in heaven to provost myself, by gramercy of justness" (*FW* 534.11–13).

In this section of the chapter, Earwicker also boasts of his many accomplishments, which include the establishment of a great city "of magnificient distances" (*FW* 539.25) and the conquest of his wife, Anna Livia Plurabelle: "I pudd a name and wedlock boltoned round her the which to carry till her grave, my durdin dearly, Appia Lippia Pluviabilla, whiles I herr lifer amstell and been" (*FW* 548.5–7). The chapter ends with the Four Old Men laughing and braying in disbelief at Earwicker: "Mattahah! Marahah! Luahah! Joahanahanahana!" (*FW* 554.10).

For additional information regarding this section, see *Letters,* III.120, 135, and 204.

**Kevin, St. (Irish, Caemgen)** (d. 618) Kevin was one of the patron saints of Dublin. Born near that city, supposedly into the royal line of the ancient Irish kingdom of Leinster, as a young man Kevin turned his back on secular life and chose instead to become a hermit living in Glendalough in County Wicklow. He subsequently founded a monastery there and served as its first abbot. Under his charge Glendalough became one of Ireland's leading monasteries. No accurate biography of St. Kevin survives, but the legendary accounts of his life include his temptation at Luggelaw and again at Glendalough by the young girl, Cathleen, who killed herself when her second effort failed. The stories also stress St. Kevin's role as a protector of animals. He died on June 3, 618, in Glendalough.

In *Finnegans Wake* Book I, chapter 8, the washerwomen at the River LIFFEY recount, in a highly stylized fashion, the apocryphal temptation of St. Kevin (*FW* 203.17–204.5). In this instance, however, the charms of the woman, now represented as A L P, prove too much: "[H]e had to forget the monk in the man so, rubbing her up and smoothing her down, he baised his lippes in smiling mood, kiss akiss after kisokushk (as he warned her niver to, niver to, nevar) on Anna-na-Poghue's of the freckled forehead" (*FW* 203.33–204.1). One of Joyce's earliest sketches in the composition of *Finnegans Wake* was of St. Kevin; he later incorporated it into Book IV (*FW* 604.27–606.12), where the saint is seen rising from the waters of new life.

**Mamalujo** This is an abbreviated form of the combination of the names of the four evangelists Matthew, Mark, Luke, and John, and the working title of an episode from *Finnegans Wake* (*FW* 383–399). The first fragment of the *Wake* to be published as a separate piece, this episode appeared under the title "From Work in Progress" in the April 1924 issue of the *TRANSATLANTIC REVIEW.* It was subsequently revised by Joyce and placed in the final version of *Finnegans Wake* as chapter 4 in Book II. As a shortened version of the names of the four evangelists, Mamalujo also stands for the Four Masters of the *Annals* of Ireland, the Four Old Men and the Four Waves of Erin.

Joyce told Harriet Shaw WEAVER that this chapter consisted of "a study of old age" (see Richard Ellmann, *James Joyce,* p. 555). The episode opens with a 13-line poem, the first 10 and the 13th lines of which all rhyme. The call of the circling gulls mocks Muster Mark's helplessness and sexual inadequacy, as Trustan steals his bride Usolde (*FW* 383.19; *cf.* TRISTAN AND ISOLDE). Lines 11 and 12 describe what Tristan will do to Isolde, and line 13 sums up: "And that's how that chap's going to make his money and mark!"

After a prose reprise of the ideas advanced in the poem, the narrative then turns to an introduction of the Four Masters—Johnny MacDougall, Marcus Lyons, Luke Tarpey, and Matt Gregory. There is a brief general account of their background, their place in Irish mythology, and their role as four old men who, like the four barons in Joseph BÉDIER's translation of *Tristan et Iseult,* spy on the lovemaking of Tristan and Isolde. Following this are individual accounts of their recollections.

Johnny MacDougall begins his disquisition by recalling a Dublin auctioneer "in front of the place near O'Clery's" (*FW* 386.20) and his sans souci youth. Johnny ends his comments by offering an account of the exit of King Mark from Isolde's room through a door and the entrance of Tristan, in his nightshirt, through a window. Much of the imagery of this passage is aquatic, with references to salt water, drowning, and the sea.

Marcus Lyons joins in next, evoking a series of important historical events. He speaks of the Flemish Armada (medieval Norman invaders of Ireland), of St. Patrick and St. KEVIN, and of a series of other real and imagined invaders and colonizers of Ireland. Marcus Lyons ends his remarks with a bemused androgynous reference to how "the four of the Welsh waves" (*FW* 390.15–16) had been divorced by their "shehusbands" (*FW* 390.20) as had been foretold in song.

Lucas (Luke) Tarpey does his part by recalling the time of mythological Irish kings. He calls to mind how the other old men had been persecuted by "Mrs. Dowager Justice Squalchman" (*FW* 390.35–36). Lucas, however, asserts that he does really not wish to dwell upon these matters but would rather "forget and forgive (don't we all?)" (*FW* 392.2).

The last of the four old men, identified here as Matt Emeritus (Matt Gregory), now comes forward, looking very much like a bumpkin from the west of Ireland, which he represents. The narrative goes into a pitiable description of him, but he never finds his own voice for a personal remembrance. The section ends with the narrator's pious wish, "God be good to us" (*FW* 393.5).

After the last of these speakers has finished his presentation, the narrative begins a reminiscence of its own, compressing recollections of Sitiric Silkenbeard, the leader of the Danish forces at the Battle of Clontarf in 1014 (whose defeat by Brian Boru, the king of Munster, marked the end of Danish hegemony in Ireland), and of the 18th-century Bartholomew Vanhomrigh, father of Jonathan SWIFT's Vanessa and Lord Mayor of Dublin. This quickly merges into more androgynous remembrances, this time of the lives of four "beautiful sister misters" (*FW* 393.17). In a fragmented fashion it traces their existence from marriage to old age.

The chapter closes with the singing of the hymn for "Iseult la belle" (*FW* 398.31–399.28). It takes the form of an epithalamion (a song in honor of the newly married), urging Isolde to forsake the old man—King Mark—and go with the younger Tristan. As the chapter comes to a close, the final image is of the Four Old Men and their donkey by the river.

As the collective name of the four old men (Matthew, Mark, Luke, and John), Mamalujo represents a recurring archetype throughout *Finnegans Wake*. It also represents an ironically amalgamated yet distinct view of the four evangelists and the authors of *THE ANNALS OF THE FOUR MASTERS*, a history of Ireland, in 1636. In various guises, Mamalujo often takes on functions similar to that of a Greek chorus, adding a measure of irony, exposition, explication, and elaboration to the events they observe.

Adaline Glasheen reports that "Joyce told [Helen Joyce, Joyce's daughter-in-law] that [Mamalujo] also stood for Mama (Nora BARNACLE), Lucia [JOYCE], Giorgio JOYCE" (*Third Census of Finnegans Wake*, p. 183). See the discussion above, under "Synopsis." For additional information surrounding Joyce's composition of the Mamalujo episode, see *Letters*, III.81, 82, and 91. Also see *Selected Letters*, pp. 296–297, where in an October 1923 letter to Harriet Shaw Weaver, Joyce sketches an initial "plan of the verses," which ends the episode (*FW* 398–399), a plan that, among other things, includes correspondences between the four evangelists and the Four Masters.

### *Mime of Mick, Nick and the Maggies, The*

This is the title of a section of *Finnegans Wake* (*FW* 219–259) published in June 1934 by the Servire Press, The Hague. This edition included illustrations by Joyce's daughter, Lucia JOYCE. In the final version of *Finnegans Wake*, it appears as Book II, chapter 1.

"The Mime of Mick, Nick and the Maggies" is presented by Shem, Shaun, and Issy (under Characters, above) in the form of a play, and takes its shape from Joyce's conception of a dramatized version of the Dublin children's game Angels and Devils, or Colors (see *Letters*, I.295). In the play Shem, portraying the character Glugg, unsuccessfully tries to answer three versions of a riddle put to him by Issy and the Maggies, who, as The Floras (or Rainbow Girls), are but multiple manifestations of Issy herself.

(Riddles are a recurring motif throughout *Finnegans Wake*; they first appear with the Prankquean in Book I, chapter 1, *FW* 21.5–23.15.) As the title of the episode suggests, the play depicts the elemental conflict between Light (= Mick = St. Michael = Shaun) and Dark (= Nick = Old Nick = the Devil = Shem), as well as between siblings.

The chapter opens with an announcement of the particulars of the play. Under the benediction of the martyr and patron saint of actors, "Holy Genesius Archimimus" (*FW* 219.9), the drama is being presented by the children of H C E and A L P every evening ("until further notice") at dusk at the "Feenichts Playhouse," Phoenix (or literally Fee Nix = no charge) Playhouse (*FW* 219.2). The play is called *The Mime of Mick, Nick and the Maggies,* and is an adaptation of material from Joseph Sheridan Le Fanu's *The House by the Churchyard.* (Le Fanu, 1814–73, was an Irish writer whose work was characterized by elements of the supernatural and mysterious.)

The cast is as follows: Glugg is played by Shem, "the bold bad bleak boy of the storybooks" (*FW* 219.24). The Floras, a variation of the 28 Rainbow Girls, are represented by the Girl Scouts from St. Bride's Finishing Establishment. The part of Izod is taken by Issy, "a bewitching blonde who dimples delightfully" (*FW* 220.7–8). Shaun, "the fine frank fairhaired fellow of the fairytales" (*FW* 220.12–13) takes the part of Chuff. The woman of the house, Ann, is played by A L P, and H C E plays Hump, the archetypal father figure and "the cause of all our grievances" (*FW* 220.27). Additional characters are represented by the customers of H C E's pub, by Kate the cleaning woman, and by Sackerson the handyman.

In a burst of metatheater, the play itself opens with a play: Chuff (Shaun) has taken the part of St. Michael the Archangel and Glugg (Shem) has assumed the role of the devil. (As befitting an archetypal representation, the identities of each of these characters shifts back and forth over the several roles that each assumes throughout the chapter.) Glugg pursues several of the Floras, but is unable to catch any of them. Abruptly, they interrupt his pursuit by turning on him. They confront him with a riddle and demand that he come up with the solution to it. Nonetheless, although he consults the Four Masters, Glugg cannot answer the puzzle.

The Floras ridicule him, and both Glugg's mental and physical discomfort increase. He feels the need to pass water, and this sensation, in turn, makes him think of an instance when he saw his mother urinating. Heedless of Glugg's uneasiness, the girls continue to press him for an answer to their riddle. In response, Glugg makes three more fruitless guesses. Feeling embarrassed and frustrated, he runs away, much to the chagrin of Izod (Issy), who has developed a great affection for him.

The Floras now dance in admiration around Chuff (Shaun). This demonstration of their affection enrages Glugg, who is still smarting from the ridicule of the girls. He returns to the group, runs amok, attacks seven little boys (representing the seven sacraments), and swears that he will have his revenge upon them all by writing stories. As he thinks of his family life and of the possibilities of a literary career, Glugg gradually calms down. A sigh from Izod makes him think that she might actually want him again, and he returns to her and to the Floras to resume the guessing game.

The competition begins again, but as before, Glugg repeatedly fails to come up with the correct answer to the girls' riddle, and again he runs away in chagrin. Chuff remains behind, and the girls begin to sing a hymn in his honor. The Floras, or the Rainbow Girls, in flowerlike fashion, begin to worship Chuff as a sun god. They cap their song of praise by offering themselves to him as they dance in an adoring circle around him. In the meantime, Glugg remains alone, sunk deep in despair.

Presently, however, Glugg rouses himself from his brooding and makes a final effort at reconciliation with the others. He publicly confesses his faults and vows to those present that he will reform his life and henceforth live as a decent man. In closing he condemns "his fiery goosemother" (*FW* 242.25) for her own behavior and for the evil influence that she exerted upon him when he was growing to maturity. Now she seems to be joining with him in a pledge to amend her own behavior.

Suddenly, someone notices that the moon has risen. The hour is late. PHOENIX PARK is full of lovers, and the time has come for the production to end. But despite H C E's threatening calls and A L P's efforts to prepare dinner, the players demur, deciding instead to continue their drama if only for a brief time. Once again Glugg runs amok among the other children, but this time he quickly breaks down and cries, frustrated over the attention that the girls give to Chuff and their obvious lack of interest in him. Glugg returns to his earlier plan to take revenge by publicizing secret information that he has acquired about them.

Izod interrupts Glugg's ranting and with seductive promises tempts him to come toward the group. However, as he attempts to move toward them, the Floras point to Glugg in revulsion. They compare him most unfavorably with Chuff, and then begin a dance. As they dance, they try to draw Glugg out by asking him teasing questions, but he only responds with crude gestures. Now led by Chuff, the Floras continue to taunt Glugg, who endures it all by focusing his mind on his desire for Izod. Glugg and Chuff confront each other, and suddenly Glugg is bested.

This new defeat throws Glugg into the depths of despair. He laments that he has no idea what will become of him or of his progeny. For a third time he has proven unable to solve the riddle, and now he has clearly lost Izod: "Evidentament he has failed as tiercely as the deuce before for she is wearing none of the three" (*FW* 253.19–20). Events now seem clearly headed for a denouement, but before the play can come to its expected conclusion, the children abruptly break off the action in anticipation of the appearance of H C E.

Taking its cue from the concerns of the children, the narrative next begins a long digression on the specific nature and origin of this father figure. A number of legends and rumors about him are recounted, and the narrative asks rhetorically why one would awaken him. It predicts ominously that "[t]he hour of his closing hies to hand" (*FW* 255.6–7). Nonetheless, instead of a dire event, A L P appears to gather together the children, stop their arguments, and set them to doing their homework before going to bed. At the sound of the shutting of the door, the curtain drops and the play ends. There is a general tumult as if it were the end of the world, and H C E is awakened. The children are sent off to study, and the chapter comes to an end.

In two letters to Harriet Shaw WEAVER (June 7, 1926, and July 15, 1926), Joyce alternately described the episode as dealing with "twilight games" and "the children's games." For most readers, however, this is not adequate to describe the chapter's depiction of the continuing human effort to exchange doubt for certainty. For additional details relating to the composition and reception of *The Mime of Mick, Nick and the Maggies,* see *Letters,* I.241–242; III.202, 304, 313, 330–331, 333, and 381. Also see the entry on *Finnegans Wake* above, particularly the section dealing with *FW* II.1 under "Synopsis or Plot Summary."

***Mookse and the Gripes, The*** A passage from *Finnegans Wake,* Book I, chapter 6 (*FW* 152.15–159.18). It was first published as one of three fragments from *WORK IN PROGRESS* (with *The Muddest Thick That Was Ever Heard Dump* and "*The Ondt and the Gracehoper,*" see both below) in August 1929 by the Black Sun Press under the title *Tales Told of Shem and Shaun* (see below).

*The Mookse and the Gripes* episode offers a Wakean rendition of the Aesop fable "The Fox and the Grapes," an extension of the conflict between Shaun (the Mookse) and Shem (the Gripes). Professor Jones tells the tale to illuminate the central idea of a lecture that he is presenting. The story focuses on a Mookse, who seems to represent a combination of English figures who had a prominent impact upon Irish history, most notably Pope Adrian IV (Nicholas Breakspear, the only English pontiff) and Henry II, the English king who, with the blessing of Adrian, invaded Ireland in 1171. The Mookse, out for a walk, confronts the Gripes, who represents prominent Irish figures, especially St. Lawrence O'Toole, bishop of Dublin at the time of the English invasion. The Gripes is hanging from a tree located on the bank of a stream directly opposite the place where the Mookse has stopped. The Mookse and the Gripes engage in a disputation that recapitulates the theological differences between the Irish Church and the Church of Rome. (The putative reason for the 12th-century English invasion—delineated in *Laudabiliter,* the papal bull issued by Adrian IV—was Irish religious heresy; there is dispute about the authenticity of the bull *Laudabiliter.*) While they are engaged in their debate, a young woman, Nuvoletta, goes past; but despite her best efforts she fails to attract their attention. The story ends inconclusively as darkness descends. The Mookse and the Gripes finally fall silent, and Nuvoletta, now in the form of rain from a cloud, disappears "into the river that had been a stream" (*FW* 159.10). (See also the entry on *Finnegans Wake,* particularly the synopsis of *FW* I.6 under "Synopsis or Plot Summary.")

***Muddest Thick That Was Ever Heard Dump, The*** A name designating the middle portion of the lessons chapter (*FW* 282.7–304.4). It was first published as one of three fragments (with *The Mookse and the Gripes* and "The Ondt and the Gracehoper") in August 1929 by the Black Sun Press under the title *Tales Told of Shem and Shaun.*

**"Norwegian Captain"** The figure of the Norwegian Captain appears as a motif running through the narrative of *Finnegans Wake.* (The individual is also recalled in passing by Leopold Bloom in the Calypso episode, chapter 4, of *Ulysses.*) The character originated in a comic story often told by Joyce's father, John JOYCE, who, according to Richard ELLMANN, had originally heard it from Joyce's godfather, Philip McCann. The story concerns a hunchbacked sea captain who attempts to order a suit from a Dublin tailor. After repeated efforts to modify the suit to the captain's physique, an argument erupts. The story culminates with the irate captain accusing the tailor of being unable to sew and the exasperated tailor accusing the captain of being impossible to fit.

This story is specifically retold in *Finnegans Wake,* Book II, chapter 3 (*FW* 309.1–332.9), and was first published as a selection from WORK IN PROGRESS in the February 1937 issue of TRANSITION.

The tale begins in an atmosphere of drunken camaraderie, in the pub owned by H C E. The radio is blaring, and the raucous behavior of the pub's patrons stops just short of a brawl.

A character known as the Norwegian Captain—who very much resembles both H C E and the Flying Dutchman—asks the ship's husband (the business agent of the ship's owner) where he might go to buy a suit of clothes. The ship's husband recommends a tailor, and the Captain is measured. When the Captain gets up to leave, the ship's husband calls out, "stop thief," but the Captain ignores him and sails away for seven years (directly evoking the image of the Flying Dutchman, an eternal wanderer who may come ashore only once every seven years).

A young man named Kersse is sent after him, but the Norwegian Captain is not afraid of him or for that matter of any of the others who are plotting to do him harm. The listeners in the meantime are getting more belligerent. They demand to know what happened to the ship's husband's daughter, and they are told that she "wends to scoulas in her slalpers" and "tumbled for his famas roalls davors" (*FW* 314.35–315.1).

The patrons call for another round of drinks, and the story continues. The Norwegian Captain returns to port for a second time, and again he encounters the ship's husband. The Norwegian Captain asks the ship's husband for a drink and a meal. The Captain orders that the food and drink be put on his bill, curses the tailor, and then leaves, once again much to the anger of the ship's husband.

In the third stage of the story, Kersse returns. Although he tries to give an account of where he has been, much of his story is drowned out by the drunken hubbub of the bar. The drunkards call out muddled curses, but little really happens. Suddenly, the radio announces that the Captain has been captured, baptized, and married to the ship's husband's daughter. The story ends with a description of their wedding celebration.

For additional details about the composition of this section of *Finnegans Wake,* see *Letters,* III.394, 399, 404, and 422.

**"Ondt and the Gracehoper, The"** An episode in *Finnegans Wake* (*FW* 414.16–419.10) that first appeared in TRANSITION in March 1928 and then in a collection of extracts from *Work in Progress* published in August 1929 by the Black Sun Press under the general title *Tales Told of Shem and Shaun.* A selection from "The Ondt and the Gracehoper"

(*FW* 417.3–419.10) also appeared the following year in a collection entitled *Imagist Anthology* 1930 edited by Ezra POUND (published in London by Chatto & Windus and in New York by Covici Friede). The final version of this episode appears as a portion of Book III, chapter 1, of *Finnegans Wake.*

Joyce modeled this passage on La Fontaine's "Fable of the Ant and the Grasshopper." It unfolds as a moral lesson told by Shaun to his "dear little cousis" (*FW* 414.18). Like La Fontaine's Grasshopper (and also like Joyce himself), the Gracehoper is an improvident individual who lives from day to day, recklessly squandering his resources. The Ondt, like La Fontaine's Ant (and similar to Joyce's brother Stanislaus JOYCE), lives a more controlled and frugal life. At the end of Joyce's story the Gracehoper is penniless and starving while the Ondt enjoys his material wealth.

The fable is more than a simple cautionary tale contrasting prudence with extravagance. It also highlights the differences in attitude and temperament between the artistic gracehoper and the middle-class ondt. The episode demonstrates that one can find a measure of venality and a degree of probity in both creatures.

The episode begins with Shaun, who has been speaking to a crowd of people, being called upon to sing a song for them. He is unwilling to comply and counters by saying that he would rather tell them the fable of the Ondt and the Gracehoper. Without giving the crowd the opportunity to refuse this offer, Shaun begins the story.

Shaun describes the Gracehoper as a creature who is content to spend his time dancing happily or "making ungraceful overtures to Floh and Luse and Bienie and Vespatilla to play pupa-pupa and pulicy-pulicy and langtennas and pushpygyddyum and to commence insects with him, there mouthparts to his orefice and his gambills to there airy processes, even if only in chaste" (*FW* 414.24–28). The Gracehoper seems a most amiable companion, willing to do almost anything to amuse those with whom he associates. He would curse to make them blush, for example, or invent salacious stories about the sexual habits of Besterfather Zeus.

The Ondt, in a clear departure from La Fontaine's fable, does not object to self-indulgence in general. But he specifically disapproves of the déclassé nature of the Gracehoper's behavior. "[N]ot being a sommerfool, [the Ondt] was thothfolly making chilly spaces at hisphex affront of the icinglass of his windhame" (*FW* 415.27–29). He wants no part of the Gracehoper, "for he is not on our social list" (*FW* 415.31).

To underscore the Ondt's snobbish materialism, the fable makes clear that as a wealthy, able-bodied fellow, he has carefully made provision for all of his tangible needs. The Gracehoper, in contrast, though no less a hedonist, has thought nothing of the future, and has rather quickly run through all of his reserves. Consequently, when the winter comes, the Gracehoper is reduced to consuming his wallpaper, swallowing his candles, and devouring 40 flights of staircases. At Christmastide, after the Gracehoper has literally eaten himself out of house and home, he decides to take a stroll. His walk brings the Gracehoper to the Ondt's home, where he sees the Ondt living in great material comfort.

The Ondt, for his part, can scarcely bear the sight of the pathetic Gracehoper, but his feelings spring not so much from compassion as from disgust. Contemplating the other's ruined condition, the Ondt tells the Gracehoper that his comfort is a result of his commercial canniness. He goes on to observe that the Gracehoper has no one but himself to blame for the troubles that presently beset him.

The Gracehoper replies to this diatribe in stereotypical artistic fashion, by reciting a long poem. The Gracehoper begins by saying that he forgives the Ondt (for what, he does not make clear), and asks him to take care of Floh, Luse, Biene, and Vespatilla. The Gracehoper assures the Ondt that he bears him no ill will and indeed accepts his fate with an attitude of grace and forbearance. Nonetheless, he maintains a keen view of the situation, concluding a long paean to the Ondt's material success with the question: "But, Holy Saltmartin, why can't you beat time?" (*FW* 419.8).

In the final lines of this episode, Joyce neatly reverses the middle-class morality that informs so many of La Fontaine's fables. Instead of the predictable moral, he elaborates upon the complexity of the relations between the Ondt and the Gracehoper. While freely acknowledging the general improvidence of artists, he raises pointed questions regarding purpose. If all there is to life is the fervid accumulation of material goods, then the commercial Ondt clearly is a success. If, on the other hand, one aspires to a kind of immortality, then the artist Gracehoper is the one who triumphs.

Like so much of *Finnegans Wake,* "The Ondt and the Gracehoper" introduces alternate but equally intelligible interpretive perspectives on every level. The contrast between Shem and Shaun is clear, but Joyce shows as much interest in their mutual attraction as he does in their mutual repulsion.

For additional details regarding Joyce's composition of "The Ondt and the Gracehoper" episode, see *Letters,* III.173, 176–178, and 483.

**"Phoenix Park Nocturne, A"** A short selection from *Finnegans Wake* (*FW* 244.13–246.2) that appeared in the March–June 1938 issue of the Paris journal *Verve.* It was also published four months later as "L'Esthétique de Joyce" in the October 1, 1938, issue of the Lausanne journal *Études de Lettres,* accompanied by an explication by Jacques Mercanton, who acknowledged Joyce's assistance. The passage comes from Book II, chapter 1 (*FW* 219–259), in which "The Mime of Mick, Nick and the Maggies" takes place and momentarily interrupts the action of the children's play to describe the effect of the rising moon over the zoo and other parts of PHOENIX PARK.

**Roderick O'Conor (Also Rory O'Connor or O'Conor; in Irish, *Ruaidhri ua Conchubair*)** (d. 1198) He was the last high king of Ireland, who waged an unsuccessful campaign (1170–75) to defeat the Anglo-Norman armies of Henry II led by the second earl of Pembroke, which had invaded the country at the request of a rival Irish king, Dermot MacMurrough of Leinster. After capturing DUBLIN, MacMurrough married his daughter Eva to Pembroke, who continued to fight Roderick after MacMurrough's death on May 1, 1171. After his defeat, Roderick pledged his loyalty to Henry II, and in return was given control over the territory outside the English Pale, as the area around Dublin was known. In 1191 he retired to a monastery in Galway, where he died seven years later.

Joyce used Roderick O'Conor as the central figure in the first passages of *Finnegans Wake* that he composed (now *FW* 380.7–382.30, the closing portion of chapter 3 in Book II). Joyce's amalgamation of O'Conor and H C E gives the dual images of King Roderick after a palace feast and H C E after a night's drinking in his pub. This combined figure is depicted stumbling around the palace-pub, drinking the dregs of alcohol left in the glasses of others, and finally passing out (the archetypal patriarchal downfall) in a drunken stupor. He is the "last pre-electric king of Ireland" (*FW* 380.12–13).

**"Scribbledehobble"** This is the title of a notebook compiled by Joyce around 1922, during the early stages of composition of *Finnegans Wake.* It contains pages headed by the titles of his books, chapters from his works, and the short stories from *Dubliners.* Under each heading there appear ideas that elaborate on concepts suggested by, although not necessarily derived directly from, the work identified. Joyce seems to have used his previous works as starting points for meditations on the narrative topics and creative concepts to be incorporated in his new project. Many of the central themes and motifs of *Finnegans Wake* are recognizable in inchoate form in these entries, which include sketches for the tales of Roderick O'Conor, TRISTAN AND ISOLDE, St. Patrick, and St. KEVIN. The notebook itself is now held in the Lockwood Memorial Library of the State University of New York, Buffalo, and has been edited by Thomas E. Connolly and published as *Scribbledehobble: The Ur-Workbook for Finnegans Wake* (1961).

**"Shaun the Post"** This was Joyce's working name for Book III of *Finnegans Wake* (*FW* 403.1–590.30); he also called it "Shaun" or referred to it by the siglum Δ (see sigla). The name is that of a character in *Arrah-na-Pogue,* a play by Dion BOUCICAULT. An early version of most of "Shaun the Post" was serialized in *TRANSITION* magazine from the March 1928 issue to the November 1929 issue. Portions of it also appeared in book form in *Tales Told of Shem and Shaun* (1929), *transition stories: Twenty-three stories from 'transition'* (1929), *Imagist Anthology 1930,* and *Haveth Childers Everywhere* (1930).

Book III encompasses a dream whose central character is Shaun, who emerges in various forms as the embodiment of Earwicker's aspirations and his hope for overcoming the failures that have dogged his own life. The dream records Shaun's flaws as well as his virtues, and it chronicles his defeats as well as his triumphs. While the dream reveals a desire for the future, an intrusive pragmatism insistently displaces any apparent optimism.

Book III is made of four chapters. In the first, Shaun presents himself as a politician seeking election, and in this role he addresses the voters, disparaging his opponent, Shem (see Characters, above). The second chapter has Shaun, now as Jaun (a variant of Don Juan), in the company of 28 schoolgirls and their princess, ISEULT, whom he lectures on the mysteries of life. In chapter 3, Jaun has metamorphosed into Yawn, and in keeping with this name is stretched exhausted on a hill in the center of Ireland. The Four Old Men (see Characters, above) and their Ass arrive to hold an inquest. Their inquiry anatomizes his faults, and Yawn finally disappears, reforming into H C E sleeping next to his wife, A L P. In the final chapter, the couple is awakened by the cries of one of the children, whom they attend to, and then return to their bedroom to engage in an ultimately unsatisfactory effort at sexual intercourse.

For details regarding the forces shaping the composition of this segment of the book, see *Letters*, III.90, 92–93, 110n.2, 131–132, 134, 138–146, 166, 178–179, 186, and 188.

**"Shem the Penman"** This is the title Joyce gave to Book I, chapter 7, of *Finnegans Wake* (*FW* 169.1–195.6). An early version of this chapter first appeared in the Autumn/Winter 1925–1926 issue of the journal *THIS QUARTER*.

This chapter anatomizes the specific nature of Shem (see Characters, above) and the general traits associated with all artists. It examines with unflinching severity the physical and emotional weaknesses of Shem, and it represents conventional elements in his character in the basest possible terms. At the same time, even when showing him at his lowest—as when he makes ink out of his own excrement, for instance—the narrative affirms Shem's unwavering devotion to art and, through his depiction as Mercius in the final pages, to life-affirming, death-denying activities generally.

From the opening lines, the narrative of the episode emphasizes the undeniable faults of Shem's nature. "A few toughnecks are still getatable who pretend that aboriginally he was of respectable stemming . . . but every honest to goodness man in the land of the space of today knows that his back life will not stand being written about in black and white" (*FW* 169.1–8). Both in his physical deformity and in his perverted character (see *FW* 169.11–170.24)—"Shem was a sham and a low sham" (*FW* 170.25)—deficiencies dominate the reader's initial perceptions of him.

More than that, however, the narrative depicts Shem as a type of renegade. Although he may lack the dash of an iconoclast, he is always operating outside, and is antipathetic to, the bounds of society. Nonetheless, as indicated by the extended answer that the chapter provides to "the first riddle of the universe" (*FW* 170.4) that Shem asks the "yungfries," being not a man—that is, being a sham—is not necessarily a negative trait. As the narrative repeatedly asserts, Shem is not the average fellow, and the very uniqueness of his nature is revealed as a key element of his artistic temperament.

The narrative repeatedly brings negative depictions of Shem to the fore, beginning with a highly reductive and bluntly dismissive view of Shem's nature: "he was in his bardic memory low" (*FW* 172.28). Beneath the assault on Shem's character, however, a sense of a greater struggle is revealed within Shem's own consciousness as he strives to define himself as an artist. Raising the nationalist impulses that propelled Europe into World War I, the narrative chastises Shem for his lack of concern for these issues. Shem in the meantime has immersed himself in a solipsistic concern with his own nature, the better to come to grips with his own creative powers.

As a means of reinforcing many of the conflicts represented in "Shem the Penman," references to religious belief and religious heresies recur as a leitmotif that underscores the intellectual and spiritual struggle that Shem is undergoing. Like Stephen Dedalus in chapter IV of *A Portrait of the Artist as a*

*Young Man,* Shem is coming to a sense of art as the moral center of his universe and is striving to articulate more precisely the tenets of aesthetic belief by which he hopes to govern his life.

This intellectual and artistic endeavor coalesces in a brief passage, appropriately written in Latin (see *FW* 185.14–26 and the appendix on page 397), that describes a secular Eucharistic and self-consecrating ritual that confirms Shem's position as a priest of eternal imagination. Mixing together his own feces and urine, Shem consecrates a form of ink derived from wastes of his own body. (For an examination of the religious implications of such a gesture, see TRANSACCIDENTATION and TRANSUBSTANTIATION.) He uses this degraded creation in an elevated fashion to write "over every square inch of the only foolscap available, his own body, till by its corrosive sublimation one continuous present tense integument slowly unfolded" (*FW* 185.35–186.1).

With this gesture, Shem transforms himself into Mercius, a New Testament–like figure who in the final pages of the chapter is interrogated by Justius, a representative of an Old Testament conscience. Although Justius is as keen to indict Mercius as Shaun (see Characters, above) was to condemn Shem, this struggle is far less lopsided. Reflecting a self-assurance that puts him beyond danger, Mercius refuses to respond directly or in kind to Justius's brutality. In the end, the guilt-ridden efforts of Justius to inhibit Mercius have no effect. "[Mercius] lifts the lifewand and the dumb speak" (*FW* 195.5) and, temporarily at least, the affirming artist impulse triumphs.

For further information regarding "Shem the Penman," see *Letters,* III.122–123.

***Storiella as She Is Syung*** This is the name given to a portion of *Finnegans Wake* (*FW* 260.1–275.2 and 304.5–308.32) found at the opening and the closing section of the Lessons chapter in Book II, chapter 2. It first appeared in the July 1935 edition of *TRANSITION* and was also published separately by Corvinus Press, London, in 1937, with an illuminated letter drawn by Lucia JOYCE appearing at the beginning.

As its informal title, The Children's Lessons, indicates, this selection describes the children's efforts to go over their school lessons. In keeping with this pedagogical theme, the episode's actual design has the appearance of a heavily annotated scholarly work. The body of text is in the center of the page, with footnotes at the bottom and comments in the margins. Each of these groups of text has its distinct voice. The voices of the left and right marginalia, as Joyce points out in a July 1939 letter to Frank BUDGEN (*Letters,* I.406), shift positions at about the midpoint of the chapter, taking, as it were, the opposite sides of their original commentaries. Joyce also comments in the same letter that *Finnegans Wake* "pp. 260 et seq" seem "the most difficult" for readers.

The lessons of *Storiella as She Is Syung* begin with an ambiguous discussion of the process of creation, adducing various theories on the origin of the universe. This leads into a rambling chronicle of the pursuit of women by men, which is then seen acted out in the nursery, highlighting incipient sexuality and sexual taboos. *Storiella* is interrupted here by a variety of discussions on such topics as history, mathematics, geometry, and letter writing. It is also in this section that some of the sigla Joyce used when composing *Finnegans Wake* can be found (see *FW* 299.F4). The sigla in the footnote on page 299 represent, respectively, H C E, A L P, Issy, the Four Old Men, the title of the book, Shaun, and Shem. The main narrative is taken up again at the end of the chapter, where there is a long list of topics that have been studied, and it ends with the children being called down from the nursery to their dinner.

The chapter opens with a comment on an ontological presence that is every bit as puzzling as the riddle of the Prankquean (to which the text itself alludes in the paragraph that follows). "As we there are where are we are we there from tomtittot to teetootomtotalitarian." Almost at once the commentators in the marginalia begin their responses. On the right, in a voice like that of Shaun, one annotator summarizes the statement into a simpler form: "UNDE ET UBI" (where and when). On the left, in a tone that calls to mind Shem, the other elaborates and specifies questions of creation to associate them with a patriarchal figure very much like H C E: "With his broad and hairy face, to Ireland a disgrace." And the first footnote, sounding very much like Issy, contributes a digressive, subjective comment on sexual relations with the patriarch.

From this initial floundering on the question of origins, the text quickly turns to the identification of various intellectuals who have pursued some aspect of the question, weaving the names of historians, scientists, philosophers, artists, and other great thinkers into the narrative. This, in turn, produces an awareness of how little one actually knows of the world one inhabits, and leads to a consideration of myth and religious belief as sources of understanding. After a broad survey of theologians, the narrative jumps to a specific evocation of the TRISTAN AND ISOLDE legend associated with PHOENIX PARK. The narrative moves from idea to idea without settling upon any truly satisfactory method of resolving its questions.

Attention next shifts to the behavior of the children, focusing on the boys studying the struggles between the Romans and the Huns. This, however, quickly gives way to their efforts to enact variations on creation myths, which merge into manifestations of sexual curiosity and precocity. In this way the nursery becomes the microcosmic reflection of the fundamental forces of love and war that have shaped human history.

As the implications of this primordial association are pursued by the narrative, a series of metaphoric representations of courage, wisdom, and sensuality proceeds in quick succession. This section ends with a survey of buildings in their capacity as monuments to human achievement. The crude association of the erection of an edifice and blatant sexual desire underscores how fundamental this inquiry remains.

At the end of the chapter (*FW* 304.5), *Storiella as She Is Syung* takes up the response of Dolph (Shem) to a blow from Kev (Shaun). The assault upon Dolph comes directly out of Kev's indignation over the information that Dolph has given them all about the act of procreation and its association with their mother. Rather than letting matters escalate, however, Dolph refuses to return Kev's blow and instead makes every effort to make peace.

As the Lessons chapter draws to a close, the children review the individuals and the topics touched upon by their studies. When their mother calls them to supper, they respond first with a primal recitation of numbers from 1 to 10 and then with the Nightletter. In this missive, they send their best wishes to "Pep and Memmy and the old folkers below," and with that the chapter concludes.

For additional information relating to *Storiella as She Is Syung*, see *Letters*, III.386, 397, 406, 407, 422, 424, and 427.

***Tales Told of Shem and Shaun*** An amalgamation of three distinct episodes from *Finnegans Wake* that Harry and Caresse Crosby persuaded Joyce to let them publish together in book form in August 1929 under the imprint of their Black Sun Press in Paris. A fragment of these episodes was published a year later in a London *Imagist Anthology*, under the title "From 'Tales Told of Shem and Shaun'; Three Fragments from *Work in Progress*." The collection consists of early versions of *The Mookse and the Gripes* (*FW* 152.15–159.18), the middle portion of the Lessons chapter (*The Muddest Thick That Was Ever Heard Dump*, *FW* 282.7–304.4), and "The Ondt and the Gracehoper" (*FW* 414.16–419.10). For additional information see *Letters*, III.189 and 193.

***Two Tales of Shem and Shaun*** This is an abbreviated form of the selection from *Finnegans Wake* entitled *Tales Told of Shem and Shaun* published by FABER AND FABER in December 1932, and it contains *The Mookse and the Gripes* (*FW* 152.15–159.18) and the story of "The Ondt and the Gracehoper" (*FW* 414.16–419.10). For additional information concerning the appearance of "Two Tales of Shem and Shaun," see *Letters*, III.267.

## CONTEMPORARY REVIEWS OF *FINNEGANS WAKE*

Prior to its publication in book form in 1939, *Finnegans Wake* was known as *Work in Progress*. From April 1924, fragments of *Work in Progress* began to be published in different journals or separately as booklets. One such review of a fragment published in the April 1927 issue of *transition* was Desmond McCarthy's "Affable Hawk," which appeared in the *New Statesman* xxix (May 14, 1927), p. 151:

> 'Here say figurines billycoose arming and mounting. Mounting and arming bellicose figurines see here. Futhorc, this liffle effingee is for a firefling called flintfortfall. Face at the eased! O I fay! Face at the Waist! Ho, you fie! Upwap and dump em, ace to ace. When a part so ptee does duty for the holos we soon grow to use of an allforabit.'
>
> In the case of the above passage, however, we need not feel any sympathetic pain; for the writer, so far from being an aphasiac, is a man remarkable for a command of words. It is a passage from Mr. James Joyce's new work now in progress; and so far from standing out from the first thirty pages printed in the April number of *Transition* [*sic*], published by the Shakespeare Co., it is characteristic of their texture. But though every deformation of word and sentence in this passage is intentional and deliberate, it should no more provoke laughter than the attempt of the unfortunate sick man to state that he took his dog out in the morning. It should disgust. The taste which inspired it is taste for cretinism of speech, akin to finding exhilaration in the slobberings and mouthings of an idiot . . . How poor, too, the sense of fun, if fun it can be called, which sustains the author through the labour of composing page after page of distorted rubbish!

The American poet William Carlos Williams lived in Paris in the 1920s and knew Joyce. An admirer of Joyce's work, Williams contributed an essay to *Round His Factification for Incamination of Work in Progress* and offered one of the early comments on *Work in Progress*, "A Note on the Recent Work of James Joyce," published in *transition*, No. 8 (November 1927), pp. 149–154. (This short essay was reprinted in Williams's *Selected Essays*, 1954, pp. 75–79):

> Joyce has carried his writings this far: he has compared us his reader with God. He has laid it out clean for us, the filth, the diseased parts as a priest might do before the Maker. I am speaking of his style. I am referring to his broken words, the universality of his growing language which is no longer English. His language, much like parts of Rabelais, has no faculties of place. Joyce uses German, French, Italian, Latin, Irish, anything. Time and space do not exist; it is all one in the eyes of God—and man. . . .

The following is an excerpt from "James Joyce's Jabberwocky" by Paul Rosenfeld, one of the first reviews of *Finnegans Wake.* It was published in the *Saturday Review of Literature* (May 6, 1939), 10–11:

> . . . In the face of the wit and mysterious poetry with which the book is strewn, and all the reasons for foreseeing its future greater intelligibility, we close it without a great feeling of enthusiasm . . . It is cold and cerebral in comparison with that of a veritable 'radical' like Gerard Manley Hopkins. The pressure of passion and driving necessity frequently seems absent. And too often we have the sense of repletion and a mark overshot. . . .

An unsigned review titled "The Progress of Mr. Joyce" was published in the *Times Literary Supplement,* May 6, 1939, 265–266:

> . . . A sympathetic and patient reader can get stimulation and entertainment out of such literature. But he will only get from it a fraction of what was in Mr. Joyce's mind. There is only one person who can fully understand and appreciate this stupendous work, or can tell us truly how splendid it is or is not; and that person is Mr. Joyce himself. . . . Mr. Joyce is of course abundantly justified if he is content with the satisfaction of art for art's sake, and a splendid audience of one. But in so far as he aims at communication—and why else publish a book?—how serious a drawback that he should require a method which interposes such barriers between his most appreciative readers and his own fertile mind. . . .

Joyce's friend the poet and playwright Padraic Colum wrote a review of *Finnegans Wake* that appeared in the *New York Times,* May 7, 1939, 1, 14:

The problem of the writer of today is to possess real words not ectoplasmic words, and to know how to order them. They must move for him like pigeons in flight that make a shadow on the grass, not like corn popping. And so all serious writers of English today look to James Joyce, who has proved himself the most learned, the most subtle, the most thorough-going exponent of the value-making word. From his early days Joyce has exercised his imagination and intellect upon the significance of words, the ordering of words. . . .

The following is from the author and critic Malcolm Muggeridge's review of *Finnegans Wake* that appeared in *Time and Tide,* May 20, 1939, 654–656:

. . . Considered as a book, and considering the object of a book to be by means of written symbols to convey the author's emotions or thoughts to the reader, *Finnegans Wake* must be pronounced a complete fiasco. Such a word as "bababadalgharaghtakamminarronnkonnbronntonnerronntuonnthunntrovarr-hounawns kawntoohoohoordenenthurnuk!" is not merely senselesss, it is absurb. How many mornings Mr. Joyce devoted to coining this particular word, I do not know; perhaps it only took him one morning, or just an hour or so; but in any case he was wasting his time as surely as, more surely than, a village idiot trying to catch a sunbeam. . . .

From Alfred Kazin's review of *Finnegans Wake,* which appeared in the *New York Herald Tribune,* May 21, 1939, 4:

In reality *Finnegans Wake* is a stupendous improvisation, a great pun. . . . Words take on dozens of associations, all equally firm, real, clever; the punning becomes a galvanic needle on the sloth and fat of conventional language and thinking. . . .

Richard Aldington's review of *Finnegans Wake* appeared in the *Atlantic Monthly,* June 1939, clxiii, n.p.:

. . . . Common honesty compels this reviewer to state that he is unable to explain either the subject or the meaning (if any) of Mr. Joyce's book; and that, having spent several hours a day for more than a fortnight in wretched toil over these 628 pages, he has no intention of wasting one more minute of precious life over Mr. Joyce's futile inventions, tedious ingenuities, and verbal freaks.

. . . Translated into native Tasmanian, this book should have a well deserved sale.

The following is from an unsigned review of *Finnegans Wake* that was published in the *Irish Times,* June 3, 1939, 7:

The author appears to be doing something which has no relation to the reader of a work of fiction; nothing coherent comes out of all these words; it is a game which only Mr. Joyce can play, for he alone knows the rules, if there are any. He will take a word and twist and turn it, and chase it up and down through every language that he knows—English, French, German, Gaelic, Latin, Greek, Dutch, Sanscrit, Esperante.

. . . The writer may come to it to dig for words amidst the ruins of the novel, but the form of "Ulysses" and the content of it which could be imitated are not here. This book could be imitated only by Mr. Joyce himself. It may appear, therefore, in the ultimate view, that, although after "Ulysses" he had no more to say, in "Finnegans Wake" he went on saying it.

The following is by the writer and critic Mary Colum, wife of Padraic Colum and friend of Joyce; her review, "The Old and the New," appeared in *Forum and Century* cii (October 1939), 158–163:

Joyce's *Finnegans Wake* represents, for good or for ill, the very last word, up to the present and maybe for a long time in the future, in the development of the novel . . .

*Finnegans Wake* is the revelation of the goings on in that part of the mind which contains the raw and confused materials of consciousness, and the events of the whole book take place in the minds of people who are in a state of dream, whether sleeping or waking. As we spend at least one third of our lives in sleep and over two thirds of it in some state of dream, it is fitting that some writer should devote himself to exploring what takes place in our minds and emotions during those periods; it is fitting, if we are to give any allegiance to the modern conception of literature as an attempt to portray the whole of man. . . .

The following brief—and humorous—statement is from Walter Rybert's "How to Read *Finnegans Wake*," published in *New Horizons* iii (November/December 1940):

> The first requirement in reading *Finnegans Wake* is a revision in reading habits. Be "given time to read" is one, or "take it easy." It can't be done while hanging on a strap or sitting in a railway station. You've got to be where you won't be ashamed to laugh out loud, murmur "ah!" or satisfy the desire to read something of what you've just discovered to an appreciative listener, preferably feminine. An easy chair, nothing else will do, is essential. A pint of grog will be helpful.

The following observation on *Finnegans Wake* is from *A Literary History of England*, edited by Albert C. Baugh (New York: Appleton-Century-Crofts, Inc., 1948), p. 1562:

> The distortions and convolutions of language transcend the extreme limits of intelligibility. Single sentences are brilliant, ingenious, amusing, or profound. The extraordinary linguistic acrobatics may hold the reader's attention for a while. But before long, light dies before Joyce's "uncreating word" "and universal Darkness buries All." Joyce has retired so far within himself as to be beyond reach.

Eugène Jolas, the American writer, editor, and, with his wife, Maria Jolas, and Elliot Paul, founder of *transition*, published "Homage to the Mythmaker" in *transition*, No. 27 (May 1938), 169–175, a year before the publication of *Finnegans Wake;* the following is a brief excerpt:

> *Work in Progress* is "a compendium, an encyclopedia of the entire mental life of a man of genius," a definition which Wilhelm Schlegel posited, more than a hundred years ago, for the novel of the future.

## *Pomes Penyeach* (1927)

This is the title of a collection of 13 poems written by Joyce over a 12-year period, from 1912 through 1924, and published on July 5, 1927, by Shakespeare and Company, Sylvia BEACH's Paris bookshop that had also published *Ulysses* in 1922. ("Tilly," the first poem of the collection, however, dates back to 1903; 11 were previously published; see below.) The poems are generally on personal and autobiographical topics and touch upon a variety of themes and emotions. Most of the verses were written in TRIESTE between 1912 and 1915; others were written in ZURICH between 1915 and 1919 and in PARIS after 1920. In October 1932, a limited holograph facsimile edition of the poems was published in London by Desmond Harmsworth, with the text illuminated by letters that Joyce's daughter, Lucia, designed. In a December 1931 correspondence with his benefactor Harriet Shaw WEAVER, Joyce indicated that his idea of having Lucia involved in the preparation of the text would help her get through the fragile emotional state she was suffering (see *Letters* I.308–309); it would be to no avail.

The title of the collection seems to evoke the slurred pronunciation of a street hawker crying his wares to a passing crowd—poems penny each. However, a more plausible interpretation is offered by Padraic COLUM: "A word for 'apples' [*pommes* in French] was imposed on 'poems' in the title, giving the sense of windfalls bought at a wayside stall" (*Our Friend James Joyce*, p. 80). Ezra POUND, however, did not see much merit in the poems. In a February 1927 letter to Weaver, Joyce noted that Pound, who read two of the poems at Joyce's request, commented: "They belong in the bible or the family album with the portraits" (*Letters* III.155). Although *Pomes Penyeach* was generally ignored by contemporary reviewers and the public, the reviews it did receive were favorable. Today, the collection has particular historic interest, but this interest should not obscure the value of the poetry. The emotions in *Pomes Penyeach* express personal and powerful sentiments that Joyce was experiencing at the time that he was composing the verses. The poems were also easily adaptable to music—as were those in *Chamber Music*—and in 1933, six years after their publication, *The Joyce Book,* edited by Herbert Hughes, appeared with a musical setting for each poem. (For further details, see *The Joyce Book* below.)

## THE POEMS OF *POMES PENYEACH*

The following order of the poems follows that of the published text.

**"Tilly"** This is the opening poem of the collection. The title means the 13th in a baker's dozen, a gratuitous extra. (The word *tilly,* according to the OED, comes from the Irish word *tuilleadh,* meaning an additional quantity. In *Our Friend James Joyce,* Padraic Colum mentions: "As the price of the little volume was a shilling, one expected to find twelve poems in it, one for each penny. Actually there were thirteen, the additional one being named 'Tilly.' In this Joyce was being obscurely local: the extra half-cup of milk that the milkman left in the Dublin householder's jug in the morning was a 'tilly'—something unpaid for" [80]. Also see Colum's "James Joyce as Poet" in *The Joyce Book,* p. 14, and *U* 1.398–399 where the old milkwoman who arrives at the MARTELLO TOWER in the morning pours "a measureful and a tilly.") The poem was first titled "Cabra," after the DUBLIN district where the Joyce family lived at 7 St. Peter's Terrace from late October 1902 until late March 1904. (During a portion of this time, December 1902 through April 1903, Joyce himself was living in Paris.) "Cabra" was written soon after the death of his mother, May JOYCE, on August 13, 1903, and Joyce considered including it in *Chamber Music* (*Letters,* II.181). Around 1919, Joyce changed the title to "Ruminants" and then to "Tilly" when he significantly revised the poem before it was published in 1927. (The subscript to the poem in *Pomes Penyeach* reads: Dublin, 1904.)

The first two stanzas of the poem depict a vivid image of a cattle driver "with a flowering branch" pressing his herd homeward as the sun is setting on a cold winter night. In the third and last stanza, the speaker of the poem appears to be at rest stretched out by the fire at home, but is in fact in anguish: "I bleed by the black stream / For my torn bough!" (11–12). Focusing on the image of the torn bough and on allusions to Virgil, Ovid, Dante, and others, Robert Scholes argues that the poem is "about betrayal and exile, about the contrast between the contented ruminants who are located specifically in Cabra, Ireland, and the speaker, bleeding from his torn bough by some nameless dark stream" (*In Search of James Joyce,* 96). Richard Ellmann and Chester G. Anderson interpret the poem biographically. Ellmann suggests that it reflects Joyce's feelings at the time of the death of his mother (*James Joyce,* 136–137), and Anderson sees it as reflective of Joyce's relationship with his college and university classmate J. F. BYRNE ("James Joyce's 'Tilly,' " *Publications of the Modern Language Association of America,* 73, 1958, 285–298).

**"Watching the Needleboats at San Sabba"** This is the second poem in order of appearance in the collection. A needleboat, as Padraic Colum explains, is the Galway term for a boat with a pointed prow (*The Joyce Book,* ed. Herbert Hughes, 14). In his note on this poem, J. C. C. Mays offers other explanations. The popular name arose from the way these single sculls "appeared to jump ahead of each other in races like shuttles or needles," or the term may be slang for a randan, "a clinker-built single sculling boat used by beginners or as a pleasure boat" (*James Joyce: Poems and Exiles,* 288–289). According to Richard Ellmann, Joyce wrote the poem on September 7, 1913, after watching his brother Stanislaus compete in a boat race at San Sabba, an area just outside of Trieste on the Adriatic coast. "As the scullers pulled towards shore," Ellmann writes, "they began to sing an aria from Puccini's *La Fanciulla del West.* Joyce plays lugubriously on the last line: '*e non ritornero più*' " (*James Joyce,* 347). This line from Puccini is echoed in the last line of each of the poem's two stanzas, and Joyce conflates the singing of the scullers with a deeper lament for the passing of time and the loss of youth.

On September 9, 1913, Joyce sent the poem as a gift to his brother and the other members of the rowing club (see *Letters,* II.323–324). It was later published in the September 20, 1913, issue of the *Saturday Review.* (For further details, see *Letters,* II.352 and III.276.) There appears to be a discrepancy in the date of this poem. The subscript to the poem in the published text of *Pomes Penyeach* reads: Trieste, 1912. In his preface to volume 1 of *The James Joyce Archive,* A. Walton Litz speculates that the 1912 date is too early; this and other inconsistencies in dates regarding the poems may have arisen from a lapse of memory or from Joyce's intention to achieve greater "coherence to the pattern of emotional development traced by the poems" (xl). (For the music, see Ruth Bauerle, *The James Joyce Songbook,* pp. 124–126a.)

**"A Flower Given to My daughter"** This is the title of the third poem in the collection; it was composed by Joyce in Trieste in 1913 and first published in the May 1917 issue of *Poetry.* The poem subtly reveals a romantic sentiment toward a young woman who has shown kindness to his daughter through the gift of a flower. Passages throughout the posthumously published *Giacomo Joyce* (1968) (see Miscellaneous Works), a notebook Joyce kept at that time, indicate Joyce's secret infatuation with an unidentified person. One notation refers specifically to an incident when this person gave Lucia JOYCE the flower that occasioned the poem. In his introduction to *Giacomo Joyce* (*GJ* xii) and in his biography *James Joyce* (p. 342), Richard ELLMANN suggests that this girl may have been Joyce's student Amalia Popper. Peter COSTELLO disputes Ellmann's claim and argues that the young woman in the poem is probably a composite of several students (see *James Joyce: The Years of Growth,* 1882–1915, p. 308). John McCourt, however, in *The Years of Bloom: James Joyce in Trieste 1904–1920,* supports Ellmann's contention (pp. 202–203).

**"She Weeps over Rahoon"** This poem appears fourth in the collection. Joyce composed it after he and Nora visited the grave of Michael BODKIN at Rahoon, Ireland, in the summer of 1912. (The date in the subscript to the poem: Trieste, 1913.) Bodkin, who died from tuberculosis, was the Galway sweetheart of Nora BARNACLE and the model for Michael Furey, whose memory Gretta Conroy evokes in the closing pages of the *Dubliners* short story "The Dead." "She Weeps over Rahoon" records the voice of a woman as she commemorates her dead lover and reminds her current lover of their own mortality. The image of the rain that falls softly on Rahoon echoes that of the softly falling snow at the end of "The Dead." Joyce is consciously connecting the two pieces and the emotions that they call to mind. This poem, along with "On the Beach at Fontana" and "Alone," appeared in the November 1917 issue of *Poetry.*

**"Tutto è Sciolto"** This is the title of the fifth poem in the collection. "Tutto è Sciolto"—"All is lost now" in English—is taken from an aria in the second act of Vincenzo Bellini's opera *La Sonnambula* (*The Sleepwalker*). The aria is sung by the distraught Elvino when he discovers his fiancée, Amina, in Count Rodolfo's bedroom, which she entered when sleepwalking. (Bellini was one of Joyce's favorite operatic composers.) Written in Trieste on July 13, 1914, the poem describes the speaker's recollections of a young girl whom he has known; an aura of failed seduction permeates the last lines of the verse. The emotion of loss expressed in the poem and by its title may also relate to two separate incidents in Joyce's life. The first occurred in 1909 when he was in Dublin without Nora. Joyce was told by his former university classmate Vincent COSGRAVE that in 1904 he was betrayed by Nora, who had surreptitiously dated him without Joyce's knowledge. This false claim so upset Joyce that he accused Nora of infidelity and rejected her protestations until his trusted friend J. F. Byrne and his brother Stanislaus intervened. The second incident, in 1914 in Trieste, relates to Joyce's failed attempt at an affair with his student Amalia Popper. The poem also appeared with "Simples," "Flood," "Nightpiece," and "A Flower Given to My Daughter" in the May 1917 issue of the American journal *Poetry.*

Allusions to Bellini's aria also occur during the Sirens episode (chapter 11) of *Ulysses,* when Richie Goulding whistles the music of that song when he is dining with Leopold Bloom in the Ormond

Hotel. References to "All is lost now" subsequently recur throughout the narrative as the aria becomes a motif evoking Bloom's general feelings of loss and despair over his relations with his wife, Molly, and of his dismay over her impending affair with Blazes Boylan. (For the music, see Ruth Bauerle, *The James Joyce Songbook,* pp. 119–123.)

**"On the Beach at Fontana"** This is the sixth poem in the collection, written around 1914 in Trieste. With "Alone" and "She Weeps over Rahoon," it was first published in the November 1917 issue of *Poetry.* "On the Beach at Fontana" recalls a swimming excursion near Trieste that Joyce took with his son and underscores the experience of a moment of intense paternal love that inspired an epiphany of Joyce's affections toward him. In one of his Trieste notebooks (reprinted in *The Workshop of Daedalus,* collected and edited by Robert Scholes and Richard M. Kain), Joyce described the deep feeling of love that he sought to capture in the lines of his poem: "I held him in the sea at the baths of Fontana and felt with humble love the trembling of his frail shoulders."

**"Simples"** This, the seventh poem in the collection, was written in Trieste in 1915. Just as "On the Beach at Fontana" describes a moment that evokes Joyce's great affection for his son, this poem describes his daughter's gathering herbs in a Trieste garden and captures an instant in which Joyce feels a profound love for her. At the same time, a note of ambiguity in the final stanza suggests that the speaker feels a measure of apprehension over the powerful hold that the child has on his emotions.

With "Tutto è Sciolto," "Flood," and "A Flower Given to My Daughter," "Simples" was published in the May 1917 issue of *Poetry.*

**"Flood"** The title of the eighth poem in the collection. Written in Trieste around 1915, "Flood" was first published with "Tutto è Sciolto," "A Flower Given to My Daughter," and "Simples" in the May 1917 issue of *Poetry.* The poem dwells upon frustrated desire in a tone closer to self-pity than to seduction and reiterates an erotic theme found in some of the poems of *Chamber Music.*

**"Nightpiece"** This, the ninth poem in the collection, was written in Trieste in 1915. Joyce drew inspiration for this particular poem from a dream that he recorded in his journal *Giacomo Joyce.* (For the specific passage, see *James Joyce: Poems and Shorter Writings,* ed. Richard Ellmann, A. Walton Litz, and John Whittier-Ferguson, p. 235). The dream conflates a recollection of a visit that Joyce made to the cathedral of Notre Dame in Paris during Good Friday devotions in 1903 with his romantic interest in one of his language students in Trieste. Richard Ellmann identifies the student as Amalia Popper. The poem betrays a sense of gloom and bleakness culminating in an emptiness captured by the word *voidward,* a neologism that the OED now cites from this poem. (The passage from *Giacomo Joyce* also connects to Joyce's fiction. The description of Paris that Stephen Dedalus calls to mind in chapter 3, the Proteus episode, of *Ulysses* is a similar depiction of the city and, as J. C. C. May points out, the British Museum owns a manuscript, *Archive* I 196–197, that links "Nightpiece" with Joyce's treatment of the Tristan and Isolde story in *Finnegans Wake* II.4 [*James Joyce: Poems and Exiles,* p. 294].)

At the urging of Ezra Pound, Harriet Monroe published "Nightpiece" and four other poems by Joyce—"Simples," "Tutto è Sciolto," "Flood," and "A Flower Given to My Daughter"—in the May 1917 issue of the journal *Poetry.*

**"Alone"** This is the title of the 10th poem in *Pomes Penyeach.* It was written in Zurich in 1916 and first published in the November 1917 issue of the American periodical *Poetry.* Like many of the other poems in the collection, "Alone" expresses a speaker's wistful, indolent mood. It also represents an instance of passive eroticism similar to that found throughout the posthumously published *Giacomo Joyce,* composed around 1914 in Trieste.

**"A Memory of the Players in a Mirror at Midnight"** The 11th poem in the collection was written in Zurich in 1917. It follows the same imagist structure that had attracted the interest of Ezra Pound to the poem "I hear an army" in *Chamber Music.* "A Memory of the Players in a Mirror at

Midnight" is an observation on the anguish of aging and draws directly upon Joyce's involvement with the Zurich-based amateur theatrical company, the ENGLISH PLAYERS, during World War I. (For additional details regarding this poem, see *Letters* II.445–446 and 462.)

**"Bahnhofstrasse"** This is the 12th poem in the collection. The poem was composed in Zurich in 1918, after Joyce's first attack of glaucoma on Zurich's Bahnhofstrasse in August 1917. The imagery in the opening line of the poem underscores Joyce's reaction to this initial eye problem, which is coupled with the realization of lost youth. The poem's pensive mood reflects Joyce's twofold concern about his growing blindness and the process of aging.

**"A Prayer"** This, the 13th and last poem in *Pomes Penyeach,* was written in Paris in May 1924. The first poetic work that Joyce wrote in six years, it records a lover's address to his mistress. Charged with a tone of submission and passivity, the poem's effect is to evoke, albeit much less explicitly, a sexual ethos similar to the sadomasochistic fantasies of Leopold Bloom that unfold in the brothel of Bella Cohen during the Circe episode, chapter 15, of *Ulysses.*

## RELATED TITLES AND A BOOK

**"Cabra"** This is the title of a poem Joyce wrote sometime after the death of his mother on August 13, 1903. The poem was revised in 1919 and retitled "Ruminants." Joyce later rewrote the poem yet again, renaming it "Tilly," and placed it first in *Pomes Penyeach.* See "Tilly" above.

***Joyce Book, The*** This volume, published by the Sylvan Press in 1933 and edited by Herbert Hughes, contains musical settings of *Pomes Penyeach.* In addition to the settings and the editor's note, the book also includes a portrait of James Joyce drawn by Augustus John, a prologue by James Stephens, a brief discussion of Joyce as poet by Padraic Colum, and an epilogue by Arthur Symons. The composers, with the poems they set to music, are E. J. Moeran, "Tilly"; Arnold Bax, "Watching the Needleboats at San Sabba"; Albert Roussel, "A Flower Given to My Daughter"; Herbert Hughes, "She Weeps over Rahoon"; John Ireland, "Tutto è Sciolto"; Roger Sessions, "On the Beach at Fontana"; Arthur Bliss, "Simples"; Herbert Howells, "Flood"; George Antheil, "Nightpiece"; Edgardo Carducci, "Alone"; Eugene Goossens, "A Memory of the Players in a Mirror at Midnight"; C. W. Orr, "Bahnhofstrasse"; and Bernard van Dieren, "A Prayer."

**"Ruminants"** This is the intermediate title of a poem that eventually appeared as "Tilly" in *Pomes Penyeach.* See "Tilly" above.

## REVIEWS OF *POMES PENYEACH*

Known by the pseudonym Æ, George RUSSELL signed the following review of *Pomes Penyeach* with the initials Y. O.; the review appeared in the *Irish Statesman* (July 23, 1927) 478:

> . . . There is nothing in the new book quite so exquisite as the best lyrics in *Chamber Music.* The poet seems to have been aware that in his youth he had created something which perhaps became more beautiful in retrospect in his imagination because the full strength of his intellect had since been devoted to writing the most realistic novels of our generation, and his early verse may have littered in memory with the irridescence of a shell if a thought of it had come up when he was writing the meditations of Mrs. Bloom. . . .

The American critic Edmund Wilson published a review of the volume in *New Republic* lii, no. 673 (October 26, 1927), p. 268:

> . . . In these thirteen new poems, Joyce has outgrown the imitation of his early masters and caused the influences to contribute to a kind of lyric unmistakably original and with far more color and complexity than the songs in *Chamber Music.* There is not much of it, but it is real poetry—perhaps some of the purest of our time—and a single strain of its music is enough to strike dumb whole volumes which we may previously have pretended to take seriously. . . .

Robert Hillyer's review of *Pomes Penyeach* appeared in the *New Adelphi* i. no. 3 (March 1928), p. 264:

> One critic in America, slavishly devoted to the cult of the later Joyce, praised these lyrics extravagantly, far, far beyond their actual merits which are, indeed, high enough. . . . The truth is that one cannot sincerely admire both these simple lyrics and *Ulysses:* they were written by two opposed personalities, one the sensitive youth who composed the poems, the other, the weary man who bestowed on them the title *Pomes Penyeach.*

# *A Portrait of the Artist as a Young Man*

This is the title that Joyce gave to his first published novel, derived, as noted below, from the shorter version given to an earlier prose piece. Joyce composed *A Portrait of the Artist as a Young Man* over the course of seven years, and, although it represented a significant advancement from earlier work, it undeniably grew out of a long-standing plan for a *Kunstlerroman* (novel about the development of an artist) whose early manifestation appears in the surviving fragments of the novel *Stephen Hero,* which was abandoned within a year or so after Joyce had left Dublin in favor of work on *Dubliners.*

## COMPOSITION AND PUBLICATION HISTORY

Joyce probably began serious composition of *A Portrait of the Artist as a Young Man* shortly after completing the last story in *Dubliners,* "The Dead." He was still working to finish the novel when, in January 1914, he sent the first chapter to Ezra POUND. The reaction of Pound was instantaneous and enthusiastic. He sent it off to the avant-garde London periodical the EGOIST, and pressed for its publication there. Pound's intervention not only had an immediate impact on Joyce's chances to put his novel before the public, it also made Joyce known to Harriet Shaw WEAVER, then working as the business manager at the *Egoist,* who until the end of Joyce's life would prove to be an unswerving supporter and both a financial and emotional bulwark for the family.

At Pound's urging and with the support of Weaver and others *A Portrait of the Artist as a Young Man* appeared in serialized form in the *Egoist* from February 1914 to September 1915. Throughout the process, Joyce rushed to complete its composition to keep up with relentless publishing deadlines. Subsequently, Weaver, who had become convinced of Joyce's genius, endeavored to bring out the novel in book form. She had great difficulty finding an English printer willing to set it into type, and, as an alternative, Pound hit on the idea of having it appear in the United States and then importing copies back to Great Britain. Consequently, the American publisher B. W. HUEBSCH brought it out as a book on December 29, 1916.

The vagaries of publication, while doubtless frustrating to Joyce at the time, mirror the complex creative evolution of the novel. What began as a rather predictable narrative form growing out of the tradition of the writings of popular 19th-century English novelists evolved into a work that now stands as one of the foremost examples of the modernist impulse in literature. In consequence, it is useful at this point to trace the stages through which this creative project moved, from its conventional beginning through a series of progressively more radical imaginative revisions, to come to a clearer sense of the work that readers now know.

The first stage in the composition of *A Portrait of the Artist as a Young Man* began in 1904, eight months before Joyce left Ireland for his lifetime of self-imposed exile on the Continent. On January 7 of that year, Joyce completed an extended prose meditation entitled "A Portrait of the Artist" that he hoped to publish in the Irish literary magazine *Dana* (see Miscellaneous Works). Although the editors of that journal had initially asked Joyce for a contribution, when they received this amalgamation of fictional narrative and philosophic exposition, they declined to print it. One of the magazine's editors, W. K. MAGEE, later explained his logic for opposing bringing out "A Portrait of the

Artist" by saying to Joyce that "I can't print what I can't understand" (*James Joyce,* p. 147).

Almost immediately after this rejection, Joyce drastically reconfigured his plans for the essay. Rather than simply revising it to expand upon or clarify its central principles, he decided to use its central concern, the development of the artistic temperament in the claustrophobic atmosphere of Ireland, as the basis for a book-length work of fiction. In this new form, he planned to express himself through a strictly realistic format, in an account of artistic maturation provisionally entitled *Stephen Hero.*

In this version of the novel that would eventually become *A Portrait of the Artist as a Young Man,* Joyce intended to trace the evolution of the life of his artist-figure, Stephen Daedalus (as he was then known), from infancy to well past his university days. The project clearly captured his imagination, for Joyce worked steadily on composing *Stephen Hero* for about a year and a half. Then, in June 1905, when he was, by his own account, about halfway through the composition of the work, Joyce abandoned it and turned his full attention to the completion of the *Dubliners* stories.

In the absence of a clear declaration of his purpose in giving up on the project, at least in the form it initially took, one can only speculate on the reason for Joyce's decision. Nonetheless, there are clues, both biographical and textual, that allow one to come to a general sense of his motivations. Joyce had already completed a number of the stories that would make up the *Dubliners* collection, and even a cursory comparison shows their narratives as far more technically sophisticated than *Stephen Hero*'s. When he found himself locked into the conventional and formally restrictive style typical of the 19th-century English novel made popular by Scott, Dickens, Thackeray, and others, Joyce quite likely became frustrated with what he could express and how he could explore the creative options that he came to see as increasingly important. He consequently abandoned that prescriptive form of narrative in favor of an approach with more open-ended interpretive alternatives.

At the same time, the narrative concerns outlined in *Stephen Hero* remained compelling. Thus, when Joyce went back to the task of composing a novel-length bildungsroman, an account of development from childhood to adulthood (although some would consider it a *Kunstlerroman,* a novel of the development of the artist, as well), the issues that animated the earliest form of this work, "A Portrait of the Artist," remained the center of narrative concern, albeit in radically reconfigured form.

In 1907, after completing "The Dead," the last story of *Dubliners,* Joyce once again took up the task of writing a novel of maturation. Composition of his short stories had given him a far more sophisticated sense of the narrative potential of highly personalized accounts of ordinary events. To exploit this potential he discarded the limitations of the realistic form and experimented with a looser and formally more flexible style, now recognizable as a characterizing feature of English MODERNISM, that relied heavily on the active participation of readers in the process of forming a unified narrative. In this fashion, the traditionally structured *Stephen Hero* went through the stylistic metamorphosis into *A Portrait of the Artist as a Young Man* while retaining the thematic concerns of the earlier composition.

With this redirection of form and recommitment to content foremost in his consciousness, Joyce worked on this novel for the next seven years. In the process, he transformed a conventional narrative approach into a unique fictional account while keeping the issues of artistic development in Ireland as the essential concerns. When the *Egoist* began serializing *A Portrait of the Artist as a Young Man* in February 1914, Joyce was well on his way toward completing his transformation into a modernist writer. In mid-1915, shortly before the last chapters were due to appear in the *Egoist,* he finished the last revisions to his manuscript and in the process he put behind him the specter of conventional narrative forms that had been featured in his earliest writing.

## COMMENTARY AND SYNOPSIS

In its final version *A Portrait of the Artist as a Young Man* stands in very distant relation to *Stephen Hero,* the work from which it was derived, but its link to this ur-work remains a useful measure of its achievement. The episodic format and concern with the consciousness of its protagonist in *A Portrait of the Artist as a Young Man* announce a modernist disposition absent from the surviving fragments of *Stephen Hero* even as they express the concern, apparent in Joyce's earliest writing, for the difficulty in defining an artistic identity in an unremittingly parochial world. The narrative's supple oscillation between detached objectivity and an empathetic awareness of Stephen's most intimate thoughts, desires, and apprehensions shows a discursive sophistication not present in its predecessor while at the same time they mark the maturing artistic vision of an author now firmly in control of descriptive patterns only partially comprehended before.

When it began to appear in serial form in 1914, *A Portrait of the Artist as a Young Man* seemed to display far greater affinity, both formally and thematically, with *Dubliners* than with *Stephen Hero.* Nonetheless, the fundamental thematic features that shaped the narrative trajectory of the earlier prose work retain pride of place in its successor. Like *Stephen Hero, A Portrait of the Artist as a Young Man* chronicles the life of an emerging artist, Stephen Dedalus (essentially the same character who appeared in the earlier work, with a slight modification in the spelling of his surname). The discourse follows the gradual maturation of Stephen from his infancy, through his primary, secondary, and university education, to the eve of his departure from Ireland. It displays a similar fascination with the most mundane elements in Stephen's life, and it asserts the same presumption of distinction in his nature.

Unlike *Stephen Hero,* however, *A Portrait of the Artist as a Young Man* avoids the imaginative constraints and mechanical accounts that can grow out of NATURALISM by not attempting a detailed sequential account of Stephen's life. Instead, it introduces epiphanic moments to give the narrative a unique discursive rhythm, breaking up the action into discrete episodes and drawing readers into the action to resolve the apparent disunities of the fragmented accounts. As a result, the narrative feels free to move abruptly from chapter to chapter and even from scene to scene, while trusting to the reader the obligation to make the connections among them.

Of course, that is not to say that anarchy reigns. The overall narrative is united thematically, and the story that is driving events traces with increasing insistence Stephen's growing alienation from the inflexible social, cultural, and creative environments in Ireland that threaten first to circumscribe and then to stifle the imagination of the young artist.

The narrative features withdrawal but not defeat—ultimately privileging an interpretive strategy that parallels the techniques of "silence, exile, and cunning" that in the final chapter Stephen announces as his weapons of self-defense. In a carefully choreographed sequence of events, culminating in the final chapter, the narrative records Stephen's progressive disillusionment with the central institutions defining the nature of Irish-Catholic society: the family, the church, and the nationalist movement. The striking feature of this movement lies in the way that its restrained development mimics the gradual enlightenment that comes out of most human experience. Thus, through a skillfully orchestrated sequence of events stretched over the five chapters of the novel, Stephen successively comes to a greater and greater sense of each institution as an oppressive and inhibitive force, antipathetic to all that he has come to value in his life. As a result, he turns with increasing determination from society and toward art. As noted already, critics have come to see *A Portrait of the Artist as a Young Man* as a paradigmatic modernist novel, a work of fiction that cleanly breaks from earlier artistic conventions and that establishes a commitment to an aesthetic vision as a moral value, but the very label runs the risk of limiting one's sense of Joyce's achievement. Rather than see the work as a benchmark in literary history, it is far more useful to consider the source of its continuing impact on contemporary readers. Given the episodic structure of the discourse, this approach is best accomplished through a chapter-by-chapter survey. However, a slight detour is first necessary.

### Epigraph

*A Portrait of the Artist as a Young Man* stands as Joyce's only published work preceded by an epigraph: *Et ignotas animum dimittit in artes.* The passage comes from Ovid's *Metamorphoses,* and it can be translated as "he turned his mind to unknown arts." It records the response of Daedalus, the fabulous artificer, when told by King Minos of Crete that he and his son would not be allowed to leave the island. Daedalus in turn produced the wax wings that allowed him and Icarus to soar away but that also led to his son's death when the young man flew too close to the sun and the wax melted. This epigraph traces wonderfully the narrative movement of each chapter, which ends on a high note only to be brought low by the depressing image or scene that introduces the next chapter. Even more to the point for readers, the epigraph stands as an open invitation to interpretive freedom. The vague pronoun of the phrase (it becomes masculine only because of Ovid's context) and the image of imaginative exploration invite all readers, men and women, to open their minds to new ways of seeing.

The epigraph also serves as a good reminder of the provisionality of the novel's title. This is "a" portrait, with the indefinite article providing a sense of the openness and subjectivity of the narrative. Further, a portrait by its very nature reflects as much of the perceiver as it does of the subject. Thus, even before one begins to read, Joyce has offered ample warning that those who approach the text seeking definitive meaning or a prescriptive reading will only succeed in creating a great deal of frustration for themselves.

### *Chapter 1*

Chapter 1 immediately enforces the need for the interpretive flexibility suggested by the title and epigraph. It announces its groundbreaking intentions by opening the novel with an arresting departure from conventional narrative forms: an abrupt introduction into the experiences of the work's central character that demands immediate and sustained reader involvement. The fractured recapitulation of the fairy tale that Stephen's father, Simon Dedalus, tells to his young son, nicknamed Baby Tuckoo—"Once upon a time and a very good time it was . . ."—challenges traditional interpretive methods and announces a new role for the reader. From these first few lines, the source of the speaker and function of the narrative come into question. This is not to say that the narrative is flawed but rather that it is intentionally incomplete or ambiguous. Joyce self-consciously sustains a range of interpretive options within his discourse by allowing the reader to resolve or complete such moments in the narrative. The reader quickly sees that, from early on, much of the meaning of the novel will derive directly from his or her own interpretive choices, without the usual authorial guidance. Further, these decisions have a provisionality that allows readers to reconfigure the meaning of the novel every time they encounter it.

Immediately following this opening, readers encounter the disturbing and disorienting images of fear and punishment. As young Stephen cowers under a table, he learns that the consequences of disobedience have mythic authority: "Eagles will come and pluck out his eyes." At the same time, as the phrase "Pull out his eyes Apologize" is repeated in a singsong fashion, the reader must decide if this represents the voice of authority hammering home the lesson or the consciousness of an already rebellious Stephen throwing back the threat in a mocking tone.

Already, two key features of the narrative have become evident to readers. The voice that recounts the experiences of Stephen Dedalus, while not exactly Stephen's consciousness, has at all times a keen sense of Stephen's feelings. Further, that voice articulates its views in a vocabulary roughly equivalent to what one would expect from Stephen at whatever age he is when the discourse recounts specific experiences or attitudes. This gives readers a powerful sense of the maturation process even as it conveys a feeling of intimate knowledge of the developing attitudes of the central character.

Finally, these first two pages of the novel provide a brief introduction of the central themes that *A Portrait of the Artist as a Young Man* will take up—the roles of family, Catholicism, and nationalism in the formation of identity. None are developed in any detail, but that too suits the structure that Joyce has chosen. Just as the very young Stephen will only be aware of these institutions in very general and unformed fashion, readers glimpse their significance in his consciousness without a specific idea of their effect.

Next, the narrative goes on to describe life at Stephen's first school, CLONGOWES WOOD COLLEGE, the prestigious institution that marks the beginning of Stephen's association with the Jesuits. In the process, the discourse begins to outline for the reader the particular character traits that will set Stephen apart from others, and the challenges that he will face in his efforts to sustain the uniqueness of his nature in a society that emphasizes conformity.

Stephen feels the predictable homesickness and disorientation of a very young boy sent away from home. He finds himself frustrated by being the butt of jokes—when Wells asks him if he kisses his mother, Stephen is chagrined to learn that there is no answer that will not produce ridicule. At the same time he comes to take pride in his budding intellectual abilities and in his growing sense of how he is expected to behave. (When he becomes ill after Wells shoulders him into the muddy water of the square ditch, he keeps the schoolboy code of silence.) While a hasty reading might suggest that Stephen is simply an outsider shunned by his classmates, a more careful assessment shows a young boy carefully making his way in a complex world. He gains a measure of respect from his fellows even as he also shows his callowness.

The chapter ends with two well-known episodes that underscore the complexity of Stephen's world. In the first, readers see the fragility of the structures that seemingly support and nourish the young boy. In the second, we get a good sense of the resilience of Stephen in the face of injustice.

The Christmas dinner scene begins with deceptive good cheer. In an upbeat tone it announces a pleasant rite of passage, Stephen's first opportunity to eat a holiday meal with the adults rather than with the other young children. However, the cheerfulness that initially characterizes the narrative quickly dissipates with the outbreak of a bitter argument over Charles Stewart PARNELL between Stephen's father and Mr. Casey, supporters of Parnell, and Dante Riordan, an ardent nationalist who nonetheless follows the dictates of the hierarchy of the Catholic Church in condemning Parnell as an adulterer. The quarrel captures stark divisions among political, social, and spiritual goals without offering a clear sense of right and wrong in the dispute. The argument ends with a paradoxical inversion of stereotypical roles—the men are in tears and Dante boisterously exits the room shouting her defiance—and it leaves Stephen wondering which if any of the Irish institutions invoked by both sides during the bitter confrontation—family, church, and nationalist movement—can be trusted.

The chapter concludes with a description of maltreatment and melioration that inverts the pattern of the Christmas dinner scene. Back at Clongowes Wood, some time after the Christmas recess, an aura of confusion and resentment permeates the world of the boys at school. Some older students have done something so serious that the Jesuit teachers have responded with a series of repressive punishments applied to everyone. In a wonderfully developed interchange in which the boys try to puzzle out the cause of the turmoil, Joyce captures both the naïveté and the bravado of the group. One of the students, Athy, claims to know the cause of the turmoil, and sententiously announces that the older boys were "smugging." Though no one knows the meaning of the word, including the reader, all the others nod as if the situation was now crystal clear. (The word in fact is a neologism that Joyce employs to make his point. It allows one to imagine whatever one wishes rather than contend with a narrative that strictly details the offense. Once again, this underscores Joyce's intention to give the reader an integral role in completing the meaning of the text.)

The incident, whatever it may be, has also shaken the Jesuits at Clongowes Wood, and their reaction is to redouble discipline at the school. As a result of overzealous efforts to make an example of any and all offenders, Stephen, who cannot participate in lessons because his glasses have been broken, finds himself unfairly pandied by Father Dolan, the prefect of studies. (Pandying consisted of a series of sharp blows administered on the hands with a leather strap.) Stephen and his classmates feel the injustice of Father Dolan's act, and his schoolfellows press Stephen to seek redress. When he goes to the rector, the Rev. John Conmee, SJ, to complain of this treatment, Stephen receives assurances that it will not recur. Conmee's solicitous treatment of Stephen stands as an important, if underrated, element of the narrative. Joyce does not seek to evoke a Dickensian world that sets oppositions in stark contrast. Stephen's break from social institutions comes gradually because, despite their flaws, the narrative records ample instances of their meliorating behavior. Thus, the chapter ends with Stephen feeling a genuine sense of triumph, for events have reaffirmed, for Stephen at least, the predictable order that social institutions can be said to bring to our lives, Of course, for readers, with the advantage of detachment and hindsight, the resemblance between order and authoritarianism stands out all too clearly and presages conflicts to follow. Nonetheless, the narrative's unwillingness here to oversimplify the complexity of human interaction signals its sophisticated sense of the development of Stephen's identity.

### *Chapter 2*

Chapter 2, like all subsequent chapters, opens with a marked shift in narrative tone from euphoria to depression. The first image one encounters reasserts one of the narrative's favorite forms, inversion. Uncle Charles, the elderly relative who had been unable to intervene in chapter 1 to prevent the harsh conflict at the Christmas dinner, is now banished by Stephen's father to a building behind the main house to smoke. Although in itself, the act seems trivial, it introduces themes of isolation and humiliation that will soon characterize the fortunes of the Dedalus family.

Throughout the summer in the south Dublin suburb of Blackrock, where the family has moved, Stephen gradually becomes aware of the changes in the world around him. The narrative establishes a seemingly innocent routine in Stephen's life, even as it introduces disconcerting images such as that of Mickey Flynn, the track coach in appalling physical condition. Stephen comes to realize that unspecified obstacles will prevent him from returning to Clongowes Wood in the fall, and even more serious problems quickly become evident. Seeking less expensive housing, the Dedalus family soon moves again into Dublin proper, and the discourse begins to make direct reference to Simon Dedalus's growing financial concerns that will accelerate over the remainder of the novel.

In the midst of this unsettled time, Father Conmee, the former rector at Clongowes Wood College, who had come to Stephen's aid at the end of chapter 1, again steps in to provide assistance. This time he does so by securing for Stephen (and probably Stephen's brother Maurice) a scholarship to the prestigious Jesuit school, BELVEDERE COLLEGE, in Dublin. (Father Conmee's kindness is recounted secondhand by Simon Dedalus, who ran into Conmee on the street and who evidently persuaded the priest to intervene for Stephen. During this encounter, Conmee has also given Simon an account of Stephen's visit after the pandying episode. As Simon retells the anecdote, Conmee comes across as less sympathetic and more amused than Stephen or perhaps the reader had realized. The priest's recollection, as it is recounted by Simon to Stephen and the rest of the Dedalus family, has a dual function. It reminds readers of the highly subjective point of view that the narrative presents as it reflects Stephen's views of the world, and it draws us once again into an active engagement with the text, leaving it to us to decide how, if at all, this very different impression of events affects Stephen's sense of the occasion.)

In the episodic fashion that characterizes the narrative, the discourse abruptly shifts its attention to Stephen's renewed academic career. At Belvedere, Stephen has quickly established his intellectual prowess and become one of the more notable students. In contrast to his rather diffident role at Clongowes Wood, at Belvedere Stephen has assumed the position of class leader, although he still maintains a measure of aloofness. This transition, however, has not gone completely smoothly, and the middle portion of the chapter chronicles a series of events that highlight Stephen's intellectual and social rivalry with his classmate Vincent Heron.

As a striking contrast to Stephen's success at Belvedere, the narrative also recounts the continuing financial deterioration of the Dedalus family. A trip that Stephen takes to Cork with his father to sell off the last of the Dedalus family property there to pay Simon's accumulated debts highlights the consequences of Mr. Dedalus's profligacy. At the same time, it shows, through his father's drunken competitiveness with his son, a growing distance between Stephen and his family. At the same time, the narrative introduces ironic parallels between the father's and the son's handling of money. In the penultimate section of chapter 2, the discourse offers an extended account of Stephen's spendthrift ways as he squanders the prize money of 33 pounds (roughly equivalent to $5,000 at current exchange rates; see Appendix VIII for a detailed account of monetary values) that he had won as a school prize.

The closing episode unfolds with startling abruptness an account of a strangely passive Stephen apparently experiencing sexual initiation with a Dublin prostitute. (The narrative does not make clear whether Stephen had previously been to a prostitute, but his intense excitement and palpable nervousness make it seem unlikely.) As the final paragraph makes clear, it is the prostitute who initiates all of the action, while Stephen, with an artistlike detachment, both experiences and records the scene.

### *Chapter 3*

By the beginning of chapter 3 Stephen's initial sensual euphoria has now become a near mechanical process of satiation. His imagination now takes as much pleasure contemplating the possibility of stew for dinner as recalling the gratification offered by the prostitutes he has known. In this chapter the narrative focuses almost exclusively on giving an account of a religious retreat that the boys at Belvedere have to make, and it specifically foregrounds the sermons preached by the retreat master, Father Arnall.

Although the retreat receives a rather melodramatic representation, heightened by the selective attentiveness of Stephen's overactive imagination, the liturgy itself was a long-established practice and, as Joyce would have known, one held in particular esteem by the Jesuits. (The Society of Jesus was the first religious order that made the retreat obligatory for its members.) The format of the

The Martello Tower in Sandycove, where Stephen Dedalus, the protagonist of *A Portrait of the Artist as a Young Man,* lives in *Ulysses* *(The Irish Tourist Board)*

retreat described in chapter 3 follows the standard approach prescribed at that time by the church. It has the retreat master leading the boys toward personal assessments through a series of meditations on death, the Last Judgment, Hell, Purgatory, and Heaven.

The narrative plays a selective and possibly misleading role in its account of the retreat in which Stephen participates. It reports verbatim portions of the sermons, and then counterpoints the priest's words with Stephen's reactions to them. To anyone unfamiliar with the practice, it might seem that these passages cover the entire retreat. To the contrary, what we see in the text is a reflection of the factors that most hold Stephen's attention: pride and guilt. As a result, emphasis falls on representations of guilt and punishment.

Despite the actual breadth of the retreat format, in passage after passage, Stephen dwells exclusively upon the consequences of his mortal sins with something akin to morbid pleasure, and this state of mind brings him to a form of repentance, based almost exclusively on a mixture of conceit over the presumed magnitude of his sins and fear of retribution as a consequence, that highlights the conclusion of the chapter. (One Joyce scholar, Professor James R. Thrane, has shown that Joyce derived much of the text of Father Arnall's sermons from a devotional work entitled *Hell Opened to Christians, To Caution Them from Entering into It* written in 1688 by an Italian Jesuit, Father Giovanni Pietro Pinamonti. An English version of the work was published in Dublin in 1868, and it may very well have served as the basis for similar sermons that the young Joyce heard at Belvedere during retreats that he made.)

The primary motivation for Stephen's repentance offers important insights into his nature. Though remorse plays at the margins of Stephen's feelings and a fear of punishment has a significance in Stephen's decision to repent, pride stands as the dominant impulse in the chapter. Pride initially leads Stephen to feel that his sins are too grave for forgiveness. As the retreat sermons unfold, his pride makes him feel as if every word were directed at him. His pride causes him to dream of a personal vision of hell, like the great saints mentioned by Father Arnall. And pride leads him to imagine reconciliation not through his own approach to the Eucharist but rather with the Body of Christ coming to him: "The ciborium had come to him."

### Chapter 4

At the same time, despite these reservations about the nature of his reconciliation with the church, Stephen's gesture of repentance seems sincere. Indeed, this marks a time of genuine happiness for Stephen. However, predictably, the initial gratification derived from the renewed practice of his faith has become a habitual adherence to a mechanistic routine by the time chapter 4 begins. The episode opens with a detailed account of the near-masochistic regime of spiritual exercises and acts of self-denial that Stephen has formulated for himself in an effort to atone for his sins. Nonetheless, despite the fervor characterizing Stephen's commitment to piety, this scheme rapidly degenerates into a series of perfunctory, emotionless practices emphasizing the mortifications of the flesh rather than the spiritual enlightenment that is the real goal of these acts.

In a scene that raises a number of problematic issues relating to belief and service, the narrative focuses attention on the impact of religion on the life of a prospective artist. As one would expect in the tight-knit atmosphere of the school, Stephen's piety has come to the attention of the director of studies at Belvedere. He meets with Stephen and asks the young man to consider the possibility of a vocation to the priesthood, specifically as a member of the SOCIETY OF JESUS. As in the retreat sermons, much of what the director says, particularly about the sacramental powers that priests enjoy, appeals to Stephen's pride. Likewise, one does well to remember that the narrative emphasizes Stephen's perspective, so hasty judgments about the manipulative quality of the suggestion oversimplify the dynamics of the exchange. Indeed, at one point, the director very bluntly urges careful consideration, for an ill-conceived decision to become a priest would be disastrous. In any case, the director's suggestion precipitates a crisis of conscience in Stephen. He conducts a rigorous, probing consideration of the values that actually inform his nature and weighs them against the demands that such a full commitment to the church would place upon him. Ultimately, the confining life and rigorous discipline of the priesthood runs contrary to his perceived need for experiences to feed his creative impulses. This brings him to a decision to break with the church (a course of action made explicit in the next chapter) and choose art over religion as his life's vocation.

The chapter ends with a passage that has come to be seen as a crucial moment in Stephen's artistic development: the embodiment of the creative possibilities offered by his choice through the vision of a young girl wading in the waters of Dublin Bay. As Stephen walks along Dollymount Strand he sees a young woman, whom critics have come to label the Birdgirl, standing knee deep in the water. The beauty of this image has an aesthetic rather than an erotic impact on him that ultimately confirms for him the absolute correctness of his choice. It marks an EPIPHANY in which Stephen realizes how much he wishes for the power to evoke through his writing the same sense of pleasure he feels as he contemplates the girl's beauty.

### *Chapter 5*

As with the other moments of exhilaration that have ended previous chapters, this exuberance disappears with the opening of chapter 5. The scene in a tenement shows the tawdry, even desperate, daily life of the Dedalus family as they struggle to sustain themselves through increasing economic hardship. With harsh criticism of Stephen from Simon Dedalus opening the chapter and his mother's plea for him to return to the church near its end, Stephen's growing alienation from his family brackets a series of episodes marking his break with Ireland and his full commitment to art.

Clashes with authority have marked every stage of Stephen's development. Here the narrative methodically traces Stephen's final rejection of the institutions that have endeavored to set his moral direction—Irish nationalism, the Catholic Church, and the family. In this fashion it lays out his reasons for breaking with each, and then leaves it to the reader to decide how close Stephen has come to achieving his goal of being an artist.

The first formative force the narrative addresses is patriotism. To his friend Davin (the only character in the novel to call Stephen familiarly by a diminutive of his first name—Stevie), Stephen explains that he cannot give himself over to the Irish nationalist movement. In Stephen's opinion the history of hypocrisy and betrayal that surrounds Irish patriotic endeavors precludes any rational human being from giving his loyalty to this cause.

Before going on to address Stephen's break with other Irish institutions, the narrative offers a sketch of the values governing the alternative approach to life that the young man has embraced. To Vincent Lynch, a fellow student at UNIVERSITY COLLEGE, DUBLIN, Stephen outlines the tenets of the aesthetic theory that have come to replace Catholic dogma as the moral center of his universe. This is a section full of the self-importance and sententiousness that can at times dominate Stephen's nature. Wisely, the narrative punctuates Stephen's pedantic and humorless disquisition with Lynch's interjection of his sardonic views and his complaints of the hangover that plagues him. Although the sinuousness of the aesthetic theory itself challenges readers, it raises a larger interpretive issue, namely, to what degree one should apply the values expressed by Stephen to the novel in which they appear. Joyce wisely does not force the issue, but no complete interpretation of the book can ignore the need to come to some resolution of this question.

After the dry examination of artistic values, the narrative returns to the core issues of social environment. Talking to another friend and confidant, Cranly, also a classmate at University College, Dublin, Stephen touches on his religious alienation when he explains his break with his mother over his unwillingness to profess publicly his Catholic faith by making his Easter duty. While Lynch, suffering from the effects of a heavy night of drink, was a distracted and often disinterested listener, Cranly provides a very different response. Although he evinces no greater loyalty to Irish institutions than does Stephen, Cranly does maintain a cynical pragmatism that challenges Stephen's idealistic approach. For Cranly, appearances mean little, and so apparent acquiescence to the authority of the family, church, and state will have little effect upon him. He offers Stephen the alternative of accommodation, and the logic behind his reasoning shows how tempting his suggestions must have been. In the end, however, Stephen rejects Cranly's approach, and in doing so he forecloses the possibility of continuing to live in Ireland.

Near the end of the chapter, the narrative makes a final, radical shift in form, and introduces direct evidence of Stephen's artistic maturation. In a series of diary entries, readers see Stephen's summation of his views on Ireland and art, and they can judge from this written evidence how close Stephen has come to attaining his ambition. As Stephen completes his account of his emancipation from Irish cultural institutions, he utters a paradoxical declaration that neatly sums up his imaginative condition. On the point of leaving the claustrophobic atmosphere of Ireland to go to Paris, he nonetheless affirms his inextricable connection to his cultural, spiritual, and imaginative heritage, declaring: "I go to encounter for the millionth time the reality of experience and to forge in the smithy of my soul the uncreated conscience of my race" (*P* 252–253). Stephen will not come to a full sense of this dependence upon Ireland as an inspiration for his art until the pages of *Ulysses,* but this statement clearly announces the direction in which his development is headed.

Although readers in Joyce's time may not have realized it, *A Portrait of the Artist as a Young Man* has established itself as the foremost example of English modernism in the canon. As one expects from a modernist work, it offers a thorough critique of the key social institutions that seek to shape the life of its central character—in Stephen's case the family, the church, and the state (in the form of Irish nationalism). With deft attention to detail, the narrative traces, in the five chapters of the novel, the gradual lessening of influence exerted by each institution. It avoids the melodramatic sunderings chronicled by some of the lesser modernists like D. H. Lawrence, and instead presents an account of Stephen's cumulative sense of the inadequacy of the institutions in the world around him. As an alternative to the absence of valid guidance and support from these entities, the narrative shows the growing confidence of the artist's ego as the valid benchmark for guiding behavior. Also in the modernist tradition, the narrative develops in an episodic, open-ended form that actively draws readers into the completion of its meaning.

Although pre-draft material for this work is not as abundant as what is available for *Ulysses* and *Finnegans Wake,* the holograph manuscript of *A Portrait of the Artist as a Young Man* is currently held by the NATIONAL LIBRARY OF IRELAND as a result of the generosity of Joyce's longtime friend and benefactor Harriet Shaw WEAVER.

***Helpful Annotations***

Don Gifford and Robert J. Seidman, *Notes for Joyce: Dubliners and A Portrait of the Artist as a Young Man.* See the appendix on page 405 for a selected bibliography.

## CHARACTERS

**Arnall, Father** He is a Jesuit priest who first appears in chapter 1 of *A Portrait of the Artist as a Young Man.* As Stephen Dedalus's Latin teacher at CLONGOWES WOOD COLLEGE, he exempts Stephen from his studies after Stephen breaks his eyeglasses. However, when the prefect of studies, Father Dolan, enters Father Arnall's classroom and unjustly accuses the boy of being an "idle little loafer" (*P* 50), Father Arnall does not defend Stephen when he is pandied. Later, in chapter 3 of the novel, Father Arnall reappears to give the sermons during the retreat conducted when Stephen is at BELVEDERE COLLEGE. The fierce tone that Father Arnall adopts during the retreat is strikingly different from his classroom demeanor at Clongowes, but in fact the outline of the sermons comes from a very detailed program that all retreat masters of Joyce's day would have followed.

**Brigid** In *A Portrait of the Artist as a Young Man,* Brigid is a servant in the Dedalus household. Although she does not appear in the novel, while lying sick in the infirmary at CLONGOWES WOOD COLLEGE the young Stephen DEDALUS recalls the words of a song about death and burial that Brigid had taught him (*P* 24). (Joyce gives this name to two different fictional characters, both of whom are family servants; see also Characters under *Exiles.*)

**Butt, D., SJ** In *Stephen Hero* Father Butt is identified as the dean of students at UNIVERSITY COLLEGE, DUBLIN, where he also teaches English. He probably reappears lighting the fire in the Physicans Theatre episode of chapter 5 of *A Portrait of the Artist as a Young Man,* although in that novel the dean of students is not identified by name. Most likely, Joyce modeled his depiction of Father Butt on his recollections of the Rev. Joseph DARLINGTON, SJ, who was the dean of studies and a professor of English at University College, Dublin when Joyce attended (1898–1902).

**Casey, John** He appears in the pivotal Christmas dinner scene in chapter 1. There, he and Simon Dedalus argue with Mrs. Riordan (Dante) over the proper role of the Catholic Church in Irish politics, and, in particular, he condemns the church's repudiation of Charles Stewart PARNELL. The Fenian John KELLY, a friend of John Stanislaus JOYCE, James's father, served as the model for John Casey.

**Charles, Uncle** He is Stephen Dedalus's elderly, maternal granduncle. Uncle Charles is present at the Christmas dinner when John Casey, Mr. Dedalus, and Dante Riordan argue over Charles Stewart PARNELL. Chapter 2 opens with a request by Stephen's father that Uncle Charles smoke his "black twist" tobacco in the outhouse, a shed behind the main building, to which the old man good-naturedly agrees. Later the narrative describes Stephen spending much of his time in Blackrock during the early part of the summer with Uncle Charles. Joyce based Uncle Charles on William O'Connell, a prosperous businessman in Cork who was a maternal uncle of Joyce's father.

**Clery, Emma** She is a young woman, specifically identified by name in *Stephen Hero,* who is the object of Stephen Daedalus's romantic fantasies there. In *A Portrait of the Artist as a Young Man,* she may be the E—— C—— with whom the young Stephen Dedalus rides home on a tram after a children's party at Harold's Cross, and whom he is tempted to kiss. She seems to appear throughout the novel both as Stephen's idealized vision of Irish womanhood and as a representation of the Irish society's stereotypical attitudes of and toward women against which Stephen rebels. In chapter 3, during the retreat, Stephen imagines that Emma is with him in an encounter with the Blessed Virgin (*P* 116). Near the end of the novel (*P* 252) Stephen describes his awkward meeting with an unnamed young woman in Grafton Street who seems very like Emma, sympathetic to Stephen's problems yet a bit afraid of his unconventional attitudes. In *Monasterboice,* a play by Padraic COLUM about Joyce's quest for artistic identity, Colum uses the name *Emma* for the girl who accompanies Joyce to the monastery at Monasterboice, and Colum attributes to her qualities similar to those that so attracted Stephen Dedalus to Emma in *A Portrait of the Artist as a Young Man.*

**Conmee, Rev. John, SJ (1847–1910)** He was an actual Jesuit priest and the rector at CLONGOWES WOOD COLLEGE from 1885 to 1891. In 1893, Father Conmee arranged for both Joyce and his brother Stanislaus to attend BELVEDERE COLLEGE on scholarships. According to Herbert Gorman, Joyce received comfort from Father Conmee and described him to Gorman as "a very decent sort of chap." Conmee was appointed prefect of studies at Belvedere College (1891–92), prefect of studies at UNIVERSITY COLLEGE, DUBLIN (1893–95), superior of St. Francis Xavier's Church (1897–1905), provincial (1905–09), and rector of Milltown Park (1909–10).

Fictional versions of Conmee appear in both *A Portrait of the Artist as a Young Man* and *Ulysses.* In the first chapter of *A Portrait of the Artist as a Young Man,* Stephen Dedalus appeals to Father Conmee after being unjustly accused of idleness and pandied by Father Dolan. In the second chapter, Simon Dedalus relates having met Father Conmee, and announces that the priest has promised to intervene to obtain a scholarship for Stephen (and possibly his brother Maurice) to attend BELVEDERE COLLEGE. See also Characters under *Ulysses.*

**Cranly** He appears in both *Stephen Hero* and in chapter 5 of *A Portrait of the Artist as a Young Man.* Cranly is a close friend of Stephen's, and a classmate at University College, Dublin. Cranly provides pragmatic advice on how to get along in the claustrophobic world of Dublin. During an extended walk around the city they discuss religious belief and family relations. Cranly is modeled on Joyce's mild-mannered friend and confidant, John Francis BYRNE.

**Dante** See Riordan, Mrs.

**Davin** He is a character who appears in chapter 5 of *A Portrait of the Artist as a Young Man.* Davin is one of Stephen Dedalus's classmates at UNIVERSITY COLLEGE, DUBLIN. He is a nationalist who comes from rural Ireland, a devout Catholic, and a sexually chaste young man. In this respect, Davin stands as Stephen's polar opposite. The contrast allows Davin to serve as a foil for Stephen's attitudes, giving the reader a clear sense of the changes that have occurred in Stephen as he matures physically, emotionally, and psychologically over the course of the novel and as his literary aspirations develop. At the same time, despite their very different backgrounds and views, Davin enjoys a particularly close friendship with Dedalus, and he is the only person outside the family in the book to address Stephen by his first name. (In fact he uses the diminutive, Stevie, that no one else does.) The character of Davin is modeled on Joyce's friend and university classmate George CLANCY, who is also the model for the character of Madden who appears in *Stephen Hero.*

**Dedalus, Katey** She is one of Stephen Dedalus's younger sisters, appearing in both *A Portrait of the Artist as a Young Man* and in a more extended role in *Ulysses.* In chapter 5 of *A Portrait,* Mrs. Dedalus asks Katey to prepare the place for Stephen to wash, and she in turn asks her sister Boody. See also, Characters under *Ulysses.* (See the appendix on page 402 for the Dedalus family tree.)

**Dedalus, Simon** He appears in both *A Portrait of the Artist as a Young Man* and *Ulysses.* Simon Dedalus is the improvident and alcoholic father of Stephen Dedalus and the head of the Dedalus household. Like his precursor (Mr. Simon Daedalus in *Stephen Hero*), Joyce modeled Mr. Dedalus's character on that of his own father, John Stanislaus JOYCE.

The consequences of Mr. Dedalus's financial and social ruin significantly shape much of the material and emotional circumstances informing the life of Stephen Dedalus in *A Portrait of the Artist as a Young Man* and *Ulysses.* In spite of Mr. Dedalus's failures, his intolerant temperament, his resentments, and his strong political and religious opinions, he is nonetheless presented as a witty raconteur and amiable socializer. His ability to tell a good story and sing a good song in pleasing tenor voice makes him a pleasant companion at least for those not dependent upon him for financial support. Throughout Stephen has ambivalent feelings for his father, and readers repeatedly see the danger for Stephen of becoming a Dublin character like Simon Dedalus.

*A Portrait of the Artist as a Young Man* begins with direct references to Mr. Dedalus's storytelling and singing, talents that make a lasting impression on the young Stephen and readers as well. As the novel develops and his financial circumstances worsen, he recedes into the background, relinquishing his role as head of the family and becoming merely a disruptive influence in the lives of his wife and children. In the final chapter, when asked about his father by Cranly, Stephen sardonically sums up the life of Simon Dedalus with a dismissive series of labels: "A medical student, an oarsman, a tenor, an amateur actor, a shouting politician, a small landlord, a small investor, a drinker, a good fellow, a storyteller, somebody's secretary, something in a distillery, a taxgatherer, a bankrupt and at present a praiser of his own past" (*P* 241). See also, Characters under *Ulysses.* (See the appendix on page 402 for the Dedalus family tree.)

**Dedalus, Stephen** He is the central character of *A Portrait of the Artist as a Young Man* and a major character in *Ulysses.* Both his surname and given names have symbolic significance. *Stephen* was the name of the first Christian martyr, stoned to death for his religious convictions (see Acts 7:55–60). *Dedalus* (or *Daedalus* as the name appears in *Stephen Hero*) was the mythical "fabulous artificer" who made feathered wings of wax with which he and his son Icarus escaped imprisonment on the island of Crete. (Icarus, however, flew too close to the sun; the wax melted, and he plunged into the Ionian Sea and drowned.) Like the first Christian martyr with whom he shares a given name, Stephen, in advancing a new cause, breaks from tradition and faces persecution by his peers. Like Dedalus, he must use artifice and cunning to escape his own imprisonment—by the institutions of the family, the church and Irish nationalism. Stephen writes in his diary: "Old father, old artificer, stand me now and ever in good stead" (*P* 252–253).

Although he does not narrate the novel, his point of view shapes the perspective of the work. As the central consciousness of *A Portrait of the Artist as a Young Man*, Stephen's actions and attitudes set the pace and frame the development of the discourse. The book traces Stephen's intellectual, artistic, and moral development from his earliest recollections as "Baby Tuckoo" through the various stages of his education at CLONGOWES WOOD COLLEGE, BELVEDERE COLLEGE, and UNIVERSITY COLLEGE, DUBLIN, to his decision to leave Ireland for the Continent. The novel also follows the decline of the Dedalus family from upper-middle-class respectability to abject poverty, noting the progressive alienation of Stephen from his family as an almost inevitable consequence.

These deteriorating economic conditions develop rapidly in the second chapter, punctuated by the family's move into Dublin and Simon Dedalus's disastrous trip to Cork, accompanied by Stephen, to sell off the last of the family property. Given these events, it is no surprise that Stephen's distancing from his family occurs in a direct and linear fashion. However, his relations with the church are characterized by a much greater degree of uncertainty and vacillation. After a period of unrestrained sexual indulgence while at Belvedere, Stephen returns to the church, terrified by the images conjured up during the sermons at the retreat recounted in chapter 3. As a consequence, Stephen embarks upon a rigorous penitential regimen. However, he finds that the prescribed spiritual exercises do not give him the satisfaction for which he had hoped. By the end of chapter 4, with his erotically charged aesthetic vision of the young woman wading, the Birdgirl on Dollymount Strand, Stephen has given himself completely over to art.

In the final chapter, a number of Stephen's college classmates attempt in different ways to integrate him into the routine of Dublin life and thus bring him under the sway of dominant Irish social, cultural, religious, and political institutions. Davin seeks to enlist him in the nationalist cause. Vincent Lynch proposes small-scale debauchery as a means of sustaining himself in the suffocating atmosphere of Dublin middle-class life. Cranly, with perhaps the most seductive temptation, suggests that Stephen adopt the hypocrisy of superficial accommodation as a way of liberating himself from the censure of his fellow citizens. Stephen rejects all of these alternatives and remains devoted to his artistic vocation.

As the novel closes, he is about to leave Dublin to live in Paris, to attempt "to fly by those nets" of nationality, language, and religion and, as he writes in his diary, "to encounter for the millionth time the reality of experience and to forge in the smithy of my soul the uncreated conscience of my race" (*P* 203, 252–253). The Daedalus motif of the cunning artificer is alluded to here and culminates in these last lines of *A Portrait of the Artist as a Young Man*. See also Characters under *Ulysses*. (See the appendix on page 402 for the Dedalus family tree.)

**Dolan, Father** He is the unsympathetic prefect of studies at CLONGOWES WOOD COLLEGE who appears in chapter 1. His role as prefect of studies makes him an assistant to the rector and puts him in charge of the academic program. In Joyce's novel, Father Dolan seems to be acting as a dean of discipline as well. He appears near the end of chapter 1 where he accuses Stephen Dedalus of having broken his eyeglasses on purpose to avoid studying. As a punishment for this supposed transgression, Father Dolan pandies Stephen. (That is, he hits the young man's hands with a leather-covered pandybat.) Joyce modeled this character on Father James Daly, who served as prefect of studies when Joyce was attending Clongowes Wood and who reportedly punished Joyce in this way. (See also Conmee, Rev. John, SJ, above.)

**Doyle, Reverend Charles, SJ** He appears in chapter 2, identified as one of the Jesuit teachers at

BELVEDERE COLLEGE, though Stephen Dedalus does not study under him. The fictional Father Doyle is modeled on an actual faculty member of the same name. In 1921, Joyce wrote to Father Doyle enquiring about Belvedere House, the name by which the school had been called before it became Belvedere College. (For details, see *Letters*, III.49–50.)

**E—— C——** These are presumably the initials of Emma Clery, the subject of a youthful poem written by Stephen and the girl with whom he seems to be enamored for most of the novel. In *Stephen Hero*, the narrative refers to her by her full name and not just by her initials.

**Flynn, Mike** He is Stephen Dedalus's running coach, appearing very briefly at the beginning of chapter 2. Flynn is identified as an old friend of Stephen's father and is called the trainer of some of the most successful runners in modern times. Flynn was the proponent of a particularly rigid running style that Stephen had to follow: "his head high lifted, his knees well lifted and his hands held straight down by his sides" (*P* 61).

**Ghezzi, Rev. Charles, SJ** He is a Jesuit priest and the professor of Italian at UNIVERSITY COLLEGE, DUBLIN, under whom Joyce studied the works of DANTE ALIGHIERI, Gabriele D'ANNUNZIO, and other Italian writers. Joyce would also often discuss with Father Ghezzi philosophical issues pertaining to Giordano BRUNO and the aesthetics of St. THOMAS AQUINAS. Ghezzi served as a model for Father Artifoni, Stephen Daedalus's Italian instructor in *Stephen Hero*. In *A Portrait of the Artist as a Young Man*, however, Joyce used Father Ghezzi's actual name for the character. In chapter 5 in the diary entry of March 24, Stephen Dedalus refers to his instructor as "little roundhead rogue's eye Ghezzi" (*P* 249).

**Henry, Rev. William, SJ** He was the actual rector of BELVEDERE COLLEGE during Joyce's time there. He also instructed Joyce in Latin. Additionally, according to Joyce's biographer Peter Costello, Father Henry also directed the Sodality of Our Lady, to which James Joyce was admitted on December 7, 1895, and of which he was elected prefect, or head, on September 25, 1896. Throughout *A Portrait of the Artist as a Young Man*, Henry is never referred to by name but always by the title "the rector" or "the director." In chapter 3, he speaks to Stephen Dedalus's class about their forthcoming retreat, and in chapter 4, after a prolonged discussion he invites Stephen to consider a priestly vocation. This is a key scene, for Jesuits are prohibited from actively recruiting someone to join the order, and critics have debated whether Father Henry oversteps his authority in what he says to Stephen. (Father Henry also served as the model for Father Butler in the *Dubliners* story "An Encounter.")

**Heron, Vincent** He appears in chapter 2 in the contradictory roles of Stephen Dedalus's aggressive rival and putative school friend at BELVEDERE COLLEGE. In its description of him, the narrative puns upon Heron's name by describing his "mobile face, beaked like a bird's" (*P* 76), employing the avian imagery prevalent throughout the novel. This particular group of metaphors often indicates a threatening presence, as in the opening scene in which Stephen is menaced by the image of an eagle pulling out his eyes (*P* 8).

In keeping with this pattern Heron, too, takes the role of a threatening figure in Stephen's life. Heron embodies the narrow-minded, entrenched attitudes of the middle-class lifestyle that increasingly presents itself in opposition to Stephen's gestures of independence. During their first encounter, Heron demonstrates this antipathy for any sort of autonomous thinking. He clumsily tries to force Stephen to admit that the poet Byron was heretical and immoral by instigating an attack by two other classmates on Stephen (*P* 81f). Later, as the reader observes near the end of chapter 2, Heron will become more polished in his efforts to force Stephen into conformity, just as Stephen will become more adept at using his wit to sidestep such attempts.

**Lynch, Vincent** He is a character who appears as a student at UNIVERSITY COLLEGE, DUBLIN, in both *Stephen Hero* and *A Portrait of the Artist as a Young*

*Man,* and later as a medical student in *Ulysses.* In *Stephen Hero,* Lynch serves as a sounding board for Stephen Daedalus, facilitating the exposition of his views on women and the Catholic Church. In chapter 5 of *A Portrait of the Artist as a Young Man,* he listens to Stephen's disquisition on aesthetics, and his acerbic comments, growing out of his hungover condition, punctuate Stephen's disquisition and prevent it from becoming pedantic. Joyce's Dublin friend Vincent COSGRAVE was the model for Lynch.

**MacCann** He is a character, identified only by his surname, who appears in chapter 5. The narrative depicts MacCann as the most vocal political activist at UNIVERSITY COLLEGE, DUBLIN. MacCann champions the cause of pacifism, and bristles at Stephen Dedalus's refusal to sign a document that he is circulating praising the efforts of Czar Nicholas to promote universal peace. Joyce modeled MacCann on Francis SHEEHY-SKEFFINGTON, a friend and University College classmate.

**McGlade** He is a character who appears only briefly in chapter 1. The narrative identifies McGlade as one of the prefects at CLONGOWES WOOD COLLEGE. From the conversation between Stephen Dedalus and the other boys, it appears that he is associated at least marginally with the boys who are involved in the notorious SMUGGING incident.

**Moonan, Simon** He is a character who appears in the first chapter, identified by the narrative as one of the older boys at CLONGOWES WOOD COLLEGE and a favorite of "the fellows of the football fifteen." An aura of homoeroticism surrounds Moonan, although nothing more specific than innuendo appears in the story. Because Moonan is one of the boys implicated in the smugging incident, he faces a flogging as punishment. He may also be the Moonan who is referred to in chapter 5 as a fairly dull student who has nonetheless passed his exams at UNIVERSITY COLLEGE, DUBLIN.

**Moran, Father** This is the name of a priest who appears in both *Stephen Hero* and *A Portrait of the Artist as a Young Man.* In both novels his expression of nationalist sentiments and his friendship with Emma Clery arouse equal measures of disdain and jealousy in Stephen Dedalus.

**Riordan, Mrs.** She is one of the characters who appears in chapter 1, where she is called "Dante." (A corruption of "auntie," the name "Dante" is a term of familiarity and affection.) Though not an actual blood relation, Mrs. Riordan is a widow who has lived for a time in the Dedalus household, apparently as a governess. Despite the benevolence implied by her name, for the young Stephen Dedalus she stands as a harsh authority figure. At one point in the opening pages of the novel, the narrative goes so far as to make her menacing. When Stephen's mother asks him to apologize for some unspecified misbehavior, Dante threateningly adds: "O, if not, the eagles will come and pull out his eyes" (*P* 8). Her attitude epitomizes the narrow-minded religious and political views Stephen will later in life reject.

Mrs. Riordan also plays a key role in the Christmas dinner scene. There she is portrayed as headstrong and intolerant, with inflexible religious and political views that make her unsympathetic to the recently disgraced Irish political leader Charles Stewart PARNELL. After a violent dinner-table argument with Simon Dedalus and John Casey over the Irish rejection of Parnell after his adulterous affair with Kitty O'SHEA became a matter of public knowledge, Mrs. Riordan stalks out of the room and disappears from the narrative.

Mrs. Riordan's character is based upon that of Mrs. "Dante" Hearn CONWAY, a woman originally from Cork who came into the Joyce household in 1887 as a governess. Like her fictional counterpart, Mrs. Conway had a bitter fight (with John JOYCE and his Fenian friend John KELLY) over the character of Parnell during the Joyce family Christmas dinner in 1891. She seems to have left the Joyces shortly thereafter. (See also Characters under *Ulysses.*)

**Tate, Mr.** He is a character who appears in chapter 2 in *A Portrait of the Artist as a Young Man* as the English master at BELVEDERE COLLEGE, and in

*Stephen Hero* where he is identified, in passing, as Stephen Daedalus's English professor at UNIVERSITY COLLEGE, DUBLIN. In chapter 2 of *A Portrait,* Mr. Tate good-naturedly calls attention to a putative line of heresy in one of Stephen's class essays, thereby unwittingly precipitating Stephen's confrontation after school with his rival Vincent Heron and two other bullies. The character of Mr. Tate is based upon one of Joyce's English teachers at Belvedere, Mr. George Dempsey, who taught at the college from 1884 to 1923.

**Temple** See Characters under *Stephen Hero.*

**Vance, Eileen** She is a character who appears in the first two chapters of *A Portrait of the Artist as a Young Man.* She lives in Bray and is the neighbor and childhood friend of Stephen Dedalus. Stephen's attraction to Eileen is tempered by Dante Riordan's admonition not to play with her because the Vances are Protestant. Joyce based this character on his recollections of a childhood playmate of the same name.

**Wells, Charles** He is a minor character who appears both in *Stephen Hero* and in *A Portrait of the Artist as a Young Man.* When Stephen first meets him in chapter 1 of *A Portrait,* Wells is a bully at CLONGOWES WOOD COLLEGE. Wells embarrasses Stephen by asking the boy if he kisses his mother good night and then ridiculing the answer. The narrative also implies that Wells is responsible for the illness that sends Stephen to the infirmary because Wells was the one who had pushed Stephen into the square ditch (the cesspool behind the dormitory) and implores the young boy not to reveal that fact. See also Characters under *Stephen Hero.*

## CONTEMPORARY REVIEWS OF *A PORTRAIT OF THE ARTIST AS A YOUNG MAN*

Excerpt from an unsigned review, "A Study in Garbage," *Everyman,* February 23, 1917, p. 398:

> Mr. James Joyce is an Irish edition of Mr. Caradoc Evans [Welsh author, 1878–1945]. These writers, that is to say, have made it their business in life to portray the least estimable features of their respective countrymen, Irish or Welsh. Mr. Joyce's new book, *A Portrait of an Artist as a Young Man* is an astonishingly powerful and extraordinary dirty study of the upbringing of a young man by Jesuits, which ends—so far as we have been at all able to unravel the meaning of the impressionist ending—with his insanity. The description of life in a Jesuit school, and later in a Dublin college, strikes one as being absolutely true to life—but what a life! Parts of the book are perhaps a little too allusive to be readily understood by the English reader. On pp. 265–6, there is an account of what happened at the Abbey Theatre, Dublin, when The *Countess Cathleen,* by Mr. W. B. Yeats, was put on, but the fact is darkly hidden. Mr. Joyce is a clever novelist, but we feel he would be really at his best in a treatise on drains. . . .

Excerpt from a review by H. G. Wells, "James Joyce," *Nation* xx (February 24, 1917), pp. 710, 712:

> . . . . [*A Portrait of the Artist as a Young Man*] is a book to buy and read and lock up, but it is not a book to miss. Its claim to be literature is as good as the claim of the last book of *Gulliver's Travels.*
>
> It is no good trying to minimize a characteristic that seems to be deliberately obtruded. Like Swift and another living Irish writer, Mr. Joyce has a cloacal obsession. He would bring back into the general picture of life aspects which modern drainage and modern decorum have taken out of ordinary intercourse and conversation. Coarse, unfamiliar words are scattered about the book unpleasantly, and it may seem to many, needlessly. If the reader is squeamish upon these matters, then there is nothing for it but to shun this book, but if he will pick his way, as one has to do at times on the outskirts of some picturesque Italian village with a view and a church and all sorts of things of that sort to tempt one, then it is quite worth while. And even upon this unsavory aspect of Swift and himself, Mr. Joyce is suddenly illuminating. He tells at several points how his hero

Stephen is swayed and shocked and disgusted by harsh and loud sounds, and how he is stirred to intense emotion by music and the rhythms of beautiful words. But no sort of smell offends him like that. He finds olfactory sensations interesting or aesthetically displeasing, but they do not make him sick or excited as sounds do. This is a quite understandable turn over from the more normal state of affairs. Long ago I remember pointing out in a review the difference in the sensory basis of the stories of Robert Louis Stevenson and Sir J. M. Barrie; the former visualized and saw his story primarily as picture, the latter mainly heard it. We shall do Mr. Joyce an injustice if we attribute a normal sensory basis to him and then accuse him of deliberate offense.

But that is by the way. The value of Mr. Joyce's book has little to do with its incidental insanitary condition. Like some of the best novels in the world it is the story of an education; it is by far the most living and convincing picture that exists of an Irish Catholic upbringing. It is a mosaic of jagged fragments that does altogether render with extreme completeness the growth of a rather secretive, imaginative boy in Dublin. The technique is startling, but on the whole it succeeds. Like so many Irish writers from Sterne to Shaw Mr. Joyce is a bold experimentalist with paragraph and punctuation. He breaks away from scene to scene without a hint of the change of time and place; at the end he passes suddenly from the third person to the first; he uses no inverted commas to mark off his speeches. The first trick I found sometimes tiresome here and here, but then my own disposition, perhaps acquired at the blackboard, is to mark off and underline rather fussily, and I do not know whether I was so much put off the thing myself as anxious, which after all is not my business, about its effect on those others; the second trick, I will admit, seems entirely justified in this particular instance by its success; the third reduces Mr. Joyce to a free use of dashes. One conversation in this book is a superb success, the one in which Mr. Dedalus carves the Christmas turkey; I write with all due deliberation that Sterne himself could not have done it better; but most of the talk flickers blindingly with these dashes, one has the same wincing feeling of being flicked at that one used to have in the early cinema shows. I think Mr. Joyce has failed to discredit the inverted comma. . . .

Review by A. Clutton-Brock, "Wild Youth," *Times Literary Supplement,* no. 789 (March 1, 1917), pp. 103–104:

> If we begin by some complaining of the title of this book, it is only because it may turn some people away from it. Others may be put off by occasional improprieties—there is one on the very first page; and it is useless to say that people ought not to be put off by such things. They are; and we should like the book to have as many readers as possible. It is not about the artist as a young man, but about a child, a boy, a youth. As one reads, one remembers oneself in it, at least one reader does; yet, like all good fiction, it is as particular as it is universal. . . .
>
> . . . [Stephen Dedalus] has not enough egotism to have any values, and when the book ends suddenly he is setting out to find some. But for all that he is not futile, because of the drifting passion and the flushing and fading beauty of his mind. Mr. Joyce gives us that, and therefore gives us something that is worth having. It is wild youth, as wild as Hamlet's, and full of wild music.

Excerpt from the review by "A. M.," "A Sensitivist," *Manchester Guardian,* no. 22,018 (March 2, 1917), p. 3:

> When one recognizes genius in a book one can perhaps best leave criticism alone. . . . There are many pages, and not a few whole scenes, in Mr. Joyce's book which are undoubtedly the work of a man of genius, nevertheless, it leaves us combative. The reader—who is as much ignored, and as contemptuously, as it is possible for him to be in a printed work—revolts and asserts himself from time to time, and refuses to sit down passively under the writer's scorn. Once criticism is let loose, it finds range enough and many marks to hit.

Nor for its apparent formlessness should the book be condemned. A subtle sense of art has worked amidst the chaos, making this hither-and-thither record of a young mind and soul . . . a complete and ordered thing. There are ellipses, though, that go beyond the pardonable. A little too much is asked of the even eager reader in the way of understanding situations that have not been led up to, and obscure allusions. One has to be of the family, so to speak, to 'catch on.' This is part of one distinguishing feature of the book—its astounding bad manners. About this one must speak frankly at the start and have done with it. Not all the scenes are touched by genius. Some read like disagreeable phonographic records of the stupid conversations of ill-born and ill-bred youths, compact of futile obscenities, aimless outrages against reasonable decencies—not immoral, but non-moral in a bad-mannered fashion. Perhaps Mr. Joyce wants to show what may be, and often is, the ugly background of fairer things which consent astonishingly to grow in a sordid neighbourhood. Well, there is too much of this background. Also, an idiosyncrasy of Stephen, the central figure of the book—and some of his companions seem to share it—is a passion for foul-smelling things. A doctor could put a definite name to this disease, not an interesting one to the general reader, though Mr. Joyce by his insistence on it seems to think the contrary. One is driven to the conclusion that this gifted and very modern writer who rejects old theories so contemptuously is slave to a new and particularly stupid one.

At the end Stephen has not yet proved his title to the name of artist, but is still looking for a formula to work by. He is a sensitivist. For heat and cold and discomfort, for the atmosphere of persons and companies, he has extra-subtle senses. For the pace of the world, for the things of the soul, too, he has a rare keenness of feeling, and his interpreter gives these exquisite expression. Mr. Joyce's literary gift is beyond praise. At his best he is a master. His methods are hard to define. It is almost without narrative that he depicts inimitably the condition of the Dedalus family in its prosperity and the nameless squalor which it falls into when fortune fails. Lounging feebly among this squalor we find Stephen, helpless against the ruin, but with life in him, the life of the mind, keenly concerned for intellectual experience and for a faith his mind can live by. All this is true and pathetic. True also to this kind of youth is the half-expressed notion that mainly by sin he is to win his way to mental salvation. So convenient a theory for the lounger! Yet Stephen is better than his theory. Among the new-fangled heroes of the newest fiction devoted to the psychology of youth he is almost unique in having known at least once a genuine sense of sin and undergone a genuine struggle. There is drama in Stephen. The struggle might conceivably recur, and from the lounger emerges the man and the artist.

Excerpt from a review by Francis Hackett, "Green Sickness," *New Republic* x, no. 122 (March 3, 1917), pp. 138–139.

There is a laconic unreasonableness about the ways of creators. It is quite true that the Irish literary revival was beginning to be recognized at precisely the period of Mr. Joyce's novel, and it is also true that his protagonist is a student in Dublin at the hour of the so-called renaissance, a writer and poet and dreamer of dreams. So perverse is life, however, there is scarcely one glimmer in this landscape of the flame which is supposed to have illuminated Dublin between 1890 and 1900. If Stephen Dedalus, the young man portrayed in this novel, had belonged to the Irish revival, it would be much easier for outsiders to 'place' him. The essential fact is, he belonged to a more characteristic group which this novel alone has incarnated. One almost despairs of conveying it to the person who has conventionalized his idea of Ireland and modern Irish literature, yet there is a poignant Irish reality to be found in few existing plays and no pre-existent novel, presented here with extraordinary candor and beauty and power. . . . It is only when a person with the invincible honesty of James Joyce comes to write of Dubliners as they are, a person who is said to be mordant largely because he isn't mushy, that the discrepancy between the people and the myth [the myth that the southern 'Irish are a bright and witty people'] is apparent. When one says Dubliners as 'they are', one of course is pronouncing a preference. One is simply insisting that the Irishmen of James Joyce are more nearly like one's own estimate of them than the Irishmen of an amiable fabulist like George Birmingham. But there is the whole of the exquisite *Portrait of the Artist as a Young Man* to substantiate the assertion that a proud, cold, critical, suspicious, meticulous human being is infinitely more to be expected among educated Catholic Irishmen than the sort of squireen whom [the Anglo-Irish writer Charles] Lever [1806–1872] once glorified. If this is a new type in Ireland, come into existence with the recent higher education of Catholics, one can only say that it is now by far the most important type to recognize. Bernard Shaw suggested it in the London Irishman, Larry Doyle, who appeared in "John Bull's Other Island," but the main character of the present novel is much more subtly inflected and individualized than Larry Doyle, and is only said to belong to a type to intimate that his general mode is characteristic. . . .

A novel in which a sensitive, critical young man is completely expressed as he is can scarcely be expected to be pleasant. "A Portrait of the Artist as a Young Man" is not entirely pleasant. But it has such beauty, such love of beauty, such intensity of feeling, such pathos, such candor, it goes beyond anything in English that reveals the inevitable malaise of serious youth. Mr. Joyce has a peculiar narrative method, and he would have made things clearer if he had adopted H. G. Wells's scheme of giving a paragraphed section to each episode. As the book is now arranged, it requires some imagination on the part of the reader. The Catholic 'retreat' also demands attentiveness, it is reported with such acrimonious zeal. But no one who has any conception of the Russian-like frustrations and pessimisms of the thin-skinned and fine-grained Irishman, from early boarding school onward, can miss the tenacious fidelity of James Joyce. He has made a rare effort to transcend every literary convention as to his race and creed, and he has had high success. Many people will furiously resent his candor, whether about religion or nationalism or sex. But candor is a nobility in this instance.

Unsigned review, "A Dyspeptic Portrait," *Freeman's Journal,* April 7, 1917, n.p.:

Great literature . . . does not spring easily from the mood of satiety and disgust. Yet the mood is all too common amongst a certain section of modern novelists. Man delights them not nor woman neither; like Hamlet. "This brave o'erhanging firmament, this magestical roof fretted with golden fire," appears to them "a foul and pestilential congregation of vapours." The high priest of the school is Huysmans—the earlier Huysmans—who paraded before Europe, not as Byron did "The pageant of a bleeding heart," but of a tortured liver. With most of his disciples the pose has no reality; the blue devils dance in their pages merely to shock the bourgeois. Mr. Joyce, however, takes himself more seriously. The starting thing in his work is not the mimicry of Huysmans' methods—anybody with a deft pen can manage that—but the similarity of outlook; and the result is a book nearer to [Huysmans'] "En Menage" then anything written in English. "A Portrait of the Artist" has notable positive merits. Mr. Joyce's prose is masterly in its terseness and force; even his most casual descriptions haunt the mind by their vividness and wonderful economy of line. What he sees he can reproduce in words with a precision as rare as it is subtle; the pity is, that in one of his own phrases the memory of these things has too often "coated his palate with the scum of disgust." Take, for instance, this vignette of a tea-table.

He pushed open the latchless door of the porch and passed through the naked hallway, into the kitchen. A group of his brothers and sisters was sitting round the table. Tea was nearly over, and only the last of the second watered tea remained in the bottom of the small glass jars and jam pots which did service for tea-cups. Discarded crusts and lumps of sugared bread, turned brown by the tea which had been poured over them, lay scattered on the table, and little wells of tea lay here and there on a board, and a knife with a broken ivory handle was struck through the pith of a ravaged turnover.

Had it been a description of the desolation of No Man's Land on the Somme or the Yser, the horror could hardly have been laid on more thickly, and all through the book food is scarcely mentioned without the same shudder of disgust, which is more reminiscent of the pangs of dyspepsia than of the joy of art. Had the author confined himself to this particular form of ugliness it would not have been so bad, but, as Whistler said of Oscar Wilde, that he could not keep out of the area, so Mr. Joyce plunges and drags his readers after him into the slime of foul sewers. He is not, indeed, like Mr. George Moore, who points to the iridiscence as a proof of the beauty of corruption. Mr. Joyce knows better, but despite his repulsion his pen, instead of pointing to me stars overhead, is degraded into a muck-sake. This is due in a measure to a false theory of aesthetics, but it springs even more from temperamental defects. Tennyson, on his salad days, wrote "The Confessions of a Second-rate Sensitive Mind," and the description would make an admirable subtitle for "A Portrait of the Artist as [a] Young Man." The great masters have not been blind to the aspects of life that Mr. Joyce exploits, but they see them in their true perspective and do not dwell on them to the exclusion of everything else. They know the value of proportion and the importance of sanity and clear judgment and realise that to see life steadily one must see it whole. It is an accident that Mr. Joyce's book should have Dublin as its background. A youth of the temperamental quality of his Stephen Dedalus was bound to react just as sharply against any other environment; had he been brought up in an English cathedral town or an American industrial centre he would have pilloried them in just as repellant a fashion. Yet English critics, with a complacency that makes one despair of their intelligence, are already hailing the author as a typical Irishman, and his book as a faithful picture of Irish life. It would be just as accurate to declare that DeQuincey's "Opium Eater" embodied the experience of the average English youth or that Carlyle's splenetic railings reflected the emotions of Victorian England.

Excerpt from a review by J. C. Squire, "Mr. James Joyce," *New Statesman* ix (April 14, 1917), p. 40:

> His prose instrument is a remarkable one. Few contemporary writers are effective in such diverse ways; his method varies with the subject-matter and never fails him. His dialogue (as in the remarkable discussions at home about Parnell and Stephen's education) is as close to the dialogue of life as anything I have ever come across; though he does not make the gramophonic mistake of spinning it out as it is usually spun out in life and in novels that aim at a faithful reproduction of life and only succeed in sending one to sleep. And his descriptive and narrative passages include at one pole sounding periods of classical prose and at the other disjointed and almost futuristic sentences.
>
> . . . This is not everybody's book. The later portion, consisting largely of rather dull student discussions, is dull; nobody could be inspired by the story, and it had better be neglected by any one who is easily disgusted. Its interest is mainly technical, using the word in its broadest sense; and its greatest appeal, consequently, is made to the practising artist in literature. What Mr. Joyce will do with his powers in the future it is impossible to conjecture. I conceive that he does not know himself: that, indeed, the discovery of a form is the greatest problem in front of him. It is doubtful if he will make a novelist.

Excerpt from an unsigned review of *A Portrait of the Artist as a Young Man* in *Irish Book Lover*, April–May 1917, viii, nos. 9–10, p. 113:

> . . . Mr. Joyce is unsparing in his realism, and his violent contrasts—the brothel, the confes-

sional—jar on one's finer feelings. So do the quips and jeers of the students, in language unprinted in literature since the days of Swift and Sterne, following on some eloquent and orthodox sermons! That Mr. Joyce is a master of a brilliant description style and handles his dialogue as ably as any living writer is conceded on all hands, and, oh! the pity of it. In writing thus he is just to his fine gifts? Is it even wise, from a worldly point of view—mercenary, if you will—to dissipate one's talents on a book which can only attain a limited circulation?—for no clean-minded person could possibly allow it to remain within reach of his wife, his sons or daughters. Above all, is it Art? We doubt it.

From John Quinn, "James Joyce, A New Irish Novelist," *Vanity Fair,* May 1917, viii, no. 3, pp. 48, 128:

The book places James Joyce in the same rank with James Stephens and John M. Synge.

From John Macy's review, "James Joyce," *The Dial* lxii, No. 744 (June 14, 1917):

Joyce's work is outspoken, vigorous, original, beautiful.

From a review of *A Portrait of the Artist as a Young Man* published in the *Times* and reprinted in *Extract from Press Notices of* A Portrait of the Artist as a Young Man *by James Joyce (The Egoist,* Ltd.: London: 1916):

Like all good fiction it is as particular as it is universal. . . . Mr. Joyce can make anything happen that he chooses. He can present the external world excellently. . . . No living writer is better at conversations. . . . It is more real than real talk. . . . It is wild youth, as wild as Hamlet's, and full of wild music.

From Margaret Anderson's note on *A Portrait of the Artist as a Young Man* published in *The Little Review* iii. (No. 10 [April 1917]), pp. 9–10.

This James Joyce book is the most beautiful piece of writing and the most creative piece of prose anywhere to be seen on the horizon today. It is consciously a work of Art in a way that *Jean-Christophe* made no effort to be; it is such head and shoulders above *Jacob Stahl* or Gilbert Cannan's *Mendel* that one must realize those books as very good novels and this as something quite more than that. It can be spoken of in terms that apply to *Pelle the Conqueror,* but only in this way: each is a work of Art and therefore not to be talked of as lesser or greater; but while *Pelle* is made of language as it has been used the *Portrait* is made of language as it will come to be used. There is no doubt that we will have novels before long written without even as much of the conventional structure of language as Mr. Joyce has adhered to—a new kind of 'dimension in language' which is being felt in many places and which George Soule has illustrated beautifully in an article in *The New Republic.*

But that isn't the most important thing. The interest in *Pelle* is in the way its stories are told. The interest in the *Portrait* is in the way its aesthetic is presented. . . .

## *Stephen Hero* (1944)

This is the title of the novel begun by Joyce on his 22nd birthday, February 2, 1904, shortly after the editors of DANA had rejected his essay "A Portrait of the Artist" because they deemed its contents unsuitable for their magazine. Textual evidence suggests that Joyce reworked much of the essay and incorporated it into the novel. Indeed, it is useful to see *Stephen Hero* as a transitional work from the aesthetic manifesto of "A Portrait of the Artist" to the creative achievements of *A Portrait of the Artist as a Young Man.* At the same time, readers need to make clear distinctions between Joyce's initial effort to write a novel-length prose fiction and the work that appeared in print a decade after the project began. Although it is evident that *Stephen Hero* includes many of the same characters and incidents that later appeared in *A Portrait of the Artist as a Young Man,* this earlier work takes a much more literal, realistic approach to the subject, with none of the stylistic innovations that make *A Portrait* the prototypical modernist novel. *Stephen Hero* stands as an important document in tracing Joyce's creative development, but its literary value, whatever that might be, remains distinctly separate from what he accomplished in *A Portrait of the Artist as a Young Man.*

What should be kept in mind is that *Stephen Hero* marks Joyce's first steps as a fiction writer. By April 1904, Joyce had completed the first 11 chapters of the book, and he continued writing even after he began the stories that would make up *Dubliners.* By the time he ceased work on *Stephen Hero* in June or early July 1905, he had written 914 manuscript pages, "about half the book" by his own estimate (*Letters,* II.132). Joyce turned his back on the traditional, 19th-century novel form manifested in *Stephen Hero* when, in September 1907, he began *A Portrait of the Artist as a Young Man.* Nonetheless, for whatever reason, he retained at least a portion of the *Stephen Hero* manuscript. An apocryphal story surrounding this manuscript—that Joyce out of despair over publication problems had thrown it into the fire only to have it rescued by Nora—was circulated by Sylvia Beach in her 1935 catalogue and later by Herbert Gorman in *James Joyce* (196). In fact, the manuscript that Joyce, sometime in 1911, had thrown into the fire out of anger over publication problems with *Dubliners* was that of *A Portrait of the Artist as a Young Man,* and it was retrieved not by Nora but by his sister Eileen. (For further details, see *Letters,* I.136; John J. Slocum and Herbert Cahoon, *A Bibliography of James Joyce,* 136–137; and Richard Ellmann, *James Joyce,* 314.)

An overview of the extant narrative may not fully explain Joyce's apparent disdain for the work. However, it does give one a sense of why he would wish to remove it from his canon. *Stephen Hero* is like none of the other prose fiction that Joyce produced over his lifetime, although it does anticipate themes found in Joyce's later works: Stephen's emerging artistic consciousness, for example, and the conflicts he faces within the confines of his social and religious environment. Some critics, such as Thomas E. Connolly, caution readers that *Stephen Hero* should be "the last of the Joyce texts" to be read, for only then will it be useful, and that it "should not be considered as a fragment of a novel, nor even as the first draft of a novel, because it does not fit into the genre of a novel at all" ("*Stephen Hero,*" in Zack Bowen and James F. Carens, eds., *A Companion to Joyce Studies,* 232). Others may agree with Theodore Spencer in his introduction to *Stephen Hero* that the fragment "can stand on its own merits as a remarkable piece of work" (18). The stylistic and narrative innovations that one associates with Joyce's other writing from *Dubliners* through *Finnegans Wake* are absent from *Stephen Hero.* In spite of the limitations of the work, *Stephen Hero* is of importance to the understanding of Joyce's growth as a writer.

## SYNOPSIS

The existing fragment of *Stephen Hero* opens with a truncated chapter beginning in mid-sentence. (Hans Walter Gabler has since renumbered the chapters of the novel, and this has resulted in a slight variation from the form of the work edited first by Theodore Spencer and then later by John J. Slocum and Herbert Cahoon. This entry uses Gabler's numbering system, with the original chapter number given in parentheses. For details of Gabler's argument for renumbering, see his essay "The Seven Lost Years of *A Portrait of the Artist as a Young Man.*" The opening narrative describes the president of UNIVERSITY COLLEGE, DUBLIN, and refers to the university bursar and to Father Butt, the dean of the college. Much of the remainder of this first fragment deals with the college life of Stephen Daedalus, as Joyce spelled the name throughout this novel (see under Characters, below) and specifically with Stephen's budding reputation as a unique and formidable intellect based upon his work in Father Butt's English composition class: "It was in this class that Stephen first made his name" (*SH* 26).

The next chapter, 16, offers a more concrete indication of Stephen's ability by detailing the elaborate compositional exercises undertaken by Stephen as a means of honing his creative skills. As a way of contextualizing his struggle for artistic identity, it goes on to describe his often uneasy relations with other students who are bemused by Stephen's taste and behavior. The narrative also highlights Stephen's increasing lack of interest in his classes. The chapter provides evidence of Stephen's sophistication when it touches upon specific Continental writers—Maeterlinck, IBSEN, Turgenev—whose works influenced Stephen's views on art, and by extension it highlights the intellectual and artistic distance between him and others at the university.

Chapter 17 touches upon Stephen's home life and upon his efforts to prepare an essay. It also shows, in Stephen's exchanges with Madden (a variation on the Davin character who will appear in *A Portrait of the Artist as a Young Man*), his unwillingness to submit even to a minimal degree to the authority of Irish nationalism. At this same time, Stephen begins to study Irish. This may seem to conflict with his attitude toward Irish nationalism, but as the narrative quickly reveals he is seeking in this indirect way to gain favor with a girl, Emma Clery. (In *A Portrait of the Artist as a Young Man,* she is referred to only by her initials, E—— C——.)

Chapter 18 (18 and 19 in the old system) describes Stephen's meeting with Charles Wells, an old classmate from CLONGOWES WOOD COLLEGE. (Wells will subsequently appear in chapter 1 of *A Portrait* as the bully who pushes Stephen into the square ditch, though he has no further involvement in that novel's narrative.) Wells is studying for the priesthood at the seminary in Clonliffe, though their exchange makes it seem a pragmatic rather than an idealistic choice. The narrative then goes on to describe Stephen's essay "Drama and Life" and his efforts to interest friends in his aesthetic views. This is an important juncture, for it draws attention to Stephen's desire to gain acceptance as much as to declare his imaginative independence. Despite the iconoclastic tone of his ideas, Stephen does not articulate them simply to shock or distance others. Rather, he sees these views as essential to an aesthetic system upon which he intends to base his own work and which he strongly wishes his peers would embrace. The chapter ends with Stephen and the president of UCD discussing the president's objections to Stephen's essay, which Stephen had planned to present as a lecture to the Literary and Historical Society.

Without clearly resolving the issue of the president's objections, chapter 19 (20 old system) offers an account of the presentation of Stephen's paper and of the responses, both hostile and laudatory, that it elicits from his fellow students. There is also a description of Stephen's refusal to sign the "testimonial of admiration for . . . the Tsar of Russia" (*SH* 114). The chapter concludes with discussions between Cranly and Stephen about the Catholic Church.

Chapter 20 (21 old system) traces Stephen's growing friendship with Cranly, and outlines his growing alienation from the institutional aspect of Roman CATHOLICISM. Like Stephen, Cranly takes a cynical view of much that goes on within the university community, and he shows little patience for the docile hypocrisy of his classmates. Unlike Stephen, however, Cranly contents himself with expressions of disdain and aloofness, and does not endeavor to make direct challenges to university authority. In juxtaposition to the way these views are developed in *A Portrait of the Artist as a Young Man,* through detailed conversations with Cranly, readers of *Stephen Hero* first see directly the conflict that arises between Stephen and his mother, who is deeply concerned about her son's loss of faith, and then hear the elaboration of his position through exchanges with Cranly.

Chapter 21 (22 old system) shows Stephen temporarily without the moral support of Cranly, who has gone to Wicklow, and the absence underscores how different Stephen remains from most of the others at the university. The narrative reinforces this view through its account of Stephen's desultory courtship of Emma Clery. As with the discourse on Stephen's artistic views, exchanges with Emma reflect Stephen's desire for acceptance even as they highlight his unwillingness, even inability, to change to accommodate the views of others.

Chapter 22 (23 old system) brings home the harshness of the Daedalus family's life and Stephen's sense of alienation particularly from his father, with a poignant description of the death and burial of Stephen's sister Isabel, whose illness was announced in the preceding episode. The chapter goes on to describe Stephen's second year at the university as a time of growing restlessness. Chapter 23 (24 old system) deals with the publication of a new college magazine, which Joyce based on the magazine ST STEPHEN'S. It also describes the final break between Stephen and Emma Clery over his rejection of conventional courtship and his frank avowal of sexual desire.

Chapter 24 (25 old system) shows Stephen's continuing intellectual attraction to the Catholic Church, despite his obvious unwillingness to submit to its authority. An analogous conflict with what Stephen sees as illegitimate authority occurs in his deteriorating relations with his father. There is also an EPIPHANY, similar to the one that ends the *Dubliners* short story "Araby," which leads him to compose "The Villanelle of the Temptress." (In *A Portrait of the Artist as a Young Man*, Stephen composes a poem of the same name after an erotic dream.) Finally, Stephen describes to Cranly his emerging aesthetic theory. (This passage is similar to the conversation Stephen Dedalus has with Vincent Lynch in chapter 5 of *A Portrait*.) Chapter 25 (26 old system) describes the final weeks before the end of the college's spring term.

The continuous narration of the manuscript ends here. However, the 1963 edition of *Stephen Hero* contains additional manuscript pages that begin to describe the events of the summer Stephen spent with Mr. Fulham, his godfather and benefactor, in Mullingar. Nothing like this made it into *A Portrait of the Artist as a Young Man*.

## PUBLICATION HISTORY

While living in Paris, Joyce gave the manuscript of *Stephen Hero* to Sylvia BEACH, who subsequently sold it to the Harvard College Library in 1938. In 1944, with permission of the Harvard College Library and Joyce's executors, Theodore SPENCER first published a manuscript fragment under the title *Stephen Hero*. Spencer did this despite a letter dated April 22, 1939, and written by Paul LÉON to Spencer on Joyce's behalf expressing Joyce's uneasiness at the prospect of this fragment being published. What Spencer actually intended, however, remains unclear, for he assured Joyce that he did not plan to publish the manuscript. On May 8, 1939, he had convinced David Fleischmann, George Joyce's stepson and hence Joyce's stepgrandson, to write to Paul Léon and offer him Spencer's assurances that he did not wish to publish the manuscript. (Both letters are part of the Joyce-Léon collection housed at the NATIONAL LIBRARY OF IRELAND, first made available in April 1992. For further details, see *The James Joyce Paul Léon Papers*, p. 117.) Additional pages of *Stephen Hero* subsequently appeared and were incorporated into the revised version of *Stephen Hero*, edited by John J. SLOCUM and Herbert CAHOON, and published in 1963.

## HELPFUL ANNOTATIONS

Marc A. Mamigonian and John Noel Turner, "Annotations for *Stephen Hero*," *James Joyce Quarterly* 40 (Spring 2003), 347–518.

Portions of the *Stephen Hero* manuscript are held by Harvard University, Yale University, and Cornell University.

## CHARACTERS

**Artifoni, Father** He is a character who appears in *Stephen Hero*. Artifoni teaches Italian to Stephen Daedalus at UNIVERSITY COLLEGE, DUBLIN. He is modeled on Joyce's Italian instructor there, Rev. Charles GHEZZI, SJ. However, Joyce took the surname for this character from his employer at the Berlitz school in POLA, Signor Almidano Artifoni. (See also Artifoni, Almidano, in Characters under *Ulysses*.)

**Butt, D., SJ** He appears as the dean of students at UNIVERSITY COLLEGE, DUBLIN, where he also teaches English. Although the dean of students is not identified by name in chapter 5 of *A Portrait of the Artist as a Young Man*, that character is probably also Father Butt, for the scene there replicates Stephen's encounter with Father Butt in the opening pages of the *Stephen Hero* fragment. Joyce probably modeled his depiction of Father Butt on his recollections of the Rev. Joseph DARLINGTON, SJ, dean of studies and professor of English at University College when Joyce attended (1898–1902).

**Clery, Emma** She is the conventional young woman who is the object of Stephen Daedalus's romantic fantasies. In chapter 23 (24 old system), Stephen shocks her with the bluntness of his proposition that they engage in a night of sexual gratification and then part forever.

**Cranly** In *Stephen Hero* and *A Portrait of the Artist as a Young Man* Cranly appears as a close friend of Stephen Dedalus. In *Stephen Hero* Cranly provides the audience for Stephen's discussion of his ideas on aesthetics. Cranly is modeled on Joyce's friend and confidant, John Francis BYRNE.

**Daedalus, Isabel** She is a younger sister of Stephen Daedalus, whose illness colors the Daedalus family life for the first half of the manuscript. Because of poor health, Isabel is asked to leave her convent and return home to live, much against her father's wishes. Not long after her return, she dies. The end of chapter 21 and the beginning of chapter 22 (22 and 23 old system) of the novel vividly narrate her death and its effect on Stephen and the Daedalus family. Joyce based the incident of Isabel's death on the untimely demise of his brother George, who died in 1902.

**Daedalus, Maurice** See Maurice.

**Daedalus, Mrs** She is Stephen Daedalus's mother. In chapter 18 (19 old system), Stephen reads her his essay on IBSEN and later gives her a few of Ibsen's plays to read. In chapter 20 (21 old system), she is upset when she learns that Stephen is no longer a practicing Catholic. Mrs. Daedalus is the prototype of May Dedalus, the mother in *A Portrait of the Artist as a Young Man.* In both works, she stands as a figure who, despite the increasing poverty that oppresses the family, upholds traditional values and shields her son from his father's criticism.

**Daedalus, Simon** He stands as the titular, if ineffectual, head of the Daedalus household in *Stephen Hero,* and precursor of Simon Dedalus in *A Portrait of the Artist as a Young Man* and *Ulysses,* in which the classical spelling of the surname is modified. Mr. Daedalus's domineering personality and his improvident and alcoholic ways are modeled on those of Joyce's father, John Stanislaus JOYCE. In *Stephen Hero,* Simon Daedalus is portrayed as a type rather than as a character. He is an angry and embittered man who resents his own family and whose social and financial downfall he blames on others. The narrator's exposition of Mr. Daedalus's character, as found, for example, in chapter 19 (20 old system) is much more direct and less skillfully crafted than in either *A Portrait of the Artist as a Young Man* or *Ulysses.*

**Daedalus, Stephen** He appears as the central character in Joyce's unfinished novel, *Stephen Hero.* In essence the same figure, albeit with a more subtly evolved identity, appears in *A Portrait of the Artist as a Young Man* and *Ulysses* with the spelling of the name *Daedalus* modified to *Dedalus.*

It remains important to keep in mind that, just as the Stephen Dedalus of *Ulysses* differs somewhat from his namesake in the previous novel, the Stephen Dedalus of *A Portrait of the Artist as a Young Man* represents an evolution from the Stephen Daedalus of *Stephen Hero.* Although, as with *A Portrait,* Joyce intended *Stephen Hero* to trace the maturation of his central character from childhood to young adulthood, because only a fragment of the work has survived we see the protagonist only during his university period. Nonetheless, if we contrast him with the Stephen of chapter 5 of *A Portrait,* he emerges as stiffer, less complex, and surely less articulate.

**John, Uncle** He is one of Stephen Daedalus's two maternal uncles. He puts in a brief appearance in *Stephen Hero* (*SH* 166) during the family's mourning over the death of Isabel Daedalus. At the Daedalus home, he criticizes in sanctimonious fashion the immoral books available in Dublin bookstores, only to be ridiculed by Stephen's brother, Maurice Daedalus. Joyce used his maternal uncle, John Goulding (the brother of Richie Goulding, see Characters under *Ulysses*), as a model for this character.

**Keane, Mr** He appears in *Stephen Hero* as a leader (editorial) writer for the *FREEMAN'S JOURNAL* and a professor of English composition at UNIVERSITY COLLEGE, DUBLIN, where he is one of Stephen Daedalus's teachers. Although he does not appear in *A Portrait of the Artist as a Young Man,* an analogous character, Professor Hugh MacHugh, does appear in the Aeolus episode (chapter 7) of *Ulysses.*

MacHugh, however, seems to be more a visitor to than an employee of the *Freeman's Journal,* and while he clearly knows Stephen, no specific university connection is made. (See also MacHugh, Hugh, in Characters under *Ulysses.*)

**Madden** He appears in *Stephen Hero* as a student from Limerick with outspoken nationalist sympathies. Madden is a friend of Stephen Daedalus at UNIVERSITY COLLEGE, DUBLIN, where he is "recognized as the spokesman of the patriotic party" (*SH* 39). Madden serves as a foil for Stephen's (and most likely Joyce's) views on Irish nationalism. Joyce probably drew the details of his character from features of his friend George CLANCY. In chapter 5 of *A Portrait of the Artist as a Young Man,* the figure of Madden is replaced by Davin, a student with similar nationalist sentiments. (See Clancy in Characters under *A Portrait of the Artist as a Young Man* and also in Characters under *Ulysses.*)

**Maurice [Dedalus/Daedalus]** He is the younger brother of Stephen Daedalus; glancing references are made to him as well in *A Portrait of the Artist as a Young Man* and *Ulysses,* where he is called Stephen's whetstone.

*Stephen Hero* offers a more detailed sense of the relationship between the brothers. Specifically, it shows how while growing up Stephen uses Maurice as a sounding board upon which to test his emerging aesthetic and artistic views. Joyce's brother Stanislaus JOYCE, who had often critiqued his brother's efforts during Joyce's early writing career, clearly served as the model for Maurice, and according to Richard ELLMANN, Stanislaus was disappointed to see that many references to the character Maurice were dropped when Joyce revised *Stephen Hero* into *A Portrait of the Artist as a Young Man.*

**Moran, Father** He is a priest who appears in both *Stephen Hero* and *A Portrait of the Artist as a Young Man.* Although he expresses nationalist sentiments and his friendship with Emma Clery arouses a measure of jealousy in Stephen Daedalus, his character is never developed beyond that of a type.

**Temple** He is a character who appears in both *Stephen Hero* and *A Portrait of the Artist as a Young Man.* Temple is an acquaintance of Stephen Daedalus, who, with Stephen, attends UNIVERSITY COLLEGE, DUBLIN. The character of Temple was based on a Dublin medical student, John Elwood, whom Joyce came to know through Oliver St. John GOGARTY.

**Wells, Charles** When Stephen is at UNIVERSITY COLLEGE, DUBLIN, he encounters Wells, who by that time has become a seminarian pursuing his studies for the priesthood at the Clonliffe seminary. When at Clongowes, Joyce had two classmates with the last name of Wells.

# *Ulysses* (1922)

This is Joyce's mock-heroic, epic novel. It celebrates the events of one day (June 16, 1904) in the lives of three Dubliners, the novel's main characters: Leopold Bloom, his wife, Molly Bloom, and Stephen Dedalus (see Characters, below). This June day is known to Joyceans everywhere as BLOOMSDAY. Published on Joyce's 40th birthday (February 2, 1922), *Ulysses* is a landmark in 20th-century literature and a watershed in the history of the novel, and, next to *Finnegans Wake,* it stands as Joyce's most sustained and innovative creative effort.

## COMPOSITION BACKGROUND AND PUBLICATION HISTORY

Joyce began writing *Ulysses* in late 1914 or early 1915, a time marked by major transitions in his literary career and in his private life: *Giacomo Joyce* was written some time in 1914, *Dubliners* was published in June 1914; *Exiles* was finished in 1915 (published in 1918); and *A Portrait of the Artist as a Young Man* (previously serialized in the EGOIST) was published in book form in the United States by B. W. HUEBSCH in December 1916. In 1915, the Joyce family moved from TRIESTE to ZURICH, where they resided for four years before moving to PARIS in July 1920 after a brief return to Trieste in October 1919.

Joyce wrote steadily on his novel while in Zurich; however, both financial and health problems interrupted his work during the time he spent there. Joyce managed to support his family by giving language lessons and through public and private subsidies of his income. Through the efforts of Ezra POUND and William Butler YEATS, Joyce was awarded a grant in 1915 from the Royal Literary Fund, and, beginning in 1917, Harriet Shaw WEAVER started providing Joyce with financial support on a regular basis that lasted throughout his life. Mrs. Harold McCormick (Edith Rockefeller) also provided financial assistance from early 1918 to the fall of 1919. Nonetheless, the Joyce family's finances were at times precarious. Furthermore, while in Zurich, Joyce suffered serious eye troubles and in August 1917 underwent the first of his several eye operations, after which he and his family spent several months in Locarno, where the climate was milder. Despite all this, Zurich stood as a pleasant and productive time.

Joyce's original idea for a story called *Ulysses* goes back to 1906 (see *Letters,* II.190). It was to be included in *Dubliners* and to feature a Mr. (Alfred H.) HUNTER, an actual Dubliner who Joyce believed was Jewish (see *Letters,* II.168). But because of unfavorable circumstances in Joyce's life at that time, the story, as he explained in 1907 to his brother Stanislaus, "never got any forrader than the title" (*Letters,* II.209). This initial idea, however, remained with Joyce for eight or nine more years before it began to take shape in a radically new way, forming the foundation of the novel. By June 1915 Joyce had prepared an outline of *Ulysses* that contained 22 chapters (rather than its present 18) and had completed one chapter. On a postcard to Stanislaus, Joyce commented: "The first episode of my new novel *Ulysses* is written. The first part, the Telemachiad, consists of four episodes: the second of fifteen, that is, Ulysses' wanderings: and the third, Ulysses' return home, of three more episodes" (*Selected Letters,* 209). By 1918 *Ulysses* began to appear serially in the American journal the *LITTLE REVIEW.* A year earlier, Ezra POUND, the journal's European correspondent, had lent his assistance to Joyce, and the journal's editor, Margaret ANDERSON, realized early on that Joyce's work would be the finest writing she would ever print. Fourteen installments of the novel—from the Telemachus episode (chapter 1) to the first part of the Oxen of the Sun episode (chapter 14)—were published in 23 successive issues from March 1918 through September–December 1920. Pound was also instrumental in getting portions of *Ulysses* published in Harriet Shaw WEAVER's London periodical, the *EGOIST.* But this journal printed only three episodes and a portion of a fourth (Nestor, Proteus, Hades, and The Wandering Rocks), which appeared from its January–February 1919 through December 1919 issues. Publication of installments eventually ceased because Weaver could not find an English printer who was willing to risk prosecution to set the type for any of the other chapters. (Printers in England were as liable as publishers and authors.)

James Joyce after one of a series of operations performed on his eyes *(James Joyce Collection, Beinecke Rare Book and Manuscript Library, Yale University)*

As Joyce's creative ideas matured over the eight-year period in which he composed the novel, both its form and its content changed considerably. Even after portions of *Ulysses* were serialized, Joyce's composition process continued to evolve. He extensively expanded some sections of the work, revised others, and made overall structural and stylistic alterations to suit his current thinking. But other modifications of the text also occurred. During the *Little Review* serialization, Ezra Pound and Margaret Anderson made unauthorized deletions. They believed that some passages, if published, would lead to legal problems. Their strategy, however, did not work. Four issues of the *Little Review* were eventually seized and burned by the U.S. Post Office, causing Joyce to remark in a February 1920 letter to Harriet Shaw Weaver: "This is the second time I have had the pleasure of being burned while on earth so that I hope I shall pass through the fires of purgatory as quickly as my patron S. Aloysius" (*Letters,* I.137; Joyce's confirmation name was Aloysius). In September 1920, the New York Society for the Suppression of Vice filed a legal complaint against the Nausikaa episode, which appeared in the July–August 1920 issue of the *Little Review.* The case was brought to court and tried, and in February 1921, Margaret Anderson and her coeditor, Jane HEAP, were found guilty of publishing obscenity, fined $50 each, and prohibited from publishing any further episodes of *Ulysses.* Their attorney was John QUINN, a New York lawyer and patron of the arts who in 1917 had purchased from Joyce the manuscript of *Exiles.* He was also acquiring *Ulysses* manuscripts. Although Quinn disliked Anderson, Heap, and their magazine for, in his opinion, exploiting artistic talent, he nevertheless did his best to win the case, knowing that failure could prevent the book from being published altogether. Quinn's defense attempted to demonstrate the novel's virtual incomprehensibility. The tactic was straightforward but unconvincing to the three judges. The two defendants themselves were also upset with his strategy, and Joyce was bewildered. Quinn's biographer, B. L. Reid, and others, however, have suggested that Quinn actually laid the foundation for Judge John M. WOOLSEY's 1933 court decision to lift the ban on the novel.

The decision rendered against the *Little Review* and its coeditors as well as the earlier reluctance of printers to set type for individual portions of *Ulysses* presaged the difficulties Joyce would face in publishing the final version of the novel. As the work neared completion, he made a number of unsuccessful attempts to find a publisher and was on the point of giving up when in 1921 Sylvia BEACH offered to publish it under the imprint of her Paris bookstore, SHAKESPEARE AND COMPANY. By aggressively pursuing subscribers for the first edition, Beach managed to secure sufficient capital to finance the project. She also found a printer in Dijon, Maurice DARANTIERE, who not only agreed to print the work as it stood but who willingly provided Joyce with multiple galley proofs (sheets printed for checking and correcting purposes) so that he could carry on the process of revising and expanding his novel almost to the day of its publication. In late June 1921, about eight months before the publication of *Ulysses,* Joyce estimated that he had spent approximately 20,000 hours in writing the novel (*Letters,* I.166). He often worked 16 hours a day on it (*Letters,* I.170).

Beach continued to bring out successive editions of *Ulysses* throughout the 1920s, although commercially it does not seem to have been a very profitable enterprise. The EGOIST PRESS in London brought out the first British edition, printed in France in October 1922. In 1932, after difficult negotiations between Joyce and Beach, the Odyssey Press in Germany (with locations in Hamburg, Paris, and Bologna) took over publication on the European continent. Odyssey issued four impressions between December 1932 and April 1939, and corrected typographical errors in the text, making its edition one of the most reliable. In 1934 RANDOM HOUSE, through the shrewd efforts of its cofounder Bennett CERF and his legal counsel Morris Ernst, brought out the first American edition of *Ulysses,* about a month after Judge Woolsey's decision on December 6, 1933, to lift the ban on its appearance in the United States (see the appendix on page 392). In 1936 the London publisher John Lane published the BODLEY HEAD edition, the first British edition of *Ulysses* to be printed in Britain. In 1984 Hans Walter Gabler and a team of German editors produced the first major revision of the work, published as a "critical and synoptic" edition in three volumes by GARLAND Publishing in New York and London. Two years later a single-volume trade edition of *Ulysses* based on Gabler's revised text was published by Random House (see GABLER EDITION). Almost immediately after the lapse in European copyright protection in 1992, a number of publishing houses issued editions of

*Ulysses.* These, however, generally relied on previous editions for their texts, and, as of the date of this writing, while several scholars announced large-scale editing projects, none successfully published a full-scale revision of *Ulysses* equaling Gabler's (see the appendix on page 381). Subsequently, between 1993 and 1996 the European Union extended copyright protection to 70 years after the author's death. In 1998 the United States Congress enacted similar legislation. This means that any proposed new editions of *Ulysses* as of this writing can appear only with the permission of the literary executors of Joyce's estate.

One finds ample evidence of Joyce's process of composition of *Ulysses* in material held by various institutions in the United States and England. The final holograph manuscript of *Ulysses* is held by the Rosenbach Foundation of Philadelphia (see the ROSENBACH MUSEUM AND LIBRARY). Notebooks that Joyce used are at the British Library and at the University Library at the State University of New York at Buffalo. Other prepublication material is held by the Houghton Library at Harvard University, the Cornell University Library, the University of Wisconsin–Milwaukee Library, the Firestone Library at Princeton University, the Harry Ransom Humanities Research Center at the University of Texas, and the Morris Library at Southern Illinois University. *The* JAMES JOYCE ARCHIVES, vols. 12–27, published by Garland, contain most of the extant notes, drafts, typescripts, and proofs for *Ulysses.* In 2002, the NATIONAL LIBRARY OF IRELAND acquired additional prepublication material for *Ulysses.*

## STRUCTURE AND SYNOPSIS OF *ULYSSES* (SEE APPENDICES FOR *ULYSSES* SCHEMA)

The formal structure of *Ulysses* is based on a compositional framework that appears every bit as complex as its publishing history. There are three major parts of the novel. The Telemachia consists of three episodes: Telemachus (chapter 1), Nestor (chapter 2), and Proteus (chapter 3). This section focuses on Stephen Dedalus, and, as in HOMER's *ODYSSEY,* it places emphasis upon a young man's search for his father and the transition from childhood to adult life. *Telemachiad* (spelled with a final *d*) is the traditional term for the first of three divisions of Homer's *Odyssey,* divisions that Joyce adapted for *Ulysses.*

*The Wanderings of Ulysses* is an informal designation for the middle section of *Ulysses,* chapters 4 through 15, consisting of Calypso, Lotus-Eaters, Hades, Aeolus, Lestrygonians, Scylla and Charybdis, The Wandering Rocks, Sirens, Cyclops, Nausikaa, Oxen of the Sun, and Circe. The phrase underscores the idea of exile, a central feature of this portion of the narrative, which traces the peregrinations of Leopold Bloom (see Characters, below) around Dublin on June 16, 1904, from the time he leaves his home (chapter 4, Calypso) until he rescues Stephen Dedalus at the end of the Circe episode (chapter 15). As a term, *The Wanderings of Ulysses* derives from the notion behind the Greek word *Nekuia,* a traditional subdivision of HOMER's *ODYSSEY,* which deals with the wanderings and adventures of ODYSSEUS. Although in a September 1920 letter to John Quinn, speaking of the threefold division of the novel, Joyce used the term *Odyssey* to designate this middle part of the novel, the phrase *Wanderings of Ulysses* has become the accepted designation (see *Letters,* I.145). It calls attention to Bloom's constant activity during the day, accurately characterizing what is happening in this portion of the novel.

*Nostos* is Joyce's informal designation for the third and final section of *Ulysses. Nostos* is a Greek term meaning homecoming. In Homer's *Odyssey,* it designates the third and final section of the epic, ODYSSEUS's return to Ithaca after his adventures following the Trojan War. Nostos comprises three chapters: Eumaeus (chapter 16), Ithaca (chapter 17), and Penelope (chapter 18). This subdivision of the novel is an ironic evocation of Odysseus's return home, his meeting with his son Telemachus, his reunion with his wife, Penelope, and his repossession of his kingdom after he defeats her suitors. Joyce's adaptive use of Homer's epic in general and of Nostos in particular is a comic transformation of the Greek hero *Ulysses* into the modern-day Dubliner Leopold Bloom. Though Joyce does not strictly adhere to the Homeric ordering of the chapters, he felt sufficiently tied to the association that, for the benefit of a few early commentators of *Ulysses,* he produced schemas or diagrams showing the novel's Homeric analogies and correspondences (see *Ulysses* schema, in the appendix on page 392). Joyce also strongly encouraged Stuart GILBERT, the first critic to write a book-length commentary on *Ulysses,* to exploit the parallels between the novel and Homer's epic by using terms from the *Odyssey* to identify the chapters of *Ulysses.*

Other important structural elements pertain to the compositional framework of the novel. *Ulysses* begins in the modernist tradition. In the Telemachia, the consciousness of a single character, Stephen Dedalus, exerts a formative effect upon the shape of the discourse, but it soon advances beyond this pattern, one that Joyce established in *A Portrait of the Artist as a Young Man.* In The Wanderings of Ulysses and Nostos, the narrative focus shifts frequently among multiple characters, causing at times what poststructuralist critics would identify as an *indeterminacy* of narrative voice. These diverse perspectives illuminate the consciousnesses of a number of characters. They validate seemingly contradictory points of view within the narrative, and by doing so displace the primacy of the traditional, single point of view.

The events of *Ulysses* are presented with the same emphasis on narrative pluralism and thematic multiplicity accorded to individual perspectives. Thus, while *Ulysses* records a sequence of mundane events in the lives of ordinary Dubliners over the course of a typical late spring day in 1904, the intimate view given the reader of the characters, their thoughts, and their social behavior reveals these events as far richer and more significant than their quotidian nature seems to indicate. These Dubliners wake in the morning and begin a round of daily activities that encompasses the whole spectrum of life. They eat and drink throughout the day and evening, discharge bodily wastes, bathe, shop, attend mass, bury the dead, work, get annoyed, argue, perform acts of kindness, wander about, greet one another, sing, write letters, frequent pubs and get drunk, become vitriolic, read books, engage in sexual acts, commit adultery, give birth, visit brothels, get tired, and go back to bed. Joyce transforms a day in the life of DUBLIN into art, and the Dubliners Leopold and Molly Bloom and Stephen Dedalus into representatives of all humanity.

But from a different perspective, June 16, 1904, is not just another ordinary Dublin day in the lives of Bloom, Molly, and Stephen. In the Telemachus episode (chapter 1), for instance, the reader learns that two men are searching Dublin Bay for the body of a drowned man (*U* 1.669–677). As the narrative unfolds, the reader becomes aware of Stephen's apparent decisions to depart from the MARTELLO TOWER where he is living with Buck Mulligan and to quit his teaching job at the Dalkey boys' school run by Garrett Deasy. In her monologue in the Penelope episode (chapter 18), Molly seems to suggest that her adultery earlier in the day with Blazes Boylan marked a highly unusual experience in her marital life. Bloom's involvement in a barroom quarrel in the Cyclops episode (chapter 12) is very much out of character for this otherwise thoughtful and philosophic person. The drunken debauchery of the nonviolent Stephen and his friends in the Circe episode (chapter 15), while arguably an inevitable consequence of their drinking, culminates in a noteworthy scuffle in front of a brothel much out of character for the usually physically timorous Stephen. And, finally, the late-night visit of Stephen to Bloom's house at No. 7 ECCLES STREET in the Ithaca episode (chapter 17) and the latter's invitation to remain there occasions a display of hospitality that goes well beyond ordinary civility.

Without descriptive elaboration, the novel also includes allusions to historical, social, cultural, and geographic features of Ireland of a magnitude and accuracy that set it apart from conventional narratives. Joyce claimed that if Dublin were to disappear, it could be rebuilt (at least in its 1904 version) from his description of it in *Ulysses* (see Frank Budgen, *James Joyce and the Making of Ulysses,* pp. 67–68). Despite its hyperbole, that statement captures the essence of the book's extratextual accomplishments. In its near-encyclopedic representation of turn-of-the-century Irish culture, Joyce's novel fully acclimates its reader to the elements that shaped its characters. This achievement, however, goes beyond allusive virtuosity. Multiple and diverse references allow *Ulysses* to operate on several levels, including that of traditional narrative. This is one of the novel's greatest strengths: its ability to sustain varied and sometimes contradictory interpretations, amply rewarding the application of a broad range of literary categories and critical methodologies, such as MODERNISM, POSTMODERNISM, and psychoanalytic theory, without foreclosing any other modes of reading. This openness to diverse interpretation becomes apparent from the very beginning of the novel.

The initial three episodes of *Ulysses*—Telemachus, Nestor, and Proteus—focus on Stephen Dedalus. Joyce had already written at length about Stephen in *A Portrait of the Artist as a Young Man*, and many readers familiar with that novel may feel tempted to take up where it left off. Certainly, in the Telemachiad, Stephen is continuing his quest to become an artist along fairly predictable lines. His exchanges in the Telemachus episode (chapter 1) with Buck Mulligan make it clear that he remains aloof and disdainful of common ambition. In his talk with his employer Garrett Deasy in the Nestor episode (chapter 2), it becomes evident that Stephen measures himself against a personal standard that concedes little to the everyday material values of the world. Finally, as his daydreams on Sandymount Strand indicate, during the Proteus episode (chapter 3) he takes a romantic, imaginative view of the life that surrounds him.

At the same time, the Telemachiad gives ample evidence that Stephen has also grown more complex and introverted, and that he appears less likely to fulfill his artistic ambitions and achieve the kind of recognition he anticipated in *A Portrait*. In his reaction to the behavior of the old milkwoman who visits the Martello Tower during the Telemachus episode, for example, Stephen demonstrates a clear longing for the approval of his countrymen that he seemed to disdain earlier. In his ruminations on his student Cyril Sargent in the Nestor episode, Stephen shows a heretofore hidden capacity to empathize with others. And as he walks along the beach in the Proteus episode, his sardonic, self-mocking recollections of his early pretensions as an author show a detachment and a sense of humor nowhere evident in *A Portrait of the Artist as a Young Man*.

Although Stephen reappears in several subsequent episodes throughout the rest of *Ulysses*, a radical shift in the narrative focus occurs in part 2, The Wanderings of Ulysses, which begins with the fourth chapter, the Calypso episode, and in the process it opens the novel to a range of concerns that would have been impossible to address had the emphasis remained solely on Stephen. The novel moves back to eight o'clock, the time of the Telemachus episode, and introduces Leopold Bloom, a Dublin Jew who works as a newspaper advertisements canvasser. The obvious differences between Bloom and Stephen quickly signal a new narrative direction. Although both struggle with the role of outsider, in fact in the tiny Dublin world that both men inhabit, conventional ethnic stereotyping and all-too-common Irish prejudices isolate Bloom to a far greater degree than do the artistic aspirations of Stephen. With Bloom the focus of the reader's attention moves from the concerns of a youthful, penurious, iconoclastic artist to those of a middle-aged, middle-class, middlebrow family man who has a deep affection and concern for his wife, his daughter, and a host of others. Bloom's inability to ignore and unwillingness to confront his wife's adultery and his daughter's sexuality are among the domestic tensions that shape his day. As a result, much of the remaining action of the novel centers around Bloom's efforts to keep himself from dwelling on these concerns.

Like the three chapters of the Telemachia, the first three chapters of this section give readers a glimpse of the domestic, public, and interior personae of the central character. Calypso introduces the reader to Bloom's life with Molly. The Lotus-Eaters episode (chapter 5) provides access to Bloom's way of thinking as he begins his day with a leisurely stroll around Dublin's city center to kill some time before attending the funeral of a friend, Paddy Dignam. And the Hades episode (chapter 6) shows Bloom's often ineffectual efforts to interact with his fellow Dubliners.

The Aeolus episode (chapter 7), set in the offices of the *FREEMAN'S JOURNAL*, begins the process of alternating the experiences of Bloom and those of Stephen and also introduces the first of the distinctive stylistic variations, in this case the headlines, that will punctuate the remainder of the narrative. The next episode, Lestrygonians (chapter

8), turns attention back to Bloom and the dominant style of the narrative as he moves about the city center before lunching at DAVY BYRNES'S PUB. In Scylla and Charybdis (chapter 9) the narrative again introduces stylistic variations as it reverts to Stephen Dedalus holding forth at the NATIONAL LIBRARY OF IRELAND. The Wandering Rocks episode (chapter 10), with its segmented narrative and concurrent interpolations, moves perspective back from the intense scrutiny of the central characters to remind readers of the vivid backdrop provided by the daily life of Dubliners.

The opening of the next episode, Sirens (chapter 11), with its opera-like overture, brings attention back to Bloom while continuing stylistic experimentation. As the time for Boylan's visit to Molly approaches, the narrative gives readers a clear sense of Bloom's heightened anxiety. This erupts graphically in the Cyclops episode (chapter 12), when he throws aside his usual meekness and confronts a barroom bully (the Citizen) in BARNEY KIERNAN'S pub. It continues in the next episode, Nausikaa (chapter 13), when Bloom deviates from the usual discretion that he displays in public when he wanders onto Sandymount Strand and masturbates as he watches a young woman, Gerty MacDowell, expose her legs and undergarments to him. It also marks the most radical shift in style to that point, as the first half of the chapter mimics the tone of popular romantic novels. As this section of the novel moves toward a conclusion, the narrative form becomes even more challenging. The stylistic pastiche of the Oxen of the Sun episode (chapter 14) imitates forms of English writing from medieval times to the present. It also reflects both the reckless condition of Stephen, by now quite drunk, and the deep depression of Bloom as they come together at the Holles Street Maternity Hospital. These thematic and stylistic markers recur in NIGHTTOWN, Dublin's red-light district, during the Circe episode (chapter 15), but the emotional tone shifts as both Bloom and Stephen experience cathartic confrontations with the sources of their suffering.

The final section of the novel both moves toward resolution and underscores the ambiguity of the narrative condition. The Eumaeus episode (chapter 16) reinstates the reader's sense of the isolation both Stephen and Bloom feel as they speak at cross-purposes in desultory conversation in a cabman's shelter. The Ithaca episode (chapter 17), related in a question-and-answer format, shows the final efforts of Bloom and Stephen to reconcile themselves to their respective lots in life before separating. Then in a stylistic and thematic tour de force the novel closes with the Penelope episode (chapter 18), a long rambling INTERIOR MONOLOGUE as Molly contemplates her life with Bloom, her childhood in Gibraltar, the events surrounding her adultery, and her plans for the future.

## HELPFUL ANNOTATIONS

Weldon Thornton, *Allusions in Ulysses: An Annotated List* and Don Gifford and Robert J. Seidman, *Ulysses Annotated: Notes for James Joyce's Ulysses.* See the appendix on page 405 for other helpful titles.

## THE CHAPTERS OF *ULYSSES*

### *Telemachus*

This is the first episode of *Ulysses* as well as the initial chapter in the Telemachia section. A version of this chapter first appeared in print when it was serialized in the March 1918 issue of the *LITTLE REVIEW.* According to the SCHEMA (see *Ulysses* schema, Appendix on page 392) that Joyce loaned to Valéry LARBAUD, the scene of the episode is the MARTELLO TOWER. The time at which the action begins is 8 A.M. The art of the chapter is theology. The episode's symbol is the heir. And its technique is narrative (young).

The Telemachus episode derives its name from the son of ODYSSEUS who, after 20 years of awaiting his father's return to Ithaca, restlessly initiates the action of *THE ODYSSEY* by defying the suitors of his mother, Penelope, and setting off in search of his father. In a similar fashion, Stephen Dedalus (see Characters, below), who has already left his father's house "to seek misfortune" (*U* 16.253), as he later tells Leopold Bloom in the cabman's shelter during the Eumaeus episode (chapter 16), begins the day unconsciously searching for a spiritual father and still in mourning for his mother, who died nearly a year earlier.

In keeping with Stephen's aloof and sometimes indolent nature, it is Buck Mulligan who initiates the action of the novel by cajoling Stephen to adopt a more pragmatic, less overt program of intellectual rebellion than the stringent and serious-minded one that he is pursuing. Stephen's carefully constructed reply, which hints at a rivalry between the two and skirts engagement with the issue of his public persona, instead introduces one of the novel's major themes, an inquiry into the nature of paternity and of creativity. After acquainting readers with the unacknowledged competition between Stephen and Mulligan, the Telemachus episode lays out a number of other important themes associated with Stephen throughout the novel: his sense of loss and his feelings of guilt related to the death a year earlier of his mother, his dissatisfaction with his present life without a clear sense of alternatives, his nagging desire for recognition by his fellow Dubliners, and his frustration over his apparent inability to fulfill his artistic ambitions.

"Stately, plump Buck Mulligan came from the stairhead . . ." (*U* 1.1). With these words the day of June 16, 1904, opens for the reader. There, on the roof of the Martello Tower in SANDYCOVE, pausing while shaving to give his blessing to all that he surveys, Mulligan presents a portentous beginning that signals a tone of self-mockery and of self-awareness that will run throughout the narrative discourse. By opening the chapter and the book with a parody of a Catholic priest reciting the opening prayer of the Latin mass: "*Introibo ad altare Dei*" (I will go unto the altar of God; *U* 1.5), he plays upon a ritual familiar to most Irish of the day with a flippant tone that both acknowledges and dismisses a central feature of Irish culture, its Catholic heritage. Mulligan continues his mummery by mimicking the act of consecration of the Eucharist and pretending to effect his own form of TRANSUBSTANTIATION. It is a typical gesture for him. Mulligan is outrageous and irreverent among those who will take no offense, but, unlike Stephen, he remains careful not to display his impudent wit before those who might not be amused.

Stephen Dedalus appears on the scene immediately thereafter, and, for readers of *A Portrait of the Artist as a Young Man*, intimations of a sequel to that work seem at this point quite strong. Stephen, who at the close of Joyce's last novel stood metaphorically poised, like ICARUS, to take flight from Ireland, is now, like Hamlet, back in his native country, sitting glumly on the gun rest at the top of the tower. He has in the interval been to Paris, but has returned to his native city, recalled a year earlier by an unintentionally comical telegram that announced with the initial word mistyped the sad news of the impending death of his mother: "Nother dying come home father" (*U* 3.199). Now, dressed in black as a sign of his continuing mourning (and of his morbid Hamlet fixation), Stephen watches Mulligan shave and listens to him pontificate about plans to Hellenize Ireland through an infusion of Classical culture: "Ah, Dedalus, the Greeks! I must teach you" (*U* 1.79).

As this discourse continues, Mulligan patronizes Stephen about his clothes, his demeanor, his poverty, his art, and his general reputation around DUBLIN. To all this, Stephen replies with a laconic wit, noticeably absent in *A Portrait of the Artist as a Young Man*, that shows an awareness of Mulligan's competitiveness and an assurance of being more than capable of holding his own against Mulligan (a medical student): "He fears the lancet of my art as I fear that of his" (*U* 1.152).

Beneath this seemingly lighthearted early-morning banter, evidence of a rivalry between the two young men gradually emerges for readers. At first it is manifested subtly, by Stephen's coolness when he reminds Mulligan of an offhand and thoughtless remark made nearly a year before, shortly after the death of Stephen's mother, which Stephen still recalls with umbrage. As the narrative develops, however, it becomes obvious that larger and longer-lasting concerns are the source of a continuing sense of friction in the relations between the two young men.

While it is never clearly or fully delineated, the antagonism that hovers at the margins of their conversation seems to arise from a competitiveness based upon artistic ambition and dedication. Even the relatively brief opening chapter has already shown that both Stephen and Buck are clever and entertaining, and both have ambitions beyond simply being barroom wits. Markedly different attitudes, however, condition their approaches to manifesting creative abilities and to gaining public recognition.

Stephen has given himself over completely to art and shows no regard for public sentiment or expectations. Mulligan, on the other hand, frankly and unashamedly seeks the renown afforded by art that is popular and easily accessible, and he is unwilling to sacrifice material comfort and social approval for artistic principle. Thus, although he is bawdy in certain circumstances—the "Ballad of Joking Jesus" (*U* 1.584–587, 589–592, 596–599), which he recites near the end of the chapter, attests to this—he is always careful to gauge his audience and to adjust his performance to suit its tastes. (As for the ballad itself, Joyce received a version of this poem in 1905 from his friend Vincent COSGRAVE, who claimed that he had gotten it from Oliver St. John GOGARTY, the model for Buck Mulligan.)

As the episode unfolds, it quickly becomes apparent that this rivalry between Stephen and Mulligan has been exacerbated considerably by the intrusive presence in the Martello Tower of the Englishman Haines, Mulligan's Oxford classmate. Haines, a modern version of the archetypal English invader of Ireland, has come in the role of an intellectual colonist; he wishes to study the effects of the IRISH LITERARY REVIVAL. His enthusiasm for Irish folk tradition ironically counterpoints Stephen's disenchantment with Irish culture and politics. Stephen is schooling himself in Continental intellectual currents.

On his trip across the Irish Sea, however, Haines has lost none of the imperial insensitivity that had for generations fostered among the Irish an intense animus toward the British. Haines's attitude toward Stephen is even more patronizing than Mulligan's, and he views most other Irish whom he encounters with a mixture of amusement, condescension, and suspicion. Haines's unself-conscious ANTI-SEMITISM only underscores the fundamental chauvinism and cultural intolerance that underlie his nature. On a more mundane level, Stephen's personal distaste for Haines and his Anglo-Saxon attitudes has been considerably aggravated this morning by lack of sleep, caused by Haines's "raving and moaning to himself about shooting a black panther" (*U* 1.61–62) as he slept.

Haines, in fact, becomes the embodiment of many of the conditions that trouble Stephen throughout the Telemachus chapter. His self-congratulatory, condescending view of the Irish becomes most apparent in the interchange among himself, Mulligan, Stephen, and the old woman who delivers milk during their breakfast in the tower. It serves as a bitter reminder to Stephen of both Ireland's second-class status within the British Empire and the maddening subservience evident among so many of his countrymen toward the very people who oppress them. In this interchange, Stephen's natural reticence causes him to be overlooked as the old woman is shamelessly obsequious toward Haines, who speaks to her in Irish, and self-consciously polite toward Mulligan, who only grudgingly pays for the milk she has delivered: "a voice that speaks to her loudly . . . me she slights" (*U* 1.418–419). While Stephen normally would care little about such a person's opinion, this one stings him, for both metaphorically and literally she represents Ireland and its potential response to him and his art.

After breakfast, despite the superior tone that he has unconsciously adopted toward Stephen, Haines still seeks to explore, with unfeigned curiosity, the paradoxical makeup of the Irish intellectual. As the three men walk toward the 40-foot hole for Mulligan's swim, the obtuse and humorless Haines and the mordant Stephen engage in an animated discussion revolving around the English treatment of the Irish. Stephen is in a ticklish position, for, as he made clear in his exchanges with Davin in chapter 5 of *A Portrait of the Artist as a Young Man,* he certainly does not wish to embrace conventional nationalist sentiments. At the same time, he can hardly abide Haines's willful suppression of the English role in creating the political troubles that have circumscribed Irish life for centuries.

Stephen wittily resolves this dilemma by a deft metaphorical evocation of the problem confronting him. He speaks of his sense of isolation and oppression in a clever epigram that sums up his problem without entrapping him in clichéd political rhetoric: "I am a servant of two masters . . . an English and an Italian. . . . And a third . . . there is who wants me for odd jobs" (*U* 1.638, 642). Although Stephen here refers to the obedience demanded by the English colonial authorities and by the Roman Catholic Church, and somewhat obliquely to the pull of Irish nationalism, Haines, the devotee of Irish culture, is frankly baffled by the allusions and can acknowledge them only by offering the tepid, self-deluding observation that "[i]t seems history is to blame" (*U* 1.649).

Arriving at the 40-foot hole, Stephen's sense of displacement grows. Feeling alienated both from Mulligan and from the prospect of their continuing to share accommodations, Stephen sees his options being foreclosed even as the day itself is only beginning. The episode ends with Stephen relinquishing his key to the Martello Tower; and as he leaves Mulligan and Haines, he has a heightened sense of his own alienation.

For additional details concerning the Telemachus episode, see *Letters,* II.126–127, 187n.1, 206n.1, 218n.3, 414, and III.240 and 284.

### *Nestor*

This is the second episode of *Ulysses* and the second chapter in the Telemachia section of the novel. A version of the episode first appeared in serialized form in the April 1918 issue of *The* LITTLE REVIEW, and it was also published in the January–February 1919 issue of the EGOIST. According to the SCHEMA (see *Ulysses* schema in the appendix on page 392) that Joyce loaned to Valéry LARBAUD, the scene of the episode is the school in Dalkey, about 15 minutes southeast of the MARTELLO TOWER, run by Garrett Deasy (see Characters, below). The time at which the action begins is 10 A.M. The art of the chapter is history. The episode's symbol is the horse. And its technic is catechism (personal).

The informal title of the chapter refers to Odysseus's old comrade Nestor, the master charioteer who fought by his side during the siege of Troy. After leaving the family home in Ithaca to search for news of his father, Odysseus's son, Telemachus, in book III of *The Odyssey,* first seeks out Nestor in the hope of learning his father's fate. Although Nestor can give the young man little information relating specifically to the return of Odysseus, he treats his old friend's son with honor, and tells Telemachus what he has learned of the homecomings of other Greek heroes who had fought at Troy. The stark contrast between this archetypal wise man and the fatuous Garrett Deasy reminds readers of the mock-heroic undertone of the narrative and underscores how alone Stephen is in a world in which crass materialism and smug self-satisfaction now masquerade as attributes of wisdom.

Like Telemachus in Ithaca, Stephen Dedalus finds himself surrounded by hostile males—the sardonic Buck Mulligan and the obtuse Englishman, Haines—in his fortress home, the MARTELLO TOWER. In leaving, however, Stephen does not come across support elsewhere. Instead he encounters the recalcitrant, naive anti-intellectualism of the upper-middle-class students at Garrett Deasy's private school in Dalkey. Like the surly young men whom Stephen teaches, Deasy, too, seems to harbor a measure of animosity toward Stephen, but his more obvious role is to provide an ironic analogue to Homer's Nestor by offering Stephen Dedalus inappropriate advice on the practical management of his affairs, financial and otherwise. With such contrasts, the chapter presents an impressionistic view of Stephen's public self, or at least his professional self, and it demonstrates that this facet of his life is no more satisfactory than the private one outlined in the previous chapter.

In its opening pages, the Nestor episode underscores Stephen's ineffectuality in the classroom as he struggles to maintain a modicum of order among a group of boys who have no interest in the rote drill by which he attempts to lead them through the day's lessons. Their lack of attention mirrors Stephen's own boredom. As the INTERIOR MONOLOGUE of the opening scene makes evident, his mind seems as detached from the curriculum as those of his students. While the grinding routine of recitation moves forward, he distracts himself by evoking first the elaborate panorama of the victory of Pyrrhus at Asculum won at a great cost and then by imagining, with an interest bordering on voyeurism, the details of the social lives that await the boys he is now teaching.

As the class progresses, however, it becomes apparent that a good portion of the problems that Stephen faces in the classroom relates quite simply to his own social awkwardness. Although he tries to win over the boys through his wit, they are at a loss as to how to respond to the allusion that Stephen makes to the Kingstown pier as a disappointed bridge or to his riddle with the enigmatic answer, "The fox burying his grandmother under a hollybush" (*U* 2.115). In the end his behavior simply puzzles and embarrasses them. He cannot quite succeed as either a teacher or an entertainer, and his students are all too happy to run off to the playing field at the end of the period.

After the class has left to play field hockey, Stephen remains in the room for a few moments to tutor one of his students, Cyril Sargent, who has fallen behind in his math studies. In his helplessness and his isolation Sargent may evoke for some readers images of the young Stephen as a student at CLONGOWES WOOD COLLEGE in the first chapter of *A Portrait of the Artist as a Young Man.* Stephen himself makes this connection and briefly calls to mind incidents from his own school days. In consequence, he responds to Sargent's helplessness with perhaps greater patience and sympathy than he might otherwise have shown.

The differences between student and teacher, however, are much greater than any similarity. While both the young Stephen and Cyril Sargent must endure the indignities of their physical weakness, Stephen as a boy had the advantage of a quick wit, an active intelligence, and the courage of his convictions. The last of these qualities eventually earned for him the respect of his classmates when he went to complain to Father John Conmee, the rector of Clongowes Wood College, about the unfair punishment that he had received from Father Dolan. Sargent, in contrast, stands out as dull, stupid, and perpetually fearful, as helpless and timid intellectually as he is physically.

Nonetheless, Stephen sustains the parallels between them that he sees by calling up an image of Sargent's mother as a woman fearlessly protecting her feeble boy from the threats of the world. The picture is entirely Stephen's invention, but it underscores for readers at least the reverence that he still has for motherhood and by extension his veneration for the memory of his own mother. Indeed, in the Circe episode (chapter 15), Stephen's hallucination, in which his mother appears to remind him of the care that she gave him when he was a child, reveals not her feelings but the guilty remorse that Stephen himself experiences.

After sending a still-baffled Sargent off to participate reluctantly in field hockey with the rest of his class (again evoking images from chapter 1 of *A Portrait of the Artist as a Young Man* when Stephen too was unenthusiastic about playing sports), Stephen goes to Deasy's office to collect his salary. As Deasy pays Stephen, he cannot resist incorporating an abbreviated lecture on economics into the proceedings; but his evocation of "the proudest word you will ever hear from an Englishman's mouth . . . *I paid my way*" (*U* 2.244–245, 251) shows not only Deasy's inability to count (four words, not one) but also his severe misunderstanding of Stephen's temperament and national loyalties.

Deasy, in fact, is himself far more disposed to the English than to the Irish in his sentiments, although he tries to link his Unionist views with a broad commitment to Irish heritage and culture. In the abstract, such an argument might have merit, but inaccuracies in Deasy's recapitulation of Irish history undermine much of the force of his sentiments. Most notably, Deasy mistakenly thinks that his ancestor Sir John Blackwood supported union with the United Kingdom when in fact he opposed it, and the pedantic and misogynistic schoolmaster confuses the roles played by both MacMurrough and O'Rourke in bringing about the English invasion of Ireland by the forces of Henry II.

The chapter concludes with a final idiosyncratic gesture on Deasy's part. He gives Stephen a letter that he has written warning the public at large of the dangers to Irish cattle posed by a potential epidemic of hoof-and-mouth disease. Although skeptical about such an effort, Stephen agrees to approach some editors whom he knows about publishing the letter in various newspapers and journals. (In the Aeolus episode [chapter 7] he is successful in getting Myles Crawford to insert it in the FREEMAN'S JOURNAL, and in the Scylla and Charybdis episode [chapter 9] he speaks to an evasive George Russell, who is unsure whether he will be able to print it in DANA.) In another example of the emergence of a self-deprecating sense of humor, Stephen, in anticipation of Buck Mulligan's reaction to this act of goodwill, characterizes himself ironically as "the bullockbefriending bard" (*U* 2.431).

Despite this demonstration of kindness on Stephen's part, the final lines of the chapter underscore the cultural, intellectual, and emotional gulf between him and Deasy. As Stephen is leaving the school, Deasy, echoing the ANTI-SEMITISM of Haines but with a trace of coarse humor, asserts that the reason that Ireland never persecuted the Jews is "because she never let them in" (*U* 2.442). To this unvarnished, unembarrassed prejudice, Stephen makes no response.

Stylistically, the Nestor episode offers a sustained development of the interior monologue technique introduced in the opening episode, Telemachus. Nestor also renews the images of alienation and restiveness that emerged in the opening chapter as features of Stephen's character (and before that, in the final chapters of *A Portrait of the Artist as a Young Man*). Additionally, in the imaginative digressions Stephen allows himself—while conducting his class, tutoring Sargent, or listening to Deasy—the narrative makes readers aware of Stephen's creative potential, and in this fashion offers some validation of his artistic claims, a topic that will be elaborated on in the next chapter, the Proteus episode.

Although one could hardly read it as autobiographical, events in Nestor are loosely based on Joyce's own experiences in the classroom during his brief stint at the Clifton School in Dalkey in 1904. The school's founder and headmaster during Joyce's tenure was the idiosyncratic Francis Irwin, who provided a model for Deasy. The interest in hoof-and-mouth disease, however, was Joyce's, not Irwin's. In 1912, an Ulsterman living in Trieste, Henry N. Blackwood Price, another figure who contributed to the character of Deasy, made Joyce aware of its seriousness, and Joyce subsequently wrote "Politics and Cattle Disease," a short article published in the September 10, 1912, issue of the *Freeman's Journal* (see *The Critical Writings of James Joyce*). (The article is unsigned, but a letter from Joyce's brother Charles to Stanislaus JOYCE identifies Joyce as the author.) For additional details concerning this episode, see *Letters*, II.223n.2, 286, 300n.8, 413, and 415.

### *Proteus*

This is the third episode of *Ulysses* and the final chapter in the Telemachia section. A version of this chapter first appeared in serialized form in the May 1918 issue of the *LITTLE REVIEW*, and was subsequently published in the March–April 1919 issue of the *EGOIST*. Margaret ANDERSON, one of the editors of the *Little Review*, later recalled that when she first saw the opening lines of Proteus she exclaimed: "This is the most beautiful thing we'll ever have."

According to the SCHEMA (see *Ulysses* schema, Appendix on page 392) that Joyce loaned to Valéry LARBAUD, the scene of the episode is Sandymount Strand, a beach to the east of the Ringsend section of Dublin, just to the south of the River Liffey. The time at which the action begins is 11 A.M. The art of the chapter is philology. The episode's symbol is the tide. Its technic is monologue (male).

The Proteus episode derives its informal designation from the name of the Greek god Proteus, the "Ancient of the Sea." Proteus served as the herdsman of the sea god Poseidon. He would change his shape to avoid answering questions. In book 4 of *The Odyssey*, Menelaus tells Telemachus how he ambushed Proteus, catching the god by surprise, and then hung on to him as Proteus rapidly transformed himself into a series of different creatures and objects. By retaining his hold throughout these metamorphoses, Menelaus was able to compel Proteus, as a condition of release, to reveal how Menelaus should placate the gods so they would allow him to return home.

Joyce elaborates upon this characteristic to enforce the concept of creative fluidity that recurs throughout the chapter, reflected generally in the protean quality of the imaginative conceptions that pass in rapid succession through the consciousness of Stephen Dedalus (see Characters, below) as he walks along the beach toward the center of DUBLIN. In a series of vividly evoked images, Stephen's mind jumps nimbly from remembrances of his aunt and uncle's household, to recollections of his half-hearted efforts at medical studies in Paris, to assessments of his own artistic abilities and pretensions, to meditations on the Irish national heritage. Stephen's thoughts, mimicking the multiple forms taken by the Greek god in Homer's epic, range over the breadth of his nature without fixing him in a single role.

The opening line of Proteus, a meditation on the relation between the human imagination and physical reality, captures Stephen's unsettled and introspective state of mind: "Ineluctable modality of the visible: at least that if no more, thought through my eyes. Signatures of all things I am here to read . . ." (*U* 3.1–2). From this declaration, Stephen moves to a recollection of odds and ends of philosophical and aesthetic critiques from Jacob Boehme, ARISTOTLE, Samuel Johnson, George BERKELEY, G. E. Lessing, and William Blake. Through this selective recapitulation of their ideas, he endeavors to articulate his own views about art, perception, and beauty. With these few sentences the narrative underscores for readers the challenge that the arcane references and diverse philosophical perspectives will pose to interpretation.

As he nears Strasbourg Terrace and the residence of his aunt and uncle, Stephen's thoughts turn momentarily from the application of aesthetic values to the domestic affairs of his Aunt Sally and his Uncle Richie Goulding. In a clever piece of narrative misdirection, Joyce has Stephen imagine the reception that he would receive were he to call upon the Gouldings. Stephen unfolds the scene with such evocative skill that one realizes that Stephen is merely imagining the events of the visit after he has walked past the Goulding house and decided that he will not stop to visit his aunt and uncle after all.

Stephen quickly moves from thoughts of his relations to an assessment of his ambitions and accomplishments. His sardonic commentary makes clear that he has no illusions about what he has done with his life over the past few years. As he dwells upon the disparity between the achievements that he had foreseen and what he has actually done, the reader becomes aware that somewhere between *A Portrait* and the beginning of *Ulysses*, Stephen has acquired a highly refined sense of humor, which allows him a detached and even ironic view of himself.

In an easy transition Stephen moves from considering his early creative ambitions to recollecting his stay in Paris. Acknowledging his artistic pretensions, he is reminded of the self-conscious pride he once took in the idea of living the life of the expatriate artist. "Just say in the most natural tone: when I was in Paris, *boul'Mich'*. . ." (*U* 3.178–179). However, with the juxtaposition of memories of his frustrations in France and those of the sad fate of the old expatriate Fenian Kevin Egan, Stephen makes clear that his romanticized sense of his life in Paris is as illusory as that of his achievements as an artist.

At this point the material world begins to intrude upon Stephen's reveries, allowing him to return to considerations of the relation between perception and reality introduced in the opening pages. He sees two cocklepickers, a man and a woman, rambling along the beach. After enduring the mundane indignity of being frightened by their dog, Stephen begins to integrate them into his imagination by a process of free association. He posits for the pair a gypsy existence possibly more exotic and certainly tawdrier than their actual lives seem to be. On the surface it stands as a harmless daydream. Nonetheless, these images demonstrate to readers once again the evocative power and artistic promise that emerge from Stephen's offhanded and unplanned creative manifestations.

These efforts offer particularly revealing aspects of Stephen's nature, for, near the close of the chapter when he consciously tries his hand at artistic production, the result seems contrived and painfully flawed. In an attempt to express aesthetically the feelings that have been running through his head throughout his walk along the beach, Stephen writes hastily on a scrap of paper torn from the letter Garrett Deasy had given him earlier that morning in the Nestor episode (chapter 2). He produces the opening lines of a highly stylized and extremely derivative poem that incorporates the worst excesses of the SYMBOLIST MOVEMENT. Although readers will not see all four lines of Stephen's composition until the Aeolus episode (chapter 7), the snatches that occur here are enough to show that Stephen is far more effective when he works unself-consciously.

Stephen's manifestations of his creativity become even more elemental and degraded as the episode moves toward its conclusion. In the final pages, the narrative underscores the sardonic view of creative ambition that Stephen has shown throughout the chapter, relentlessly lampooning the aura of sanctity with which some reverently surround the creative gesture. As the narrative returns from the ethereal world of philosophical reflection to the mundane world of physical materiality, it records Stephen's final acts of production: urinating and picking his nose.

Proteus brings to an end the extended introduction (or reintroduction if one has read *A Portrait of the Artist as a Young Man*) of Stephen Dedalus. In three carefully balanced chapters, the narrative has laid out a view of Stephen's social, public, and private selves, with each manifestation standing distinct from the other two. Taken together they form a highly complex but ultimately accessible view of his nature. In some ways, perhaps, the Telemachia represents a false start to the novel, for after this intimate portrait of Stephen, the narrative goes back temporally and begins again at 8 A.M. with an equally intimate portrait of Mr. Leopold Bloom.

Nonetheless, this section serves important stylistic and contextual functions. It establishes the central elements and concerns informing Stephen's nature—his artistic ambition, his sardonic view of himself, his sense of loss over the death of his mother, his insecurity over his own identity—and, in laying out this diverse consciousness, it sets his character in tension with, and not in opposition to, that of Bloom's equally complex, if less cultivated, personality. Together with Molly Bloom these figures split the focus of the narrative in a fashion characteristic of MODERNISM and POSTMODERNISM.

For further details regarding the Proteus episode, see *Letters*, II.28, 49, 148, 222, and 416, and III.193.

### *Calypso*

This is the fourth episode of *Ulysses*, and the first chapter in the novel's middle section known as The Wanderings of Ulysses. A version of the Calypso episode first appeared in serialization in the June 1918 issue of the LITTLE REVIEW. It is in this episode that Joyce introduces Leopold Bloom and his wife, Molly Bloom (see Characters, below).

As detailed in book 5 of *The Odyssey*, Calypso is the goddess who, at the time the poem opens, has held Odysseus captive on her island of Ogygia for more than seven years. At the intercession of Athena, Zeus compels Calypso to allow Odysseus to depart the island and to resume his journey to Ithaca. Joyce alludes to this story through an analogy between the marital relations of Bloom and Molly and the captive/captor relationship of Odysseus and Calypso. Bloom's complicit bondage appears in the uxoriousness that emerges early in the chapter. He dotes upon every aspect and attends to every whim of his wife, and his obsessive recollections throughout the day of his life with her underscore the hold that Molly has upon him.

According to the SCHEMA (see *Ulysses* schema in the appendix on page 392) that Joyce loaned to Valéry LARBAUD, the scene of the episode is the Bloom house at No. 7 Eccles Street. The time at which the action begins is 8 A.M. The episode's organ is the kidney; the art is economics; the symbol is the nymph. And the technic of the episode is narrative (mature).

The obvious, though ironic, analogue with *The Odyssey* has Molly as a reflection of the female figure, Calypso. The narrative, however, inverts the parallel in that Molly so captivates her husband that she can compel him, albeit reluctantly, to leave home for the day so that she can carry out her assignation with Blazes Boylan. Set predominantly in Bloom's house, the episode's action takes place at the same hour as the action of the Telemachus episode (chapter 1). In fact, the first six episodes of *Ulysses* mirror each other structurally—public, domestic, and internal lives—and chronologically—Telemachus/Calypso (8 A.M.), Nestor/Lotus-Eaters (10 A.M.), and Proteus/Hades (11 A.M.). These parallel arrangements inevitably invite critical comparisons between Stephen Dedalus and Leopold Bloom. Although these two main characters perceive and assess the world in radically different ways, they have enough in common to link together not only important aspects of their personalities, but also important aspects of the novel itself.

In his chapter on *Ulysses* in *A Companion to Joyce Studies*, Zack BOWEN offers a concise analysis of the thought patterns of Stephen and Bloom, pointing out their differences as well as their interconnectedness. According to Bowen, Stephen's is a world governed mostly by the dynamics of inner

A painting of 7 Eccles Street, the address of Leopold and Molly Bloom in *Ulysses.* Painted by Flora H. Mitchell *(Croessman Collection of James Joyce, Special Collections/Morris Library, Southern Illinois University)*

psychological perception, while Bloom's life is animated by perception of exterior reality (see Bowen, p. 447ff). "But, curiously enough, though Bloom's thoughts stem from different things and lead to different conclusions," Bowen observes,

> they become intricately interwoven with Stephen's. Also, the two share experience with or interest in a number of common topics. For example, cattle, Ireland, politics, women, music, and literature play a great part in the thoughts of both men (p. 448).

By the time the chapter ends, the reader has become aware that this episode does more than simply establish temporal parallels to those preceding it. It introduces broader associations by focusing on issues concerning Bloom that parallel those dominating Stephen Dedalus's consciousness: an ambiguous sense of paternity, a lingering sorrow over the losses of his son and his father, and apprehensiveness regarding his immediate future. Bloom tends to take a more practical, even banal, view of life than does Stephen, but both of them begin the day of June 16, 1904, with unsettled minds troubled by similar concerns. Stephen too is dominated by thoughts of paternity, by the loss of his mother, and his own apprehensiveness regarding his artistic future.

However, these links are not immediately apparent. Indeed, the Calypso episode initially underscores the differences between the aloof and ascetic Stephen and the cordial (if alienated) and pedestrian Bloom. It opens with a vivid description of Bloom's sensual nature: "Mr. Leopold Bloom ate with relish the inner organs of beasts and fowls. He liked thick giblet soup, nutty gizzards, a stuffed roast heart, liver slices fried with crustcrumbs, fried hencods' roes. Most of all he liked grilled mutton kidneys which gave to his palate a fine tang of faintly scented urine" (*U* 4.1–5). Just as the opening words of chapter 1—"Stately, plump Buck Mulligan . . ." (*U* 1.1)—play with language, the first line of the opening of the second part of the novel, The Wanderings of Ulysses, does the same. The word *relish* in the sentence can mean that Mr. Leopold Bloom eats with a sense of delight and zest or that the inner organs of beasts and fowls that he eats are flavored with a savory condiment; further, both interpretations together may be correct.

In keeping with this culinary introduction, the narrative emphasizes Bloom's domestic side, placing him in the kitchen preparing breakfast for Molly, who is still in bed. He thinks about kidneys, gives milk to the cat, and contemplates the feline nature. But before bringing Molly her tray, he decides to step out to Dlugacz's butcher shop to purchase a pork kidney for his own breakfast. As he prepares to leave the house he hears the brass quoits of the bed jingle and is reminded of Gibraltar, where both Molly and the bed are from. (Though seemingly unimportant at the time, this sound recurs during Bloom's hallucinations in the Circe episode [*U* 15.1136].)

Nothing that Bloom does, however, is arbitrary. On the way out the door, he meticulously checks his hatband to make sure that the white slip of paper with "Henry Flower" on it—Bloom's nom de plume in his clandestine correspondence with Martha Clifford—is still safely hidden there. Before quietly closing the hall door, Bloom realizes he does not have the latchkey and leaves it partially open. He later forgets it again when leaving for the day.

As Bloom walks along Dorset Street, the narrative, with dispassionate irony, gives the reader a sense of Bloom's active and erotic imagination. For example, while he is being waited on at Dlugacz's, Bloom is in a hurry to follow the female servant from the house next door who has been waited on before him. "Mr. Bloom pointed quickly. To catch up and walk behind her if she went slowly, behind her moving hams. Pleasant to see first thing in the morning. Hurry up, damn it. Make hay while the sun shines" (*U* 4.171–173). As Dlugacz laboriously fills his order, Bloom's voyeurism comes to the surface when he lets his mind picture the maid's possible assignations with policemen in the park.

Bloom returns home to find two letters, and a card in the morning post. The letters arouse contrasting and ambivalent feelings in him. One, from Blazes Boylan to Molly, confronts Bloom with evidence of the event that he will endeavor to suppress all day long—his wife's impending infidelity. The other, a letter from his daughter Milly, who now works as a photographer's assistant in Mullingar, evokes in him a sense of his love for both wife and daughter, while raising concern over Milly's own emerging sexuality as well as for Molly's unfaithfulness. (See Milly Bloom in Characters.)

After Bloom reads Milly's letter, he brings Boylan's letter and the card from Milly to Molly on her breakfast tray. Later, when he returns to their bedroom, Bloom sees a strip of the torn envelope of Boylan's letter showing from under the pillow—an image that will haunt him during the day. He asks about the songs she will be singing in her forthcoming concert tour with Boylan. One, a duet with J. C. Doyle, is "Là ci darem" from Mozart's *Don Giovanni,* and the other is the popular "Love's Old Sweet Song"; allusions to these pieces will recur in Bloom's thoughts throughout *Ulysses.* Molly asks Bloom about the meaning of METEMPSYCHOSIS, a word that she found in Amye Reade's *Ruby: The Pride of the Ring,* a mildly pornographic, sadomasochistic novel. Bloom defines it in several different ways. It is a word that comes from the Greek, he says, meaning "the transmigration of souls" (*U* 4.341–342) or "reincarnation" (*U* 4.363).

During Bloom's pedantic clarification of the word, Molly turns her attention to matters relating more directly to her own pleasure. She has a taste for soft-core pornography, and she instructs Bloom to purchase a book by the erotic author Paul de KOCK—"Nice name he has" (*U* 4.358)—a writer whose novels she has previously enjoyed. Then, abruptly, Molly smells something burning, and Bloom remembers the kidney that he put on the fire. He hastily returns to the kitchen to save his own breakfast from incineration.

While Bloom is eating, he gives himself the pleasure of a leisurely perusal of Milly's letter. However, the experience produces as much anxiety as satisfaction. Having just celebrated her 15th birthday, Milly begins by thanking him for "the lovely birthday present . . . my new tam," and promises to write Molly thanking her for a "lovely box of creams" (*U* 4.398–400). She goes on to tell of life at the photographer's shop in MULLINGAR, noting that the store was busy one fair day when "all the beef to the heels were in" (*U* 4.402–403), a phrase that recurs as a motif throughout the novel. (This phrase, in use in Mullingar, in a cattle-raising district of Ireland, refers to women with stocky legs [see Don Gifford, *Ulysses Annotated,* p. 79]. Milly appears to apply it unself-consciously with little sarcasm or irony.) Bloom's concern is raised further when Milly mentions her interest in a young student called Bannon and then goes on to make an innocently ironic reference to Blazes Boylan by confusing him with the author of the song "Those Lovely Seaside Girls," yet another tune that will echo in Bloom's thoughts later in the day.

Near the end of the episode, in a scene that shocked Ezra Pound and a number of Joyce's other supporters, Bloom defecates in the privy in his yard. This heightened NATURALISM is not simply an example of the narrative's (and Joyce's) cloacal preoccupation. It confronts each of us with our own assumptions about what should or should not be recorded in the narrative, and as a result of this confrontation makes us much more aware of the subjective approach that we bring to the act of reading.

While moving his bowels, Bloom reads Mr. Philip Beaufoy's story "MATCHAM'S MASTERSTROKE" in the journal *TITBITS*. Bloom is impressed with the payment that Beaufoy received for his efforts, and he considers writing a similar story with Molly as his inspiration. (This is one of a series of get-rich-quick schemes that passes through Bloom's mind over the course of the day.)

The implicit sensuality of Beaufoy's story and the association that Bloom makes between it and Molly turn his thoughts to her meeting with Boylan set for that afternoon, an event that Bloom repeatedly and unsuccessfully tries to drive from his consciousness throughout the course of *Ulysses*. Perhaps because he fears their assignation will have consequences beyond the day, Bloom begins to wonder about Boylan's financial condition (*U* 4.528–529). He characteristically refuses to dwell on the matter, however, and turns his mind to more immediate, pragmatic concerns. With a form of closure appropriate to the setting, Bloom tears "away half the prize story sharply" (*U* 4.537) and wipes himself with it. On leaving, the bells of St. George's Church remind him of the impending funeral of Paddy Dignam (*U* 4.551) and serve as a transition for the reader to subsequent chapters.

### *Lotus-Eaters*

This is the fifth episode of *Ulysses* and the second in the Wanderings of Ulysses section. It was serialized in the July 1918 issue of the *LITTLE REVIEW*.

According to the schema (see *Ulysses* schema, Appendix on page 392) that Joyce loaned to Valéry LARBAUD, the scene of the episode is the Turkish bath that Leopold Bloom visits before he attends the funeral of Paddy Dignam (see Characters, below), although much of the chapter's action takes place prior to that on the streets of Dublin as Bloom goes from place to place, and the narrative breaks off before he actually reaches the bath. The time at which the action begins is 10 A.M. The organ of the chapter is the genitals. The arts of the chapter are botany and chemistry. The episode's symbol is the Eucharist. And its technic is narcissism.

The informal title of this episode comes from book 9 of Homer's *Odyssey*, where Odysseus and his men encounter the Lotus-Eaters, people who live in a somnambulant state of forgetfulness as a result of eating the narcotic lotus flowers. When Odysseus and his crew arrive on land, the Lotus-Eaters treat them with great friendliness, but their hospitality is double-edged. The crew members who eat the lotus flower become lethargic and lose all desire to return to their homeland, and Odysseus has to compel them back to their ships by force.

The Lotus-Eaters episode presents the first extended view of Bloom's public persona, yet its narrative remains dominated by his private concerns. Thoughts of his wife, Molly, recur throughout the episode, as they will all day long, and time and again the reader sees Bloom filtering his sense of the world through his relations with Molly. For example, late in the chapter, the comparisons that C. P. M'Coy attempts to make between his wife, Fanny M'Coy, and Molly stir both Bloom's indignation and his insecurity. At the same time, a tremendous level of self-control circumscribes all of Bloom's actions. His flirtatious epistolary affair with Martha Clifford, for example, anticipates both his voyeurism and his caution, for he makes it clear that he has no wish to go beyond the discreet pleasure that he derives from his mildly salacious correspondence. This is one of several instances in the chapter that reinforce the reader's sense of Bloom's self-containment, for despite his frequent encounters with various acquaintances throughout the chapter, one sees many instances of Bloom's pronounced aloofness and intentional isolation from his fellow Dubliners.

Throughout the chapter Leopold Bloom wanders in a desultory manner around the area near Trinity College and the quays south of the River LIFFEY. Although he does run a few errands, in keeping with the chapter's informal title Bloom moves about lethargically as he passes the time until he must attend Paddy Dignam's funeral. His first recorded response in the chapter—choosing to say nothing to the young boy who is smoking—is in keeping with this theme and consistent with his character: he combines sensitivity and concern with a prudent inclination to avoid taking action.

Moving south of the river from the quays, Bloom calls in at the Westland Row Post Office to collect a letter from Martha Clifford addressed to him under his pseudonym, Henry Flower. Martha had initially written to Bloom in answer to a dummy ad that he had placed for clerical help; the tone of their letters seems quickly to have shifted from professional to personal and by now she has become a far more intimate correspondent. As he leaves the post office, and before he can read the letter, Bloom encounters C. P. M'Coy, whose business experiences are roughly similar to Bloom's and whose wife, Fanny M'Coy, a soprano like Molly Bloom, has gained a measure of local renown with her singing. M'Coy seems to be affected by the same torpor that has inhibited Bloom and he prolongs their conversation through remarks on implicit parallels between their lives. Aware of M'Coy's reputation as a sponger and suspicious that his friendliness is simply a prelude to some sort of importunate proposal, Bloom resists accepting the analogy that M'Coy draws between them, and coolly keeps him at arm's length.

After parting from M'Coy, Bloom finds a secluded spot in Cumberland Street where he scans Martha Clifford's letter. Its contents make it clear to readers that Bloom is carrying on an epistolary affair with the woman, and reading between the lines reveals certain aspects of Bloom's sexual nature. In responding to Bloom's most recent letter, Martha Clifford opens with a titillating allusion—"I do wish I could punish you for that" (*U* 5.244). Some sort of discipline fetish seems to be at the heart of their mutual attraction, and she presses for the opportunity to meet him face to face.

Certain aspects of Martha's letter obviously give Bloom pleasure. He clearly enjoys a voyeuristic satisfaction at the mild suggestiveness of her writing, and he takes further pleasure from the memories of other women that this letter stimulates. He also feels a measure of gratification in comparing Martha (as he imagines her) with Molly. At the same time, Bloom's reaction to the suggested meeting makes it clear that he has no wish to let the relationship become more involved and no intention of complicating his life by actually meeting with this young woman.

After carefully tearing up the envelope in which Martha Clifford's letter arrived (but saving the letter itself, as he has saved all her previous letters), Bloom enters All Hallows Church. Still killing time before Dignam's funeral, he sits down in one of the pews and dispassionately observes the end of a Mass. He thinks to himself, "Good idea the Latin. Stupifies them first" (*U* 5.350–351). Bloom's condescending attitude toward CATHOLICISM and his fundamental ignorance of Catholic ritual make it clear that, despite his being baptized before his marriage to Molly, his allegiance to the church is nominal at best.

At the conclusion of Mass, Bloom leaves the church and wanders down to the end of the street to the establishment of F. W. Sweny, Chemists, where he refills Molly's order for body lotion and buys a bar of lemon soap that he will use at the Turkish baths located around the corner. Leaving Sweny's shop, Bloom encounters the layabout Bantam Lyons. Lyons seems to have little real interest in talking to Bloom, but he does wish to consult Bloom's newspaper for the latest racing news. When Bloom tells him to keep the paper because he was about to throw it away, Lyons assumes that Bloom is coyly giving away a tip on Throwaway, a horse entered in the Ascot GOLD CUP race being run that day, and he rushes off to place a bet on the horse. However, Lyons subsequently loses his nerve and so misses cashing in when Throwaway wins at 20 to 1.

The chapter ends with a languorous image that, in keeping with the theme of the episode, is evoked through Bloom's imagination (though a quick reading may miss this fact): Bloom decides to go to the Turkish bath on Leinster Street, and in the final paragraph the narrative records his anticipation of the pleasure he will feel as he immerses himself in the water there.

The Lotus-Eaters episode introduces a number of images—lemon soap, the Gold Cup race, the horse Throwaway—that recur throughout *Ulysses* and provide the novel with a measure of contextual stability. The same form of INTERIOR MONOLOGUE that characterizes the narrative in the preceding four chapters dominates the style of this chapter. The Lotus-Eaters episode provides a detailed representation of Bloom's psyche, and expands the reader's understanding of his role in the novel. Nonetheless, much of what motivates Bloom's behavior and shapes his perception of the world remains hidden.

For additional details, see *Letters,* II.268 and 449.

### *Hades*

This is the sixth episode of *Ulysses,* and the third chapter in the Wanderings of Ulysses section. Its earliest version was serialized in the September 1918 issue of the LITTLE REVIEW.

In book 10 of *The Odyssey,* when seeking to discover a means to reach Ithaca Odysseus is instructed by Circe to seek the counsel of the blind seer, Tiresias, in Hades, the abode of the dead ruled by Hades, the brother of Zeus. In book 11, after the necessary ritual sacrifices, Odysseus descends into Hades. There the ghost of Tiresias appears. He explains to Odysseus that Poseidon is preventing him from returning immediately to Ithaca, and he cautions Odysseus about the many dangers that he must still face on his journey. Tiresias also prophesies that Odysseus will recapture his home and live a long and contented life. Before Odysseus departs from the land of the dead, he meets the ghosts of other important figures as well as that of his mother. Thematic parallels between this chapter in *The Odyssey* and the analogous episode in Joyce's *Ulysses* highlight and comment upon the kinds of struggles that Leopold Bloom will encounter during the day of June 16, 1904, before he returns to recapture his home from the intruder, Blazes Boylan (see Characters, below).

According to the SCHEMA (see *Ulysses* schema in the appendix on page 392) that Joyce loaned to Valéry LARBAUD, the scene of this episode is the graveyard at GLASNEVIN Cemetery. The time at which the action begins is 11 A.M. The organ of the episode is the heart. The art of the episode is religion. Black and white are its colors. Its symbol is the caretaker. And its technique is incubism, a neologism suggesting something spectral, as an incubus.

The chapter opens in front of the home of the deceased Paddy Dignam in Sandymount. Martin Cunningham, Jack Power, and Simon Dedalus, followed by Bloom, enter a hired carriage and join the funeral procession that is about to begin its journey across the city to Glasnevin Cemetery. As they wait in silence for the carriage to move, Bloom finds that he is sitting uncomfortably on the cake of lemon soap in his hip pocket that, in the previous episode, Lotus-Eaters, Bloom had purchased at Sweny's the chemist. Once the carriage starts moving, the men gaze out the windows at passersby and comment with approval on people lifting their hats in respect for the deceased Dignam. Bloom sees Stephen Dedalus, who is on his way from Sandymount Strand to the office of the FREEMAN'S JOURNAL. Noticing that he is dressed in black, Bloom assumes that he too is in mourning. Bloom mentions to Simon that his "son and heir" (*U* 6.43) is walking by, causing Mr. Dedalus to deprecate Buck Mulligan as a cad and belittle his brother-in-law Richie Goulding as a worn-out joker given to drink. The image of a son and heir causes Bloom to consider momentarily how it might have been had his own child Rudy lived. In Bloom's mind, this thought is then associated with the moment of Rudy's procreation: "Must have been that morning in Raymond terrace she was at the window watching the two dogs at it by the wall. . . . Give us a touch, Poldy. God, I'm dying for it. How life begins" (*U* 6.77–81). The themes of the father-son relationship and the eros-thanatos conjunction, central to the novel, converge at this point in the chapter. Even the messy condition of the carriage seats—crumbs and other evidence suggesting that, à la *Madame Bovary,* sexual activity recently took place there—contributes to the picture (*U* 6.97–108).

The cab stops at the Grand Canal, one of the several waterways in the episode corresponding to the rivers in Hades. Bloom sees the Dogs' Home and begins to think of his father's last wish to provide for his old dog, Athos. The desultory conversation in the cab turns to Ben Dollard's singing of "The Croppy Boy" the night before and to Dan Dawson's speech printed in the newspaper. The topic of singing prompts Bloom to think of Blazes Boylan, whose planned assignation with Molly later in the afternoon haunts Bloom all day. At that moment, an ironic coincidence occurs. Boylan is spotted by Cunningham walking past and is saluted by Bloom's companions. Talk then turns to the forthcoming concert tour Boylan and Molly will give together. (Although Bloom explains these plans in detail, here and throughout the novel, he never refers to Blazes Boylan by name.) Bloom himself cannot attend because of his plans to visit Ennis on the anniversary of his father's death. On seeing Reuben J. Dodd, the moneylender, Bloom is reminded of a comic story involving Dodd and his son. Upset over his father's decision to break up his relationship with a girl by sending him to the Isle of Man, Reuben J. Jr. jumped into the River LIFFEY only to be saved from drowning by a boatman, to whom Dodd senior gave a miserly tip of a silver florin (two shillings; see the appendix on page 430 for monetary values). Simon Dedalus's comment—"One and eightpence too much" (*U* 6.291)—causes much laughter among the men in the carriage. The story contains yet another reference to the father-son theme. The conversation of the party, however, keeps returning to the serious subject of death. Mr. Power, unaware at this time that Bloom's father had committed suicide, judges that type of death to be particularly disgraceful. The sensitive Cunningham intervenes, and Bloom contemplates the church's refusal to offer Christian burial in cases of suicide and infanticide. (One who commits suicide, with no sign of repentance prior to death, is excluded from church burial; infanticide, however, does not in itself incur excommunication and does not prevent one from being buried in a Catholic cemetery. The misinformation about infanticide is an example of Bloom's inadequate understanding of church law.) Having realized Cunningham's intentions, Bloom, in turn, thinks sympathetically of Cunningham's plight, living with an alcoholic wife.

The carriage next stops because cattle and sheep, being driven to slaughter the next day, are blocking its passage. The ever practical Bloom asks why these animals cannot be taken by special tram to the boats, freeing up the thoroughfare. This thought leads him to mention that there should also be special trams transporting funeral processions directly to the cemetery, an idea to which Martin Cunningham adds that such a practice would prevent a hearse from capsizing and sending a coffin to the road (*U* 6.415–416). At Crossguns Bridge, the carriage traverses the Royal Canal, northwest of Dublin. Since the canal continues out to the town of MULLINGAR, Bloom makes the connection with Milly and speculates on the wisdom of making a surprise visit there to see her. Nearing Glasnevin cemetery, the procession passes the stonecutter's yard of Thos. H. Dennany, "monumental builder and sculptor" (*U* 6.462), and the tenantless house where a murder had been committed. After going through the cemetery gates, the carriage stops and the men exit, with the fastidious Bloom quickly shifting the lemon soap from Sweny's to his handkerchief pocket before he steps out. Bloom and the others watch the mourners attending a child's funeral pass by and wait for Paddy Dignam's coffin, which they carry into the chapel, followed by friends, the undertaker Corny Kelleher, and Dignam's son. To forestall further embarrassing remarks about suicide, Cunningham whispers to Mr. Power that Bloom's father poisoned himself, while Bloom asks Mr. Kernan about Dignam's insurance and his widow and children. In conversation with Ned Lambert, Mr. Dedalus gives further background about the family, explaining that Dignam had worked for the solicitor John Henry Menton but lost his job through drink.

After they enter the chapel, Father Coffey begins the prayers for the dead, and Bloom speculates: "Makes them feel more important to be prayed over in Latin" (*U* 6.602). At the end of the service, the coffin is taken out by the gravediggers followed by the mourners, and the narrative presents a series of vignettes related to diverse Irish attitudes toward death. Mr. Dedalus on passing near his wife's grave begins a self-indulgent expression of sorrow that ignores any responsibility for causing his wife's early death. Mr. Kernan, a Protestant converted to CATHOLICISM, offers Bloom, also a convert, a disapproving assessment of Father Coffey's performance and of the service. John Henry Menton asks Ned Lambert who Bloom is, not having remembered meeting him years ago at Mat Dillon's, but vividly recalling Molly. The caretaker,

John O'Connell, greets the mourners and tells them a joke about two drunks looking for a friend's grave. At the gravesite, Bloom begins to think about jokes the dead might like to hear and calls to mind the gravediggers' scene in *Hamlet*. Stepping back to count the number of mourners, Bloom is at 13 until he counts the unknown man in a mackintosh. As dirt is thrown on the coffin, Bloom fears that Dignam might still be alive: "No, no: he is dead, of course. Of course he is dead" (*U* 6.866–867). But the possibility of burying someone alive makes Bloom contemplate safety measures that might be taken. The reporter, Joe Hynes, compiling an account of the funeral for the paper, approaches Bloom to ask him, without any obvious irony, for his Christian name. After answering, Bloom, at Charley M'Coy's request in the Lotus-Eaters episode (*U* 5.169–170), gives Hynes M'Coy's name to include in the newspaper. When Hynes asks about the unknown fellow, whom Bloom identifies as wearing a mackintosh, Hynes assumes that to be his name. It later appears as M'INTOSH in the *Telegraph* account that Bloom points out to Stephen in the cabman's shelter in the Eumaeus episode (chapter 16).

Still linking birth and death, Bloom sees the coffin band being coiled by one of the gravediggers, and this suggests to him a navel cord, an image used earlier by Stephen Dedalus in the opening of the Proteus episode (*U* 3.36). As Bloom is leaving the cemetery, he considers the monuments and questions the prudence of spending money for them, money which could better be used for the living. Significantly, in contrast to melodramatic companions like Simon Dedalus, it is to the living that Bloom's mind continually turns throughout the chapter, and here, once again, his thoughts are in affirmation of "warm fullblooded life" (*U* 6.1005). Upon meeting John Henry Menton on the way out, Bloom points out the dinge in the man's hat, only to be snubbed by him. Nonetheless, with a renewed sense of life, Bloom enters the world of the living.

Hades marks the first sustained view that the reader has of Bloom's public life. It shows him isolated in the midst of men whom one would initially assume to be his friends. At the same time, as Hades unfolds the episode insinuates an idea about the men that will be elaborated throughout the narrative. All the Dubliners who appear in these pages suffer from a sense of alienation as powerful, if not as overt, as Bloom's. Though bound together on the surface by the routines of cordiality and camaraderie, these men in fact share little besides a taste for alcohol and a bitter view of the world. In fact, as the reader observes Bloom more closely over the course of the day, it becomes evident that despite the tendencies of the others to regard him as marginal to Dublin life he, more successfully than any of them, has adapted himself to the harsh emotional and physical demands of the world that they all inhabit.

For further information on circumstances surrounding the composition of this episode, see *Letters*, II.32n.1

### *Aeolus*

This is the seventh episode in *Ulysses* and the fourth chapter in the Wanderings of Ulysses section. An early version was serialized in the October 1918 issue of the LITTLE REVIEW.

Book 10 of *The Odyssey* gives an account of Aeolus, the god of the winds, attempting to help Odysseus reach his homeland, Ithaca, by confining all adverse winds in a bag. Odysseus's crew, seeking booty that they assume Odysseus has hidden from them, open the bag and release the winds, causing their ship to be blown back to the island of Aeolia. When Odysseus returns a second time to ask for assistance, he is rebuffed and sent away by Aeolus. The long-winded conversations of the Dubliners occupying this episode offer an obvious analogue to the Homeric original.

According to the SCHEMA (see *Ulysses* schema in the appendix on page 392) that Joyce loaned to Valéry LARBAUD, the scene of the episode is the office of the FREEMAN'S JOURNAL. The time at which the action begins is noon. The organs of the chapter, not surprisingly, are the lungs. The art of the chapter is rhetoric. The color is red. The episode's symbol is the editor. And its technic is enthymemic (that is, like a syllogism containing an implied or unstated premise).

In this chapter the garrulous men who gather in the newspaper offices to provide, with their hot air, an ironic evocation of this Homeric episode include Simon Dedalus and Ned Lambert (see Characters, below), who come to the offices after attending the funeral of Paddy Dignam in the morning. Others, like Lenehan and Professor MacHugh, have wandered in during the course of the morning. From their conversations, however, it quickly becomes clear that most of these men have little to occupy their time. Leopold Bloom—anxiously collecting information regarding the advertisement that he wishes to sell to the tea, wine, and spirit merchant Alexander Keyes—is a striking exception to this condition, and consequently he becomes a target for the voluble ridicule of the loafers in the office. The imagery of windiness embodied in the garrulous dialogue of these loafers is enhanced by such seemingly mundane actions as the opening and closing of doors. Adding a note of anarchy to the scene, Myles CRAWFORD, editor of the *Evening Telegraph,* punctuates the conversations with his drunken interruptions.

The action of the chapter begins when Bloom encounters John "Red" Murray, an employee of the *Freeman's Journal.* Murray has located a previously published Keyes advertisement for Bloom to show as a sample to Joseph Patrick Nannetti, the newspaper's production foreman. While Bloom talks to Murray, William Brayden, the owner of the paper, enters the offices, and Red Murray takes note of the purported resemblance of Brayden's face to popular images of "Our Savior" (*U* 7.49). Bloom, however, thinking of Christ speaking with Mary and Martha, pictures a different face, one more like that of Mario, a tenor well known to Dublin opera buffs of the day, famous for singing the aria "M'appari" in Flotow's MARTHA.

This association is typical of many occurring throughout *Ulysses.* In this instance, Bloom's introduction of the Flotow aria into the narrative anticipates Simon Dedalus's rendition of the same aria in the Ormond bar in the Sirens episode (*U* 11.587–751) (chapter 11). The opera's title is also the first name of the woman (Martha Clifford) with whom Bloom is carrying on a clandestine correspondence.

On his way to Nannetti's office with his copy of the Keyes ad, Bloom sees Joe Hynes, who has arrived ahead of him, apparently to deliver his account of the Dignam funeral. While Hynes arranges with Nannetti for the publication of the story, Bloom introduces the issue of identity by contemplating the oddity that Nannetti has never visited Italy: "Strange he never saw his real country. Ireland my country" (*U* 7.87). The irony of this seemingly unself-conscious observation will not be lost to careful readers. Bloom—though he was born in Dublin and became a Catholic in order to marry Molly Bloom—is viewed by his fellow Dubliners as a Jew and a foreigner in his own land, an outsider tolerated but not accepted. Nannetti—whose Italian antecedents ostensively seem as foreign in parochial Dublin as Bloom's—is well established as a city councillor, an insider, who may even become Lord Mayor of Dublin (*U* 7.106). (This theme of identity recurs throughout the narrative, and it comes to the foreground in a dispute between Bloom and the Citizen in the Cyclops episode.)

As Hynes is about to leave the newspaper offices, Bloom, for the third time (*U* 7.119), subtly tries to remind him of the three-shilling debt that he owes, but this effort comes to nothing. Bloom next shows the Keyes advertisement to Nannetti and explains the need to add a pair of crisscrossed keys as an emblem at the top of the ad. The concern for keys is another example of thematic (and symbolic) correspondence in the novel. Bloom, like Stephen Dedalus (also an outsider, who has given up his key to Buck Mulligan in the Telemachus episode [chapter 1]), is himself keyless this day. Nannetti agrees to the advertisement but wants a three-month renewal, a difficult business challenge for Bloom. He will later get the keys symbol from a Kilkenny newspaper at the National Library (see the Scylla and Charybdis episode [chapter 9]) and get a promise for renewal, but only for two months (*U* 7.973). (As with so many instances in the novel, a modernist aversion to unambiguous resolution brackets Bloom's efforts.)

On his way out, Bloom watches Old Monks neatly set the type, which he reads backwards, reminding Bloom of his father, Rudolph, reading the Hebrew letters right to left in the Haggadah at Pesach (Passover) (*U* 7.206–207). Bloom's consciousness emerges as fundamentally linked to a

Jewish rather than to a Catholic identity, and this disposition, despite Bloom's sporadic resistance, becomes more strongly defined as the day goes on. Instead of taking a tram to visit Keyes, who might not be in, Bloom decides to go into the editorial office of the *Evening Telegraph* to use the phone. As he enters, Bloom is startled by a screech of laughter coming from Ned Lambert, and then he hears the voice of Professor MacHugh softly saying "The ghost walks" (*U* 7.237), a comment that—given the Shakespearean affectations of Stephen Dedalus manifest throughout the morning—can be seen as an ironic evocation of the ghost of Hamlet's father allied to the insubstantial Bloom, and a reminder of the pervasive father-son theme throughout the novel. Soon after this introductory line, MacHugh reinforces these associations with still another allusion to Hamlet (*U* 7.325).

The dominant form of expression in the chapter, however, is not drama but oratory, and when the men in the newspaper offices attempt to take up this rhetorical mode their endeavors only underscore their shortcomings. Ned Lambert, Professor MacHugh, and Simon Dedalus, for example, repeatedly refer to the efforts of noted speakers, often in strikingly accurate recollections. These men, however, cannot go beyond crude parodies. Ned Lambert, for instance, mockingly reads the patriotic and flowery speech of the well-to-do baker, Dan Dawson, made the previous evening. This in turn evokes satiric responses from both Simon Dedalus and Professor MacHugh. Later, MacHugh recalls the speech John F. Taylor had made at the college historical society in response to Justice Gerald Fitzgibbon's attack on the Irish language movement. Despite his desire to pay homage to Taylor's disquisition, MacHugh's rendition comes across as a pompous, heavy-handed caricature.

The bombast of the characters, however, reflects only the most overt and least sophisticated forms of expression under consideration. A subtle rhetoric of gesture shapes the narrative action every bit as profoundly as the verbal exchanges so much in evidence. For example, when the solicitor J. J. O'Molloy comes in to see Miles Crawford about a loan, the doorknob hits Bloom's back and he must step aside. O'Molloy's entrance in effect usurps Bloom's place, symbolically anticipating the moment later in the day when Bloom will be forced to step aside metaphorically to let Blazes Boylan into his house.

As the chapter unfolds, gestures often define Bloom's position and continually underscore the power of unspoken discourse. When Bloom attempts to approach Crawford about using the telephone to contact Keyes, Crawford, in a drunken fuddle, ignores Bloom's advance and launches into abusive greetings to all present.

In other associative action, Lenehan, who was with Crawford in the inner office, enters waving pages from *Sport* and offering a sure tip on Sceptre in the GOLD CUP race. In fact, that race at Ascot will be won by the dark horse, Throwaway, a long shot. As readers learn more details of the race and see their links to various characters, sexual connotations begin to emerge. For example, one can see the cup as symbolizing feminine sexuality and phallic Sceptre as evoking the masculine. One might speculate further that Bloom, the dark outsider, like Throwaway, will ultimately achieve the victory over the sure thing, Boylan, Molly's lover. Bloom is the one with more spunk (see the Penelope episode [chapter 18] *U* 18.168), and it is he who will occupy the winner's circle by the end of the Ithaca episode in chapter 17, (see *U* 17.2332). Bloom will continue to lie in Molly's bed.

After his phone call, Bloom exits to seek Keyes at Dillon's auction rooms in Bachelor's Walk. Crawford is glad to get rid of him. Meanwhile, Mr. Dedalus and Ned Lambert have left for a drink. While the remaining men critically assess ancient Rome's contribution to civilization, Mr. O'Madden Burke enters followed by Stephen Dedalus, who, fresh from his walk along Sandymount Strand, appears with the letter concerning hoof-and-mouth disease that Garrett Deasy had asked him to have printed. The editor attempts to persuade Stephen to join the newspaper trade, ignoring Stephen's real ambitions as an artist. Crawford is reminded of Ignatius Gallaher's great achievement in covering the PHOENIX PARK MURDERS. The conversation briefly turns to literature, a topic very much on Stephen's mind, but soon reverts to oratory, the central subject of this episode, and to the debate between Taylor and Fitzgibbon on the revival of the Irish language.

On Stephen's invitation (*U* 7.885–886), the group leaves the newspaper offices to go to a pub. (Lenehan suggests Mooney's, but it remains unclear whether the others actually pay any attention to him or simply go there because of its proximity.) As they are walking, Bloom, back from his meeting with Keyes, catches up to Crawford, who had earlier refused to answer Bloom's phone call to the office with a question about the Keyes ad (*U* 7.670–673). Crawford again irritably dismisses Bloom, calling to mind a Homeric parallel with the rebuke that Aeolus gave Odysseus on their second meeting. Once more, Bloom is left standing alone.

On the way to Mooney's, Stephen endeavors to demonstrate his creative talents by telling his story, "A PISGAH SIGHT OF PALESTINE OR THE PARABLE OF THE PLUMS," yet another form of oratory. Unfortunately, in contrast to his father, Stephen has not developed the practiced narrative delivery of a barroom raconteur, and the story receives a lukewarm reception from both MacHugh and Crawford. The chapter ends with this failure.

Although the episode is full of the witty exchanges that distinguish much of *Ulysses*, perhaps the most striking feature of the Aeolus episode is stylistic: The headings that subdivide the narrative with a range of commentaries—straightforward, sardonic, comic, or serious—on the material that follows punctuate the narrative in a fashion that cannot be ignored with a form that cannot be readily explained. They resist a naturalization into conventional interpretive approaches, and many critics see these headings, which were inserted in a late draft of the chapter, as overtly marking the point at which the structure of this novel undergoes a radical formal change. (These headings did not appear in the version of "Aeolus" serialized in the October 1918 issue of the *LITTLE REVIEW.* Joyce began adding them and making other changes elsewhere in the text some time in the late summer of 1921.) Because they are so emphatically disjoined from the rest of the narrative, the headings call attention to the act of reading, making the reader aware of the protocols one must follow in the attempt to derive meaning from Joyce's work. Further, they signal the beginning of a process of stylistic evolution—a formal shifting from chapter to chapter—that characterizes the rest of the work.

Both from a stylistic and from a contextual perspective Aeolus was clearly one of Joyce's favorite episodes. It offers an open testimony of the break with conventional narrative that goes on from the first page of the novel but which the reader can accept only after the six chapters of acclimatization that precede it. As a reflection of the fondness that he felt, Joyce chose to read selections from this chapter, from the sections entitled "Impromptu" and "From the Fathers" (*U* 7.812–840 and 841–870), when he made a phonograph recording of a portion of *Ulysses* in Paris in 1924. For additional information on this episode, see *Letters,* III.111n.l, 142n.3, and 262n.2.

### *Lestrygonians*

This is the eighth episode of *Ulysses* and the fifth in the Wanderings of Ulysses section. An earlier version of it was serialized in the January and February–March 1919 issues of the *LITTLE REVIEW,* although the January issue was confiscated by U.S. postal authorities because of complaints of obscenity made about the *Ulysses* excerpt (see *Letters,* II.448).

According to the SCHEMA (see *Ulysses* schema in the appendix on page 392) that Joyce loaned to Valéry LARBAUD, the scene of the episode is Leopold Bloom's lunch in DAVY BYRNE's pub. The time at which the action begins is 1 P.M. The organ of the chapter is the esophagus. The art of the chapter is architecture. The episode's symbol is constables. And its technic is peristaltic.

Joyce took the informal title of his episode from book 10 of *The Odyssey,* in which Odysseus describes a frightening encounter with the cannibalistic Lestrygonians. With the exception of the ship commanded by Odysseus, the entire fleet is trapped in a bay by Antiphates, the king of the Lestrygonians. The ships are destroyed, and the men are devoured. Only Odysseus and his crew escape.

In the Lestrygonians episode images of eating dominate the narrative, and they serve to underscore the predatory elements inherent in the urban life in the novel. The chapter follows the movements of Leopold Bloom after he leaves the *FREE-*

MAN'S JOURNAL office, the scene of the Aeolus episode (chapter 7). Although he is still ostensibly pursuing the ad from Alexander Keyes, Bloom is in fact listlessly trying to distract himself from thoughts of Molly's impending adultery with Blazes Boylan.

Nearly every character and event in the chapter, however, seems to conspire to thwart his desire to avoid confronting her infidelity. As the Lestrygonians episode opens and Bloom walks down O'Connell Street toward the LIFFEY bridge, a throwaway (an advertising flyer) announcing the imminent appearance in Dublin of an American religious revivalist, "Dr. John Alexander Dowie restorer of the church in Zion," is placed in his hand (*U* 8.13–14). The throwaway reminds him of Dowie's teachings on polygamy (and also recalls the GOLD CUP racehorse Throwaway). This by association turns Bloom's mind briefly, but tellingly, back to Molly and Boylan. It brings on a moment of panic, when Bloom unwillingly speculates on the possibility that Boylan could have a venereal disease, a horrific idea that Bloom quickly suppresses by considering the possible etymological derivations of the word PARALLAX.

Once across the O'Connell Bridge and heading south on Westmoreland Street, Bloom attempts to fill his mind with memories of happier times with Molly. While doing so, he encounters Josie Breen, an old friend of Molly's and the wife of the lunatic Denis Breen. Bloom learns from Josie of her husband's latest mania, his rage at being sent a mocking postcard inscribed simply with the initials U.P. (This becomes yet another of the narrative's conundrums, for it never explains what the phrase means.) Paradoxically, thinking about Mrs. Breen's chaotic life has a calming effect on Bloom, distracting him from his own anxieties. Their talk then shifts to the confinement of Mina Purefoy and the impending birth of her ninth child.

After leaving Mrs. Breen, Bloom continues south, skirting the edge of the TRINITY COLLEGE campus, and prepares to enter Grafton Street, at this time filled with the lunchtime crowd. Spurred by his conversation with Josie Breen, Bloom thinks of various other Dubliners and their unhappy family situations. These thoughts lead him to a more general consideration of the harshness of life in the city, and he wonders at the cruel humor of the men who mock Denis Breen. Bloom turns from this rather detached contemplation of human suffering to considering the more personal pain that comes from losing a child at birth. (In the Calypso episode, [chapter 4], he explicitly references the death of his son, Rudy Bloom [*U* 4.420]. The narrator in the Ithaca episode, chapter 17, records further details of Rudy's birth and death 11 days later [*U* 17.2280–2282]; also see the Oxen of the Sun episode [chapter 14] [*U* 14.271–272].) From this image, Bloom turns his thoughts to the brutishness of Dublin police constables, and in consequence thinks of the shiftiness of Corny Kelleher, whom he suspects of being a police informer. Finally, his mind goes back to a series of events illustrating the uncertain loyalties of the Irish toward their political leaders, specifically Charles Stewart PARNELL.

As Bloom walks into Grafton Street, "gay with housed awnings" (*U* 8.614), he is momentarily distracted by the hurly-burly of the street filled with people on their lunch breaks. He recalls his own hunger, and he walks into Duke Street where he looks in at the Burton, a restaurant, thinking to get a meal. The heavy sensuality of the lunchtime crowd there assaults both Bloom and the reader, and the gross manners and coarse behavior of the diners send Bloom back to the street. After a moment's hesitation, he turns and crosses to a more tranquil venue, Davy Byrne's: "Moral pub," he thinks to himself (*U* 8.732).

Inside Davy Byrne's, Bloom orders a gorgonzola cheese sandwich and a glass of burgundy and falls into conversation with the barfly Nosey Flynn, to whom he mentions Molly's forthcoming singing engagements. Although Bloom tries to talk about the tour while avoiding reference to Blazes Boylan, Flynn unconsciously forces the issue by bringing up Boylan's recent financial success in promoting the Myles Keogh–Percy Bennett boxing match. With that Bloom finishes his sandwich, and, as he leaves the pub, a number of men who have just entered the bar are turning their minds to what has become one of the dominant topics of the day, the question of who will win the Gold Cup race. The fiscally cautious Bloom has no interest in betting, but in the minds of other Dubliners—spurred by the salacious gossip of Lenehan—Bloom, Throwaway, and the Gold Cup race will later form a curious conjunction in the Cyclops episode (chapter 12).

Immediately upon walking out of the pub, Bloom encounters a blind stripling, a piano tuner by trade, who will reappear in the Wandering Rocks episode (chapter 10), return to the Ormond Hotel at the close of the Sirens episode (chapter 11), and finally emerge as a hallucination in the Circe episode (chapter 15). Bloom helps the young man cross Dawson Street, and guides him north to Molesworth Street. Then, walking east on Molesworth Street, he sees Blazes Boylan on Kildare Street. As the chapter ends, Bloom, flustered by the idea of running into the man who he knows will later in the day cuckold him, quickly ducks into the National Museum.

After the emphasis on Bloom's public persona in the preceding chapter, Aeolus, the narrative of the Lestrygonians episode refocuses attention on Bloom's private thoughts and concerns. Nonetheless, despite the privileged perspective afforded to readers by the INTERIOR MONOLOGUE technique of most of the chapter, the narrative itself yields little clear insight into Bloom's personal feelings. As he has done from the Calypso chapter onward, Bloom struggles to suppress thoughts of the day's most momentous event, Blazes Boylan's four o'clock visit to Molly, but at every turn he encounters someone or something to remind him of it.

Paradoxically, through the understated manner by which it makes us aware of his suffering, the narrative subtly emphasizes Bloom's acute pain. It also touches upon the complexity of Bloom's situation and raises questions about his response to Molly's adultery, including the choices open to him. From Bloom's unwillingness to confront these issues, the reader begins to sense the broader, far-reaching consequences of Molly's adultery and the difficult position in which Bloom finds himself. While living with the knowledge of her infidelity is painful, he must know that acknowledging her behavior would certainly produce a confrontation, which might provoke a split with Molly and bring to an end a life that Bloom finds satisfying in so many ways. Thus, on closer examination Bloom's willful denial seems less an act of timidity and more an act of resignation by one who has carefully weighed the options.

On the formal level, Joyce has structured the episode around metaphors of eating and nourishment. Because the chapter takes place over the lunch hour, it is no surprise that most of the characters who appear in the Lestrygonians episode make some reference to food, have it on their minds, or are eating. Images of food so permeate the chapter that readers find associations even when the narrative does not explicitly make them, as in the homophonic correspondence that occurs when Bloom thinks: "Molly looks out of plumb" (*U* 8.618–619).

The thematic significance of the food imagery, however, has a more fundamental function, turning on its evocation of basic appetites and the impulse for consumption. There is a clear analogy between the coarse images of the diners lunching at the Burton and the fierce, predatory way Dubliners rend and consume the spirits and reputations of their fellow citizens. This in turn reinforces the sense of Bloom as persecuted and put-upon, not only by Boylan and Molly, who make him a cuckold, but also by so many other Dubliners whom he meets over the course of the day and who treat him with varying degrees of disdain.

### *Scylla and Charybdis*

This is the ninth episode of *Ulysses,* and the sixth of the Wanderings of Ulysses section. An early version of the chapter appeared in serialization in the April and May 1919 issues of the LITTLE REVIEW.

According to the SCHEMA (see *Ulysses* schema in the appendix on page 392) that Joyce loaned to Valéry LARBAUD, the scene of the episode is the NATIONAL LIBRARY OF IRELAND. The time at which the action begins is 2 p.m. The organ of the chapter is the brain. The art of the chapter is literature. The episode's symbols are Stratford and London, the two locations associated with Shakespeare. Its technic is dialectic.

The chapter derives its name from the dual perils, described by the enchantress Circe in book 12 of *The Odyssey*—the six-headed monster Scylla and the whirlpool Charybdis. In choosing to avoid the more unpredictable and far more dangerous hazard, the Wandering Rocks, Odysseus confronts instead the twin challenges of Scylla and Charybdis between which Odysseus must navigate after leaving Circe's island. The challenge involves more than overcoming danger. It forces Odysseus to make a life-and-death decision regarding his crew. Rather than risk the possible loss of the entire ship by sailing near the whirlpool, Charybdis, he elects to sail close to the lair of the ferocious Scylla, although in doing so Odysseus intentionally sacrifices six of his crew whom the six-headed monster will seize and devour.

The Scylla and Charybdis episode in *Ulysses* itself emphasizes the need to make choices and the inevitability of having to skirt danger in order to succeed, though these are of an intellectual rather than a physical nature. The chapter takes place in the office of the director of the National Library of Ireland. There Stephen Dedalus presents his theory of the creative forces in the work of William SHAKESPEARE to a small (and sometimes hostile) group of Dublin intelligentsia, made up at various times of Thomas Lyster, the chief librarian; Richard Best, another librarian; John Eglinton (William MAGEE), an assistant librarian; the writer and editor George RUSSELL (AE); and Buck Mulligan.

The narrative is organized around Stephen's presentation of his Shakespeare theory, previously mentioned to Mulligan's English friend, Haines, in the Telemachus episode (chapter 1). Stephen's talk seems to be a desperate attempt to impress these men with his erudition and perhaps to show them the mistake that was made when he was not invited to the literary evening scheduled to take place that night at the home of George MOORE. This drive for recognition becomes most evident with the appearance of Buck Mulligan, who attempts to command attention with an improvised comic performance. Within a short time, a thinly veiled competition for the approbation of their shared audience emerges between the two young men. Despite these efforts, however, the episode ends with little apparent change in the attitude of either Russell or Eglinton and with the rivalry of Stephen and Mulligan lurching forward under the ambiguous cover of a dubious friendship.

Like the opening of the novel, the chapter begins in an epic mode, in medias res, with Stephen holding forth in front of Lyster, Best, Eglinton, and Russell. From the start of the episode, it is clear that Stephen's views already have begun to provoke the animosity of Eglinton and Russell, both of whom respond to Stephen's remarks by pontificating about the nature of Irish art. Stephen can bear their highly critical commentaries with equanimity only by carrying on an internal, unvoiced dialectic that pointedly rebuts and rebukes their assessments. Stephen's mind rages at the rapid succession of slights and insults offered by Russell and Eglinton, and his intellect conjures up a number of equally tart rejoinders. At the same time, he is fully aware of the power they exert within local intellectual circles, so he holds his anger in check and keeps his thoughts to himself. Instead of lashing out, he replies to their derision with studied politeness while determinedly endeavoring to turn the discussion back to his theory on the nature of Shakespeare's creativity and to its consequent effect upon Shakespeare's process of composition.

Stephen's disquisition, in fact, shows more scholarship than creativity. It is a mix of ideas liberally drawn from a number of well-known Shakespearean critics of the day—most notably George Brandes, Frank Harris, and Sidney Lee, whose work Joyce consulted while composing the chapter. The resultant conglomeration of ideas, suppositions, and facts forms not so much a lucid argument as an occasion for the display of Stephen's wide-ranging knowledge of diverse details of Shakespeare's life and work.

Stephen's talk moves widely and freely around accurate and apocryphal biographical details that serve as the foundation for broad, far-reaching metaphors of conception, birth, and paternity. On the surface these allusions convey Stephen's scholarly erudition, but they also betray his own profound insecurity when forced to confront issues like the sources of artistic creation and the extent of an artist's imaginative debt to his predecessors. Stephen's relentless focus upon intellectual independence, his near-obsessive concern with artistic influences, and even his passing reference to Christian heresies on the Trinity all relate to his desire to establish himself as an independent artistic force.

Despite the intensity of Stephen's feelings and the intellectual dexterity of his argument, however, the response from his audience is at best mixed. Russell seems openly hostile to Stephen's approach, and he does not hesitate to voice his broad dissatisfaction with Stephen's methods of interpretation. In a more punctilious though no less disruptive fashion, Eglinton objects to Stephen's treatment of diverse literary and biographical details that emerge during the talk, repeatedly interrupting Stephen's exposition to carp about various points in an aggressively querulous tone.

Stephen, though his mind is raging at these insults, maintains a polite façade. Nonetheless, his disquisition has no more than minimal impact upon his audience. While Best and Lyster remain polite, if somewhat distracted, Russell abruptly decides that he has heard enough and rudely gets up to leave. Stephen continues his presentation despite Eglinton's sniping, but the force clearly seems to have gone out of the young man's argument. When Mulligan abruptly enters the director's office, however, Stephen's tone changes markedly.

Mulligan's irreverence punctures the solemnity that has stifled the discourse up to this point. His bawdy humor counters the sententiousness of Eglinton and challenges Stephen to work that much harder to hold the attention of the audience. As the conversation continues, both Stephen's and Buck's roles as performers become quite clear, as does their competition for their listeners' approval.

In the end, however, the efforts of both prove fruitless. The humorless Eglinton is unmoved by Mulligan's buffoonery and at the same time is unwilling to disregard his resentment of Stephen to take a comprehensive view of the argument. When the talk is finished, Eglinton pointedly asks Stephen if he believes his own theories. Stephen, at this point no longer disposed to restrain himself, provocatively answers no. Eglinton takes the reply at face value—rather than as an acknowledgment of the subjectivity of all criticism and all art. As a result, with a pronounced measure of satisfaction, he dismisses all that Stephen has said.

As Buck and Stephen are leaving the library, the mercurial Mulligan once again shifts his ground to play a double role. In a vulgar poem, he mocks Eglinton's solemnity and speculates on his inclination toward masturbation. Continuing that theme, he expresses his desire to write a play entitled "Everyman His Own Wife, or A Honeymoon in the Hand." With an abrupt shift in tone, he then voices his admiration of Stephen for standing his ground against the pompous Dublin literati even as he chides his friend for his lack of delicacy. Mulligan pragmatically advises Stephen to mix a greater measure of diplomacy into his artistic demeanor: "Couldn't you do the Yeats touch?" (*U* 9.1160–1161). In a final mercurial twist, when Bloom and Mulligan pass on the portico of the library, the latter cannot resist anti-Semitism and calculated crudeness. "The wandering jew . . . O, Kinch, thou art in peril. Get thee a breechpad" (*U* 9.1209–1212).

Over the course of this chapter, Joyce has gone to great pains to integrate the formal and contextual features of the struggle among Stephen, Russell, and Eglinton, into a skillfully arranged dramatic framework. A series of literary puns and dramatic allusions give a structure to the Scylla and Charybdis episode that both reinforces its Shakespearean topic and also reminds readers of its own dialectical process. Stephen's unvoiced concerns about his own creative potential, about his guilt over his mother's death, and about his uneasy relations with his father mirror the concerns he articulates about Shakespeare's life and creative methods and about his own artistic reputation.

The chapter also highlights another theme that has been running through the narrative: Stephen's pressing need to gain the esteem of his fellow Dubliners. With "A PISGAH SIGHT OF PALESTINE, OR THE PARABLE OF THE PLUMS," the story that he relates to Myles Crawford and Professor Hugh MacHugh in the offices of the *Freeman's* JOURNAL during the Aeolus episode (chapter 7), we begin to see evidence in Stephen of the urge to perform and to be taken seriously. His holding forth on Shakespeare is another manifestation of that drive, and in the Oxen of the Sun episode (chapter 14) and the Circe episode (chapter 15), he will again attempt to gain public recognition. (In these latter instances, however, his drunkenness makes his efforts more laughable than anything else.)

For further details relating to the Scylla and Charybdis episode, see *Letters*, II.38n.1, 108n.1, 110, 436, and 448n.2, and III.73.

***Wandering Rocks, The***

This is the 10th episode of *Ulysses* and the seventh in the Wanderings of Ulysses section. An earlier version was serialized in the June and July 1919 issues of the *LITTLE REVIEW,* and the first half of the episode also appeared in the December 1919 issue of the London journal the *EGOIST.*

According to the SCHEMA (see *Ulysses* schema, Appendix on page 392) that Joyce loaned to Valéry LARBAUD, the scene of the episode is the streets of DUBLIN. The time at which the action begins is 3 P.M. The organ [*sic*] of the chapter is blood. The art of the chapter is mechanics. The episode's symbol is the conglomeration of the citizens of the city. Its technic is the labyrinth.

The name derives from Joyce's modification of the term *Planktai,* or Clashing Rocks, the group of drifting boulders that Odysseus, in book 12 of *The Odyssey,* avoids when after leaving the island of the enchantress Circe, he chooses instead to sail his ship in the direction of the monster Scylla and the whirlpool Charybdis.

Using a narrative strategy that expands the scope of the discourse, the Wandering Rocks episode samples diverse elements of Dublin life. Its montagelike narrative moves around the city and, through a series of rapidly unfolding vignettes, shifts the reader's attention away from the central characters of the novel—Leopold Bloom, Stephen Dedalus, and Molly Bloom. It unfolds in 19 brief scenes, which for the most part feature relatively minor characters, many of whom have been introduced over the course of the first nine chapters. In this episode they are seen performing the mundane activities that make up their lives from day to day.

The chapter begins with Father John Conmee, SJ, a character already familiar to readers of *A Portrait of the Artist as a Young Man,* attempting to find a place for one of the sons of the late Paddy Dignam at the O'Brien Institute for Destitute Children in Artane. As with so many individuals in Joyce's fiction, even a brief exposure reveals the complexity of the character. Although he has set out to do a good deed, Conmee's INTERIOR MONOLOGUE, as he travels toward Artane, shows him to be rather pleased with himself and perhaps a bit of a snob. At the same time, his meeting with the three schoolboys from BELVEDERE COLLEGE recalls Conmee as the rector who was extremely kind to the young and frightened Stephen Dedalus at CLONGOWES WOOD COLLEGE at the close of the first chapter of *A Portrait.* The depiction sets the tone for representations of figures throughout the chapter and indeed over the course of the novel. Joyce's characters are not simple or reductive. Rather, they manifest the same contradictory traits and impulses found in most individuals.

The narrative continues to unfold through a series of short scenes that reinforce readers' impressions of—or that provide new information about—a number of characters. In the next vignette, Corny Kelleher stops his work for a casual conversation with a police constable, an incident that suggests without confirming the validity of Bloom's earlier suspicion that Kelleher is a police informant. Immediately following this exchange, the narrative abruptly shifts to a description of a one-legged sailor begging along ECCLES STREET. When he passes under the Blooms' window, he receives a coin tossed out by Molly. At the same time, three children of Simon Dedalus—Katey, Boody, and Maggy—gather in their tenement in the Cabra section of the city for a late afternoon meal of pea soup given to them by a nun from the Sisters of Charity, whose convent is located to the east on Gardiner Street.

Simultaneously, on the other side of the River LIFFEY, Blazes Boylan stops at Thornton's on Grafton Street to purchase a basket of fruit, potted meat, and port to send to Molly. As he places his order and flirts with the girl behind the counter, the narrative gives the reader the first direct view of Boylan, unadulterated by the salacious gossip of other Dubliners or the apprehensive thoughts of Bloom. Nearby, Almidano Artifoni, Stephen Dedalus's former music teacher, stops near TRINITY COLLEGE to talk with Stephen about the latter's chances to develop a career as a singer. Artifoni's affectionate concern and Stephen's respectful politeness show a very different side of the young man's nature than readers have seen to this point. While this conversation is occurring, in another part of Dublin Miss Dunne, Blazes Boylan's secretary, receives a call from her employer inquiring about the details of the concert tour that he is planning for Molly Bloom. From Miss Dunne's response to Boylan's questions, it appears that the tour will be a far more modest undertaking than either Bloom or Molly has assumed. By this point in the chapter, readers are becoming accustomed to the narrative's synchronous representations. It is a deft rhetorical achievement, breaking the conventional linear bonds of description to show concurrently how much is occurring across the city.

The overlapping scenes also underscore the connections, some perceived and some unconscious, between many of the Dubliners mentioned in the novel. Back on the north side of the Liffey, an amateur historian, Rev. Hugh C. Love (the man who has had a writ issued to the impecunious Father Bob Cowley) is being taken by Ned Lambert on a tour of the old chapter house of St. Mary's Abbey on Capel Street. Although famous as the site where Silken Thomas (Thomas Fitzgerald, Lord Offaly) expressed his defiance of the authority of Henry VIII, in Joyce's time the building housed the seed merchants Messrs. Alexander & Co. South of the river again, Lenehan and C. P. M'Coy walk toward the Liffey discussing Tom Rochford, whom they have just left, and gossiping about Bloom and Molly. While this is going on, Bloom stops at a seedy bookstore near the quays and buys a mildly pornographic book, *Sweets of Sin,* for Molly.

On the opposite side of the river again, Stephen's sister Dilly Dedalus meets her father near Dillon's auction rooms by the O'Connell Street Bridge, and she browbeats her father into giving her a bit of money to buy food for the family. At the same time, the tea vendor Tom Kernan celebrates a recent sale by stopping for a drink at the establishment of William C. Crimmins, tea, wine, and spirit merchant. Shortly after her confrontation with Simon Dedalus, Dilly meets Stephen at a bookstall south of the Liffey. She is buying a used French primer with some extra money that her father gave her for milk and a bun. Simon Dedalus, in the meantime, has walked down to the Ormond Quay where he meets Father Bob Cowley and Ben Dollard.

Simultaneously, Martin Cunningham, Jack Power, and John Wyse Nolan—on a mission of charity similar to that of Father Conmee—are on their way to meet with the sub-sheriff, Long John Fanning, in an effort to raise money for the Dignam family. Meanwhile, Buck Mulligan and his English friend Haines are having an afternoon snack in the Dublin Bakery Company's tearoom at 33 Dame Street. There, as Haines fusses over the quality of the cream, Mulligan allows himself the pleasure of ridiculing Stephen's literary ambitions. Near Merrion Square, a local eccentric, Cashel Boyle O'Connor Fitzmaurice Tisdall Farrell, collides with the blind stripling piano tuner first seen in the Lestrygonians chapter. And Patrick Dignam, Paddy's son, walks along Nassau Street, heading home with a package of porksteaks from Mangan's butcher shop.

In the final two sections of The Wandering Rocks chapter, through a technique that enables a reprise of the main events of the chapter, the narrative rushes the reader through the city as it follows the course of a viceregal cavalcade from the viceroy's residence in PHOENIX PARK to Pembroke Township near Ringsend to oversee the opening of the Mirus Bazaar. As the cavalcade passes through the streets of Dublin, the reader is brought up to date on the location of many of the characters already mentioned in the episode. It also introduces other figures into the action—M'Intosh and Gerty MacDowell, for example—who have played or will play a part in the development of the narrative.

At first glance, the structure of the Wandering Rocks episode seems to revert to an earlier, less experimental form than some of the chapters immediately preceding it, echoing the dominant style of the first six chapters of the novel. However, its self-conscious manipulation of temporal and spatial elements proves to be very different from anything that has occurred previously. For example, the narrative reintroduces the throwaway handed to Bloom at the beginning of an earlier episode—Lestrygonians (chapter 8)—announcing the arrival of Alexander Dowie. Bloom has thrown it into the river, and, as it floats down the Liffey, one sees in its movements on the ebb and flow of the waterway an evocation of the rising and falling tempo of life across the city. One also sees in its presentation the intricacy of detail with which Joyce weaves together the novel's seemingly disparate and insignificant activities into a larger artistic unity.

Further, throughout the episode, the narrative evokes a sense of simultaneity by integrating events occurring on one side of the city into scenes taking place in completely different locations. This effect of ongoing action is enhanced as details of one scene continue to appear in subsequent scenes. In addition, The Wandering Rocks also underscores the variety of Dublin life, as it proffers a series of brief but significant glimpses into the lives of a number of minor characters.

For additional details regarding The Wandering Rocks episode, see *Letters*, I.149, II.66, 193 and 436, and III.68.

***Sirens***

This is the 11th episode of *Ulysses*, and the eighth in The Wanderings of Ulysses section. An earlier version first appeared in a two-part serialization in the August and September 1919 issues of the LITTLE REVIEW.

According to the SCHEMA (see *Ulysses* schema in the appendix on page 392) that Joyce loaned to Valéry LARBAUD, the scene of the episode is the concert room of the Ormond Hotel. The action begins at 4 P.M. The organ of the chapter is the ear. The art of the chapter is music. The episode's symbols are the barmaids. And its technic is the *fuga per canonem*, that is, a fugue according to a rule (*canon*) or instruction.

The chapter derives its name from an incident in book 12 of *The Odyssey*, in which man-eating creatures, half women and half fish, recline upon rocks and sing to Odysseus and his crew, tempting them toward shipwreck and death. Having been warned of this danger by the enchantress Circe, Odysseus has plugged the ears of his crewmen with wax so that they will not hear the Sirens' song; but, curious about the nature of their voices, Odysseus has had himself tied securely to the mast of the ship and has ordered his men not to release him under any conditions until the ship has passed the Sirens' rocks.

The Sirens episode takes place in the Ormond Hotel and begins with what, if it were a musical composition, would be termed an overture, a 63-line introduction that provides a synopsis of the central events of the chapter in much the same way that the overture of a symphony or opera introduces the major musical themes and motifs characterizing a particular work. In keeping with this format, variations on the topics of music, performance, seduction, and destruction provide the contextual format for the rest of the chapter. Listening and observation stand out, making passive modes of behavior, paradoxically, the characterizing gestures of the episode: The barmaids observe customers coming and going, as does the deaf waiter, Pat. Customers watch the barmaids and each other. And, at the close of the chapter, nearly everyone's eyes are fixed upon Ben Dollard as he sings "The Croppy Boy."

The opening scene focuses on the two barmaids, Lydia Douce and Mina Kennedy. Critical opinion remains divided as to the identity of the chapter's title characters, but whether these women do or do not have all the attributes of Homeric sirens, they are quite able to destroy men, figuratively if not literally. From Lydia's remark at the beginning of the chapter ("He's killed looking back" [*U* 11.77]) to her curt reprimand of the young boy bringing them their tea, to her ridicule of the chemist in Boyd's, she seems well able to deal scornfully with any man whom she encounters. Mina, though less outspoken, proves equally adept when it comes to rebuffing Lenehan's half-hearted effort at flirtation.

Whether they are able to captivate men, on the other hand, seems much less certain. Lydia is clearly interested in garnering notice, and makes several efforts to hold the attention of various men who wander into the bar. She flirts with Simon Dedalus and later with the solicitor, George Lidwell, and she brazenly snaps her garter for the amusement of Blazes Boylan and Lenehan. In each instance, however, Miss Douce only manages to hold the interest of these men for a relatively short time before they wander. Mina Kennedy displays even less inclination toward flirtation. She shows absolutely no interest in teasing exchanges with men, and seems tacitly to disapprove of Lydia's behavior on that score. Even taken together, the women lack the requisite abilities to charm and destroy that one finds in their Homeric models.

Additionally, the Sirens analogue becomes further strained as the reader realizes that these women have no discernible musical talent. With the dubious exception of Lydia Douce's garter snapping, the men who inhabit the bar—from the blind stripling who earlier in the day tuned the piano, to Simon Dedalus and Father Bob Cowley who play it, to Ben Dollard who sings to its accompaniment—provide the musical entertainment that appears throughout the chapter. It is their efforts, in fact—especially Dollard's singing near the end of the chapter—that draw the attention of the other men at the Ormond.

In oxymoronic fashion, watching and listening emerge as the dominant activities of characters in the chapter. Both Leopold Bloom and Richie Goulding, who are eating an early supper in the dining room that adjoins the bar, embody those traits. They more or less silently observe a parade of men, many of whom Bloom had encountered earlier in the day, pass through the hotel bar, including Blazes Boylan. Ironically, seeing that Boylan is dallying in the bar with Lenehan and Miss Douce makes Bloom more active than he has been for most of the chapter, as he seems to fret that Boylan might very well be late for his four o'clock assignation with Molly Bloom.

Bloom's interest in Boylan, however, is quickly diverted. While he and Richie Goulding eat their dinner, Ben Dollard begins to sing "All is lost now," the tenor solo from BELLINI's opera *La sonnambula.* Simon Dedalus next sings "M'appari," the tenor solo from Flotow's opera, *MARTHA.* As the performance unfolds, it begins to exert a soothing influence. Bloom becomes a bit sentimental and melancholy, as he thinks regretfully of the estrangement between the brothers-in-law Simon Dedalus and Richie Goulding. This in turn leads Bloom back to recollecting his own affairs. He quickly writes a note in response to the letter he had received earlier from Martha Clifford. She is, however, a pale substitute for Molly, thoughts of whom cause Bloom to imagine Boylan traveling inexorably toward Bloom's house on ECCLES STREET.

In the closing pages of the chapter Ben Dollard performs "The Croppy Boy" to the rapt attention of all, save perhaps Bloom and the solicitor George Lidwell. Both men are watching Lydia Douce—again attempting to play the Siren as best she can—keeping time to the song by stroking the beerpull in a masturbatory fashion. The final musical note of the chapter, however, is a comic one, and it is sounded by Bloom, at that point on the street outside the Ormond Hotel, as he vents the gas that has built up from the cider that he drank with his dinner: "Pprrpffrrppffff" (U 11.1293).

As with food imagery in the Lestrygonians episode, music recurs throughout the chapter as an insistent leitmotif. Songs and melodies punctuate, counterpoint, and even exacerbate the feelings of Bloom and other characters. Additionally, like the songs of the Sirens in Homer's *Odyssey,* the music of this chapter has a powerfully evocative effect. It creates a range of emotions and responses. More significantly, the musical emphasis reconstitutes the formal structure of the narrative. Beginning with the opening 63 lines (the same number as that of the headings in the Aeolus episode [chapter 7]), the discourse of the Sirens episode continually veers away from the conventional narrative framework, with the lyrics and melodies of the music in the bar continually overlapping and sometimes displacing the thoughts of various characters.

For additional information surrounding this chapter, see *Letters,* I.129; II.301, 347, 431, 436, and 440; and III.13.

### Cyclops

This is the 12th episode of *Ulysses,* and the ninth chapter in the novel's middle section known as The Wanderings of Ulysses. An earlier version was serialized in four issues of the *LITTLE REVIEW* (November 1919, December 1919, January 1920, and March 1920).

The chapter takes its informal title from a confrontation, described by Odysseus in book 10 of *The Odyssey,* between himself and his crewmen and the one-eyed giant, Polyphemus. In this episode, Odysseus and his men land in Sicily and begin to explore the island. When they arrive at the cave of Polyphemus, the Cyclops (one-eyed monster), they are taken prisoner, and the Cyclops eats six of the men. Odysseus tricks the Cyclops into getting drunk, puts out his eye with the sharpened end of a stake, and escapes to sea with the remainder his men. From the apparent safety of his boat Odysseus smugly mocks the blinded Cyclops, who hurls a boulder at them as their ship sails away. Joyce, through the mock-heroic cadences of the narrative, transforms Homer's story of reckless daring into a farcical misadventure.

According to the SCHEMA (see *Ulysses* schema in the appendix on page 392) that Joyce loaned to Valéry LARBAUD, the scene of the episode is BARNEY KIERNAN's pub, located on Little Britain Street. The time at which the action begins is 5 P.M. The organ [*sic*] of the chapter is the muscle. The art of the chapter is politics. The episode's symbol is the Fenian. (The Fenian Brotherhood was a 19th-century Irish nationalist and revolutionary group.) Its technic is gigantism.

Bloom has agreed to meet Martin Cunningham at Barney Kiernan's to arrange a visit to Paddy Dignam's widow to discuss what benefits might accrue from her late husband's insurance policy. However, until the closing pages, Bloom himself plays a relatively minor role in the chapter, for the episode steps back from the narrative's heretofore close account of Bloom's day to take a broad view of the Irish nationalist temperament. The action centers on the vituperative observations of the principal narrator, who makes every character in the chapter a target for his caustic abuse. At the same time, a carnivalesque voice produces a running comic parody, interspersed throughout the chapter, of the action unfolding for the reader.

The first voice is that of the unnamed sponger and process server who appears in the opening lines and accompanies Joe Hynes on his way to meet the Citizen (modeled on the Fenian Michael CUSACK) at Kiernan's. They are to discuss hoof-and-mouth disease, the topic at the meeting of cattle traders attended by Hynes earlier in the day. The second speaker, intruding into the narrative through a series of interpolations in a variety of parodic styles, mock-heroically inflates the action of the chapter, affirming Joyce's humorous treatment of the material.

The pub itself, like the cave of Polyphemus, is a bleak haven for chauvinism and self-delusion. Its dreary atmosphere reinforces the xenophobia of many of its denizens, nurturing rigid nationalistic attitudes inimical to Bloom's broad-minded internationalism and making conflict inevitable between the Citizen and Bloom. The heightened intolerance compels Martin Cunningham, at the end of the episode, to lead Bloom out of the bar to prevent a physical confrontation.

The chapter opens with the unnamed narrator encountering Joe Hynes. The narrator has been chatting with a retired police officer and may himself be a police informant. Nonetheless, Joe, who had been paid earlier in the day at the office of the *FREEMAN'S JOURNAL*, invites the unnamed man to go to Kiernan's for a drink and a chat with the Citizen. Before all this comes to pass, however, several interpolations have appeared in the narrative. The first is a legalistic rendering of the debt that Michael E. Geraghty owes Moses Herzog (one that the narrator has tried unsuccessfully to collect). The second and third digressions describe in idyllic terms the area surrounding the pub, as if it were a mythic location.

Upon entering Kiernan's, Joe exchanges a series of RIBBONMEN signs with the Citizen. The gestures and phrases that pass between them highlight the preoccupation with Irish nationalism that dominates the conversations of most of the men in the bar. These exchanges also prepare the way for another departure from the subject that describes the Citizen in the idealized terms of an ancient hero in Irish folklore.

Joe quickly orders a round of drinks for the narrator and the Citizen. When Alf Bergan enters the pub, the talk moves in desultory turns from Denis Breen, to Bloom, to a fellow in Mountjoy prison about to be hanged. In each instance, the pub loungers take a measure of satisfaction in hearing of the miseries of others, like that of the Dignam family. Their conversation is suddenly interrupted by the entrance of a drunken Bob Doran, who at first only dimly comprehends the news of the death of Paddy Dignam and then becomes quite belligerent over it. Contrasting with and undercutting Doran's maudlin response is narrative digression, offering a highly stylized account of a spiritualist encounter with the soul of Dignam speaking to those left behind.

In the midst of all this, Bloom enters the bar, and though he refuses Hynes's offer of a drink he does accept a cigar. Bergan, meanwhile, begins to tell the story of H. Rumbold, master barber and part-time hangman. Talk of executions leads to talk of the hanged man's erection, and the narrative then interpolates a parody of Bloom explaining the phenomenon medically. The Citizen assertively turns the conversation back to nationalism, and that leads to another interpolation, a long parodic account of the execution of an Irish patriot under circumstances greatly resembling the death of Robert Emmet, who in 1803 unsuccessfully attempted to foment an Irish uprising against the British.

As the conversation continues, the Citizen's animosity toward Bloom and the unnamed narrator's unvoiced ill will toward everyone come to dominate the narrative. Joe Hynes continues to buy rounds of drinks, and Bloom's marginal relationship with the rest of the men in the bar becomes all the more obvious. Narrative interpolations continue to comment sardonically on the proceedings in a range of styles that restate, in ironic form, the views being offered in the bar.

Eventually the talk turns to the Keogh-Bennett boxing match that Blazes Boylan had recently promoted; the mention of Boylan predictably increases Bloom's discomfort. At the same time, it provides a wonderful opportunity for a discursive account of the prizefight in lurid journalistic style. The appearance of J. J. O'Molloy with Ned Lambert brings up a discussion of recent court cases, and the ever malevolent Citizen takes the opportunity to interject a series of anti-Semitic slurs that Bloom ignores.

The entrance of Lenehan, bemoaning the results of the GOLD CUP race, briefly turns the talk to betting. The Citizen, however, cannot bear to have the conversation stray from Irish nationalism and English imperialism, and he launches into British efforts to stifle Irish trade. This leads Ned Lambert to make a sarcastic observation about the British navy's role in protecting Ireland from its enemies, and that in turn brings the talk to the topic of corporal punishment in the navy. This unlikely subject gives the reader a strong sense of just how upset Bloom is. Instead of assuming what one would expect his position to be—opposition to brutality—he seems to seek out a confrontation with the Citizen by contradicting the latter's negative opinion of the heavy-handed nature of British military justice.

This inversion of attitudes, however, does not last long. The Citizen quickly takes up again his defense of the ideal of physical force, especially in the nationalist movement. In response, Bloom calls into question the efficacy of these tactics, leading the Citizen to challenge Bloom's right to call himself Irish. Bloom, however, will not back down, and continues to affirm the value of love as "the opposite of hatred" (*U* 12.1485). With that final salvo, Bloom leaves the pub to look for Martin Cunningham at the courthouse.

As soon as Bloom has gone out the door, Lenehan begins to spread the implausible rumor that Bloom has won a great deal of money betting on the Gold Cup race and has gone off to collect his winnings. When Bloom returns, purportedly with the money from his wager, and fails to buy drinks for the house, the outraged Citizen picks a fight. Bloom is oblivious to the immediate source of this hostility. Nonetheless, he is in no mood to mollify a drunken anti-Semitic bully and responds with equal belligerence. Martin Cunningham, who has arrived during Bloom's absence and is having a drink, hustles Bloom out the door. From the carriage, Bloom uses the concept of identity to turn the Citizen's prejudices against him: "Your God was a jew. Christ was a jew like me" (*U* 12.1808–1809). The outraged Citizen follows and throws a biscuit tin at the car in which Bloom is now riding—a gesture that directly emulates the moment in *The Odyssey* when the Cyclops hurls a stone at the departing *Ulysses*—and the chapter comes to an end. Zack Bowen, who has written extensively on comedic elements in *Ulysses,* considers this episode one of the most humorous in all literature.

Formally, the Cyclops episode introduces another variation in the narrative style. For the first time, the voice of a first-person narrator is heard, as the unnamed bill collector imbues the narrative with his highly subjective bitterness. In counterpoint to this unrelieved hostility, a series of comic interpolations break into the main narrative, offering equally subjective, and highly sardonic, commentaries on the events in the pub and the topics under discussion as they are represented by the narrator. Readers relying on conventional interpretive strategies, or traditional habits of reading, are presented with a direct challenge to the validity of their assumptions.

Contextually, the narrative develops in an equally complex fashion. One finds clear evidence of the tremendous emotional effect on Bloom caused by Molly's adultery. His belligerent exchange with the Citizen shows that, for the moment at least, he has become far less cautious than we have come to expect and more likely to challenge slights than to ignore them. The pain Bloom feels from his awareness of Molly's infidelity, occurring simultaneously to the action of the Cyclops episode, makes him far more sensitive to the needs of others, leading to behavior that men like the Citizen clearly do not understand. In a broad sense, however, one also begins to see the stark alienation endured by most of the men encountered in the narrative. Despite the passionate nationalist rhetoric that resounds throughout the chapter, the isolation of these individuals from any real community is evident, as are their desperate efforts to avoid recognizing this condition and its implications.

For additional comments regarding this episode, see *Letters,* I.126; II.451–452 and 455; III.18n.1, 55, and 252. George Antheil began composing an opera based on this Cyclops episode of *Ulysses;* see the appendix on page 381.

### *Nausikaa*

This is the 13th chapter of *Ulysses,* and the 10th in The Wanderings of Ulysses section of the novel. An earlier version was serialized in the April 1920, May–June 1920, and July–August 1920 issues of the LITTLE REVIEW. The U.S. postal authorities seized the July–August issue, which contained the concluding portion of the Nausikaa episode. (Although a portion of the "Oxen of the Sun" episode [chapter 14] appeared in the *Little Review* in the September–December 1920 issue, furor over the publication of episodes like Nausikaa brought about the cessation of the novel's serialization and exacerbated the problem of finding a publisher for the novel.)

According to the SCHEMA (see *Ulysses* schema in the appendix on page 392) that Joyce loaned to Valéry LARBAUD, the scene of the episode is the rocks on Sandymount Strand. The time at which the action begins is 8 P.M. The organs of the chapter are the eye and the nose. The art of the chapter is painting. The episode's symbol is the virgin. And its technics are tumescence and detumescence.

The Nausikaa episode derives its informal name from that of the young princess who appears in book 6 of *The Odyssey.* Nausikaa and her handmaids have gone to the beach with laundry from the palace. There she comes across the exhausted Odysseus, who, after leaving Calypso's island on his way back to Ithaca, has been shipwrecked and washed ashore on a beach in the land of the Phaeacians. Nausikaa promises to give Odysseus her protection, and she brings him to the court of her father, the king.

The Nausikaa episode is set on Sandymount Strand, in the area near Ringsend in southeast Dublin, and it recalls Stephen Dedalus's walk on the same stretch of beach earlier in the day—specifically, at around 11 A.M., during the Proteus episode (chapter 3). Its action also evokes parallels to Stephen's encounter, at least a half dozen years earlier, with the Birdgirl on Dollymount Strand, just north of the River Liffey, at the close of the fourth chapter of *A Portrait of the Artist as a Young Man.* However, while watching the young woman wading in the surf moved Stephen to aesthetic inspiration, viewing Gerty MacDowell's exhibitionism only stimulates Bloom's masturbatory gratification.

As the chapter opens, Leopold Bloom has just come from a visit with Martin Cunningham to the widow of Paddy Dignam (an event that takes place outside the narrative, during the time that elapses between the Cyclops and Nausikaa episodes). He has wandered down to the beach seeking some form of diversion that will allow him to postpone his inevitable return home to Molly. The chapter divides itself nearly evenly between alternating points of view, presenting first a depiction of events from the highly romanticized perspective of Gerty MacDowell (or from a point of view that seems very similar to hers, though critics do not agree on the source of the narrative voice) and then from Bloom's.

In the first half of the chapter, in a stylized fashion the narrative introduces readers to the consciousness of Gerty, a lower-middle-class young woman whose behavior throughout the episode establishes her as a modern-day analogue to the Homeric Nausikaa. Gerty is sitting on the beach with two of her friends, Edy Boardman and Cissy Caffrey, passing the time on a warm summer evening and minding Edy's baby brother and Cissy's two younger brothers, Tommy and Jacky.

Using a tone that approximates the style and ethos of contemporary romantic fiction (which Joyce read in great quantity to prepare for the Nausikaa episode), this portion of the chapter focuses on Gerty as it describes her life and thoughts. It offers in minute detail an account of the elements that make up her daily routine and of the factors that influence her view of life and romance. Despite the intimacy and frankness of these revelations, however, they present little evidence that Gerty possesses any profound vision of the world she inhabits. Her near-obsessive concern for things like toiletries and undergarments seems banal. Additionally, the purple prose in which the narrative is cast heightens the irony implicit in its account of Gerty's prosaic daily routine and her predictable ambition to find a nice young man to marry.

There is a sharp distinction between the style of the narrative and the way Gerty and her friends actually speak when they are quoted directly. Nonetheless, the almost complete domination of the narrative by sentimental romanticism suggests more about Gerty than anything openly represented in the narrative. It leaves the reader to decide whether the narrative voice itself mocks Gerty's simplistic views or if Gerty has resolutely blotted out the ugly aspects of her world by this naively idealized perspective.

In either case, it is evident that Gerty has a disposition to filter the often harsh reality of her world. This inclination is most apparent when she begins to speculate about Bloom's private life. Gerty notices Bloom because he has been watching her from a distance. His attention both piques her curiosity and disposes her toward a favorable opinion of him. As a result, she perceives a very different figure from the one to whom readers have become accustomed. By blending images from sentimental fiction and speculation from her own daydreams, Gerty conjures up a Byronic history for Bloom more suited to a character in a romance novel than to the "prudent member" (*U* 12.211), as Joe Hynes refers to Bloom in the previous episode, Cyclops (chapter 12).

As the initial section of the chapter draws to a close, the various topical threads—romanticism, denial, and environmental coarseness—combine to illuminate for the reader the motivations behind Gerty's behavior. When her friends run down the beach to view the fireworks marking the close of the Mirus Bazaar, Gerty remains where she has been sitting. As she leans back on the rock, as if to watch the pyrotechnic display, she in fact makes a fully calculated effort to expose her underwear to Bloom. As he masturbates—an act that the narrative suggests Gerty seems well aware of—her mind is full of the action of the fireworks, which the narrative describes in a manner that suggests that she too is achieving sexual climax. As Gerty limps away from the beach, the contrast between the way she seems to think and how she actually behaves highlights what has by now become a common narrative strategy: the reader is left to resolve seeming contradictions in the narrative in order to create a unified understanding of the text.

During the second portion of the chapter, the narrative reverts to a tone more typical of the book thus far. For the first time in the chapter, Bloom is identified by name, and through variations on the technique of FREE INDIRECT DISCOURSE the narrative makes its way into his consciousness. In a form of sardonic recapitulation, Bloom's mind unconsciously reviews many of the same topics that engaged Gerty's interest earlier in the episode, and in so doing provides an ironic commentary on many of Gerty's observations.

At the same time, an inflection noticeably different from that of previous chapters informs the rhythm of Bloom's thoughts as they periodically break into the narrative discourse. His assessments of Gerty, especially in the light of her lameness, which he notices only as she is walking away (*U* 13.771), take a far harsher attitude than the reader has come to associate with him. To some degree, his attitude and manner reflect a coarseness that one can associate broadly with his quasi-public masturbation, a form of sexual assertiveness and retaliation provoked by Molly's adultery. Specifically, it demonstrates the deadening emotional effect that thoughts of Molly's affair with Blazes Boylan have had upon Bloom over the course of the day. As if to underscore this fact, during much of the remainder of the Nausikaa episode Bloom thinks of women in a far more cynical fashion than he does at any other time in the novel. He reflects on the gamut of female foibles that he has observed over the course of his life, but shows none of the empathy so characteristic of his customary judgment of others, especially women. He recovers this empathy in the next episode, Oxen of the Sun (chapter 14), when he visits the Holles Street Maternity Hospital to inquire about Mrs. Mina Purefoy, who has been in labor for three days.

While readers quickly note that the pain that Bloom feels over his wife's infidelity is very close to the surface of his awareness, he employs a variety of physical and intellectual tactics to avoid confronting it directly. The narrator, on the other hand, despite apparent sympathy for Bloom, shows far less hesitancy to face the events of the day. As the beach darkens, the now visibly tired Bloom can no longer avoid recollections of Molly. His thoughts turn willy-nilly to the enormity of what has happened that afternoon in his house, and the narrative underscores Bloom's growing shame when the chapter ends with three stanzas of the derisive treble refrain "Cuckoo," sounded from the clock on the mantelpiece in the rectory of Mary Star of the Sea parish. This device bluntly emphasizes what Bloom has been aware of throughout the chapter but has avoided facing: He is now a cuckold.

The Nausikaa episode offers yet another variation on Joyce's efforts at stylistic experimentation. Its first half is dominated by a tenor and diction radically different from the discursive tone to which the reader has become accustomed. These disparities renew for the reader the questions about the relationship between voice and narration that have arisen in preceding chapters. The question most in need of resolution is one of origination: whether the discourse is moved forward by a single narrator who employs multiple voices, or by multiple narrators each with its own voice. While the distinction may initially seem without great consequence, in fact the perception of a diverse but unified consciousness as opposed to a collection of independent entities will greatly affect the reader's interpretation of the episode.

The chapter also personalizes issues of deprivation and degradation previously considered only peripherally by the narrative. The examination of Gerty enforces upon the reader a sense of the dull and often degrading life of lower-middle-class Dublin women at the turn of the century. In the process, by illuminating the narrow range of options open to women and young girls from Dilly Dedalus to Milly Bloom, it gives one a clearer and indeed more chilling sense of the harsh and unforgiving world in which they lived. Along the same lines, the Nausikaa episode specifically underscores the numbing and coarsening effect that Molly's adultery has upon Bloom.

For additional details, see *Letters,* I.134; II.428, 431, and 458; III.27–30 and 280.

### *Oxen of the Sun*

This is the 14th chapter of *Ulysses* and the 11th in The Wanderings of Ulysses section. An earlier version of the first portion of the episode was published in the September–December 1920 issue of the LITTLE REVIEW, the last excerpt to appear before the United States postal authorities forced the magazine to discontinue publication.

According to the SCHEMA (see *Ulysses* schema, Appendix on page 392) that Joyce loaned to Valéry LARBAUD, the scene of the episode is the Holles Street Maternity Hospital. The time at which the action begins is 10 P.M. The organ of the chapter is the womb. The art of the chapter is medicine. The color of the chapter (a category that Joyce used infrequently in the schema) is white. The episode's collective symbol is mothers. And its technic is embryonic development.

The Oxen of the Sun episode derives its title from an incident recounted by Odysseus in book 12 of *The Odyssey.* After leaving Circe's island and passing by first the Sirens and then Scylla and Charybdis, Odysseus and his shipmates land on the island of the sun god, Helios, to spend the night. Knowing well the potential for retribution they could face for annoying Helios, Odysseus makes the crew swear that they will not harm the god's cattle grazing there. Unfortunately, adverse weather strands the men on the island and eventually their supplies run low. When Odysseus goes off to pray, his crew takes advantage of their leader's absence, slaughters the animals, and feasts upon them. As punishment for this sacrilege, when the ship leaves the island, Zeus hurls a lightning bolt killing all of the crew save Odysseus.

The action of the episode is more subdued than most of its predecessors. It follows Leopold Bloom as he visits the hospital to inquire about the condition of Mina Purefoy. He finds a raucous group of young men, getting progressively drunker in one of the rooms off the hospital wards, and quietly joins the party, watching without really taking part in the festivities.

The Oxen of the Sun episode presents perhaps the most challenging compositional approach to appear thus far in *Ulysses*. Formally, it is a highly compressed stylistic survey of English prose, beginning with an amalgamation of Latin and Irish. The discourse then shifts successively to forms that mimic Anglo-Saxon (Old English), to Middle English, and to a style similar to that of Sir Thomas Malory's *Morte d'Arthur,* which dates from the 15th century.

The narrative next imitates a range of 16th- and 17th-century styles, beginning with prose resembling that of John Bunyan in *Pilgrim's Progress.* From there it turns to evocations of the styles of the 17th-century diarists John Evelyn and Samuel Pepys. These give way to simulations of such early 18th-century writers as Daniel Defoe, Addison and Steele, and Jonathan Swift, and thence to the emerging 18th-century novel form practiced by Laurence Sterne and Henry Fielding. After this, the discourse attempts to bring to mind the political rhetoric made famous by well-known parliamentary orators such as Edmund Burke and Richard Brinsley Sheridan. Then, returning to fiction, the narrative takes up the gothic form, popular for the last four decades of the 18th century and well into the 19th. This is followed by an expository style modeled on the work of early 19th-century essayists Charles Lamb, Thomas DeQuincey, and Thomas Babington Macaulay. As the chapter draws to a close, imitations of the Victorian prose of Charles Dickens, Cardinal Newman, Walter Pater, and John Ruskin appear. In its final pages, the chapter breaks away from its literary prose models and lapses into a near-unintelligible conglomeration of Dublin *patois.*

This formal tour de force reflects the equally complex thematic progression of the chapter. After leaving Sandymount Strand at the end of the Nausikaa episode (chapter 13), Leopold Bloom finds himself still unwilling to return to Molly. He walks northward in the general direction of his home on Eccles Street but stops near Merrion Square at the Holles Street Maternity Hospital to inquire after Mina Purefoy, who is in labor and about to give birth to her ninth child. At the hospital, Bloom encounters a group of drunken men—among them Stephen Dedalus, Vincent Lynch, and Lenehan—who are carousing in a room set aside as a refectory.

The men have been drinking ale, presumably purchased with Stephen's money, and, in keeping with their surroundings, they have been discussing a range of matters relating to procreation, contraception, pregnancy (and various conditions leading to its termination), and birth. Although several of the men offer coarse opinions of sexual desire and fulfillment, Stephen holds himself aloof and at various points in the exchange launches into attacks upon birth control, abortion, and medical procedures that put the life of the child at risk to preserve that of the mother. At first glance, these positions themselves may seem inconsistent with Stephen's general way of thinking, but two significant elements explain his motivation. He has been thinking about creation, albeit artistic, all day long, and his insistence on the primacy of the child over the mother is consistent with his view of the primacy of art (or the artist) over its social matrix. Moreover, Stephen has also been holding forth all day long, and wishes to continue to do so. In a room full of shouting, drunken men, one way to grab their attention is to take a position no one else holds.

Thus, as he did at the newspaper offices of the FREEMAN'S JOURNAL in the Aeolus episode (chapter 7) and at the NATIONAL LIBRARY OF IRELAND in the Scylla and Charybdis episode (chapter 9), Stephen attempts to demonstrate his intellectual and imaginative abilities through a public performance of sorts. By this time, however, he is so drunk that the distinguishing feature of his talk is incoherence. Additionally, the drunkenness of those listening to him leads to a great many combative interruptions, a great many rambling asides, and a general lack of attentiveness.

Throughout the clamor, Bloom maintains a watchful silence. He avoids drinking (discreetly disposing of the alcohol pressed upon him so that he gives no offense through his refusal), and skirts direct involvement in the arguments unfolding around him. Bloom is not completely detached from what is going on, however. As he follows Stephen's movements, he develops a paternal concern for the young man, who is quite obviously too drunk to care for himself. (Bloom has been thinking about his own deceased son, Rudy, all day long, which doubtless disposes him to feel anxiety over Stephen's welfare.) This solicitous interest will prompt Bloom to follow Stephen when, in the Circe episode (chapter 15), the young man goes off in the company of Lynch to Bella Cohen's Nighttown brothel.

At an apparent lull in the conversation, Lenehan mentions seeing Garrett Deasy's letter in the evening paper. That turns the conversation to hoof-and-mouth disease, then to papal bulls, and next, by analogy, to the 12th-century invasion of Ireland by the English (sanctioned by the papal bull *Laudabiliter*, issued by the only English pope, Adrian IV, born Nicholas Breakspeare). In a somewhat garbled fashion, the men in the room review the central events of the English subjugation of Ireland. The conversation becomes more animated until the arrival of Buck Mulligan fresh from George MOORE's literary party, referred to during the Scylla and Charybdis episode (chapter 9), provides a new topic.

Mulligan is far more sober than anyone else in the room, save Bloom, and he immediately begins to exploit his position. He suppresses the conversation and begins to act the entertainer by relating his scheme of retiring to Lambay Island to become "Fertiliser and Incubator" for all Ireland. Although this provokes the expected response, his performance is interrupted by the entrance of nurse Callan who announces that Mina Purefoy has just given birth to a son. This news leads predictably to a round of coarse speculation on sexual habits, first on those of the Purefoys and then on those of humanity in general, and from there to a series of anecdotes relating to malformed births. Mulligan attempts to regain control of the conversation, but his efforts are disrupted by Haines, who appears and hastily arranges a later meeting with Mulligan at the Westland Row Station.

At this point the narrative briefly reverts its attention from the public discourse to Bloom's thoughts. Possibly motivated by the sight of the young men carousing, Bloom thinks of his own youth and of his first sexual experience. From there his thoughts turn to his present condition and to his sexual anxieties about his wife, Molly, and his daughter, Milly. In the meantime Lynch and Stephen are talking about their own schooldays, and Lynch takes the opportunity to offer a gratuitous jibe at Stephen's artistic pretensions.

The discussion next drifts to the degeneration of the human condition, made all the more sententious and unfathomable by the participants' drunkenness. With the ale they have brought into the hospital exhausted, the young men rush off to Burke's, the nearest public house, hoping for a few drinks before the 11 P.M. closing. At Burke's, in a jarring displacement of the discourse, the form shifts from its imitation of the various styles of English literary prose to a series of conversations conducted in nearly incomprehensible Dublin slang. As the group leaves the bar and begins to disperse, Stephen invites Lynch to accompany him to Nighttown, and the episode concludes.

As the narrative unfolds, the chapter shows great creative dexterity. The Oxen of the Sun episode employs a wealth of engaging metaphors drawn from the procreative process of conception, gestation, and birth. The chapter is written in a succession of English literary styles, from the medieval to the early 20th century, making it difficult to follow. It consists of long rambling discussions of birth, abortion, contraception, and conception, with a great deal of drunken digression. Joyce integrates these tropes into a protean discourse that derives its shape and cohesion from the continually evolving styles of English literary prose. With these elements the narrative is able to touch upon topics that illuminate the novel's broader concerns about artistic creativity and individuality.

The episode's stylistic progression has a dual significance. It offers convincing evidence of Joyce's creative virtuosity, showing his mastery of virtually any prose form imaginable. Additionally, when the structure of language degenerates into near-gibberish at the end of the episode, it demonstrates forcefully the importance of style to give order to linguistic expression. There is a dramatic contrast between the elevated tone of the discourse filtered through the various literary prose forms and the baser, virtually unintelligible, vernacular that is presented seemingly without the imaginative mediation of the artist. (Of course, this ostensibly unmediated style is itself a formal representation of great skill.)

As Joyce himself noted, the structure of the Oxen of the Sun also evokes the rhythm of the nine-month gestation of human pregnancy. This framework allows him to develop the analogy between material and imaginative creativity in a unique fashion. As the chapter explores the implications of biological reproduction, the complexities informing Stephen's struggle to evolve as an artist become much more evident. The same analogy also addresses the function of literary tradition in the creation of language, thus helping to clarify what Stephen must do to earn the critical esteem for his imaginative endeavors that he so desperately seeks throughout the novel. About two and a half years after *Ulysses* was published, Joyce's brother Stanislaus, commenting on the first fragment of *Finnegans Wake* to appear in print, identifies the Oxen of the Sun episode as anticipating the language of Joyce's new work. "I have received," Stanislaus wrote to his brother in August 1924, "one installment of your yet unnamed novel in the Transatlantic Review. I don't know whether the driveling rigmarole about half a tall hat and ladies' modern toilet chambers (practically the only things I understand in this nightmare production) is written with the deliberate intention of pulling the reader's leg or not. You began this fooling in the Holles Street episode in ULYSSES . . ." (*Letters*, III. 102–103).

For additional information regarding the Oxen of the Sun episode, see *Letters,* I.139–140; II.458–459 and 464–466; and III.16, 33, and 365.

### *Circe*

This is the 15th episode in *Ulysses,* and the 12th and final chapter in the novel's middle section known as The Wanderings of Ulysses.

In book 10 of *The Odyssey,* the hero Odysseus gives an account of his adventures with Circe, the witch who through magic transforms Odysseus's crew into swine. Her magic fails to effect a change in Odysseus because of the protective herb (identified by the Greek word *moly,* which, as Stuart GILBERT has noted, pleased Joyce as a pun on the name of Molly Bloom) Odysseus was given by the god Hermes. Eventually, Odysseus triumphs over Circe and forces her to restore his men to their human form. The struggle that highlights the middle portion of the chapter between Leopold Bloom and Bella Cohen corresponds to this encounter.

According to the SCHEMA (see *Ulysses* schema, Appendix on page 392) that Joyce loaned to Valéry LARBAUD, the scene of the episode is the brothel run by Bella Cohen in NIGHTTOWN. The time at which the action begins is midnight. The organ [*sic*] of the chapter is the locomotor apparatus. The art of the chapter is magic. The episode's symbol is the whore. Its technic is hallucination.

At first glance the structure of the Circe episode appears to take a straightforward form, that of a play. However, the shift in interpretive procedure that this requires leads to a very different way of understanding the action of the episode. In reading plays, one must supply the unifying links between characters and action that the narrative voice provides in fiction. This model means that many of the events earlier in the day will be cast into radically different forms and represented by drastically dissimilar perspectives. While stage directions and dramatis personae are clearly indicated, they rarely give one a fully formed sense of the direction of the action, nor is it always possible for readers to determine which characters are present in the episode and which are hallucinations. Thus, the episode repeatedly foregrounds an ambiguity that will challenge any interpretation, and ultimately the reader's procedure for deriving meaning is shown to be a highly subjective process. Further, as one moves through the chapter, it becomes increasingly evident that distinctions between reality and illusion are not easily defined and that a surreal world has displaced one's perception of the "real" events being narrated.

After leaving Burke's pub at the end of the Oxen of the Sun episode (chapter 14), Vincent Lynch and Stephen Dedalus go to the Mabbot Street entrance of Nighttown (the red-light district of the city) at around midnight. The episode opens with a description of the area that is immediately undermined: "stunted men and women [who] squabble" and "grab wafers between which are wedged lumps of coral and copper snow" (*U* 15.5, 6–7) become children sucking ices. The swift reversal calls into question the accuracy of the reader's initial impressions. At the same time, the genuine grotesqueness of the deaf-mute idiot described after this introduction presents one with a sense of how deformed reality can become. Then, when Cissy Caffrey and Edy Boardman—earlier represented as relatively innocent young girls in the Nausikaa episode (chapter 13)—reappear in this episode as prostitutes, the reader realizes that he or she must struggle to determine the reliability of any perception derived from the narrative in this chapter.

Stephen and Lynch, however, seem unaffected by this distorted world. Indeed, they move blithely through this carnivalesque atmosphere giving little heed to their surroundings. Stephen, in fact, seems to be attempting to take up the discussion that the two had on aesthetics in the final chapter of *A Portrait of the Artist as a Young Man*. Lynch, on the other hand, has his mind only on the women whom Stephen has promised to purchase and gives at best grudging attention to the disquisition.

Bloom, out of concern for Stephen's condition, has followed the pair from the Holles Street Hospital only to lose them in the crowd at the entrance to Nighttown. Unlike the oblivious Lynch and Stephen, Bloom seems disoriented, and the text represents his senses as hyper-attuned to the environment of Mabbot Street. After he is almost hit by a tram (*U* 15.183–197), a series of apparent hallucinations begins. However, the episode so deftly integrates these experiences into the storyline that the reader is often hard-pressed to distinguish the hallucinations from what is really occurring.

For example, Jacky and Tommy Caffrey, the twin boys who appear on the beach in the Eumaeus episode, collide with Bloom shortly before he encounters the spirits of his father, Rudolf Bloom, and his mother, Ellen Bloom. The latter are clearly figments of Bloom's imagination, momentarily dominating thoughts that have been triggered by his shame at being in the wrong place with the wrong people: "I told you not go with drunken goy ever," says the vision of Bloom's father (*U* 15.253–254). The status of the twins, as real figures or apparitions, remains unclear.

Both encounters, however, sharply underscore Bloom's unease over his rejection of his parents' values while at the same time preparing the reader for a series of subsequent encounters that Bloom has with women. Guilt and carnal appetites become recurring themes in the episode. First a vision of his wife, Molly, reminds Bloom (and us) of his uxorious and masochistic tendencies. Then successive encounters with Bridie Kelly and Gerty MacDowell foreground Bloom's premarital and extramarital sexuality, while the appearance of Molly's friend Josie Breen, who confronts Bloom about his presence in Nighttown, touches upon the range of Bloom's fantasies.

Mrs. Breen fades away, and a parade of Nighttown denizens appear, including the English soldiers Private Carr and Private Compton. They will become Stephen's adversaries late in the episode. Bloom, for a moment, ponders what he is doing in that part of the city at that time of night, and then, after momentarily wavering, determines to continue his efforts to help Stephen: "What am I following him for? Still, he's the best of that lot. If I hadn't heard about Mrs. Beaufoy Purefoy I wouldn't have gone and wouldn't have met. Kismet. He'll lose that cash" (*U* 15.639–642).

As he thinks about Stephen's money, Bloom considers his own wasted purchases a few moments earlier—on a pig's crubeen and a sheep's trotter (*U* 15.155–161)—which he now feeds to a dog that has been following him (*U* 15.657–675). This gesture brings Bloom to the attention of two police officers. When accosted by them, Bloom stammers that he is "doing good to others" (*U* 15.682). When questioned by the officers, who ask for his name and address, Bloom gives several false answers. This prevarication stimulates further hallucinations that elaborate upon Bloom's sense of guilt. First, Martha Clifford confronts Bloom as her betrayer; then Myles Crawford appears to praise Bloom, but immediately Philip Beaufoy, author of "MATCHAM'S MASTERSTROKE," accuses him of plagiarism (*U* 15.810–855). A trial ensues, during which Bloom's former maid, Mary Driscoll, accuses him of sexual misconduct (*U* 15.867–893).

J. J. O'Molloy, the solicitor who, earlier in the Aeolus episode (chapter 7), had tried to get a loan from Myles Crawford appears here as Bloom's legal counsel. O'Molloy's defense is based on Bloom's utter incompetence, once again providing the opportunity for a review of his faults. Mrs. Yelverton Barry, Mrs. Bellingham, and the Honourable Mrs. Mervyn Talboys appear as witnesses to accuse Bloom of further wrongdoings in a trial that now seems centered on revealing Bloom's sexual fantasies and sense of shame. Bloom desperately resorts to the alibi of attending the funeral of Paddy Dignam, and after an extended disquisition by Dignam himself Bloom's hallucination dissipates.

Still in pursuit of Stephen, Bloom proceeds through Nighttown. He hears someone playing a piano, and thinking that it might be Stephen at the keyboard, he stops in front of Bella Cohen's brothel. Bloom has in fact found the place where Stephen and Lynch have gone in search of the prostitute Georgina Johnson. On the steps, Bloom is accosted by one of Bella's girls, Zoe Higgins.

After he finds out from her that Stephen is inside, Bloom gets ready to enter the whorehouse, but first a series of hallucinations occur. Zoe's request for a cigarette produces a pedantic reply that in turn leads to a vision of Bloom as Lord Mayor of Dublin. In a rise and fall that evokes the political career of Charles Stewart Parnell, Bloom's fantasy allows him to articulate all the schemes for social welfare that have run through his mind over the course of the day. As he continues to talk, popular sentiment turns against Bloom, and a group of doctors headed by Buck Mulligan assist him as he gives birth to "eight male yellow and white children" (*U* 15.1821–1822). Finally as Bloom takes on the role of a Christ-like scapegoat bearing the sins of Ireland, the hallucination ends.

After all these delays, Bloom finally joins Stephen and Lynch in the parlor of the bordello. There a drunken Stephen attempts to entertain the assembled prostitutes, and he and Bloom experience a series of hallucinations that continue to recapitulate the major themes of the novel as well as emphasize important psychological and sexual concerns of these two characters. Stephen's inebriation produces a muddled religious fantasy that plays off images of the Antichrist and Armageddon against the conventions of Catholic dogma.

Next, Bloom's grandfather, Lipoti Virag, appears, renewing Bloom's sense of shame and degradation with a coldly clinical analysis of the whores in the bordello. Virag gives way to Henry Flower, Bloom's alter ego, and this marks a transition to Stephen's hallucination of Almidano Artifoni appearing to supervise his efforts at singing. While Lynch and the whores conduct an ostensibly normal conversation, both Bloom and Stephen drift in and out of their respective fantasies.

When Bella Cohen, the "massive whoremistress" (*U* 15.2742), enters the room, Bloom slips into an extended hallucination centering on his sexuality. Bella experiences a metamorphosis into the masculine Bello, and Bloom in turn finds himself transformed into a female prostitute. Bello accuses Bloom of all of the peccadillos that have haunted his subconscious, and he struggles to cope with the shame and the masochistic pleasure produced by their revelation. Bloom submits to one humiliation after another until he is confronted with the Nymph from the picture that hangs in his bedroom. The Nymph too piles one humiliation on top of another as she reveals Bloom's innermost secrets and desires. However, when Bloom's back trouser button unexpectedly pops off, the hallucination has a marked shift in tone. Bloom chases off the Nymph, and then coldly reestablishes himself before the once again feminine Bella. As in other scenes in the chapter, one is hard-pressed to mark the exact transition from fantasy to reality.

The narrative next turns the reader's attention to Stephen, as Bella demands money to cover the cost of their entertainment. Bloom steps in to see that Stephen is not cheated, and he temporarily takes charge of Stephen's money. Stephen barely takes note of Bloom's kindness, and instead when Lynch mentions the word "Pandybat" (*U* 15.3666) he slips into reveries of his childhood. Father Dolan and Father Conmee, characters from *A Portrait of the Artist as a Young Man*, appear in quick succession.

While Zoe attempts to calm an increasingly agitated Stephen, Bloom has a particularly unpleasant fantasy involving Blazes Boylan and Molly. In an elaborate depiction of Molly's adulterous afternoon, Bloom envisions not simply his own cuckolding but also his role as impotent witness and even facilitator of the event. The hallucination combines a bawdiness and poignancy that underscores Bloom's complex reactions to Molly's infidelity.

In the meantime, Stephen has been entertaining the whores with tales of his brief time in Paris. His descriptions become more extravagant and produce visions of his father and Garrett Deasy. Zoe suggests a dance, and, as Stephen whirls around the room, an apparition of his dead mother appears before him. It is a significant event, for it crystallizes many of the emotions and much of the guilt that have dogged him throughout the day.

The shock of seeing this vision of his mother proves to be too much for Stephen. He strikes out at the lamp above his head, and runs into the street in a panic, unmindful of the disorder he has caused. Bloom methodically calms Bella Cohen, pays for the damage that Stephen has caused, and follows the young man outside. There he finds Stephen embroiled in a confrontation with two British soldiers—Privates Carr and Compton—over a supposed insult to Cissy Caffrey. Bloom tries his best to defuse the situation, but the drunken Stephen stubbornly refuses to be led off. An array of phantasms representing various nationalistic tendencies punctuates the text, and it is not always clear whether they originate in Stephen's or Bloom's imagination. Finally, an equally drunk and highly enraged Carr knocks Stephen down. Bloom steps in to prevent further violence and, with the help of Corny Kelleher and two commercial travelers, manages to prevent Stephen's arrest for public drunkenness (*U* 15.4787–4907).

The episode ends with Bloom attempting to revive Stephen, who lies unconscious on the street. While doing so, Bloom sees a vision of his own dead son, Rudy (*U* 15.4956–4967). Thus, part 2 of *Ulysses* comes to an end by confronting the reader with a series of father-son images but without offering the closure that one finds in the novel's Homeric analogue, when Odysseus returns to Ithaca and meets his son.

Circe, with its dramatic structure, marks a radical departure from the formal prose style of the rest of the novel and indeed from most conventional narratives. Critics have found analogies to these fantastic representations in works like Gustave FLAUBERT's *La Tentation de Saint Antoine* (The temptation of St. Anthony) and the *Walpurgisnacht* from Goethe's *Faust*. However, Joyce's representations retain a psychological uniqueness distinct from other writings. In the hallucinations that occur through the chapter, both Stephen and Bloom consider issues that have concerned them during the day. These now appear without the amelioration of Stephen's and Bloom's normal psychological defenses. As they face traumatic issues in their most direct confrontations in the novel, the reader is able to elaborate upon the impressions that have accumulated over the preceding 14 chapters. This episode recapitulates many of the novel's motifs. The critic Hugh KENNER has observed that by the end of the Circe episode Bloom "seems a changed [man], courageous, ready of mind. Like a psychoanalysis without an analyst," Kenner continues to elaborate upon the change "—apparently what Joyce understood by 'catharsis'—Circe's rummaging amid the roots of his secret fears and desires has brought forth a new self-possession, and the man who lost his head at the Citizen's taunts [see Cyclops] and had to be whisked off amid jeers, pursued by a mangy dog and a flying biscuit-box, has managed Stephen's assailants with aplomb" (*Ulysses* [revised ed., 1987], p. 127). The Circe episode, then, is as much a revitalization of Bloom's inner self as it is a recapitulation of the novel's motifs and the day's events.

Because of its unique structure, the Circe episode has been seen as having the potential for a creative existence independent of the rest of the work. The best-known effort to exploit this feature occurred in 1958 when Burgess Meredith directed an off-Broadway production of *Ulysses in Nighttown,* a dramatization of this episode adapted for the stage by Marjorie Barkentin. Joyce's old friend, the poet Padraic COLUM, also assisted in the production. In 1974, the play was produced on Broadway. (For further information, see the appendix on page 381.) For additional information on Joyce's views of this episode, see *Letters,* I.141, and 144; II.126–127; and III.9, 11, 15, 18–19, 21, 24, 26, 30–32, 35, 38, 43, 51, 53, and 104–105.

### *Eumaeus*

This is the 16th chapter of *Ulysses* and the opening episode of the third and final division of the book, Nostos or Homecoming.

The episode derives its name from book 14 of *The Odyssey.* In that portion of the epic poem Odysseus, disguised as an old beggar, arrives at the hut of his faithful servant Eumaeus, a swineherd, whose hospitality provides emotional as well as physical comfort to the weary traveler. Odysseus, made up as the old beggar, spins yarns about his travels and about associations with Odysseus that delight the old servant. It is only to his son, Telemachus, that the putative beggar reveals his true identity, and together Odysseus and the young man plot revenge against the suitors who are importuning Penelope and despoiling their property. Deception plays a prominent role in this passage of *The Odyssey,* as it does throughout this chapter of *Ulysses,* for in each instance the narrative underscores how easily both language and appearances can conceal, as well as reveal, true identity.

According to the SCHEMA (see *Ulysses* schema in the appendix on page 392) that Joyce loaned to Valéry LARBAUD, the scene of the Eumaeus episode is the cabman's shelter reputedly run by James Fitzharris, the former Invincible (also known as "Skin-the-Goat"). The time at which the action begins is after midnight. The organs [*sic*] of the episode are the nerves. The art of the episode is navigation. The episode's symbol is the sailors. And its technic is narrative (old).

After the exhausting psychological traumas that they endured in the Circe episode (chapter 15), Leopold Bloom and Stephen Dedalus retreat to the cabman's shelter at Butt Bridge, rumored to be run by Fitzharris, the reputed driver of the getaway car during the PHOENIX PARK MURDERS, political assassinations that took place on May 6, 1882. Just as the true identities of the shelter's proprietor and many of its denizens remain open to debate, throughout the chapter the validity of a range of seemingly straightforward perceptions is constantly challenged by shifting, ambiguous perspectives. Ideas are fragmented, intentions are misunderstood, and language itself seems to break down into clichés, as if the very narrative is too fatigued to conduct an imaginative discourse.

The Eumaeus episode opens with a sly parody of formulaic, clichéd description as Bloom brushes shavings off Stephen and helps him with his hat and ashplant "in orthodox Samaritan fashion" (*U* 16.03). The line plays the hackneyed image of the Good Samaritan off against the contradictory description of the breakaway Samaritan sect as orthodox. From its opening, the narrative of the chapter signals to attentive readers that it will manipulate the very misprisions of trite language to create a meaningful and artistically skillful discourse.

From NIGHTTOWN Stephen and Bloom make the short journey to the cabman's shelter under Butt Bridge. Although they are physically together at this juncture (embodying the recurring father/son theme of *Ulysses*), intellectually and psychologically Stephen and Bloom remain far apart. Stephen, still recovering from a night of drinking and the assault of Private Carr, has turned his thoughts to Ibsen. Bloom, on the other hand—acutely aware of the lateness of the hour, his own fatigue, and his incipient hunger—has concentrated his mind on the pleasant smell emanating from James Rourke's nearby bakery.

Bloom begins the first of several unsuccessful efforts to engage Stephen in conversation by gently suggesting the possible consequences of Stephen's reckless behavior. Before his words can have any effect, however, the two encounter the first of several characters who interrupt their discourse. As they pass under the Loop Line Bridge, Stephen endeavors to avoid being seen by a building site watchman, Gumley, a friend of his father, but he is shortly accosted by a penniless and homeless acquaintance, John Corley (a principal character in the *Dubliners* story "Two Gallants"). Stephen's attitude toward Corley is ambivalent at best. He sarcastically suggests to Corley that he apply for a job as a "gentleman usher" in the boys' school at Dalkey, the job that Stephen has apparently decided to leave. Before they separate, however, Stephen searches his pockets for money and, to Corley's surprise, hands over one of his two half-crowns. (See the appendix on page 430 for further information on monetary values.)

As they continue walking, the differences in temperaments between Bloom and Stephen become even more apparent. Just outside the cabman's shelter, they pass a group of Italian ice cream vendors. As they enter the building, Bloom cannot resist commenting upon the beauty of the Italian language. Stephen, on the other hand, sardonically notes that they are bickering over money.

Once they are seated inside, Stephen's lassitude and Bloom's pensiveness become even more apparent. In a matter of moments, their desultory conversation is interrupted by W. B. Murphy, a sailor who has been dominating the talk in the cabman's shelter with tall tales about his adventures at sea. Murphy's occupation as a seaman and his appearance in the Eumaeus episode suggest associations with Odysseus, but discrepancies in his stories call his integrity into question and give him the role of a false or pseudo-Odysseus figure. (A fine irony obtains here as well, for although Odysseus was noted for his ability to fabricate stories, the "lies," the word that Joyce uses in a February letter to Frank BUDGEN [see *Letters*, I.60], told by Murphy are so transparent that Bloom manages a running commentary on their falseness that counterpoints Murphy's entire monologue.)

After asking Stephen's name, Murphy claims to have known a man named Simon Dedalus, a sharpshooter who "toured the wide world with Hengler's Royal Circus" (*U* 16.412). Murphy expands on this recollection to talk of his own experiences in the Orient and in South America. All of his accounts, however, rely upon generalities, and he seems disturbed to the point of belligerence when pressed by Bloom for details.

The sight of an old streetwalker passing back and forth outside the cabman's shelter distracts everyone's attention and breaks Murphy's monopoly on the conversation. Bloom resumes his conversation with Stephen, and, after a series of rambling remarks, Bloom attempts to turn the conversation to Molly. Stephen, however, still shows little interest in sustaining the dialogue. In consequence, as the talk in the shelter meanders on, Bloom slips deeper into his own thoughts, recalling the exploits of the Invincibles and specifically the Phoenix Park murders even as he is telling Stephen the story of his own encounter with the Citizen that afternoon. Stephen expresses his distaste for both violence and Irish nationalism and underscores his disinterest with abrupt rudeness by telling Bloom: "We can't change the country. Let us change the subject" (*U* 16.1171).

With this rebuke, Bloom again lapses into silent contemplation and begins to speculate on the reasons behind Stephen's behavior. Eventually he decides "to pen something out of the common groove. . . . *My Experiences . . . in a Cabman's Shelter*" (*U* 16.1229–1231). Seeking a diversion, he spots a copy of the *Telegraph* lying near him, picks it up, and reads Joe Hynes's account of the funeral of Paddy Dignam, which contains a misprint of Bloom's name as "L. Boom." Further, to Bloom's amusement, although neither Stephen Dedalus nor C. P. M'Coy attended the funeral both of their names appear in the account, as well as that of M'Intosh (*U* 16.1259–1261). Stephen then takes up the paper, reading Garrett Deasy's letter on hoof-and-mouth disease that Myles Crawford had published at Stephen's request earlier in the day (see Nestor and Aeolus). This offers the opportunity for a brief exchange, but Stephen soon falls silent again.

One of the men in the shelter mentions Charles Stewart PARNELL, and this sets Bloom's mind off on his recollections of the dead statesman. From consideration of Parnell's political activity, Bloom inevitably moves to Parnell's adulterous affair with Kitty O'SHEA and to the furor surrounding its revelation. Given his own fraught domestic circumstances, Bloom is surprisingly sympathetic to Parnell's position in this matter, demonstrating his profound ability to suppress associations painful to him. Nonetheless, these ruminations do recall Molly to his mind, and this recollection in turn leads Bloom to show Stephen her picture and ask his opinion of her beauty. As the torpid Stephen gazes dumbly at the photograph, Bloom continues to think sympathetically of Parnell and Kitty O'Shea, remembering the abuse Parnell endured as the Irish people expressed their indignation over his sexual misconduct.

While the hallucinations of Circe seemed to bring Bloom's pain to the surface, these painful considerations appear cathartic. In short order he suggests that Stephen accompany him home, pays for their coffee and bun, and guides the young man out the door. Talking about music as they walk toward Bloom's home at 7 ECCLES STREET, a new familiarity develops between them, and, for a time, a sense of shared affinities. Thus the episode ends.

For some years it has been a critical commonplace that the Eumaeus episode, with its emphasis on clichés and exhausted language, reflects the fatigue that Joyce must have felt after the enormous effort of composing the Circe episode (chapter 15). More recently, however, scholars have come to see that the trite and hackneyed dialogue is yet another instance of Joyce's virtuosity as a writer. In forging the language of the chapter from the most mundane elements of everyday speech, he conveys the profound exhaustion felt by all of the men in the cabman's shelter in a style that paradoxically demonstrates a sophisticated creative approach. At this time of night none is capable of fresh or imaginative expression. Here, as elsewhere in *Ulysses,* Joyce's ability to play upon conventional forms of narrative—and the reader's expectations—enables him to use familiar material in new and illuminating ways.

On the textual level, the narrative also reiterates the central concerns of the day for Bloom and Stephen as it moves toward the climactic decisions (or the deferral of those decisions) that will occur in the Ithaca episode (chapter 17). Stephen's listlessness and passivity remind us that he has run out of options, and he now faces the unpleasant prospect of returning to Buck Mulligan in the MARTELLO TOWER and to his teaching job at Garrett Deasy's school in Dalkey. It is clear that neither situation appeals to him. The narrative also recalls for us that Bloom too faces a distasteful experience, as the time nears when he must return home and confront the evidence of his wife's adultery. These rather depressing circumstances make the sudden familiarity of Bloom and Stephen more understandable than it would otherwise have been.

As does its counterpart in *The Odyssey,* the Eumaeus episode of *Ulysses* marks a pause in the narrative. It allows two of the work's central figures a few moments' rumination on the choices that lie ahead, and it provides for the reader an unhurried review of the circumstances and feelings that have driven these men through the day. While Joyce's chapter does not produce a plan of action as decisive as that concocted by Odysseus and his son, it brings Stephen and Bloom together, and points them toward the most satisfying courses of action open to them.

For further information, see *Letters,* I.143–144, 148, 154, 160, and 178–179; and III.38 and 448.

### *Ithaca*

This is the 17th episode in *Ulysses* and the second in the novel's final section, Nostos.

According to the SCHEMA (see *Ulysses* schema in the appendix on page 392) that Joyce loaned to Valéry LARBAUD, the scene of the episode is Leopold Bloom's house at No. 7 ECCLES STREET. The time at which the action begins is after midnight. (More precisely, it is probably closer to one o'clock.) The organ [*sic*] of the chapter is the skeleton. The art of the chapter is science. The episode's symbols are comets. And its technic is catechism, an impersonal and confessional question-and-answer format.

Joyce took the title of the Ithaca episode from the name of the native land of Odysseus. This choice underscores the theme of homecoming that dominates this chapter. For the Greek hero, returning to Ithaca means both the successful completion of his 20-year odyssey and the restoration of his authority at home, which was threatened by the suitors for his wife, Penelope. Ithaca signals for Odysseus reaffirmation of authority, reunion with his wife and son, and repossession of his lands.

Leopold Bloom's return to 7 Eccles Street produces more ambiguous results. After aimlessly wandering about the city for most of the day, he has spent the latter portion of the evening in epical or mock-epical tasks, rescuing Stephen Dedalus from near-arrest in NIGHTTOWN in the Circe episode (chapter 15) and unsuccessfully trying to sober him up at the cabman's shelter in the Eumaeus episode (chapter 16). Bloom brings Stephen home with him at around 2 A.M. Over cocoa in the kitchen, the two men, exhausted from the day but still not ready for sleep, engage in a rambling discourse on a range of random topics.

Because the narrative is set in a rigid question-and-answer pattern from which it never deviates, the reader may have trouble comprehending how events unfold in the chapter. The difficulty does not come from the complexity of the rhetorical structure, for Joyce has cast the narrative in a format derived from that conventionally followed in Catholic catechisms and many of the textbooks commonly used in the primary schools of the day. (Richmal Mangnall's *Historical and Miscellaneous Questions, for the Use of Young People*, a work that Joyce had in his TRIESTE library and doubtless drew upon as a model, is a book of this sort.) Rather than offer a linear account of what transpires in Bloom's home, the episode's voluminous detail piles undifferentiated fact upon fact to such a degree that one begins to feel a sort of fatigue analogous to that which Stephen and Bloom are experiencing.

After just a few pages, simply maintaining a fundamental grasp of what the narrative unfolds becomes a chore. The questions and answers that form the discourse in this highly artificial fashion introduce a range of topics in a fairly desultory fashion. The sensitive reader can still trace the development of action within the chapter, but, perhaps more significantly, the very digressiveness of their interchanges underscores for such a reader the deep emotional scars that both men have acquired and the need that both have to skirt painful topics, both from that day and from the course of their lives.

Numbed by the events of June 16, particularly Molly's adultery, Bloom nonetheless continues to feel a deep love for his wife and concern over what will happen to their marriage because of her infidelity. Moreover, he endures an ongoing sorrow over his father's suicide, and he feels a deep unease and frustration over his inability to do anything about his daughter's burgeoning (and if she is like her mother, potentially reckless) sexuality. Stephen, though still a bit drunk, has a keen sense of the foolishness of his behavior throughout the day, and he remains profoundly insecure over his role as an artist and troubled by guilt over the circumstances of his mother's death.

The episode opens with Bloom and Stephen walking through the deserted city streets from the cabman's shelter, where the action of the Eumaeus episode transpired, back to Bloom's house. The narrative records, in a general way, the substance of their conversation, and, draws analogies to similar walks and similar conversations that both men have had with other friends. When the two men arrive at Bloom's house, Bloom finds that he has forgotten to bring the latchkey (something that he had reminded himself to avoid in the Calypso episode [chapter 4]). Rather than awaken Molly, he climbs over the area railing and enters the house on the lower level through the kitchen. From there he walks up to the ground floor, opens the front door, and brings Stephen (who has been waiting on the front steps) through the hallway and downstairs to the kitchen.

Once they are in the kitchen, Bloom assumes the role of the host and begins to make cocoa for Stephen and himself. Throughout these preparations, the narrative describes in great detail the mundane physical elements, kinetic phenomena, and municipal arrangements that contribute to Bloom's ability to draw water, bring it to a boil, and use it to make cocoa. The narrative also sums up Bloom's feelings on entering his house for the first time since Molly's assignation with Blazes Boylan. Specifically, Bloom takes careful note of the various signs pointing to Boylan's presence in the house earlier in the day, but he avoids further speculation on the events of the afternoon by thinking instead of the GOLD CUP horse race.

At this point, the narration, as if in response to Bloom's growing discomfort over the evidence of his wife's infidelity, offers another distraction, an account of the details of Bloom and Stephen's acquaintance. As the conversation continues, it touches randomly upon diverse interests and opinions held by the two men, and sketches recollections of events that mark the ordinary routines of both men's earlier lives. Throughout this exchange, Bloom's thoughts relentlessly return to his family, primarily to Molly, though with increasing frequency to Milly. His reflections show the depth of his love for both women, but they also underscore his unwillingness to confront painful aspects of their lives.

Bloom at this point seems ready for sleep, and he offers to let Stephen spend the night in the room adjacent to the bedroom that he and Molly share. Although Stephen hastily declines, he does so with uncharacteristic good grace. The two men next tentatively agree that Stephen will give Italian lessons to Molly, and in return she will offer him vocal lessons. Furthermore, they make tentative plans to "inaugurate a series of static, semistatic and peripatetic intellectual dialogues" (*U* 17.964–965). Bloom then leads Stephen into the back garden. Both men contemplate the early morning sky and then, together, urinate, after which Stephen leaves.

Bloom returns to the house, and, when he accidentally bumps his head against the walnut sideboard (an image ironically and unintentionally presaged by Stephen 15 hours earlier in the first paragraph of the Proteus episode [chapter 3]), he notices that the furniture in the front room has been moved around. This and detritus scattered about undeniably reinforce Boylan's disruptive presence in the house that afternoon. After taking this in with equal measures of stoicism and denial, Bloom mechanically straightens up the house, and prepares to go to bed. Overlaying all this, he reconsiders the events of the day, carefully noting his successes and failures, income and expenditures, tasks accomplished and those left undone.

This routine has an important psychological function. It moves toward a reintegration into the familiar pattern of life with Molly. More important, as Bloom moves through the house, he also faces, in his own oblique and muted fashion, the incontrovertible fact that Molly has spent the afternoon committing adultery in their bed with Blazes Boylan. In his most daring and least evasive gesture of the day having to do with his wife, Bloom allows himself to speculate on the various courses of action that he might take in the light of her infidelity. Although he vividly imagines what his life might be like should he decide to abandon her and leave Dublin, he comes to no definite decision regarding what he ultimately will do.

When Bloom finally climbs into his bed, he faces the last indignity of the day: further evidence of Boylan's earlier presence and of Molly's lack of concern over his learning of her adultery in the form of crumbs under the covers and a dried semen stain on the sheet. Resolved to do nothing, at least for the present, Bloom follows his usual bedtime routine and kisses "the plump mellow yellow smellow melons of [Molly's] rump." This gesture arouses him sexually and awakens her.

As Bloom is lying down with his head at Molly's feet—evidently his customary position in bed—she awakens and begins to question him about how he has spent his day. Bloom replies with a highly edited and in some cases patently untrue account of his movements since he left the house that morning. Though Molly has her suspicions about Bloom's veracity, which become evident from her recollections of the conversation in the Penelope episode (chapter 18), she makes no direct challenge to this account. Eventually, Bloom slips off to sleep as the day ends for him.

As the penultimate chapter, Ithaca recapitulates the central issues of the novel. It reminds the reader of the numerous matters that have haunted: both Stephen and Bloom throughout the day. Stephen's barely repressed guilt over his mother's death, his resentment over the failure of his fellow Dubliners to recognize his artistic abilities, his feelings of insecurity and lack of direction. Bloom's deep sadness over the deaths of his father, Rudolph Virag, and his son, Rudy Bloom; his concern over his daughter, Milly, and her incipient sexuality; the agony that he feels over the adultery of his wife; and his longing for a quiet, well-ordered life all emerge in the narrative's account of his thoughts, despite his effort to suppress all painful references.

The chapter demonstrates Joyce's unparalleled ability to fashion a coherent and compelling narrative from a rhetorical form as overtly artificial and unpromising as the question-and-answer. More significantly, by its obvious artificiality, the form of the Ithaca episode reminds us that *Ulysses* is a work of experimental fiction demanding that its readers participate in the creation of its meaning. The stylistic self-consciousness of the chapter highlights the self-reflexivity of the narrative throughout the entire novel.

For further details relating to the Ithaca episode, see *Letters,* I.175; II.97n.1 and 202n.2; and III.39, 43, 45–46, 48–49, and 51–52.

***Penelope***

This is the 18th chapter of *Ulysses,* the third and final episode of the Nostos section, and the conclusion of the book.

According to the SCHEMA (see *Ulysses* schema in the appendix on page 392) that Joyce loaned to Valéry LARBAUD, the scene of the episode is Molly and Leopold Bloom's bed. The time at which the action begins is indeterminate (though it is probably around two in the morning). The organ [*sic*] of the chapter is the flesh. The episode's symbol is the earth. And its technic is monologue (female). There is no art for the chapter.

The Penelope episode takes its name from the wife of Odysseus who waited 20 years for her husband's return from the Trojan War. More specifically, the chapter's title calls to mind book 23 of *The Odyssey,* in which Penelope is awakened and told that her husband has returned and killed all of the suitors who were occupying her house. Despite this seemingly welcome turn of events, Penelope takes a cautious approach to this strange man who has suddenly appeared in her home. She demands that he verify his identity by answering a question about the position of their bed known only to her husband. When he replies correctly, they are finally reunited.

The Penelope episode finally offers readers an extended and highly personal exposure of Molly Bloom's nature, and it takes the form of a rambling monologue presented in eight long, unpunctuated segments (which critics commonly designate as sentences). Each segment/sentence, a riot of orthographic and grammatical anarchy with misspellings, neologisms, and malapropisms abounding, is stamped with Molly's unique voice. Each reflects on much of the same material, as Molly moves randomly from personal recollections to speculation on the future to running commentary on various characters who have appeared in the preceding chapters.

Just as Joyce's epic (or mock-epic) novel begins in medias res, its final chapter opens in the same abrupt manner. With the phrase "Yes because he never did a thing like that before" (*U* 18:1), the narrative drops us in the midst of Molly's assertive INTERIOR MONOLOGUE, leaving us scrambling to catch up with her often mysterious references and her erratic train of thought. The opening lines also initiate the signature syntactic form that punctuates the discourse throughout the chapter by using "yes" to begin and end Molly's soliloquy.

The reader's abrupt introduction to Molly's monologue also underscores her own surprise at Bloom's wish as he was falling asleep at the end of the Ithaca episode (chapter 17), that she serve him breakfast in bed in the morning. From her initial amazement at this request, she jumps into a series of freewheeling associations that grow out of her perception of Bloom's relations with various women. These associations, in turn, cause her to begin thinking about Blazes Boylan and about his surreptitious advances prior to their climactic afternoon together. This chain of recollections initiates an associative pattern that will recur throughout the chapter: thoughts of her afternoon with Boylan inevitably lead Molly into an increasingly exaggerated graphic evocation of the day's sexual encounters. Paradoxically, this section also initiates another ruminative cycle as Molly begins a struggle with her conscience about her adultery (see *U* 18.134–135) and attempts to cope with the personal guilt that she bears for it. (Later in her monologue, she places full blame on Bloom: "its all his own fault if I am an adulteress" [*U* 18.1516], but even here her assertion seems hollow and unsure.)

In analyzing what has just transpired, Molly tries to assess Boylan's feelings for her and her own for him. Not surprisingly, given what the narrative has revealed about Boylan's materialistic nature, she takes what seems a frankly mercenary track. "If I only had a ring with the stone for my month a nice aquamarine Ill stick him for one and a gold bracelet" (*U* 18.261–262). Molly's thoughts of Boylan's behavior lead to comparisons with Bloom, and these lead her into recollections of Bloom's courtship, distinguished by the near obsessive fascination that he had for her. This memory in turn makes her recall British army lieutenant Stanley Gardner, a young man whom Molly had met in Dublin and with whom she carried on an affair that may or may not have been consummated. Gardner later died of enteric fever in South Africa during the Boer War, and Molly cherishes his memory. Thoughts of Gardner and the army also remind Molly of her early life in the British military garrison at Gibraltar, where her father, Brian Tweedy, was stationed.

Molly's mind turns to her own sensuality and to assessments of her sexual attractiveness. She reiterates this concern throughout the chapter, and the reader begins to see a clear connection between men's responses to her and her own sense of self-worth. At the same time, despite her preoccupation with physical beauty, Molly sustains a calculated detachment when considering the effects of sensuality. From a careful appraisal of Boylan's fascination with her breasts, to a judicious consideration of the shape of men's genitals, to a dismissive judgment of Bloom's cache of pornographic pictures, to frank bemusement over Bloom's wish to put her breast milk in his tea, Molly ranges unself-consciously over the erotic and sensuous side of her life with a candid enjoyment of her appetites.

The sound of a distant train whistle breaks up her sexual reverie and brings Molly's mind back to her life at Gibraltar, where she spent her childhood, as she remembers her friendship with Hester Stanhope. Molly reminisces about the confidences that she shared with the older woman, and recalls the loneliness she felt when Hester and her husband left Gibraltar. Both in what she recalls and in the obvious gaps in her memory, grim aspects of Molly's childhood become increasingly evident. The pleasure that she took in Dublin life when she first arrived further underscores how difficult her Gibraltar childhood must have been, particularly without the comfort of a mother (whose disappearance from the family is never explained) and friends her own age.

Thoughts of her childhood and adolescence bring Molly to remember her first male admirer, Harry Mulvey, a lieutenant in the Royal Navy whom she met at Gibraltar. Molly's emerging sexual curiosity and open sensual enjoyment distinguish her encounter with him, but, as with her recollection of Hester Stanhope, the details that she can still call to mind of their one day together suggest just how little actually must have occurred during that period of her life. From Mulvey her thoughts return once more to another military man, Stanley Gardner, emphasizing the deep affection that she retains for him.

Molly shifts her attention to more mundane matters as she begins to plan her routine for the next day. With characteristic pragmatism she attempts to calculate the long-term consequences of Bloom's new bid for attention in his request that she make his breakfast. Her mind calls up a series of anecdotes about Bloom, and she good-naturedly chafes at the trials of living with a man so eccentric. With less equanimity, however, Molly also begins to think about Milly and the tension caused in the household by her daughter's emerging sexuality. An aura of competition is evident in Molly's recollections, perhaps because they contain an unwelcome reminder of her aging. With these thoughts running through her mind and with the realization that her period is beginning (*U* 18.1105), Molly goes to the chamber pot to urinate, an event described with earthy humor in a jumbled evocation of the opening lines of Robert Southey's "The Cataract of Lodore": "O how the waters come down at Lahore" (*U* 18.1148) (Molly confuses the title).

Molly's jocularity evaporates abruptly as she wonders "is there anything the matter with my insides" (*U* 18.1149). Although she does not wish to dwell upon it, from her attitude and remarks it is evident that she is worried that she may have some serious gynecological problem. This form of denial, seemingly at odds with the brisk and confident approach to life that Molly usually takes, offers a subtle insight into the complexity of her nature. Turning her thoughts away from this mysterious and disturbing complaint, Molly again recalls events from her courtship with Bloom. These memories in turn provoke another digression, focusing on the idiosyncrasies, sexual and otherwise, of men in general. But, as seen earlier (*U* 18.85–89), her inclination to fantasize about seducing some young boy makes the urges that she describes here in men seem all too human and certainly no more coarse than her own. As she fantasizes about Stephen Dedalus and taking Italian lessons from him, she momentarily thinks of her own deceased son, Rudy Bloom, who died as an infant 11 years before.

Despite all her emphasis on sensuality, what Molly really wants from men remains unclear. Certainly, it goes beyond simple physical gratification, for, although she recalls with great pleasure and in fond detail the vigor of Boylan's lovemaking, she also takes deep offense at what she perceives as his lack of genuine respect for her. Molly shows an almost ingenuous sensitivity about male attitudes and behavior, a reminder that, both growing up in Gibraltar and living with Bloom, she has led a relatively sheltered life. Despite her seeming obsessive concern with men and sex, Molly's practical experience appears limited. Her own recollections demonstrate that she certainly is not the promiscuous slattern that gossips like Lenehan or Simon Dedalus make her out to be, and in many ways she displays an openness and lack of cynicism that call to mind the simple, lonely girl who grew up in the military garrison on Gibraltar.

As her soliloquy and the novel itself draw to a close, Molly begins to show her fatigue, and the narrative reflects the confused amalgamation of her thoughts and sensations. Nonetheless, certain fundamental feelings assert themselves clearly to the very end, including the desire to reveal her infidelity to Bloom: "Ill let him know if thats what he wanted that his wife is fucked yes and damn well fucked too up to my neck" (*U* 18.1510–1511). At the same time, her defensiveness when she recollects some man in the audience yelling "adulteress" at a singer during an opera (*U* 18.1118–1119), suggests that she does feel a measure of guilt and that the boldness of her previous statements is, to some extent, a bluff.

In fact, Molly's needs are strikingly similar to those manifested in the mind of Gerty MacDowell during the Nausikaa episode (chapter 13). Like Gerty, Molly seeks an idealized combination of sentiment and desire that in all likelihood no man could give her. The romantic element in Molly's nature grows increasingly evident over the course of her soliloquy and leads her to recollect key events in her courtship by Bloom, specifically the moment on HOWTH when Bloom proposed to her. Her thoughts return to the same gesture of affirmation (though perhaps with a very different emphasis) with which the chapter began: ". . . . and yes I said yes I will Yes" (*U* 18.1608–1609).

Despite its relatively narrow range of topics, Molly's soliloquy allows the reader a full and varied look at her consciousness. It offers her perspective on her adultery with Blazes Boylan. It highlights the central events in her life at Gibraltar. It elucidates her relations with her daughter and gives some insight into her abiding if ambivalently articulated grief over the death of her infant son. Most important, it presents a detailed picture of her marriage to Leopold Bloom.

The Penelope episode offers the reader a view of Molly that is in striking contrast to Bloom's uxorious perspective or the salacious representations of the Dubliners who talk about her throughout the day of June 16. Her monologue does not completely rebut the picture of Molly as a self-centered, self-indulgent, coquettish woman, but it does show her character as much subtler than her detractors realize, and it gives the reader a clearer understanding of what lies behind the profound hold that she has on Bloom's emotions.

In a more general sense, the Penelope episode can be considered a tailpiece to the novel, whose immediate action ends with Bloom's drifting into sleep at the closing of the previous episode, Ithaca. Its freewheeling form underscores the openness to a variety of readings that Joyce intends throughout the book. In considering numerous incidents that have been alluded to earlier in the novel, Molly alters our perceptions through her understanding of them and their significance. Even when Molly gives herself over to an ecstatic recollection of Bloom's proposal of marriage on the Hill of Howth, Joyce refuses to impose any sort of narrative closure, as though to assert the narrative ambiguity of life itself, and as a result critics continue to debate what precisely Molly affirms here and how the reader is to take it.

For further details regarding the Penelope episode, see *Letters,* I.164, 168, 170; II.72 and 274; and III.39, 48–49, 51, 57, 253, and 398, and *Selected Letters,* 284–285.

## CHARACTERS

**Artifoni, Almidano** In The Wandering Rocks episode (chapter 10), Artifoni appears as the music teacher who encourages Stephen Dedalus to continue to develop his singing voice so that one day he might perform professionally. The name of this character was taken from Signor Almidano Artifoni, the director of the Berlitz schools in Trieste and Pola where Joyce was an English-language instructor.

**Bannon, Alec** Bannon is a student and a friend of Buck Mulligan, first mentioned at the end of the Telemachus episode. He appears in The Oxen of the Sun episode (chapter 14) when he accompanies Mulligan to the Holles Street Hospital. He is subsequently part of the group that goes to Burke's pub, and there, within the hearing of Leopold Bloom, he speaks to Mulligan about Milly Bloom, whom he has met in Mullingar. Overhearing this conversation, Bloom is disturbed, for earlier in the day, in the Calypso episode (chapter 4), he had read, with some uneasiness, Milly's letter in which she says she has met a young student, whom he now takes to be Bannon. When Bannon realizes that Bloom is Milly's father, the young man slips away.

**Bergan, Alf** He is one of the drinkers who patronize BARNEY KIERNAN'S pub and participate in the discussions in the Cyclops episode. In the Lestrygonians episode, Bloom speculates that either Bergan or Richie Goulding is the practical joker responsible for the disturbing postcard—with the message "U.P." printed on it—sent to Denis Breen (*U* 8.257–258, 320), read as "U.P.: up." Alf Bergan was modeled on an actual Dublin resident, Alfred Bergan, who was an assistant to the city's sub-sheriff and a friend of Joyce's father. Alfred Bergan's recollections probably provided the source for the text of the hangman's letter that appears in the Cyclops episode (*U* 12.415–431).

**Best, Richard** He is a fictionalized version of the assistant to the actual director of the National Library in Dublin when Joyce was a young man. He later became the head librarian. He lived from 1872 to 1959. In the novel Best demonstrates a measure of sympathy for Stephen's efforts in the lively philosophical and literary discussion on Shakespeare that takes place in the Scylla and Charybdis episode.

**Bloom, Ellen (Higgins)** She is the deceased mother of Leopold Bloom. Bloom thinks of her throughout the day, often in a fashion similar to—but without the intensity of—Stephen Dedalus's recollections of his mother. Bloom's memories mingle affirmations of her love for him with the awareness that he has sometimes caused her pain. She appears in one of Bloom's hallucinations during the Circe episode (chapter 15).

**Bloom, Leopold** Bloom, or Poldy as Molly calls him, is the 38-year-old Dubliner whose daylong journey around that city on June 16, 1904—now commemorated as BLOOMSDAY—forms the narrative core of *Ulysses.* He is the husband of Molly Bloom and father of Milly and Rudy Bloom. In his wanderings about Dublin and his encounters with its citizens, Bloom emerges as a modern-day Odysseus figure. As a Jew and the son of an immigrant, he is typed as a foreigner and considered an outsider by many in the provincial world of Irish society. As he moves about Dublin, Bloom is preoccupied with his wife's impending adultery and mindful of his daughter's budding sexuality. He also feels a continuing, deep grief over the death, 11 years earlier, of his son, Rudy, and over the suicide of his father, Rudolf Virag (who had changed the family name to Bloom).

Bloom first appears in the Calypso episode, where the reader sees his uxorious devotion to his wife, Molly, and becomes aware of his complex inner life. The chapter balances Bloom's morning routine of preparing breakfast for himself and Molly against his vivid sexual fantasies and poignant concerns for his wife and his daughter, Milly. The next episode, Lotus-Eaters, depicts the public side of Bloom as he moves about Dublin running errands

A painting of Leopold Bloom, a main character in *Ulysses* *(Paul Joyce)*

and preparing to attend the funeral of an acquaintance, Paddy Dignam; in this chapter the reader also learns of Bloom's epistolary affair with Martha Clifford when he retrieves a letter from her at the Westland Row post office. In the Hades episode, Bloom accompanies a group of mourners to GLASNEVIN Cemetery where Paddy Dignam is being buried. Here the reader's sense of Bloom's isolation is starkly enforced by the often rude and insensitive treatment he receives from the other mourners.

For the remainder of the day, Bloom moves about the city unwilling to go home and desperate to keep his thoughts from dwelling on Molly's impending adultery with Blazes Boylan. He visits the offices of the *FREEMAN'S JOURNAL* in the Aeolus episode, where again the majority of the men whom he encounters are either rude or indifferent to him, and lunches at DAVY BYRNE's pub during the Lestrygonians episode. When he ducks into the National Museum to avoid Boylan and then crosses the yard to the National Library, Bloom encounters Stephen Dedalus and Buck Mulligan on the steps at the end of the Scylla and Charybdis episode. After wandering down to the quays during the Wandering Rocks episode, he obtains a pornographic book (*The Sweets of Sin*) for Molly. In the Sirens episode, Bloom dines with Richie Goulding at the Ormond Hotel (and sees Boylan leave for his assignation with Molly). A short time later, Bloom confronts the xenophobic Citizen at BARNEY KIERNAN'S pub in the Cyclops episode, then in the Nausikaa episode he masturbates on Sandymount Strand while watching Gerty MacDowell. From there he goes to the Holles Street Maternity Hospital to check the condition of Mina Purefoy, but ends up, throughout the Oxen of the Sun episode, watching Stephen and his friends drunkenly carouse in the refectory. In the Circe episode, after following Stephen to NIGHTTOWN, Bloom goes through a series of degraded hallucinations at Bella Cohen's bordello. The action comes to a head when a drunken Stephen is knocked down by a British soldier outside a whorehouse, and Bloom cares for the young man. During the Eumaeus episode Bloom takes Stephen to a cabmen's shelter in an unsuccessful attempt to get the drunken young man to eat. Subsequently, in the Ithaca episode, Bloom brings Stephen home to 7 ECCLES STREET, gives him cocoa, and offers the homeless young man a bed. When Stephen declines his invitation to spend the night, Bloom sees the young man off through the back garden and then, after a brief consideration of the events of the day, finally goes to bed.

In his cultural background, his psychological attitudes, his material condition, Bloom can be read as a modern Everyman figure—*l'homme moyen sensuel*—whose life reflects the traumas of the contemporary world from which the narrative of *Ulysses* emerges. He is also a complete man, as Joyce explained in a conversation with his Zurich friend Frank BUDGEN. "I see [Bloom]," Joyce said, "from all sides, and therefore he is all-round in the sense of your sculptor's figure. But he is a complete man as well—a good man" (*James Joyce and the Making of Ulysses*, p. 17). The classical literary model for the complete man is, of course, Odysseus, whose endurance and return home are his ultimate triumphs. The adventures of this epic figure provide the archetypal basis for much of the comic action in *Ulysses.* But Joyce also drew from other individuals—biographic as well as literary—in his creation of Leopold Bloom, figures that include himself and his father, John Stanislaus JOYCE.

Although the dominant element in Bloom's identity is his Jewishness, in the strictest sense, as defined by Jewish tradition, Bloom is not a Jew. Although his father was Jewish, his mother was not, and he was not circumcised. His background adds to the ambiguity of his antecedents. He grew up among Jews and in a limited way he learned Jewish customs, traditions, and religious rituals. In a series of gestures toward integration into the relatively homogeneous Dublin society, made first by his father and then by himself, Bloom was first baptized as a Protestant and then again, before marrying Molly, as a Catholic. However, in the assessment of most Dubliners, he is still a Jew, and in his own thoughts he identifies with his Jewish ancestry.

These conditions enforce Bloom's status as an outsider, an identity that emerges in tension with his Everyman identity throughout the text. Bloom stands both inside and outside Dublin society, getting a complex, PARALLAX view of it. The alternate perspectives also shape the way the reader understands the ethos of *Ulysses.* Further, Bloom's ambivalent self-identity exerts an important, though understated, influence on the self-perceptions of numerous other characters whom he (and the reader) encounters in Joyce's novel.

Thus, the cosmopolitan, multicultural, religiously diverse, politically pluralistic, sexually conflicted character known as Leopold Bloom is as much a representative as an individual. Time and again in the narrative, he serves not only to highlight the attributes of others but also as a means to illuminate the Dublin mentality. While he never achieves the status of a fully accepted member of society, he wonderfully underscores (both by what he does and by what he chooses not to do) the attitudes, attributes, and experiences that constitute the lives of his fellow Dubliners.

(See the appendix on page 402 for the Bloom family tree.)

**Bloom, Marcus J.** He was an actual Dublin dentist of Joyce's day whose name appears in The Wandering Rocks episode. He is not related to Leopold BLOOM.

**Bloom, Milly (Millicent)** She is the 15-year-old daughter of Leopold Bloom and Molly Bloom. She does not take part in the action of the book directly, but rather is presented through her letter to Bloom and the thoughts of her parents. Milly's birthday is June 15, the day before the action described in *Ulysses.* On June 16, 1904, she is living in the town of MULLINGAR in central Ireland, where she is an apprentice to a photographer and where she has met Alec Bannon, a young student whose acquaintance with Milly causes Bloom to feel a measure of fatherly concern.

In the Calypso episode, Bloom reads her birthday thank-you letter (*U* 4.397–414), and, in the Oxen of the Sun episode she is described to Buck Mulligan by Bannon, citing some of the same language Milly has used to describe the women of Mullingar, as "a skittish heifer, big of her age and beef to the heel" (*U* 14.502–503). She also figures in Molly's monologue in the Penelope episode.

The narrative invites readers to draw parallels between her emergent sexuality, her attractiveness, and her physique, and those traits characterizing Molly at the same age. The analogy offers some insight into Molly's complex personality, and it elaborates upon the intricacies of the Bloom family life. Further, as the object of her father's affection and concern, the figure of Milly allows the reader insight into the range of attitudes that inform Bloom's conscience.

(See the appendix on page 402 for the Bloom family tree.)

**Bloom, Molly** She is the voluptuous 33-year-old wife of Leopold Bloom, mother of Milly Bloom, and concert soprano. She was born Marion Tweedy in Gibraltar on September 8, 1870 (the Feast Day of the Nativity of the Blessed Virgin Mary), and she moved to Dublin with her father, Major Brian Tweedy, when she was about 16 years old. Her mother, Lunita Laredo, either died or left home when Molly was a young child.

If Leopold Bloom represents the complete man, Molly Bloom stands for the complete woman. From the first faint sound of her voice answering "Mn" (that is, "No") to Bloom's question concerning breakfast in the Calypso episode to her final ecstatic "Yes"—the novel's last word—in the Penelope episode, Molly's presence slowly and pervasively emerges as an archetypal embodiment of the feminine. Hers is a spiritual and physical presence that affirms the whole of *Ulysses.* In a letter to Frank BUDGEN dated August 16, 1921, Joyce discussed his broad intentions in writing Penelope and explained some of the chapter's structural components. He emphasized that the episode "begins and ends with the female word *yes*"—it is the "*clou,*" the star turn of the whole novel—and that the words *because, bottom, woman,* and *yes* express the chapter's four cardinal points: "the female breasts, arse, womb and cunt." In this letter, Joyce also included the German phrase "Weib. Ich bin der [*sic*] Fleisch der stets bejaht" ("Woman. I am the flesh that continually affirms [assents]"). Richard ELLMANN sees this as a play upon the line from Goethe's *Faust,* "I am the spirit that always denies" (see *Selected Letters,* p. 285).

Though physical sensations dominate Molly's consciousness, it is language, uninhibited and often without clear direction, that defines her. Molly's monologue in Penelope—eight long unpunctuated sentences—shows a spirited mind reflecting on the course of her life and desires. The complexity of these sentences, which build upon one association after another, is magnified by the rapid shifts in Molly's thoughts. In her monologue, she touches upon a wide range of seemingly unrelated biographical events: her childhood in Gibraltar, her sexual experiences with Lieutenant Mulvey 18 years earlier and other sexual encounters real and imagined, her liaison with Blazes Boylan earlier in the day, and her marriage to Bloom.

Over the course of the narrative, the character of Molly oscillates from evocative archetype to complex individual. For most of the first 17 chapters she is seen through the consciousness of Bloom and the comments of a series of other Dublin men, with their recollections more often than not highlighting their sexual inadequacies rather than offering insights into her nature. Among them, they conjure up almost every conceivable variation of the Madonna/whore stereotype. Not surprisingly, for much of the novel Molly also plays upon the reader's inclinations toward sexual stereotyping. In the final chapter, however, she confounds all generalizations (both positive and negative) and emerges as a highly complex individual. The reader is offered glimpses into her enigmatic and often contradictory consciousness—she is alternately coarse and squeamish, sensuous and modest, calculating and artless. No single aspect captures her nature, no series of traits sums her up. Her soliloquy leaves the reader with a range of rich impressions that must be reconciled to arrive at an understanding of *Ulysses* as a whole.

(See the appendix on page 402 for the Bloom family tree.)

For further discussion of Molly's background and nature, see James Card's *An Anatomy of "Penelope"* and Richard Pearce's *Molly Blooms: A Polylogue on "Penelope" and Culture Studies.*

**Bloom, Rudolph** He is the father of Leopold Bloom. He came to Ireland as a Hungarian Jewish immigrant, and changed his name from Rudolf Virag (the Hungarian name for flower) to Rudolph Bloom. After the death of his wife, Rudolph committed suicide in the town of Ennis by poisoning himself. To commemorate the anniversary of his father's death, Leopold plans to go to Ennis, coincidentally at the same time that his wife, Molly, proposes to go on a concert tour with Blazes Boylan. Throughout *Ulysses,* Bloom often thinks of his father as "poor papa."

(See the appendix on page 402 for the Bloom family tree.)

**Bloom, Rudy** He is the dead son of Leopold and Molly Bloom. Throughout *Ulysses,* Bloom thinks frequently of Rudy, who lived for only 11 days (from December 29, 1893, to January 9, 1894), and of the psychological, physical, and emotional losses that he sustained with the child's death. The Circe episode ends with Bloom seeing an apparition of the child. Recollections of Rudy and of his death also provide a powerful emotion in Molly's monologue in the Penelope episode, in which Molly shows how deeply she still feels the effect of his loss, and her response underscores how imperfectly both she and Bloom have reconciled themselves to their tragedy.

(See the appendix on page 402 for the Bloom family tree.)

**Boardman, Edy** She is a minor character who appears with her friends Cissy Caffrey and Gerty MacDowell on Sandymount Strand in the Nausikaa episode. Edy is minding a young brother in a stroller. She reappears briefly at the beginning of the Circe episode though it remains unclear whether it is in person or as a hallucination.

**Boylan, (Hugh) Blazes** Although his actual appearance in the novel is brief, he remains a pivotal character in *Ulysses.* Boylan is a well-known and popular Dublin advertising man and impresario. He is an acquaintance of Leopold Bloom, and on June 16, 1904, he becomes the lover of Molly Bloom. Boylan's coarseness and animal vitality stand in antithesis to Bloom's more sensitive nature, and the contrast provides the immediate rationale for Molly's infidelity. Bloom spends much of the day avoiding encounters with Boylan and suppressing thoughts of his liaison with Molly. Boylan is also arranging a concert tour for Molly, although the reader senses that the scope of the tour will not live up to his grand promises.

In the novel's final episode, Penelope, Molly's recollections of Boylan and of the day that they have spent together provide a much fuller picture of him and of their relationship. Despite the physical gratification that she has taken from their encounter, her reservations about Boylan and her admiration for aspects of Bloom's nature become quite evident over the course of her monologue. As a result, although Molly continues to feel a strong sensual attraction for him, by the end of the episode, Boylan's flaws have become all too evident to her.

**Breen, Denis** He is a mentally unbalanced character who appears sporadically throughout the narrative of *Ulysses.* Throughout the day, Breen wanders around the city seeking legal counsel in order to file a complaint against the prankster who sent him a card with "U.P." written on it, possibly meant as a cryptic disparaging comment on Breen's sexuality, "you pee," "up," or "under proof," a distilling term signifying a weak or unsatisfactory product. (The precise insult contained on the postcard, and for that matter its precise meaning, have long been debated among Joyce scholars.) In the Lestrygonians episode, Leopold Bloom sees Breen carrying two heavy law books. In the Cyclops episode, Breen is ridiculed by the patrons in BARNEY KIERNAN'S pub when they spy him walking by. Breen stands as a contrast to Bloom. Although both men are outsiders, Bloom has reconciled himself to the life that he finds himself living while Breen lashes out wildly at everything around him.

**Breen, Mrs. Josephine** She is the wife of Denis Breen, a friend of Molly Bloom, and possibly an old flame of Leopold Bloom. In the Lestrygonians episode, she confides in Bloom about her husband's postcard and about her concern for her husband and her family. Like Denis Breen in relation to Bloom, Josie Breen stands as a contrast to Molly.

**Caffrey, Cissy** She is a minor character and friend of Gerty MacDowell and Edy Boardman. In the Nausikaa episode she appears with them on Sandymount Strand, where Leopold Bloom is lingering after visiting Paddy Dignam's widow in Irishtown.

**Carr, Pvt. Harry** He is one of the drunken British soldiers wandering around NIGHTTOWN during the Circe episode. He gets into a fight with Stephen Dedalus over a supposed insult to King Edward VII. The real-life model for Carr was a staff member of the British Consulate in Zurich, Henry Carr, who with Joyce belonged to the ENGLISH PLAYERS and who was involved in an acrimonious lawsuit (1918–19) with Joyce over the cost of a pair of trousers purchased for a performance of Oscar WILDE's *The Importance of Being Earnest.*

**Citizen, The** This is the name given to one of the central characters of the Cyclops episode. Though he is little more than a barfly, the Citizen dominates the scene in BARNEY KIERNAN'S pub. No one can ignore his loud, aggressive demands that every conversation be turned back to a celebration of the Celtic past and a condemnation of English imperialism. The Citizen is modeled on the Irish nationalist, Michael CUSACK, and he proffers a belligerent ultranationalist political philosophy (tinged with xenophobia) to anyone within earshot. His crude and volatile nature manifests itself most obviously in his marked antipathy for Bloom. In his outbursts in the bar, he mingles ANTI-SEMITISM with anger in his suspicion that Bloom has won a large sum of money on Throwaway in the GOLD CUP race. The Citizen takes offense when he believes that Bloom is mean-spiritedly refusing to buy a round of drinks to celebrate. The final scene in the episode, in which the Citizen throws a biscuit tin at the jaunting car taking Bloom away, provides a harsh burlesque of the image of Irish manliness to which the Citizen continually refers.

**Clifford, Martha** She is an offstage character who is first introduced in the Lotus-Eaters episode. Martha is a freelance typist and the woman with whom Leopold Bloom (under the pen name of Henry Flower, Esq.) carries on a clandestine and mildly titillating correspondence. In the letter that she sends to Bloom, Martha underscores her growing affection for him through the flattened petals of a yellow flower that she has enclosed. During the Sirens episode, Bloom writes in response to her letter. She actually appears, in a manner of speaking, in one of Bloom's hallucinations in the Circe episode. The model for this character may have been Marthe Fleischmann, a Zurich acquaintance with whom Joyce corresponded.

**Cohen, Bella** She is the portly madam who runs the brothel in NIGHTTOWN visited by Stephen Dedalus, Vincent Lynch, and Leopold Bloom during the Circe episode. Midway through the chapter, in one of Bloom's sadomasochistic hallucinations, Bella metamorphoses into Bello, and he/she performs a series of sadomasochistic humiliations in which Bloom, now changed into a woman, both fears and delights.

**Conmee, Rev. John, SJ** Father Conmee was the rector of CLONGOWES WOOD COLLEGE when Stephen Dedalus attended it. In *Ulysses,* Father Conmee appears in the Wandering Rocks episode where he is intent on obtaining a place for young Patrick Dignam, the orphaned son of Paddy Dignam, at the O'Brien Institute for Destitute Children in Fairview.

See also Characters under *A Portrait of the Artist as a Young Man.*

**Corley, John** In the Eumaeus episode, Corley appears as a homeless derelict, wandering the streets, jobless and looking for a place to sleep. Stephen Dedalus recognizes him and lends him some money. According to Richard ELLMANN, Corley was the name of one of of Joyce's Dublin acquaintances. He was the eldest son of a police inspector.

See also Characters under "Two Gallants" in *Dubliners.*

**Crawford, Myles** Crawford is the fictional editor of the *EVENING TELEGRAPH.* His drunken disquisitions punctuate the dialogue of the Aeolus episode. Stephen Dedalus brings him Mr. Deasy's letter on hoof-and-mouth disease to be published in the paper. Though dismissive of Deasy, Crawford shows a genuine interest in Stephen's talents and tries to draw the young man into a career in journalism by recounting the exploits of the newsman Ignatius Gallaher. At the same time, Crawford is impatient with and even rude to Leopold Bloom, who has come into the office to try to sell Crawford an advertisement.

**Cunningham, Martin** Cunningham, a Dublin Castle official, appears as a minor character in several episodes of *Ulysses,* including Hades, The Wandering Rocks, and Circe; he plays an important role in the Cyclops episode when he rescues Leopold Bloom from a barroom fracas by leading him out of BARNEY KIERNAN'S pub just as Bloom is about to be attacked by the Citizen.

See also Characters under "Grace" in *Dubliners.*

**Deasy, Garrett** He is the headmaster of the school in Dalkey, a seaside resort southeast of Dublin, where Stephen Dedalus teaches. Deasy appears in the Nestor episode, where he is portrayed as misogynistic, anti-Semitic, and a pro-British imperialist. Knowing that Stephen has literary connections, Deasy gives him a letter relating to the threat of hoof-and-mouth disease to Ireland's cattle in the hope that Stephen will be able to have it published in some of the city's newspapers and magazines (see "Politics and Cattle Disease" in *The Critical Writings of James Joyce*). It later appears in the *Evening Telegraph,* as recounted in the Eumaeus episode.

**Dedalus, Boody** She is one of Stephen Dedalus's sisters. Although only briefly seen in the Wandering Rocks episode, her shabby appearance stands as a mute testimony to the family's destitution.

(See the appendix on page 402 for the Dedalus family tree.)

**Dedalus, Dilly (Delia)** She is one of Stephen Dedalus's younger sisters. In the Wandering Rocks episode, she confronts her father on the street to demand money to buy food for the family. This scene (*U* 10.643–716) and one that follows soon after showing her speaking with Stephen by the cart containing secondhand books (*U* 10.854–880) indicate the impoverished condition into which the Dedalus family has fallen. It also underscores the self-centeredness of Stephen's artistic vocation. He clearly understands his family's desperate condition, but he has made the long-term decision not to allow family obligations to deter him from the pursuit of his own creative ambitions and the short-term choice to privilege his drinking over their hunger.

(See the appendix on page 402 for the Dedalus family tree.)

**Dedalus, Katey** She appears in the Wandering Rocks episode, returning home with Boody after an unsuccessful attempt to sell Stephen's books to get money for food (*U* 10.258–297). Here and elsewhere in the chapter, the poverty of the Dedalus household is clearly evident.

See also Characters under *A Portrait of the Artist as a Young Man.*

(See the appendix on page 402 for the Dedalus family tree.)

**Dedalus, Mrs.** She is the long-suffering wife of Simon and mother of Stephen. When *Ulysses* begins, she has been dead for nearly a year. Nonetheless, she appears in one of Stephen's hallucinations during the Circe episode, and it provokes the violent reaction that leads him to damage one of Bella Cohen's lampshades.

See also Mrs. Daedalus under Characters in *Stephen Hero.*

(See the appendix on page 402 for the Dedalus family tree.)

**Dedalus, Simon** He appears in both *A Portrait of the Artist as a Young Man* and *Ulysses.* Simon is the improvident and alcoholic father of Stephen Dedalus and the head of the Dedalus household. Like his precursor (Mr. Simon Daedalus in *Stephen Hero*), this character is modeled on Joyce's father, John Stanislaus JOYCE. Mr. Dedalus's spiral into financial and social ruin significantly shapes much of the material and emotional circumstances of the life of Stephen Dedalus in *A Portrait of the Artist as a Young Man* and *Ulysses.* In spite of Mr. Dedalus's failures, his intolerant temperament, his resentments, and his strong political and religious opinions, he is nonetheless presented as a witty raconteur and amiable socializer. His ability to tell a good story and sing a good song in pleasing tenor voice make him a pleasant companion.

Although father and son never encounter one another in *Ulysses,* Mr. Dedalus appears throughout the narrative. He is first seen in the Hades episode, in which he rides to the funeral of Paddy Dignam with Leopold Bloom, Martin Cunningham, and Jack Power and denigrates Buck Mulligan for his bad influence on Stephen. The Aeolus episode finds him hanging about the offices of the *FREEMAN'S JOURNAL* and leaving for a drink only moments before Stephen arrives. Later, in the Wandering Rocks chapter, his daughter Dilly Dedalus approaches the inebriated and now disagreeable Mr. Dedalus to ask him for money to buy food for the family. He reluctantly gives her a shilling, and then, in a flash of transitory remorse, adds two pennies so that she can buy something for herself. In his last actual appearance, in the Sirens episode, he is heard singing popular songs in the bar at the Ormond Hotel. Simon remains in Stephen's thoughts for much of the day, and he emerges as one of Stephen's hallucinations near the end of the Circe episode. Despite the sardonic characterization of Simon Dedalus, Joyce takes care to represent as well the charming and witty qualities that made him (and John Joyce, his model) so popular throughout Dublin.

See also Characters under *A Portrait of the Artist as a Young Man*.

(See the appendix on page 402 for the Dedalus family tree.)

**Dedalus, Stephen** He is the hero of *A Portrait of the Artist as a Young Man* and a major character in *Ulysses*. His names have symbolic significance. St. Stephen was the name of the first Christian martyr, persecuted for his convictions (see Acts 7:55–60), and Dedalus (or Daedalus) was the mythical artificer who made feathered wings of wax with which he and his son Icarus escaped imprisonment on the island of Crete. (Icarus, however, flew too close to the sun; the wax melted, and he plunged into the Ionian Sea and drowned.) Like the Christian martyr, Stephen faces persecution by his peers, or at least feels he does, and, like Dedalus, he must use artifice and cunning to escape his own imprisonment—by the institutions of the family, the church, and Irish nationalism. As Stephen writes in his diary: "Old father, old artificer, stand me now and ever in good stead" (*P* 252–253).

After an extended representation in *A Portrait of the Artist as a Young Man* that concludes with his impending departure for Paris, Stephen reappears in *Ulysses*, having been called back to Dublin by the death of his mother and kept there by a combination of penury and inertia. In *Ulysses*, he does not command the same attention that he did in the previous novel. By this time Joyce had come to feel that Stephen's nature did not allow for much further character development and so devoted much more consideration and space to Leopold Bloom. Nonetheless, Stephen occupies large portions of the novel, especially in the first three chapters.

The narrative opens in Telemachus with a series of exchanges between a disgruntled Stephen and a self-absorbed Buck Mulligan, the friend with whom he lives in the MARTELLO TOWER in Sandycove. In the Nestor chapter, Stephen is shown at work, teaching, or at least attempting to teach, at Garrett Deasy's school for young boys in Dalkey. After Stephen is paid by Deasy, the narrative follows him along Sandymount Strand in the Proteus episode, walking toward Dublin and mulling over his future.

Stephen reappears sporadically throughout the rest of *Ulysses* as he spends the day drinking up much of his salary and trying to demonstrate his artistic powers to an ever-changing audience of Dubliners. At the newspaper office in the Aeolus episode, Stephen tries unsuccessfully to hold the attention of Myles Crawford and others through a flawed recitation of his story, "A PISGAH SIGHT OF PALESTINE, OR THE PARABLE OF THE PLUMS" that ends up being spoiled by a poorly delivered punch line. In the office of the director of the National Library in the Scylla and Charybdis episode, he finds himself equally unsuccessful in his attempts to impress a representative group of Dublin's literati—George Russell, John Eglinton, Richard Best, and Thomas Lyster—with a disquisition on Shakespeare.

By the time he appears at the Holles Street Maternity Hospital in the Oxen of the Sun episode, Stephen has become so drunk that his attempts at demonstrating his wit prove feeble and almost incoherent. After treating his friends to a final round of drinks at Burke's pub just before closing time, Stephen and Lynch go off to NIGHTTOWN in search of Georgina Johnson, a prostitute who has apparently captured his drunken imagination.

At this point, the themes of paternity and familial devotion that have appeared sporadically throughout the novel move into the center of the narrative with the convergence of Stephen and Bloom. After encountering Stephen at the Holles Street Maternity Hospital during the Oxen of the Sun episode, Bloom, motivated by a paternal concern, follows him in an attempt to keep him out of trouble. In the Circe episode, Stephen wanders about the parlor of Bella Cohen's bordello, drunkenly explaining his aesthetic views and hallucinating about his dead mother. A final hallucination frightens Stephen so much that he breaks a lampshade, runs out into the street, encounters two British soldiers who are just as drunk as he, and is promptly knocked down. Bloom comes to his rescue, prevents his arrest, and determines that Stephen find a safe place to spend the night.

In the Eumaeus episode, Bloom takes Stephen to a cabman's shelter to help him recuperate, though as drunkenness gives way to fatigue Stephen often proves to be a less than charming companion. Then, in the Ithaca episode, Bloom takes Stephen home with him to 7 ECCLES STREET. On the walk to Bloom's house and later in the kitchen, the two engage in a wide-ranging conversation, doubtless more interesting to Bloom than to Stephen. Their colloquy ends when Stephen politely declines the offer of a bed for the night and walks out of Bloom's garden and out of the novel. While the conflicts that Stephen and Bloom feel regarding the roles of fathers and sons remain unresolved, their interaction has given readers a keen view of the complex psychological features constituting their characters.

See also Characters under *A Portrait of the Artist as a Young Man.*

(See the appendix on page 402 for the Dedalus family tree.)

**Dignam, Master Patrick Aloysius** He is the eldest son of the late Paddy Dignam. In the Wandering Rocks episode, Master Dignam muses over the events of the day and reluctantly returns home after purchasing port steaks for the family's dinner. While walking, he reflects with a mixture of curiosity and awe upon his father's last words to him and on how his father looked after he died.

**Dignam, Paddy (Patrick T.)** He is the deceased Dubliner whose funeral at GLASNEVIN Cemetery Leopold Bloom attends during the Hades episode. Dignam's death and burial form a motif throughout *Ulysses.* Allusions to his mortality animate the action early in the narrative, and serve as a reference point for characterization and plot throughout. A good part of Bloom's public activity throughout the day of June 16, 1904, centers on his concerns for the Dignam family and the payment of Dignam's insurance policy to them.

**Dillon, Mat** He is an offstage character in *Ulysses.* He is a friend of Leopold Bloom and of Molly Bloom's father, Major Brian Tweedy. In the Sirens episode, Bloom remembers having seen Molly for the first time at Dillon's residence in Terenure, a well-to-do middle-class district on the south side of Dublin.

**Dlugacz, Moses** He is the Hungarian Jew (as indicated by his surname) and pork butcher who owns the shop in Upper Dorset Street where Bloom buys a kidney for his breakfast in the Calypso episode.

**Dodd, Reuben J.** He is a minor figure in Ulysses. He is an accountant and a parsimonious moneylender, well known to men like Simon Dedalus, Martin Cunningham, and several of the others attending the funeral of Paddy Dignam. During the Hades episode, Paddy Dignam's funeral cortege passes Dodd walking near Daniel O'Connell's statue, prompting Leopold Bloom's inadequate effort to tell the story of Dodd's response to the attempted suicide of his son, Reuben J. Dodd Jr. The young man attempts to drown himself by jumping into the River Liffey. A boatman saves him, and Dodd Sr gives the man a paltry tip of a florin (two shillings); see the appendix on page 430 for a detailed description of monetary values. " 'One and eightpence too much,' Mr. Dedalus said drily" (U 6.291).

There was an actual Dublin resident with that name in 1904, when the novel takes place. Although in reality he was a Roman Catholic, in the novel the anti-Semites in Paddy Dignam's funeral cortege, who blindly associate money-lending with Jewishness, speak of his fictional counterpart as if he were a Jew. (See ANTI-SEMITISM.)

**Dodd, Reuben J., Jr.** He is the son of Reuben J. Dodd. He does not appear directly in the novel, but is referred to by other characters. Shortly before June 16, 1904, distraught over an unhappy love affair, the younger Dodd attempts suicide by jumping into the River LIFFEY but is saved from drowning by a boatman. The restrained expression of gratitude by his father, Reuben J. Dodd Sr., becomes the source of an amusing anecdote recalled by Leopold Bloom in the Hades episode.

**Doran, Bob** He first appears as a central character in "The Boarding House." The married Bob Doran reappears, "on one of his periodical bends," throughout the narrative of *Ulysses.* In the Cyclops episode, he threatens to create a nasty scene in BARNEY KIERNAN'S pub when he hears the news of the death of Paddy Dignam.

See also Characters under "The Boarding House" in *Dubliners*.

**Douce, Lydia** She appears in the Sirens episode, one of the barmaids at the Ormond Hotel. At the opening of the episode, she and Miss Kennedy are looking out the window, viewing the viceregal procession. During the chapter she distinguishes herself as an inveterate flirt, trying to impress Blazes Boylan by snapping her garter and George Lydell by provocatively stroking the beer pull.

**Driscoll, Mary** She never actually appears in the novel, but did serve for a time as a domestic and former servant in the Bloom household. When Leopold Bloom took a sexual interest in her, she was fired by Molly (see *U* 18.55–77). In the Circe episode, Mary Driscoll appears in one of Bloom's hallucinations, participating in a trial during which she accuses him of attempting to seduce her.

**Egan, Kevin** He is a Fenian (that is, a member of a secret Irish and Irish-American group intent on overthrowing British rule in Ireland) living in self-imposed exile and working as a printer in Paris. In the Proteus episode, Stephen Dedalus recalls time spent with him in Paris (*U* 3.163–264). Joyce modeled Egan's character after Joseph Casey, an Irish expatriate whom he knew in Paris at the turn of the century.

**Eglinton, John (1868–1961)** This is the pseudonym adopted by William Kirkpatrick Magee, an essayist and assistant librarian at the NATIONAL LIBRARY OF IRELAND in the early part of the 20th century. His brief time as editor of the literary magazine *DANA* coincided with its rejection of Joyce's essay "A Portrait of the Artist." In the Scylla and Charybdis episode, Eglinton is an active participant in the discussion on Shakespeare. Magee is the author of *Irish Literary Portraits* (1935), which contains a brief assessment of Joyce.

**Fanning, Long John** He is a minor character in *Ulysses*, modeled on Long John Clancy, a sub-sheriff of DUBLIN in 1898. Fanning appears in the Wandering Rocks episode, when Martin Cunningham visits him to solicit a contribution to a fund for the Dignam family. References to him also occur in the Aeolus episode of *Ulysses* and in the *Dubliners* short story "Grace."

**Farrell, Cashel Boyle O'Connor Fitzmaurice Tisdall** He is a character derived from an actual Dublin eccentric nicknamed Endymion, after the youth in Greek mythology loved by the moon goddess, Selene. In the Lestrygonians episode, he passes by Leopold Bloom conversing with Mrs. Josie Breen, who, upon seeing him walking outside the lampposts (that is, in the street), comments that her husband "will be like that one of these days" (*U* 8.304). Cashel Boyle O'Connor Fitzmaurice Tisdall Farrell appears again in the Wandering Rocks episode, and in the Circe episode, he is in a hallucination, where a reference is made to his monocle.

**Fitzharris, James "Skin-the-Goat"** This is the name of a member of the INVINCIBLES who participated in the 1882 PHOENIX PARK MURDERS as the driver of one of the getaway cars. In the Eumaeus episode, the man who runs the cabman's shelter at Butt Bridge where Stephen Dedalus and Leopold Bloom stop after their excursions in NIGHTTOWN is reputed to be "Skin-the-Goat."

**Fleming, Mrs.** She never actually appears in *Ulysses*, but is identified as a woman who does household chores for the Bloom family. Bloom thinks of her during the Hades episode, as does Molly during her monologue in the Penelope episode.

**Flower, Henry, Esq.** This is the nom de plume used by Leopold Bloom to disguise his real identity in his clandestine correspondence with Martha Clifford. At the beginning of the Lotus-Eaters episode, Bloom goes to the Westland Row post office and, after handing the postmistress a calling card with his pseudonym printed on it, he receives a letter from Martha addressed to Henry Flower, Esq. Soon after, Bloom surreptitiously reads the letter, which he has secreted within the folds of a newspaper (*U* 5.237–259). Martha's correspondence, with seemingly unself-conscious irony, contains the flattened petals of a yellow flower. The narrative is much more aware of the potential for wordplay and sardonically invokes Henry Flower's name at several points in the novel, including the Sirens, Circe, and Ithaca episodes, reminding readers of the slightly ridiculous aspects of Bloom's double life.

**Flynn, Nosey** He is an acquaintance of Leopold Bloom and a habitué of DAVY BYRNE'S PUB. See also Characters under "Grace" in *Dubliners.*

**Garryowen** This is the name of the mean-tempered dog accompanying the Citizen in the Cyclops episode. Garryowen, however, belongs to Gerty MacDowell's grandfather, Grandpa Giltrap, though the narrative never explains why the dog is with the Citizen. The name also alludes to an Irish ballad, "Garryowen." For further information, see *The James Joyce Songbook,* edited, with a commentary, by Ruth Bauerle.

**Goulding, Richie** He is Stephen Dedalus's maternal uncle, and a man intensely disliked by his brother-in-law, Simon Dedalus. Goulding, a practical joker apparently ruined by drink, is a legal clerk for the firm of Collis and Ward. In the Proteus episode, Stephen walks along Sandymount Strand and contemplates visiting his Uncle Richie. In the end he decides not to. In the Lestrygonians episode, Richie Goulding is one of two people who come to Leopold Bloom's mind as the possible author of the postcard with "U.P." written on it that has so upset Denis Breen (*U* 8.257 and 8.320). Later, in the Sirens episode, Goulding joins Bloom at the Ormond Hotel for an early dinner. He also appears in one of the hallucinations during the Circe episode.

**Haines** He first appears in the Telemachus episode. He is an Oxford friend and guest of Buck Mulligan at the MARTELLO TOWER, where Stephen Dedalus is also temporarily lodging. Haines takes the role of the prototypical patronizing English tourist visiting Ireland to study what he sees as its quaint folkways. Haines's ANTI-SEMITISM (*U* 1.666–668), like that of Mr. Garrett Deasy in the Nestor episode, gives a broad grounding to the particularized treatment that the outcast Leopold Bloom will encounter time and again during the day of June 16, 1904. He also is seen in the Wandering Rocks episode having tea with Mulligan at the Dublin Baking Company, and he looks in briefly at the Holles Street Maternity Hospital to arrange to meet Mulligan at the Westland Row Station.

Joyce based Haines's disturbing dream of a black panther, which greatly upsets Stephen, on an actual incident that occurred to Samuel Chenevix Trench, an English friend of Oliver St. John GOGARTY, the model for Buck Mulligan. Joyce met Trench while briefly staying with Gogarty at the Martello Tower, and modeled Haines on him.

**Higgins, Zoe** She appears in the Circe episode as a young prostitute at Bella Cohen's brothel. She accosts Leopold Bloom when he pauses in front of the brothel while searching for Stephen Dedalus, whom he can hear playing the piano inside. In the encounter, Zoe takes from Bloom's trouser pocket a shriveled potato he keeps as a talisman. Coincidentally, her surname is the same as Bloom's mother's maiden name.

**Hynes, Joe** He is a newspaper reporter who appears in Hades to write an account of Paddy Dignam's funeral. He takes the names of the mourners and jots down the name of an unknown person in a mackintosh as M'Intosh, a name that appears in Hynes's account of the funeral published in the edition of the *Telegraph* (*U* 16.1248–1261) that Leopold Bloom reads in the cabman's shelter during the Eumaeus episode. As the reader learns in Aeolus, Hynes owes Bloom three shillings, which he seems in no hurry to repay. (See the appendix VIII for a detailed account of monetary values.) Later, he appears again in the Cyclops episode, where he treats the Citizen and the chapter's unnamed narrator to several rounds of drinks at BARNEY KIERNAN'S pub. He does, however, buy Bloom a cigar in Barney Kiernan's pub during the Cyclops episode. Hynes also appears in a hallucination in the Circe episode.

See also Characters in *Dubliners.*

**John, Uncle** He is one of Stephen Dedalus's two maternal uncles, mentioned in a disparaging aside by Simon Dedalus during the Wandering Rocks episode (chapter 10).

See also Characters under *Stephen Hero.*

**Johnson, Georgina** She is a Dublin prostitute who never actually appears in the narrative but whom Stephen Dedalus thinks of and mentions several times during the course of the day. She is apparently a favorite of his, in part at least because of her claim that she is the daughter of a clergyman. In the Circe episode, when he visits the brothel of Bella Cohen, Stephen learns that she has supposedly married a commercial traveler, Mr. Lambe of London, and that she has left Dublin and, presumably, her profession.

**Kelleher, Cornelius ("Corny")** He is a character who appears at several key points in the narrative of *Ulysses.* Kelleher works for Henry J. O'Neill, a Dublin carriage maker and undertaker, and the narrative hints that Kelleher also serves as a police informer. Kelleher is in charge of the arrangements for the funeral of Paddy Dignam at GLASNEVIN Cemetery—the central event of the Hades episode.

Kelleher makes two more brief appearances that provide strong circumstantial evidence that he is an informer. In the Wandering Rocks episode, his talk with a police constable who had "seen that particular party" (*U* 10.225) gives the impression that Kelleher is in regular contact with the police. Later in the evening, during the Circe episode, Kelleher takes the lead in dissuading two Dublin police constables on the point of arresting Stephen Dedalus after his altercation in NIGHTTOWN with two English soldiers. (Bloom's clumsy efforts have only antagonized the policemen, so Kelleher's intervention at this point proves to be crucial.)

**Kelly, Bridie** She is a young woman, perhaps a prostitute, who never actually appears in the narrative. She is mentioned in the Oxen of the Sun and is in a hallucination in the Circe episode. She is identified as the woman responsible for the sexual initiation of young Leopold Bloom in an encounter on Hatch Street.

**Kennedy, Mina** She is a character who appears at several points in the narrative of *Ulysses.* She is identified, often sardonically, with the color gold: "Bronze by gold, miss Douce's head by miss Kennedy's head. . . . Sadly she twined in sauntering gold hair behind a curving ear" (*U* 11.64, 81–83). Miss Kennedy is first mentioned in passing during the Wandering Rocks episode, and then she appears at some length in the Sirens episode, working with Lydia Douce as a barmaid in the Ormond Hotel. She seems to be older and far more reserved than Miss Douce, whose playful vulgarity and easy willingness to flirt with the male customers stands in contrast to Miss Kennedy's more self-contained demeanor.

**Keogh, Mrs.** She is the superannuated cook at the brothel owned by Bella Cohen in the NIGHTTOWN district. A minor character, Mrs. Keogh surfaces in the Circe episode to help the whores subdue Leopold Bloom during his hallucinatory transformation into a young prostitute.

**Kernan, Tom** He is a tea salesman and, like Bloom, a man who converted to CATHOLICISM to marry. He is among the mourners at Paddy Dignam's funeral, and during the funeral service he makes it clear to Leopold Bloom that his religious loyalties remain with the Church of Ireland (the Irish version of the Anglican Church). There are occasional references to Kernan throughout the narrative, and he reappears in the Wandering Rocks episode having a drink to celebrate a sale he has just negotiated. In the Sirens episode, he joins the men gathered in the Ormond Hotel bar. He also appears in hallucinations in Circe. Kernan's character, according to Richard ELLMANN (*James Joyce,* pp. 22, 133n), seems to have been based on an amalgamation of John JOYCE and Ned Thornton, a neighbor of the Joyce family when they lived on North Richmond Street in Dublin in 1895. See also Characters under "Grace" in *Dubliners.*

**Keyes, Alexander** Keyes is a prosperous grocer and tea, wine, and spirit merchant. Although he never actually appears in the narrative (he does walk on in several hallucinations in Circe), he plays a central role in shaping Bloom's movements during the middle of the day. Bloom spends a good portion of it trying to secure the renewal of a newspaper advertisement for Keyes's business in the *FREEMAN'S JOURNAL*. While by no means conclusive, Bloom's lack of success with Keyes does provide a rough measure of his abilities as an ad canvasser.

**Kiernan, Barney** He is the owner of the pub (BARNEY KIERNAN'S) on Little Britain Street in which the Cyclops episode takes place. Kiernan himself never makes an appearance in the episode and, according to the narrator of the chapter, is an inmate of the House of St. John of God in Stillorgan Park, County Dublin, an insane asylum. The narrative hints that he may be suffering from delirium tremens: "he's out in John of God's off his head, poor man" (*U* 12.55).

**Lambert, Ned (Edward J.)** He is a character in *Ulysses* who first appears as one of the mourners at the funeral of Paddy Dignam in the Hades episode. In the Aeolus episode, Lambert lingers in the *EVENING TELEGRAPH* office over the noon hour before going off for a drink with his friend Simon Dedalus. During the Wandering Rocks episode, Lambert gives Rev. Hugh C. Love a tour of the old St. Mary's Abbey, the site of Silken Thomas's renunciation of his allegiance to Henry VIII and now a grain storehouse where Lambert works. Still later, he stops in for a drink at BARNEY KIERNAN'S pub during the Cyclops episode, and finally appears in a hallucination in Circe.

**Laredo, Lunita** She is the mother of Molly Bloom. Although details of her background remain obscure, her surname and hints dropped by Molly during her soliloquy in the Penelope episode suggest that Lunita Laredo was of Spanish and Jewish ancestry. Although Molly seems to have only vague recollections of her mother, she recalls the beauty of her mother's name and speculates on the similarity of their natures. The narrative does not clearly explain the circumstances surrounding Lunita Laredo's courtship by Major Brian Tweedy or even the couple's marital status, but it suggests that she either died when Molly was very young or deserted Molly and her father while they lived in Gibraltar.

**Lenehan, T.** He first appears in the Aeolus episode of *Ulysses* where he shows his practiced skills as a hanger-on, lighting cigarettes and thereby obtaining one for himself, telling banal jokes to remind others of his presence and insinuating himself into the group that goes off to Mooney's pub, where Stephen Dedalus has proposed to buy a round of drinks. In the Wandering Rocks episode, one sees another side of Lenehan, a chameleon-like willingness to assume the attitudes of whomever he is with. As he strolls along chatting with the coroner's secretary C. P. M'Coy, he tells a salacious story about Molly Bloom, but when he notes M'Coy's disapproval Lenehan quickly changes his tone. In the Sirens episode, his toadying to Blazes Boylan goes beyond even that displayed when he was currying the favor of Corley in "Two Gallants." And in the Cyclops episode, as he maligns Bloom purely out of spite, one sees that he is willing to resort to any level of slander and gossip in order to cultivate the attention of others. He continues his role as hanger-on when he joins the drunken medical students in the refectory of the Holles Street Maternity Hospital in Oxen of the Sun. He also is in several hallucinations in Circe. In his every appearance in Joyce's work, Lenehan embodies the self-serving amorality that lies beneath the congenial and sociable facade maintained by so many of the characters in the novel. Joyce presumably modeled Lenehan on Michael Hart, a Dublin friend of his father. See also Characters under "Two Gallants" in *Dubliners*.

**Lynch, Vincent** Although his character is established as a friend of Stephen's in appearances in both *Stephen Hero* and *A Portrait of the Artist as a Young Man*, in *Ulysses*—especially in the Oxen of the Sun episode—Lynch takes a more antagonistic position. As a representative of Stephen's generation, the group against which Stephen's achievements will ultimately be measured, Lynch stands as a reminder of what Stephen has not yet accomplished. In the Circe episode, Lynch accompanies Stephen to the whorehouse run by Bella Cohen in NIGHTTOWN, but he deserts Stephen when the latter becomes involved in a confrontation on the street with two British soldiers. Joyce's Dublin friend Vincent COSGRAVE was the model for Lynch. See also Characters under *A Portrait of the Artist as a Young Man*.

**Lyons, [Frederick M.] "Bantam"** He is a Dublin layabout who appears at several points throughout *Ulysses.* The narrative introduces Lyons when he encounters Leopold Bloom outside Sweny's chemist shop during the Lotus-Eaters episode, and mistakenly believes that Bloom is encouraging him to bet on Throwaway, a horse running that day in the GOLD CUP race. In the Lestrygonians episode, while having a drink in DAVY BYRNE'S PUB with several men who are looking for a tip on the race, he tells them of Bloom's supposed tip. Later in the day, Lenehan resurrects this rumor, and uses it to provoke the altercation between Bloom and the Citizen in BARNEY KIERNAN'S pub at the end of the Cyclops episode. Lyons himself fails to back Throwaway, the long-shot winner of the Gold Cup, and his remorse is all too evident when he appears lamenting his indecision in Burke's pub near the end of the Oxen of the Sun episode.

Although it is not entirely clear from the context, Bantam Lyons may be the same Lyons who appears as a political canvasser in the *Dubliners* short story "Ivy Day in the Committee Room."

**MacCann** He does not actually appear in *Ulysses,* but he is recalled as a creditor by Stephen during the Nestor episode (chapter 2). Although his name here is Philip McCann, his character remains essentially the same.

See also Characters under *A Portrait of the Artist as a Young Man.*

**MacDowell, Gerty** She is the young woman first introduced into the narrative briefly near the end of the Wandering Rocks episode. Her primary appearance occurs in the Nausikaa episode, where she arouses Leopold Bloom's sexual fantasies as he stands watching her with her friends, Edy Boardman and Cissy Caffrey, during the early evening on Sandymount Strand. Before that, however, Gerty's thoughts and impressions dominate the first part of the chapter and reflect the prose style of popular women's magazines at the beginning of the 20th century. The narrative voice, if not identical with Gerty's, mimics (some might even say parodies) Gerty's thoughts and the general cultural discourse that has shaped her consciousness. It offers the reader opinions of Bloom, of Gerty's friends, and of life in Dublin from the highly stylized perspective of a young, poorly educated, lower-middle-class city girl whose imagination is dominated by images from the popular press, a perspective different from any in the narrative thus far. (In the second half of the chapter, Joyce gives Bloom's view of many of the same things.) It also sets up expectations about the nature of Gerty herself that subsequent events both confirm and contradict.

During the course of these reflections, Gerty becomes aware of, fascinated with, and eventually quietly aroused by Bloom's persistent and open interest in her. When the fireworks display at the Mirus Bazaar begins, Gerty uses the wish to get a better view as an excuse to shift her position, enabling her to excite Bloom by revealing her undergarments to him. The degree to which Gerty acknowledges to herself what she is doing seems open to question, but it is clear that she knows exactly what Bloom is doing.

As Gerty watches Bloom masturbate, the narrative describes her reaction in terms strongly suggesting that she also is experiencing a sexual climax. This instance of Gerty's own sexual assertiveness undermines the tacit assumption of innocence created by the apparent naïveté of the narrative that precedes it and forces readers to reexamine whatever impressions of Gerty they may have formed in the highly stylized and sentimental first half of the chapter, and from her apparently ingenuous behavior prior to exposing herself to Bloom. Later, in the Circe episode, a hallucination of Gerty again appears to Bloom as a manifestation of his sexual guilt.

**MacHugh, Professor Hugh** He is a decayed academic who appears in the office of the *FREEMAN'S JOURNAL* during the Aeolus episode. He is also included in one of the hallucinations in Circe. Although his remarks are characterized by a mordant wit and a great deal of pedantry, the narrative offers no evidence that his title represents anything more than an honorific exaggeration of MacHugh's tenuous affiliation with Irish education. Nonetheless, clear analogies exist between MacHugh and Mr. Keane, a character in *Stephen Hero,* who is identified as the professor of English composition at UNIVERSITY COLLEGE, DUBLIN, and as a leader (editorial) writer for the *Freeman's Journal*.

**Madden, William** He is a medical student and friend of Buck Mulligan. He may be intended as the same character as the Madden in *Stephen Hero*, who appears as Davin in *A Portrait of the Artist as a Young Man*.

See also characters under *Stephen Hero* and *A Portrait of the Artist as a Young Man*.

**M'Coy, C. P. (Charley)** He is a character appearing in the Lotus-Eaters episode and in the Wandering Rocks episode and in several hallucinations in Circe. Although presented as an analogue to Leopold Bloom, M'Coy's life also shows some similarity to that of Simon Dedalus. As a young man he was a tenor of some reputation. He worked as a clerk for the Midland Railway, a canvasser for advertisements for the *IRISH TIMES* and the *FREEMAN'S JOURNAL* (as did Bloom), a town traveler for a coal firm, a private inquiry agent, a clerk in the office of the sub-sheriff, and, on June 16, 1904, secretary to the city coroner. Because of this job, he cannot attend the funeral of Paddy Dignam. (He must attend to a drowning in Dublin Bay.) Consequently, when he meets Bloom in the Lotus-Eaters episode, M'Coy asks Bloom to have his name listed among the mourners (*U* 5.172–173). Bloom's willingness to comply comes, in part at least, from his hope that M'Coy will help to secure a railroad pass for him to travel to MULLINGAR to see his daughter, Milly Bloom (*U* 4.453).

Like Simon Dedalus, M'Coy is sometimes down on his luck, a fact highlighted in the *Dubliners* story "Grace." M'Coy, who plays the buffoon for the company, is treated coolly by Jack Power, who remembers that M'Coy had borrowed luggage from him "to enable Mrs. M'Coy to fulfill imaginary engagements in the country" (*D* 160) and had then pawned the luggage. In *Ulysses* Leopold Bloom thinks of this trick when speaking to M'Coy during the Lotus-Eaters episode (chapter 5; *U* 5.148–149), which puts him on his guard for a similar request, and again at various times throughout the day (*U* 11.972; 13.789; 16.524).

**M'Coy, Fanny** She is a character referred to in several episodes of *Ulysses* and in the *Dubliners* story "Grace." The wife of C. P. M'Coy, Fanny earns some money giving piano lessons to children as well as occasionally performing as a concert singer. Like Molly Bloom, she is a soprano.

The obvious parallels between the musical careers of Fanny M'Coy and Molly Bloom put the two into professional competition, an idea that preoccupies Bloom in the Sirens episode and Molly in the Penelope episode. These allusions to Fanny M'Coy also serve to clarify both the relative success that Molly has enjoyed in pursuing her musical career and the rather narrow range of options open to Dublin women of their age and class who wish to find an alternative to managing domestic affairs.

**M'Intosh** He is an anonymous character who first appears in the Hades episode at the burial of Paddy Dignam. He is given his eponymous name when Bloom identifies him by the mackintosh raincoat he is wearing; Joe Hynes, inattentively making a list of mourners for the evening edition of the paper, the *Telegraph*, takes the reference to the coat to be the man's surname. Like other motifs, the man in the mackintosh is referred to throughout *Ulysses*. M'Intosh appears at the end of the Wandering Rocks episode, crossing the path of the viceregal cavalcade in Lower Mount Street. He shows up again in Burke's pub at the end of the Oxen of the Sun episode. And he even inhabits one of Bloom's hallucinations in the Circe episode.

There has been a great deal of scholarly speculation about the identity of the man in the mackintosh. Guesses (informed and otherwise) range from James Duffy, a central figure in the *Dubliners* story "A Painful Case," to James Joyce himself. His true identity probably has less significance than the ambiguity his occasional presence evokes.

**Milly** See Bloom, Milly.

**Molly** See Bloom, Molly.

**Mooney, Polly** She is the wife of Bob Doran. References to her in the Cyclops episode (chapter 12) of *Ulysses* indicate that Polly has begun to take on many of her mother's shrewish and calculating features.

See also Characters under "The Boarding House" in *Dubliners*.

**Mulligan, Malachi "Buck"** Mulligan is the first character to appear in *Ulysses*. Stephen Dedalus lives with Mulligan in the MARTELLO TOWER located in SANDYCOVE, south of the city. He is at once Stephen's rival and confidant.

As a successful medical student and writer who is beginning to be noticed by the Dublin literati, Mulligan leads a public life that stands in sharp contrast to that of Stephen's, who lives a hand-to-mouth existence and remains on the periphery of the local artistic community. The literary party given by the novelist George MOORE on June 16, 1904, to which Mulligan but not Stephen receives an invitation illustrates the degree of Stephen's alienation from, and Mulligan's acceptance by, the Dublin literary establishment. Mulligan's success comes, to some degree at least, from a greater willingness than Stephen's to modify his public persona to accommodate public opinion. Mulligan represents the kind of artist that Stephen might become were he to compromise himself in that way. At the same time Mulligan is clearly aware of Stephen's unswerving commitment to artistic integrity and is self-conscious about his own willingness to adapt himself and his artistic views to those of the company he keeps.

The narration of *Ulysses* plays upon the ambiguities of their friendship by juxtaposing Mulligan and Stephen at key points throughout the day. The book opens on the rooftop of the Martello Tower as Mulligan is declaiming to Stephen on the nature of Irish art and aesthetics (see Telemachus episode). Later in the day, at the National Library—during the Scylla and Charybdis episode—Mulligan interrupts Stephen's disquisition on Shakespeare and, through coarse humor and slapstick clowning, attempts to capture the attention of those listening to Stephen. In the Wandering Rocks episode, Mulligan has tea with Haines, an Oxford friend and houseguest introduced in chapter 1, to whom he denigrates Stephen's ambitions and abilities. Stephen and Mulligan meet again at the Holles Street Maternity Hospital—in the Oxen of the Sun episode—where Mulligan openly ridicules Stephen, who by this point is far too drunk to offer a coherent response. In the whorehouse of Bella Cohen—during the Circe episode—images of Mulligan invade Stephen's hallucinations.

The Dublin writer, wit, and physician, Oliver St. John GOGARTY, is widely regarded as the model upon whom Joyce drew for the character of Buck Mulligan. Like Stephen and Buck, Gogarty and Joyce were friendly rivals in Dublin, and for a very short time they had lived together in the same Martello Tower in Sandycove that serves as the fictional home of Stephen and Buck. They had a falling out before Joyce left Dublin, and, despite Gogarty's subsequent efforts at reconciliation, the breach remained for the rest of Joyce's life. After the publication of *Ulysses,* Gogarty vehemently denied any similarities between himself and the fictional figure in Joyce's novel, but most Dubliners from that era, especially those who knew them both, see the parallels as quite close and regard Joyce's Mulligan as an instance of Joyce's using his fiction as an opportunity to repay old slights.

**Murphy, W. B.** He is a character who appears in the Eumaeus episode. Murphy, who claims to have been originally from Carrigaloe Station near Cork, purports to be a seaman who has traveled extensively around the world for the past seven years. His astonishing tales of his travels call to mind the sort of exaggerations with which Shakespeare's Othello charmed Desdemona, and evidence that he has not actually experienced most of the adventures that he relates accumulates almost as rapidly as he recounts the tales. In his role as a wanderer separated from his wife, Murphy mimics in a distorted form the archetypal Odysseus figure embodied by Leopold Bloom. Whatever he may or may not be, in his glib ability to tell a story appropriate to the general direction of the conversation, Murphy does represent a proto-Ulysses figure in the novel's mock-epic cosmos.

**Nannetti, Joseph Patrick (1851–1915)** He was an actual turn-of-the-century Dublin politician whom Joyce incorporated into *Ulysses*. An Irishman of Italian descent, Nannetti served as a member of Parliament from 1900 to 1906, and he was Lord Mayor of Dublin from 1906 to 1907. The fictional version of Nannetti appears as the print shop foreman of the FREEMAN'S JOURNAL in the Aeolus episode of *Ulysses,* and he is subsequently referred to at several other points in the narrative. For Leopold Bloom, Nannetti's life and accomplishments represent both a consolation and a rebuke. Nannetti's foreign heritage, like Bloom's, makes him stand out among the homogeneous Dubliners. However, to a far greater degree than Bloom, Nannetti has earned both the respect and the esteem of his adopted countrymen, as demonstrated by his election to public office. (Joyce parenthetically alludes to the real-life Nannetti's Italian nationality and mayoralty in "Ireland, Island of Saints and Sages," a 1907 lecture delivered in Italian in Trieste. See *The Critical Writings of James Joyce.*)

**Power, Jack** Power is among the group of mourners—including Simon Dedalus, Tom Kernan, Martin Cunningham, and Leopold Bloom—at the funeral of Paddy Dignam in the Hades episode. In the Wandering Rocks episode Powers accompanies Martin Cunningham to the office of sub-sheriff Long John Fanning in an effort to raise money for Dignam's family. Finally, in the Cyclops episode, he meets with Martin Cunningham, Leopold Bloom, and J. T. A. Crofton at BARNEY KIERNAN'S pub before visiting Dignam's widow to advise her about the dead man's insurance policy.

See also Characters under "Grace" in *Dubliners.*

**Purefoy, Theodore** He is a DUBLIN character who never actually appears in the narrative but is referred to in the Lestrygonians episode and the Oxen of the Sun episode. Purefoy also is in one of the hallucinations in the Circe episode. He is the husband of Wilhelmina ("Mina") Purefoy and an acquaintance of Leopold and Molly Bloom.

As a Protestant with a good job as an accountant at the Ulster Bank, Purefoy is the image of Presbyterian steadiness and conformity. At the same time, he has fathered nine children, implying a sensuality in contrast to his public demeanor. This dissimilarity is hinted at during Bloom's conversation with Josie Breen in the Lestrygonians episode and is asserted directly in the bawdy talk of the drunken medical students in the Oxen of the Sun episode. It occurs again in a highly distorted fashion in Bloom's hallucination in the Circe episode.

**Purefoy, Mrs. Wilhelmina ("Mina")** She is a character mentioned at several points in *Ulysses,* identified as the wife of Theodore Purefoy and an acquaintance of Leopold and Molly Bloom. In the Lestrygonians episode, Bloom learns from Josie Breen that Mrs. Purefoy has been admitted to the Holles Street Maternity Hospital, and in the Oxen of the Sun episode he goes there with the intention of inquiring after her condition. While Bloom is there, Mrs. Purefoy gives birth to her ninth child, a son, Mortimer Edward.

**Riordan, Mr.** He is the husband of Mrs. Dante Riordan. In her monologue in the Penelope episode, Molly Bloom mentions him with the implication that he deserted his wife.

**Riordan, Mrs. Dante** In *Ulysses* she is referred to simply as the Mrs. Riordan who had lived at the City Arms Hotel where she knew the Blooms. When Bloom passes the MATER MISERICORDIAE HOSPITAL in the Hades episode, he recalls that she died in the hospital's ward for incurables (*U* 6.375–378). Both the unnamed narrator in the Cyclops episode and Molly Bloom in the Penelope episode comment upon the amount of time that Leopold Bloom spends currying favor with her in the hope of inheriting money after her death. While the narrator of Cyclops is content to ridicule Bloom, Molly pours equal scorn on Mrs. Riordan. She takes a cynical view of Mrs. Riordan's piety, though she does admire the woman's intelligence and her independence.

Mrs. Riordan's character is based upon Mrs. "Dante" Hearn CONWAY, a woman originally from Cork who came into the Joyce household in 1887 as a governess. Like her fictional counterpart, Mrs. Conway had a bitter fight (with John JOYCE and his Fenian friend John KELLY) over the character of PARNELL during the Joyce family Christmas dinner in 1891. She seems to have left the Joyces shortly thereafter.

**Sargent, Cyril** He appears in the Nestor episode of *Ulysses,* a student at the school of Garrett Deasy in Dalkey where Stephen Dedalus teaches. Sargent immediately attracts Stephen's attention as a weak and ineffectual student, both physically and intellectually inferior to his classmates. Although Stephen sees parallels between himself and Sargent, a careful reader will find that their differences are more significant than their similarities, and Stephen's association has a metaphysical rather than a physical or intellectual basis. This is all the more evident when Stephen conjures up images of a loving and protective mother—much like his own mother, May Dedalus—and imagines how this woman must have cared for Sargent and endeavored to shelter him from the harsh realities of an unfeeling world (*U* 2.139–150). On close examination one sees that Sargent actually bears little resemblance to Stephen, lacking both his wit and his precociousness, at least as demonstrated in *A Portrait of the Artist as a Young Man.* The comparison that Stephen makes underscores, more than anything else, the guilt that Stephen feels over his own mother's death, a recurring theme throughout the novel.

**Skin-the-Goat** See Fitzharris, James.

**Throwaway** This is the name of the racehorse, ridden by W. Lane, who was the long-shot winner of the Ascot GOLD CUP race held on June 16, 1904, the day on which *Ulysses* takes place. Though he never appears, throughout the narrative, Throwaway is mentioned repeatedly by racing-obsessed Dubliners. Because of a misperception by Bantam Lyons in the Lotus-Eaters episode and an unfounded remark made by Lenehan in the Cyclops episode, a rumor circulates that Leopold Bloom placed a bet on this horse at odds of 20 to 1 and consequently won a great deal of money. This misunderstanding indirectly leads to Bloom's confrontation with the Citizen in BARNEY KIERNAN'S pub. A portrait of Throwaway appeared on the front page of the October 1985 (No. 18) issue of the *James Joyce Broadsheet* and again in the 1991 *Joyce Studies Annual* (p. 107).

**Tweedy, Major Brian Cooper** He is the father of Molly Bloom, née Tweedy. Before moving with Molly to Dublin after retiring from the army, Tweedy seems to have been a former officer of the British army who served in the garrison on Gibraltar. It was there that his daughter Molly was born and lived until young adulthood. It is unclear whether Tweedy married Molly's mother, Lunita Laredo, before or after Molly's birth. (Recent criticism has speculated that Tweedy was more likely not an officer but a sergeant major.)

**Virag** This is the original family name of Leopold Bloom and is also the Hungarian word for *flower.* After leaving Hungary and settling in DUBLIN, Leopold's father, Rudolf, had the family name changed by deed poll (see Rudolph Bloom). References to Virag and wordplay based upon associations with flowers, such as Bloom's pseudonym, Henry Flower, occur throughout *Ulysses.*

## CONTEMPORARY REVIEWS OF *ULYSSES*

George Rehm, *Chicago Tribune* (European Edition), February 13, 1922:

> "*Ulysses,* long attended upon, waited for these several years with bated breath or hopeful curiosity has at last appeared.
>
> What it will mean to the reader is a question. Too many are the possibilities of this human flesh when finally in contact with the crude, disgusting and unpalatable facts of our short existence. One thing to be thankful for is that the volume is in a limited edition, therefore suppressed to the stenographer or high school boy. But another thing to be thankful for is that it might be the precursor to a new understanding of the printed word, a new 'coup de grace' for the salacious prudishness of our present day conventions. Great harm can be done or great good will be done by Ulysses. . . .
>
> All known borders encircling the hemisphere of literature have been traversed with a cynical grin tossed to worldly criticism. Religion, government, ideals, life and death, all are scathingly ridiculed. I am shocked, so will you be, but I am also disturbed to find I am so easily shocked. . . .

The theme of Ulysses might be outlined as the thoughts and reflections of a number of characters, some ordinary, some extraordinary, but all genuine. The rawness of expression, the employment of words chosen from the seamy, filthy side of our vocabulary, may seem without excuse, but it is true that the prized volumes of our latter-day geniuses are permitted to repose in honored manner on library shelves only by means of a subtler turning of word and phrase. . . .

Where is the value? Better to wait a few generations. Give the Phillistine an opportunity to rise above his level or disappear. Allow worthy judges to pass sentence on such a work, be it masterpiece or rot, and so prevent the usual mauling and manhandling invariably accorded to a comparable production by our dearly beloved public.

In all events, it is fitting to extend congratulations to Shakespeare and company and Sylvia Beach for having finally published the book.

Sisley Huddleston, "Ulysses," *Observer,* (March 5, 1922):

No book has ever been more eagerly and curiously awaited by the strange little inner circle of book-lovers and literateurs than James Joyce's Ulysses. It is folly to be afraid of uttering big words because big words are abused and have become almost empty of meaning in many mouths; and with all my courage I will repeat what a few folk in somewhat precious cenacles have been saying—that Mr. James Joyce is a man of genius. I believe the assertion to be strictly justified, though Mr. Joyce must remain, for special reasons, caviare to the general. I confess that I cannot see how the work upon which Mr. Joyce spent seven strenuous years, years of wrestling and of agony, can ever be given to the public. . . .

Obscenity? Yes. This is undoubtedly an obscene book; but that, says Mr. Joyce, is not his fault. If the thoughts of men and women are such as may be properly described as obscene then how can you show what life is unless you put in the obscenity? This may not be your view or mine, but if it is Mr. Joyce's he has no option but to fulfill his mission as a writer. . . .

The expectation that these difficulties and the belief in the exceptional genius of Mr. Joyce aroused in the restricted circles of literary craftsmen is, in my experience, unprecedented. Those who have read the earlier books of Mr. Joyce have realised that here is a man who can write. 'We are mighty fine fellows nowadays,' cried Stevenson, 'but we cannot write like Hazlitt!' and many of us have felt like that about Joyce. There are phrases in which the words are packed tightly, as trim, as taut, as perfect as these things can be. There are fine ellipses in which a great sweep of meaning is concentrated into a single just-right sentence. There is a spot of colour which sets the page aglow. There is a point of light which gives life to the world as the lamp-lighter gives sudden life to the street. Here is erudition transfigured by imagination. . . .

Mr. Joyce's style is such that it is sometimes difficult to distinguish between what is taking place externally and what is taking place internally. The internal action is put on the same plane as the external action. Mr. Joyce indicates both with infinite humour and with extraordinary precision. . . .

S. P. B. Mais, "An Irish Revel: And Some Flappers," *Daily Express* (March 25, 1922):

. . . Reading Mr. Joyce is like making an excursion into Bolshevist Russia: all standards go by the board. . . .

J. Middleton Murry, *The Nation & Athenæum,* April 22, 1922:

. . . "Ulysses" has form, a subtle form, but the form is not strong enough to resist overloading, not sufficient to prevent Mr. Joyce from being the victim of his own anarchy. . . .

Arnold Bennett, "James Joyce's *Ulysses,*" *Outlook* (London) (April 29, 1922):

. . . James Joyce is a very astonishing phenomenon in Letters. He is sometimes dazzlingly original. If he does not see life whole he sees it piercingly. His ingenuity is marvellous. He has wit. He has a prodigious humour. He is afraid of naught. And had heaven in its wisdom thought fit not to deprive him of that basic sagacity and that moral self-dominion which alone enable an artist to assemble and control and fully utilise his powers, he would have stood a chance of being one of the greatest novelists that ever lived.

Edmund Wilson, *New Republic,* (July 5, 1922):

> Yet, for all its appalling longueurs, *Ulysses* is a work of high genius. Its importance seems to me to lie, not so much in its opening new doors to knowledge—unless in setting an example to Anglo-Saxon writers of putting down everything without compunction—or in inventing new literary forms—Joyce's formula is really . . . nearly seventy-five years old—as in its once more setting the standard of the novel so high that it need not be ashamed to take its place beside poetry and drama. *Ulysses* has the effect at once of making everything else look brassy. Since I have read it, the texture of other novelists seems intolerably loose and careless; when I come suddenly unawares upon a page that I have written myself I quake like a guilty thing surprised. The only question now is whether Joyce will ever write a tragic masterpiece to set beside this comic one.

Cecil Maitland, "Mr. Joyce and the Catholic Tradition," *New Witness* xx (August 4, 1922):

> . . . No one who is acquainted with Catholic education in Catholic countries could fail to recognise the source of Mr. Joyce's 'Weltanschauung'. He sees the world as theologians showed it to him. His humour is the cloacal humour of the refectory; his contempt the priests' denigration of the body, and his view of sex has the obscenity of a confessor's manual, reinforced by the profound perception and consequent disgust of a great imaginative writer.
>
> If we consider Mr. Joyce's work from this point of view, it becomes clear that while his study of humanity remains incomplete, the defect is not due to any inherent lack of imagination on his part. Rather it arises from the fact that to a Catholic who no longer believes that he has an immortal soul, fashioned in the image of God, a human being becomes merely a specially cunning animal. I suggest then that Mr. Joyce's failure is not his own, but that of the Catholic system, which has not had the strength to hold him to its transcendentalism, and from whose errors he has not been able to set himself free.

Alfred Noyes, "Rottenness in Literature," *Sunday Chronicle* (October 29, 1922):

> I have picked out *Ulysses* because it brings to a head all the different questions that have been perplexing literary criticism for some time past. There is no answer possible in this case. It is simply the foulest book that has ever found its way into print. It has received columns of attention from many of our leading journals, and its author has been proclaimed a slightly mad genius perhaps, but still a genius.
>
> The writing of the book is bad simply as writing, and much of it is obscure through sheer disorder of the syntax. But—there is no foulness conceivable to the mind of madman or ape that has not been poured into its imbecile pages. . . .

T. S. Eliot, "*Ulysses,* Order and Myth," *Dial* lxxv (November 1923):

> . . . I am not begging the question in calling *Ulysses* a 'novel' and if you call it an epic it will not matter. If it is not a novel, that is simply because the novel is a form which will no longer serve; it is because the novel, instead of being a form, was simply the expression of an age which had not sufficiently lost all form to feel the need of something stricter. . . .

# Miscellaneous Works

The category "miscellaneous works" is meant to identify several lesser-known pieces in Joyce's oeuvre. With few exceptions, notably *Giacomo Joyce, Letters of James Joyce,* and *Selected Letters of James Joyce,* all these works are short and relatively insignificant. The titles are included here to assist the general reader in identifying these unfamiliar works, which are sometimes referred to throughout this volume and occasionally found in the secondary literature on Joyce. The entries in this section also provide an added perspective on Joyce's writings, especially those written during the early years of his maturation as an artist.

**"Balia"** This is the title given to a posthumously discovered Latin poem attributed to Joyce. The classicist R. J. Schork unearthed the ballad after noticing a reference to it in the "Unidentified Manuscripts, Letters and Papers" section of Robert E. Scholes's *The Cornell Joyce Collection: A Catalogue* (1961). Schork published its full Latin text with a translation, commentary, and discussion of the manuscript in the spring 1991 issue of *The James Joyce Literary Supplement,* and argued that this four-stanza Latin poem was composed by Joyce sometime around 1902. The title of the ballad is taken from the heroine's name, Balia, a virgin seduced and betrayed by a soldier. Balia's suicide torments the guilt-ridden lover, from whom her ghost exacts 20 gold sovereigns in reparation. In departing, the ghost scornfully says:

> Farewell, you sweetheart of a mercenary,
> farewell!
> You and your decrees mocked Balia's fate.
> Farewell, my penny-wise lover, farewell!
> See if you can find another playmate.

A few years after the publication of "Balia" in *The James Joyce Literary Supplement,* Wes Davis discovered the ballad's author, George Henry Glasse, and the original place and date of publication, *Gentleman's Magazine,* August 1805. The manuscript ascribed to Joyce is, as Davis explains, "a virtual transcription of Glasse's text" ("'Balia' *Inventa:* The Source for Joyce's Latin Manuscript," *James Joyce Quarterly* 32 [Spring/Summer 1995] 742; Davis's discussion is followed by Schork's translation of the poem as it appeared in *Gentleman's Magazine.* Also see, Schork's *Latin and Roman Culture in Joyce,* 1997, p. 9).

***Before Sunrise*** This is the English title of Joyce's translation of Gerhart HAUPTMANN'S play *VOR SONNENAUFGANG.* When he and his father were visiting MULLINGAR during the summer of 1900, Joyce undertook the task of translating the play as a linguistic and aesthetic exercise. He also translated Hauptmann's *Michael Kramer* during this period. Hauptmann's dramatic style very much suited the aesthetic views Joyce held at the time, and the challenge of rendering Hauptmann's German dialogue into evocative English touched upon Joyce's linguistic and artistic ambitions. In 1978 the Huntington Library published this translation, with an introduction by Jill Perkins, under the title *Joyce and Hauptmann: Before Sunrise.*

***Brilliant Career, A*** This is the title of Joyce's first play; it is not extant. In *MY BROTHER'S KEEPER,* Joyce's brother Stanislaus gives a brief description of the play and its background. It was a realistic prose work in four acts, written when Joyce was with his father in MULLINGAR during the summer of 1900. This was a period when Joyce was intently reading IBSEN, especially *When We Dead Awaken, A Doll's House, An Enemy of the People,* and *The League of Youth.* These are all plays that deal with love, sacrifice, and politics, and presumably they influenced *A Brilliant Career.*

According to Stanislaus's summary of the play, Paul, a young doctor, forsakes his love for Angela and marries another woman who, he believes, will advance his career. He is successful and becomes mayor of a small town. When a plague hits the town, he responds heroically with the help of an unknown woman, later revealed to be Angela. Paul realizes too late that his career means nothing next to his love for her. However, Angela rejects him, and he is left alone when the curtain falls.

On August 30, 1900, Joyce sent this play to the critic William ARCHER in London. Archer's response was quick and direct. He replied on September 15, 1900, saying that he found the play difficult to follow and suggested that Joyce "choose a narrower canvas" (*Letters,* II.9). The only surviving part of the play is the title page, which Archer copied onto the letter Joyce sent him (*Letters,* II.7 n.5):

'A Brilliant Career'
drama in 4 acts

—To—
My own Soul I
dedicate the first
true work of my
life.

**"Buy a book in brown paper"** This is the title of a six-line poem by Joyce (in the rhyme scheme aaa b cc) written as a blurb and printed on the dust jacket of the 1930 two shilling FABER AND FABER edition of *Anna Livia Plurabelle,* which became book 1, chapter 8 of *Finnegans Wake* (*FW* 196.1–216.5). This humorous verse in mock *Finnegans Wake* style entreats the reader to buy a copy and read about Anna Livia, who "ebb[s] music wayriver she flows." (See also Anna Livia Plurabelle under Characters in the *Finnegans Wake* section.)

**"Centenary of Charles Dickens, The"** An essay written by Joyce, in English, on April 24, 1912, at the University of Padua as part of an examination to qualify him to teach English in the Italian secondary school system. The extemporaneous essay emphasizes an historical view of Dickens and his work. The essay was discovered by Louis Berrone, and published in *James Joyce in Padua.* (See also "The Universal Literary Influence of the Renaissance.")

**"Christmas Eve, A"** This is the title of an unfinished short story that Joyce began writing in the fall of 1904 after he and Nora left Dublin. He abandoned this piece to begin a different story entitled "Hallow Eve," which was eventually published in *Dubliners* as "Clay." Joyce had planned to send "Christmas Eve" to the *Irish Homestead* (see *Letters,* II.70). The surviving story fragment was published, with an introduction by John SLOCUM and Herbert CAHOON, in *The James Joyce Miscellany, Third Series* (1962). Tom Callanan is the central character in the story. He works as a clerk in a solicitor's office on Wellington Quay, Dublin. Hooper, a minor character, works as a clerk in a solicitor's office in Eustace Street, and visits Tom Callanan. Katsey is the daughter of Tom and Mrs. Callanan. Her character, however, does not appear in "Clay."

**"Commonplace"** This is the title of a no longer extant poem that Joyce wrote around 1901 and sent with several others to the drama critic William ARCHER. In his critique, Archer commented that "Commonplace" was one of the poems that he liked best. Joyce's brother Stanislaus maintains that "Commonplace" was the original title of the second poem in *Chamber Music,* "The Twilight Turns from Amethyst" (see *My Brother's Keeper,* pp. 150 and 151).

**"Curious History, A"** This is the title of Joyce's account of the delay (which lasted more than eight years, from April 1906 to June 1914) in the publication of *Dubliners* (1914) from the first commitment he received for its printing to its long overdue appearance. In this explanation Joyce details the obstacles he faced from publishers who objected to certain passages in the book. This account was first published, with a short preface by Ezra POUND, in the January 15, 1914, issue of the EGOIST magazine. It was later reprinted as a promotional broadside by Joyce's New York publisher, B. W. HUEBSCH, on May 5, 1917.

"A Curious History" contains a collation of two letters by Joyce, one dated August 17, 1911, and the other November 30, 1913 (see *Letters,* II.291–293 and 324–325). The first was an open letter that Joyce sent to a number of Irish newspapers. It was published in part in the *Northern Whig* (August 26, 1911) and in full in *Sinn Féin* (September 2, 1911). The second, which was an expanded version of the first, was sent to Ezra Pound in November 1913. According to Richard ELLMANN, Joyce updated "A Curious History" to serve as a preface to *Dubliners,* but his publisher, Grant RICHARDS, objected to its inclusion. ("A Curious History" is published in Pound/Joyce: *The Letters of Ezra Pound to James Joyce* (ed. Forrest Read; New York: New Directions, 1970), pp. 20–23.)

In "A Curious History," Joyce reviewed the events that caused the eight-year delay in the publication of *Dubliners.* At its heart is Joyce's objection to any form of censorship forced upon authors publishing in Great Britain and Ireland. Joyce explained that the delay began some 10 months after he signed a contract in 1906 with the London publisher Grant Richards. After agreeing to accept the collection, Richards decided that he wanted to omit "Two Gallants" from the collection and alter passages in other stories. Joyce refused, and after prolonged negotiations Richards rescinded his agreement to publish.

In 1909 Joyce signed a new contract with the Dublin publishers MAUNSEL & CO., but early in 1910 this firm also objected to certain passages and demanded either radical changes or omissions in "Ivy Day in the Committee Room," a story that they believed contained pejorative allusions to King Edward VII. Again Joyce refused to make changes unless he could add an explanatory note and disclaimer. Denied that alternative, Joyce sought legal counsel and even the opinion of King George V (the successor to the recently deceased Edward VII), to whom he sent a copy of the disputed passage. (In a letter to Joyce, the king's secretary said "it is inconsistent with rule for His Majesty to express his opinion in such cases.") After further negotiations with Maunsel, Joyce—assuming that the collection would finally be published—reluctantly acquiesced to their requests, which also included omitting "An Encounter" and passages in other stories, as well as changing the actual names of businesses and locations. In addition to these radical changes in *Dubliners,* Maunsel asked Joyce to pay £1,000 as a security deposit. Joyce refused. They accepted Joyce's counteroffer to pay 60 percent of the cost of printing the first edition, which Joyce had planned to sell through his brother, Stanislaus; but in 1912 when Joyce went to Dublin to sign the contract, he was informed that the printer, John FALCONER, would not surrender the copies to him, that the type was destroyed, and that all copies would be burned. (Printers in Ireland and England at this time could, like authors and publishers, be held liable and prosecuted for works they produced.) The next day, Joyce left Ireland, never to return, and took with him a single copy of the printed text which he managed to get from the publisher. Joyce eventually signed a second contract with Grant Richards in March 1914, and the full text of *Dubliners* was finally published in June of that year.

"A Curious History" is included in full in Robert Scholes and A. Walton Litz, editors, *Dubliners: Text, Criticism and Notes,* New York: Viking Press, 1969, pages 289–292.

***Dream Stuff*** This is the title of a play in verse that Joyce began to write around 1900. Only a few lines of a song from the play are extant. Richard ELLMANN quotes them in his biography of Joyce:

In the soft nightfall
Hear thy lover call,
Hearken the guitar!
Lady, lady fair
Snatch a cloak in haste,
Let thy lover taste
The sweetness of thy hair . . .

(*James Joyce,* p. 80)

**"Et Tu, Healy"** This is the title of a no longer extant poem that Joyce wrote at the age of nine in commemoration of the death of Charles Stewart PARNELL on October 6, 1891. The title, an allusion to Caesar's dying line "*Et tu, Brute?*" in Shakespeare's *Julius Caesar* 3.1.78, refers to the politician Timothy Healy, a longtime supporter of Parnell, who ultimately led the forces of the Irish Parliamentary party in rejecting Parnell's leadership after the Kitty O'SHEA affair. Although Richard ELLMANN, through information supplied by Joyce's brother Stanislaus, has in his biography given a general description of the poem, no copy of it exists, and its exact content is unknown (*James Joyce,* pp. 33–34). Also see the *Dubliners* short story "Ivy Day in the Committee Room"; *Letters,* I.295; Stanislaus Joyce, *My Brother's Keeper,* p. 46; and *James Joyce: Poems and Shorter Writings,* edited by Richard Ellmann, A. Walton Litz, and John Whittier-Ferguson, pp. 71 and 257.

**"Final Peace, The"** This is the title of a poem, now lost, that Joyce wrote around 1901 and sent to the drama critic William ARCHER to critique. In a September 1901 correspondence with Joyce, Archer pointed out that this poem was one of the five poems he liked best of the selection Joyce had sent him to read. The others were "Wanhope," "Commonplace," "The Passionate Poet," and "Tenebrae." See *Letters,* II.10.

***Giacomo Joyce*** This is the title that appears on the front cover of a short collection of sketches recording Joyce's infatuation with one of his younger female students in TRIESTE. (Though Richard Ellmann, on page xii of his introduction to the posthumously published edition of the work claims the title was not in Joyce's hand and that Joyce never used this Italian form of his name, John McCourt, in *The Years of Bloom,* p. 198, cites evidence that refutes this assertion.) The text itself consists of observations and expressions of erotic feeling toward this unknown person (who may have been Amalia POPPER), which were carefully written out on large, heavy paper sometime around 1914 and posthumously published by the Viking Press, with an introduction and notes by Richard ELLMANN, in 1968. Internal evidence suggests that Joyce began collecting impressions for this journal even before 1914, perhaps as early as 1911. For example, the subject matter and imagery of the poem "A Flower Given to my Daughter," dated 1913, Trieste, also appears as a brief entry in *Giacomo Joyce.* After completing this work, Joyce apparently returned to it for material to use in subsequent writings. One can, in fact, find specific examples of ideas and images found in these sketches assimilated into *A Portrait of the Artist as a Young Man, Exiles,* and *Ulysses.* For specific examples of Joyce's use of *Giacomo Joyce* in these works, see Ellmann's notes in *Giacomo Joyce,* pp. xxxi–xxxvii. (Also see *James Joyce: Poems and Shorter Writings;* Vicki Mahaffey's discussion of *Giacomo Joyce* in *A Companion to Joyce Studies,* edited by Zack Bowen and James F. Carens, pp. 387–420; and John McCourt, *The Years of Bloom: James Joyce in Trieste 1904–1920,* pp. 196–206.)

**"Hallow Eve"** The original title of an early version of the *Dubliners* short story "Clay." Joyce finished the story in early January 1905; it was the fourth story to be written for *Dubliners.* He sent it to his brother Stanislaus for publication in the *IRISH HOMESTEAD,* which had previously published "The Sisters," "Eveline," and "After the Race," but that rejected "Hallow Eve." Before September 1905, Joyce rewrote it and changed the title; he again worked on the story in November 1906.

**"James Joyce Ad-Writer."** This identifies lines written in connection with the publication in London of "Haveth Childers Everywhere." It appeared in the March 1932 issue of *TRANSITION.*

**"Last Supper, The"** This is the title of a proposed mock-heroic short story that Joyce had planned for inclusion in *Dubliners* but which he never wrote because, as he notes vaguely, "circumstances were [not] favourable" (*Letters,* II.209). It was to focus on Joe MacKernan, the son of one of Joyce's Dublin landladies.

See also *Letters,* II.194.

***Letters of James Joyce*** This is the title of a collection of many, though by no means all, of the extant letters written by James Joyce and, in selected instances, of a few important pieces of correspondence to him from friends and associates. The *Letters of James Joyce* first appeared in 1957 in a single volume edited by Joyce's friend Stuart GILBERT. They covered the author's adult life from 1901 to 1940. Richard ELLMANN edited two additional volumes of correspondence, which appeared in 1966 under the title *Letters of James Joyce,* volumes II and III. Volume II contained letters from 1900 to 1920, and volume III printed letters from 1920 to 1941, that Gilbert had not published. With volume I, this material provided wide-ranging and detailed information that had heretofore been available only in piecemeal form in the GORMAN (1939) and Ellmann (1959; revised 1982) biographies.

Both Gilbert and Ellmann decided to omit from this collection material they considered either too personal or simply irrelevant. Some of that material now appears in Selected Letters of James Joyce, edited by Ellmann and published in 1975. Nonetheless, a fair number of Joyce letters remain uncollected and unpublished. A detailed list of this correspondence was compiled by Richard B. Watson and Randolph Lewis and published in the *JOYCE STUDIES ANNUAL* (1992).

***Michael Kramer*** This is the title of a play written by the German dramatist Gerhart HAUPTMANN in 1900. The Ibsen-like emphasis on social realism in Hauptmann's dramas very much interested Joyce at this time, and during the summer of 1900, which Joyce spent with his father in MULLINGAR, he translated this play and an earlier Hauptmann work, *Before Sunrise,* into English, primarily as a linguistic exercise. He later submitted his translations to the Irish Literary Theatre, where they were turned down by William Butler YEATS in 1904.

***Moods*** This is the title that Joyce gave to a collection of his youthful poems, written in the mid-1890s. The verses from this work are now generally believed to be lost. Nonetheless, a few scholars have offered the view that some of the fragments of early poems by Joyce that appear in the commonplace book of Stanislaus JOYCE, now at the library of Cornell University, may be from this collection. (The commonplace book contains quotations from authors both modern and ancient that Stanislaus compiled.) (See also *Shine and Dark.*)

**"O fons Bandusiae"** This is the opening line ("O source of Bandusia") of Horace's Ode III.13, which Joyce translated as part of his Latin studies at BELVEDERE COLLEGE when he was around 14 years old. The translation has been published both in Herbert GORMAN's *James Joyce* and in Richard ELLMANN's *James Joyce.* In the study chapter of *Finnegans Wake,* Joyce alludes to the same Ode: "that fount Bandusian" (*FW* 280.31–32).

**"Passionate Poet, The"** This is one of a collection of five poems, all now lost, that Joyce sent to the critic William ARCHER in the late summer of 1901. After reading them, Archer replied to Joyce in a tone that attempted to offer both encouragement and useful advice: "In all of these I see very real promise. But do pray let me beg you not to cultivate metrical eccentricities such as abound especially in the opening lines of the collection" (*Letters* II.10). (The other poems that Joyce sent to Archer were "The Final Peace," "Wanhope," "Commonplace," and "Tenebrae.")

**"Portrait of the Artist, A"** This is the title of a brief prose sketch commissioned by the Irish magazine *DANA* and completed by Joyce on January 7, 1904. When *Dana* editors John EGLINTON and Frederick Ryan saw the essay, they declined to print it; Eglinton later explained that "I can't print what I can't understand" (*Ellmann's James Joyce,* 147). Their rejection led to Joyce's decision to expand the work into a novel, first under the title *Stephen Hero* and then ultimately, after major revisions, *A Portrait of the Artist as a Young Man.*

In the hybrid literary form that Joyce adapted to this work, "A Portrait of the Artist" combines fictional narrative and philosophical exposition, and this amalgamation leads to a dramatized description of the evolution of artistic sensibilities in the consciousness of an unnamed young man. The essay contains the seeds of incidents and of ideas that Joyce subsequently elaborated more fully in *A Portrait of the Artist as a Young Man.* The mood that dominates the encounter of Stephen Dedalus with the Birdgirl at the end of chapter 4 or the views that emerge from his discussion of religion with Cranly near the close of chapter 5 both have their genesis in this work. The essay is most notable for its glimpse of aesthetic values that Joyce would articulate in later works and for its identification of themes that would form the central concerns of *A Portrait of the Artist as a Young Man.*

Joyce wrote "A Portrait of the Artist" in an exercise book that had previously belonged to his sister Mabel. Years later (in 1927 or 1928), at Joyce's request, Stanislaus JOYCE made a typescript copy of the holograph to present to Sylvia BEACH. Both versions of "A Portrait of the Artist" are now held by the Cornell University Library. The essay was first published by Richard M. KAIN and Robert SCHOLES in the *Yale Review* and again in their book *The Workshop of Daedalus;* it also appears in *A Portrait of the Artist as a Young Man, Text, Criticism, and Notes,* edited by Chester G. ANDERSON, pp. 257–266.

**"Realism and Idealism in English Literature (Daniel Defoe–William Blake)"** See "Verismo ed idealismo nella letteratura inglese (Daniele Defoe–William Blake)."

***Selected Letters of James Joyce*** This is a collection of Joyce's correspondence edited by Richard ELLMANN and published in 1975. The bulk of the letters that appear in this volume were written by Joyce, but selected correspondence from a few others—William ARCHER, Lucia JOYCE, Paul LÉON, and John SULLIVAN—containing material relevant to Joyce are also included. Most of the correspondence had already appeared in the three-volume edition *Letters of James Joyce,* but this collection contains 10 new letters and portions of a number of other letters published previously in abridged form.

In preparing this edition, Ellmann chose to include highly personal and explicitly sexual material from letters Joyce wrote to Nora BARNACLE when he was visiting Ireland in 1909. Some readers have found the contents of these letters to be quite shocking, and Joyce's grandson, Stephen JOYCE, has been highly critical of the editorial decision to include them in unabridged form. Ellmann defended his action on the grounds that unauthorized copies of these letters had been in circulation for a number of years, and that these, combined with rumors about the contents of the letters, had produced a distorted sense of what the correspondence really contained. He claimed that his aim in publishing them was to dispel misconceptions and to let readers reach their own conclusions about the letters.

***Shine and Dark*** This is the title of a collection of poems written by Joyce around 1900. Although most of these early verses have been lost, some seem to have been preserved on the verso leaves of a commonplace book belonging to Joyce's brother Stanislaus, now held at the Cornell University Library. These fragments were gathered and published by Richard ELLMANN, A. Walton Litz, and John Whittier-Ferguson in *James Joyce: Poems and Shorter Writings.* According to Stanislaus, "Villanelle of the Temptress," a poem written by Stephen Dedalus near the close of chapter 5 of *A Portrait of the Artist as a Young Man,* came originally from *Shine and Dark.*

***Silhouettes*** This is the title given to a series of prose sketches Joyce wrote when he was a student at BELVEDERE COLLEGE. Though none survive, a description of one of the sketches by Stanislaus JOYCE in his memoir, *My Brother's Keeper,* suggests that they followed a pattern and structure similar to those Joyce would subsequently employ in writing his epiphanies. (See EPIPHANY.)

**"Tenebrae"** This is one of five no longer extant poems that Joyce sent to the critic William ARCHER in the late summer of 1901. After reading these verses, Archer offered Joyce encouraging criticism but also cautioned him against "metrical eccentricities" (see *Letters,* II.10). The other four poems were "The Passionate Poet," "The Final Peace," "Wanhope," and "Commonplace."

**"Universal Literary Influence of the Renaissance, The"** This is the English title of "L'Influenza Letteraria Universale del Rinascimento," an essay written by Joyce on April 24, 1912, at the University of Padua as part of a qualifying examination to teach English in the Italian secondary school system. The extemporaneous essay offers a wide-ranging historical view of art and aesthetics tracing the impact of figures like DANTE through the centuries down to artists like Richard Wagner. The essay was discovered by Louis Berrone, and published in Berrone's book, *James Joyce in Padua.*

See also "Centenary of Charles Dickens, The."

**"Verismo ed idealismo nella letteratura inglese (Daniele Defoe–William Blake)"** This is the title of two lectures that Joyce presented at the Università Popolare Triestina in March 1912; only a fragment of the lecture on Blake appears to have survived. Both pieces are published in *James Joyce: Occasional, Critical, and Political Writing,* edited by Kevin Barry and translated by Conor Deane. The lecture on Daniel Defoe is in two parts; the first offers a brief survey of the political and literary history of England during the 16th century. Joyce then explains that Defoe, one of the earliest English novelists, was the first English author whose work was independent of foreign influences. He finally discusses Defoe's struggles and literary achievements. In the few extant pages of the fragment of the lecture on Blake, Joyce touches upon the effects of Blake's artistic visions and on particular moments of his life, including the kindness that he showed toward a consumptive art student (a student suffering from tuberculosis), his relationship with his wife, his mysticism, and his indebtedness to Michelangelo and Swedenborg.

**"Wanhope"** This is one of five no longer extant poems that Joyce sent to the critic William ARCHER in the late summer of 1901. After reading these verses, Archer offered Joyce encouraging criticism but also cautioned him against "metrical eccentricities" (see *Letters,* II.10). The other four poems were "The Passionate Poet," "The Final Peace," "Tennebrae," and "Commonplace."

# PART III

# *Related Persons, Places, and Ideas*

**Abbey Theatre** The Abbey, as it is popularly called, is an internationally renowned repertory playhouse operating in DUBLIN for more than a century. It came into existence as an offshoot of the IRISH LITERARY REVIVAL. In 1904 Miss Annie Fredericka Horniman, an Englishwoman and friend of the poet and playwright William Butler YEATS (one of the Abbey's first codirectors), financed the reconstruction of the then unoccupied Mechanics' Institute, located in Abbey Street. It was intended

Old Abbey Theatre, Dublin *(Irish Tourist Board)*

to serve as the home for the Irish National Theatre Society, founded in 1902 as a successor to the IRISH LITERARY THEATRE, established by Yeats, Lady Augusta GREGORY, and Edward Martyn in 1899 to promote Irish drama. On December 27, 1904, the Abbey Theatre opened with three one-act plays: Yeats's *On Baile's Strand* and *Cathleen ni Houlihan* and Lady Gregory's *Spreading the News.* A public subscription in 1910 purchased the theater for the company, and in 1925 the newly established Irish Free State (now the Republic of Ireland) awarded the Abbey an annual subsidy that continues to this day. In 1951 a fire destroyed the original building, and a modern replacement was constructed on the same site. The Abbey played an important part in the revival of Irish drama that began in the 1960s, and it continues to exert a strong influence on the Irish and the international theater.

At the same time, the Abbey has not proven to be particularly interested in Joyce's work. *Exiles,* his only extant play, was rejected by Yeats in August 1917, because it did not evoke Irish folk drama and was not the type of play that Yeats believed could be performed well by the company. To date, Joyce's play has never been performed at the Abbey. Previously, Yeats had rejected Joyce's translations of two plays by the German dramatist Gerhart HAUPTMANN: *VOR SONNENAUFGANG* (Before Sunrise) and *Michael Kramer* (see Miscellaneous Writings). These translations, undertaken in 1901 during the summer that Joyce spent in MULLINGAR, were returned to him two months before the Abbey Theatre opened.

**Adam and Eve's** This is a Catholic church in DUBLIN under the administration of the Franciscan fathers, located on Merchant's Quay on the south bank of the River LIFFEY. Its official name is the Church of St. Francis of Assisi. The opening line of *Finnegans Wake* begins with a reference to this church: "riverrun, past Eve and Adam's" (*FW* 3.1). The reversed order of the church's popular name is an indication that other reversals are to occur, that throughout the *Wake* the narrative current will flow against conventional expectations, altering the reader's perception of time and space. In Joyce's short story "The Dead," Adam and Eve's is the church where Julia Morkan, Gabriel Conroy's elderly aunt, is the principal soprano.

**AE** See RUSSELL, GEORGE.

**Anderson, Chester G.** (1923– ) Anderson is a well-known Joyce scholar and the author of *James Joyce and His World* (1967), a pictorial biography that shows the close relationship between Joyce's life and his art, and *James Joyce* (1998), a brief biography that does much the same. More significantly, however, Anderson is the editor of *A Portrait of the Artist as a Young Man: Text, Criticism, and Notes* (1968), the Viking edition of Joyce's novel and the first major reappraisal of the text since its publication in 1916. He is also the author of "Joyce's Verses" in *A Companion to Joyce Studies* (1984), edited by Zack BOWEN and James F. Carens. Anderson has been a professor of English at the University of Minnesota since 1968. He now holds the rank of professor emeritus.

**Anderson, Margaret C.** (1886–1973) She was an American publisher, book reviewer, author, and editor. She was born in Indianapolis, Indiana, on November 24, 1886. She left college after a year and in 1908 moved to Chicago to pursue a career as a journalist. In the spring of 1914 she launched the literary magazine the *LITTLE REVIEW.*

Under her editorship and that of her associate, Jane HEAP, the *Little Review* serialized portions of Joyce's *Ulysses* in 23 issues between March 1918 and December 1920, at which time the magazine was forced by the New York Society for the Suppression of Vice to cease publishing installments of the novel, on the grounds that the work was obscene. The legal action was provoked by the July–August 1920 issue, containing the last part of the Nausikaa episode (chapter 13). In her autobiography, *My Thirty Years' War* (1930), Anderson gives a detailed account of the obscenity trial that ended with the agreement that the *Little Review* would cease its serialized publication of *Ulysses.*

***Annals of the Four Masters, The*** This is the English title of a 17th-century account, written in Irish, of the history of Ireland from its earliest period to 1616. Bryan Geraghty published an English translation by Owen Connellan in Dublin in 1846. The work, originally known as *The Annals of Donegal* and then as *The Ulster Annals,* was compiled at the Franciscan monastery in Donegal between 1632 and 1636 by Michael O'Clery, who was assisted by Peregrine O'Clery, Conary O'Clery, Peregrine O'Duigenan, and Fearfesa O'Mulconry. Whether in fact there were four, five, or even more authors may be questioned (the specific names and number of authors attributed to the work vary slightly), but the number four is given preference in the title that now identifies the *Annals.*

In *Finnegans Wake,* a reference to the *Annals* first appears on page 13, line 31: "annals of themselves timing the cycles of events grand and national," followed on the next page by an obscure allusion to the names of the four masters: "Now after all that farfatch'd and peragrine or dingnant or clere lift we our ears" (*FW* 14.28). Later in *Finnegans Wake,* Joyce clearly refers to their names: "Peregrine and Michael and Farfassa and Peregrine" (*FW* 398.15). In addition to these more or less explicit references to the authors of the *Annals,* the four masters appear in different guises throughout the *Wake.*

**Anstey, F.** This is the pseudonym used by Thomas Anstey Guthrie (1856–1934), the English humorist, novelist, and dramatist. His satiric novel VICE-VERSA, *or a Lesson to the Fathers* (1882), about the transformation of a father into his son and vice-versa, was adapted for the stage by Edward Rose. Joyce appeared in a production of the play at BELVEDERE COLLEGE, probably in May 1898, and he played the part of the schoolteacher in a manner that reportedly included parodying the mannerisms of the Rev. William HENRY, SJ, then Belvedere's rector. This play likely serves as the model for the unnamed production in which Stephen Dedalus appears in chapter 2 of *A Portrait of the Artist as a Young Man.*

**Antient Concert Rooms** This is a performance hall and meeting place located at 42$^1/_2$ Brunswick (now Pearse) Street in Dublin. The Antient Concert Rooms originally served as the offices of the Dublin Oil and Gas Company; the site has subsequently housed a bookstore and a cinema. The first performance of the National Theatre Society, which later became the ABBEY THEATRE company, took place there in 1902, and on August 27, 1904, Joyce sang there in a concert with John MCCORMACK and others. The Antient Concert Rooms is the setting for the musical performances in the *Dubliners* short story "A Mother." (The spelling of the name of the hall is a rare variant of Ancient.)

**anti-Semitism** This is a term referring to any form of prejudice against and hostility toward Jews as members of an ethnic group or as adherents of the Jewish faith. The issue of anti-Semitism is a complex one for Joyce critics. It is sometimes raised because a number of characters throughout *Ulysses* express virulent anti-Semitic feelings in their actions and speech, particularly with respect to Leopold Bloom. This, however, has no bearing on Joyce's views but rather reflects a larger Irish (and European) cultural consciousness of Jews as "Christ-killers" and cursed wanderers guilty of deicide. The violent outburst of anti-Semitism that occurred in the Limerick riots in 1904 would have been very much in the public mind of the Dubliners in the novel, arousing in some the anti-Semitic sentiments that find their way into *Ulysses,* which takes place on June 16 of that year.

In the first chapter of *Ulysses,* the Telemachus episode, the Englishman Haines comments that he does not want to see his country taken over by German Jews. At the end of the Nestor episode (chapter 2) of *Ulysses,* the Anglo-Irishman Garrett Deasy, in conversation with Stephen Dedalus, displays an offhanded anti-Semitic bias when he distorts Irish history and makes light of the anti-Semitism in his own country. At the end of the Cyclops episode (chapter 12), anti-Semitism reaches a virulent crescendo in the Citizen's heated argument with Leopold Bloom, who, though putatively converted to Catholicism, thinks of himself as a Jew and whose father, as many of his friends and acquaintances know, was a Jew. In his anger over Bloom's retorts, the Citizen hurls a biscuit tin at the departing Bloom. In each of these depictions, Joyce demonstrates the virulence of the prejudice and the repulsive manner in which it is expressed so that readers have no choice but to confront the intellectually and spiritually debilitating aspects of such hatreds.

**Archer, William** (1856–1924) When Joyce was a young man, Archer enjoyed a reputation as a well-known drama critic, journalist, translator, and playwright. He was born in Perth, Scotland, and spent much of his childhood in Norway, where his grandparents had settled. For most of his adult life he lived in London, where he helped establish Henrik IBSEN's reputation. His translation of *Pillars of Society* was the first of Ibsen's plays to be performed in England. Archer went on to publish the collected works of Ibsen and by the outbreak of World War I was one of the most influential critics in London.

On April 23, 1900, Archer wrote Joyce to inform him that Ibsen was very pleased to read a review written "by Mr. James Joyce" for the *FORTNIGHTLY REVIEW* on April 1, 1900, entitled "Ibsen's New Drama," Joyce's first published work. Joyce was delighted by this recognition, and when he and his father traveled to London in May he was able to meet Archer and thank him personally. In August Joyce sent Archer the manuscript of his play *A Brilliant Career* (now lost). Over the course of the next year, he also sent Archer several poems. In a letter to Joyce dated September 15, 1900, Archer commented on *A Brilliant Career*: "Taking it simply as a dramatic poem, I cannot help finding the canvas too large for the subject" (*Letters* II.8). In writing about the poems, he sought to be both supportive and useful in his criticism. Over the years, Joyce and Archer kept in sporadic contact, and in 1915 and again in 1917 Joyce called upon Archer for assistance in having *Exiles* produced in London. Archer, however, offered little support for this project.

For further details of their relationship see *Letters*, I.51, 86, 94, and 104; II.7–8, 9–11, 16–17, 25, 196, 207, 335, 368–369, 374, 386, 401, and 420; and III.112.

**Aristotle** (384–322 B.C.) With Plato and Socrates, Aristotle is one of the most influential Greek philosophers from the Classical period. Aristotle's ideas provided the basis of the Thomistic SCHOLASTICISM that shaped much of Joyce's Jesuit education. Joyce read Aristotle's *De Anima* (On the soul) and *Metaphysics* while in Paris in 1903. (An oblique reference to this reading at the Bibliothèque Sainte-Geneviève appears through the recollections of Stephen Dedalus in the Nestor episode, chapter 2 of *Ulysses.*) During his visit to Paris in February and March of 1903, Joyce recorded his impressions of Aristotle in a notebook, carefully dating and signing each entry. (See "Aesthetics" in *The Critical Writings of James Joyce.*) His concerns, like those in the 1904 "Pola Notebook" on Aquinas's notion of the good and the beautiful, focused exclusively on aesthetics. Patterned on the rhetorical style of Aristotle, the notebooks show a conscious effort to clarify key ideas that would emerge as central points in the discussions of aesthetic theory found in *Stephen Hero* and *A Portrait of the Artist as a Young Man.*

**Aristotelian concepts** These ideas appear throughout *Ulysses,* especially at the beginning of the Proteus episode (chapter 3), in which Stephen Dedalus's thoughts weave in and out of Aristotle's theory of vision, and Stephen recalls DANTE's depiction of Aristotle as *maestro di color che sanno* (master of those who know) (*Inferno* IV.131). (Joyce earlier used this phrase from Dante to conclude his review "Aristotle on Education.") During the discussion on SHAKESPEARE in the Scylla and Charybdis episode (chapter 9) of *Ulysses,* Stephen's mind momentarily wanders to Aristotle's notion of actuality and the term *entelechy* (actualization), a theme that recurs throughout the discussion. In this chapter Stephen also recollects Aristotle's exile following the death of his student Alexander the Great, an event of particular significance to Stephen, who, at this time, is considering exile from Dublin and Ireland. See also ARISTOTLE.

**Ascot** See GOLD CUP.

**Atherton, James S(tephen)** (1910– ) Atherton is an esteemed British Joyce scholar, former lecturer at Wigan District Mining and Technical College, Wigan, England, and visiting professor at the State University of New York at Buffalo in 1965. In 1959, Atherton published *The Books at the Wake: A Study of Literary Allusions in James Joyce's Finnegans Wake,* a work he revised and expanded in 1974. *The Books at the Wake* is a detailed study of the written sources Joyce used when composing *Finnegans Wake* and of the function these sources play in his work. It had a seminal impact on Joyce scholarship, providing an important foundation for a range of subsequent studies of the diverse literary influences on Joyce's last work. Atherton also wrote the introduction and notes to the 1965 Heinemann edition of *A Portrait of the Artist as a Young Man.*

**Augustine** (354–430) St. Augustine was the bishop of Hippo in northern Africa from 396 until his death and one of the most creative and influential thinkers in Western Christianity. He is well known for the chronicle of his spiritual growth that appears in his autobiography, *The Confessions.* One of Augustine's most lasting influences was in the formulation of Trinitarian theology and doctrine, central to the Catholic education that Joyce (whose middle name was Augustine) received in his Jesuit schools.

This familiarity with Augustine and Augustinian thought led to numerous references in Joyce's writings. In "Drama and Life," a paper he presented while still at University College, Dublin, in January 1900, Joyce quotes from Augustine's *Contra Epistolam Parmeniani* (Against the Letter of Parmenianus), III.24, to make the point that all art must be free of judgment; art is not to be used for moral teaching. In *A Portrait of the Artist as a Young Man,* Father Arnall, in one of his terrifyingly impassioned sermons in chapter 3 of *Portrait,* draws upon elements from St. Augustine's teachings to instill in the minds of Stephen and his classmates at BELVEDERE COLLEGE the fear of eternal damnation.

In the section "From the Fathers" in the Aeolus episode, chapter 7, of *Ulysses,* Stephen Dedalus, well aware of Augustine's position as one of the great rhetoricians of his time, recalls a passage from St. Augustine's *Confessions* that provides an explanation of the corruption of the good. By extension, Stephen applies Augustine's stinging commentary to the corrupt state of journalistic rhetoric, and in this fashion provides himself with an argument against accepting Myles Crawford's invitation to become a newspaperman.

Joyce's use of Augustine also extends to what is perhaps Augustine's most important theological doctrine, that of the Trinity. Along with the writings of St. THOMAS AQUINAS, Augustine's teachings concerning the relationship among the Father, Son, and Holy Spirit form the theological foundation of Western Christian belief, a concept that Joyce parallels in the paternity motif so evident throughout *Ulysses.* In the Scylla and Charybdis episode, for example, Stephen spends much time supporting conventional Catholic teaching by advancing an Augustinian-Thomistic view of the Trinity. Stephen's concern for fatherhood has profound aesthetic implications. An analogy between Augustine's Trinitarian doctrine of filial generation (God the Father has begotten his Son) and the artist's literary generation discloses the spiritual nature of literary creation. It also discloses the distinction between, and oneness of, the artist and the work. In *Finnegans Wake,* Joyce includes a reference to Augustine as "Ecclectiastes of Hippo" (*FW* 38.29–30), and alludes to the passage quoted in "Drama and Life" (*FW* 593.13–14).

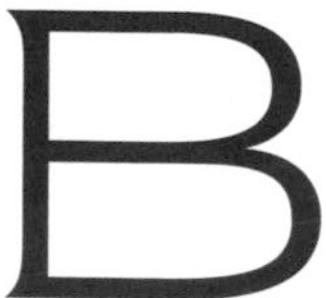

**Balfe, Michael William** (1808–1870) He is an Irish composer and singer who enjoyed fame as a composer of operas. In Paris, Balfe met the Italian composer Gioacchino Rossini, who was instrumental in establishing a position for him at the Théâtre des Italiens, and in whose *Il barbiere di Siviglia (The Barber of Seville)* Balfe sang the part of Figaro. Only a few of Balfe's own works are performed today, primarily in Ireland, and he is best known for *The Bohemian Girl* (1843).

Songs from his operas such as *The Siege of Rochelle* (1835), *The Bohemian Girl,* and *The Rose of Castille* (1857) were well known to the Irish public in Joyce's day. At the end of Joyce's short story "Clay," Maria sings the first verse of "I Dreamt That I Dwelt" from *The Bohemian Girl,* and in *Ulysses,* allusions to all three of these operas occur, especially in the Aeolus and Sirens episodes. In Aeolus, the editor Myles Crawford intones two lines of an aria from *The Rose of Castille* (*U* 7.471–472). The opera's title is spelled *Castile* in the novel, and Lenehan puns on the opera's title when he asks: "What opera resembles a railwayline?" (*U* 7.514)—his answer, "*The Rose of Castile*. . . . Rows of cast steel" (*U* 7.591). Almost like a leitmotif, this pun reverberates elsewhere in the novel. It occurs in Sirens, the Oxen of the Sun, and Circe, where Bloom is accused of plagiarizing it (*U* 15.1730–1734).

**Balzac, Honoré de** (1799–1850) He was a French novelist and the author of many realist works portraying French society and its customs. Balzac distinguished himself as a prolific writer and a keen observer of human affairs and behavior. In *La comédie humaine (The Human Comedy),* Balzac created a series of more than 90 interconnected novels and short pieces that encompass a variety of subjects, characters, and literary techniques. In his 1903 essay on Henrik IBSEN's play *Catilina,* Joyce criticizes Balzac for his lack of precision. Nonetheless, one finds a subtle allusion to Balzac's *La peau de chagrin* (*The Wild Ass's Skin,* part of *The Human Comedy*), allied to Oscar WILDE'S *The Picture of Dorian Gray,* in a passage about the artist in *Finnegans Wake:* "the squidself which he had squirtscreened from the crystalline world waned chagreenold and doriangrayer in its dudhud" (*FW* 186.6–8).

**Barnacle, Nora** (1884–1951) She was Joyce's wife, born in Galway on March 21, 1884. Her father was a baker who drank heavily, and her mother was worn down with the struggle to make ends meet for a large family. When she was five years old, Nora went to live with her grandmother, and, after her parents' separation, her mother's brothers took an increasingly central role in her life. Nora left school at the age of 13, and began a series of menial jobs. It was also during her adolescence in Galway that she became close to Michael BODKIN, a student at University College, Galway. Bodkin would later become the model for Michael Furey in Joyce's *Dubliners* short story "The Dead." Another young acquaintance, Willy Mulvey, became a model and the namesake for the first young man with whom Molly Bloom became involved in *Ulysses.* Nora's friendship with Mulvey so enraged her uncle Tommy Healy that he gave her a brutal beating over it; the following week, Nora left Galway for Dublin, where she found work as a chambermaid at FINN'S HOTEL.

Within a few months of her arrival in Dublin, the 20-year-old Nora met Joyce on June 10, 1904. She went walking with him at Ringsend on Thursday, June 16, the date Joyce later immortalized as the day on which *Ulysses* takes place. Their courtship intensified over the summer, and Joyce's letters and the recollections of friends and family make it clear that in this relatively short time Joyce fell deeply in love with her. At the same time, Joyce rejected the institution of marriage and the Catholic Church's imposition of its authority on family life in Ireland. As a result both of his unwillingness to live according to the conventions of Irish society and his desire to experience the intellectual and artistic freedom that he imagined existed on the Continent, in October of that year Joyce left Ireland with Nora.

Until he established himself as a writer, Joyce hoped to earn a living as a language teacher, working for the Berlitz schools. In consequence he and Nora traveled across Europe—first to a job in POLA and then early in 1905 to TRIESTE. (Both cities at that time were part of the Austro-Hungarian Empire.) For Nora, a young woman with no knowledge of Italian or German, little money, and both her husband's drinking and her own pregnancy to cope with, the time was indeed daunting. On July 27, 1905, George JOYCE was born in Trieste, and, while family life never became conventional, George's birth settled the Joyces into a bourgeois pattern of existence.

The combined pressures of his creative restlessness and precarious financial conditions, created to a large degree by Joyce's profligacy, punctuated their early years together. In July 1906, Nora, George, and Joyce went to Rome in a fruitless nine-month search for more stable circumstances. In March 1907 the family returned to Trieste, where on July 26 Nora gave birth to their second child, Lucia JOYCE, in a pauper ward. Over the next few years, as Joyce continued to write steadily and developed a following of language students, the family's living conditions began to improve.

In 1909, however, a crisis arose that put Nora's relationship with Joyce to a severe test. While Joyce was in Dublin, Vincent COSGRAVE, one of his classmates from UNIVERSITY COLLEGE, DUBLIN, intimated that he had enjoyed an intimate relationship with Nora in 1904 during the time that she and Joyce were courting. Fortunately, another former UCD classmate, J. F. Byrne, and Joyce's brother Stanislaus, writing from Trieste, succeeded in persuading Joyce that such claims were without foundation, and Joyce and Nora were reconciled when he returned home. Sexual tension surrounding the marriage, however, remained strong. A few years later, in 1911 or 1912, a Trieste friend, Roberto PREZIOSO, attempted to seduce Nora, and when she told Joyce he angrily confronted Prezioso and publicly humiliated him. (According to biographer Richard Ellmann, Joyce encouraged Prezioso's attentions up to the point of admiration but not seduction.)

As Nora entered her 30s, her life with Joyce settled into a predictable pattern. Despite the family's frequent moves, the rhythm of daily life became fairly well established. In 1915 the Joyces, who held British passports, had to leave Trieste for neutral Switzerland, but by this time Nora had learned to cope with such displacements. When World War I ended they returned briefly to Trieste before moving in 1921 to Paris, where they lived for almost 20 years.

The 1920s and 1930s marked a period during which Joyce received growing recognition of his work, as well as increasing financial rewards. (Joyce's "spendthrift habits," as he himself termed them, prevented the family from ever achieving complete economic security.) Other concerns, however, soon came to command the family's attention. Nora's apprehensiveness over Joyce's drinking and other health problems grew over the years, and their daughter, Lucia, evinced a growing emotional instability—diagnosed as schizophrenia—as she reached adulthood.

After having lived together for nearly 27 years, Joyce and Nora were legally married on July 4, 1931, to protect the inheritance rights of their children. While their gesture provided for the material well-being of George and Lucia, they found themselves incapable of halting their daughter's psychological deterioration. Throughout the 1930s, both James and Nora Joyce did whatever they could to find a cure for Lucia, but no form of treatment proved successful. In the end Nora had little choice but to accept her daughter's schizophrenia with resignation.

In December 1939, some three months after the outbreak of World War II, the Joyces left Paris for the French countryside. They lived in various locations outside Paris for almost a year, attempting to secure travel permits that would allow the entire family to go to Switzerland. In the end they had to leave without Lucia, who by this time was hospitalized, and in late December 1940 they moved to ZURICH with their son George and their grandson, Stephen.

On January 13, 1941, within a month of their arrival, Joyce died, and, for the first time in almost four decades, Nora found herself without him. She remained in Zurich, living with George in straitened circumstances, but, as had been the case for more than 30 years, the friendship and generosity of Harriet Shaw WEAVER saw her through these difficult times. Nora died in Zurich on April 10, 1951, and was buried in Fluntern cemetery, though there was not space for her to be interred next to Joyce. However, in 1966 they were reburied next to one another.

For people outside the Joyce family, the impact of Nora upon Joyce's personal and artistic life is impossible to calculate. Richard Ellmann's biography of Joyce and Brenda Maddox's biography of Nora make clear the central position that Nora occupied as the anchor of Joyce's emotional, sensual, domestic, public, and creative worlds. At the same time, as evidenced by the markedly different tone of these works and by the harsh reaction of members of the Joyce family to Maddox's depiction of Nora, one can see that no single view of Joyce's wife can do her justice.

At the most rudimentary level it is clear that Nora became the model for aspects of a number of women who appear in his works. She appears most notably as Gretta Conroy in "The Dead," as Bertha in *Exiles,* as Molly Bloom in *Ulysses,* and as Anna Livia Plurabelle in *Finnegans Wake.* In addition, a lifetime spent with Nora doubtless influenced Joyce's depiction of women in his work from *Dubliners* to *Finnegans Wake.* Beyond all this, however, her continuing regard for him as a man, not as an artist, must have sustained him during even the most difficult of times. For further information, see Brenda Maddox, *Nora: The Real Life of Molly Bloom.*

**Barney Kiernan's** This is a pub located on Little Britain Street, Dublin, and the setting for the Cyclops episode of *Ulysses.* Although a range of drinkers patronize the pub, the most noticeable one, the Citizen, holds forth nationalistically on a variety of subjects. The bombast of this customer brings out the worst in the natures of others, and it gives the pub an unpleasant atmosphere. The Citizen's xenophobia and ANTI-SEMITISM foment an angry resentment of Leopold Bloom, a feeling compounded by the rumor spread by Lenehan that Bloom has won a great deal of money on the Gold Cup race and is reluctant to treat the bar patrons to a round of drinks with his winnings. Eventually the Citizen provokes a quarrel with Bloom, who is in the pub waiting to meet Martin Cunningham, with whom he is going to visit the widow of Paddy Dignam.

**"Battaglia Fra Bernard Shaw e la Censura, La. 'Blanco Posnet Smascherato' "** See *The Critical Writings of James Joyce.*

**Beach, Sylvia** (1887–1962) She was an American-born expatriate who became a Paris bookseller. In 1922, Beach assumed the role of the first publisher of *Ulysses,* which was released under the imprint of her bookstore, SHAKESPEARE AND COMPANY. Throughout the 1920s, her bookstore was a meeting place for English and American expatriates, and she gave assistance—financial, emotional, and professional—to many writers, including Ernest Hemingway, Sherwood Anderson, H. D., and Katherine Anne Porter. Additionally, during the 1920s, Beach acted informally as Joyce's business manager and as one of his principal benefactors. As a gesture of gratitude for her assistance, Joyce assigned to her world rights to *Ulysses;* but in late 1931 she was persuaded to relinquish those rights to allow Joyce to pursue more lucrative publishing deals. In 1932 she and Joyce had a falling-out. As a result, Joyce's close friend, Paul LÉON, assumed Beach's role as Joyce's unofficial business manager. Although Joyce and Beach later effected a reconciliation of sorts, they were never again as close as they once had been.

For further information, see Noel Riley Fitch's *Sylvia Beach and the Lost Generation: Literary Paris in the Twenties and Thirties,* and Sylvia Beach's *Shakespeare and Company.*

**Beckett, Samuel (Barclay)** (1906–1989) Beckett was a poet, novelist, dramatist, short-story writer, and translator. Although Beckett was born in Foxrock, a southern suburb of Dublin, he lived most of his adult life in Paris. The exact date of Beckett's birth is disputed, but he claimed the portentous day of Good Friday, April 13. Beckett received his B.A. with honors in French and Italian from TRINITY COLLEGE, DUBLIN, in 1927.

Beckett had already read and admired *Ulysses* by the time he traveled to Paris and met Joyce in October 1928. A close association between the two writers developed over a 19-month period. Between 1928 and 1930, when Joyce's eyesight was failing, Beckett aided him in numerous ways, including running errands and taking dictation for *Work in Progress.* Some scholars have suggested that certain passages in the *Wake* may actually reflect Joyce's attitude toward Beckett, particularly *FW* 112.3–6 and 467.18–32.

Beckett at this time also became a vocal supporter of Joyce's latest work. His "Dante . . . Bruno . Vico . . Joyce" is the first essay in OUR EXAGMINATION ROUND HIS FACTIFICATION FOR INCAMINATION OF WORK IN PROGRESS (1929), the collection of critical writings intended to spark interest in the fictional effort that would become *Finnegans Wake.* Each dot in the title represents a century, and in this shorthand fashion Beckett identifies his sense of the intellectual tradition that joins Joyce's final work with the writings of critical and creative forebears going back six centuries. The essay centers its attention on Vico's "dynamic treatment of Language, Poetry and Myth," but it also judiciously draws upon concepts manifest in the writings of Dante (and, to a lesser extent, Bruno) to establish the imaginative continuity of Joyce's experiments. This was Beckett's first published essay, and later that year it appeared, together with his first short story "Assumption," in the literary magazine *TRANSITION.*

Irish playwright Samuel Beckett *(Irish Tourist Board)*

In December 1929, Beckett, along with several others, was asked by Joyce to translate into French the Anna Livia Plurabelle section of *Work in Progress* (now in *Finnegans Wake,* book 1, chapter 8. The translation was published in *La Nouvelle Revue Française* on May 1, 1931). Their close association came to an unfortunate end in May 1930. After she mistook attention paid to her father for an affection for her, Beckett was forced to tell Joyce's daughter, Lucia JOYCE, that he was not romantically interested in her. Joyce took his daughter's part and his attitude toward Beckett cooled noticeably.

Beckett eventually returned to Ireland and took his M.A. in French from Trinity in 1931. Although he wrote a critical study of Proust in 1931, Beckett did not pursue an academic position. Instead, he spent a good deal of time traveling in Ireland, France, England, and Germany, and visited Joyce whenever he passed through Paris. When Beckett settled in Paris in 1937, he and Joyce resumed their friendship and remained close until the latter's death.

Although his Irish citizenship would have enabled Beckett to remain safely in France during the German occupation in World War II, he did not join his country in remaining neutral. On the contrary, Beckett became a member of the French Resistance in 1941, and in 1942 he went into hiding in unoccupied France to escape arrest by the Gestapo. In 1945 while visiting his homeland, Beckett volunteered for service in the Irish Red Cross and returned to France to work as an interpreter at a military hospital in Saint-Lô.

From 1947 onward Beckett wrote primarily in French, later translating his French works into English. His plays *Waiting for Godot* (1952), *Endgame* (1957), and *Krapp's Last Tape* (1958) are especially well known, as are the novels that make up a trilogy: *Molloy* (1951), *Malone Dies* (1952), and *The Unnameable* (1953). An agonizingly stark view of the human condition, in which neither hope nor despair seems to reside, is at the core of Beckett's vision of life. He was the recipient of many literary awards, including the Nobel Prize in Literature in 1969.

For further information see Deirdre Bair's *Samuel Beckett: A Biography.*

**Bédier, Joseph** (1864–1938) Bédier was a French medievalist whose *Tristan et Iseult* (1918), a retelling of the *Romance of Tristan and Iseult,* was Joyce's main source for the story as he adapted it for *Finnegans Wake.* In a June 1926 letter to Harriet Shaw WEAVER, Joyce underscored the importance of this book by singling it out as a source that would help her comprehend passages of the *Wake:* "I shall send you Bédier's *Tristan et Iseult* as this too you ought to read" (*Letters,* I.241).

See also TRISTAN AND ISOLDE.

**Beja, Morris** (1935– ) Beja is an American Joyce critic, an emeritus professor of English at Ohio State University in Columbus, and the executive secretary and past president of the INTERNATIONAL JAMES JOYCE FOUNDATION. He is the author of many articles and books, including the biography *James Joyce: A Literary Life* (1992) and *Epiphany in the Modern Novel* (1971), an examination of the creative processes of Joyce, Woolf, and other modernist writers. He also edited *James Joyce: Dubliners and A Portrait of the Artist as a Young Man: A Selection of Critical Essays* (1973) and several collections of essays from various James Joyce symposia. With more than three decades of work devoted to Joyce, Beja's scholarship traces the changing theoretical and contextual issues that have characterized Joyce studies and provides a source of intellectual continuity and stability for several generations of students.

**Bellini, Vincenzo** (1801–1835) A contemporary of Rossini's, Bellini was an Italian operatic composer whose music was a favorite of Joyce's. In the Sirens episode, chapter 11, of *Ulysses,* allusions to Bellini's *La sonnambula* (1831) underscore Bloom's struggles to reconcile himself to his wife's impending adultery. Evocations of the love triangle from Bellini's *Norma* (1831) that appear in the Cyclops episode (chapter 12) represent a more oblique but equally emphatic introduction of the same concern.

**Belvedere College** This is a well-known and highly respected Jesuit school still in operation and housed on Great Denmark Street, Dublin, in a converted mansion originally built for the second earl of Belvedere, George Rochfort, in 1775. The SOCIETY OF JESUS purchased the building in 1841 for use as a school. Joyce attended Belvedere from 1893 to 1898, and he drew upon his memory of certain events, classmates, and teachers as the basis of his description of Stephen Dedalus's experiences in the middle portion of *A Portrait of the Artist as a Young Man.* In chapter 3 of *A Portrait,* for example, Joyce draws upon personal recollections to evoke the rhythms of daily activities and the cadences of minatory sermons given during the annual retreats conducted for the students. Earlier, in chapter 2, he evokes the atmosphere of the annual Whitsuntide play, drawing on the performance of F. ANSTEY'S play *VICE-VERSA* in which Joyce performed in May 1898 during his last year at Belvedere.

Joyce (center, wearing mortarboard) with the cast of *Vice-Versa* (Belvedere College, Dublin)

**Ben of Howth** This is a hill, over 555 feet high, located on the Howth peninsula, several miles northeast of Dublin, which forms the northern shore of Dublin Bay. On top of this hill is an ancient stone cairn that according to Irish legend, is believed to be the head of FINN MACCOOL, the great warrior in the Fenian cycle of Irish mythology; Finn is the sleeping giant beneath Dublin, and his feet are the hills in PHOENIX PARK. At the end of chapter 3 in book 1 of *Finnegans Wake* (*FW* 75.1–7), Joyce associates cairns, stones, and Howth with H. C. Earwicker, the work's hero, who is closely identified with Finn MacCool. Ben of Howth is also the setting of Leopold Bloom's marriage proposal to Molly Bloom (see Characters under *Ulysses*), vividly remembered by Bloom in the Lestrygonians episode (chapter 8) of *Ulysses,* and again by Molly in the Penelope episode (chapter 18).

**Benstock, Bernard** (1930–1994) He was a prominent American Joyce critic, cofounder in 1987 and editor of the *JAMES JOYCE LITERARY SUPPLEMENT.* Among Benstock's numerous, highly regarded books are *Joyce-again's Wake: An Analysis of Finnegans Wake* (1965), *Approaches to Ulysses: Ten Essays* (1971, edited with Thomas F. STALEY), *Approaches to James Joyce's Portrait: Ten Essays* (1977, edited with Staley), *James Joyce: The Undiscovered Country* (1977), *Who's He When He's at Home: A James Joyce Directory* (1980, with his wife, Shari Benstock), *James Joyce* (1985), and *Narrative Contexts in Ulysses* (1991). As one of the founders of the JAMES JOYCE FOUNDATION and of the biennial James Joyce Symposia, Benstock combined the critical insights evident in his writings with generous efforts to foster an intellectual atmosphere that encouraged younger scholars to develop their own work from a variety of critical approaches. Benstock taught at Louisiana State University, Kent State University, the University of Illinois, the University of Tulsa, and the University of Miami.

**Bérard, Victor** (1864–1931) He was a well-known French classical scholar who translated

Homer's ODYSSEY. In his scholarly work *Les Phéniciens et l'Odyssée* (The Phoenicians and *The Odyssey*), Bérard posited Semitic antecedents for the Greek epic, and examined a number of correspondences of epic events with commercial sites and trading routes important to the ancient cultures of the Mediterranean basin. Bérard's work attracted a great deal of attention when it first appeared in 1902, and his assertions about the impact of the Phoenician commercial culture on Homer held Joyce's interest as he wrote *Ulysses,* a novel whose central character, Leopold Bloom, also has Semitic roots.

**Berkeley, George** (1685–1753) Berkeley was a noted Anglo-Irish philosopher and clergyman, a major figure in Irish intellectual history, known for his original thought in several fields. Berkeley was a protégé of Jonathan SWIFT. He lectured in divinity, Greek, and Latin at TRINITY COLLEGE, Dublin, before being ordained in the Church of Ireland (the Irish branch of the Anglican Communion) in 1710. He lived in the British colony of Rhode Island from 1728 to 1731, and was appointed bishop of Cloyne in Ireland in 1734.

Berkeley's philosophical work was centered in the field of epistemology, the study of knowledge and reality. He stands as a leading exponent of philosophical idealism, opposed to mechanistic thinkers like Descartes and Newton and materialists like Hobbes and Spinoza. His main argument is perhaps best summarized in his assertion that "to be is to be perceived." Berkeley maintained that the objects of sense perception have no knowable existence outside the mind that perceives them; working from this premise, he reasoned that all reality ultimately consists of ideas in the mind of God.

In *Finnegans Wake,* Berkeley appears as Balkelly, the archdruid who wears a "heptachromatic sevenhued septicoloured roranyellgreenlindigan mantle" (*FW* 611.6–7)—a phrase that evokes the image of the rainbow, a biblical symbol of rebirth and promise. He argues with St. Patrick about perception and truth (*FW* 611.2–612.35). Berkeley is also one of a

Sandymount Strand, 1952, Dublin *(Irish Tourist Board)*

number of philosophers whom Stephen Dedalus calls to mind as he walks along Sandymount Strand in the Proteus episode (chapter 3) of *Ulysses*.

**Besant, Annie Wood** (1847–1933) She was a British Theosophist and social reformer. Because of the early death of her physician father, she grew up in constrained financial conditions. At 19, she married a clergyman, Frank Besant, but she soon began to question fundamental Christian beliefs. She separated from her husband in 1870 and in the mid-1870s began writing for the radical journal *National Reformer*, immersing herself in issues relating to marriage and women's rights. Throughout the 1880s she turned to political reform, especially relating to women's issues. In the late 1880s, Besant was introduced to the work of Mme Helena BLAVATSKY, and by 1889 she had become an avid follower of Blavatsky's teachings. Besant went to India in 1894, became president of the Theosophical Society in 1907, and wrote many books and essays on THEOSOPHY. Joyce's Trieste library contained two of her works, *Une introduction à la théosophe* and *The Path of Discipleship*, indicating some interest in her ideas. In the Scylla and Charybdis episode (chapter 9) of *Ulysses*, Theosophical ideas associated with Besant's writings, such as the sacrificial fire and esoteric life, enter the thoughts of Stephen Dedalus (*U* 9.61–71).

**Blake, William** (1757–1827) An early English romantic poet, William Blake was also an engraver, painter, and mystic. *Songs of Innocence* (1789), *The Marriage of Heaven and Hell* (1790–1793), and *Songs of Experience* (1794) are three of his most commonly known works, and Dante's *Divine Comedy* and the Book of Job are two of the famous works that he illustrated. In March 1912, Joyce delivered a lecture on Blake (and another on Daniel Defoe) at the Università Popolare Triestina. In his lecture on Blake, Joyce questions Blake's mysticism and examines the artistic influences on his art. (See Miscellaneous Works, "Verismo ed idealismo nella letteratura inglese (Daniele Defoe–William Blake.")

**Blamires, Harry** (1916– ) English writer and critic who in 1966 published *The Bloomsday Book: A Guide through Joyce's Ulysses*, a detailed introduction to *Ulysses* designed for the uninitiated reader. The book's extensive commentary, although helpful to the new reader, tends toward the reductive and is not always accurate, though he did revise the book extensively in 1988. Blamires, who was principal lecturer in English and later dean of arts and sciences at King Alfred's College, Winchester, England, has also published other critical works (including guides to John Milton's *Paradise Lost* and T. S. Eliot's *Four Quartets*) as well as works of fiction and theology.

**Blavatsky, Helena Petrovna** (1831–1891) She was born in Russia to a noble family. She had an unhappy childhood and married at the age of 17, though she ran away from her husband after three months of marriage. Over the next 10 years she traveled through Tibet and India and eventually became a spiritualist. She returned to Russia and a tentative reconciliation with her husband, but her traveling continued. In 1873 she immigrated to New York and in 1875 with the help of Henry Steele Olcott formed the Theosophical Society. Blavatsky was a famous figure in her day. She toured Europe, America, Egypt, and India developing and preaching THEOSOPHY, an esoteric belief system combining mysticism, the concept of universal brotherhood, and doctrines concerning the laws of nature. Among her books are *Isis Unveiled* (1877) and *The Secret Doctrine* (1888), which deal with occult doctrines, spiritualist themes, and esoteric knowledge.

At several points in *Ulysses* Stephen Dedalus alludes to Mme Blavatsky and to *Isis Unveiled*. In the Proteus episode (chapter 3) as well as the Scylla and Charybdis episode (chapter 9) Stephen's thoughts turn to that book when mention is made of the Theosophical meeting to be held that night. Other references to Mme Blavatsky and her doctrines occur in the novel.

Theosophical teachings were well known among the Dublin literati and, partly because of the theosophical emphasis on spiritual rebirth, formed part of the impetus behind the IRISH LITERARY REVIVAL. AE (George RUSSELL) and John EGLINTON, who appear in the Scylla and Charybdis episode of

*Ulysses*, were at one time affiliated with the Dublin Lodge of the Theosophical Society, as was the playwright and poet William Butler YEATS. See also Annie Wood BESANT.

**Bleibtreu, Karl** (1859–1928) He was a German critic, playwright, and historical writer. Bleibtreu propagated the idea that SHAKESPEARE's plays were written by Roger Manners, fifth earl of Rutland (1576–1612). One finds an allusion to this theory in the Scylla and Charybdis episode (*U* 9.1073–1077). This reference is a rare anachronism in *Ulysses*, which is set in the Dublin of 1904, for Bleibtreu did not publish his ideas until 1907 (in *Die Lösung der Shakespeare-Frage: Eine neue Theorie* [The Solution of the Shakespeare Question: A New Theory]). Joyce was introduced to Bleibtreu's work through a Zurich friend, Claud W. Sykes, in 1918. Joyce wrote to Bleibtreu, who was also living in Zurich at that time, for details concerning the theory and its date, and the two men eventually met.

**Bliss, Arthur** (1891–1975) He was an English composer, born in London and educated at Rugby and Cambridge. Bliss set Joyce's poem "Simples" to music for *The Joyce Book* (1933). He was one of 13 composers who contributed to that volume. In a letter to his son, George, Joyce said that Bliss's setting of the poem pleased him very much and that he considered Bliss one of the best composers to have set his poems to music. Bliss held the post of Master of the King's Music and is best remembered today for his score for the film version of H. G. Wells's novel *Things to Come* (1936).

For additional details, see *Letters*, III.287 and 338.

***Bloom*** This is the title of Sean Walsh's highly impressionistic cinematic representation of *Ulysses*. It was released in 2004, and takes a very different approach to the narrative than does Joe Strick's 1967 realistic rendition. The screenplay of the film compresses many of the events of Joyce's novel, and the sometimes fragmented dialogue makes it difficult for anyone not already familiar with the work to comprehend what is unfolding in the action.

See also the appendix on page 381.

**Bloomsday** June 16, the day in 1904 on which the action of *Ulysses* takes place and since 1924 a date celebrated by admirers of *Ulysses* and James Joyce worldwide. Joyce set *Ulysses* on this particular date to commemorate a significant day in his life. It was on Thursday, June 16, 1904, in the Ringsend district of Dublin, that he first went walking with Nora BARNACLE. In a letter written on June 27, 1924, to Harriet Shaw WEAVER, Joyce mentioned "a group of people who observe what they call Bloom's day—16 June. They sent me hortensias, white and blue, dyed" (*Letters*, I.216). (White and blue are the colors of the Greek flag and the colors chosen by Joyce for the cover of *Ulysses* when it was first published.) Bloomsday has become an international celebration—probably the only one devoted to a single literary work—that includes readings of *Ulysses*, performances of Joyce's works, festivities, and scholarly gatherings.

**Boccaccio, Giovanni** (1313–1375) He was an Italian poet, prose writer, and man of letters. A prolific author, Boccaccio influenced the whole of European literature, and, with Petrarch, he was an instrumental force behind the Italian Renaissance. His most famous work is *The Decameron* (1348–1353), a collection of stories told over 10 days by a group of people fleeing the Black Death. Characters in *The Decameron* are alluded to in the Scylla and Charybdis episode (chapter 9) of *Ulysses*. At one point, Stephen Dedalus refers to Boccaccio's dim-witted Calandrino as "the first and last man who felt himself with child" (*U* 9.836–837). This comment immediately precedes Stephen's opinion that fatherhood "is a mystical estate" (*U* 9.838), a concern much on Stephen's mind throughout the day and echoed in different ways in his conversations on aesthetics and SHAKESPEARE's *Hamlet*.

**Bodkin, Michael** He was a student at University College, Galway, who courted Nora BARNACLE for a time but contracted tuberculosis and died. Bodkin was Joyce's model for the figure of Michael Furey in "The Dead," a story in *Dubliners*. In *EXILES*, the reference to an early lover of Bertha also alludes to Bodkin's relationship with Nora, as does Joyce's poem "She Weeps over Rahoon."

**Bodley Head, The** This was the name of the British publishing firm that is now part of the Random House publishing empire. The Bodley Head issued the first edition of *Ulysses* to be printed in England. A limited edition of 1,000 copies was published in October 1936, and a second printing followed in September 1937. For its text, The Bodley Head used the second impression of the Odyssey Press edition of *Ulysses* (October 1933). In 1960 The Bodley Head edition was reset and was used as the setting text for the 1961 RANDOM HOUSE edition. In 1993 The Bodley Head published an edition of *Ulysses* based on the 1986 Random House text, prepared by Hans Walter GABLER as part of the critical and synoptic edition of *Ulysses*, published in 1984 by Garland Publishing Company. Bruce Arnold's *The Scandal of Ulysses: The Sensational Life of a Twentieth-Century Masterpiece*, offers a comprehensive discussion and review of the publication history of the novel.

***Book of Kells, The*** This is an elaborately illustrated calf vellum manuscript of the Four Gospels. Its Latin text, written mostly in Insular Majuscule calligraphy, is interspersed with illuminated pages of human and mythic figures. The exact date of the manuscript is unknown, although the end of the eighth or the beginning of the ninth century is a plausible date. It is believed to have been created at the Columban monastery in Kells, County Meath. The manuscript is now in the library of Trinity College, Dublin.

The many unique ornamental features of *The Book of Kells* appealed to Joyce, and there are numerous direct allusions in book 1, chapter 5, of *Finnegans Wake* (*FW* 119.10–123.10) to its ornament, lettering, place of origin, and "Tunc" page. Subtle references appear elsewhere in the *Wake*. The Tunc page of *The Book of Kells* contains, in the shape of an X (symbol of the cross), the crucifixion text from the Gospel according to St. Matthew: *Tunc crucifixerant XRI* [*STUM*] *cum eo duos latrones* (Then they crucified with Christ two thieves). This crucifixion motif becomes an image for Joyce's notion of the artist, as expressed, for instance, in Shaun's execrations against his brother, Shem, in book 1, chapter 7, of *Finnegans Wake:* "O, you were excruciated, in honour bound to the cross of your own cruelfiction! (*FW* 192.17–19).

Richard ELLMANN notes that in December 1922, when Joyce was already engaged with the new work that would become *Finnegans Wake,* he sent Harriet Shaw WEAVER a facsimile copy of some pages of *The Book of Kells* with a commentary by Sir Edward [O']Sullivan, as a Christmas present (see *James Joyce*, p. 545).

***Book of the Dead, The*** This is a colloquial name given to the Papyrus of Ani, a collection of Egyptian funerary texts dating from between 2400 B.C. and 1700 B.C. It is also known as "The Chapters of Coming-Forth-by-Day" (Joyce alludes to this title in *FW* 493.34–35). The collection includes magic formulas inscribed within the Egyptian crypts, as well as hymns to the Sun god, Ra. These formulas were thought to be ways of ensuring a safe and peaceful journey into the next world. *The Book of the Dead* also contains a section known as "The negative confession," referred to several times in the *Wake*. (Spoken by the supplicant before the god Osiris, the negative confession states the offenses one has avoided committing.) A popular English edition, transliterated, translated, and with an introduction by E. A. Wallis Budge, was first published in 1895.

In *The Books at the Wake: A Study of the Literary Allusions in James Joyce's Finnegans Wake* (1959), James S. Atherton devotes a chapter (pp. 191–200) to this important Egyptian text in Joyce's work and posits that Joyce used Budge's version. In chapter 4 of *Joyce's Book of the Dark: Finnegans Wake* (1986), John Bishop provides an extensive discussion of Joyce's use of *The Book of the Dead* and of its "vital presence" (p. 86) in the *Wake*. An awareness of Joyce's allusions to *The Book of the Dead* greatly enhances interpretative possibilities. For example, references to the *mastaba* tombs, where material relating to *The Book of the Dead* was found, appear as "Mastabatoom, mastabadtomm" (*FW* 6.10–11).

**Boucicault, Dion[ysius Lardner]** (1822–1890) He was an Irish actor and playwright, born in Dublin and educated at the University of London.

Boucicault was a significant figure in 19th-century Irish drama, and his many plays were well received in London, Dublin, and New York. They include *The Colleen Bawn; or The Brides of Garryowen* (1860) and *Arrah-na-Pogue; or The Wicklow Wedding* (1864).

Throughout *Ulysses* and *Finnegans Wake,* Joyce alludes to Boucicault and to several of his plays, in particular, to *Arrah-na-Pogue* (Nora of the Kiss), a play in which Nora (a lower-class heroine) helps her imprisoned foster brother (the upper-class hero) escape by way of a message she transfers to him through a kiss. Nora later marries Shaun the Post, a humorous character of her own social class. In *Finnegans Wake,* the name of H. C. Earwicker's son Shaun the Post is only the most obvious of many allusions to this play. In the opening pages of *Finnegans Wake,* book 2, chapter 4, for example, Tristan is seen cuddling and kissing Iseult by the Four Old Men, who are reminded of Arrah-na-Pogue and Dion Boucicault (see *FW* 384.17–386.11). In *Ulysses,* an allusion to the play occurs when Bloom in the Lestrygonians episode (chapter 8) recalls an earlier romantic and passionate time with Molly on HOWTH: "Ravished over her I lay, full lips full open, kissed her mouth. Yum. Softly she gave me in my mouth the seedcake warm and chewed" (*U* 8:906–907). Molly too in the Penelope episode (chapter 18) of *Ulysses* remembers that same incident (*U* 18:1574).

**Bowen, Zack** (1934– ) He is an American Joyce critic, author, president of the JAMES JOYCE SOCIETY from 1978 to 1986, professor of English at the University of Miami, Coral Gables, and humorous bel canto performer of Joyce songs. More than any other critic, Bowen is responsible for the rising interest in Joyce's integration of music into literary forms. Bowen's *Musical Allusions in the Works of James Joyce: Early Poetry through Ulysses* (1974) marked a watershed in Joyce criticism, illuminating for the first time the calculated and complex play of music among the multilayered referential implications of Joyce's prose. In addition to his own interpretive insights, Bowen's scholarship has provided a solid foundation for numerous other studies in this area. Among his other works is *Ulysses as a Comic Novel* (1989); he also edited the *Irish Renaissance Annual* (1980–83).

**Boyle, Robert, SJ** (1915–1998) He was an American Joyce critic and author of numerous studies of Joyce's artistic exploitation of Catholic theology, such as Joyce's use of Trinitarian and Eucharistic imagery, essential to an understanding of Joyce's aesthetics. Father Boyle regularly contributed essays to scholarly journals such as the *JAMES JOYCE QUARTERLY,* and to collections of Joyce criticism. He also contributed to the *New Catholic Encyclopedia.* His writings included *James Joyce's Pauline Vision: A Catholic Exposition* (1978), a book that builds upon his earlier discussions of Joyce, and *Metaphor in Hopkins* (1961). In 1981 he retired from full-time teaching in the English department at Marquette University.

**Boyne, Battle of the** The battle at which the army of James II, the deposed Roman Catholic Stuart king of England, Scotland, and Ireland, was defeated by the Protestant forces of his Dutch-born son-in-law William III on July 1, 1690, at the River Boyne, three miles west of Drogheda. Forced into exile in France by the Glorious Revolution of 1688 after three years on the English throne, James had sought to win back the crown with the help of French and Irish troops. In 1690 he landed in Ireland, hoping to use it as a base from which to return to England, but the outcome at the Boyne frustrated his plans. He fled to France soon after this defeat, although his Jacobite forces fought on unsuccessfully in Ireland for another year. Protestants (Orangemen) in Northern Ireland annually celebrate the Battle of the Boyne as a victory for their cause. The historical implications of the Battle of the Boyne were a living part of Joyce's Irish heritage and a conscious part of his individual experience.

Allusions to the Battle of the Boyne and references to the WILD GEESE (supporters of James II who subsequently emigrated from Ireland) recur throughout *Ulysses:* in the section "Shindy in Well-known Restaurant" of the Aeolus episode (chapter 7), in the Cyclops episode (chapter 12), and in the Circe episode (chapter 15). In *Finnegans Wake* book

1, chapter 7 (*FW* 185.6), Joyce uses a variation of the phrase, "wildgoup's," to describe the literary artist's necessary exile from Ireland in order to create and publish without censorship. Joyce himself became an exile after 1904 and, except for two visits in late 1909 and one in the summer of 1912, never returned to Ireland. In April 1907 at the Università Popolare in Trieste, Joyce delivered a lecture in Italian entitled "Irlanda, Isola dei Santi e dei Savi" ("Ireland, Island of Saints and Sages"), in which he touches upon the economic and political conditions of his homeland and laments the inevitable flight of many of Ireland's citizens, "wild geese" who leave their country more barren and less promising every year. This concern reappears in Robert Hand's newspaper article on Richard Rowan toward the end of Joyce's play *Exiles*.

**Bray** This is a seaside suburb south of Dublin. Joyce's family lived in Bray at 1 Martello Terrace from 1887 to 1891.

**Brion, Marcel** (1895–1984) Brion was a French author, critic, art historian, and contributor to *OUR EXAGMINATION ROUND HIS FACTIFICATION FOR INCAMINATION OF WORK IN PROGRESS*. Brion's essay, "The Idea of Time in the Work of James Joyce"—translated from the French by Robert SAGE and the only essay in the volume not originally written in English—begins by explaining the importance of time both as a concrete reality and as an essential component in all great works of art.

Brion's conceptual basis is closer to the Greek notion of *kairos* (time as event) rather than to *chronos* (time as measurement). At one point, he compares Joyce and Proust, for both incorporate time as a dominant aspect of their work. But time for Joyce, Brion notes, in contrast to Proust, is not a separate element, autonomous and external. It is the elementary aesthetic principle in Joyce's writings and at the heart of *Work in Progress,* whose structure attests to Joyce's reliance on Giambattista VICO's cyclical theory of time. Like Einstein, Brion concludes, Joyce demonstrates the relativity of time.

**Brown, Gordon** This is the stage name Joyce chose for himself when he was in his late teens and thought of becoming an actor. According to his brother Stanislaus JOYCE, Joyce picked this name because of his high esteem for the Renaissance philosopher Giordano BRUNO.

**Browne, Rev. Henry, SJ** Father Browne was a Jesuit faculty member at UNIVERSITY COLLEGE, DUBLIN, during the time Joyce was a student there. As an adviser of the college magazine ST STEPHEN'S, in 1901 he prohibited the publication of Joyce s essay "The Day of the Rabblement" in the journal. In response, Joyce and Francis SHEEHY-SKEFFINGTON, a fellow student whose essay on the status of women at the university had also been rejected, published their work independently in a broadside entitled "Two Essays."

**Bruno, Giordano** (1548–1600) Bruno was an Italian Renaissance philosopher and poet born Filippo Bruno at Nola, near Naples. In 1565 he entered the Dominican monastery in Naples (where St. Thomas Aquinas had taught), which had become a center of the Inquisition, and took the name Giordano. He fled to Rome in 1576 after being accused of heresy. The Nolan, as Bruno called himself, spent the next 16 years challenging philosophical orthodoxy, offering anti-Aristotelian ideas, and confronting intellectual intolerance. He traveled and lectured in northern Italy, Switzerland, France, England, and Germany before returning to Venice in 1591. Soon after his return, Bruno was betrayed by his Venetian benefactor and student, Giovanni Mocenigo, and handed over to the Inquisition. He was transferred to Rome, where he was convicted of heresy and imprisoned for eight years before being burned at the stake on February 16, 1600.

Bruno's Hermetic ideas concerning magical religion and his cosmological theories of an infinite universe and other inhabited worlds, as well as his critical attitude and unorthodox quest for truth, all had a significant impact on 17th-century European thought. Eventually he was hailed as a martyr for intellectual freedom and inquiry, and by the end of the 19th century a statue had been erected in his honor on the Campo de' Fiori, the site of his death. Among his many works, *Spaccio de la bestia trionfante* (*The Expulsion of the Triumphant Beast,* 1584), dedicated to the English poet Sir Philip Sidney, may be the best known. It was primarily for this work, which deals allegorically with social evils and proposes a moral and religious renewal, that the Inquisition demanded Bruno's imprisonment and execution. However, the exact grounds for declaring him a heretic remain unclear, for records of his trial are missing.

Joyce was sympathetic to Bruno for personal as well as philosophical and artistic reasons. His affinity for and interest in this innovative and daring philosopher began early and continued throughout his life. When he was in his late teens and thinking of becoming an actor, he chose "Gordon BROWN" as a stage name in honor of Bruno. Joyce began his 1901 essay, "The Day of the Rabblement," with a quotation from the Nolan. Joyce's 1903 review of J. Lewis McIntyre's *Giordano Bruno,* entitled "The Bruno Philosophy," contains enthusiastic comments about Bruno, and certain passages foreshadow ideas that Joyce would later incorporate into *Finnegans Wake,* such as the union of opposites apparent in the dualism of the Shem-Shaun relationship. (See Shaun and Shem under Characters in *Finnegans Wake.*) This concept of opposites, to which Joyce refers in a letter to Harriet Shaw WEAVER dated January 27, 1925, ultimately forms an integral part of the *Wake:* "Bruno Nolano (of Nola) another great southern Italian was quoted in my first pamphlet *The Day of the Rabblement.* His philosophy is a kind of dualism—every power in nature must evolve an opposite in order to realise itself, and opposition brings reunion etc etc" (*Letters,* I.226). Other allusions to Bruno occur in *A Portrait of the Artist as a Young Man* (chapter 5) and at several points in *Ulysses,* particularly in the Nestor episode (chapter 2).

**Budgen, Frank** (1882–1971) He was a close friend of Joyce and author of *James Joyce and the Making of Ulysses* (1934), a straightforward first-hand introduction to Joyce's novel. Born in England, Budgen spent a period as a merchant seaman before he settled in Paris to study painting. During World War I he moved to ZURICH, where he met Joyce in 1918. Budgen contributed to *OUR EXAGMINATION ROUND HIS FACTIFICATION FOR INCAMINATION OF WORK IN PROGRESS* an essay entitled "James Joyce's *Work in Progress* and Old Norse Poetry," which focuses on Joyce's adaptation of the Edda form in *Finnegans Wake.* His autobiography, *Myselves When Young,* published in 1970, contains reminiscences of Joyce.

Budgen was the first to admit that he lacked the training of a professional literary critic. Nonetheless, his close friendship with Joyce during much of the period when *Ulysses* was being written gave him remarkable insights into Joyce's process of composition. His recollections have become an invaluable scholarly tool for subsequent generations of Joyce critics seeking to understand the creative process that informed Joyce's writing.

**Burgess [Wilson], [John] Anthony** (1917–1993) Burgess was a prominent British novelist, critic, composer, translator, and editor, who also published under the pseudonym Joseph Kell. He is probably best known to readers for his novel *A Clockwork Orange* (1962; revised edition, 1963). However, Burgess also did a great deal of language-oriented criticism of Joyce's work, especially *Finnegans Wake.*

Specifically, he edited *A Shorter Finnegans Wake* (1966), a condensation of the *Wake* with an introduction and selections from the text interspersed with commentaries. He wrote an extended (but uneven) critical study of *Ulysses* and *Finnegans Wake* entitled *Re Joyce* (1965; published in England as *Here Comes Everybody: An Introduction to James Joyce for the Ordinary Reader*), as well as *Joysprick: An Introduction to the Language of James Joyce* (1973). Burgess also wrote the musical *The Blooms of Dublin,* which was broadcast on BBC radio as part of the Joyce centenary in 1982.

**Byrne, John Francis** (1879–1960) He was a fellow student, friend, and confidant of Joyce's during their time at the university. Although the mild-mannered Byrne was Joyce's classmate at BELVEDERE COLLEGE, they did not become close friends until their days at UNIVERSITY COLLEGE, DUBLIN. At UCD Byrne began to take Stanislaus Joyce's place as sounding board and whetstone to Joyce's creative endeavors. Before making the decision to leave Ireland and elope to the Continent with Nora

Joyce (right) with his friends John Francis Byrne (center) and George Clancy (left) *(Croessman Collection of James Joyce, Special Collections/Morris Library, Southern Illinois University)*

BARNACLE in October 1904, Joyce consulted Byrne on the wisdom of such a move. From 1908 to 1910 Byrne lived with two cousins at 7 Eccles Street in Dublin—the address Joyce later designated as the residence of Leopold and Molly Bloom in *Ulysses*.

When Joyce returned to Ireland in 1909, he visited Byrne at the Eccles Street address. On one evening Byrne arrived home very late, accompanied by Joyce. When he reached into his pocket for his front door key, Byrne realized that he had left it in another pair of trousers. In order not to disturb his sleeping cousins, Byrne climbed over the area railings to get in through the back door. Joyce incorporated this incident into the Ithaca episode (chapter 17) of *Ulysses*. There Leopold Bloom also forgets his latchkey and must let himself and his companion Stephen Dedalus in without disturbing Molly using the same procedure of climbing over the area railings. See also Cranly under Characters in *Stephen Hero*.

In 1910, Byrne emigrated to the United States and found work there as a journalist. He became the financial editor of the *Daily News Record* of New York from 1929 to 1933 and wrote under the pseudonym J. F. Renby. In 1953 Byrne published his memoirs, *The Silent Years*, in which he records his recollections of conversations with Joyce that he relates to Joyce's fiction.

# C

**Cahoon, Herbert** (1918–2000) He was, with John J. SLOCUM, the first American bibliographer to offer a detailed compilation of Joyce's works. In 1954 he was appointed director of library services and curator of autograph manuscripts at the Pierpont Morgan Library in New York City. With Slocum, Cahoon compiled *A Bibliography of James Joyce,* published in 1953. Although it has been supplemented by more recent bibliographical studies, this work remains an invaluable research tool for anyone seeking information on the publication history of Joyce's work up to 1950. It also contains a very useful section on Joyce's manuscripts. The few omissions in the book do not diminish its otherwise comprehensive and accurate lists. New editions and translations of Joyce's works have, of course, appeared since 1950, and the reader must consult other bibliographies for information on these.

***Calendar of Modern Letters, The*** This was a literary journal founded by Edgell Rickword, Bertram Higgins, and Douglas Garman in London to promote contemporary literature. It was published from March 1925 to March 1926 as a monthly and from April 1926 to July 1927 as a quarterly. The journal was scheduled to publish a version of the Anna Livia Plurabelle section of *Finnegans Wake* (book 1, chapter 8) in 1925, but the journal's printers judged the passage to be obscene and refused to set the text. Joyce withdrew the chapter and subsequently had it published in the October 1, 1925, issue of *Le Navire d'argent.*

**Callanan, Ellen** She was Joyce's maternal great-aunt and the model for Miss Kate Morkan in "The Dead." With her daughter, Mary Ellen Callanan, and her sister, Julia Lyons, she operated the "Misses Flynn School" at 15 Usher's Island, where lessons in piano, voice, dancing, and deportment were offered.

**Callanan, Mary Ellen** She was a second cousin of Joyce and the model for the music teacher Mary Jane in "The Dead." She was the daughter of Ellen CALLANAN.

**Campbell, Joseph** (1904–1987) He was an American author, critic, and authority on folklore and mythology. Campbell was also the husband of the dancer-choreographer Jean ERDMAN. His best-known works are probably *The Hero with a Thousand Faces* (1949; revised 1980) and *The Masks of God* (4 vols., 1959–68).

Campbell's deep interest in the significance of myth in modern life and art led him to study the works of Joyce. With Henry Morton ROBINSON, Campbell published *A Skeleton Key to Finnegans Wake* in 1944, the first full-length (and extremely influential) study of Joyce's final work. *A Skeleton Key* offers an analysis of the *Wake*'s structural division, a detailed summary of its plot, and a paraphrase of its text. Although it is now thought by some critics to have overemphasized the *Wake*'s mythic dimensions, *A Skeleton Key* was, for many years, one of the leading secondary sources used by readers of *Finnegans Wake.*

**Catholicism** Although its influence has diminished somewhat in recent years, the Roman Catholic Church in Ireland has been for centuries a dominant political, cultural, and religious force in Irish society. (The fact that Joyce's Catholicism came out of a tradition untouched by the sweeping reforms of the Vatican II Council makes many Catholic allusions difficult to grasp even for those who are practicing members of the church.) Indeed, in part because of its long suppression by British colonial regimes, during Joyce's time and for many years after the church exerted a paramount influence on the attitudes and behavior of the Irish people. Joyce was born, reared, and educated in a culture permeated by Catholicism. When he was six and a half, he began his formal education at CLONGOWES WOOD COLLEGE and later attended BELVEDERE COLLEGE, both of which were run by the Jesuits (see SOCIETY OF JESUS). He was well aware of the powerful effects that the church's pervasive presence had on Irish life. By his early 20s, Joyce voiced a passionate dissatisfaction with Catholic religious doctrines and the larger church-dominated social system that he believed victimized the citizens of Ireland. He rejected the authority of the church and claimed that it "is still, as it was in the time of Adrian IV [Nicholas Breakspear, the only English pope, 1154–59], the enemy of Ireland" (*Letters*, II.187).

Joyce did not, however, minimize the place of religion in his work. In numerous ways—many not at all complimentary to the church—his writings reflect the Catholic culture in which his mind was formed. A notable example is the sequence of sermons in chapter 3 of *A Portrait of the Artist as a Young Man,* in which Father Arnall presents a fearfully vivid description of hell and eternal punishment that derives, in part, from St. AUGUSTINE's *City of God.*

References to the Mass, the sacraments, funeral rites, veneration of saints, the cult of the Blessed Virgin Mary, religious retreats, sermons, and other Catholic practices abound in Joyce's work. They function not as decorative devices but as important representations of his overall thematic intentions. As a result, even such a seemingly inconsequential fact as the birthday of Molly Bloom can be charged with religious irony, for September 8 is the feast day of the birth of the Blessed Virgin Mary.

The Catholic images and symbols that occur throughout Joyce's writings evoke powerful emotional resonances and sustain his often subversive artistic purposes. At the same time, it would be a mistake to read these allusions as exclusively dismissive of the images that they evoke. For example, as early as the 1904–05 broadside, "The Holy Office," a satiric poem in which he ridicules writers of the IRISH LITERARY REVIVAL and defends his realistic and straightforward approach to literature, Joyce chose a title that alludes to the church bureau that was responsible for maintaining doctrinal standards and that possessed essentially the same authority as the Inquisition. The Congregation of the Holy Office was established in the 16th century to be a reforming force in the church, and Joyce believed his writings would likewise exert a reforming influence in literature.

Moreover, knowledge of the specific practices and imagery of Irish Catholicism also enhances readings of Joyce's canon. In "The Sisters," for example, with no sense of satire or ridicule, the young narrator is led to ponder the grave duties of a priest toward maintaining confessional secrecy and administering the Eucharist. In "Araby," on the other hand, the pious naïveté of the narrator emerges as he recalls how he imagined carrying his "chalice safely through a throng of foes" while hearing "the shrill litanies of shop-boys" and "the nasal chanting of street-singers." In a more neutral tone, the narrative of the story "Grace" metaphorically parallels the church's teachings on the fall of humanity and the need for redemption that can be effected only through the Catholic Church.

Major sections of *A Portrait of the Artist as a Young Man,* such as Stephen Dedalus's discussions on religion and art, his attitude toward and rejection of Christianity, and his acceptance of an artistic vocation, reflect an ingrained Catholic consciousness, though by no means an acceptance of all of those views. Indeed, the flaws of parochial Irish Catholicism appear evident in the attitude of Mrs. Riordan (Dante) at the Christmas dinner scene in chapter 1 of *Portrait,* when she defends the church's role in Irish politics and supports without question or hesitation its part in the downfall of Charles Stewart PARNELL.

The first character to speak in *Ulysses,* Buck Mulligan, mockingly intones the Introit (the entrance song) of the Catholic Mass in its pre-Vatican II Latin form. Throughout the whole of this work, Joyce exploits the church's liturgy, teachings, rites, and traditions. Stephen Dedalus's speculations on the nature of art and literature reveal a Scholastic education situated squarely within the Catholic theological tradition (see SCHOLASTICISM). As the narrative unfolds, his intellectual positions and rational analyses often reflect a religious and theological approach to the resolution of issues with which he is concerned.

The archetypal fall of humanity and resurrection stand as two of the most important images in *Finnegans Wake.* Because they have profound religious and theological overtones, they serve as handy metaphors for understanding the significance of the seemingly mundane struggles that unfold in the narrative. Such allusions pervade the narrative, but it remains important to note that the first passages Joyce composed for the *Wake,* although they were placed in the last chapter of the book, include sketches on St. KEVIN and St. PATRICK, suggesting Joyce's intentions from the start to fill the discourse with theological allusions. (See also THOMAS AQUINAS.)

**Cavalcanti, Guido** (ca. 1255–1300) Cavalcanti was born into an influential Florentine family and studied under the philosopher Brunetto Latini, who earlier had been a teacher of DANTE ALIGHIERI. Approximately 50 of Cavalcanti's poems have survived, most of them dominated by themes of love, and many critics judge him as second only to Dante among the poets of his time, though opinions may be influenced by Dante's generous praise of Cavalcanti's writings. Cavalcanti was one of the writers whom Joyce studied at UNIVERSITY COLLEGE, DUBLIN, as part of his training in Italian. In 1915, Ezra POUND sent a copy of his translation of Cavalcanti's poems, *The Sonnets and Ballate of Guido Cavalcanti* (1912), to Joyce, and the book is still in Joyce's Trieste library, now held by Harry Ransom Humanities Research Center of the University of Texas at Austin. (Compare Pound's September 12, 1915, letter to Joyce in *Pound/Joyce: The Letters of Ezra Pound to James Joyce, with Pound's Essays on Joyce,* p. 57.)

**Cecilia Street Medical School** This is the informal name of the Royal University Medical School on Cecilia Street in Dublin. Joyce briefly attended this institution in the autumn of 1902, when he was contemplating a career in medicine. After deciding to abandon this course of study, he left for Paris under the pretense of continuing his pursuit of a medical degree there.

**Cerf, Bennett** (1898–1971) Cerf was an American editor and one of the most influential publishing figures of his time. In 1927, Cerf and Donald S. Klopfer founded RANDOM HOUSE. In January 1934, as a consequence of a court verdict the previous autumn, Random House became the first American publishing house to issue an authorized edition of *Ulysses.* It was Cerf who hired the attorney Morris Ernst to argue the case against the ban on *Ulysses* in the United States. On December 6, 1933, the Hon. John M. WOOLSEY rendered his landmark decision (reprinted in the appendix on page 392). In his book *At Random: The Reminiscences of Bennett Cerf* (1977), Cerf devotes a chapter to an account of his decision to publish *Ulysses,* describing the effort to mount a successful legal challenge to the ban on Joyce's book, and detailing his dealings with Joyce.

For further information see *Letters,* III.241–244, 259, 263, 269, 291, 295, 302, 314–315, 320, 328, and 351.

**Chapelizod** The word literally means the "chapel of Iseult." Chapelizod is a district in the western suburbs of DUBLIN between the River LIFFEY and the southwestern edge of PHOENIX PARK, where the chapel itself is located. Chapelizod is the Dublin locale of the tragic Tristan and Isolde romance, which Joyce incorporates as one of the major motifs and unifying themes throughout *Finnegans Wake.* One of the important geographical locations in the *Wake,* it is where H. C. Earwicker and his family live. Chapelizod is also the suburb where Mr. James Duffy resides in "A Painful Case" in *Dubliners.*

**Clancy, George** (1879–1921) He was a fervent Irish nationalist who was a close friend and fellow student of Joyce's at UNIVERSITY COLLEGE, DUBLIN. At UCD Clancy was an active member of the GAELIC LEAGUE and a vocal supporter of Home Rule. This deep involvement in nationalist politics continued after graduation, and during the War of Independence Clancy was killed by the Black and Tans, an auxiliary force of the Royal Irish Constabulary, while serving as lord mayor of Limerick. Clancy is the model for Madden in *Stephen Hero* and for Davin in *A Portrait of the Artist as a Young Man.*

**Clongowes Wood College** This is a well-known and highly respected boys' preparatory school, still in operation, run by the SOCIETY OF JESUS, and located in County Kildare, west of Dublin. Clongowes Wood College was founded in 1814 by the Rev. Peter KENNY, SJ, In Joyce's time, Clongowes Wood was considered to be the best Catholic school in Ireland. Joyce was six and a half when he entered Clongowes in September 1888 as a boarder, and he remained a student there until John Joyce's inability to pay the tuition forced James's withdrawal in June 1891. Joyce's fictional character Stephen Dedalus also attended the school as a boarder for a short time and, like Joyce himself, left when his family could no longer afford the fees. Some of Stephen's earliest childhood memories in *A Portrait* are of Clongowes and its "wide playgrounds . . . swarming with boys" (p. 8),

Joyce (third row, second from left) with classmates, including friend George Clancy (middle row, in front of Joyce) and Constantine Curran (first row, far right), and faculty at the University College class of 1902

Clongowes Wood College *(Irish Tourist Board)*

and it is the setting for much of the action in chapter 1.

**Colum, Mary Maguire** (1885–1957) She was an Irish-American literary critic who grew up in Sligo, was part of the political and literary scene of Dublin in the first decade of the new century, married Padraic COLUM in 1912, and emigrated with him to New York in 1914. She coauthored, with her husband, *Our Friend James Joyce* (1958), a lively retelling of their encounters with Joyce, whom they knew in Dublin and Paris. A fine critic and essayist, Mary Colum contributed essays and reviews to the *New Republic* and *Saturday Review,* and in 1941 she wrote an essay rebutting Oliver St. John GOGARTY's attack on Joyce. Her book *Life and the Dream* (1947) contains recollections of the literary circles she frequented.

**Colum, Padraic** (1881–1972) Colum, an Irish poet and playwright associated with the IRISH LITERARY REVIVAL, was born at Columkille in County Longford. During the first decade of the new century, he achieved a measure of success as a poet and playwright for the ABBEY THEATRE. As a young man, Joyce felt a measure of jealousy over the attention that Colum received from established writers like W. B. YEATS and George MOORE. Joyce alludes to him in the satiric broadside "The Holy Office," and Colum appears as "Patrick What-do-you-Colm" in the broadside "Gas from a Burner." This sense of rivalry greatly diminished once Joyce had begun to receive a measure of literary recognition. Joyce makes additional reference to Colum in the Scylla and Charybdis episode (chapter 9) of *Ulysses,* where it is pointed out that he is one of several contributors to AE's *New Songs, a Lyric Selection.*

Although he emigrated to the United States in 1914, during the 1920s and 1930s Colum and his wife, Mary, spent time in London and Paris and saw a great deal of the Joyces. In their memoir *Our Friend James Joyce* (1958), they offered a highly sympathetic view of Joyce's life. Colum wrote an introduction to the 1951 edition of Joyce's play *Exiles,* praising it as a "watershed" work and clearly situating it in Joyce's canon. Colum also wrote a Noh play (using the form of the classical Japanese drama), *Monasterboice* (1966), which deals with Joyce's emergent identity as an artist.

***Contact (Contact Collection of Contemporary Writers)*** Literary journal edited in Paris by Joyce's friend Robert McAlmon. In May 1925 it published an excerpt from WORK IN PROGRESS. The passage is now a part of *Finnegans Wake* (*FW* 30.1–34.29).

**Conway, Mrs. "Dante" Hearn** She was the biographical source for the character Mrs. ("Dante") Riordan, who appears in the first chapter of *A Portrait of the Artist as a Young Man* and in *Ulysses* is referred to as a former neighbor of Leopold and Molly Bloom. The actual Dante Conway joined the Joyce household as a governess to the children soon after they moved to Bray, south of Dublin, in 1887. According to Richard ELLMANN, one of Joyce's biographers, Mrs. Conway's life closely resembled that of her fictional counterpart, and her departure from the Joyce household followed an argument over Charles Stewart PARNELL similar to that described in *A Portrait.*

**Cornell University Library** In 1957 the Cornell University Library purchased a significant amount of Joyce material from Nellie Joyce, the widow of Joyce's brother Stanislaus JOYCE. Holdings at Cornell include fragments of early poetry, a manuscript of *Chamber Music*, a typescript of an early sketch of *A Portrait of the Artist as a Young Man*, and working drafts of *Ulysses*. The collection also includes personal correspondence, photographs, and various editions of Joyce's works.

The collection contains 63 manuscripts, including working drafts and typescripts of *Ulysses*. Also significant among the manuscripts are some of his early essays, fragments of his "lost" juvenile poetry, his earliest essay, "Trust not Appearances" (1897), the earliest known manuscript of *Chamber Music*, a typescript of the first brief sketch of *A Portrait of the Artist as a Young Man*, and a journal entitled "My Crucible" kept by Stanislaus Joyce from 1903 to 1905.

There are more than 300 letters, postcards, and telegrams in the Cornell Joyce Collection. These include those written by James Joyce to his family, documenting his difficult winter in Paris in 1902–03, and nearly 100 letters from Joyce to his brother Stanislaus, covering the years 1904 through 1907. He also began writing "The Dead" and first conceived the idea for *Ulysses* during this period. The collection also contains intimate correspondence between Joyce and his wife, Nora, mostly written in 1909 during two trips to Ireland that Joyce took while Nora remained in Trieste. Other correspondence in the collection includes letters to or relating to Joyce by Ezra POUND, Harriet Shaw WEAVER, Grant RICHARDS, W. B. YEATS and Lady GREGORY, Arthur SYMONS, Elkin MATHEWS, George Bernard Shaw, and Oliver GOGARTY. There are also 175 letters between several members of the Joyce family, including Joyce's father, brothers, and his aunt Josephine Murray.

There is a published catalog of the collection: *The Cornell Joyce Collection,* a catalog compiled by Robert E. Scholes (Ithaca, N.Y.: Cornell University Press, 1961).

**Cosgrave, Vincent** (ca. 1882–1927) Cosgrave was a college friend of Joyce's who served as the model for the character of Vincent LYNCH in *A Portrait of the Artist as a Young Man* and in *Ulysses*. The fictionalized version of Cosgrave is depicted, particularly in *Ulysses,* as a betrayer and a Judas figure, perhaps echoing Joyce's sentiment for his real-life counterpart. Cosgrave may also be the model for Robert HAND in *Exiles*.

While Joyce was visiting Dublin in 1909, he heard from Cosgrave the salacious story that during the time Joyce and Nora BARNACLE were courting, she and Cosgrave had enjoyed an intimate physical relationship. The news stunned Joyce, who wrote immediately to Nora who was in Trieste with their children. Her shocked response to the charge and the urgings of both Stanislaus JOYCE and J. F. BYRNE to discount any slanders heard from Cosgrave finally convinced Joyce of the ludicrousness of the claim. Nonetheless, he felt deeply embarrassed by his temporary loss of faith in Nora and deeply resented Cosgrave's malevolent efforts to destroy his family life.

**Costello, Peter** (1946– ) Costello is an Irish writer and a biographer whose *James Joyce: The Years of Growth, 1882–1915* (1992) is intended for the general reader. In it, Costello attempts to offer a fresh approach to Joyce's life up to the age of 33 and to present a new view of a complex literary personality. He challenges much of what has been accepted about Joyce's early life. Costello's familiarity with Dublin life and his access to local records have enabled him to offer correctives to a number of the details in Richard ELLMANN's award-winning biography. Among Costello's other works pertaining to Joyce and his milieu are *The Heart Grown Brutal: The Irish Revolution in Literature from the Death of Parnell to the Death of Yeats, 1891–1939* (1978), *Clongowes Wood: A History of Clongowes Wood College, 1814–1989* (1989), and *Dublin Characters* (1989). His novel, *Leopold Bloom: A Biography* (1981), is an extrapolation from *Ulysses* that relies heavily on Joyce to flesh out the imagined details of the life of Leopold Bloom.

***Criterion, The*** (1922–39) London-based literary review founded by Lady Rothermere, wife of the newspaper magnate Viscount Rothermere; the journal was edited by T. S. ELIOT. In the July 1925 issue, a fragment of *WORK IN PROGRESS* (*FW* 104.1–125.23) was published. Joyce's poem "Ecce Puer," celebrating the birth of his grandson Stephen and mourning the death of his father, was published for the first time in the January 1933 issue of the *Criterion.*

**Croce, Benedetto** (1866–1952) He was an Italian philosopher, historian, and literary critic. In Joyce's time, he was best known for his *Aesthetic as Science of Expression and General Linguistic* (1922), a study of aesthetics in which art is considered as the expression of the imagination. (His late work, *History as the Story of Liberty* [1941], gained international renown for its anti-Fascist position.) Croce was popular among a number of Joyce's language students in Trieste, and according to Richard ELLMANN, Joyce took a particular interest in Croce's commentary on Giambattista VICO. Georges Borach, a Zurich friend of Joyce's, recalled Joyce saying in 1917 that "all the great thinkers of recent centuries from Kant to Benedetto Croce have only cultivated the garden." Croce was one of the many writers and intellectuals who in 1927 signed a petition protesting Samuel ROTH's unauthorized publication of *Ulysses* in the United States.

**Curran, Constantine** (1882–1971) Curran was a UNIVERSITY COLLEGE, DUBLIN, classmate of Joyce's and a lifelong friend. Though he shared Joyce's interest in the Continent, Curran remained in Dublin, and during the late 1920s and early 1930s wrote theater criticism for George RUSSELL's *Irish Statesman.* Eventually, he became registrar of the High Court. (Curran is the photographer who took the well-known picture of a young James Joyce standing in front of a greenhouse. When asked later what he had been thinking when the photo was taken, Joyce confessed that he was wondering if he could touch Curran for a loan.) Despite a difference in temperaments, Joyce respected Curran's views. In June 1904, Joyce showed the manuscript of *Stephen Hero* to Curran, which the latter praised. However, later that summer when Joyce sent Curran a copy of "The Holy Office" for publication in ST STEPHEN'S magazine, Curran, then editor, had to refuse it. According to Richard Ellmann, Curran served as a model for Gabriel Conroy. Curran kept in touch with Joyce for the rest of his life, and recalled their days in Dublin in a memoir, *James Joyce Remembered* (1974).

**Cusack, Michael** (1847–1907) He was originally from the Burren in County Clare. A teacher by profession, he was better known as an ardent Irish nationalist and an enthusiastic supporter of traditional Irish sports. With Maurice Davin he founded the GAELIC ATHLETIC ASSOCIATION (1884). Cusack served as Joyce's model for the chauvinistic Citizen in the Cyclops episode of *Ulysses.*

# D

**dada** This is the name of an artistic and literary movement that flourished in Europe during and just after World War I. Its proponents severed the relationship between idea and statement and dedicated themselves to subverting causal logic and conventional aesthetics. Dada was founded in ZURICH in 1916 by artists from around Europe—notably the Romanian poet Tristan Tzara and the French painter Jean (Hans) Arp—as a reaction against the inability of conventional civilized, rational art and aesthetics to prevent the madness of the Great War. Although Tzara's time in Zurich coincided with Joyce's, there is no evidence that they knew each other. (This did not prevent playwright Tom Stoppard from writing a comedy, *Travesties,* based upon the postulated friendship of Joyce, Tzara, and Lenin in Zurich in 1916.)

**Daedalus, Stephen** This is the name under which Joyce published some of his earliest works ("The Sisters," "Eveline," and "After the Race," all of which first appeared in the *IRISH HOMESTEAD* in 1904). As a young man, Joyce also signed some of his letters with this name. See also Characters under *Stephen Hero.*

***Daily Express*** This Dublin newspaper was published between 1851 and 1922. Its pro-British reputation is alluded to in "The Dead" when Molly Ivors jokingly calls Gabriel Conroy a "West Briton" because his book reviews have appeared in it. In 1902 and 1903 Joyce, like his fictional counterpart, wrote many reviews for the *Daily Express.* (These have been reprinted in *The Critical Writings of James Joyce.*) Of particular note is Joyce's harsh assessment, in a March 26, 1903, review, titled "The Soul of Ireland," of *Poets and Dreamers* by Lady Augusta GREGORY. Joyce's comments so disturbed the *Daily Express* editor, Ernest V. Longworth, that he took the unprecedented step of having it printed over Joyce's initials so as to disclaim any responsibility for it. (At that time reviews in his newspaper were customarily anonymous.) In the Scylla and Charybdis episode (chapter 9) of *Ulysses,* the incident is recalled when Buck Mulligan chides Stephen Dedalus for the same act:

> —Longworth is awfully sick, [Mulligan] said, after what you wrote about that old hake Gregory. O you inquisitional drunken jewjesuit! She gets you a job on the paper and then you go and slate her drivel to Jaysus. Couldn't you do the Yeats touch? (*U* 9.1158–1161)

**Daly, Father James** He was the prefect of studies at CLONGOWES WOOD COLLEGE when Joyce was a student there (September 1888 to June 1891). Father Daly came to Clongowes in 1887 and was the model for Father Dolan, who appears in chapter 1 of *A Portrait of the Artist as a Young Man* to punish Stephen unjustly. As prefect, Daly was an academic assistant to the rector and responsible for the curriculum.

***Dana: An Irish Magazine of Independent Thought*** (1904–1905) *Dana* was a short-lived Irish journal coedited by Fred Ryan and John

Eglinton (the latter being the pen name of W. K. MAGEE). The journal's title was taken from the name of the Celtic goddess of fertility and wisdom. In 1904, Joyce submitted his essay "A Portrait of the Artist" for publication in *Dana,* but it was rejected. However, his poem "My love is in a light attire (*Chamber Music,* VII) was published in *Dana* a few months later in August 1904. After 12 monthly issues the journal ceased publication.

**D'Annunzio, Gabriele** (1863–1938) He was an Italian poet, playwright, novelist, war hero, adventurer, and political leader, prominent from the 1880s through the 1920s. His extravagant style of living put him in debt and forced him to flee to France in 1910. He returned to Italy when World War I broke out, saw active service, and lost an eye in aerial combat. After the war he led an attempt to seize Fiume (now Rijeka, in Croatia) for Italy and became a leading supporter of Mussolini and the Fascists. In 1921 he retired to his home on Lake Garda to spend his last years writing. He died from a stroke on March 1, 1938, and received a state funeral from the Fascist government.

As a student at UNIVERSITY COLLEGE, DUBLIN, Joyce first read D'Annunzio's work. Joyce became a lifelong admirer of his prose style, which most subsequent critics have found gaudy and affected. In 1937, Joyce sent his copy of one of D'Annunzio's plays to the author to be autographed by him, a compliment Joyce seldom accorded any writer. (For further information concerning D'Annunzio, see *Letters,* II.19, 76, 80, 85; III.110, 392.)

**Dante Alighieri** (1265–1321) He was an Italian politician, poet, and author whose many works in Italian and Latin include *Commedia (Divine Comedy)* and *La Vita Nuova (The New Life)*. Dante was born in Florence, and he became the first important poet to write in the Italian vernacular language rather than in Latin. Joyce studied Dante and considered him to be one of the supreme writers. Both Dante's power as a poet and his fate as an exile from 1302 on, during which time he wrote the *Divine Comedy,* played significant roles in Joyce's literary imagination, as is evident from the many allusions to him throughout Joyce's works. Dante traveled throughout France and then spent the last decade of his life in northern Italy. He died in Ravenna in 1321.

Joyce freely integrates Dante into all his writings. An extensive and detailed list of Dante allusions in Joyce's work appears in an appendix in Mary T. Reynolds's *Joyce and Dante* (pp. 223–329).

**Darantiere, Maurice** (1882–1962) He was a French printer in Dijon who set the first edition of *Ulysses,* published by Sylvia BEACH's SHAKESPEARE AND COMPANY in 1922. Because of Joyce's many handwritten additions to the page proofs, Darantiere, who was not fluent in English, found himself extremely hard pressed to meet the scheduled publication date of February 2 (Joyce's 40th birthday). Richard ELLMANN has estimated that these emendations increased the length of *Ulysses* by as much as a third. Inevitably, given the language barrier and Joyce's innovative narrative approach errors in transmission occurred. A well-known example of this occurs in the text of the telegram Stephen Dedalus receives in Paris, telling him of his mother's illness. Joyce's rendering of this reproduced a misprint that had occurred in the real-life telegram he himself had received about his mother: "Nother dying come home father." The printer, thinking this was Joyce's error, changed "Nother" to "Mother," and so it remained in all subsequent editions until restored in the GABLER EDITION of 1984 (*U* 3.199). Despite the mistakes, through the combined patience of Darantiere and generosity of Sylvia Beach, Joyce was able through this elaboration to increase immeasurably the aesthetic power of the work.

***Dark Lady of the Sonnets, The*** This is the title of a 1910 comedy written by George Bernard Shaw. Mistaking Queen Elizabeth for his dark lady, Shakespeare attempts to make love to her. Once he recognizes who she is, he implores her to fund a National Theatre, but to no avail. She explains that the time will be right in 300 years. When the Zurich theater company The ENGLISH PLAYERS staged a version in 1918, Joyce wrote the program notes. (See "Programme Notes for the English Players.")

**Darlington, Rev. Joseph, SJ** He was the dean of studies and professor of English at UNIVERSITY COL-

LEGE, DUBLIN, when Joyce was a student there between 1898 and 1902. Father Darlington is the model for Father D. Butt, SJ, in *Stephen Hero,* and most likely for the unnamed dean of studies and professor of English at University College in *A Portrait of the Artist as a Young Man.*

**Davitt, Michael** (1846–1906) Davitt was a prominent 19th-century Irish nationalist. In 1865 he joined the Irish Revolutionary Brotherhood and became its secretary in 1868. Davitt was sent to an English prison in 1870 for his efforts to smuggle arms into Ireland. He was paroled in 1877, and two years later he organized the Land League, a group that sought economic relief for tenant farmers. Davitt subsequently brought Charles Stewart PARNELL into the league as its president, and the two men combined to make land reform and Home Rule the dominant issues on the Irish political scene. Their alliance worked well to advance Irish interests in the British Parliament throughout the 1880s. However, when Captain William O'SHEA divorced his wife, Katherine O'SHEA, because of her affair with Parnell, the Irish Parliamentary party split over the issue of continuing to support Parnell. Davitt was among those who demanded that Parnell step down from his leadership position. Davitt was elected to Parliament several times in the 1890s, and resigned in 1899 in protest over the Boer War. He published *The Fall of Feudalism in Ireland; or The Story of the Land League Revolution* (1902), a book that Joyce had in his Trieste library.

In *A Portrait of the Artist as a Young Man,* Dante Riordan signals her nationalism in part through her two hair brushes. One has a green velvet back (subsequently removed after the Kitty O'Shea scandal), symbolizing Parnell. The other has a maroon velvet back for Davitt. (While the green is an obvious symbol of Ireland, the choice of maroon for Davitt remains a mystery.)

**Davy Byrne's pub** This is the "moral" pub where Leopold Bloom has lunch (a Gorgonzola cheese sandwich and a glass of burgundy) in the Lestrygonians episode of *Ulysses.* The pub, which is still serving drinks and food, is located just south of Trinity College at 21 Duke Street, a short walk from the National Library of Ireland to the east and the Grafton Street shopping area to the west.

***Dead, The*** This is the title of a cinematic adaptation of the *Dubliners* story of the same name. The film was made in 1987 by John Huston—the last film he directed before his death—and its screenplay was written by his son Tony Huston. Gretta Conroy was played by the director's daughter Anjelica Huston and Gabriel Conroy by the Irish actor Donal McCann. An all-Irish cast of supporting actors evokes the ethos of turn-of-the-century Dublin. Although a few narrative details are missing from the film, overall it is faithful to Joyce's story, and has received a great deal of praise from film critics and Joyce scholars alike.

**Defoe, Daniel** (1660–1731) He was an English novelist, journalist, satirist, political operative, and pamphleteer. Among his best-known works are the novels *Robinson Crusoe* and *Moll Flanders* and his fictionalized account of the bubonic plague in England in 1665, *A Journal of the Plague Year.* Defoe's realism, that is, his use of common events and speech patterns, appealed to Joyce. In 1912, Joyce gave a lecture in two parts on Defoe's narrative style ("Daniel Defoe") at the Università del Popolo in Trieste.

Although his close friend Frank BUDGEN quotes Joyce claiming to have owned Defoe's complete works and to have read every line of them, connections between Joyce's writing and Defoe's prose obtain on only the broadest level. While Joyce may have found encouragement in Defoe's writing for efforts to present imaginative constructs through colloquial images, artists like FLAUBERT proved to have a much more lasting effect upon Joyce's creative consciousness.

The text of Joyce's Trieste talk was translated by Joseph Prescott and was published in *Buffalo Studies* 1 (December 1964).

**Dempsey, George Stanislaus** He was a teacher and English master at BELVEDERE COLLEGE when Joyce was a student there. Dempsey served as the model for Mr. Tate, the English master who appears in both *A Portrait of the Artist as a Young Man* and *Stephen Hero.*

**Divine Comedy** This is DANTE ALIGHIERI's epic poem, one of the major poetic works in Western literature and the first to be written in a vernacular language rather than Latin. When it was completed in 1321, the work's title was *Commedia.* However, by the 16th century it was referred to as *Divina Commedia.* The poem begins on the evening of Maundy Thursday, when the poet finds himself lost "in a dark wood," and ends a week later at sunset on the Thursday after Easter. The poem narrates the ascent of the poet from hell through purgatory to heaven. It is written in *terza rima,* three-line stanzas, or tercets, interlinked by a common rhyme scheme: aba/bcb/cdc, etc.

*The Divine Comedy* stands roughly at the midpoint between the classical epic tradition, exemplified in the works of HOMER and Virgil, and the adaptations of that form that Joyce would develop in *Ulysses.* In its combination of the religious and the secular, the noble and the mundane, and its penetrating commentary on the forces of contemporary civilization, *The Divine Comedy* is a model for Joyce's work. More than any direct structural correlation, however, Dante's imaginative virtuosity, his awareness of the condition of exile that permeates the poem, and his critical response to powerful institutions offered strong creative paradigms for Joyce to follow.

The most overt claim to a connection between the *Divine Comedy* and the works of Joyce comes from Stanislaus JOYCE, who asserts that in the *Dubliners* story "Grace," with Tom Kiernan's literal and metaphoric fall and eventual putative redemption, Joyce parodies the threefold structure—hell, purgatory, and heaven—of Dante's poem. The literalism of Stanislaus's claim aside, one finds more insight into Joyce's work by tracing the broad artistic affinities, outlined above, between the two writers. For a comprehensive study, see *Joyce and Dante: The Shaping Imagination* by Mary T. Reynolds and *Joyce, Dante, and the Poetics of Literary Relations: Language and Meaning in Finnegans Wake* by Lucia Boldrini.

**Dixon, Vladimir** (1900–1929) Born in Sormovo, Russia, Dixon was the son of a naturalized American, Walter Frank Dixon, who was from England, and a Russian mother, Ludmilla Ivanova Bidzhevskaia. Dixon joined the U.S. Army in 1918, and because he was versed in several languages served as one of General Pershing's translators. When World War I ended, Dixon studied at M.I.T. and Harvard, where he received a B.S. in 1921 and a master's degree in 1922. In 1923, he was working as an auditor for the Singer Company at its European headquarters in Paris. While in the city, Dixon read early fragments of *WORK IN PROGRESS* as they began to appear in the April 1927 issue of *TRANSITION.* Fascinated especially by Joyce's use of language, Dixon wrote a letter, dated February 9, 1929, in the style of *Finnegans Wake* and sent it to Joyce in care of Sylvia BEACH's bookstore, Shakespeare and Company. Dixon's letter was included as the last piece in *OUR EXAGMINATION ROUND HIS FACTIFICATION FOR INCAMINATION OF WORK IN PROGRESS.* Both Beach and Richard ELLMANN erroneously believed that the letter was written by Joyce himself; see Beach's memoir, *Shakespeare and Company,* p. 178, and *Letters,* III.187. (Under the sleuthing of the *James Joyce Quarterly* editor, Robert Spoo, the journal devoted much of its Spring 1992 issue to Dixon [vol. 29].)

**Dowland, John** (1563–1626) Dowland was born in London, possibly of Irish origin. He was an accomplished composer and lutenist but failed to win a position in royal service, allegedly because of his Catholic faith. He compiled several books of songs between 1597 and 1612. In *Giacomo Joyce, Stephen Hero, A Portrait of the Artist as a Young Man,* and *Ulysses* Joyce mentions him as an artistic paragon. According to Stanislaus JOYCE, Joyce admired Dowland's songs and copied out many of them. Joyce's CHAMBER MUSIC is written in a lyrical form that owes much to Dowland.

**Dublin** This is the capital city of Ireland and the major Irish Sea port, where James Joyce was born and grew up. The Irish *dubh linn* means "black pool." The Irish name for the city is *Baile Átha Cliata,* "Town of the Ford of Hurdles." Located on Dublin Bay on the east coast of Ireland, Dublin was founded as a trading post by Viking invaders in 841, although there were earlier Celtic settlements on the site. The River LIFFEY flows through the center of Dublin from west to east; south of the city are the Wicklow Mountains.

The city of Dublin plays a prominent role in the writings of Joyce and provides the cultural backdrop and central geographical motif for most of his work. In a letter to his London publisher, Grant RICHARDS, dated October 15, 1905, Joyce hinted at the emotional, psychological, and spiritual significance Dublin had for him and its importance in his stories: "I do not think that any writer has yet presented Dublin to the world. It has been a capital of Europe for thousands of years, it is supposed to be the second city of the British Empire and it is nearly three times as big as Venice. Moreover, . . . the expression 'Dubliner' seems to me to have some meaning and I doubt whether the same can be said for such words as 'Londoner' and 'Parisian' both of which have been used by writers as titles" (*Letters,* II.122).

Almost a year later, in a letter dated September 25, 1906, to his brother Stanislaus, Joyce again expressed his feeling for the city that he both loved and hated: "Sometimes thinking of Ireland it seems to me that I have been unnecessarily harsh. I have reproduced (in *Dubliners* at least) none of the attraction of the city for I have never felt at my ease in any city since I left it except in Paris. I have not reproduced its ingenuous insularity and its hospitality. The latter 'virtue' so far as I can see does not exist elsewhere in Europe. I have not been just to its beauty: for it is more beautiful naturally in my opinion than what I have seen of England, Switzerland, France, Austria or Italy" (*Letters,* II.166).

In *Ulysses* Dublin is so vividly and accurately reproduced that several books, such as Cyril Pearl's *Dublin in Bloomtime: The City James Joyce Knew,* William York TINDALL's *The Joyce Country* (which includes references to Joyce's other works), Clive HART and A. M. Leo Knuth's *A Topographical Guide to James Joyce's "Ulysses"* (2 vols.), and Jack McCarthy's *Joyce's Dublin: A Walking Guide to Ulysses,* have been published to aid readers in visualizing the city and the allusions Joyce makes to it. This evocative power has a practical source, for, when writing *Ulysses,* Joyce made extensive use of *Thom's Directory* (1904), which contained the names of Dublin's citizens, businesses, and their addresses.

In *Finnegans Wake,* Dublin is the geographical counterpart to H C E and his family, and the Scandinavian element in Dublin's history provided Joyce with material he used throughout the work. Further, in several places in *Finnegans Wake,* Joyce uses variations of the city's motto: *obedientia civium urbis felicitas*—obedience of the citizens is the happiness of the city; see, for example, *FW* 23.14–15; 140.6–7; 277.8; and 540.25–26.

Joyce wrote most vividly of Dublin after he had left it, using it as a key feature in virtually all of his works. His depiction of Dublin's citizens, streets, neighborhoods, shops, public houses, churches, parks, culture, politics, and history is unsurpassed in Irish literature. Throughout his life, Joyce's affection for Dublin never dwindled, and he often fondly referred to it as "dear dirty Dublin" and as the seventh city of Christendom.

**Dujardin, Edouard** (1861–1949) He was a French writer, poet, and editor. His novel *Les lauriers sont coupés* (1887)—published in English as *We'll to the Woods No More*—was the first to use the INTERIOR MONOLOGUE, a technique that Joyce developed in his works, and which he brought to its apogee as a literary device in Molly Bloom's monologue in the Penelope episode (chapter 18) of *Ulysses.* Although Dujardin had slipped into obscurity even in Joyce's time, the notoriety that surrounded *Ulysses* brought a renewal of attention to his works. For additional information, see *Letters,* I.283 and 287–289; II.154 and 409; and III.98, 152, 191–192, 195, 197, 247–248, 270, 286, and 433–434.

**Eccles Street** This is a street in northwest DUBLIN, just off Dorset Street, where Joyce's friend John Francis BYRNE lived, at no. 7. Joyce appropriated this address for Leopold Bloom, the protagonist of *Ulysses*. Number 7 Eccles Street is the scene of the Calypso episode, the Ithaca episode, and the Penelope episode. The house itself no longer exists, but the door from number 7 is now at the James Joyce Centre on North Great George Street.

7 Eccles St., Dublin, home of Leopold and Molly Bloom in *Ulysses*, as it appears today *(Irish Tourist Board)*

***Egoist, The*** This is the name of a little magazine founded by Dora Marsden in England in 1911 and originally called *The Freewoman*. At the urging of Ezra POUND and John Gould Fletcher, Marsden and the journal's shareholders decided on December 23, 1913, to change the name to *The Egoist* to signal a broader scope for the journal, shifting its emphasis from a strictly feminist periodical to one that would become a vehicle for imagist poetry and criticism. Harriet Shaw WEAVER was its editor from July 1914 until the journal stopped publication in 1919.

"A Curious History," Joyce's description of his long and involved struggle to have *Dubliners* published, appeared in the January 15, 1914, issue. Between February 1914 and September 1915 *The Egoist* serialized *A Portrait of the Artist as a Young Man*, and between January and December 1919, a few episodes of *Ulysses*. Other writers associated with *The Egoist* included T. S. ELIOT, who served as assistant editor, Pound, H. D. (Hilda Doolittle), and Rebecca West.

**Egoist Press** The press was established by Harriet Shaw WEAVER in 1920, shortly after the *Egoist* ceased publication in 1919. Its edition of *Ulysses*, a run of 2,000 copies, printed from the plates of the original SHAKESPEARE AND COMPANY edition, was the second printing of the novel, though it contained eight pages of errata. It was printed in Dijon by Maurice DARANTIERE, the printer of the Shakespeare edition, and mailed from Paris by John RODKER, an associate of Weaver, directly to individuals who had ordered copies as well as to the press offices in London. The volume is referred to as the first British (or English) edition because the Egoist Press was based in London. In January 1923, Rodker published a second British edition of the novel, again in Paris. The press went out of business in 1924 and turned over its titles to Jonathan Cape.

**Eliot, T(homas) S(tearns)** (1888–1965) He was an American-born poet, essayist, dramatist, and critic. Eliot was educated at Harvard and Oxford, and in 1914 he moved to London. He became a British citizen in 1927. Eliot served as an assistant editor of the EGOIST (1917–19) and helped found the CRITERION, which he also edited (1922–39). In 1948, Eliot received the Nobel Prize in literature. One of the dominant figures in 20th-century literature, his poetry, plays, and criticism include *The Love Song of J. Alfred Prufrock and Other Observations* (1917), *The Sacred Wood* (1920), *The Waste Land* (1922, the same year as *Ulysses*), *The Use of Poetry and the Use of Criticism* (1933), *Murder in the Cathedral* (1935), *The Idea of a Christian Society* (1939), *Four Quartets* (1943), *The Cocktail Party* (1950), and *Complete Poems and Plays* (1952).

Eliot first met Joyce in Paris in August 1920. (Wyndham LEWIS, who had been traveling with Eliot, describes their meeting in his memoir *Blasting and Bombardiering.*) In November 1923 Eliot's seminal three-page essay "*Ulysses*, Order, and Myth"—one of the first published critiques of Joyce's novel—appeared in the *Dial* magazine. In this highly influential article, Eliot focused on Joyce's structural use of Homeric myth and parallels. "In using the myth," Eliot comments, "in manipulating a continuous parallel between contemporaneity and antiquity, Mr. Joyce is pursuing a method which others must pursue after him. They will not be imitators, any more than the scientist who uses the discoveries of an Einstein in pursuing his own, independent, further investigations. It is simply a way of controlling, of ordering, of giving a shape and a significance to the immense panorama of futility and anarchy which is contemporary history."

The friendship between Joyce and Eliot grew over the years, although doubtless a measure of rivalry persisted. In 1925 Joyce parodied *The Waste Land* in a letter to Harriet Shaw WEAVER, and did so, again more publicly in *Finnegans Wake* (*FW* 135.6–7, 235.9–12, 236.12–13). Although the two men differed greatly in temperament, Eliot remained a strong advocate of Joyce's work, even after others like Ezra POUND withdrew their support because of *Finnegans Wake.* Eliot, in fact, was an early supporter of *Finnegans Wake,* publishing "Fragment of an Unpublished Work," a section of *Finnegans Wake* book 1, chapter 5 (*FW* 104–125), in the July 1925 issue of the *Criterion.* Eliot was one of the many authors who signed the statement protesting Samuel ROTH'S unauthorized serialization of *Ulysses* in the United States. In 1934, when Joyce was seeking a British publisher for *Ulysses,* Eliot, who had by then joined the editorial board of FABER AND FABER, explained in a letter to Joyce why that house would be unable to publish the novel. (Eliot and the firm feared prosecution.) Nonetheless, in the end Faber did bring out the British edition of *Finnegans Wake,* and, as letters in the Joyce-LÉON papers at the National Library of Ireland attest, Eliot worked steadily, albeit with an editor's perspective, to see that the volume appeared. (See *Letters,* III.14 and 300–301.)

**Ellmann, Richard** (1918–1987) He was an American Joyce critic, editor, and biographer. His award-winning biography of Joyce was first published in 1959. An enlarged revision appeared in 1982, the centennial of Joyce's birth. Ellmann also edited the second and third volumes of the *Letters of James Joyce,* an edition of *Selected Letters of James Joyce,* a collection of previously unpublished sketches, GIACOMO JOYCE, and, with Ellsworth MASON, *The Critical Writings of James Joyce.* Ellmann edited *My Brother's Keeper* by Stanislaus Joyce, James's brother. Although Ellmann published several critical books on Joyce—most notably *Ulysses on the Liffey* (1972) and *The Consciousness of James Joyce* (1974)—his reputation as a Joyce scholar rests on the biography and on his editions of Joyce's letters and other writings.

The biography, in particular, stands as a singular contribution to Joyce studies. It grew out of close ties that he had formed with Joyce's family, most notably Stanislaus Joyce, and it combines a wealth of personal detail with an excellent overview of Joyce's career. Ellmann's powers as a stylist make the book both accessible and enjoyable, though lately some critics have expressed the view that Ellmann's ties with Stanislaus Joyce gave the biography a stilted perspective.

In addition to his work on Joyce, Ellmann wrote books on William Butler YEATS and a biography of Oscar WILDE, and he edited *The Norton Anthology of Modern Poetry.* He taught at Harvard, Northwestern, Oxford, and Emory Universities.

**English Players, The** This was the name of an amateur acting troupe formed in ZURICH by Joyce and his friend the British actor Claud SYKES, in the spring of 1918. Its aim was to perform plays in English, and the founders felt that they had at least the tacit encouragement of the British consul general. Sykes assumed the role of artistic director, and Joyce took the position of business manager. On April 29, 1918, the company staged a highly successful performance of Oscar Wilde's *The Importance of Being Earnest.* In June they presented a triple bill for which Joyce wrote the program notes: *The Twelve Pound Look* by J. M. Barrie, *Riders to the Sea* by John Millington SYNGE, and *The Dark Lady of the Sonnets* by George Bernard Shaw. (Nora BARNACLE took the part of one of the daughters in the Synge play.) On September 30 the company presented Shaw's *Mrs. Warren's Profession,* and on December 3 they staged Stanley Houghton's *Hindle Wakes.* Late in the year, Joyce left the English Players, although he wrote the program notes for the March 1919 production of Edward Martyn's *The Heather Field.* In April 1919 the company put on *The Mollusc* by Hubert Henry Davies. The company's plans to perform Joyce's *Exiles* never materialized. Apparently the company continued at least into the next year, for Joyce makes mention of it in a January 3, 1920, letter to Frank Budgen. (See *Letters,* I.134.)

**epicleti** This is a term that Joyce may have used in an August 1904 letter to his former classmate Constantine P. CURRAN to characterize the short stories he was writing at that time (see below for an explanation of the possible confusion caused by Joyce's handwriting): "I am writing a series of epicleti—ten—for a paper. I have written one ["The Sisters"]. I call the series *Dubliners* to betray the soul of that hemiplegia or paralysis which many consider a city" (*Letters,* I.55). The meaning of this word, however, is not certain.

The term seems to be a Latin transliteration of the Greek adjective, *epicletos,* a word related to the noun *epiclesis,* which means an invocation or a calling down upon. At the consecration of the Mass, the *epiclesis* is the invocation to the Holy Spirit to descend upon the bread and wine and transform them into the sacramental body and blood of Christ. This ancient liturgical prayer, still part of the Greek Orthodox tradition, is no longer used in the Roman Catholic liturgy. *Epiclesis* can also mean an accusation against a person and its variant, *epicletos,* can refer to an accused summoned before a court. The term *epicleti* (as a genitive singular) can mean the collection of stories about the accused, or (as a plural adjective) it can mean those whom Joyce has accused and summoned to trial by presenting them in *Dubliners.*

Joyce, however, might not have actually used the word *epicleti* in his letter to Curran, even though its concept may convincingly reflect Joyce's attitude at the time of writing *Dubliners.* Wolfhard Steppe offers a plausible argument to this effect in his article "The Merry Greeks (With a Farewell to *epicleti*)," where he contends that Joyce actually wrote the word *epiclets* (little epics) and not *epicleti,* a misreading of Joyce's handwriting. Further confusion of the term *epicleti* can occur if it is misunderstood as a synonym for EPIPHANY, a very different theological concept known to Joyce and used by him.

**epiphany** From the Greek work *epiphaneia,* meaning *apparition* or *revelation.* An epiphany is a sudden and transitory manifestation of deity. The word connotes the manifestation of the essence of something previously hidden; it can also imply a message to benefit others. In the Catholic Church, the Feast of the Epiphany, celebrated on January 6, commemorates the manifestation of Christ's divinity to the Magi, or the gentile world. Epiphany is one of the first theological terms that Joyce exploited for literary purposes in his fiction (also see EPICLETI, TRANSUBSTANTIATION, and TRANSACCIDENTATION). For Joyce, the word *epiphany* designated a moment of spiritual revelation or showing forth of one's true self. In *Stephen Hero,* the narrator explains what Stephen Daedalus means by the term: "By an epiphany he meant a sudden spiritual manifestation, whether in the vulgarity of speech or of gesture or in a memorable phase of the mind itself. He believed that it was for the man of letters to record these epiphanies with extreme care, seeing that they themselves are the most delicate and evanescent of moments" (*SH* 211). The Italian writer and Joyce critic Umberto Eco suggests that sometime around 1900 Joyce may have gotten the idea for the term from reading Gabriele D'Annunzio's *L'Epifania del Fuoco* (The epiphany of fire).

What constitutes an epiphany remains highly subjective, but Joyce never defined it any more precisely than his sense of it as a "showing forth," an idea, perhaps, similar to what Sean O'Faolain would term "the point of illumination." Indeed, the epiphany is a moment of individual revelation, and its precise features may vary from person to person. The epiphanies in *Dubliners,* for example, depend as much on the perceptions of the reader as they do on the form and content of the stories. Joyce recorded epiphanies in a notebook that he carried with him, and he later used some of these in *Stephen Hero* and *A Portrait of the Artist as a Young Man.* (These epiphanies have been reprinted in *The Workshop of Daedalus,* edited by Robert SCHOLES and Richard M. KAIN, and in *James Joyce: Poems and Shorter Writings.*)

**Epstein, Edmund L[loyd]** (1931– ) He is an American Joyce critic, linguist, and founding editor (1957–61) of the *JAMES JOYCE REVIEW.* Epstein, after teaching for a time at Southern Illinois University, has spent most of his academic life as a professor of English at Queens College of the City University of New York and at the Graduate Center, City University of New York. His work has provided an intellectual foundation for several generations of Joyce scholars. His sensitivity to the nuances of language and his skill at close reading have made his work, from his pioneering essays of the 1950s to the present, a rich and valuable source of approaches to Joyce's complex narrative forms.

Epstein's articles have appeared in scholarly journals as well as in book-length studies of Joyce. He is the author of *The Ordeal of Stephen Dedalus: Conflict of the Generations in James Joyce's* A Portrait of the Artist as a Young Man (1971) and *Language and Style* (1980), a study of stylistics and narrative strategies. Epstein has also edited *A Starchamber Quiry: Joyce Centennial Volume 1882–1982* (1982) and, with Richard F. Peterson and Alan M. Cohn, *Work in Progress: Joyce Centenary Essays* (1983). He also founded and edited the journal *Language and Style* until it ceased publication in 1991.

**Erdman, Jean** (1916– ) She was an American dancer, choreographer, and teacher. After five years with the Martha Graham Dance Company, Erdman left in 1943 to found the Jean Erdman Dance Group, which became the Jean Erdman Theatre of Dance in 1960. With her husband, Joseph CAMPBELL, whom she married in 1938, she founded Theater of the Open Eye in 1972.

Among her many works, she adapted, choreographed, directed, and staged *The Coach with the Six Insides,* an allegorical comedy based on *Finnegans Wake* and blending elements from all performing arts. The title is taken from *Finnegans Wake* 359.24. The music is by Teiji Ito. The play had its premiere in New York City at the Village South Theatre in November 1962. It portrays the life cycle of Anna Livia Plurabelle. "One might describe the essence of *The Coach with the Six Insides,*" Erdman has said, "as the play of all elements of human existence with the inevitable truths of nature." It won several awards for the best Off-Broadway play of the 1962–63 season.

***Evening Telegraph*** This was one of the major Dublin newspapers of Joyce's time. When Joyce was in Dublin in 1909, he visited the offices of the *Evening Telegraph* on several occasions, and he incorporated his impressions into the Aeolus episode (chapter 7) of *Ulysses.* In 1901, the newspaper had praised Joyce's acting in Margaret Sheehy's play *Cupid's Confidante,* performed at the ANTIENT CONCERT ROOMS on January 8, 1901. In September 1909 the newspaper printed Joyce's "Bernard Shaw's Battle with the Censor," a review of Shaw's *The Shewing-up of Blanco Posnet* (now reprinted in *The Critical Writings of James Joyce*), which Joyce had originally written for the Italian paper *Il* PICCOLO DELLA SERA.

# F

**Faber and Faber** This was the London publisher of several fragments or episodes from *WORK IN PROGRESS: Anna Livia Plurabelle* (the first British edition, published as a booklet, 1930); *Haveth Childers Everywhere* (the first British edition, published as a booklet, 1931); *Two Tales of Shem and Shaun* (first British edition, published as a booklet, 1932); *The Mime of Mick Nick and the Maggies* (published as a booklet, 1934); *Pomes Penyeach* (first British edition, 1933); and finally the complete *Finnegans Wake* (1939). Because of his close ties with Joyce, T. S. ELIOT, then an editor at Faber and Faber, provided a great deal of assistance and support for this project. Much of the correspondence between Joyce and Eliot has been saved in the James Joyce–Paul Léon papers held by the National Library of Ireland. (Detailed descriptions of this material appear in the catalogue compiled by Catherine Fahy, pp. 171–189.)

Since Joyce's death Faber and Faber has also published the British editions of his letters, and a number of collections of essays on or by Joyce. The list has included *Introducing James Joyce: A Selection of Joyce's Prose* by T. S. Eliot (1942); *Corrections of Misprints in Finnegans Wake* (1945); *Letters of James Joyce* (Volume I), edited by Stuart GILBERT (1957); *The Critical Writings of James Joyce,* edited by Ellsworth MASON and Richard ELLMANN (1959); and *Letters of James Joyce,* Volumes II and III, edited by Richard Ellmann (1966).

For further information regarding Joyce and Faber and Faber, see *Letters,* III.202, 209, 241n.1, 292–293, 300–301, 320–321, 389, 397, and 424.

**Falconer, John** He was a Dublin publisher, printer, and wholesaler of stationery, employed by the publisher MAUNSEL & CO. to print an edition of *Dubliners.* In 1912, he destroyed the proof sheets of *Dubliners* after learning of Maunsel's decision not to publish. (Printers at this time in Ireland could be held liable and prosecuted for the works they produced.) Joyce subsequently composed the broadside "Gas from a Burner," satirizing the actions of Maunsel and Falconer. Despite Falconer's obstruction, Joyce was able to obtain a complete set of proofs from the publisher.

**Feshbach, Sidney** (1931– ) He is an American Joyce critic and past president of the JAMES JOYCE SOCIETY; he was a professor of English at City College, City University of New York, from 1970 until his retirement in 1994. A graduate of Columbia University, where he studied under William York TINDALL, Feshbach, who has stressed the development of character as an organizing principle in *A Portrait of the Artist as a Young Man,* is representative of a generation of critics who effectively combined perceptive textual analysis and firmly grounded scholarship. Their ability to interpret based on close reading of a text as well as a consideration of its context helped open the way for the diverse cultural, social, and historical criticism that came to the foreground during the 1980s. With William Herman, Feshbach coauthored "The History of Joyce Criticism and Scholarship" in *A Companion to Joyce Studies.* He has also published on Wallace Stevens and Marcel Duchamp.

***filioque*** This is a Latin theological term literally meaning "and from the Son." *Filioque* refers to the divine procession of the Holy Spirit from the Father *and* the Son, as from a single principle, and it is therefore central to the Western church's conception of the Trinity. In the late sixth century, the Latin church added the term to the Nicene-Constantinopolitan Creed. The addition was not immediately accepted everywhere in the Western church (its use in the liturgy, for example, was not approved by Rome until sometime in the second decade of the 11th century), and the Greek Orthodox Church never accepted it. The clash over the theological term was the grounds for the schism between East and West in 1054.

In the fable of the Mookse and the Gripes in *Finnegans Wake* (*FW* 152.15–159.18), Joyce parodies the *filioque* dispute as the cause of separation between the Mookse (the Latin West) and the Gripes (the Greek East); the specific passage, on page 156, intensifies the filial opposition between Earwicker's two sons, Shem (Gripes) and Shaun (Mookse). In a letter to Frank BUDGEN, Joyce through his daughter, Lucia, refers to the creed and the *filioque* clause as it appears in *Finnegans Wake* (see *Letters,* III.284–285).

**Finegan, Tim** This is the name of the hod carrier and central character in the traditional Irish ballad "FINEGAN'S WAKE."

**"Finegan's Wake"** This is the title of an Irish ballad about a hod carrier named Tim FINEGAN; sometimes spelled "Finigan's Wake." There are many versions of this ballad; the original writer is unknown, but the ballad dates from the 19th century.

Born with the love of liquor, Tim falls from a ladder one morning and is thought to be dead. When a row breaks out at his wake, some liquor splashes onto his head and he awakes, leaping from his bed saying "D'ye think I'm dead?" Joyce derived the title of his book *Finnegans Wake* from this ballad, but without the apostrophe, and he uses the ballad's theme of death and resurrection throughout the book's mythic substructure. Allusions to the ballad occur frequently in the *Wake* and in one place it is even identified (FW 607.16).

**Finn MacCool (Irish *Fionn Mac Cumhail*)** (d. circa 284) Finn was the legendary warrior-leader of the Irish *Fianna* (bands of warriors), tribal hero, and a central figure in the Ossianic cycle of Irish heroic tales, the bravest and most generous of the warriors who served King Cormac. In Irish folklore, Finn and his band achieved mythological status; they possessed superhuman powers that allowed them victory in warfare and contact with the Celtic otherworld. Finn was also a master builder, responsible, at the request of St. Lawrence O'Toole, for constructing the cathedral at Lund in Sweden. Because he had at one time held the Salmon of Wisdom, Finn had only to suck his thumb to receive enlightenment. (According to Adaline GLASHEEN, the Salmon of Wisdom is the incarnation of Fintan MacBochra, the only Irish survivor of the Flood. He became a god of wisdom in the Celtic otherworld [see *Third Census of Finnegans Wake,* p. 95].)

Finn lends his name to the title of Joyce's last work, *Finnegans Wake.* As an archetypal figure, Finn is an avatar of the book's central figure, H C E. Joyce intended for the title to educe both the Irish and the Nordic origins of Earwicker's character. The name *Finn* at once alludes to Scandinavian ancestry and to the Irish giant who lies sleeping beneath the Dublin landscape, with his head forming the BEN OF HOWTH and his feet protruding as two hills near PHOENIX PARK, while Irish history runs through his mind. As Joyce explained in a March 1940 letter to his friend the Belgian poet, novelist, and critic Fritz Vanderpyl, Finn again wakes through Earwicker's mock-heroic transfiguration: "the title of [*Finnegans Wake*] signifies at once the wake and the awakening of Finn, that is, of our legendary Celto-Nordic hero" (*Letters,* III.473). The hero's name also appears in the mutated form of "Finnish Make Goal" (*FW* 374.21). Louis O. Mink observes that the identification of Finn MacCool with the sleeping giant below Dublin is Joyce's invention (see *A Finnegans Wake Gazetteer,* p. 291).

Numerous direct references to Finn MacCool and to variants on the name—Huckleberry Finn, FINN'S HOTEL, Tim FINNEGAN, Fingal—insure the reader's continual awareness of Finn. As with most patriarchal types depicted in *Finnegans Wake,* characterizations of Finn MacCool repeatedly call to mind the figure of H C E, representing both the formidable and the comic elements in him. Both Finn and H C E convey a measure of power that can be quite intimidating to those around them; and, at the same time, in their demeanor and actions, they also display a degree of buffoonery that continually undercuts whatever authority they strive to establish.

**Finn's Hotel** This was the hotel on 1 and 2 Leinster Street in central Dublin where Nora BARNACLE was working when she met Joyce in 1904. It may be cryptically alluded to in *Finnegans Wake:* "—.i. .'. . o. . 1." (*FW* 514.18).

A collection of short pieces found in the manuscript of *Finnegans Wake* was to have been published under the title *Finn's Hotel,* edited by Danis Rose, by the VIKING PRESS in 1993, but the project met with severe opposition from the Joyce estate and never appeared. Although Rose maintains that these pieces, which include "King Roderick O'Conor" and "Tristan and Isolde," were intended by Joyce to be separate short works, other scholars believe they are Joyce's initial sketches for *Finnegans Wake,* which he began to compose in 1923.

**Flaubert, Gustave** (1821–1880) He was a renowned French novelist and short story writer whose narrative style is marked by detached impersonality and precise descriptive observation. Joyce demonstrated a familiarity with Flaubert's writings as early as his 1901 essay "The Day of the Rabblement" and his 1902 essay "James Clarence Mangan." Flaubert's platonic description of beauty as the splendor of truth and his concept of the role of the artist in his art as analogous to that of God in creation helped shape Joyce's own aesthetics and narrative strategy. Joyce described the stories in *Dubliners* as having been written "in a style of scrupulous meanness," that is, in a rigorously realistic style, detached, unsentimental, and unsparing. This style led Ezra POUND in 1915 to compare Joyce with Flaubert (and Stendhal). An allusion to Flaubert's use of Plato occurs as well in chapter XVIII (XIX old system) of *Stephen Hero.* In chapter 5 of *A Portrait of the Artist as a Young Man* Stephen Dedalus discusses these aesthetic principles with Vincent Lynch. After quoting Plato and Aquinas on the nature of beauty, Stephen, borrowing from Flaubert's letter to Mlle Leroyer de Chantepie, concludes that "the artist, like the God of the creation, remains within or behind or beyond or above his handiwork, invisible, refined out of existence, indifferent, paring his fingernails." In the notes for *Exiles* Joyce explains his use in the play of an aesthetic idea underscoring a shift "from the lover or fancyman to the husband or cuckold" that he adapted from reading Flaubert's *Madame Bovary.* Flaubert's novel *La tentation de Saint-Antoine (The Temptation of Saint Anthony; or, A Revelation of the Soul)* figures among the significant sources behind the hallucinatory style of the Circe episode (chapter 15) of *Ulysses.*

**Ford, Ford Madox** (1873–1939) He was an English novelist, critic, and editor. He was born Ford Hermann Hueffer, though he is often called Ford Madox Hueffer. In either case, he changed his name to Ford Madox Ford in 1919. Under Ford's editorship in April 1924, the *TRANSATLANTIC REVIEW* became the first journal to publish an excerpt from *Finnegans Wake* (*FW* II.4.383–399). This passage, known as "Tristan and Isolde" (one of the earliest sections of the *Wake* composed by Joyce), appeared under the title "From Work in Progress." *WORK IN PROGRESS,* the provisional title of *Finnegans Wake,* was originally suggested by Ford (see *Letters,* I.405) and subsequently used by Joyce until the book was published in 1939. An important novelist in his own right, Ford is best known for his novel *The Good Soldier* (1915) and the World War I tetralogy *Parade's End* (1924). He was also closely associated with Ezra POUND, Joseph Conrad, and Henry James.

***Fortnightly Review, The*** This is the name of an English literary journal that published reviews and serialized novels. It was founded in 1865 and lasted until 1954, 20 years after it changed its name to *The Fortnightly.* Joyce's first publication, "Ibsen's New Drama," appeared in the April 1, 1900, issue.

**Francini-Bruni, Alessandro** Francini-Bruni was the assistant director of the Berlitz school in POLA, when Joyce, who taught English there during 1904 and 1905, first met him. According to Richard ELLMANN, Francini added his wife's surname, Bruni, to his own in order "to distinguish himself from the multitude of other Francinis." A friendship developed between him and Joyce, with Francini-Bruni helping Joyce perfect his Italian. Their close relationship continued in Trieste when both moved there in 1905. In 1922, Francini-Bruni published a lecture entitled *Joyce intimo spoliato in piazza* (Joyce stripped in public), containing his recollections of Joyce's time in Trieste. However, the lecture was not a tribute to Joyce, as one might expect, for in it Francini-Bruni ridiculed some of Joyce's ideas and his manner of teaching at the Berlitz School in Trieste. A brief account of this lecture is found in Herbert GORMAN's *James Joyce,* and translated excerpts appear in Richard Ellmann's *James Joyce.* The essay was published in full in the *James Joyce Quarterly* 14 (Winter 1977) 127–159; also in the same issue is Francini-Bruni's "Recollections of Joyce," 160–168. Also see Letters, III.58–59, 102.

**free indirect discourse** This is a term designating a stylistic technique that occurs throughout Joyce's writing. It integrates into a dominant narrative voice the linguistic traits of another, leaving the reader to determine who is speaking. One sees this method at work in the opening sentence of the *Dubliners* story "The Dead": "Lily, the caretaker's daughter, was literally run off her feet." Since the narrative goes on, in its very precise language, to show that Lily, though greatly overworked, actually stays on her feet, one begins to look for the source of this hyperbole. A few lines of direct speech from Lily gives one a sense of her inclination to take such a cliché to its extreme, and it makes her a likely source for the sentiments of the first line.

The late Hugh Kenner identified one form of this technique at work in *A Portrait of the Artist as a Young Man,* and called it "the Uncle Charles Principle." While some readers have taken Kenner's remarks as signaling the discovery of a new narrative approach, in fact, the more widely accepted free indirect discourse occurs throughout Joyce's fiction from *Dubliners* through *Finnegans Wake.*

***Freeman's Journal, The*** This was the name of a Dublin newspaper founded in 1763 and published until 1924. Leopold Bloom works as an advertising canvasser for the fictional version of the paper in *Ulysses,* and much of the action in the Aeolus episode of that novel takes place in its offices.

A review of Joyce's *Chamber Music* appeared in the actual *Freeman's Journal* in 1907, and an editorial, probably written by Joyce, entitled "Politics and Cattle Disease," was published in the newspaper in 1912. (This editorial, which Joyce parodies in *Ulysses,* is reprinted in *The Critical Writings of James Joyce.*) A facsimile of the June 16, 1904 (BLOOMSDAY), edition of the paper has been issued by Chelsea Press in London.

**futurism** This was the term used to identify a short-lived revolutionary movement in European art and literature that stressed freedom of expression and the overthrow of past literary and artistic conventions. It began in 1909 with the publication in the Paris newspaper *Le Figaro* of the futurist manifesto, written by the Italian poet Filippo Tommaso Marinetti. Futurism emphasized, and strove to represent (through conventional artistic means), what its practitioners regarded as the essential modern qualities of movement, energy, and power, especially as expressed through machinery. Futurism was among the earliest of 20th-century modernist art movements that rejected traditional aesthetics and included some social content. Others include cubism, DADA, expressionism, and surrealism. Joyce had a copy of a reprint of Marinetti's 1909 manifesto in his Trieste library. According to Frank BUDGEN, Joyce at one time queried him as to whether the Cyclops episode (chapter 12) in *Ulysses* was futuristic, to which Budgen replied: "Rather cubist than futurist. . . . Every event is a many-sided object . . ." (*James Joyce and the Making of Ulysses,* p. 153).

**Gabler, Hans Walter** See GABLER EDITION.

**Gabler Edition** This is the common designation of a revised edition of *Ulysses* prepared by the German Joyce scholar and textual critic Hans Walter Gabler (b. 1939), with Wolfhard Steppe and Claus Melchior, and published in three volumes under the title *Ulysses: A Critical and Synoptic Edition,* by Garland Publishing in 1984. In his foreword, Gabler states that his version, the only critical edition of *Ulysses,* "offers a new original text" that corrects "well over 5,000 departures from the author's own text as established from the documents of composition." Not only are the relatively simple matters of erroneous spellings and improper punctuation corrected but omitted material is restored. For instance, the Gabler text includes a passage in the Scylla and Charybdis episode (*U* 9.429–431) that is not found in the original 1922 edition or any subsequent edition of *Ulysses* until this one. This addition informs a passage in which Stephen Dedalus sees an apparition of his mother in the Circe episode (U 15.4192–4193). (The question of whether the omission was intended by Joyce is a matter of dispute.) This edition of *Ulysses* quickly began to replace earlier editions of the novel in scholarly research and was for a time referred to as "the corrected text," implying a definitive work. The 1986 Random House one-volume edition (Gabler's text without the critical apparatus) was advertised as such. (This text was also published by the BODLEY HEAD in Britain.)

Gabler's was a monumental accomplishment in textual studies. Nonetheless, in 1985 a then-unknown scholar, John Kidd, launched an aggressive attack on Gabler's approach to textual emendations, charging that Gabler's scholarship was faulty and that he had introduced new errors into the text. Four years after the publication of Gabler's edition, Kidd published "An Inquiry into *Ulysses: The Corrected Text*" in *The Papers of the Bibliographical Society of America* (82 [December 1988]: 411–584). In the June 1993 issue of that journal Gabler published a rebuttal, "What *Ulysses* Requires," that set Kidd's critique in perspective. Although he proposed to publish his own version of the novel, Kidd's edition of *Ulysses* has yet to appear in print. Most readers of *Ulysses* will not notice the textual differences from one version of the novel to another. The *JAMES JOYCE QUARTERLY* identifies both the Gabler edition and the 1961 Random House edition as standard editions. However, the Gabler edition, though not perfect, is usually considered the best version of *Ulysses* currently available. It has endured close scrutiny, and despite the controversial charges against, no other edition has supplanted it.

**Gaelic Athletic Association** This is an Irish nationalist organization, still in existence, founded by Michael CUSACK in 1884 with the aim of promoting Gaelic field sports (hurling, Irish football) as a way of securing the continuity of Irish identity. Although the G.A.A. did not have direct ties with militant organizations, most of its members sympathized with the Fenians, who used the association as a recruiting ground. In the Cyclops episode, allusions to the Gaelic Athletic Association and Irish sports intensify the reader's awareness of the nationalist feelings that run throughout the narrative.

**Gaelic League** This is the name of a literary and political association founded in 1893 by the writer, scholar, and statesman Douglas Hyde, who later became the first president of the Republic of Ireland (1938–45). Part of the larger national Irish revival of the late 19th and early 20th century, the league strove to restore Gaelic (Irish) as the literary and spoken language of Ireland and to advance Irish nationalism, culture, and literature. Among other activities, the league held meetings and made instruction in Irish available to all who were interested. Hyde wrote one-act plays that were translated into English by Lady GREGORY and that were dismissed by Joyce as "dwarf-drama . . . [,] a form of art which is improper and ineffectual" (*CW* 104; from Joyce's "The Soul of Ireland," a review of Lady Gregory's *Poets and Dreamers*).

Although Joyce was well aware of the league and even attended some of its meetings, the precise nature and extent of his involvement is disputed and remains uncertain. There are conflicting accounts in Richard ELLMANN's *James Joyce* and in Peter Costello's *Joyce: The Years of Growth 1882–1915*.

**Garland Publishing, Inc.** Garland is the American publisher of *The* JAMES JOYCE ARCHIVES (under the general editorship of Michael GRODEN) and of *Ulysses: A Critical and Synoptic Edition* in three volumes (the GABLER EDITION, prepared by Hans Walter Gabler with Wolfhard Steppe and Claus Melchior). Taken together, the *Archives* and the Gabler *Ulysses* have radically altered the course of textual criticism of Joyce's canon.

**Gilbert, Stuart** (1883–1969) He was a British critic, translator, and close friend of Joyce, whom he met in Paris in 1927 after retiring from the (British) Indian Civil Service. His translations include *The Stranger* by Albert Camus, and in collaboration with Auguste Morel and Valéry Larbaud, he participated in producing the French translation of *Ulysses* in 1929. This close work on *Ulysses* led Gilbert to write a critical work on the novel. With Joyce's assistance, Gilbert produced *James Joyce's Ulysses* (1930), one of the first book-length studies of the novel, an influential book written at a time when the novel itself was not easily obtainable. In his discussion, Gilbert stressed the significance of the Homeric framework of *Ulysses,* and the importance of source material such as Victor BÉRARD's *Les Phéniciens et l'Odyssée* and A. P. Sinnett's *Esoteric Buddhism,* from which Joyce derived key ideas.

Gilbert also contributed essays to OUR EXAGMINATION ROUND HIS FACTIFICATION FOR INCAMINATION OF WORK IN PROGRESS (1929), to *A James Joyce Yearbook* (edited by Maria JOLAS, 1949), and to *James Joyce: Two Decades of Criticism* (edited by Seon Givens, 1948), and he also edited volume 1 of Joyce's letters. In *Our Exagmination,* Gilbert's essay, "Prolegomena to *Work in Progress,*" discusses Giambattista VICO's philosophy of history and language and its relevance to understanding WORK IN PROGRESS. He appends a brief commentary on selected word-structures in the work.

In 1993, Thomas F. Staley and Randolph Lewis edited *Reflections on James Joyce: Stuart Gilbert's Paris Journal,* a stark, personal view of Joyce recorded over a period of five years (January 1, 1929–March 26, 1934). Gilbert's frank comments reveal his inner frustrations and an embittered attitude that grew out of what he saw as Joyce's temperamental and idiosyncratic behavior.

**Glasheen, Adaline** (1920–1993) She was an American Joyce critic and author. Glasheen taught at Wheaton College in Norton, Massachusetts, and was a visiting lecturer at the State University of New York at Buffalo. Her writings on Joyce include *A Census of Finnegans Wake: An Index of the Characters and Their Roles* (1956), a revised *Second Census of Finnegans Wake* (1963), and a further revised *Third Census of Finnegans Wake* (1977). In this work, Glasheen gives a synopsis of Joyce's last book; an invaluable chart, "Who Is Who When Everybody Is Somebody Else," which identifies and interrelates the characters in *Finnegans Wake;* and a comprehensive alphabetical list identifying and locating proper names found throughout the *Wake.* The *Third Census* is an expansion of the previous two editions of her work. It focuses on specific details of characters, providing readers of *Finnegans Wake* with an invaluable guide to research. In 2001 *A Tour of the Darkling Plain: The Finnegans Wake Letters of Thornton Wilder and Adaline Glasheen* appeared. It consists of a near-obsessive gathering of detailed correspondence between Wilder and Glasheen regarding their views on Joyce's last work. Though the text is peppered with interesting observations, they are often difficult to disinter from the mass of quotidian details.

**Glasnevin** This is an area directly east of Drumcondra on the north side of DUBLIN and the name often used throughout *Ulysses* as a synonym for Prospect Cemetery, located there. This cemetery, the final resting place of Paddy Dignam, is the setting for much of the Hades episode. It is at Dignam's graveside in Glasnevin where the mysterious M'Intosh makes his first appearance.

**Gogarty, Oliver St. John** (1878–1957) Irish physician, poet, playwright, novelist, essayist, and member of the Irish senate, known for his caustic wit, ribald humor, and penchant for practical jokes. Joyce first met Gogarty at the NATIONAL LIBRARY OF IRELAND in late December 1902, and a close friendship quickly developed. In September 1904 Joyce stayed with Gogarty for a time at the MARTELLO TOWER in Sandycove, where Samuel Chenevix Trench, the model for Haines in *Ulysses,* was also staying. At this time, however, Joyce seems to have had a falling-out with Gogarty. Gogarty was one of the individuals lampooned in Joyce's satirical poem "The Holy Office." When he learned of this, Gogarty determined to break with Joyce. Once Joyce had left Ireland for the Continent, however, Gogarty made several overtures towards reconciliation. He renewed these efforts when Joyce visited Ireland in 1909. Joyce spurned him and continued to see Gogarty as an adversary.

Gogarty nonetheless had a pronounced impact upon Joyce, and he became the model for a number of figures in Joyce's fiction. Goggins in *Stephen Hero* is a clear evocation of Gogarty, as is Robert Hand in *Exiles.* The best-known representation of Gogarty in Joyce's writings remains "stately, plump Buck Mulligan," who is introduced in the opening sentence of *Ulysses.*

Gogarty remained in Ireland and established himself as a well-known surgeon and as a man of letters. After the appearance of *Ulysses,* Gogarty spent a good deal of time denying any connection between himself and the fictional Buck Mulligan, but much to his chagrin over the years, he became increasingly well known not for his own literary accomplishments but for his association with Joyce and with *Ulysses.* He nonetheless retained a flair that made him a Dublin character for decades. In one well-known instance during the Irish civil war, he escaped capture by a group of IRA soldiers by swimming across the Liffey (an incident that, according to Richard ELLMANN, greatly amused Joyce). In gratitude Gogarty donated a pair of swans to the city, though the swans themselves may have been ambivalent about making their home in the highly polluted river.

In 1939, Gogarty moved to the United States, occasionally returning to Ireland for visits. Gogarty's memoir, *As I Was Going down Sackville Street,* contains reminiscences of Joyce.

**Gold Cup, The** This is a two-and-a-half-mile horse race held annually at the Ascot Meeting near London. In the Gold Cup race that took place at 3:00 P.M. on Thursday, June 16, 1904, Sceptre was the favorite, but the race was won by Throwaway, a 20-to-1 long shot. This race has thematic importance as a thread running throughout *Ulysses,* and its unexpected outcome becomes initially an amusing and eventually a contentious topic of discussion in the Cyclops episode.

**Gonne, Maud** (1866–1953) She was an Irish actress, revolutionary, and in 1921 the first emissary of the Irish Free State to France. Known for her beauty, she was pursued for decades by the poet and playwright William Butler YEATS, who made her the subject of several poems and plays. During his first trip to Paris, Joyce, on Yeats's behalf, had planned to visit Gonne but never did. In the Proteus episode (chapter 3) of *Ulysses*, Stephen Dedalus, as he is reminiscing about Paris, calls her and her lover M. Millevoye to mind (*U* 3.233).

**Gorman, Herbert [Sherman]** (1893–1954) Gorman was an American newspaper reporter, critic, and writer. He was the author of the first biography of Joyce, *James Joyce: His First Forty Years* (1924), written with a good deal of help (and a measure of censorship) from Joyce himself. Over the 1930s, Gorman expanded his material, publishing *James Joyce* in 1939 (revised, 1948). His examinations of Joyce's life and works were supplanted in 1959 by Richard ELLMANN's more extensive biography (revised in 1982), which was written with the use of material unavailable to Gorman and without the restrictions under which Gorman worked. Today, the two Gorman biographies give a greater sense of how Joyce wished himself to be seen than of how his contemporaries actually saw him. Gorman also wrote the introduction to the Modern Library edition of *A Portrait of the Artist as a Young Man* (1928).

**Gotham Book Mart** In 1920 Frances Steloff opened the Gotham Book Mart in New York City's diamond district. The Gotham subsequently moved to 41 West 47 Street, and in 2004 it moved again to 16 East 46 Street. From its inception the Gotham was a center for avant-garde literature, and Steloff made a point of acquiring the works of controversial authors like Joyce, D. H. Lawrence, Henry Miller, and countless others. When *Finnegans Wake* was published in May 1939, Steloff organized a launch of the book at the Gotham. A great number of literary figures attended as mourners, and Steloff took the part of the grieving widow. In his biography of Steloff, W. G. Rogers reports that Eugene JOLAS later claimed that Joyce himself was quite pleased to hear of the celebration. In 1947 Steloff cofounded the JAMES JOYCE SOCIETY, and the meetings of the society continue to be held at the Gotham at its location at 16 East 46 Street.

**Gregory, Lady (Née Isabella Augusta Persse)** (1852–1932) She was an Irish playwright, essayist, cofounder in 1898 with William Butler YEATS and Edward Martyn of the IRISH LITERARY THEATRE, and a leading figure in the IRISH LITERARY REVIVAL. Lady Gregory was born in Galway the seventh daughter of Frances and Dudley Persse. She married Sir William Henry Gregory, former governor of Ceylon and then Member of Parliament for Galway, in 1880. Lady Gregory began writing in 1892 after the death of her husband. She collected and translated a great deal of Irish folklore, and composed a number of plays and tales based upon peasant life. In 1904, Lady Gregory helped establish the ABBEY THEATRE in Dublin and became one of its directors. For the last 40 years of her life she was a prominent patron of such Irish writers as Yeats, John Millington SYNGE, AE (George RUSSELL), Douglas Hyde, Sean O'Casey, and others who frequently gathered at her home, Coole Park, in the west of Ireland.

Irish playwright, and cofounder of the Irish Literary Theatre, Lady Gregory on her estate, Coole Park *(Irish Tourist Board)*

Joyce first met Lady Gregory in 1902 through his early association with Yeats. She tried to help him in his plans to go to Paris to study medicine by introducing him to E. V. LONGWORTH, the editor of the *DAILY EXPRESS*, for whom Joyce would subsequently write a number of book reviews. The work did not always suit Joyce's temperament, but he undertook it nonetheless.

Despite this kindness, Joyce showed his independence from her influence and that of the Irish Revival in general when Longworth asked him to review Lady Gregory's book on Irish folklore, *Poets and Dreamers*. This review, entitled "The Soul of Ireland" and reprinted in *The Critical Writings of James Joyce*, appeared in the March 26, 1903, issue of the *Daily Express*. In a patronizing dismissal of the topic, Joyce credits Lady Gregory for doing the best she could with very unpromising material. Apparently not satisfied with this, Joyce included in his satirical broadside, "The Holy Office," an allusion to Lady Gregory as one of Yeats's "giddy dames" (*CW* 150).

While one may question Joyce's tact in dealing with his benefactor, the review and the poem underscore the position in which he found himself vis-à-vis established figures such as Lady Gregory. Asserting his independence as an artist, Joyce would not allow himself to fall under the sway of someone with strong artistic views of her own. Lady Gregory represented the very forms of Irish art that Joyce sought to overcome, and her money and generosity only made her a clear and present danger to the aesthetics that he sought to nurture. If he now seems ungrateful, one must consider his position as a young man without great resources struggling against a tremendous pressure to conform.

**Gresham Hotel** This is a fashionable Dublin hotel (still in operation) located on Sackville Street (now O'Connell Street). In the *Dubliners* story "The

The Gresham Hotel in Dublin, the location of the final scene in Joyce's "The Dead" *(Irish Tourist Board)*

Dead," Gabriel and Gretta Conroy stay here after attending the annual dinner-dance given by Gabriel's aunts, the Misses Morkan. For Irish readers of Joyce's generation, Gabriel's decision to stay here would subtly have enforced his comfortable middle-class status. The Conroys' room in the Gresham is the setting for the last scene in "The Dead," where Gabriel's epiphanic vision of his soul swooning into "that region where dwell the vast hosts of the dead" (*D* 223) concludes the story and the collection.

**Griffith, Arthur** (1871–1922) Griffith was an Irish journalist, the editor of the *United Irishman* from 1899 to 1906, and a politician. Griffith was the major force behind the founding of the Irish nationalist movement Sinn Féin (We Ourselves) in 1905, a movement with the goals of political and economic independence from the United Kingdom that Joyce would favorably discuss in his essay "Fenianism: The Last Fenian."

On December 11, 1902, Joyce wrote a review entitled "An Irish Poet" that appeared in the *DAILY EXPRESS*. His disapproving critique of William Rooney's patriotic *Poems and Ballads* provoked a defensive response from Griffith, whose nationalist sensibilities were offended. However, he lent support to Joyce in September 1911, when his *Sinn Féin* was one of two newspapers to publish Joyce's letter concerning the problems he was having publishing *Dubliners* (see "A Curious History" under Miscellaneous Works). Griffith eventually became, in 1922, the first president of the Dail Eireann (Irish parliament) in the Irish Free State.

The narrative of *Ulysses* repeatedly makes reference to Griffith, and at one point in the Cyclops episode (chapter 12), the unnamed narrator suggests that Bloom has acted as an adviser of Griffith (*U* 12.1574).

**Groden, Michael** (1947– ) Groden is an American Joyce scholar and textual critic who has spent much of his academic life teaching in Canada. He is general editor of *The* JAMES JOYCE ARCHIVES (63 volumes, 1977–80), and author of *James Joyce Manuscripts: An Index to the James Joyce Archive* (1980) and *Ulysses in Progress* (1977). He has written the afterword to the BODLEY HEAD edition of *Ulysses* (1993), a reprint of the 1984 *Ulysses* text edited by Hans Walter Gabler (see GABLER EDITION), and has edited (with Martin Kreiswirth and Imre Szeman) *The Johns Hopkins Guide to Literary Theory and Criticism* (2nd edition, 2005). He has also edited (with Jed Deppman and Daniel Ferrer) *Genetic Criticism: Texts and Avant-textes* (2004). Groden currently teaches at the University of Western Ontario.

With his work on Joyce's process of composing *Ulysses*, analyzing the drafts and revisions that each chapter went through, and his editorship of the *Joyce Archives* series, Groden has become one of the most prominent textual critics in contemporary Joyce studies, frequently consulted by libraries and museums.

**Guinness brewery** This is the brewery of Arthur Guinness and Sons adjacent to the River Liffey in Dublin, established in 1759 and famous for its porter and stout. After Arthur's son Sir Benjamin Lee Guinness took the business over in 1825, the brewery began a very successful export trade. Until recently the Guinness Company was the largest employer in Ireland. The Guinness brewery and its products provide an important backdrop in several of Joyce's works. At the end of the Lessons chapter in *Finnegans Wake*, "A Visit to Guinness' Brewery" is listed as one of the essay topics for the Earwicker children, Shem, Shaun, and Issy (*FW* 306.30–307.1). In a letter to Harriet Shaw WEAVER dated January 13, 1925, playing on Dubliners' fondness for stout (a dark beer), Joyce facetiously asks "what the Irish word for Guinness's vineyard's beverage would be. It is *lin dub* or *dub lin*" (in Irish, *dublin* means "dark pool") (*Letters*, I.224).

# H

**Halper, Nathan** (1907–1983) He was an American Joyce critic, author, art critic, and gallery owner, born in Manhattan and educated at Columbia University. In 1983, shortly before he died, he directed with Patrick A. McCarthy the second Provincetown (Massachusetts) James Joyce Symposium (June 12–16). Halper has contributed essays, periodicals, and books on Joyce, and is the author of *The Early James Joyce* (1973), an introduction to Joyce, and *Studies in Joyce* (1983), a collection of essays, mostly on *Finnegans Wake.* Although he was not a professional Joycean, Halper contributed greatly to Joyce studies with his enthusiasm for the work, his keen observations, and the encouragement he gave to others.

***Hamlet*** This is one of Shakespeare's greatest tragedies. Its central character is forced to avenge the death of his father. In *Ulysses,* Stephen Dedalus's affected way of dressing and his ongoing mourning for his dead mother—introduced in the Telemachus episode—represent a conscious effort to form a parallel between his life and Hamlet's. The library discussion in the Scylla and Charybdis episode revolves around Shakespeare and this play, using it to establish various themes running through the narrative, such as remorse, filiation, paternity, and adultery. For example, the discussion of the theme of paternity in *Hamlet* in Scylla and Charybdis leads into broader considerations that relate both to Stephen's behavior and to Bloom's association with him. As this theme appears throughout *Ulysses* it resonates on several levels that enhance the narrative.

**Hanley, Miles** (1893–1954) He was a linguist at the University of Wisconsin, Madison, who took an early interest in Joyce's work. Hanley published the extremely helpful *Word Index to James Joyce's Ulysses* in the late 1930s. Although it is not completely accurate and is based on the 1934 Random House edition of *Ulysses,* with its many errors, the *Word Index* has nonetheless remained an important resource for examining the linguistic and thematic structure of Joyce's novel. In some ways it has been superseded by *A Handlist to James Joyce's Ulysses* (prepared by Wolfhord Steppe with Hans Walter Gabler), which, through a computer-generated word count, gives a far more accurate account of the 1984 GABLER EDITION. Nonetheless, Hanley's was a pioneering work that still offers a useful guide for scholars.

**Harrington, Timothy C.** (1851–1910) Harrington was the lord mayor of Dublin from 1901 to 1904 and a friend of John JOYCE, James's father. Harrington was a Parnellite, loyal to the memory of Charles Stewart PARNELL and to Parnell's views on the struggle for Irish independence. He refused to receive the king on his royal visit to Ireland along with refusing a knighthood while lord mayor of Dublin. In November 1902, Harrington wrote an open letter of commendation attesting to Joyce's character. On several occasions, Joyce used the letter as a reference when he was seeking employment on the Continent.

**Harry Ransom Humanities Research Center** The Humanities Research Center was founded in 1957, on the Austin campus of the University of Texas by the vice president and provost Harry Huntt Ransom. It was built upon existing collections of rare books acquired by the university over the previous 60 years. The center began to acquire Joyce holdings in 1958 with the purchase of the library of T. E. Hanley. This acquisition pointed the center toward its mission of developing collections in 20th-century literature. In 1979 the director, Decherd Turner, added James Joyce's Trieste library to the center's holdings. And since succeeding Turner in 1988, the current director, Thomas STALEY, has continued to supplement the Joyce and Joyce-related material. The center has prepublication material—including holographs, drafts, and page proofs—for *Ulysses, Finnegans Wake,* and *Pomes Penyeach,* correspondence relating to publishing, personal papers, a number of editions of Joyce's works, and material relating to Joyce studies. The papers in the John Rodker archive include unpublished letters from Joyce, copies of Rodker's essays on Joyce, rare editions of the second and third printings of Ulysses, and materials documenting Rodker's involvement in these publications. The archive of Stuart Gilbert includes his diary, notes, and journals, along with drafts of critical works and translations, and many letters from Joyce.

**Hart, Clive** (1931– ) Hart is an Australian Joycean and critic who has spent much of his academic life teaching in England. Of the generation of Joyce scholars who came to prominence in the 1960s, Hart is the foremost authority on *Finnegans Wake.* Among his writings, two invaluable and influential books stand out: *Structure and Motif in Finnegans Wake* (1962), a study of the structural patterns and thematic design of the *Wake,* and *A Concordance to Finnegans Wake* (1963). With Fritz SENN, Hart edited *A Wake Digest* (1968), a collection of notes and short essays, most of which were first published in *A Wake Newslitter.* He was also an original trustee of the International James Joyce Foundation. Hart retired from teaching at the University of Essex in 1998.

**Hauptmann, Gerhart J. R.** (1862–1946) He was a German dramatist and novelist, recipient of the Nobel Prize in literature in 1912. His play *Vor Sonnenaufgang* (Before sunrise), written in 1889, helped introduce NATURALISM into the German theater. Hauptmann's play was influenced by Henrik IBSEN and, as did many of Ibsen's works, it caused considerable controversy at its first performance.

Hauptmann's naturalistic drama, with its emphasis on social protest and realistic representation of working-class conditions, appealed to Joyce, who at that time had pronounced Socialist sympathies, and as a linguistic exercise he translated *Vor Sonnenaufgang* and another play, *Michael Kramer,* in the summer of 1901. While it is not clear how proficient Joyce felt he was in German, he nonetheless sent the translations to William Butler YEATS to be performed by the Irish National Theatre Society in Dublin. In October 1904 Yeats rejected the plays and commented: "I gave them to a friend who is a German scholar to read some time ago, and she saw, what indeed you know yourself, that you are not a very good German scholar. . . . Nor do I think it very likely we could attempt German work at present. We must get the ear of our public with Irish work" (Richard Ellmann, *James Joyce,* p. 178).

**Hayman, David** (1927– ) Hayman is an American Joyce critic, textual scholar, and translator. He has taught at the Universities of Texas and Wisconsin, and since 1998 has been professor emeritus in the department of comparative literature at the University of Wisconsin, Madison. Besides contributing to numerous journals and books, Hayman has written and edited several excellent critical works on Joyce, which include *Joyce et Mallarmé* (2 vols., 1956), *A First-Draft Version of Finnegans Wake* (1963, edited), *Ulysses: The Mechanics of Meaning* (1970; revised and expanded, 1982), *James Joyce's Ulysses: Critical Essays* (1974, edited with Clive Hart), *In the Wake of the Wake* (1978, edited with Elliott Anderson), and *The Wake in Transition* (1990). Hayman was also the guest editor of a *Finnegans Wake* special issue of the *James Joyce Quarterly* (Spring 1965). He is coeditor of the 25 *Finnegans Wake* volumes in the JAMES JOYCE ARCHIVES (1977–80). In *Ulysses: The Mechanics of Meaning,* Hayman developed the concept of the arranger as an attempt to explain Joyce's innovations in the narrative strategies of the novel, although in the light of later studies the term is somewhat reductive. At the time Hayman proposed it, the "arranger" served as a useful starting point for discussions of narrative voice.

**Healy, Timothy M.** (1855–1931) Healy was an Irish politician from Cork widely acknowledged as both brilliant and controversial. For many years Healy acted as a staunch supporter of Charles Stewart PARNELL, calling him "the uncrowned king of Ireland." When the Kitty O'SHEA, scandal broke, however, Healy eventually turned against him. Healy publicly accused Parnell of theft, disapproved of his relations with Kitty O'Shea, and joined forces with anti-Parnellites to defeat him. When Joyce was nine years old he composed a poem, no longer extant, entitled "Et Tu, Healy," condemning Healy as a betrayer. For the next three decades Healy was something of a political maverick, but after the formation of the Irish Free State he was appointed the first governor-general, a position representing the Crown to the new Irish government.

**Heap, Jane** (1887–1964) Heap was born in Kansas and moved to Chicago to study at the Art Institute. She was a painter, critic, and coeditor (with Margaret Anderson) of the *LITTLE REVIEW,* which she eventually took over from 1923 to 1929. Earlier, the *Little Review* had serialized portions of Joyce's *Ulysses* in 23 issues between March 1918 and December 1920. Publication of *Ulysses* ceased when the New York Society for the Suppression of Vice prohibited the magazine from publishing any further installments of the novel.

***Heather Field, The*** This is the title of a play by Edward Martyn. It received its premiere in May 1899 as the second production of the Irish Literary Theatre. Martyn's drama was heavily influenced by Ibsen's plays, and, like Ibsen, Martyn has a protagonist in an unhappy marriage confronting the inevitability of ruin. Carden Tyrrell is set on cultivating a heather field. He borrows large sums of money that he is unable to repay, and loses his mind.

In 1919, despite his ambivalence toward peasant drama, Joyce encouraged the ENGLISH PLAYERS to produce this in an effort to give greater exposure to Irish theater. Joyce wrote the program notes to this play; they were later published as "Programme Notes for the English Players" in *The Critical Writings of James Joyce.* Of the four program notes Joyce wrote, the one on Martyn's *The Heather Field* is by far the longest and most detailed.

**Henry, Rev. William, SJ** He was the rector of BELVEDERE COLLEGE under whom Joyce studied Latin. According to Joyce's biographer Peter Costello, Father Henry also directed the Sodality of Our Lady, to which James Joyce was admitted on December 7, 1895, and of which he was elected prefect, or head, on September 25, 1896. Father Henry also served as the model for Father Butler in the *Dubliners* story "An Encounter." See also Characters under A *Portrait of the Artist as a Young* Man.

**Hermetic Society** This was a Dublin society, made up of poets and writers, whose aim was to promote the study and practice of mysticism based on the body of occult doctrine associated with Hermes Trismegistus, a being identified by neo-Platonists and mystics with the Egyptian god Thoth; various mystical writings were attributed to him as early as the third century A.D. The Dublin Hermetic Society derived its name from a similar society in London; it should not be confused with the poetic movement called hermeticism in early 20th-century Italy. The Hermetic Society was formed in 1885 by Charles Johnston and others associated with the Irish Literary Revival. In 1886, it was superseded by the more famous Theosophical Society, but years later the poet AE (George RUSSELL) revived its name. Allusions to the Hermetic Society are made in the Aeolus and Scylla and Charybdis episodes.

**Homer** The name given to the eighth or ninth century B.C. Greek poet to whom authorship of *The ODYSSEY* and *The Iliad* is traditionally ascribed.

The Howth countryside, an important location in *Finnegans Wake* and *Ulysses* *(Irish Tourist Board)*

Nothing is known of his life or birthplace, or even if he actually existed. How and where these epic poems were composed, their possible oral sources, and their true authorship are disputed and may never be conclusively resolved. The view of the "unitarian" critics holds that each poem has a unity that can be attributed to a single artistic consciousness, though it does not necessarily follow that both poems were written by the same author (or authors). Notable differences exist between the poems. *The Odyssey,* for instance, possesses a much tighter structural integrity than *The Iliad.*

Homer's work holds a prominent place in Western literary tradition, and his influence was especially strong on 17th-, 18th-, and 19th-century English writers, of whom Joyce was an intellectual heir. Joyce's indebtedness, however, differs from those of other artists. To suit his artistic purposes, Joyce took the universal and perennial themes of *The Odyssey* and shaped them into a modern epic. Structural techniques such as the flashback, assimilation of songs into the text, and multiple or parallel lines of action, all found in *The Odyssey,* can also be found in Joyce's *Ulysses.* Further, the *Ulysses* SCHEMA developed by Joyce as an organizational plan for the novel contains key words designating dominant themes of each chapter (see *Ulysses* schema in the appendix on page 392). These underscore his use of Homer's *Odyssey* within each episode and remind readers of the larger structural parallels between Joyce's work and Homer's.

**Horace** (65–8 B.C.) He was a Roman satirist and lyric poet whose *Ars Poetica (Art of Poetry)* heavily influenced neoclassical writers in English during the 18th century. See "O fons Bandusiae" under Miscellaneous Writing.

**Howth** This is the name of a peninsula several miles northeast of DUBLIN on the northern part of

Dublin Bay. It is the site of Howth Castle and of BEN (hill) OF HOWTH, a hill over 555 feet high with an ancient cairn on top.

Howth and, more particularly, associations by Bloom and Molly with it play a prominent role in *Ulysses.* They both think of the rhododendrons at HOWTH CASTLE. In the Lestrygonians episode (chapter 8) Leopold Bloom, while in DAVY BYRNE'S PUB, is reminded of the time he and Molly first kissed on Ben of Howth. In the Penelope episode, Molly recalls the same incident, remembering how she got Bloom to propose to her. In the Nausikaa episode, the Hill of Howth provides the background to the action.

*Finnegans Wake* opens with an allusion to "Howth Castle and Environs" (*FW* 3.3). The initials of these words provide the first reference to the work's hero, Humphrey Chimpden Earwicker (H C E) and suggest Earwicker's identification with the Dublin landscape and with the sleeping giant FINN MACCOOL, whose head is said to form the Hill of Howth. (His feet form the hills near PHOENIX PARK.) As the chapter proceeds, this identification becomes more apparent. In a November 1926 letter, which contains a version of the opening paragraph of the *Wake,* Joyce explained key words to Harriet Shaw WEAVER and stated that Howth is pronounced "Hoaeth" and comes from the Danish *Hoved,* meaning "head" (*Letters,* I.247).

**Howth Castle** Since 1177, it has been the home of the St. Lawrence family. The present castle was built in 1564, and much of it was reconstructed in the 18th century. It is located on the HOWTH peninsula, north of Dublin Bay. Its gardens are open to the public. In the third line of *Finnegans Wake,* Joyce refers to "Howth Castle and Environs," which is also the setting for the story of the

Howth Castle *(Irish Tourist Board)*

Prankquean and Jarl van Hoother found in *Finnegans Wake* (21.5–23.15). This story is based on the legend of the 16th-century Irish pirate, Grace O'Malley (see synopsis of *FW* I.1 [3–29] in the *Finnegans Wake* entry), who stopped at the castle for lodging when the earl of Howth was having dinner. Refused entry, she kidnapped the earl's son and kept him until the earl promised that the castle doors would always remain open during dinner.

**Huebsch, B. W.** (1876–1964) Huebsch was a well-known New York editor and publisher. After working as a lithographer and studying art in the evening at Cooper Union, he opened a publishing house in 1902 and began a successful business. In 1925 the firm merged with the newly founded VIKING PRESS. Huesbch brought to Viking a backlist that included D. H. Lawrence and Sherwood Anderson as well as Joyce.

Huebsch was the American publisher of many of Joyce's works: *Chamber Music* (1918), *Dubliners* (1916, 1917), *A Portrait of the Artist as a Young Man* (1916), *Exiles* (1918), and "A Curious History (1917); he also published Herbert GORMAN's *James Joyce: His First Forty Years* (1924). In April 1921, Joyce withdrew *Ulysses* from B. W. Huebsch (see *Letters* III.40) because, after the outcome of the LITTLE *REVIEW* trial in February 1921, the publisher wanted changes made in the text. Joyce's working relationship with Huebsch, however, was much more productive and congenial than it had been with previous publishers, and it was through Huebsch that Joyce's works were eventually published by the Viking Press. To show his appreciation to Huebsch, Joyce stipulated in his contract with Viking for *Finnegans Wake* that:

> If at any time during the continuance of this agreement Mr. B. W. Huebsch should sever his connection with the said Viking Press and either set up publishing on his own account or acquire interest in another firm of publishers than the Viking Press, then the said Author shall have the option of transferring the benefits of this contract to such new firm.

This provision in Joyce's contract was never invoked. For Huebsch's comments on his publishing the works of Joyce, see "Oral History: B. W. Huebsch," edited by A. Nicholas Fargnoli, *Dictionary of Literary Biography Yearbook: 1999*, pp. 193–219.

**Hunter (Alfred H.)** This is the name of a Dubliner known to the Joyce family who was the model for the central character in an unwritten short story Joyce planned to call "*Ulysses*" and add to the *Dubliners* collection. The idea for the story came to Joyce while he was in Rome in the fall of 1906. In a postscript to a letter to his brother Stanislaus, Joyce wrote: "I have a new story for Dubliners in my head. It deals with Mr. Hunter" (*Letters,* II.168). That December, Joyce asked Stanislaus for information about Hunter (see *Letters,* II.198). According to Richard ELLMANN, Joyce "frequently said in later life" that "his book *Ulysses* had its beginnings in Rome" and that the otherwise unidentified Hunter was "rumoured to be Jewish and to have an unfaithful wife" (*Letters,* II.168n.4).

# I

**Ibsen, Henrik** (1828–1906) Ibsen was a Norwegian dramatist, widely acknowledged as the first great modern playwright. Ibsen's emphasis on psychological drama in his plays from *Brand* (1866) through *When We Dead Awaken* (1899) radically reconstituted contemporary expectations about dramatic form.

As early as his student days at BELVEDERE COLLEGE, Joyce demonstrated an outspoken enthusiasm for Ibsen's plays and for the reconsideration of artistic premises that these works demanded. Despite the intellectual conservatism of the school, Joyce sustained this ardor throughout his years at UNIVERSITY COLLEGE, DUBLIN. On January 20, 1900, Joyce read before the LITERARY AND HISTORICAL SOCIETY of University College an essay entitled "Drama and Life," which showed the impact upon him of Ibsen and of advanced continental artistic thinking generally.

In this work Joyce strove to distinguish drama from other forms of literature and, profoundly shocking his conservative listeners, set the figure of the dramatist outside the conventional moral strictures by which middle-class audiences judged theatrical efforts. The paper caused a predictable furor, but this was nothing compared to the astonishment of his teachers and classmates when the prestigious London journal *FORTNIGHTLY REVIEW* published an essay by Joyce entitled *Ibsen's New Drama* in its April 1, 1900, issue. (Joyce was paid 12 guineas for this essay.) The essay focused on Ibsen's latest play, *When We Dead Awaken,* and much to Joyce's delight, it led to recognition from Ibsen (who sent his thanks via his English translator William ARCHER) and to a three-year correspondence with Archer, who did a great deal to encourage Joyce's early artistic efforts. (In 1930, the essay was reprinted in book form by the Ulysses Book Shop, London.)

As Joyce matured as an artist and found his own voice, he drew upon Ibsen less for creative encouragement than for psychological inspiration. In Joyce's mind, Ibsen remained the model of the artist who defies conventional creative approaches and who remains true to the demands of an individual aesthetic. Thus, although one finds Ibsen's social concerns and psychological realism subsumed by other features in Joyce's work, in a subtle and lasting way Ibsen remained a presence throughout Joyce's intellectual life. (See *Letters,* I.51–52; II.3–4, 7, 81–84, 86, 91, 104–105, 146, 157, 166–167, 182–183, 187, 191, 196, 201, 205, and 366; and III.55,389–391, and 453.)

**Icarus** This is the name of a figure in Greek mythology, the son of DAEDALUS, the fabulous artificer described by OVID in the *Metamorphoses.* When told by King Minos that he would not be permitted to leave the island of Crete, Daedalus fashioned two pairs of wax wings with feathers, one for himself and one for Icarus, to use to escape. The wings successfully carried them away from the island, but Icarus, ignoring his father's instructions, became intoxicated by the thrill of flying, and foolishly ventured too close to the sun. The wax wings melted, and Icarus fell into the sea and drowned.

In *A Portrait of the Artist as a Young Man* (and to a lesser extent in both *Stephen Hero* and in *Ulysses*) Stephen Dedalus reflects the dual characteristics of Icarus and Daedalus. With his artistic ambitions, Stephen aspires to the status of fabulous artificer, but his inexperience and enthusiasm cause him to reach beyond his capabilities and in consequence to fall short of his goal. Although mentioned specifically only once in Joyce's work (*Ulysses* 9.953), Icarus hovers over the narratives of both *A Portrait of the Artist as a Young Man* and *Ulysses* as an image of the danger that an immature artist must face. The irony of Stephen's bearing the name of the father while all too often replicating the failings of the son typifies the way Joyce explores issues like creativity, paternity, and artistic achievement; that is, it introduces multiple perspectives to complicate what might in other hands have been a clear-cut, linear narrative.

**imagist movement** This was a literary group defined and created by Ezra POUND between 1909 and 1918 to provide a broad and coherent intellectual basis for the aesthetic assumptions characterizing the type of poetry that held his interest at the time. Much like the romantics of the previous century, the imagists generally sought to write poetry that used the language of common speech, to avoid clichés and find instead precise words to convey meaning. Imagists also wished to create new rhythms with which to convey their new poetic mood, and to exercise absolute freedom in their choice of subjects. And finally, they strove to present images—definite pictures, often harsh in their outlines—believing that these were the very essence of poetry. Though the movement per se no longer exists, its goal of conveying an image in poetry without any real concern for meter remains popular.

Although Pound freely applied the term to others, such as Richard Aldington and H. D. (Hilda Doolittle), he broke away from the movement after a quarrel with Amy Lowell, ridiculing what she practiced as "Amygism." The imagist movement, however, provided the basis for Pound's contact with Joyce, when Pound sought and obtained permission to publish a poem from *Chamber Music*, "I Hear an Army," in his 1914 poetry anthology entitled *Des Imagistes*. At the same time, while features in Joyce's early work seemed to coincide with the imagist credo, Joyce's determination to push those ideas to the limit—in, for example, the outhouse scene at the end of the Calypso episode (chapter 4) of *Ulysses*—caused a break with the aesthetically more conservative Pound.

**interior monologue** This term designates a narrative technique that seeks to evoke for the reader a sense of the thought process in the mind of a character. Interior monologue represents the consciousness through a succession of images and concepts unimpeded by logical transitions, syntactical and grammatical accuracy, or sequential cognitive development. The seemingly anarchic structure of interior monologue places greater demands upon a reader's attention and interpretive skills than do more conventional narrative approaches, but it also affords a more intimate representation of character.

Instances of this technique appear in Joyce's writings as early as *Dubliners* (in the opening paragraph of "The Sisters" and the last paragraphs of "The Dead," for example) and *A Portrait of the Artist as a Young Man* (at consistent intervals throughout the narrative, from the Baby Tuckoo episode that opens the book to the diary passages at the end of chapter 5). Interior monologue is a dominant stylistic feature in *Ulysses*. At various points the narrative represents through this technique the ruminations of Stephen Dedalus, Leopold Bloom, and Molly Bloom. The longest sustained example of interior monologue occurs in the Penelope episode (chapter 18), where the entire chapter is given over to Molly Bloom's inner thoughts. Because of its radical narrative forms, interior monologue has proven to be more difficult to discern in *Finnegans Wake*. Nonetheless, it remains a part of Joyce's creative process there as well. (See for example the opening pages of I.7.) According to Joyce, Valéry Larbaud coined the term *interior monologue*; see Joyce's November 19, 1923, letter to Harriet Shaw Weaver (*Letters*, III.83; also see George Moore's letter to Joyce in *Letters*, III.197). For an analogous yet distinct narrative method, see STREAM OF CONSCIOUSNESS.

**International James Joyce Foundation** Formerly known as the James Joyce Foundation, it is a scholarly organization founded in 1967 (at the First International James Joyce Symposium, held in Dublin) by Bernard BENSTOCK, Fritz SENN, and Thomas F. STALEY to promote Joyce studies internationally. The foundation acts as the coordinating body for the biennial James Joyce Symposia, and it publishes the JAMES JOYCE NEWESTLATTER (formerly the *James Joyce Foundation Newsletter*), a publication providing its members with information on Joyce scholarship, conferences, symposia, and related matters.

**Invincibles, the** This is the name of a 19th-century Irish radical republican terrorist organization. Known also as the Irish National Invincibles or the Invincible Society, it was a breakaway group from the Irish Republican Brotherhood, founded in 1881 during the Land League agitation. On May 6, 1882, the Invincibles carried out the PHOENIX PARK MURDERS, killing the newly arrived chief secretary for Ireland, Lord Frederick Cavendish, and his undersecretary, Thomas Henry Burke, an act condemned by the Irish nationalist statesman Charles Stewart PARNELL. In January 1883, 17 Invincibles were arrested by British authorities and in June of that year five of them—Joe Brady, Daniel Curley, Tim Kelly, Michael Fagan, and Thomas Caffrey—were executed. James Carey, who had informed against them, was subsequently murdered by another Invincible, Patrick O'Donnell, on July 29, 1883, on board the *Melrose* shortly after the ship left Cape Town for Natal. O'Donnell was brought back to England and hanged for this crime on November 17, 1883. No further terrorist incidents attributed to the Invincibles occurred after this date.

The proprietor of the cabman's shelter in the Eumaeus episode of *Ulysses* is reputed to be James "Skin-the-Goat" Fitzharris, one of the Invincibles who participated in the Phoenix Park murders.

***Irish Homestead, The*** This was a weekly Dublin newspaper, founded in 1895 and associated with the Irish Agricultural Co-operative Movement. In 1923 it merged with the *Irish Statesman*. In 1904, George RUSSELL (AE) invited Joyce to submit work for possible publication in the paper, then edited by H. F. Norman. (A year later Russell took over as editor, a post he would hold until the 1923 merger.) Joyce rapidly responded with a series of short stories, early versions of works that would later form part of *Dubliners*. The *Irish Homestead* subsequently published "The Sisters" (August 13, 1904), "Eveline" (September 10, 1904), and "After the Race" (December 17, 1904), but Russell declined to use "Clay" and discouraged Joyce from further submissions. In *Ulysses* it is referred to as Pigs' paper (*U* 9.321).

**Irish Literary Revival** This is the name given to a literary movement that began late in the 19th century and remained a significant force shaping the direction of Irish writing into the second decade of the 20th century. The revival coincided with the emergence of figures such as George RUSSELL (AE), William Butler YEATS, Lady Augusta GREGORY, and John Millington SYNGE to national and international eminence, and played a material part in the development of their reputations.

While these figures and others were talented individually, they also understood the literary and political potential of the growing interest in Irish language and indigenous culture. There emerged a pronounced link between the practice of art (especially literature) and the nationalist movement. With the reintroduction by Standish O'Grady and others of heroic legends and mythological tales, authors and readers came to recognize the creative and political potential in the Irish culture. This awareness quickly spread beyond literature to take in the range of the Irish folk tradition, including arts, crafts, and sports.

While Lady Gregory actively nurtured the intellectual climate necessary to sustain this interest through her own transcriptions and adaptations of Irish folklore and tales—as well as through her considerable financial assistance—others, Synge in particular, drew upon the lives of contemporary Irish peasants as a rich source for artistic expression. Other literary figures, such as Padraic COLUM, Austin Clarke, James Starkey (Seamus O'Sullivan), Oliver St. John GOGARTY, and James STEPHENS, are also identified with the movement. The failure of the 1916 Easter Rising signaled the end of the revival, although a number of writers who had been influenced by it—most notably Lennox Robinson and Sean O'Casey—gained artistic recognition in the late 1910s and the 1920s.

Although Joyce himself briefly took Irish language lessons, he generally dissociated himself from the revival and its nationalistic preference for Irish art over all else simply because of its native origin. At various places in his writings, Joyce offers diverse views of the revival. While these views were not completely unsympathetic, they show his keen awareness of its artistic and intellectual limitations. "A Mother," for example, clearly demonstrates the ease with which individuals such as Mrs. Kearney and to a lesser extent her daughter Kathleen Kearney subordinated the idealistic aims of the revival to personal ambition and advancement. Joyce's depiction of the young nationalist Davin, Stephen Dedalus's classmate, in *A Portrait of the Artist as a Young Man,* reflects a highly sympathetic view of an individual committed to the nationalistic sentiments of the revival, but it also raises genuine questions about the sincerity of a broad segment of supporters of the movement. And, in the figure of the Citizen in the Cyclops episode (chapter 12) of *Ulysses,* Joyce offers a penetrating and acerbic portrait of the corruption that results from the combination of rabid, mindless nationalism and vague allegiance to the aims of the revival.

**Irish Literary Theatre** See ABBEY THEATRE.

***Irish Times*** This was and remains a leading Irish daily newspaper, published in Dublin. In Joyce's time it had the reputation of being unflinchingly pro-British. While he was away in Paris from 1902 to 1903, Joyce repeatedly tried to earn money by selling articles on Paris and Parisian life to this paper. The April 7, 1903, issue carried his essay "The Motor Derby: Interview with the French Champion (from a correspondent)," which focused on Henri Fournier, the leading contender for the James Gordon Bennett Cup, an automobile race to be held in Dublin that July. The article provided Joyce with background that he would incorporate into his *Dubliners* story "After the Race." After he had left Ireland permanently, Joyce relied on the *Irish Times* as a source of information about Ireland.

**Iseult** She is the young and very beautiful Irish princess who, according to medieval legend, was betrothed to King Mark of Cornwall. After inadvertently drinking a love potion that was meant to be used to ensure her fidelity to her future husband, Iseult and Sir Tristan, the knight sent by King Mark to escort her across the Irish Sea to Cornwall, fall tragically in love with one another. The tragedy of their love and of King Mark's jealousy is a recurring theme in western European literature, particularly in works by Mallory, Wagner, and Tennyson (see TRISTAN AND ISOLDE). Iseult is the same figure for whom Chapelizod—the Chapel of Iseult, an area of western Dublin—is named. In *Finnegans Wake,* Joyce uses Iseult as one of the central models for the character of Issy. As a woman of fatal beauty with a seductiveness she can neither avoid nor control, she sets up the possibility for both straightforward and ironic analogues to Issy, the daughter of Humphrey Chimpden Earwicker, which greatly enhance the multiplicity of Issy's nature.

***Isis Unveiled*** This is the title of a book outlining the fundamental tenets of Theosophical belief, written by Helena Petrovna BLAVATSKY in 1877. *Isis Unveiled* was Blavatsky's first book, and it offered what was to become a highly popular introduction to THEOSOPHY. In it Blavatsky criticizes contemporary science and religion, and as an alternative to these disciplines offers the Theosophical contention that mysticism is the best way to attain true spiritual insight. Although no solid evidence exists that Joyce read this work, Joyce's curiosity about Theosophy and the book's popularity make it likely that Joyce was at the very least familiar with its contents.

**Ivy Day** This is the name given to a day once informally observed as the anniversary of the death (October 6, 1891) of the Irish statesman Charles Stewart PARNELL, the late 19th-century champion of the cause of Home Rule for Ireland. In remembrance of the occasion, Parnellites would wear a sprig of ivy on their coat collars. (Very few people in modern Ireland continue the commemoration of Ivy Day.) The custom and the day are touchstones for the central concerns of Joyce's *Dubliners* story "Ivy Day in the Committee Room," which examines the motives and character of Irish politics, from hypocrisy to idealism.

# J

**Jacobsen, Jens Peter** (1847–1885) Jacobsen was a Danish poet and novelist who introduced the techniques of NATURALISM to Danish literature. He subsequently gained prominence as the movement's best-known exponent in Denmark. Jacobsen exemplifies the type of writer whom the young Joyce admired and sought to emulate, and Joyce refers to him in his early essay "The Day of the Rabblement" (1901), in which Joyce illustrates the limitations of contemporary Irish literature by contrasting the innovative prose of Jacobsen's style with the more pedestrian efforts of George MOORE. After he left Ireland Joyce continued to read Jacobsen, and he had a copy of an English translation of Jacobsen's second novel, *Siren Voices (Niels Lyhne)*, in his Trieste library. Evidence from his correspondence indicates that he first read the book early in 1905. (See *Letters*, II.83.)

***James Joyce Archives*** This is the term used to identify Joyce's unpublished notebooks, manuscripts, typescripts, corrected proofs, and other prepublication material published in facsimile form in 63 volumes between 1977 and 1980 by GARLAND PUBLISHING, INC. under the general editorship of Michael GRODEN. This project contains draft material held at 21 research institutions and in several private collections including the State University of New York at Buffalo, Cornell University, Yale University, University of Texas at Austin, the British Library, the NATIONAL LIBRARY OF IRELAND, the Rosenbach Foundation, and others. Though some manuscript material is not present, like the Rosenbach holograph copy of *Ulysses* or some of the material held by private collectors, these volumes nonetheless represent an extremely important gathering of Joyce's prepublication material. For further information on Joyce manuscript holdings, see Michael Groden, comp., *James Joyce's Manuscripts: An Index*, pp. 73–105.

***James Joyce Broadsheet*** This is the name of a journal founded at University College, London, in 1980 by Richard Brown and Pieter Bekker. It continues to appear three times a year, and devotes itself primarily to reviews and occasional essays on Joyce, his work, and related topics. The journal has been published at Leeds University since 1984.

**James Joyce Foundation** See INTERNATIONAL JAMES JOYCE FOUNDATION.

***James Joyce Literary Supplement*** This is a scholarly journal founded at the University of Miami in 1987 by Bernard BENSTOCK and Zack BOWEN. Issued twice a year by the university's Department of English Graduate Program, the *James Joyce Literary Supplement* is committed to reviewing books related to Joyce and his work within six months of their publication. It also publishes short pieces on Joycean topics and events of interest.

***James Joyce Miscellany, A*** This was the title of a scholarly journal founded by Marvin Magalaner under the sponsorship of the JAMES JOYCE SOCIETY in 1957. It appeared in three volumes. The first series (1957) was published by the James Joyce Society. The second (1959) and third series (1962) were published by Southern Illinois University Press. A *James Joyce Miscellany* gave a tremendous boost to Joyce studies in the late 1950s and early 1960s. By presenting the work of well-known and highly respected Joyce scholars, including John J. SLOCUM, Herbert CAHOON, and Richard KAIN, it offered readers a sense of the diversity and achievement of contemporary Joyce scholarship. It also provided an important outlet for younger scholars whose work proved influential in the following decades.

**James Joyce Museum** See MARTELLO TOWER.

***James Joyce Newestlatter*** This is the name of the newsletter of the INTERNATIONAL JAMES JOYCE FOUNDATION, formerly titled the *James Joyce Foundation Newsletter.* It appears twice a year, with an additional issue in even-numbered years, when there is an international symposium. The *James Joyce Newestlatter* offers detailed information about current symposia and conferences devoted to Joyce, his canon, and associated topics. It also makes available selected information on the research and the publications of foundation members and on general cultural and scholarly events of interest to its readers. *Newsletter* no. 1 was published on October 20, 1969, under the editorship of Bernard BENSTOCK. Morris BEJA took over the editorship in November 1977 with issue no. 24. The name was changed to *James Joyce Newestlatter* with the September 1989 issue.

***James Joyce Quarterly*** This is the oldest continuously published scholarly journal devoted to Joyce and his work to appear on a regular basis. It was founded at the University of Tulsa in 1963 by Thomas F. STALEY. In short order the journal established itself as the most important source available of contemporary Joyce criticism. It publishes essays, notes, book reviews, letters, and bibliographies related to the study of Joyce and his work. The *James Joyce Quarterly* has published special issues devoted to selected topics of particular interest to Joyce scholars—critical theory, individual works, biography, or associated topics.

Since its inception, the *James Joyce Quarterly* has exerted perhaps the strongest and most enduring influence of any institution on the development of Joyce scholarship. It has offered timely encouragement to younger scholars while at the same time highlighting the work of established critics. It has fostered inquiry into evolving theoretical methods, from post-structuralism through feminism, Lacanian psychoanalysis, gender studies, and cultural criticism. Further, it has provided a platform for wide-ranging, often freewheeling argument on a variety of Joycean subjects, including a long-running debate on the value of various approaches to editing Joyce's texts.

***James Joyce Review*** This was the first regularly appearing journal of Joyce studies. It was founded by Edmund L. EPSTEIN, who brought out the first issue on February 2, 1957; the third and last issue was published in 1959. Like A *JAMES JOYCE MISCELLANY,* the *James Joyce Review* offered an important outlet in the 1950s for first-rate scholarship and criticism of Joyce and his canon at a time when the demand for such work far exceeded available outlets for it. *James Joyce Review* also encouraged emerging scholars by promising a venue for their research. Although the *James Joyce Review* remained in existence for only a little more than two years, it clearly set in motion a series of events—the founding of the *JAMES JOYCE QUARTERLY,* the institution of biennial Joyce symposia, and the establishment of the JAMES JOYCE FOUNDATION—that would lead to the rapid development of Joyce scholarship and criticism in the 1960s.

**James Joyce Society** This organization, established in February 1947 at the GOTHAM BOOK MART in New York City, signaled the beginning of the post–World War II surge of interest in James Joyce and his writings. Its members still regularly meet there (though the Gotham has moved its location twice since the society's founding) to hear scholarly addresses and to discuss topics relevant to Joyce and his works. T. S. ELIOT was the society's first member. John J. SLOCUM was its first president, succeeded by Padraic COLUM. Frances Steloff, founder and owner of the Gotham Book Mart, served as the society's first treasurer. According to W. G. Rogers, author of *Wise Men Fish Here: The Story of Frances Steloff and the Gotham Book Mart,* the James Joyce Society originally "aimed to introduce Joyce students to scholars, maintain a Joyce library, further the publication and distribution of his works, encourage the presentation of *Exiles,* and issue occasional bulletins." Since 1947, the James Joyce Society has expanded both its goals and its membership. Recent programs have encompassed a wide range of topics relating to Joyce's life, his work, and the writings of his contemporaries, and the society's meetings remain an important venue for any Joyce scholar. (For further information, see the society's Web site: joycesociety.org.)

***James Joyce's The Dead*** This is the title of a musical adaptation of the *Dubliners* story. It was written by Richard Nelson and Shaun Davey. It opened off Broadway in 1999 with Christopher Walken starring as Gabriel Conroy. It was moved to Broadway and won a Tony for Best Book.

**Jesuits** See SOCIETY OF JESUS.

**Joachim Abbas** (c. 1130–1202) Joachim of Flora (sometimes *Fiore* or *Floris*) was an Italian mystic, priest, abbot, and founder of the Abbey of San Giovanni in Flora, Calabria. Joachim believed that there were three epochs of world history: the past, ruled by the Father and identified with the Old Testament; the present, the age of the Son, ruled by the Catholic Church; and a future age of universal love, governed by the Holy Spirit. For this and other heretical ideas, he was condemned by the Fourth Lateran Council in 1215.

Joachim exerted a profound, if subtle, influence upon Joyce's artistic views. As early as 1904, Joyce alludes to him as Joachim Abbas rather than Joachim of Flora in both "A Portrait of the Artist" and his novel *Stephen Hero.* The term *abbas,* employed in transliteration in the Septuagint and the Greek New Testament, derives from an Aramaic root meaning "father," and it appears in Late Latin as a reference to the superior or spiritual father of a monastic community, the abbot, the *patria potestas* in Roman law. This is thought to be a significant clue to the importance of the theme of fatherhood in Joyce's writings and artistic vision. Stephen Dedalus's phrase that paternity is "a mystical estate" in the Scylla and Charybdis episode of *Ulysses* echoes an idea identified with Joachim. Joachim is clearly in the thoughts of Stephen Dedalus in the Proteus episode and again in the Wandering Rocks episode. The posthumously published *Giacomo Joyce* (1968, composed c. 1914) also contains a passage in which Joachim's name is listed along with those of the 18th-century Swedish scientist and mystic philosopher Emanuel Swedenborg and the 18th-century Spanish mystic Miguel de Molinos. In August 1906, when he was thinking of rewriting "A Painful Case," Joyce wrote to his brother Stanislaus asking him to send "the Latin quotations from the prophecies of the Abbot Joachim of Flora" (*Letters,* II.148). He did not, however, incorporate any references to Joachim into this short story.

**Joachim of Flora** See JOACHIM ABBAS.

**John Jameson & Sons** This is the name of a Dublin-based company that distills Irish whiskey (colloquially known as Jameson's), established in Dublin in the 18th century. The distillery's Dublin location and Joyce's belief that Jameson used unfiltered water from the River LIFFEY as part of its distilling process account for the whiskey's use as a recurring motif in the fall and rise of Tim FINEGAN (and all others who rise and fall) throughout *Finnegans Wake.* Whiskey (in Irish, *usquebaugh*) means "water of life," an apt association with the Liffey—the river identified with Anna Livia Plurabelle, who symbolizes life-sustaining waters.

When entertaining the (ill-conceived) notion of having James STEPHENS finish writing *Finnegans Wake,* Joyce used the distillery's initials in a 1927 letter to Harriet Shaw WEAVER: "J J and S (the colloquial Irish for John Jameson and Son's Dublin whiskey) would be a nice lettering under the title" (*Letters,* I.253–254). See also *Letters,* III.161.

**Jolas, Eugene** (1894–1952) Jolas was an American writer and editor who with his wife, Maria

JOLAS, and Elliot PAUL founded *TRANSITION* (1927–30 and 1932–39), an experimental literary magazine that published, among other things, sections of *Finnegans Wake.*

Jolas was born in Union City, New Jersey, but relatively early in his life he became disillusioned with the industrial focus of American society. Shortly after his marriage to Maria in 1925, the couple moved to Paris, where Jolas was an editor with the *Paris Tribune.* Jolas soon became acquainted with Joyce through Sylvia BEACH, but it was only after a December 12, 1926, reading of an early version of the first section of *Finnegans Wake* (an event also attended by Maria Jolas, Paul, Beach, and Adrienne MONNIER) that their friendship solidified.

In addition to editing *transition,* Jolas was a poet (his best work was collected in *The Language of Night* 1932) and translator. Jolas also contributed to *OUR EXAGMINATION ROUND HIS FACTIFICATION FOR INCAMINATION OF WORK IN PROGRESS.* His essay, entitled "The Revolution of Language and James Joyce," defends Joyce's unconventional appropriation of words and images for *WORK IN PROGRESS,* as *Finnegans Wake* was then known. He begins by answering criticisms made by the Irish author Sean O'Faolain in a review of "Anna Livia Plurabelle," which had been published in October 1928. Jolas goes on to offer several examples of how one might read Joyce's prose. He later assisted in the translation of "Anna Livia Plurabelle" into French, taking over from Samuel BECKETT, who had begun the task. This appeared in the May 1, 1931, issue of *Nouvelle Revue Francaise.* Jolas had the distinction in 1938 of being the one finally to guess the title of *Finnegans Wake,* which Joyce had kept as a closely guarded secret.

In addition to their close professional relationship, Jolas and his wife had strong personal ties to Joyce and his family. They were particularly supportive during the 1930s and the worsening of the mental illness of Lucia JOYCE, and in 1940 when the Joyces fled Paris to escape the German occupation. For additional details of the Jolas-Joyce friendship, see *Letters,* I.280, 313, 323, 325, 326, 348, 357, 363, 372, 409, 410, and 419–420; and III.148n.7, 153, 209n.8, 247n.3, 249n.3, 250–251, 254–255, 302, 306–307, 320, 359, 410, 411, 420, 423, 426, and 427.

**Jolas, Maria** (1893–1987) She was an American expatriate living in Paris who, with her husband, Eugene JOLAS, and their friend Elliot PAUL, founded *TRANSITION* (1927–30 and 1932–39), an experimental literary magazine that printed a number of episodes from *Finnegans Wake,* then known as *WORK IN PROGRESS,* from April 1927 through April–May 1938.

Maria Jolas (née McDonald) was born in Louisville, Kentucky, a great-grandniece of Thomas Jefferson. After her marriage to Eugene Jolas in 1925, the couple moved to Paris where her husband had a job as an editor at the *Paris Tribune.* There she met Joyce, with whom her husband had already become acquainted through Sylvia BEACH, on December 12, 1926, at a reading of an early version of the first section of *Finnegans Wake.*

Maria Jolas provided a great deal of emotional support for the Joyce family during the progressively worsening mental breakdown of Joyce's daughter, Lucia. She also provided invaluable help through the various stages of the production of *Finnegans Wake.* Between the Joyces' flight from Paris in December 1939 and their eventual move to Switzerland in December 1940, Maria Jolas helped them settle into the life of the village of SAINT-GÉRAND-LE-PUY in unoccupied France. In addition to her work on *transition* and her help with *Finnegans Wake,* Maria Jolas translated works by Nathalie Sarraute, Hugo von Hofmannsthal, and Gaston Bachelard. For additional details of her friendship with the Joyces, see *Letters,* I.323, 325, 331, 342, 352, 359, 372, 374, 381, 410, and 419–420; and III.148, 247n.3, 249n.3, 302, 306–307, 309, 316, 346, 352, 366–370, 377, 400, 411, 434, 458n.2, 461, 465, 472, and 484.

**Joyce Archives** See JAMES JOYCE ARCHIVES.

**Joyce, George [Giorgio]** (1905–1976) He was the first child and only son of James Joyce, born in TRIESTE on July 27, 1905, and named after Joyce's younger brother, who had died in Dublin in 1902. (Although he was given the Italian version of the name, Giorgio, at birth, he came to prefer being called George.) With his sister, Lucia JOYCE, George grew up in a home that was at times chaotic but nonetheless solidly bourgeois in character. The family often lived in impoverished conditions and moved frequently during George's early childhood, the period when his father was struggling to complete *Dubliners* and *A Portrait of the Artist as a Young Man* while earning a precarious living as a language teacher. Despite these strained material circumstances, biographical evidence indicates that George enjoyed a relatively normal childhood and that he was a great favorite of his indulgent father.

When the Austro-Hungarian authorities forced the Joyce family to leave Trieste for neutral Switzerland in 1915, the 10-year-old George was held back two grades in his school in ZURICH because he knew no German. Although he did become a champion swimmer while in Zurich, the disruption of his education caused by World War I had a pronounced negative effect on George. The family returned briefly to Trieste from October 1919 to July 1920, and this period marked the final phase of George's formal schooling. At the same time, Joyce and Nora encouraged their son to study music, and whenever possible they assisted his efforts to cultivate his considerable talent as a singer.

After the Joyce family moved to Paris in 1920, George took a job as a clerk in a bank, but he maintained his interest in singing and eventually decided to pursue a full-time musical career. He made his concert debut as a bass in Paris on April 25, 1929. Around the same time, he began a courtship with Helen Kastor Fleischman, an American divorcée 10 years his senior. The two were married on December 10, 1930, and on February 15, 1932, Helen gave birth to their only child, Stephen James Joyce, an event commemorated by George's father in the poem, "Ecce Puer."

In the mid-1930s, George and his wife frequently journeyed back and forth between Europe and America, as George tried to advance his singing career. Despite the many separations from his father that this travel entailed, the two remained close. Near the end of the decade, Helen Joyce's behavior became increasingly erratic and uncontrollable, and by 1939 she and George were living apart. By the end of that year her mental condition required hospitalization, and in May 1940, with the war complicating matters, she

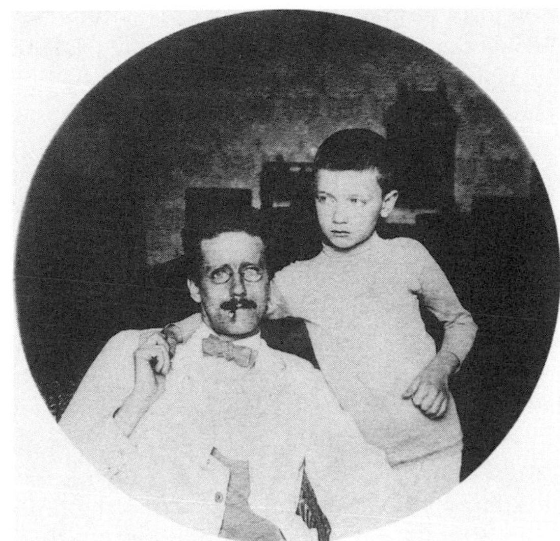

Joyce with his son, George, in Trieste, 1915

returned to the United States with her brother, Robert Kastor.

George stayed in Paris until the Germans occupied the city, and then he joined his father and mother in SAINT-GÉRAND-LE-PUY, the French village where they had taken refuge. In mid-December he traveled with his parents and his son Stephen to Zurich, Switzerland, where his father died a month later. George remained in Zurich with his mother until her death in 1951. After divorcing Helen Joyce, he married Dr. Asta Jahnke-Osterwalder in 1954, and the couple settled in Munich. George lived in Germany until his death on June 12, 1976, in Konstanz.

**Joyce, Mrs. James** See BARNACLE, NORA.

**Joyce, John Stanislaus (senior)** (1849–1931) John Stanislaus Joyce was James Joyce's father. The elder Joyce was born on July 4, 1849, of a well-to-do family in Cork and educated at St. Colman's College in Fermoy before going on to study medicine, briefly, at QUEEN'S COLLEGE, CORK. He was a popular and active student, but not particularly attentive to his studies, and he left in 1870 after his third year, without a degree. In the mid-1870s,

John Joyce went to live in Dublin. For a short time he held the position of secretary at the Dublin and Chapelizod Distilling Company. Later he became involved in Dublin politics, which led to his eventual employment in the Office of the Collector of Rates (i.e., property taxes).

In 1880 John Joyce married Mary Jane (May) Murray, and over the course of the next 13 years they had 10 children. The loss of political patronage brought about by the fall from power of Charles Stewart PARNELL and the simultaneous amalgamation of the Rates Office by the Dublin City Corporation in 1892 forced John Joyce out of his job. He received a small pension and, though he was only 43 at the time he was discharged, never held regular employment again. John Joyce did, however, take on occasional work as a solicitor's clerk (like Farrington in "Counterparts"), as a political hack (like the men in "Ivy Day in the Committee Room") and (like Leopold Bloom) as an advertising canvasser for the *FREEMAN'S JOURNAL*. In chapter 5 of *A Portrait of the Artist as a Young Man*, Stephen Dedalus sardonically chronicles for his friend Cranly the occupations and predilections of Simon Dedalus, John Joyce's fictional counterpart:

> A medical student, an oarsman, a tenor, an amateur actor, a shouting politician, a small landlord, a small investor, a drinker, a good fellow, a storyteller, somebody's secretary, something in a distillery, a taxgatherer, a bankrupt and at present a praiser of his own past. (p. 241)

Income derived from selling off what remained of the family property in Cork that John Joyce had inherited slowed his economic decline, but this period marked the beginning of the Joyce family's irreversible slide from a comfortable middle-class existence into subsistence-level poverty. As his financial situation worsened, so also did John Joyce's relations with his family. He drank heavily, verbally abused May Joyce and the children, and, on at least one occasion, physically attacked his wife. By the time of her death in 1903, the family was living in abject poverty with John Joyce making no genuine effort to hold things together. James was no longer living at home, and after their mother's death the older girls for a time took over responsibility for maintaining the house. In a relatively short time, however, the family had broken up.

Nonetheless, even after leaving Dublin in 1904 Joyce maintained close ties with his father, and John Joyce was delighted when his favorite son returned briefly to Dublin in 1909 with his grandson George. When Nora BARNACLE visited Dublin in 1912, the old man was equally pleased to see his granddaughter Lucia. Over the next two decades John Joyce continually expressed the hope that his son would again visit Dublin, but a variety of circumstances—World War I, the Irish War of Independence and subsequent Civil War, Joyce's recurring illnesses—prevented any such homecoming.

Despite all this, John Joyce retained a prominent place in his son's affections, and James tried to demonstrate those feelings in a variety of ways. In 1923, James commissioned the Irish painter Patrick Tuohy to paint a portrait of his father. In the late 1920s he several times sent friends to interview his father to gather general information about Irish life and popular culture James needed for *Finnegans Wake*. When James decided to marry in 1931 to secure rights of inheritance for George and Lucia, he chose to do so on July 4, his father's birthday. Later that same year, John Joyce became ill; he died on December 29, 1931. In response Joyce wrote "ECCE PUER," which commemorates both his father's death and the birth of his own grandson, Stephen, in February 1932. After his father died, James Joyce tried unsuccessfully to have a memorial bench erected in Dublin for him.

**Joyce, John Stanislaus (junior)** See JOYCE, STANISLAUS.

**Joyce, Mrs. John Stanislaus** See JOYCE, MARY JANE MURRAY.

**Joyce, Lucia** (1907–1982) She was the second child of James JOYCE and Nora BARNACLE. Lucia was born in TRIESTE on July 26, 1907, when Joyce was himself in the hospital suffering from rheumatic fever. Her schooling and domestic routine followed that of her brother, George, and both children coped as best they could with the irregularities that arose from the family's troubled financial condition and their status as foreigners living far from their native country.

In 1912 Nora brought Lucia to visit family in Dublin and in Galway, and within a short time they were joined by Joyce and George. In 1915 during World War I Lucia journeyed with her parents and brother to ZURICH after the local Austrian authorities compelled the family to leave Trieste. Like her brother, George, Lucia knew no German, and in consequence was forced to begin her education in Zurich by going back two grades in school. These setbacks, however, had little effect upon Joyce's view of his daughter. He was especially fond of Lucia and tended to spoil her.

Nonetheless, a note of discord was beginning to insinuate itself into the family's relations. By the time the Joyce family moved to PARIS in 1920, Lucia's behavior had become a matter of some concern to her parents. While she had not yet begun to demonstrate the mental illness that characterized her later life, certain erratic and disruptive tendencies were emerging. Doubtless, her parents chose to see many of the early signs of her illness as a temporary consequence of their somewhat nomadic existence for much of Lucia's early life. Certainly, both she and her brother felt the effects of sporadic schooling, which was often postponed until they could learn the language of the country to which their family had moved. Consequently, when in Paris she took an interest in dancing and during the late 1920s enjoyed some success in it, it may have seemed to Joyce and Nora that things had corrected themselves.

By 1929, however, instances of an agitated mental state were becoming increasingly difficult to ignore and would eventually force her institutionalization. Lucia's deteriorating condition was aggravated when in 1931 her affections for the young Samuel BECKETT, who frequently met at home with her father, were not reciprocated. (This led to a temporary rift between the two writers). But other factors contributed to her breakdown as well. Brenda Maddox speculates that George's marriage in December 1930 and his subsequent parenthood in February 1932 may have exacerbated Lucia's condition (see *Nora,* p. 279). In May of that year, Lucia was hospitalized for the first time, and for much of the decade the family searched for a physician who could help her. C. G. JUNG, the renowned Swiss psychologist, was consulted and agreed to work with her in 1934, but to no avail.

When World War II broke out, the sanatorium in Paris where Lucia was then being treated moved its patients to Pornichet in Brittany. After Paris fell to the advancing German army on June 14, 1940, Joyce determined to move his family to Switzerland. For the rest of the year he tried desperately to secure the travel papers that would allow Lucia to leave the country with them. Ultimately, he failed and Lucia had to be left behind when they moved to Zurich. After the war, Lucia was transferred to St. Andrew's Hospital in Northampton, England, where she remained until her death on December 12, 1982.

**Joyce, Mary Jane ("May") Murray** (1859–1903) She was Joyce's mother. She was born Mary Jane Murray in Dublin on May 15, 1859. Her father was an agent for wines and spirits. She met her future husband, John JOYCE, at the Church of the Three Patrons in Rathgar, where they both sang in the choir. They were married in 1880, and within a short time May Joyce was pregnant. Her first child died shortly after birth, but the next, James, was born in 1882, and nine other children followed in quick succession: Mary Alice ("Poppie") on January 18, 1884, Stanislaus JOYCE on December 17, 1884, Charles on July 24, 1886, George on July 4, 1887, Isabel on January 22, 1889, Mary Kathleen on January 18, 1890, Eva on October 26, 1891, Florence on November 8, 1892, and Mabel ("Baby") on November 27, 1893.

As John Joyce's finances deteriorated over the course of the 1890s, the burden of holding the family together, materially and spiritually, fell increasingly on May Joyce. The pressures brought about by such demands were nowhere greater than in her relations with her eldest child, James. As he grew to maturity, James felt the need to confide in his mother and to gain her approval for his artistic ambitions even as he openly challenged those institutions for which she had the deepest respect, especially the church. Although May Joyce tried very hard to offer her support for

James Joyce's mother, May Murray Joyce, drawn by Patrick Touhy *(Croessman Collection of James Joyce, Special Collections/Morris Library, Southern Illinois University)*

her son's creative aspirations, she found it difficult to reconcile her own beliefs with the growing disaffection for the Catholic Church so apparent in his reading and his writings.

Childbearing and poverty certainly weakened her health, and in 1903 she was diagnosed as having cancer. Joyce returned from Paris in April of that year to be with her. She lingered on throughout the spring and into the summer before lapsing into a coma and dying on August 13, 1903.

May Joyce was the model for Stephen Dedalus's mother in *A Portrait of the Artist as a Young Man,* as well as for her precursor in *Stephen Hero.* As Mrs. Daedalus in *Stephen Hero,* she and Stephen discuss IBSEN and religious faith in chapters 19 and 21, respectively.

The deep sorrow that Joyce felt over his mother's death found expression in Stephen Dedalus's mourning for his dead mother throughout *Ulysses.*

**Joyce, Nora** See BARNACLE, NORA.

**Joyce, P(atrick) W(eston)** (1827–1914) P. W. Joyce was an Irish linguistic scholar, born in Ballyorgan, County Limerick. He began his education in a hedge school, yet received a B.A. degree from Trinity College in 1861 and an M.A. in 1864. He went on to write *The Origin and History of Irish Names of Places* in three volumes (1869, 1875, and 1913). James Joyce alludes to this work in his satirical poem "Gas from a Burner." P. W. Joyce wrote more than a dozen other books as well. Although not related to him, James Joyce was nonetheless quite familiar with works by P. W. Joyce, which he put to good use in his own writings, including the extremely popular *English as We Speak It in Ireland* (1910), in which a number of the colloquial expressions that appear in Joyce's work are glossed.

**Joyce, Stanislaus (John Stanislaus Joyce, junior)** (1884–1955) He was James Joyce's younger brother, born on December 17, 1884. Although named after his father, throughout his life he went by the name Stanislaus—or the more familiar Stannie—especially as he became more estranged from his father. Throughout his childhood, Stanislaus Joyce was profoundly influenced by his older brother. The two spent much time together, and Stanislaus became James's confidant fairly early on. Although he did not enroll at CLONGOWES WOOD COLLEGE, possibly because the family already was experiencing financial troubles, he did attend BELVEDERE COLLEGE with his brother.

As James began to develop his artistic vision and articulate his opposition to Irish conventions and institutions, Stanislaus acted as a whetstone for his brother's ideas. Although Stannie lacked the imaginative flair of James the aspiring artist, he shared his brother's iconoclasm. As an adolescent, Stannie joined James in rebelling against the central Irish institutions of family, church, and nationalist politics. He lacked, however, James's joie de vivre, and he was particularly critical of his brother's drinking. Stanislaus recorded daily events in a diary that his brother James regularly read and mined for material for his own work. For example, many of the details that James later used for the character of James Duffy in "A Painful Case" come from Stanislaus's diary entries.

After leaving Belvedere, Stanislaus worked for a time as a clerk in an accounting office. After James eloped with Nora BARNACLE to the Continent, Stanislaus served as a reliable source of information on everyday Dublin life. He also acted as something of a local representative for James, doing what he could to forward his brother's literary aspirations. Nonetheless, James felt their separation keenly, and at his urging, Stanislaus left Dublin on October 20, 1905, to join James and his family in TRIESTE. Once there, Stanislaus took a position as a language instructor in the Berlitz School where his brother taught.

In a relatively short time, Stanislaus became a major financial support for the family, and he felt that he served as a moral curb to his brother's inclinations toward dissipation. Stannie also remained a sounding board for James's artistic work. At the same time, he came to develop his own interests, including an increasingly outspoken support for the irredentist movement, which sought the return of Italian enclaves in the Austro-Hungarian Empire, including Trieste, to Italy. After the outbreak of World War I, Stanislaus's pro-Italian political views drew the attention of the Austrian authorities, and on January 9, 1915, he was taken into government custody and interned for the rest of the war.

Near the end of 1918, Stanislaus returned to Trieste. James and his family—who during the war had gone to ZURICH, in neutral Switzerland, because of their British citizenship—also came back after the war's conclusion, and the extended family was reunited in 1919. It quickly became clear, however, that the old bonds between the brothers had weakened. Stanislaus sought to live a more independent life, while James was absorbed by the need to complete *Ulysses.* When in 1920 James left Trieste for PARIS, he and Stanislaus parted on decidedly cool terms, and their close relationship virtually ended. Over the years the brothers reconciled, but their lives moved along very different paths. Richard ELLMANN, whose biography often reflects sympathy for Stannie's perception of events, comments that Stanislaus felt his brother had taken advantage of him in Trieste. "Yet he had also been lifted away from ignominy in Dublin and given a career and an intellectual life. The debts were due and had been paid on both sides" (*James Joyce,* p. 482).

Despite his brother's departure, Stanislaus chose to remain in Trieste as a language teacher, and on August 13, 1928, he married a former student of his, Nelly Lichtensteiger. He deeply disapproved of James's work on *Finnegans Wake,* believing it to be a waste of his brother's talent. Nonetheless, he and his brother kept in contact until James's death. In the final years of his life Stanislaus became an invaluable source of information for Richard Ellmann's biography of his brother, and a volume of his own recollections—a portion of a projected larger work—was posthumously published in 1958 as *My Brother's Keeper.* Stanislaus Joyce died in Trieste on June 16, 1955, leaving his wife, Nelly, and a son, James, born on February 14, 1943.

**Joyce, Stephen** Joyce's grandson, Stephen, was born on February 15, 1932, the son of George JOYCE and Helen Kastor Fleischman. His grandfather, to

Stephen Joyce, Phillips Academy, Andover, Mass., 1950
*(Courtesy of Strother Purdy)*

commemorate this birth and the death the preceding December of his own father, wrote the poem "Ecce Puer." A letter his grandfather wrote to him (August 10, 1936, *Selected Letters*, pp. 382–384) was published as *The Cat and the Devil* (1964).

Stephen Joyce received his education in America at Phillips Academy and then at Harvard, where in 1951 he was roommates with two other grandsons of famous men, Paul Matisse and Sadruddin Aga Khan. On April 15, 1955, he married Solange Raytchine. For a number of years he worked for the Organization for Economic Cooperation and Development, the economic branch of the United Nations, and was active in and for francophone African countries. After his retirement he became fully involved as literary executor of his grandfather's estate.

***Joyce Studies Annual*** This was a scholarly journal founded in 1990 by Thomas STALEY (who had previously founded the *James Joyce Quarterly*) at the University of Texas and published by the University of Texas Press. As the preface to the first edition announced, the *Joyce Studies Annual* seeks to include material "devoted to all areas of Joyce scholarship from textual to cultural, from bibliographical to critical, from theoretical to biographical." To meet this goal the *Joyce Studies Annual* offered article-length studies, notes, and an annual bibliography of Joyce scholarship. It gave particular emphasis to analyses of the wealth of Joyce material held at the Humanities Research Center at the University of Texas in Austin. *Joyce Studies Annual* ceased publication in 2003. The editor, Thomas Staley, cited difficulties in receiving permission from the Joyce estate to publish Joyce material as the primary reason for this decision.

**Jung, Carl Gustav** (1875–1961) He was a Swiss medical psychologist, author, and an early follower of Sigmund Freud, whom he met in 1907. In 1912 Jung broke with Freud and later founded his own school of analytical psychology in ZURICH. Jung spent most of his life in Zurich, and died there on June 6, 1961.

Although Joyce maintained a skeptical view of psychological analysis throughout his life, while living in Trieste he purchased Jung's study *Die Bedeutung des Vaters für das Schicksal des Einzelnen* (The significance of the father in the destiny of the individual). While in Zurich during World War I, Joyce had a closer encounter with Jung. In 1918 a wealthy American living in Zurich, Edith Rockefeller McCormick, assumed the role of patron by settling an endowment of 12,000 Swiss francs on Joyce. The arrangement lasted for about a year and a half until Mrs. McCormick, who had become fascinated by Jung's work, pressed Joyce to undergo—at her expense—analysis by Jung. When Joyce vehemently refused, Mrs. McCormick took umbrage and withdrew her financial support.

Any ill feeling Joyce may have harbored toward Jung in consequence of this affair must have dissipated somewhat when, in 1932, Jung published " 'Ulysses': A Monologue," a psychological analysis of the work. Jung praises the novel and comments upon its difficulty but misunderstands the novel's artistic achievements, such as the linguistic brilliance of the narrative. In an August 1932 letter to Joyce, Jung acknowledged having "learned a great deal from [*Ulysses*]" (*Letters*, III.253–254). Nonetheless in several places in *Finnegans Wake*, Joyce satirizes Jung (see, for example, *FW* 115.20–24; 268.R1; and 307.3–4). Despite his antipathy for analysis and with the encouragement of Maria JOLAS, two years later Joyce, in desperation over the growing mental illness of his daughter, LUCIA, agreed to allow Jung to analyze her. The results, however, proved less than satisfactory, and in January 1935 Joyce discontinued Lucia's analysis and terminated all further contact with Jung.

**Kain, Richard M.** (1908–1990) He was an American Joyce critic and longtime teacher at the University of Louisville. His first book, *Fabulous Voyager: James Joyce's Ulysses* (published in 1947 and extensively revised in 1959), marked the beginning of the wave of post–World War II American scholarship that greatly increased the general interest in Joyce. *Fabulous Voyager* provided both an intellectual foundation and the immediate motivation for numerous critical works that appeared in its wake. Of equal or perhaps even greater importance in terms of its impact upon Joyce scholarship was an edition of early Joyce manuscripts that Kain produced in 1965 with Robert Scholes. *The Workshop of Dedalus: James Joyce and the Materials for* A Portrait *of the Artist as a Young Man* contains a great deal of writing from various stages of composition of Joyce's first published novel. Most notably among these diverse drafts, *The Workshop of Dedalus* reprints a number of the epiphanies that Joyce had composed as a young man, which figure so prominently in *Dubliners, Stephen Hero,* and *A Portrait of the Artist as a Young Man* (see EPIPHANY). The Kain-Scholes book also includes "A Portrait of the Artist," a prose sketch of 1904 that was the germ of *Stephen Hero* and *A Portrait of the Artist as a Young Man.*

**Kane, Matthew** (d. 1904) He was a Dublin friend of Joyce's father, John JOYCE. Kane was drowned in Dublin Bay on July 10, 1904. Joyce used his physical appearance and pedantic mannerisms as a model for Martin Cunningham, the generally kindly and thoughtful character in "Grace" who heads a group of men plotting to reform Tom Kernan. In *Ulysses,* he appears most prominently in the Hades episode, where he attends the funeral of Paddy Dignam; the Wandering Rocks episode; and the Cyclops episode, where he seeks to enlist the help of Dignam's friends to come to the aid of the widow and children.

**Kelly, John** (1848–1896) He was a Fenian friend of John Joyce. Kelly was sent to prison several times by the British authorities because of his LAND LEAGUE agitation. After his final release, Kelly lived for a short period in the Joyce home in Bray while he was recuperating from the deleterious effects of his incarceration. In 1891, according to Richard ELLMANN, one of Joyce's biographers, he and John Joyce participated in a loud confrontation with Mrs. Dante Hearn CONWAY during a family Christmas dinner at the Joyce home. The argument, over the Irish people's treatment of the statesman Charles Stewart PARNELL, was the source for the altercation that occurs during the Christmas dinner scene in chapter 1 of *A Portrait of the Artist as a Young Man.* Kelly is the model for John Casey, the man who in that argument sides with Simon Dedalus against Dante Riordan.

**Kenner, (William) Hugh** (1923–2003) Kenner was a Canadian-born, American-based Joyce scholar, literary critic, and authority on modernism. His many books include *Dublin's Joyce* (1955), *The Invisible Poet: T. S. Eliot* (1959), *The Pound Era* (1971), *A Reader's Guide to Samuel Beckett* (1973),

*Joyce's Voices* (1978), *A Colder Eye: The Modern Irish Writers* (1983), and *Ulysses* (revised 1987). Kenner's keen textual analysis, creative insights, and erudition have made his writings a major influence on Joyce scholarship for more than 30 years. In *Dublin's Joyce,* for example, he was the first to explain how parody underpins Joyce's works and how irony functions as a central rhetorical device in Joyce's method of composition. Offering new readings of many aspects of Joyce's *Ulysses* that relate to its Homeric parallels and structure, Kenner's *Ulysses* expands upon his earlier ideas and presents afresh a perceptive reading of the novel.

Despite his monumental contributions to Joyce studies, Kenner is best described as a polymath. In addition to literary criticism, he wrote books on mathematics, computers, geodesic domes, and comic books. Kenner taught at Johns Hopkins, the University of California at Santa Barbara, and the University of Georgia.

**Kenny, Rev. Peter, SJ** He was the founder in 1814 of the Jesuit school CLONGOWES WOOD COLLEGE—the school attended by Joyce and his fictional counterpart Stephen Dedalus. During Joyce's time at Clongowes, a portrait of Father Kenny "wrapped in a big cloak" hung in the corridor connecting the school with the Castle (the college's original building, formerly known as Castle Brown after the family that built it), where the rooms of the Jesuit community were located. (According to the Rev. Bruce Bradley, SJ, author of *James Joyce's Schooldays,* the picture is still there, hanging in the round room of the Castle.) It is down this corridor that Stephen walks when, during the closing pages of chapter 1 of *A Portrait of the Artist as a Young Man,* he goes to complain to the rector, the Rev. John CONMEE, SJ, about his unfair pandying by Father DOLAN.

**Kevin, St. (Irish, Caemgen)** (d. 618) Kevin was one of the patron saints of Dublin. Born near that city, supposedly into the royal line of the ancient Irish kingdom of Leinster, as a young man Kevin turned his back on secular life and chose instead to become a hermit living in Glendalough in County Wicklow. He subsequently founded a monastery there and served as its first abbot. Under his charge Glendalough became one of Ireland's leading monasteries. No accurate biography of St. Kevin survives, but the legendary accounts of his life include his temptation at Luggelaw and again at Glendalough by the young woman, Cathleen, who killed herself when her second effort failed. The stories also stress St. Kevin's role as a protector of animals. He died on June 3, 618, in Glendalough.

In *Finnegans Wake* Book I, chapter 8, the washerwomen at the River LIFFEY recount, in a highly stylized fashion, the apocryphal temptation of St. Kevin (*FW* 203.17–204.5). In this instance, however, the charms of the woman, now represented as A L P, prove too much: "[H]e had to forget the monk in the man so, rubbing her up and smoothing her down, he baised his lippes in smiling mood, kiss akiss after kisokushk (as he warned her niver to, niver to, nevar) on Anna-na-Poghue's of the freckled forehead" (*FW* 203.33–204.1). One of Joyce's earliest sketches in the composition of *Finnegans Wake* was of St. Kevin; he later incorporated it into Book IV (*FW* 604.27–606.12), where the saint is seen rising from the waters of new life.

**Kidd, John** See GABLER EDITION.

**Knight, E. H.** He was the manager of the Euston Hotel, London, when Joyce stayed there in January 1926. The association evidently produced a lasting impression, for Joyce subsequently referred to Knight, playing on the sound of the opening consonants in the man's name, in a letter to Harriet Shaw WEAVER; Joyce also makes a passing allusion to Knight in *Finnegans Wake* (FW 245.32). See *Letters* I.239.

**Kock, Charles Paul de** (1794–1871) He was an actual 19th-century French novelist whose "discreetly pornographic novels about Parisian life" (Don Gifford, *Annotations for Ulysses*) enjoyed great popularity in Victorian and Edwardian England. Interestingly, *Le Cocu* (The Cuckold), the single book by Kock in Joyce's Trieste library, devotes far more of the narrative to moralizing than to erotica. In his notes for *Exiles,* Joyce expresses ambivalence about Kock's fiction.

In the Calypso episode, Leopold Bloom momentarily reflects on the implications of Kock's name

(*U* 4.358) when Molly Bloom brings it up. Much later in the day, in the Sirens episode, Bloom recollects this earlier scene with Molly (*U* 11.500–501). Paul de Kock is again alluded to in the Circe episode, when Bloom is accused of attempting to send Kock's *The Girl with the Three Pairs of Stays* through the mail to Mrs. Yelverton Barry (*U* 15.1022–1024), and when Bloom's literary and sexual fantasies subtly merge through the punning designation *Poldy Koch* (*U* 15.3045), containing a hint of Molly's sexual desires and Bloom's preoccupation with them as *Paul de* becomes the homophone for *Poldy,* a name of endearment Molly uses for Leopold.

# L

**Land League** This was the name of an Irish agrarian organization that agitated for land reform by employing nonviolent tactics. It was founded on October 21, 1879, by Michael DAVITT, who quickly persuaded Charles Stewart PARNELL, leader of the Irish Parliamentary Party, to become its president. This move skillfully linked the cause of land reform to the Home Rule issue, and subsequent political pressure from the league helped bring about passage in Parliament in 1881 of Gladstone's Land Act. In amending the earlier Irish Land Act of 1870, it restricted rents and gave tenants security of tenure. Parliament also passed the Coercion Act in 1881, to counter the violence associated with the Irish Republican Brotherhood's support of Land League agitation. When Parnell was arrested on October 13, 1881, for his putatively incendiary public speeches and imprisoned in Kilmainham, the league called on all tenants to withhold rents in protest. The British government, sensitive to the organization's growing political power, used this action as an excuse to condemn the league as a criminal association and jail its leaders in 1881.

**Larbaud, Valéry (Nicolas)** (1881–1957) Larbaud was a French novelist, critic, and translator of such diverse writers as Walt Whitman, Samuel Butler, Jean Giraudoux, and Paul Claudel, as well as Joyce. Larbaud first met Joyce in Paris in December 1920 at Sylvia BEACH's bookstore, SHAKESPEARE AND COMPANY, and soon after became enthusiastically involved in promoting *Ulysses,* which Joyce was completing at that time. Larbaud, after reading portions of *Ulysses* that had been serialized in the *LITTLE REVIEW,* proposed on the book's completion to give a public lecture to help launch it. Joyce was delighted by the prospect, and in a June 24, 1921, letter to Harriet Shaw WEAVER, called Larbaud "[t]he only person who knows anything worth mentioning about the book or did or tried to do anything about it" (*Selected Letters,* p. 283). In December 1921, when Joyce was making final revisions in the text, Larbaud, with Joyce's approval, delivered the promised public lecture on *Ulysses* at Shakespeare and Company. About a month earlier, to assist him in preparing for the lecture, Joyce had lent Larbaud a SCHEMA for the novel, which outlined its techniques and Homeric parallels. Larbaud also played a major role in the French translation of *Ulysses,* published in 1929 by Adrienne MONNIER's La Maison des Amis des Livres. According to Joyce, Larbaud was the first to use the term *INTERIOR MONOLOGUE* (see *Letters,* III.83).

**"Lass of Aughrim, The"** This is the title of a well-known ballad by an anonymous author, which originated in the north of Ireland. It tells the story of a young peasant girl seduced and abandoned by Lord Gregory. When the lass appears at Lord Gregory's castle with the child that resulted from their liaison, she is turned away by his mother. Lord Gregory learns of this and pursues the lass and the child, who put to sea before he can catch up to them, leaving him helplessly to witness their drowning. According to Richard ELLMANN, Joyce heard of this ballad from Nora BARNACLE.

"The Lass of Aughrim" is the song that Bartell D'Arcy sings as guests are leaving the Morkans' annual Christmas party in Joyce's *Dubliners* story "The Dead." D'Arcy's performance deeply moves Gretta Conroy, for it calls to her mind the death of the young Michael Furey who had often sung the same song when they walked out together in Galway. Gretta's recollection in turn elicits the EPIPHANY experienced by Gabriel Conroy later that evening at the Gresham Hotel as the story closes.

For further details concerning the ballad, see Ruth Bauerle, *The James Joyce Songbook*, pp. 177–178. For Joyce's response to the ballad see *Letters*, II.240 and 242.

**Latini, Brunetto** (c. 1220–1294) Latini was a Florentine scholar of the late medieval/early Renaissance period who was instrumental in the development of early Italian vernacular poetry. He had a particularly strong influence on the work of DANTE ALIGHIERI, who acknowledged Latini's impact upon the evolution of Italian literature but who, in the 15th canto of the *Inferno*, depicts Latini as a condemned sodomist. In the Scylla and Charybdis episode (chapter 9) of *Ulysses*, Stephen Dedalus, as he faces the "miscreant eyes" (*U* 9.373) of those listening to his Shakespeare theories, recalls a line, as Don Gifford notes in *Ulysses Annotated*, from an Italian translation of Latini's *Li livres dou trésor*: "*E quando vede l'uomo l'attosca*" ("and when [the basilisk] looks at a man, it poisons him").

**Léon, Paul L.** (1893–1942) He was a close friend, with his wife Lucie Noël, of the Joyce family for the last decade that they lived in Paris. Like Joyce, Léon was an exile. He had been a professor of philosophy and sociology in his native Russia before emigrating in 1918. From 1930 to 1940 Léon greatly assisted Joyce, not as a paid secretary as some have mistakenly reported, but as a trusted consultant. Léon supervised Joyce's business and financial affairs and served as his agent or intermediary, corresponding with Harriet Shaw WEAVER, Sylvia BEACH, and others when Joyce did not wish to have direct dealings with them. Although at times Léon's tone could be imperious when responding to those he felt were putting unfair demands upon Joyce, the sincerity of his concern and devotion to Joyce and his family is beyond doubt.

In early September 1940, after Joyce and his family had fled from German-occupied Paris and before they had made their way into neutral Switzerland, Léon returned to Paris and at great personal risk—he was a Jew—collected from the Joyces' apartment a great quantity of personal and business papers. These he deposited for safekeeping with Count O'Kelly, then the head of the Irish legation in Paris. Count O'Kelly subsequently sent this material to the NATIONAL LIBRARY OF IRELAND, where it was put under seal for 50 years. (The papers became available for scholarly use in the spring of 1992, and a catalogue of the material has been compiled by Catherine Fahy, *The James Joyce–Paul Léon Papers in The National Library of Ireland.*) Léon remained in Paris, where he was arrested by the Gestapo in August 1941; he died in a concentration camp in Silesia, probably in April 1942. His wife later published an account of the friendship between these two men, entitled *James Joyce and Paul Léon: The Story of a Friendship* (1950). Also see Maria Jolas, "The Little Known Paul Léon," *A James Joyce Miscellany (Second Series)*, ed. Marvin Magalaner, 225–233.

**Lessons Chapter** This is a variation of an informal designation of Book II, chapter 2, of *Finnegans Wake* (*FW* 260–308). Others have identified the chapter as The Study Period—Triv and Quad (Joseph CAMPBELL and Henry Morton ROBINSON, *A Skeleton Key to Finnegans Wake*); Homework (William York TINDALL, *A Reader's Guide to James Joyce*); and Night Lessons (Adaline GLASHEEN, *Third Census of Finnegans Wake*). When Joyce published three fragments from WORK IN PROGRESS in the pamphlet *Tales Told of Shem and Shaun* (1929), he included a portion of this chapter (*FW* 282–304) under the title "The Muddest Thick That Was Ever Heard Dump" (see *FW* 296:20–21). In a July 1939 letter to Frank BUDGEN, Joyce explained the format of the chapter: "[T]he technique here is a reproduction of a schoolboy's (and schoolgirl's) old classbook complete with marginalia by the twins, who change sides at half time,

The office clock on the Ballast Building *(Irish Tourist Board)*

footnotes by the girl (who doesn't), a Euclid diagram, funny drawings etc" (*Letters,* I.406).

The narrative recounts the efforts of Dolph (Shem), Kev (Shaun), and their sister Issy to master their lessons, and presents an impressionistic survey of the liberal arts, including grammar, history, letter writing, politics, and mathematics. Sexual matters too are included. In the geometry lesson, for example, Dolph uses a geometrical configuration of triangles and circles (*FW* 293) to elucidate for Kev the geometry of their mother's (A L P's) vagina. For further details of this chapter, see *FW* II.2 in the *Finnegans Wake* entry.

**Levin, Harry (Tuchman)** (1912–1994) Levin was a noted American educator, critic, and professor of English at Harvard University until his retirement in 1983. His *James Joyce: A Critical Introduction* (1941) was the first book-length study written by an American of Joyce's canon to gain international attention. Levin also edited *The Portable James Joyce* (Viking, 1946), for which he wrote the introduction and notes and which remains in print more than half a century after its first appearance. Levin's early studies became the impetus for several subsequent generations of critics to explicate Joyce's work, for they showed, through close readings and thoughtful commentary on the cultural context from which the work emerged, that material which initially seemed recondite could, from the proper perspective, yield the same aesthetic satisfaction as that afforded by more conventional works. Of the reviews that Joyce read of *Finnegans Wake,* Levin's, Joyce thought, was the best (see *Letters,* III.464 and 468n.2).

**Lewis, (Percy) Wyndham** (1882–1957) Lewis was a Canadian-born artist, critic, satirist, and novelist. Lewis was educated in England, where he studied at the Slade School of Art. He later studied in Paris. In 1912, Lewis created and became a leading proponent of vorticism, a literary and artistic movement that rejected romanticism and sentimentality in art. This movement, partly inspired by cubism and futurism, lasted until around 1915. With Ezra Pound, Lewis edited the little magazine *Blast: Review of the Great English Vortex* (1914–15). Among his writings are *Time and Western Man* (1927), a critical work in which he attacks Joyce as suffering from a fixation with time, and *Blasting and Bombardiering* (1937), his autobiography, which includes a description of his and T. S. Eliot's meeting with Joyce in Paris in August 1920. In the fable of the Ondt and the Gracehoper (*FW* 414.14–419.10) Joyce defends his work in *Finnegans Wake* by satirizing Lewis as the humorless Ondt (an anagram of *Don't*) in contrast to Joyce, the prodigal Gracehoper.

Although Lewis's criticism in *Time and Western Man* clearly hurt Joyce, its long-term effect was blunted by Lewis's own loss of esteem. His early and vocal support of Fascism through books and articles alienated many. Lewis subsequently repudiated these views, but his reputation never recovered.

**Liffey** This is the name of the river that bisects the city of Dublin on an approximate west-east axis. Its Latin name is *Amnis Livia* ("the river Livia"), and its Irish name is *An Life.* The Liffey rises on a plateau between two mountains in County Wicklow, about 20 miles southwest of Dublin. Following a meandering course, it flows for about 50 miles. From its source it runs generally northwest to the Lackan Reservoir, then westward through County Kildare, gradually turning northwest and then northeast to enter County Dublin at Lexlip, from where it then flows eastward through the city to Dublin Bay.

The Liffey represents a vital force throughout Joyce's work. In all of his prose fiction it is an important landmark and an embodiment of the social, commercial, and cultural energy of the city of Dublin. In "An Encounter" (in *Dubliners*), the Liffey is both a physical and a psychological boundary for the two boys spending the day "miching" from classes in their parochial school. In *A Portrait of the Artist as a Young Man,* the Liffey is the benchmark against which the unmistakable decline of the fortunes of Simon Dedalus is measured, for once the family begins a series of removals to accommodations in less genteel sections of the city north of the river, their degraded financial situation can no longer be ignored.

In *Ulysses,* the Liffey takes on protean qualities. It is both the location and the means of the unsuccessful suicide attempt of Reuben J. Dodd Jr, recounted by Leopold Bloom and Martin Cunningham in the Hades episode (chapter 7). In the Lestrygonians episode (chapter 8) it serves as the vehicle for a clever advertising scheme for Kino's 11-shilling trousers. Later, in the Wandering Rocks episode (chapter 10), the river marks the pace of the narrative as its current carries the torn fragments of the Alexander J. Dowie throwaway from O'Connell Bridge to Dublin Bay.

Nowhere in Joyce's canon does the River Liffey have a more prominent place than in *Finnegans Wake.* It circuitously flows through the whole work from the opening passage—"riverrun, past Eve and Adam's"—to the last lines of Book IV, where in her monologue Anna Livia alludes to her life as the Liffey flowing from its source to the open sea. In *Finnegans Wake,* the river is Anna Liffey and the topographic embodiment of the work's mature female presence, Anna Livia Plurabelle. (*Plurabelle,* a word suggesting "most beautiful" or "loveliest," Joyce added to underscore the wonder and beauty of this important river.) One whole chapter of *Finnegans Wake* (I.8), which also contains the camouflaged names of more than 300 rivers, gives Anna Livia hegemony over all the rivers in the world. In its gentle yet powerful form, the Liffey conveys both the constant change and the vital continuity characteristic of Anna Livia Plurabelle, who symbolizes affirmation and renewal throughout the *Wake.* (See *Letters,* I.261 for Joyce's comments on the difficulty of composing a particular passage in *Finnegans Wake* relating to the Liffey.)

**Linati, Carlo** (1878–1949) Born in Como, Italy, Linati was an important Italian critic, translator, and writer who published in various newspapers and journals, such as *Corriere della Sera, La Stampa, Verde e Azzurro, Gazzetta Letteraria,* and *La Voce.* Among others, he translated works by D. H. Lawrence, William Butler Yeats, John Millington Synge, Charles Dickens, and James Joyce. In 1920, Linati's translations of *Exiles,* "Araby," and passages from *Ulysses* appeared in the Milan periodical *Il Convegno.* Perhaps he is best known for the *Ulysses* schema associated with his name that Joyce sent to him in September 1920. In *Ulysses on the Liffey,* Richard ELLMANN reproduces the schema both in its original Italian and in translation. (For more information, see SCHEMA and the appendix on page 392.)

**Linati schema** See LINATI, CARLO.

**Literary and Historical Society, The** This was the name of a student organization that sponsored undergraduate lectures and debates at UNIVERSITY COLLEGE, DUBLIN. It was founded by John Henry Cardinal NEWMAN, and continues to enjoy an active existence at the university. As a student, Joyce participated in debates held by the society during the 1898–99 academic year, and he was elected to its executive committee on February 18, 1899. Joyce later read two papers before the society, "Drama and Life" on January 20, 1900, and "James Clarence Mangan" on February 1, 1902.

**"Little Jim"** This is the title of an unattributed poem that Joyce had to recite before his classmates as part of the regular school exercises while a student at CLONGOWES WOOD COLLEGE. A line from the poem—"The cottage was a thatched one"—can be found in an April 25, 1925, letter to Harriet Shaw WEAVER, in which Joyce parodies the poem; see *Letters,* I.227.

***Little Review, The*** This was an American literary monthly, published irregularly between 1914 and 1929 by Margaret ANDERSON and Jane HEAP. Its pugnacious approach was made clear in its subtitle: "A Magazine of the Arts, Making No Compromise with the Public Taste." The first issue was published in March 1914. Ezra Pound, the journal's "foreign correspondent," was instrumental in getting the *Little Review* to serialize *Ulysses.* Ultimately it ran 23 installments that covered the narrative from the Telemachus episode (chapter 1; March 1918) through the first portion of Oxen of the Sun (chapter 14; September–December 1920).

Once *Ulysses* began to appear and to attract attention, distribution of the *Little Review* became increasingly difficult. Beginning with the January 1919 number (the first portion of the Lestrygonians episode), the U.S. Post Office began seizing issues on the grounds that passages from the serialized novel were obscene. On these grounds, the Post Office also confiscated the May 1919 issue (the second half of the Scylla and Charybdis episode), the January 1920 issue (the middle portion of the Cyclops episode), and the July–August 1920 issue (the concluding section of the Nausikaa episode). In September 1920 the New York Society for the Suppression of Vice lodged an official complaint with the Court of Special Sessions. John QUINN, a New York attorney and patron of the arts who had earlier corresponded with Joyce, unsuccessfully defended the journal and its editors. In February 1921, Anderson and Heap were found guilty of publishing obscenity, fined $50 each, and dismissed with the tacit understanding that no further excerpts from the novel would be published. In 1922, the *Little Review* became a quarterly. It ceased publication in 1929.

**Llona, Victor** (birth and death dates unknown) He was a critic and translator resident in Paris in the 1920s and 1930s, and a contributor to *OUR EXAGMINATION ROUND HIS FACTIFICATION FOR INCAMINATION OF WORK IN PROGRESS,* a collection of essays published by SHAKESPEARE AND COMPANY, intended as a critical response to the bewildered reception of *Finnegans Wake,* then being published in installments under the title *WORK IN PROGRESS.*

Llona's article, entitled "I Dont Know What to Call It but Its [*sic*] Mighty Unlike Prose," attempts to explain the linguistic structure of the narrative of *Work in Progress.* Despite his defense of Joyce's work, one cannot avoid the sense from Llona's own words that he, too, feels a degree of bafflement. He does affirm an unwillingness to dismiss the beauty of the writing simply because the language seems opaque. By way of suggesting a model for reading diverse elements of the work, Llona compares Joyce's efforts to those of RABELAIS. By the conclusion of the essay, however, Llona fails to convince even himself, and he falls back on a defense of *Work in Progress* based upon the work's uniqueness. In the end, he reasserts the need for the reader to accommodate herself or himself to the idiosyncratic demands of Joyce's writing.

**Lockwood Memorial Library** The Poetry Collection at the State University of New York–Buffalo stands as one of the earliest and most complete gatherings of Joyce material in the world. It is built upon the acquisition in 1950 of material left behind in Joyce's Paris apartment when he and his family left the city in 1939. It consists of important prepublication material for *Ulysses* and *Finnegans Wake,* such as the *Finnegans Wake* notebooks, holograph drafts for episodes of *Ulysses,* a notebook for *Exiles,* and 22 holograph drafts of the Epiphanies (see EPIPHANY). There are also letters, press clippings, journal articles on his works, family portraits, Joyce's library, and other personal effects (passports, canes, etc.). In 1951 and again in 1959 B. W. HUEBSCH donated page proofs of the front matter and two lists of errata for *A Portrait of the Artist as a Young Man,* as well as his correspondence with Joyce from 1915 to 1938. Also in 1959, the library received a large portion of Sylvia BEACH's personal Joyce collection. It included a holograph draft of Joyce's 1904 "Portrait" essay, 12 workbooks of *Ulysses* episodes, 1,200 pages of typescript, and 800 of galley proofs, all with additions and corrections by Joyce, printed texts (most with dedications by the author to Beach), extensive correspondence concerning Joyce's personal and business affairs, and many photographs that document Joyce's life and the Paris literary scene of the 1920s and 1930s. After Beach's death in 1962 the library received 212 letters from Joyce to Beach, further first editions signed by the author and dedicated to her, translations, and more photographs. Finally in 1968 Maria JOLAS gave the library 31 pages of six different transition galley proofs of *Work in Progress* printed and revised from

May 27, 1927, to June 1928 for transitions 4, 5, and 11–13. In 1962 Peter Spielberg published a catalogue of the collection, and at present Luca Crispi is in the process of revising it.

**Longworth, Ernest V.** (1874–1935) He was an editor from 1901 to 1904 at the Dublin newspaper the *DAILY EXPRESS* when Joyce was a young man in Dublin. In 1902, at the urging of the prominent literary patron Lady Augusta GREGORY, Longworth agreed to send books to Joyce to review while the latter was pursuing his medical studies in Paris. Like his fictional counterpart Stephen Dedalus—as Buck Mulligan caustically observes, "she gets you a job on the paper and then you go and slate her drivel to Jaysus" (*U* 9.1159–1160)—Joyce was less than gracious in repaying the favor, for he wrote an extremely harsh review of Lady Gregory's book *Poets and Dreamers*. This clearly put Longworth in an awkward position, although after some delay he did print the review. Longworth eventually quarreled with Joyce and declined to offer him further books for review.

**Luening, Otto** (1900–1996) He was an American composer, conductor, and flutist, who as a teenager studied in Zurich with the Italian composer, pianist, and conductor Ferruccio Busoni. In Zurich in 1917, Luening was introduced to Joyce through Claud W. SYKES. In his autobiography, *The Odyssey of an American Composer* (1980), Luening devotes part of a chapter to Joyce. He is one of a number of composers who have set to music poems from *Chamber Music*.

**MacCool, Finn (Fionn MacCumhal)** See FINN MACCOOL.

**Magee, W. K.** See Eglinton, John, under Characters in *Ulysses.*

**Mallarmé, Stéphane** (1842–1898) He was a French poet, a leading figure of the symbolist movement. As a young man, Joyce was a great admirer of Mallarmé's symbolist aesthetics. One finds evidence of Mallarmé's lingering influence in the *Chamber Music* poems and in a number of the *Dubliners* stories. During Stephen Dedalus's rambling discussion of SHAKESPEARE in the Scylla and Charybdis episode (chapter 9) of *Ulysses,* Joyce specifically invokes the poet as Stephen quotes Mallarmé's description of Hamlet: "il se promène, lisant au livre de lui-même" (He strolls about, reading the book of himself) (*U* 9.114).

**Mangan, James Clarence** (1803–1849) He was an Irish poet manqué who produced a large though uneven body of work. Irish history, folklore, and mythology furnish the themes for much of his writing. Mangan contributed to the *Dublin University Magazine,* the *Nation,* and the *United Irishman* but is today best remembered for his allegorical poem on Ireland, "Dark Rosaleen." As a young man, Joyce—possibly seeking to establish parallels with his own artistic life—championed Mangan's work, and he delivered an address to the LITERARY AND HISTORICAL SOCIETY OF UNIVERSITY COLLEGE, DUBLIN on February 15, 1902, entitled "James Clarence Mangan." The talk featured Joyce's assessment of Mangan's accomplishments for a new generation of Dubliners. In Joyce's fiction, Mangan serves more as a personification of the consequences of the artistic life than as a model for Joyce's vision of the Irish artist: an individual whose talents receive little or no recognition from the public and whose life ends prematurely in dissipation and despair. In his later work, especially *Ulysses,* allusions to Mangan's poetry (*U* 12.68, 12.84, 12.1264, 12.1450–1451, 14.1326, 15.1143, and 15.4338–1439) serve a dual purpose: to call to mind both a temperament that can make good artistic use of the atmosphere of Ireland and the dangers that an Irish artist faces from his homeland's ingrained hostility to art. However, these references appear in contexts that reflect Joyce's awareness of the limitations of art that depends too heavily on romanticism and sentimental nationalism.

**Margaret Mary Alacoque, Saint** (1647–1690) She was a nun of the Visitation order who spent most of her adult life at the convent in Paray-le-Monial, France. In 1675 Margaret Mary had a vision in which Christ charged her to establish devotion of His Sacred Heart. In response she worked for the establishment of the Feast of the Sacred Heart (the Friday after the Octave of the Feast of Corpus Christi) and the Litany of the Sacred Heart. In 1864, she was beatified and, in 1920, canonized a saint.

In the *Dubliners* short story "Eveline" (first composed in 1904), the narrator refers to her as *Blessed*

Margaret Mary Alacoque, the term used in the Catholic Church to indicate that an individual has reached the stage (beatification) in the canonization process just short of being declared a saint.

In *Ulysses* the narrative alludes to her in the Hades episode (chapter 6) by mentioning the Sacred Heart (*U* 6.954). Later in the Scylla and Charybdis episode, chapter 9, Buck Mulligan interrupts Stephen Dedalus's disquisition on Shakespeare with a bawdy reconstitution of her name as "Blessed Margaret Mary Anycock" (*U* 9.646).

**Martello Tower** The tower in SANDYCOVE in *Ulysses* that Malachi Mulligan and Stephen Dedalus share is one of a series of defensive fortifications built along the Irish coast by the British between 1804 and 1806 in anticipation of a Napoleonic invasion. (The name comes from Cape Martello in Corsica, where the first such tower was built, in 1794.) In September 1904, Joyce lodged for about a week as the guest of Oliver St. John GOGARTY in the Martello Tower located just south of Dublin at Sandycove, overlooking Scotsman's Bay. Today the tower has become the home of the James Joyce Museum, which contains displays of Joycean memorabilia from the turn of the century, notes for revisions to a fair copy of *Finnegans Wake* III.1–2, and a reconstruction of the living quarters that Joyce shared with Gogarty.

The Martello Tower in Sandycove, where Stephen Dedalus resided in *Ulysses* *(Irish Tourist Board)*

The Telemachus episode opens on the roof of the tower with Buck Mulligan's disquisition to a still sleepy Stephen Dedalus regarding a new aesthetic that Mulligan proposes to introduce into Ireland. Although early commentators believed that the narrative indicates that Stephen has paid the rent for the tower, in fact the passage in question is Stephen's recollection of Mulligan's assertion. This helps us understand why, on the day on which the novel takes place, Stephen feels as if his place is being usurped by Haines, Mulligan's English house guest. The tower that was built to repel invaders of Ireland now, ironically, gives shelter to one of them.

***Martha*** This is the title of an opera, written in 1847, by the German composer Friedrich Flotow (1812–83). Allusions to this work appear throughout *Ulysses*. The aria "M'appari" (translated as "When First I Saw That Form Endearing") forms part of the musical setting of the Sirens episode and provides an ironic juxtaposition to the events occurring at that moment in the life of Leopold Bloom. He is at the Ormond Hotel at the very hour of his wife Molly's assignation with Blazes Boylan. Bloom is eating and about to write to Martha Clifford. As he hears Simon Dedalus singing the aria, he thinks: "*Martha* it is. Coincidence. Just going to write. . . . How strange! Today" (*U* 11.713, 716). The lines " '*Co–ome, thou lost one! Co–ome, thou dear one!*' " (*U* 11.740–741), coupled with Bloom's thoughts, add a tone of sadness to the irony.

**Mason, Ellsworth Goodwin** (1917– ) He is an educator, librarian, rare book collector, and editor with Stanislaus JOYCE of *The Early Joyce: The Book Reviews, 1902–1903* (1955) and with Richard ELLMANN of *The Critical Writings of James Joyce* (1959). Mason is the author of *James Joyce's "Ulysses" and Vico's Cycle* (1973), among other works. In 1982 he was appointed as a consultant to the library at the University of Colorado, Boulder.

**"Matcham's Masterstroke"** This is the title of an article by Philip Beaufoy that appears in the copy of *Titbits* read by Leopold Bloom during his visit to the privy near the end of the Calypso episode. The heavy-handed melodramatic tone of the work and Bloom's calculation that Beaufoy had received three pounds, 13 shillings and sixpence for his efforts (*U* 4.505) lead him to daydream about writing such a piece himself. The image of Beaufoy recurs in the Circe episode (*U* 15.818). The appearance of this putatively successful writer of popular fiction vividly underscores Bloom's hope that through a spectacular single event he will be able to produce a material change in his fortunes. In the Oxen of the Sun episode, Bloom's musings about his house in the country run along similar lines and illustrate the same attitude.

**Mater Misericordiae Hospital** This is the largest hospital in Dublin, located at the intersection of ECCLES STREET and the Berkeley Road, within a city block of the house of Leopold Bloom. (The land upon which the actual house once stood, at 7 Eccles Street, is now occupied by flats owned by the hospital.) In Joyce's time the Mater was under the administration of the Sisters of Mercy. In the Telemachus episode of *Ulysses* Buck Mulligan speaks of doing part of his medical residency there. In the Hades episode, Bloom remembers the Mater as the place where Dante Riordan died, and also as the hospital where the young Dr. Dixon attended to Bloom's bee sting.

**Mathews, Elkin** (1851–1921) He was a well-known turn-of-the-century English publisher. He began bringing out books in 1884 in Exeter in cooperation with other antiquarian booksellers. In 1887 he moved to Piccadilly and in 1892 entered into a two-year partnership with John Lane. In 1907 his firm became the first to bring out a book by Joyce when it published his first collection of poems, *Chamber Music*. Mathews declined at that time to publish Joyce's short-story collection *Dubliners*, and did so again in 1913. He was also the first to publish W. B. YEATS, Ezra POUND, and Robert Bridges. For further information relating to Mathews's dealings with Joyce, see *Letters*, II.180, 181, 185, 206, 209–210, 219, 223–224, 224–225, 283–284, 296, 321, 323, 357, and 462.

**Matisse, Henri** (1869–1954) He was a French painter, one of the most influential artists of the 20th century. In 1935 he executed a series of six etchings, with accompanying sketches, for The Limited Editions Club's 1,500-copy run of *Ulysses*. Joyce himself said of Matisse that "he knows the French translation very well but has never been to Ireland" (*Letters*, III.314). This may account for the stylized form of the etchings that evoke *The* ODYSSEY as much as they illustrate Joyce's novel. Joyce in fact preferred the work that Lucia JOYCE had done on *Ulysses* over Matisse's. See *Letters*, I.365; III.304, 314, 317, 320, and 332.

**Maunsel & Co.** This was an Irish publishing house founded in 1905 by George ROBERTS, whom Joyce had known (and from whom he had borrowed money) in Dublin, with Joseph Maunsel Hone and Stephen Gwynn as codirectors. Maunsel & Co. expressed an interest in examining the manuscript of *Dubliners* as early as 1907, after Elkin MATHEWS rejected it. Joyce, however, did not send it to them until 1909. They accepted it in August, and Joyce signed a contract with the firm on the 19th of that month.

In 1910 Roberts, concerned that portions of *Dubliners* would give offense, began asking Joyce for changes. Negotiations over proposed emendations dragged on into 1912, and on September 5 of that year Roberts suggested as a compromise that Joyce take over the sheets of *Dubliners* that had already been printed and publish the collection himself. Joyce agreed, but the printer, John FALCONER, intervened to prevent the collection's appearance. Although he forfeited his claim to payment by his action, Falconer refused to turn the printed sheets over to Joyce. Instead, he destroyed them on September 11, 1912. (Some disagreement arose over the manner of destruction. Joyce, perhaps with the image of an auto-da-fé in mind, claimed that they were burned, but Falconer asserted that they had been given the more ordinary treatment of pulping.) The entire affair left Joyce understandably bitter, and he vented some of his anger in a satirical poem entitled "Gas from a Burner," which he wrote shortly after the printed sheets were destroyed. Maunsel & Co. continued publishing in Dublin for another 13 years. The company was liquidated in 1925. See "A Curious History" under Miscellaneous Works.

**McAlmon, Robert** (1896–1956) McAlmon was an American poet, short-story writer, and publisher who lived in Paris between the two world wars, returning to the United States only after the German occupation of France in 1940. He recollects this time in Paris in his 1938 biography (expanded in 1968 by Kay Boyle), *Being Geniuses Together.* During his time in Paris McAlmon became friends with Joyce, and he contributed an essay to *OUR EXAGMINATION ROUND HIS FACTIFICATION FOR INCAMINATION OF WORK IN PROGRESS.*

McAlmon's article, entitled "Mr. Joyce Directs an Irish Word Ballet," emphasizes the evocative instead of the representative aspect of the language of Joyce's final work. In several examples from the Anna Livia Plurabelle section of *Finnegans Wake,* McAlmon points out that, since that section does not sustain the ordinary referential meaning of various words as a more conventional narrative would, Joyce's prose requires different expectations, for it often evokes sensations rather than the significations associated with language. McAlmon also implies that there are connections to be explored between the effect of Joyce's writing and assumptions about the human subconscious that had recently gained attention through the growing popularity of psychoanalytic studies.

**McCann, Philip** See MacCann under Characters in *A Portrait of the Artist as a Young Man.*

**McCormack, John** (1884–1945) McCormack was an Irish singer, considered to be one of the world's finest tenors in the first decades of the 20th century. In 1903, at the very beginning of his musical career, McCormack won the prestigious Irish national musical competition, Feis Ceoil, and was awarded a scholarship for a year's vocal study in Italy. The next year McCormack encouraged Joyce to enter the same competition. Joyce, who possessed a fine tenor voice himself, did well when he sang two pieces that he had prepared for the occasion, but he failed at sight reading and so lost his chance for the top prize.

In a passage in the Hades episode (chapter 6) of *Ulysses,* Leopold Bloom expresses the hope that McCormack (spelled *MacCormick* in the narrative) will join the tour that Blazes Boylan proposes to organize for Molly (*U* 6.222). In drawing McCormack into the story, even obliquely, Joyce plays upon the renown that the singer had achieved by 1922 to enhance the associations that the readers would make with Boylan's fictional 1904 tour.

In the 1930s, when Joyce was championing the cause of the tenor John SULLIVAN, McCormack, because of his international prominence as a singer, took on an exaggerated importance in Joyce's mind as the figure standing in the way of Sullivan's success. If McCormack knew of this sentiment, it did not prevent him from helping George JOYCE late in 1934 when the latter was in New York looking for singing engagements. Joyce himself never lost his appreciation for McCormack's voice, and in fact listened to the tenor's recordings while in Switzerland shortly before his death. See *Letters,* I.66, 158, 231, 272, 273, 291, 343, 353, and 358; II.48n.1, and 198; III.32, 35, 36, 177, 326–330, 333, 338, 339, 345, and 356.

**McFarlin Library** Located on the campus of the University of Tulsa, the McFarlin Library has a great many of Joyce's published works, from "The Day of the Rabblement" through composition material for *Ulysses* to page proofs for *Finnegans Wake.* It also houses several important collections related to Joyce studies: the papers of Harriet Shaw WEAVER, the Paul and Lucie Léon collection, the Ellsworth MASON collection, and Richard ELLMANN's personal and professional papers. In addition, the papers of Joyce's contemporaries—Edmund WILSON, Cyril Connolly, and Rebecca West—offer insights on Joyce and his work to supplement the other material.

**McGreevy, Thomas** (1896–1967) McGreevy was a poet, critic, and, from 1940 to 1964, director of the National Gallery of Ireland. He first made Joyce's acquaintance in Paris in 1924. McGreevy resumed the friendship in 1927 after two years in London and became one of the contributors to OUR EXAGMINATION ROUND HIS FACTIFICATION FOR INCAMINATION OF WORK IN PROGRESS.

McGreevy's essay, "The Catholic Element in *Work in Progress,*" offers a highly sophisticated view of Irish Catholicism, with useful insights into Joyce's process of transforming the distinctive Catholic structures of thought in which he was brought up into the structural and thematic organization of his prose. In his essay, McGreevy devotes as much attention to the influence of Joyce's Catholic consciousness upon the composition of *Ulysses* as to its manifestations in *Work in Progress.* In addition to its ontological comments on Joyce's work, McGreevy's essay usefully demonstrates the "purgatorial aspect" of *Finnegans Wake* that enables the narrative to project a complex and often highly satirical representation of the central themes of the book.

**McHugh, Roland** (1945– ) He is a British-born Joyce critic and former curator of the James Joyce Museum (1976–77) at the MARTELLO TOWER in Sandycove, just south of Dublin. McHugh formally studied zoology and entomology at Imperial College and Sir John Cass College, both in London. With an eye for detail, McHugh focuses much of his scholarly attention on *Finnegans Wake.* His explication of phrases and words in *Annotations to Finnegans Wake* (1980; revised 1991) is a helpful source to readers on all levels. His writings also include *A Sigla of Finnegans Wake* (1976), a detailed analysis of Joyce's use of sigla found in the manuscripts and letters, and their significance to the *Wake*'s structure, and *The Finnegans Wake Experience* (1982), an introduction to the *Wake.* He has contributed to *A Conceptual Guide to Finnegans Wake,* edited by Michael H. Begnal and Fritz SENN (1974), and to *A Wake Newslitter.* He currently teaches in the School of Food Science and Environmental Health at the Dublin Institute of Technology.

**metempsychosis** This is a Greek word signifying the transfer of the soul from a dead body into that of another living thing, whether animal or vegetable. In the Calypso episode of *Ulysses,* Molly Bloom comes across the term in a novel that she has been reading, *Ruby: the Pride of the Ring,* and asks Leopold Bloom to explain its meaning. He defines the word as "the transmigration of souls" (*U* 4.342) and then adds: "Metempsychosis . . . is what the ancient Greeks called it. They used to believe you could be changed into an animal or a tree. . . . (*U* 4.375–376). As Bloom walks down Westmoreland Street during the Lestrygonians episode, he recalls Molly's unique pronunciation of the word: "Met him pike hoses she called it" (*U* 8.112) though her words are not recorded in the narrative.

**Miami J'yce Conference** A gathering of Joyceans in Coral Gables, Florida, to commemorate Joyce's birthdate. The conference began in 1987, organized by Bernard BENSTOCK, Zack BOWEN, and Patrick McCarthy. Conference themes included postcolonial Joyce, textual Joyce, nonlinear Joyce, women and Joyce, Joyce and popular culture, and other current topics in Joyce criticism. The most recent conference took place in Sarasota on February 2–4, 2006.

**modernism** When used in literature, a term that designates a movement that began in the 19th century and grew to prominence during the decades surrounding World War I. Scholars have debated its specific features, but there is general agreement about its broader characteristics, which reflect the scientific, social, and cultural changes of its day. Literary modernism constitutes a movement that interrogates the legitimacy of traditional social institutions such as the family, the church, and the state, rejecting their authority to prescribe and enforce moral standards of behavior. Instead modernism allows individuals, in literary works quite often artists, the right to disregard social norms of ethical conduct. As a corollary, perhaps, literary modernism (like modernism in other arts) is characterized by formal experimentation, entailing the use of such devices as STREAM OF CONSCIOUSNESS, ambiguity, the unreliable narrator and self-reference (the authorial highlighting of the text as fiction), breaking the illusion of verisimilitude. Styles are highly individual, varying greatly from author to author.

Scholars usually place Joyce—along with T. S. ELIOT, D. H. Lawrence, and Virginia Woolf—among the foremost proponents of modernism in English. One might certainly argue that *Dubliners* and most certainly *A Portrait of the Artist as a Young Man* fit the modernist mold. However, a great deal of debate has taken place over the issue of whether *Ulysses* is in fact a modernist or a postmodernist work, and most critics feel that *Finnegans Wake* clearly falls into the category of POSTMODERNISM.

**Molly Maguires** This is the name of a secret and often extremely violent, agrarian society formed in Ireland in the mid-1800s. This group used terror against landlords and rent collectors as a means of fighting evictions of tenant farmers unable, in hard times, to pay their rents. The Molly Maguires supposedly took their name from a widow who led a similar group that had resisted landlord exploitation in the early 1840s. (A similar, though unrelated, secret organization of American coal miners responsible for acts of terror in the coalfields of Pennsylvania and West Virginia from 1862 to 1876 took its name from this group.)

In the Cyclops episode of *Ulysses,* the unnamed narrator makes the surprising allegation that the Molly Maguires are supposedly after the ultranationalistic Citizen, "looking for him to let daylight through him for grabbing the holding of an evicted tenant" (*U* 12.1315–1316). The allusion alone is enough to call into question the sincerity of much of the Citizen's chauvinistic rhetoric, although it must be remembered that the narrator's charge is made silently and offered by the most slanderous person in the pub.

**Monnier, Adrienne** (1892–1955) She was a close friend and supporter of Joyce, and the lover of Sylvia BEACH. She owned a bookshop, the Maison des Amis des Livres, on the rue de l'Odéon across the street from Sylvia Beach's SHAKESPEARE AND COMPANY, and she was an influential figure on the French literary scene between the wars.

Early in the effort to draw public attention to *Ulysses,* Monnier was instrumental in enlisting the help of the noted French writer, critic, and translator, Valéry LARBAUD, whose lecture on Joyce and *Ulysses,* on December 7, 1921, gave Joyce's novel an important endorsement on the eve of its publication. Monnier also supported Joyce's early efforts to establish the credibility of *WORK IN PROGRESS.* In the October 1925 issue of her journal, *Navire d'argent,* Monnier brought out one of the first segments of that work, publishing what would eventually become the Anna Livia episode (*FW* I.8.196–216). In addition, in February 1929 Monnier published the first French edition of *Ulysses,* translated by Auguste Morel. On June 27 of the same year, she hosted the now famous Déjeuner *Ulysse,* a luncheon commemorating this publication and attended by Edouard DUJARDIN, Paul VALÉRY, and Samuel BECKETT, among other literary luminaries. When Sylvia Beach's friendship with Joyce cooled in the early 1930s, Monnier naturally enough sided with her and in consequence she and Joyce drifted apart.

**Monto** This was a slang term for Montgomery Street and the popular name, in Joyce's time, for Dublin's north side brothel district. It was in the Monto area, on Lower Tyrone Street, that Joyce located the fictional brothel of Bella Cohen, the setting for most of the Circe episode (chapter 15) of *Ulysses.* In *Ulysses,* Joyce designated this area "NIGHTTOWN."

**Moore, George** (1852–1933) Moore was a prominent Anglo-Irish writer of the late 19th and early 20th century. Moore was a member of the literary generation preceding Joyce's, and in many ways can be seen as Joyce's creative precursor, especially with respect to his interest in stylistics and in Continental literature. Their relations, however, were never warm. When Joyce was still a young man in Dublin, Moore kept him at arm's length, and in "The Day of the Rabblement" Joyce openly questioned Moore's abilities as a writer. Joyce alludes to their relationship in the Scylla and Charybdis episode (chapter 9) of *Ulysses,* in which Moore is described as giving a literary party to which Buck Mulligan but not Stephen Dedalus has been invited.

Nonetheless, critics have argued that *Dubliners* derived its fundamental shape, in part at least, from

Moore's work, especially his collection of short stories, *The Untilled Field* (1903). As he grew older, Joyce's attitude toward Moore mellowed. In 1916 Moore joined Ezra POUND and W. B. YEATS in a successful effort to secure Joyce a civil list grant from the British government, and over time relations between the two men became still more cordial. The two met several times in England in the autumn of 1929, and Joyce made a point of sending a wreath to Moore's funeral and of inquiring into the details of Moore's interment. For more information, see *Letters,* I.286–288, 290, 304, and 333–336; II.71, 129, 152, 154–155, 157, 162–163, and 384, 386; III.51, 192–194, and 196–197.

**Morris Library** The Morris Library on the campus of Southern Illinois University in Carbondale contains one of the earliest private collections of Joyce's books, manuscripts, and correspondence, the Harley K. Croessmann Collection. It also includes papers of Herbert GORMAN, George Goyert, Stanislaus JOYCE, and other friends of the author. The library also has material from Joyce's contemporaries such as Richard Aldington, Kay Boyle, and Black Sun Press editors Harry and Caresse Crosby. Additionally, there is a strong representation of other 20th-century Irish authors.

**Mullingar** This is a town in County Westmeath in the geographical center of Ireland. In the summer of 1900, when John JOYCE was employed there to work on voting lists, he took his son James and some of his other children with him. During this stay in Mullingar, Joyce wrote his play *A BRILLIANT CAREER,* now lost, and translated two plays by Gerhart HAUPTMANN: *Michael Kramer* and *Before Sunrise.* He also found the inspiration for two of his EPIPHANIES from the visit. Joyce used his Mullingar experiences as the basis for an episode in *Stephen Hero* in which Stephen Daedalus visits his godfather and benefactor Mr. Fulham. In *Ulysses,* Milly Bloom works in a photographer's shop in Mullingar.

**Murray, William** (1858–1912) He was Joyce's maternal uncle. William Murray was the model for Richie Goulding, Stephen Dedalus's uncle, whom Stephen recalls in the Proteus episode (chapter 3) of *Ulysses* and who dines with Leopold Bloom at the Ormond Hotel in the Sirens episode (chapter 11). Evidence from correspondence suggests that Joyce's father did not have a very high opinion of the Murray family. Joyce's wife, Nora Barnacle, shared this view (*Letters,* II.222 and 303), though Nora's disapprobation probably did not extend to William Murray's wife, Joyce's Aunt Josephine, who showed her a great many kindnesses over the years. Joyce himself enjoyed warm relations with the entire Murray family, and he was especially close to his Aunt Josephine.

**Murray, Mrs. William (Josephine Giltrap)** (1862–1924) She was reportedly Joyce's favorite aunt and his letters indicate that she remained a longtime sympathetic confidante. After he had left Dublin, she acted as a tireless researcher of the minute details that went into Joyce's works. Joyce continued to write to his Aunt Josephine for the rest of her life, and he was deeply saddened when she died in Dublin in late 1924. Mrs. Murray serves as the model for Aunt Josephine, the wife of Richie Goulding. This character appears in a vignette in chapter 2 of *A Portrait of the Artist as a Young Man* and she enters the narrative of *Ulysses* obliquely through Stephen Dedalus's recollections of the Goulding household as he walks along Sandymount Strand during the Proteus episode (chapter 3).

**Mutton, Mountainy** This was the term Joyce uses in his invective broadside, "Gas from a Burner," to identify the Irish poet Joseph Campbell (1879–1944). The name parodies the title of Campbell's collection of poems, *The Mountainy Singer,* published by MAUNSEL & CO., the firm that had reneged on its contract to publish *Dubliners* in 1912, the action that occasioned this satiric broadside.

***My Brother's Keeper*** This is the title of the posthumously published DUBLIN memoirs of Joyce's brother Stanislaus JOYCE. The book appeared in 1958, three years after Stanislaus's death. It offers a very important view of the formative years of James Joyce and of the Dublin of the 1880s through the early 1900s that shaped Joyce's imaginative consciousness. At the same time, the work bears the clear stamp of Stanislaus's own nature, presenting highly subjective, even idiosyncratic, assessments of his brother's work. (The title itself is taken from the biblical story of Cain and Abel.) Nonetheless, *My Brother's Keeper* remains an invaluable resource for those wishing to understand the extra-textual elements that contributed to Joyce's creative process.

Because these recollections represent only the first installment of a larger project intended to cover all of Stanislaus's life, it was necessary for his widow, Nellie, to engage the services of the Joyce biographer Richard ELLMANN to edit the manuscript into a format that made it suitable for independent publication.

# N

**National Library of Ireland** The National Library was established by legislation of the British Parliament, the Dublin Science and Art Museum Act, and it was founded in Dublin in 1877. The nucleus of its collection was donated by the Royal Dublin Society. Its books and facilities were housed in the Royal Dublin Society House (Leinster House) until the construction of its present building was completed in 1890.

The National Library is located on Kildare Street, immediately to the west of Leinster House (now the site of the Irish Parliament), and it stands

The National Library, Dublin *(Irish Tourist Board)*

opposite the National Museum of Ireland. In Joyce's time, the National Library served as a gathering place for students from UNIVERSITY COLLEGE, DUBLIN. (At that time UCD was located just south of the library across ST STEPHEN'S GREEN.) In consequence, Joyce set a number of episodes in the fifth chapter of *A Portrait of the Artist as a Young Man* at and around the library. The disquisition on Shakespeare that Stephen Dedalus delivers to a representative audience of Dublin literati in the Scylla and Charybdis episode (chapter 9) of *Ulysses* takes place in the director's office of the library. There is also a passing reference to "our nazional labronry" in *Finnegans Wake* (*FW* 440.5), with perhaps a neat jab at what Joyce saw as its repressive intellectual atmosphere.

The National Library has maintained strong material links to Joyce himself. It has become a focal point for scholars who come to Dublin to do research on Joyce and his work. The library is currently the repository of the *IRISH HOMESTEAD* texts of "The Sisters," "Eveline," and "After the Race." It holds the holograph version of *A Portrait of the Artist as a Young Man*. In 1992 the library received material from the estate of Paul LÉON making up the James Joyce–Paul Léon correspondence. And in 2001 and 2002, it acquired important prepublication material for *Ulysses* also from the estate of Paul Léon. In addition, the library contains a wealth of related material illuminating both Joyce's life and the life of turn-of-the-century Dublin.

**National University** This is an administrative designation for an entity established by the University Education Act of 1879. It operated under the name the Royal University from its establishment until 1909. As a purely administrative unit, the National University itself has no facilities for offering courses. Rather, it is empowered to set broad academic criteria, to examine candidates, and to grant degrees to students from the university colleges in Dublin, Cork, and Galway. (It also granted degrees for Queen's College, Belfast, now Queen's University, until the partition of Ireland after the War of Independence.) The National University also oversees six other institutions: St. Patrick's College, Maynooth; St. Patrick's College, Drumcondra; Our Lady of Mercy College, Blackrock; Mary Immaculate College of Education, Limerick; Royal College of Surgeons, Dublin; and St. Angela's College, Sligo. It is the National University that administers the exams whose results are discussed by various students in the fifth chapter of *A Portrait of the Artist as a Young Man*.

**naturalism** This is the designation for a style or school of writing that came to prominence in the 19th century, particularly under the influence of ideas generated by Darwinian biology. Broadly speaking, naturalism focuses on physical nature and material circumstances while denying the reality or significance of a spiritual or metaphysical component of humanity. From this determinist perspective, naturalism holds that while basic personal instincts are hereditary, psychological forces and social institutions—which the individual neither controls nor understands—shape and refine one's approach to life. Simply put, naturalism is REALISM plus determinism.

A number of scholars have noted evidence of naturalism in Joyce's early writings, especially in *Dubliners*. This gritty social realism permeates the narratives of such stories as "Eveline," "Two Gallants," and "Grace," and inflects the often pessimistic attitudes that dominate the lives of characters such as Farrington, Bob Doran, or James Duffy. All offer ample evidence of parallels between these stories and depictions found in widely recognized naturalistic works. Joyce surely drew some inspiration from the writings of acknowledged naturalist authors such as Honoré de BALZAC, Émile ZOLA, and Guy de Maupassant; in fact, in his early writings and in the books he acquired once he had moved to TRIESTE, one finds ample evidence of an interest in works by these authors. Nonetheless, despite these undeniable links, it would be an oversimplification to limit one's conception of Joyce's fiction to a model based exclusively upon the tenets of naturalism.

**Nelson's Pillar** This was a round column commemorating the English naval hero of the Napoleonic Wars, Admiral Lord Horatio Nelson. The 121-foot-high column surmounted by a 13-

Nelson's Pillar, a monument that used to stand on O'Connell Street in Dublin *(Irish Tourist Board)*

foot statue of Lord Nelson was erected in Dublin in 1808 in the middle of what is now O'Connell Street in front of the General Post Office, and quickly became a popular landmark. In 1966 the Irish Republican Army, resenting it as a symbol of British colonialism, blew up the pillar.

Nelson's Pillar receives passing reference throughout Joyce's writings, and it serves as the site of the anecdote—"A PISGAH SIGHT OF PALESTINE OR THE PARABLE OF THE PLUMS"—that Stephen recounts to Professor MACHUGH and Myles CRAWFORD near the end of the Aeolus episode (chapter 7) of *Ulysses.* It is the destination of "[t]wo Dublin vestals . . . [who] want to see the views of Dublin from the top of Nelson's pillar" (*U* 7.923, 931).

**Newman, John Henry** (1801–1890) Newman first gained renown as an eminent Anglican cleric, a major figure in the Anglo-Catholic Oxford Movement. Then, after his conversion in 1845, he became a leading churchman and eventually a cardinal in the Roman Catholic Church. In 1852–53, Newman became the first rector of the Catholic University of Dublin, the forerunner of UNIVERSITY COLLEGE, DUBLIN. (The lectures that he delivered in 1852 as rector-elect grew into his widely acclaimed philosophical work, *The Idea of a University.*)

Although as a student at University College, Dublin, Joyce agreed less and less with Newman's religious views, his friend Constantine Curran noted the tremendous influence that Newman's "silver-veined" prose style had on Joyce as a young man. It apparently produced a lifelong effect, for Stuart GILBERT recalls Joyce's "habit of reciting to his friends in the mellow after-dinner hour at Les Trianons or Fouquet's" passages from Newman's work (*Letters,* I.30). In his Trieste library Joyce had a copy of Newman's two-volume *Essays Critical and Historical,* and in his Paris library there was a copy of Newman's *Discourses Addressed to Mixed Congregations.* See also *Letters,* II.110 and III.365.

***New Statesman, The*** This is an influential weekly British review of politics, public affairs, and literature, founded by Sidney and Beatrice Webb in 1913. It was the organ of the Fabian Society, which espoused a peculiarly British variety of nonrevolutionary, reformist socialism, and has been informally associated with the Labour Party. These associations doubtless disposed the magazine favorably toward the NATURALISM that many readers see in Joyce's early writings. Gerald Gould praised *Dubliners* in a review in the June 27, 1914, issue of the journal, and Desmond McCarthy favorably reviewed *Exiles* in the September 21, 1918, issue. It celebrated its 90th year of publication in 2003.

**Nighttown** This is Joyce's name for the brothel district located on the north side of Dublin, which he describes in some detail in the Circe episode of *Ulysses.* Dubliners would have been unfamiliar with Joyce's term since the area was popularly known as MONTO, a shortened form of *Montgomery Street,* one of the district's principal thoroughfares. In Joyce's time, Dublin had one of the highest rates of prostitution of any European city, and the majority of the city's brothels were concentrated in the Monto area.

**Norman, Harry Felix** (1868–1947) He was the editor of *IRISH HOMESTEAD* from 1900 to 1905 when George RUSSELL took over. In 1904 after George Russell had invited Joyce to contribute to the journal, Norman published early versions of several of Joyce's stories that later appeared in *Dubliners*—"The Sisters," "Eveline," and "After the Race." Norman declined to publish an early version of "Clay" and indicated that he was not interested in any other stories from Joyce because their perspectives on Irish life were at odds with those held by the majority of his readers.

**Oblong, May** This is the name or possibly nickname of a well-known prostitute in turn-of-the-century Dublin, whom Joyce may have known. According to Adaline GLASHEEN, a variation on her name occurs in *Finnegans Wake,* where *Dublin* suggestively becomes *d'Oblong.*

**Occult, the** In general, the term includes any theories and practices relating to esoteric knowledge of the supernatural world. Aspects of the occult include alchemy, divination, magic, and witchcraft. A range of references to occult practices occur throughout Joyce's works, especially in the narrative of the Scylla and Charybdis episode (chapter 9) of *Ulysses,* which touches with biting sarcasm on fundamental elements of theosophical belief and ritual, particularly in relation to prominent characters such as George RUSSELL (AE). In *Finnegans Wake* there are a number of broad allusions to alchemy throughout the narrative, generally in analogies to artistic creation. An intense and sardonic exploration of the mysteries inherent in both alchemy and the Roman Catholic sacrament of the Holy Eucharist appears in the Latin passage on *FW* 185. This depicts Shem as the artist creating his work first by making ink from his own feces and urine, and, then, reverting to English, speaks of him as "the first till last alshemist [who] wrote over every square inch of the only foolscap available, his own body" (*FW* 185.14–36).

**O'Connell, Daniel ("The Liberator")** (1775–1847) O'Connell was the great Catholic nationalist political leader of early 19th-century Ireland. He was trained as a lawyer and called to the Irish bar in 1798 but gave as much attention to public service as to private practice. Throughout his life, O'Connell worked tirelessly for Catholic emancipation and political reform. He helped found the Catholic Association in 1823 (reorganized as the New Catholic Association in 1826), and succeeded in forcing the resolution of the issue of Catholic representation in the British Parliament by winning an election in County Clare in 1828. By reason of his religion, he was not able to take his seat until passage of the 1829 Emancipation Act.

Throughout the 1830s O'Connell attempted to work in cooperation with Whig leaders in Parliament to attain a measure of reform. As an alternate tactic, he conducted a series of mass meetings across Ireland in the early 1840s and was arrested and imprisoned for three months in 1844 on charges of seditious conspiracy. After his release, O'Connell's health began to fail and leadership of the nationalist movement passed to the more radical Young Ireland group.

A formidable political leader, O'Connell appears, along with Charles Stewart PARNELL, as an archetypal paternal figure throughout Joyce's work. A putative family connection doubtless heightened Joyce's interest in O'Connell, for one of his great-grandfathers, the Cork alderman John O'Connell, claimed to be a cousin of The Liberator, a tie that, according to Joyce's biographer Richard ELLMANN, Daniel O'Connell acknowledged numerous times during his visits to Cork.

**Odysseus** This is the name of the eponymous hero of HOMER's epic poem *The ODYSSEY,* one of the most prominent Greek heroes during the siege of Troy described in Homer's *Iliad.* Odysseus is the figure par excellence of the indefatigable hero whose steadfast courage is matched only by his cunning, which enables him to escape any crisis. As is noted in the *Odyssey,* it is Odysseus who conceives of the plan for capturing Troy through the ruse of the Wooden Horse. His character receives extended treatment in *The Odyssey,* a chronicle of his 10-year struggle to return home from Troy to Ithaca. In his attempts to propitiate Helios, whom his crew has mortally offended (by slaughtering the god's cattle), to overcome natural and man-made obstacles to his return, and to regain his rightful position of husband, father, and ruler, Odysseus provides a model of heroic behavior.

In *Ulysses,* Joyce uses the mock-heroic to construct his comic novel. Although its central character, Leopold Bloom, is humorously presented as a modern-day Odysseus figure, it would be a mistake to look for precise one-to-one correspondences between Homer's Odysseus and Joyce's Bloom, for part of the humor of *Ulysses* is in the contrast between them. Nonetheless, certain parallels obtain that do illuminate Bloom's character for the reader. Like Odysseus, Bloom is continually struggling to assert himself in an ever-hostile society. Bloom's identity (though not his life) is threatened again and again, and his self-defense relies more often than not on his psychological rather than his physical strength. Keeping Odysseus in mind while following Bloom through the travails of his day allows the reader to balance the bathos of Bloom's situation with his inherent dignity; this in turn underscores the multiplicity of perspectives through which the narrative of *Ulysses* is given. (*Ulysses* is the Roman name for Odysseus, and prior to the 20th century the name most often used in English poetry, including translations of Homer.)

**odyssey** This is the term Joyce informally employed to designate the second of the three main divisions of *Ulysses* (chapters 4–15), which he also called The Wanderings of Ulysses.

***Odyssey, The*** This is the title of an ancient Greek epic poem in 24 parts, or books, traditionally attributed to the poet HOMER. (With its companion piece, *The Iliad,* it forms the prototype for the epic genre in Western literature.) *The Odyssey* records the 10 years of wandering endured by the Greek hero ODYSSEUS after the fall of Troy. Odysseus struggles to overcome the obstacles put in his way by the god Poseidon, father of Polyphemus, who has been blinded by Odysseus (see book 9), and return to his family and home in Ithaca.

The poem begins in medias res with Odysseus trapped on the island of the nymph Calypso, who has fallen in love with him and forced him to remain with her against his will. Odysseus is able to leave only after the goddess Athena takes pity on him and intercedes for him with the god Zeus. At the same time, on Ithaca a number of suitors, assuming that Odysseus is dead, have appeared to seek the hand of his wife, Penelope. The suitors' despoiling presence has become a threat to Telemachus, the son of Odysseus, who has grown to young manhood in the 20 years that his father has been gone, and who now sets out in search of news of him.

After consulting Nestor and Menelaus, his father's former comrades at Troy, Telemachus returns to Ithaca. Meanwhile, Odysseus has been shipwrecked and cast ashore on the beach in Phaeacia. There Nausikaa, the king's daughter, finds him. Odysseus is brought to the court of Alcinous where he tells the king of his suffering in his encounters with the Lotus Eaters, whose soporific drugs threaten to enervate the crew; the Cyclops, the one-eyed Polyphemus who seeks to imprison Odysseus and his crew and to devour them one at a time; the Lestrygonians, fierce cannibals; Aeolus, the god of the winds who offers Odysseus assistance in returning to Ithaca; Circe, the enchantress who briefly transforms Odysseus's crew into swine; the Sirens, seeking through their songs to lure sailors to steer their ships onto rocks to destroy them; Scylla and Charybdis, the six-headed monster and the gigantic whirlpool between which Odysseus must sail; and the Oxen of the Sun, the cattle beloved of the god Helios that Odysseus's crew slay despite his admonitions. Alcinous sends Odysseus back to

Ithaca, where disguised as a beggar he visits his faithful swineherd Eumaeus. He learns of the suitors who are vying for Penelope's attentions and despoiling his property, and with the help of Telemachus, to whom he has revealed himself, he returns home and kills them all. After assuring Penelope of his true identity by answering correctly her question about the construction of their bed, Odysseus is reunited with his wife. He then visits his father, Laertes, as the poem ends.

As the prototype of the epic form, *The Odyssey* offers a rough formal and contextual model for the structure that frames Joyce's *Ulysses.* Although in composing his work Joyce made no effort to follow the narrative line of Homer's epic, he did use characters and scenes from the poem as the basis for significant portions of his novel. The most obvious associations are the parodic, mock-epical evocations of familiar material from Homer's poem. For a detailed breakdown of Joyce's Homeric references, see the *Ulysses* SCHEMA reprinted in the appendix on page 392.

**O'Grady, Standish James** (1846–1928) O'Grady was an Irish writer from Cork who rose to prominence in the late 19th century with his popular (and some would say popularized, or diluted) English versions of the sagas and epics of ancient Irish mythology. This work earned O'Grady the disapprobation of such literary figures as William Butler YEATS, but it nonetheless made him one of the dominant forces of the IRISH LITERARY REVIVAL. O'Grady stands out as a prime example of the kind of traditional Irish writer whose influence the young Joyce strove to overcome.

**O'Neill, Rev. George, SJ** Father O'Neill was the successor to Thomas Arnold (brother of Matthew Arnold) as professor of English at UNIVERSITY COLLEGE, DUBLIN. Both men taught Joyce, but Father O'Neill seems to have had the more lasting impact. He strongly endorsed the view promulgated by the American novelist Delia Salter Bacon (1811–1859) that Francis Bacon was the author of the plays ascribed to William Shakespeare. His adherence to this view provided Joyce with material that he lampooned in the informal discussion of *Hamlet* that Stephen Dedalus conducts at the National Library of Ireland in the Scylla and Charybdis episode (chapter 9) of *Ulysses* (*U* 9.410).

See also BLEIBTREU, KARL.

**O'Shea, Katharine ("Kitty")** (1846–1921) She was the Englishwoman whose adulterous affair with the Irish statesman Charles Stewart PARNELL precipitated a political crisis that resulted in a split in the Irish Parliamentary Party and ultimately in Parnell's downfall. Kitty O'Shea (as she became popularly known) was born Katharine Page Wood, the sixth daughter of the Reverend Sir John Page Wood of Rivenhall Place, Essex. She married Captain William Henry O'SHEA in 1867, and by him bore a son and two daughters. Kitty O'Shea became acquainted with Parnell in 1880, and in 1881 they began a love affair. Their relationship was an open secret—indeed, throughout the decade they frequently lived together for extended periods at

The Parnell Monument in Dublin *(Irish Tourist Board)*

Eltham, near London. In 1889 Mrs. O'Shea's husband, deciding that he could no longer endure the status quo, filed for divorce. Captain O'Shea's action brought the matter to general public attention, with momentous consequences for Mrs. O'Shea, Parnell, and Irish history. The resulting scandal that arose in both England and Ireland led to the formation of a diverse coalition of forces opposed to Parnell's continuing leadership of the Irish Parliamentary Party, and he was ultimately forced from power. After the divorce had been settled in the courts, a still defiant Parnell married Katharine O'Shea in June 1891, four months before his death.

Although references to Kitty O'Shea occur throughout Joyce's work, they appear perhaps most poignantly in two instances. During the argument over Parnell in the Christmas dinner scene in chapter 1 of *A Portrait of the Artist as a Young Man,* John Casey, in his "story about a very famous spit" (*P* 34–37), describes how he defended the name of Kitty O'Shea from insult. In the Eumaeus episode (chapter 16) of *Ulysses,* Leopold Bloom thinks admiringly of Parnell and then begins drawing parallels between his wife, Molly Bloom, and Kitty O'Shea—apparently suppressing the unflattering parallel between his position and that of Captain O'Shea.

Joyce's interest in Katharine O'Shea rested exclusively on the literary value he could derive from her story. Nonetheless, he must have realized the significance of her own perspective on the tragedy of Parnell, for, while he was working on *Ulysses,* he acquired her biography of her lover and husband, *Charles Stewart Parnell: His Love Story and Political Life.*

**O'Shea, Capt. William Henry** (1840–1905) Captain O'Shea was an Irish politician whose divorce suit against his wife, Katharine O'SHEA, led to the downfall of the Irish statesman Charles Stewart PARNELL. Born in Dublin, the only son of a Catholic solicitor, O'Shea attended Trinity College, Dublin, before joining the British army's 18th Hussars as a cornet (junior cavalry officer) in 1858. O'Shea retired from the army as a captain in 1862, and married Katharine Page Wood in 1867. O'Shea was elected to Parliament in 1880, representing County Clare as a member of Charles Stewart Parnell's Home Rule Party. His wife began an affair with Parnell the following year. O'Shea knew of the affair and tolerated it until 1889, when he filed for divorce, naming Parnell as corespondent. The scandal that followed brought about Parnell's fall from political power.

As the knowing cuckold, O'Shea's spirit hovers around the narrative discourse of *Ulysses.* It is especially evident in the Eumaeus episode (chapter 16), when Leopold Bloom recalls Parnell and the scandal surrounding his political demise. Although Bloom suppresses the connection between himself and O'Shea, the similarities between the two men's acceptance of their wives' infidelity in exchange for tangible benefits—for O'Shea, political position, for Bloom, the advancement of Molly's singing career—are evident.

***Our Exagmination round His Factification for Incamination of Work in Progress*** This is the title of a collection of 12 essays and two letters of protest. It was the first published critical work on *Finnegans Wake,* excerpts of which had appeared under the title WORK IN PROGRESS. Published by SHAKESPEARE AND COMPANY in May 1929, its title is taken from Book III, chapter 3, of *Finnegans Wake* (*FW* 497.2–3), where Anna Livia Plurabelle, speaking through Yawn, briefly recounts Earwicker's failures.

The idea of publishing a collection of essays that would enhance the reader's understanding of *Work in Progress* was Joyce's, and he actively encouraged each contributor. The essays, many of which focus on Joyce's poetics and use of language, were written with the intention of dispelling the aura of inaccessibility and incomprehensibility that surrounded Joyce's innovative work. Several of the essays had been previously published in *TRANSITION,* the Paris magazine in which fragments of *Work in Progress* also appeared. The contributors and their respective articles included Samuel BECKETT, "Dante . . . Bruno . Vico . . Joyce"; Marcel BRION, "The Idea of Time in the Work of James Joyce"; Frank BUDGEN, "James Joyce's *Work in Progress* and Old Norse Poetry"; Stuart GILBERT, "Prolegomena to *Work in Progress*"; Eugene JOLAS, "The Revolution of Language and James Joyce"; Victor LLONA, "I Dont

Know What to Call It But Its [*sic*] Mighty Unlike Prose"; Robert MCALMON, "Mr. Joyce Directs an Irish Word Ballet"; Thomas MCGREEVY, "The Catholic Element in *Work in Progress*"; Elliot PAUL, "Mr. Joyce's Treatment of Plot"; John RODKER, "Joyce & His Dynamic"; Robert SAGE, "Before *Ulysses*—And After"; and William Carlos WILLIAMS, "A Point for American Criticism." The two letters of protest are by G. V. L. SLINGSBY, "Writes a Common Reader," and Vladimir DIXON, "A Litter to Mr. James Joyce." The collection also contains an introduction by Sylvia BEACH, owner of Shakespeare and Company.

*Our Exagmination* provided an immediate answer to friends and critics who believed that Joyce was wasting his time and talent in writing *Finnegans Wake.* Taken as a whole, the volume's assessment of *Work in Progress* may seem uneven. Nonetheless, the individual essays provide the reader with an important overview of the various strategies for reading employed by Joyce's contemporaries, and they outline areas of concern that remain viable topics for critics of the *Wake.*

**Ovid** (43 B.C.–c. A.D. 17) He was the great Latin poet of the Augustan age. His *Metamorphoses,* VIII.188 is the source of the epigraph for *A Portrait of the Artist as a Young Man,* the only one of Joyce's works with such an opening: "Et ignotas animum dimittit in artes" (He turned his mind to unknown arts). The passage from which the line is taken describes the reaction of the mythical Daedalus, deemed "the fabulous artificer," when told by King Minos that he could not leave Crete. The prospect of what would have amounted to a lifelong captivity leads him to fabricate wings made of wax and feathers which he and his son Icarus can use to fly away from the island. The line quoted by Joyce evokes the concept of metamorphosis that occurs throughout *A Portrait of the Artist as a Young Man* (and later in *Ulysses*) as Stephen Dedalus struggles to re-form himself into an artist.

In a gesture typical of the multiplicity of Joyce's language, the line also points to the task facing the reader who undertakes an interpretation of *A Portrait of the Artist as a Young Man.* In the context of the *Metamorphoses,* the translation of the line is straightforward. The subject of the verb *dimittit* is Daedalus; it is he who turns his mind. Taken out of context, the antecedent of *dimittit* is more ambiguous since the third person singular form of the verb leaves it to the reader to determine whether it refers to the pronoun he, she, or it. Thus, Joyce may intend us to think of the subject of the sentence as the mythical Daedalus, as Stephen Dedalus, as Joyce in his role as author, or as the reader him- or herself. The ambiguity of the epigraph sets the tone of the narrative and invites us to read the remainder of the novel in any of a number of possible ways.

# P

**Palmer, G[eoffrey] Molyneux** (1882–1957) He was an English-born composer who wrote musical settings for many of Joyce's poems. Palmer received a bachelor of music degree from Oxford in 1902, and from 1904 to 1907 studied at the Royal College of Music with Sir Charles Villiers Stanford. Although raised in England, Palmer prided himself on his Irish heritage, and he always considered himself an Irish composer. Palmer began to correspond with Joyce shortly after the publication of *Chamber Music* in 1907, seeking permission to set Joyce's poems to music. From the start Joyce enthusiastically endorsed the project, and over the years he did all that he could to facilitate Palmer's work. In a December 1934 letter to his son, Joyce commented that Palmer's musical settings of the poems were in his judgment the best: "30 or 40 musicians at least have set my little poems to music. The best is Molyneux Palmer. After him are Moeran and Bliss" (*Letters*, III.340).

By 1909 Palmer had written scores for at least eight of the *Chamber Music* poems, and he sent the results to Joyce. (The manuscript of the music for "O it was out by Donnycarney" is still in the collection from Joyce's Trieste library, now at the University of Texas.) In 1910 Palmer settled in Ireland, and by 1913 had secured a post as organist at the Protestant church in Mallow, County Cork. By 1920, the multiple sclerosis that had first manifested itself when Palmer was a young man had made him an invalid, forcing him to live the remainder of his life in the care of his sisters in Sandycove. However, early in 1921 Palmer sent two more settings of *Chamber Music* poems to Joyce. In all he set to music 32 of the volume's 36 poems. Throughout the project Joyce did whatever he could to support and encourage Palmer's work. (For a more detailed account of Joyce's views, see *Letters*, I.66, 67, 69, 73–74, and 127; and II.227–228 and 223–224.)

**parallax** This is a term used in astronomy to indicate an apparent change in place or direction of movement of an object caused by a change in the point of observation. Leopold Bloom first thinks of this word in the Lestrygonians episode although, as he admits to himself, he does not quite understand its meaning (*U* 8.110–111). It underscores for the reader the concept of multiple perspectives, and recurs as a motif in the Oxen of the Sun episode, in the Circe episode, and in the Ithaca episode. The term *parallax* can easily signify the difficulty of interpretation in reading Joyce's novel. The reader's perspective continually changes with the shifts of narrative strategies and points of view.

**Paris** This is the city in which Joyce resided for the longest portion of his self-imposed exile from Ireland. Joyce first went to Paris from December 3 to 22, 1902 and, after spending the Christmas holidays in Ireland, returned from January 23 to 11, April 1903, while ostensibly pursuing his medical studies. In 1920, at the urging of Ezra Pound, Joyce returned to Paris with his family in search of a quiet place to finish *Ulysses*. Though he intended the move as only a temporary dislocation, Joyce in fact lived there for most of the final two decades of his life. It was in Paris where *Ulysses* was first published by Sylvia BEACH's SHAKESPEARE AND COMPANY and where Joyce wrote *Finnegans Wake*.

References to Paris appear sporadically in Joyce's writings. At the end of *A Portrait of the Artist as a Young Man*, Stephen Dedalus is poised to leave Dublin, although the reader only learns of his destination retrospectively, in *Ulysses*. In that novel, Paris figures most prominently in Stephen's recollections in the Proteus episode (chapter 3), when he thinks of his meeting with the Irish political expatriate Kevin EGAN, of the frustrations of a foreigner living in that city, and of the rhythm of life on the Paris boulevards. Later, during the Circe episode (chapter 15), a drunken Stephen attempts to relate jumbled anecdotes about Paris prostitutes to the women at Bella Cohen's NIGHTTOWN bordello. In *Finnegans Wake*, Joyce alludes frequently to the city and to specific locations within it.

Paris between the wars was the center of an international arts movement that included some of the leading thinkers, artists, and writers of the 20th century. It provided an intellectual haven for everyone from black American jazz musicians, pioneers of nonrepresentational abstract art and avant-garde music to exiles from Fascism and Communism; American, Irish, German, and Spanish expatriates; and others. Joyce was only one figure among many, though a major one.

**Parnell, Charles Stewart** (1846–1891) With perhaps the exception of Daniel O'Connell, Parnell was the leading Irish political leader in the last quarter of the 19th century. His great popularity led many to call him "Ireland's uncrowned king." Parnell first came to prominence when he was elected to Parliament in 1875. By 1877 he had successfully molded the often unruly and divided Irish Parlia-

A close-up of the Parnell Monument *(Irish Tourist Board)*

mentary Party into a disciplined voting bloc that came to hold the balance of political power between the Liberal and the Conservative parties in the British Parliament. Parnell used this leverage to advance the cause that dominated his concerns, the Home Rule Movement.

In 1879 Michael DAVITT founded the Irish LAND LEAGUE. Parnell, although he was himself an Anglo-Irish Protestant landlord, immediately saw its importance. He gave his support to the endeavor and agreed to become its first president. In the 1880s, after a somewhat rocky start, Parnell's political influence and general popularity grew to enormous proportions. He greatly influenced the Irish land reform legislation of 1881. At the same time, his speeches became increasingly violent. This resulted in his arrest and confinement in Kill-mainham Gaol. When Land League violence increased, the government was forced in the spring of 1882 to release Parnell as a way of meliorating civil disturbances. In alliance with Prime Minister Gladstone and the Liberal Party, Parnell was nearly successful in engineering the passage of a Home Rule Bill in 1886. On April 18, 1887, the *Times of London* published a letter purportedly written by Parnell condoning the PHOENIX PARK MURDERS. In 1889 Richard Pigott admitted under cross-examination to an investigating commission that he had forged the letter. His repeated misspelling of *hesitancy* as "hesitency" proved to be his undoing. (Joyce referred to the misspelling and to Pigott throughout *Finnegans Wake*.) Parnell was exonerated and at the peak of his power.

Later in 1889, however, his political and social position came under sudden and severe challenge. Captain William O'SHEA, one of Parnell's political associates, petitioned for a divorce from his wife, Katharine, on grounds of adultery. O'Shea named Parnell (who had been openly conducting an affair with Mrs. O'Shea for 10 years) as corespondent. The ensuing trial and scandal (Mrs. O'Shea became familiar to the newspaper-reading public as "Kitty O'SHEA") raised opposition to Parnell in both Britain and Ireland. A coalition of religious, civil, and political leaders brought pressure to bear on Parnell's associates and created a rift that for all practical purposes ended Parnell's leadership of the Irish Parliamentary Party. On December 6, 1890, Timothy Michael HEALY, a former supporter, led the bulk of the party to split from Parnell over the affair. Parnell sought to regain control through vigorously electioneering. Unfortunately, his health was broken by the strain produced by those events, and Parnell died on October 6, 1891, a few months after marrying Katharine O'Shea. The date of his death came to be known as IVY DAY (ivy is a traditional symbol of remembrance).

Joyce's father, John JOYCE, was an ardent Parnellite and a beneficiary of his party's patronage, and his son shared this loyalty and admiration. References to Parnell and his betrayal by the Irish appear throughout Joyce's work, and they often provide the metaphors for wide-ranging critiques of the Irish character. Joyce's earliest known composition was a poem written at the age of nine, "ET TU, HEALY," decrying the betrayal of Parnell by his political supporters, particularly Parnell's lieutenant Tim HEALY, in the Irish Home Rule Party. Although ELLMANN reports that Joyce's father had the poem printed, no copies survive. Nonetheless, there remains ample published evidence of Joyce's feelings for Parnell.

While in TRIESTE, Joyce wrote an article entitled "The Shade of Parnell" for the newspaper *Il PICCOLO DELLA SERA,* published in Italian in the paper's May 16, 1912, issue. It indignantly condemns the Irish willingness to abandon their long-time leader. Likewise, in his vitriolic poem, "Gas from a Burner," written to condemn the moral hypocrisy of his countrymen, Joyce cites an event from Parnell's life to epitomize Irish venality, noting that: "'Twas Irish humour, wet and dry, / Flung quicklime into Parnell's eye."

Joyce memorialized the date of Parnell's death in his *Dubliners* short story "Ivy Day in the Committee Room." There he invokes the image of Parnell to contrast the energy and idealism that animated Irish politics in Parnell's era with the cynicism and maudlin sentimentality that informs it at the time of the story. Perhaps most distinctly, Parnell serves as an important figure in chapter 1 of *A Portrait of the Artist as a Young Man.* Lying ill in the school infirmary, Stephen Dedalus dreams of Parnell's funeral. Later in the same chapter, during the well-known Christmas dinner episode, Simon Dedalus, John Casey, and Dante Riordan have a bitter fight over the morality of Parnell and the position of the Irish Catholic Church.

References to Parnell occur throughout *Ulysses.* In the Hades episode (chapter 6), several of the men attending the funeral of Paddy Dignam at Glasnevin Cemetery make a point of visiting the grave of "the Chief" before leaving the grounds. In the Eumaeus episode (chapter 16), Leopold Bloom recalls public reaction to the revelations of Parnell's adultery with Kitty O'Shea and examples of his ill treatment by the Irish people in a way that shows great sympathy for Parnell and, ironically because of Bloom's own situation, not much regard for the cuckolded husband.

In *Finnegans Wake* Parnell, the "uncrowned king" (a term purportedly coined by Timothy M. Healy, who later spearheaded the move to oust him as party leader), is one of many archetypal paternal figures, and he exemplifies the Irish national inclination, as Joyce perceived it, to betray their leaders. "As hollyday in his house so was he priest and king to that: ulvy came, envy saw, ivy conquered" (*FW* 58.5–6). Adaline GLASHEEN's *Third Census of Finnegans Wake* finds references to Parnell and to Joyce's earlier commentary on Parnell throughout the narrative. In his library in Trieste, Joyce had an anthology of Parnell's speeches entitled *Words of the Dead Chief: Being Extracts from the Public Speeches and Other Pronouncements of Charles Stewart Parnell from the Beginning to the Close of His Memorable Life.* For additional details of Joyce's view on Parnell, see *Letters,* II.3, 295, and 456–457.

**Pater, Walter** (1839–1894) Pater was a well-known 19th-century Oxford don, novelist, critic, and aesthetician. His book *The Renaissance: Studies in Art and Poetry,* with its supple articulation of an aesthetic appreciation based on the idea of art for art's sake, established important intellectual connections with Swinburne and the pre-Raphaelites. More significantly, it exerted a formative influence on several generations of Victorian and Edwardian writers, including the Irish authors Oscar WILDE (who studied under Pater at Oxford), George MOORE, and James Joyce, who was interested in Pater both for his ideas and for his influence upon Wilde.

Although Pater's direct impact upon Joyce's writing remains difficult to discern with any sort of precision, C. P. CURRAN, Joyce's classmate and lifelong friend, ventured the opinion that "Pater, I am pretty sure, had followed the 'silver-veined' Newman in Joyce's pre-Ibsen schooldays and may have taught him how to poise an adverb" (*Joyce Remembered*). Pater certainly exerted a broad influence on the aesthetics of early MODERNISM and on modernist writers, and sometime during his stay in TRIESTE, Joyce appears to have reread Pater's novel *Marius the Epicurean* and his critical study *The Renaissance.* He acquired copies of both works during that period and took the trouble to transcribe seven passages from *Marius the Epicurean* into a notebook that he kept during 1919 and 1920. (These appear in *The James Joyce Archive,* volumes 2 and 3.)

**Paul, Elliot** (1891–1958) He was an American journalist, critic, novelist, and publisher who lived in France and Spain between the two world wars. Born in Malden, Massachusetts, Paul served in World War I and went on to Paris to work as a newspaperman on the Paris *Tribune* in 1925 where he met Eugene JOLAS. With Eugene and Maria JOLAS, he helped found *TRANSITION* (1927–30 and 1932–39), a highly experimental literary magazine that, among other things, published a number of excerpts from *Finnegans Wake.*

As a personal friend of Joyce, Paul wrote one of the essays appearing in *OUR EXAGMINATION ROUND HIS FACTIFICATION FOR INCAMINATION OF WORK IN PROGRESS.* His contribution to that collection, with the deceptively conventional title "Mr. Joyce's Treatment of Plot," stresses the structural and contextual uniqueness of *Finnegans Wake.* Taking contemporary advances in physics and mathematics as analogous achievements exemplifying his argument, Paul identifies Joyce's writing as a highly skilled representation of the non-Cartesian thinking that at the time exerted a pronounced influence within intellectual circles as an innovative mode of expression. Paul's essay was partly intended as a rebuttal of Wyndham LEWIS's highly critical *Time and Western Man.* Paul takes up the same topics covered in that work, but does so through a complimentary assessment of Joyce's approach.

**Phoenix Park** This is a 1,760-acre woodland, measuring seven miles in circumference, located on the northern banks of the River LIFFEY at the western edge of the DUBLIN city limits. Phoenix Park is the largest enclosed urban nature preserve in Europe, with a wall stretching the full seven miles around its borders. It has nine main gates, and is divided along a northwest/southeast axis by Chesterfield Road, named after the 18th-century lord lieutenant responsible for numerous improvements made within the park.

The name *Phoenix* is an English corruption of the Irish word *Fionnusige,* meaning "fair water." The land first came into English hands in 1541, and it was made a deer park in 1671 by the duke of Ormond. The duke determined the park's present size by enclosing the land with a wall to contain the deer and to hinder poaching.

A number of locations and landmarks within the park play prominent roles throughout Joyce's writings. In "A Painful Case" the park itself symbolizes the isolation of Mr. James Duffy. In *Ulysses,* Joyce makes topical allusions to the Viceregal Lodge (now the official residence of the American ambassador) in the Wandering Rocks episode (chapter 10), and to the PHOENIX PILLAR, the site of the 1882 PHOENIX PARK MURDERS, in the Eumaeus episode (chapter 16).

In *Finnegans Wake,* Phoenix Park's literal associations with the mythical bird continually evoke the theme of resurrection that is an integral part of the narrative. As a natural preserve in the midst of the city, separated from, yet surrounded by, urban life, Phoenix Park invites postmodern revisions of the Eden myth very much in keeping with the general imaginative trajectory of *Finnegans Wake.* Phoenix Park also evokes other myths and legends. The feet of the giant FINN MACCOOL, who lies sleeping beneath Dublin, form the two hills near Phoenix Park, and it is the legendary site of the Forest of Tristan into which Tristan—a recurring figure in *Finnegans Wake*—retreats in despair over the conflict between his love for ISEULT and his allegiance to King Mark, to whom Iseult is betrothed. It is also the scene of the crime that H C E is alleged to have committed. References to park landmarks—among them the WELLINGTON MONUMENT, the Zoological Gardens, and the Magazine Fort—also appear throughout the *Wake.* Each, in its own way, enhances the park's associations with historical, natural, and mythical themes in Joyce's work.

**Phoenix Park murders** This is the name given to a politically motivated killing carried out by a terrorist group in the park on May 6, 1882. The murderers, members of a nationalist society called the INVINCIBLES, ambushed two British officials, Lord Frederick Cavendish, chief secretary for Ireland, and Mr. Thomas Henry Burke, an undersecretary in Dublin Castle, and stabbed them to death near the PHOENIX PILLAR, in the area of the Viceregal Lodge. Although those involved in the killings were eventually apprehended and several executed, the incident caused an international sensation, provoked a revulsion from terrorism, and ultimately strengthened the political hand of Charles Stewart PARNELL, who had just effected a compromise with the British government over the land question. In the Aeolus episode of *Ulysses,* Myles Crawford recounts the efforts of Ignatius Gallaher to convey details of the event to the *New York World* newspaper. In the Eumaeus episode, Leopold Bloom suggests that the proprietor of the cabman's shelter that he and Stephen Dedalus visit is "Skin-the-Goat" Fitzharris, a member of the Invincibles who is rumored to have driven the getaway carriage.

**Phoenix Pillar** This is a stone column, 30 feet tall and surmounted by a stone replica of a phoenix. It was erected in PHOENIX PARK in the 18th century by Lord Chesterfield, one of the principal architects of the park's present configuration. It was the site of the PHOENIX PARK MURDERS in 1882.

***Piccolo della Sera, Il*** It was the most important daily newspaper published in TRIESTE during the time that Joyce was living in that city. Founded in 1881 by Theodor Mayer, *Il Piccolo della Sera* supported the return to Italy of Italian territory (including Trieste) that was then under the control of Austria-Hungary. Over a five-year period between 1907 and 1912, Joyce, at the invitation of Roberto PREZIOSO, then the paper's editor, wrote in Italian a series of articles on aspects of Irish history, art, and society: "Fenianism: The Last Fenian" (1907), "Home Rule Comes of Age" (1907), "Ireland at the Bar" (1907), "Oscar Wilde: The Poet of Salomé" (1909), "Bernard Shaw's Battle with the Censor" (1909), "The Home Rule Comet" (1910), "The Shade of Parnell" (1912), "The City of the Tribes" (1912), and "The Mirage of the Fisherman of Aran" (1912).

**Pigeon House, The** This is the name given to a building on the breakwater that extends into Dublin Bay from Ringsend, on the south bank of the River LIFFEY. In Joyce's time, the Pigeon House was the site of an electric generating and drainage station. The name derives from an 18th-century inn erected on the spot by a man named John Pidgeon, called Pidgeon's Inn. The Pigeon House is the destination of the two boys who go off on "a day's miching" from school in the *Dubliners* story "An Encounter."

**Pigott, Richard** (1828–1889) He was an Irish journalist who wrote a series of articles under the general title "Parnellism and Crime," published in the *London Times* beginning on April 18, 1887. The articles used forged letters to implicate the Irish statesman Charles Stuart PARNELL in the PHOENIX PARK MURDERS and in the call for the murder of landlords during the Land War of 1879–82. On September 17, 1888, at Parnell's insistence, a special parliamentary Commission of Inquiry began an investigation of Pigott's charges. On February 20, 1889, Pigott was unmasked as a forger through his misspelling of the word *hesitancy* as "hesitency," both in his personal correspondence and in the letter falsely attributed to Parnell and reprinted in the April 18, 1887, article.

The misspelled "hesitency" recurs as a significant motif throughout *Finnegans Wake,* and it is often associated with the stuttering of H C E. It is an obvious allusion to the Parnell affair and Joyce's opinion of the Irish inclination to betray their leaders. Joyce also expands on these allusions to evoke broader ideas about the effect of language and literature on our perception of the world.

Pigott fled on March 1, 1889, nine days after the revelation of his crime, and later committed suicide in Madrid. His two sons, Joseph and Francis, were fellow students of Joyce's at CLONGOWES WOOD COLLEGE at the time, and Francis was in the same class. Although the Jesuit masters tried to shield the two boys from immediate knowledge of their father's death, one of their classmates told them, and a terrible scene resulted. The two boys were withdrawn from the college that summer.

**A Pisgah Sight of Palestine, or The Parable of the Plums** This is the story recounted by Stephen Dedalus at the end of the Aeolus episode of *Ulysses.* The title is a reference to Deuteronomy 34, in which Moses "went up from the plains of Moab unto the mountain of Nebo, to the top of Pisgah," from which the Lord showed him the Promised Land before he died. A Pisgah Sight of Palestine traces the steps of a pair of middle-aged, working-class women, Anne Kearns and Florence MacCabe, "two Dublin vestals (*U* 7.923), to the top of NELSON'S PILLAR for a panoramic view of the city of Dublin. It represents for them, at least, a rather momentous undertaking, as they trek across the city from "Fumbally's lane . . [o]ff Blackpits" (*U* 7.924, 926).

Although the parable has a superficial appeal that comes from Stephen's liberal use of local color, it also shows the marked difference in Stephen's literary tastes from those of his listeners. The story's modernist structure and its ambiguous ending give it a tone very different from that to which Stephen's audience—Myles Crawford and Professor MacHugh—are accustomed. When it ends with seemingly a flat punch line, neither man knows how to react. This is one of several instances in the novel when Stephen makes an unsuccessful attempt to gain a sort of popular acclaim for his wit.

**Pola** This is a port on the Balkan coast of the Adriatic Sea 150 miles south of TRIESTE. The Austrian army captured the town in 1797, and it became the main base for the Austro-Hungarian navy after 1866. Joyce went to Pola in the late fall of 1904 after leaving Dublin with Nora BARNACLE. He found a job teaching English at the Berlitz language school recently opened there. Joyce called the city "a naval Siberia," and from almost the moment of his arrival he developed a profound distaste for it. In March 1905, Joyce and Nora moved to the more agreeable city of Trieste. Pola is now Pula, Croatia.

**Popper, Amalia** (1891–1967) She was one of Joyce's private language students in Trieste. Joyce tutored her for a year or so starting around 1908. She graduated from the prestigious Liceo Femminile and two years later, in 1910, she began her student days at the University of Florence, where she eventually met her husband, Michele Risolo. Amalia's father, Leopoldo Popper, was a well-to-do businessman of Jewish background from Bohemia and served as a model for Leopold Bloom. Richard Ellmann speculates that Amalia may have been the mystery woman of *Giacomo Joyce* or at least part of the composite figure of the Jewish female student Joyce had in mind (*James Joyce,* pp. 342 and 775n.7). In October 1929, she published a translation of "A Little Cloud" ("Una Nuvoletta") that appeared in *Il Piccolo della Sera,* the same newspaper that had published several of Joyce's articles on Irish matters between 1907 and 1912. Her interest in Joyce's short stories continued with other translations from *Dubliners.*

***Portrait of the Artist as a Young Man, A*** This is a cinematic version of Joyce's novel of the same name, directed by Joseph Strick. It was filmed in Ireland in 1977 with Bosco Hogan in the role of Stephen Dedalus and T. P. McKenna (who plays the role of Buck Mulligan in the Strick film of *Ulysses* [2]) in the role of Simon Dedalus. Its doggedly realistic mode recapitulates the narrative outline of Joyce's novel, but it fails to capture the multiple perspectives that make Joyce's narrative far more than the linear representation of a series of events. See also the appendix on page 381.

**postmodernism** This is a term used to designate a cultural and intellectual tendency that grew directly out of MODERNISM, the late 19th- and early 20th-century challenge to Victorian thinking and values. Scholars have long debated about the specific elements that constitute postmodernism, but there is general agreement about certain broad features.

Like modernism, postmodernism features an ongoing interrogation of the legitimacy of the moral authority of social institutions—the family, religion, and the state—and it resists the enforcement by them of standards of morality and conduct. Unlike modernism, postmodernism shows itself equally skeptical of the ability of individuals to act as the proper arbiters for ethical conduct. Instead it assumes the view, sometimes with nihilistic overtones and sometimes with an enlightened sense of liberation, that there are no valid objective standards against which to measure human behavior. In a very general way, literary postmodernism encourages formal experimentation, but its implementation varies greatly from author to author.

Joyce is often identified—along with his compatriot and fellow exile Samuel BECKETT—as one of the foremost postmodernists to write in English (Beckett also wrote in French). Aside from the clear determination of both writers to distinguish their work from the work of earlier writers, however, they share few, if any, stylistic similarities. Moreover, they represent two distinct tendencies of postmodernism, Joyce taking optimistic advantage in *Finnegans Wake* of the freedom from restrictions that such a movement presents, and the nihilistic Beckett continually lamenting the loss of coherence in a world now without meaning. While *Finnegans Wake* has all of the expected elements distinguishing that movement, a great deal of debate has taken place over the issue of whether *Ulysses* is a modernist or a postmodernist work. Part of the controversy, of course, grows out of the evolving nature of postmodernism itself. Nonetheless, despite changes over the decades postmodern thinking can still find the most consistent articulation of its fundamental principles in Joyce's work.

**Pound, Ezra** (1885–1972) He was an American poet and critic. Pound took the role of friend and mentor to a number of prominent modernist writers including Joyce and T. S. ELIOT. Born in Hailey,

Idaho, and raised in the Philadelphia suburbs, he attended the University of Pennsylvania from 1901 to 1903, where he met his lifelong friend William Carlos WILLIAMS. Pound transferred to Hamilton College, in Clinton, New York, from which he graduated in 1905. He returned to Penn, where he earned an M.A. in 1906 and began work on his doctorate (never completed). After teaching briefly at Wabash College in Indiana, Pound left for Europe in 1908. Arriving in London, he became friends with Ford Madox FORD and W. B. YEATS, among others, and began his promotion of a poetic movement he called imagism (see IMAGIST MOVEMENT). He published several books, including *Personae* (1909) and *The Spirit of Romance* (1910), and began writing for literary journals. By 1913, Pound had established himself as an important literary figure. He eventually became one of the most influential poets and critics of the century. Because of his eccentric political and economic views, which eventually led him to embrace Fascism and anti-Semitism and to broadcast Axis propaganda during World War II, he was also one of the most controversial. His major poetic work was *The Cantos* (published at intervals from 1925 to 1960), and he published numerous critical essays as well.

Pound made contact with Joyce late in 1913, when he wrote to ask permission to include the poem "I Hear an Army" in *Des Imagistes* (1914), a volume of imagist poems. As a result of their initial exchange, Pound became deeply interested in bringing Joyce's other work to public attention. With this in mind, he arranged for the English journal the EGOIST to serialize Joyce's novel *A Portrait of the Artist as a Young Man.* The first installment appeared in the February 2, 1914, issue (Joyce's 32nd birthday), and, although World War I made transmission of chapters from TRIESTE to London difficult, the serialization continued in 25 installments (with, as Chester ANDERSON has noted, "two *lacunae* caused by Joyce's inability to complete Chapter V on the serialization schedule") until September 1, 1915.

For the remainder of the decade, Pound did whatever he could to promote Joyce's works and to bring a measure of financial stability into Joyce's life. In February 1916 he published a favorable article on *Exiles* in the American journal *Drama.* In the same year Pound worked successfully to get the British government to award Joyce £100 from the Civil List (a fund made available by Parliament for discretionary grants by the government). In March 1918, at Pound's urging, the LITTLE REVIEW brought Joyce's *Ulysses* to general public notice by beginning a serialization of the novel with the Telemachus episode (chapter 1). Chapters from *Ulysses* continued to appear in the *Little Review* through December 1920 with the Oxen of the Sun episode (chapter 14). Publication ceased after obscenity charges were brought against the journal's editors, Margaret ANDERSON and Jane HEAP. Even with the sudden discontinuation, the serialization gave a tremendous boost to Joyce's work on the novel. Under the discipline of the publishing schedule, he completed chapters (many of which he subsequently revised) at a regular and timely pace. Furthermore, the attention garnered by these excerpts confirmed Joyce's sense of the validity of the approach that he was taking.

Despite all this effort, however, Pound's devotion to Joyce's writing began to wane. As he read more and more of *Ulysses,* Pound became disenchanted with the work. Joyce sensed this lessening of enthusiasm, and not surprisingly it created a distance between the two men. Nonetheless, Pound remained Joyce's friend and in 1920 he helped him relocate from Trieste to Paris in order to finish *Ulysses.* When Pound moved to Italy in 1924, his already conservative political inclinations and idiosyncratic economic theories grew more pronounced, turning more or less explicitly toward Fascism, which had recently triumphed in Italy. Joyce's political sentiments were antipathetic to such views, and his friendship with Pound cooled. In December 1926, Pound refused to sign the statement condemning Samuel ROTH's piracy of *Ulysses* (see *Letters* III.150n1). In the meantime, Pound was openly hostile to the fragments of *WORK IN PROGRESS* that appeared in print, and as his sympathy for Fascism grew he and Joyce drifted further apart. Nonetheless, to the end of his life, Joyce retained his respect for Pound and a sense of gratitude for the help that he had received from him. (See "Letter on Pound"; also see *Letters,* I.101,

397–398; II.352–353, 358, 387, 467–469; III.12–13, 27–28, 32–34, 47, 144–145, 155, 156, 165–166, 218–219, 239–240, 415, and 508–510. References to Pound appear throughout Joyce's letters; in particular, see *Letters,* I.76–78, 80, 84–86, 89, 91–92, 95, 99–100, 105, 121, 126, 131, 143, 149, 150, 152, 157, 161, 163, 165–166, 181, 184, 204, 234, 249, 269, 277, 281, and 296; *Letters,* II.336, 338, 340, 357, 368, 370, 376–377, 379, and 396, 403; III.15–16, 30, 41, 131, 154, 174, 217, 220, 242, 311. Also see *Letters* II.326–328, 349, 352, 354, 356, 358–360, 363–367, 372–373, 375, 381–386, 405, 413–414, and 423–424; *Letters,* III.145–146, 150n.1, and 237.)

For further information, see Hugh Kenner, *The Pound Era* (1971); Humphrey Carpenter, *A Serious Character* (1988); C. David Heymann, *Ezra Pound: The Last Rower* (1976).

**Prezioso, Roberto** (1869–1930) He was the editor of the TRIESTE newspaper *Il* PICCOLO DELLA *Sera* during the time Joyce was in Trieste. In 1905 he became one of Joyce's English-language students, and in 1907, seeking to help Joyce out of financial difficulties, Prezioso invited him to write a series of articles—ultimately extending over five years—about Ireland for publication in *Il Piccolo della Sera.* Over time, the friendship between the Joyces and Prezioso grew quite close, but sometime in 1911 or 1912, Prezioso apparently tried to seduce Nora BARNACLE, and this precipitated a confrontation between him and Joyce that brought their friendship to an end. Richard Ellmann speculates that Joyce drew upon the incident and used elements from Prezioso's character in the creation of both Robert Hand in *Exiles* and Blazes Boylan in *Ulysses.*

**Queen's College, Cork** This is one of three Queen's colleges in Ireland (the other two were in Belfast and Galway), established on December 30, 1845, as a response to popular demand for institutions of higher education open to Catholics. (The title Queen's College comes from the legislation that gave Victoria the power to endow new colleges for the advancement of learning in Ireland.) It opened in 1849, and after the passage of the University Education Act of 1879 its curriculum came under the jurisdiction of the Royal University. The university is still in existence, now called University College, Cork.

Joyce's father, John JOYCE, attended Queen's from 1867 to 1870. He was, however, more attentive to his social life than to his academics, and left the university without a degree. Joyce drew on this connection with Queen's College by making Simon Dedalus, Stephen's father, an alumnus as well. In chapter 2 of *A Portrait of the Artist as a Young Man* Simon returns to Queen's, while visiting Cork to sell off property, bringing a reluctant Stephen with him.

**Quinet, Edgar** (1803–1875) Quinet was a French poet and historian whose liberal views exerted great influence upon 19th-century French society. His first major work was a translation of Johann Gottfried Herder's *Ideen zur Philosophie der Geschichte der Menschheit* (Introduction to the philosophy of the history of humanity). From this study Joyce drew, in Clive HART's words, "the only quotation of any length to be included in *Finnegan's Wake.*" It appears in Quinet's French in the LESSONS CHAPTER of *Finnegans Wake,* (*FW* 281.4–13), and recurs in variant forms elsewhere in the narrative. The lines can be translated:

> Today, as in the time of Pliny and Columella, the hyacinth thrives in Wales, the periwinkle in Illyria, the daisy on the ruins of Numantia, and while the cities around them have changed masters and names, several having passed into nothingness, civilizations having clashed and broken, their peaceful generations have crossed the ages and come down to us, fresh and laughing as in days of battles.

These lines allude to the cyclical nature of history, whose force transcends human endeavor and gently mocks human pretensions. The ethos embodied in these lines infuses the narrative of *Finnegans Wake,* and refers specifically to Joyce's view of Irish nationalism, whose ambitions had led to so much needless suffering.

**Quinn, John** (1870–1924) He was the American attorney, patron of the arts, and collector of manuscripts, including those of Joyce's *Exiles* and *Ulysses.* In February 1921, Quinn unsuccesssfully defended Margaret ANDERSON and Jane HEAP against charges of obscenity brought by the New York Society for the Suppression of Vice for publishing part of the Nausikaa episode (chapter 13) of *Ulysses* in the July–August 1920 issue of their journal, the *LITTLE REVIEW.* Joyce, according to Richard ELLMANN, was not pleased with Quinn's legal strategy. Quinn claimed that *Ulysses* was disgusting rather than erotic, and therefore not obscene under the meaning of the law. Joyce believed this to be a missed opportunity to challenge the principle of censorship (see *James Joyce,* pp. 502–504). Quinn and Joyce met for the first time in October 1923.

For further information, see *Letters,* I.100, 103, 124, 144, 149–150, 157–158, 160–162, 164, 183, 192, 199, 204, 206–207, 208, 211, 219, 398n.1; *Letters,* II.394–396, 404–406, 447–448, 455, 459–460; *Letters,* III.17, 21–22, 27–31, 33, 40, 41, and 82.

# R

**Rabelais, François** (1483?–1553) He was the French humanist scholar, physician, and satirist best known for his *Gargantua and Pantagruel,* a bawdy chronicle of two giants, father and son. Through the exaggerated appetites and adventures of these characters and their companions, the tales ridicule the foibles, beliefs, and institutions of late medieval French society. Rabelais's employment of coarse, graphic language and his use of detailed, ludicrous catalogues that parody epic conventions are distinguishing features of his work. Such features had some influence on Joyce's *Ulysses*—in the Cyclops episode (chapter 12), for instance, and in the numerous hallucinations that punctuate the Circe episode (chapter 15)—and on *Finnegans Wake,* which contains parodies of epic conventions and medieval romances. Although Joyce, possibly afraid of seeming derivative, resisted comparisons with Rabelais, claiming not to have read him, he did have a copy of *Les cinq livres* in his Trieste library and acquired the English version, *The Works of Rabelais,* translated by Gustave Doré, sometime after moving to Paris in 1920. For additional details, see *Letters,* III.40, 44, and 74n.4.

**Random House** The is the New York publishing firm founded by Bennett CERF and Donald Klopfer in 1923. In March 1932 Cerf acquired the American publishing rights to *Ulysses* for a $1,500 advance and the promise of 15 percent royalties on the book's future earnings. As the first step in securing the legal right to publish the book in the United States, Cerf arranged to have a copy of *Ulysses* sent to him from Paris and seized by the U.S. customs authorities. With reviews pasted into it (so they could be entered into evidence and cited in defense of its literary merit), the book arrived in the port of New York in early May 1932. By this time smuggling *Ulysses* into the United States had become so routine that customs officials generally ignored any copies they came across, and it was only at the insistence of a representative of Random House that the book was seized. So began the legal challenge to the prohibition against distribution of the book in America.

The *Ulysses* obscenity trial commenced in federal court in late August 1933. Morris Ernst acted as counsel for the defense. On December 6, 1933, the Hon. John M. WOOLSEY, the presiding judge, ruled that he found nowhere in it "the leer of the sensualist," and ordered that *Ulysses* "be admitted into the United States." Typesetters began work immediately, and the first 500 copies under the Random House imprint appeared in January 1934, with the remainder of the run being printed in February. The text of this edition was the accepted standard text until the publication of the revised critical edition of Walter Gabler by Garland Publishing in 1984. This GABLER EDITION was published in 1986 as the "corrected text" in a trade edition by the Random House imprint, Vintage Books. See the appendix on page 392 for the full text of Judge Woolsey's decision.

**realism** This is the term used to identify a broad literary movement and style of writing generally seen as originating in 19th-century France with

Honoré de BALZAC. The fundamental aim of realism, which stands in opposition to romanticism, is to present an accurate representation of ordinary life. Achieving this involves the rendering of settings and characters in a fashion that evokes impressions familiar to the common reader.

Early critics often applied the term "realism" to all of Joyce's prose fiction up to and including *Ulysses.* Subsequent interpretive studies have generally dismissed the applicability of "realism" to *Ulysses*—which many prefer to consider a modernist work—and some have even questioned its use with respect to parts of *Dubliners* or *A Portrait of the Artist as a Young Man.* There is certainly a core of realistic elements in much of Joyce's fiction, but the complexities of his narrative strategies militate against the use of any particular literary style to describe his work.

**Renan, (Joseph) Ernest** (1823–1892) Renan was a French philosopher and historian whose *La vie de Jésus* (Life of Jesus), published in 1863, created a tremendous uproar in France because of the emphasis that it placed upon the humanity of Jesus in its account of the creation of Christianity. Although Renan may not have had a pronounced effect upon Joyce's aesthetic or artistic views, his ideas seem to hover about the periphery of Joyce's consciousness. Joyce initially read *La vie de Jésus* in January 1905, shortly after settling in TRIESTE (see *Letters,* II.76 and 82). Later while living in ZURICH during World War I, he acquired a copy of an English translation of the work. Joyce had also read Renan's memoirs, *Souvenirs d'enfance et de jeunesse (Memories of Childhood and Youth),* in which the author's account of his education echoes that of Stephen Dedalus in *A Portrait of the Artist as a Young Man* (see *Letters,* II.72, 110, 155, 164, and 191). In *Stephen Hero,* Joyce makes Stephen Daedalus a reader of Renan (*SH* 174–175 and 190), and in *Ulysses* Stephen mentions Renan in passing during his disquisition on Shakespeare in the National Library in the Scylla and Charybdis episode (chapter 9; *U* 9.394 and 756).

***Revue des Deux Mondes*** French literary magazine edited by René Doumic. In its August 1, 1925, issue, the *Revue des Deux Mondes* published a harsh critique of *Ulysses* by Louis Gillet entitled "Littératures Etrangères: Du Côté de chez Joyce" (Foreign literature: from Joyce's point of view). Despite the acerbic tone of this essay, Joyce was pleased that his novel had been discussed in such a prestigious journal (see *Letters,* I.232 and III.74). Gillet had subsequent reservations about his own assessment of *Ulysses,* and a friendship sprang up between the two men after Gillet wrote to Joyce apologizing for the review and assuring him that he had reconsidered his opinion (*Letters,* III.210–211). In the December 15, 1940, issue of the *Revue,* Gillet made further amends with a highly favorable appraisal of *Finnegans Wake,* which Joyce read before he died in January 1941 (see *Letters,* III.506).

**Ribbonmen** This was the name of an 18th- and 19th-century Irish rural partisan group, or its members, that advocated the use of physical force to achieve its political ends. It was similar to the WHITEBOYS, an earlier organization. The group got its name in the early 19th century, around 1826, from the green badge worn by its members. The Ribbonmen were terrorists, employing violence against landlords who, by exploiting a legal loophole in the Encumbered Estates Act, brought about large-scale evictions of tenant farmers following the famine of 1845–49. It declined in popularity after mid-century and was practically moribund when declared illegal in 1871. References to this group appear in the Cyclops episode (chapter 12) of *Ulysses,* where Joe Hynes and the Citizen exchange a series of signals that seem to derive from a secret greeting used by Ribbonmen to identify one another.

**Richards, (Thomas Franklin) Grant** (1872–1948) He was a British publisher. The son of an Oxford don, Richards worked for W. T. Stead on the *Review of Reviews* from 1890 to 1896, before setting up his own publishing firm in London in 1897. His list of publications included Samuel Butler's *The Way of All Flesh* and the work of the English classicist scholar and poet A. E. Housman, among others.

Joyce's association with Richards began in 1904 when he submitted *Chamber Music* to him. Richards declined to publish it. Undaunted, Joyce sent him the *Dubliners* manuscript late in 1905, and in February 1906 Richards accepted it. Shortly after this, however, Richards raised objections to portions of various stories. He demanded that Joyce make a number of specific deletions or modifications. Although hesitant to undertake large-scale revisions, Joyce did make some effort to address Richards's criticisms and concerns while maintaining the integrity of his work. Unfortunately, none of Joyce's proposed emendations fully satisfied the publisher. Their negotiations continued until September 1906 when Richards abruptly withdrew his offer to publish.

In late November 1913, Joyce, who was living in TRIESTE, unexpectedly received a letter from Richards regarding *Dubliners*. According to Joyce's biographer Richard ELLMANN, Richards had had a change of heart. Although he gives no further details, it seems clear in retrospect that literary tastes had finally caught up with Joyce. This time he made no objections, quickly issued a contract to Joyce, and brought the work out under his imprint in the following year.

Joyce detailed his sense of frustration over the events surrounding the publication of *Dubliners* in his open letter "A Curious History." Robert Scholes and A. Walton Litz give an account of the matter in their edition of *Dubliners*, where they collect the relevant Joyce-Richards correspondence. See *Letters*, I.59–64 and 75; II.104–105, 112, 122, 129–144, 152–153, 158, 164, 175–180, 184–185, 225, 291–293, 324–325, 327–330, and 332–341.

***Riders to the Sea*** This is a one-act play written in 1904 by the Irish dramatist John Millington SYNGE. *Riders to the Sea* explores the tragedy inherent in the harsh life faced by turn-of-the-century Aran Islanders, focusing on the sufferings endured by a single family whose men have lost their lives at sea over the course of three generations. Joyce read an early unpublished version of the play in 1903 when he met Synge in PARIS and was shown the work in manuscript form. Joyce was at first highly critical of the play, although this reaction may have sprung more from the competitiveness he felt with Synge than from critical judgment. In 1908, however, while living in TRIESTE, Joyce collaborated with Nicolò Vidacovich on translating the play into Italian. In ZURICH in 1918, Joyce persuaded Nora BARNACLE to take a part in the ENGLISH PLAYERS's production of the play. He also wrote the program notes, ending them with the following comment: "Whether a brief tragedy be possible or not (a point on which Aristotle had some doubts) the ear and the heart mislead one gravely if this brief scene from 'poor Aran' be not the work; of a tragic poet." See *Letters*, I.66–67, 95, and 117, and II.35, 212, 235, and 238; see also *CW* 250. (See also "Programme Notes for the English Players" under *The Critical Writings of James Joyce*.)

**Roberts, George** (1873–1953) He was one of the founders, with Joseph Maunsel Hone and Stephen Gwynn, of the Dublin publishing firm MAUNSEL & CO. Prior to his departure for the Continent in 1904 Joyce had known Roberts, and Roberts had at one time lent Joyce money (though at the time many in Dublin could make the same claim). Roberts's generosity did not, however, prevent Joyce from satirizing him in the broadside "The Holy Office" for his devotion to George RUSSELL (AE) as one "who loves his Master dear."

Although Roberts agreed to consider *Dubliners* for the Maunsel list in 1909, he apparently did little to advance Joyce's case with the firm over the next three years, and he raised many of the same objections that Grant RICHARDS had advanced a half-dozen years earlier. When Joyce returned to Dublin in July 1912 to attempt to force Roberts to publish the collection, the ensuing confrontation and the ultimate destruction of the page proofs for the book by the printer, John FALCONER, left him so bitter that he featured Roberts in "Gas from a Burner," a satirical piece that he wrote on the train as he returned to TRIESTE from Dublin. For additional details on this matter, see *Letters*, I.70 and II.261, 269, 287–288, 291–292, 297–298, 300–301, 303–315, 318–320, 325, and 347. (See also "A Curious History" under Miscellaneous Works.)

**Robinson, Henry Morton** (1898–1961) He was an American author of both fiction and nonfiction, including the popular novel *The Cardinal*. He is known primarily among Joyce scholars as the coauthor, with Joseph CAMPBELL, of one of the earliest studies of *Finnegans Wake,* the 1944 work *A Skeleton Key to Finnegans Wake.* The book provides a chapter-by-chapter summary, in a highly linear and subjective fashion, of the narrative events of Joyce's last work.

From its initial appearance, *A Skeleton Key to Finnegans Wake* has faced harsh attacks from numerous critics. Its emphasis on an episodic form and what some see as its reductive tendencies have proven especially maddening to those readers and critics who would give the book a post-structural reading taking critical account of reader response or the specific epistemological perspectives that many find central to an understanding of *Finnegans Wake.* Nonetheless, the Campbell and Robinson book has remained one of the most popular introductory studies of *Finnegans Wake.* This is doubtless due, in part at least, to its penchant for synopsis that, while by no means exhausting the meanings within the narrative, provides an interpretive starting point for many readers overawed by the complexities of *Finnegans Wake.*

**Rodker, John** (1894–1955) He was a British poet, novelist, and publisher who was one of the contributors to *OUR EXAGMINATION ROUND HIS FACTIFICATION FOR INCAMINATION OF WORK IN PROGRESS.* In his essay "Joyce & His Dynamic," Rodker tries to articulate a sense of the profound aesthetic impact exerted by Joyce's unique use of language. In his remarks describing the reception of Joyce's prose, Rodker's reactions prefigure the views of many contemporary readers' response to critics. In the end, Rodker claims, the impact of Joyce's words upon his readers produces nothing less than the "re-vitalizing [of] language."

In a 1920 letter, Joyce mentions Rodker as a friend, and over the following decade a number of references to him appear in Joyce's correspondence detailing Rodker's efforts to facilitate the publication of *Ulysses* and his subsequent interest in *Finnegans Wake.* Rodker founded the Ovid Press in 1920, and in 1922 and 1923 he published *Ulysses* for the Egoist Press in London. In 1928, he brought out a portion of the *Cantos* of Ezra POUND (*A Draft of the Cantos 17–27 of Ezra Pound*) under his own imprint. From 1940 to 1955 he published the complete works of Freud through the Imago Publishing Company. For additional information about Joyce's relations with Rodker, see *Letters,* I.146, 150, 157, 161, 186, 187, 196, and 271; II.423; and III.12, 15, 17, 20–21, 23, 25, 28–29, 47, 72, 153, 175–176, 290, 293–294, 296, and 299.

**Rogers, Margaret** (1927– ) Rogers is an American musician and composer who has written a series of choral pieces based on Joyce's works. "A Babble of Earwigs, or Sinnegan with Finnegan," which premiered at the Joyce conference in Milwaukee in June 1987, draws its inspiration from the general structure of *Finnegans Wake.* "The Washerwomen Duet" derives from the A L P sections of the work, especially chapter 8 in book 1. "Sirens Fugue" (written with Sigmund Snopeck) and "Sirens Duet" were inspired by the Sirens episode (chapter 11) of *Ulysses.*

**Rome** Joyce and his family lived in Rome from July 31, 1906, to March 7,1907. Joyce went to work as a clerk in a bank with the hope that this change would lead to an improvement in his financial circumstances. His position, however, turned out to be tedious and inimical to Joyce's efforts at writing. Life in Rome also proved to be far less agreeable than he had imagined and more expensive. In February 1907, Joyce gave notice to the bank, and after some vacillation about what to do, returned to TRIESTE with his family in March. For a sample of Joyce's feelings while living in Rome, see a series of letters that he wrote to his brother Stanislaus JOYCE from August 7, 1906, to March 7, 1907, *Letters,* II.144–175, 178, and 180–220.

**Rosenbach, A. S. W.** See ROSENBACH MUSEUM AND LIBRARY, THE.

**Rosenbach Manuscript** See ROSENBACH MUSEUM AND LIBRARY, THE.

**Rosenbach Museum and Library, The** Founded in Philadelphia in 1954, the museum is the former home of two brothers, Dr. A. S. W. Rosenbach, a collector of manuscripts and rare books, including Joyce's hand-written copy of *Ulysses,* and Philip Rosenbach, a collector of fine arts, furniture, and other decorative pieces. In January 1924, Dr. Rosenbach purchased Joyce's fair copy of the *Ulysses* manuscript for $1,975 at an auction at the Anderson Galleries in New York. This copy—now referred to as the Rosenbach manuscript—originally belonged to Joyce's American attorney, John QUINN, who between 1920 and 1921 had bought the manuscript in installments from Joyce for $1,200. (At the time of the auction, Quinn was dying from cancer. Joyce was not pleased when, in the previous fall, he heard from Quinn the meager amount that the manuscript was expected to fetch.) Rosenbach rejected Joyce's offer to buy back the manuscript. In a May 1924 letter to Harriet Shaw WEAVER four months after the auction, Joyce mentions that he received word from Rosenbach, who wanted to buy the corrected proofs of the novel. "When he receives a reply from me," Joyce wrote, "all the rosy brooks will have run dry.

> Rosy Brook he bought a book
> Though he didn't know how to spell it.
> Such is the lure of literature
> To the lad who can buy it and sell it.
>
> (*Letters,* I.214)

**Roth, Samuel** (1894–1974) Roth was an Austrian-born American poet, editor, and avant-garde publisher. He attended Columbia University on a faculty scholarship and published a poetry magazine, *The Lyric,* that included works by D. H. Lawrence, Archibald MacLeish, and Stephen Vincent Benét. After World War I, he opened the Poetry Bookshop in Greenwich Village. In 1921, while in England as a correspondent for the *New York Herald,* Roth wrote to Joyce expressing his admiration for Joyce's work and attempting unsuccessfully to arrange a meeting.

In 1925 Roth launched his quarterly magazine *Two Worlds* by reprinting five fragments from *WORK IN PROGRESS* between September 1925 and September 1926 (see *Letters,* III.139 and 156n.1). Although various sources disagree over the amount, it seems clear that Roth did in fact send Joyce money for these early *Finnegans Wake* pieces. According to Roth's daughter, Adelaide Kugel, these passages were printed with the permission of Ezra POUND. (Kugel has also argued that Richard ELLMANN downplayed Roth's efforts to gain Joyce's cooperation before publishing Joyce's works.) Whatever good-faith effort Roth may have made with regard to *Finnegans Wake,* however, in July 1926, Roth began to print portions of *Ulysses* in the inaugural issue of a second journal, *Two Worlds Monthly.* This publication, the first since the *LITTLE REVIEW* was forced to cease its serialization of the novel in 1920, was clearly against Joyce's wishes. It continued for 12 installments until October 1927. At Joyce's instigation, his friends Archibald MacLeish and Ludwig Lewisohn composed and circulated a document entitled "An International Protest," which was ultimately signed by 167 prominent writers. It took legal action by Joyce's American lawyers to secure an order, dated December 27, 1928, from the New York courts enjoining further publication. See *Letters,* III.151–153 for the protest letter and a list of signatures.

**Rotunda, the** This is the collective name given to a group of buildings erected in DUBLIN in 1757 by Dr. Bartholomew Mosse at the top of O'Connell Street on a site formerly known as the Barley Fields. These structures include a theater, a concert hall, assembly rooms, and a maternity hospital. Not surprisingly, the Rotunda dominates the physical and psychological typography of O'Connell Street, and references to the Rotunda recur throughout Joyce's works.

It is at the Rotunda that Mr. James Duffy meets Mrs. Emily Sinico during a musical concert at the beginning of the *Dubliners* story "A Painful Case." Near the end of chapter 5 of *A Portrait of the Artist as a Young Man,* Stephen Dedalus remembers seeing a diorama of English politicians on display in the Rotunda. In the Sirens episode (chapter 11) of *Ulysses,* the narrative makes note of the horse and car driven by Blazes Boylan passing the Rotunda as it marks his progress toward No. 7 ECCLES STREET and his assignation with Molly Bloom. References to the Rotunda, Dr. Mosse, and the Barley Fields also recur in *Finnegans Wake.*

A statue of Sir John Gray on O'Connell Street, Dublin, not far from the Rotunda *(Irish Tourist Board)*

**Ruskin, John** (1814–1900) He was an English painter, art critic, essayist, and Oxford don. Ruskin came to prominence through his association with the pre-Raphaelite Brotherhood, and his criticism had a profound impact on several generations of late Victorians, including Oscar WILDE, who studied with Ruskin at Oxford. As a young man, Joyce also fell under Ruskin's influence, taking his prose as a stylistic model. One finds a testament of his respect in an anecdote related by Joyce's brother Stanislaus. Shortly after Ruskin died on January 20, 1900, Joyce composed a tribute—never published and now apparently lost—entitled "A Crown of Wild Olive," written in imitation of Ruskin's style. Joyce took the title from Ruskin's collection of lectures on social and economic subjects, *The Crown of Wild Olives.*

**Russell, George** (1867–1935) Russell was an Irish writer and intellectual who rose to prominence at the turn of the century. He is often identified simply by his pen name, AE, which he took from the first two letters of the Latin word *aeon,* a term derived from the Greek *aion,* meaning "age" or "lifetime." Russell came from a poor Protestant family, and was largely self-educated. His early poetry brought him to the attention of W. B. YEATS, who helped him get a job as an organizer for the Irish cooperative movement. He later became editor of the *IRISH HOMESTEAD.* When he read portions of *Stephen Hero,* the novel Joyce began writing in 1904, Russell was generally impressed, and seemed inclined to foster Joyce's early literary aspirations. During the spring of 1904, when Russell temporarily served as editor of the *Irish Homestead* during the absence of H. F. NORMAN, he asked Joyce to submit a short story to the journal. (Russell would take on the position of editor in 1905.) This led to the publication of early versions of several of the stories that subsequently appeared in *Dubliners*—"The Sisters," "Eveline," and "After the Race." But because Joyce's stories were not in keeping with Russell's notion of fiction (or in Russell's view, with those of his readers), the *Irish Homestead* declined to publish "Clay," and urged Joyce to make no further submissions. Joyce blamed Russell for its rejection.

Russell was also an ardent adherent of THEOSOPHY and a member of the Dublin Lodge of the Theosophical Society. This interest is parodied by Joyce in the Scylla and Charybdis episode (chapter 9) of *Ulysses.* Russell's relations with Joyce became strained shortly before the latter left DUBLIN for the Continent in 1904, and Joyce lampooned his erstwhile supporter in the satirical ballad "The Holy Office." Although Russell responded with a number of harsh comments of his own and was dismissive of *Ulysses* when that book appeared, the feelings of both men mellowed over the years, and Russell signed his name to the 1927 protest against the pirating of *Ulysses* by Samuel ROTH. For a sampling of Joyce's feelings, see *Letters,* I.176 and 258; II.28, 58–59, 70, 78n.4, 83, 85, 170, 209, 212, and 230–231.

# S

**Sage, Robert** (1899–1962) He was an assistant editor of TRANSITION magazine and a contributor to *OUR EXAGMINATION ROUND HIS FACTIFICATION FOR INCAMINATION OF WORK IN PROGRESS.* The thesis of his essay, entitled "Before *Ulysses*—And After," is that all of Joyce's works "form an indivisible whole," and that each should be interpreted as part of a larger, unified aesthetic entity. Using evolutionary metaphors frequently, Sage offers a detailed survey of Joyce's work, focusing on how the increasing richness of language in each of his previous prose works—*Dubliners, A Portrait of the Artist as a Young Man, Ulysses*—prepares us for *Work in Progress.* In addition, Sage offers extended analyses of Joyce's representations of the central characters Anna Livia Plurabelle and Humphrey Chimpden Earwicker. He ends his essay by arguing for the accessibility of this work in progress and citing the achievements of Joyce's earlier writing as proof both that his work has always been complex and that readers have always found it rewarding nonetheless.

**Saint-Gérand-le-Puy** French village near Vichy, in an area of the country designated "Unoccupied France" during the German occupation from 1940 to 1944. In an effort to avoid anticipated fighting in and around PARIS, Joyce and Nora left the capital and moved to Saint-Gérand-le-Puy on December 24, 1939, and with the exception of two months in Vichy during the summer of 1940, they lived there for almost a year. On December 14, 1940, they left the village for ZURICH, Switzerland, where Joyce died one month later.

**St Stephen's** In Joyce's time, it was the unofficial literary magazine of UNIVERSITY COLLEGE, DUBLIN, founded in 1901. In October of that year the journal's faculty adviser, the Rev. Henry Browne, SJ, rejected Joyce's essay "The Day of the Rabblement," written in protest of the growing provincial tendencies within the Irish Literary Theater. In May 1902, the magazine published his essay "James Clarence Mangan," Joyce's ambivalent tribute to the artistic achievements of the early 19th-century Irish romantic poet.

**St Stephen's Green** This is a 27-acre park in the center of DUBLIN, south of TRINITY COLLEGE. In Joyce's time, it faced the buildings that housed UNIVERSITY COLLEGE, DUBLIN. Stephen Dedalus ironically calls it "my green," in chapter 5. The land making up the green was first set aside as a park and enclosed to allow citizens to "take the open aire" in 1670. By the 18th century, the park had become surrounded by Georgian mansions, and it enjoyed the reputation of being a fashionable place for the beau monde of DUBLIN to promenade. The park fell into disuse for most of the 19th century. In 1877, however, the deteriorating border of St Stephen's Green was replaced by wrought-iron railings and extensively relandscaped through a bequest from Arthur Guinness, Lord Ardilaun. The park quickly reemerged as a popular gathering

St Stephen's Green in Dublin *(Irish Tourist Board)*

place for Dubliners of all classes. It is mentioned throughout Joyce's works, but, because of its proximity to University College, Joyce refers to the landmark most frequently in *Stephen Hero* and *A Portrait of the Artist as a Young Man.*

In 1982, during the centenary celebration of Joyce's birth, a bust of Joyce was placed in the park.

**St. Thomas Aquinas** See THOMAS AQUINAS.

**Sandycove** This is the name given to the area south and east of DUBLIN, below Kingstown (now Dun Laoghaire) and adjacent to Dalkey. Sandycove is the location of the MARTELLO TOWER where Joyce once stayed briefly with Oliver St. John GOGARTY, and which provides the setting for the opening scene of *Ulysses* in the Telemachus episode. In the novel it is where Stephen Dedalus lives with Buck Mulligan and Mulligan's English guest, Haines. The Martello Tower is still standing and is today the home of the James Joyce Museum.

**schema** This is a rough, chapter-by-chapter conceptual framework designed to give a few early interpreters of *Ulysses* a clearer sense of the structure of the work and its parallels to the Greek epic *The Odyssey.* Joyce sketched it as a diagrammatic plan (or "scheme"). Several versions of it exist, but their variations are slight. In a September 1920 letter to the American attorney and arts patron John QUINN, Joyce offered a broad outline that divides *Ulysses* into three major parts paralleling the traditional tripartite division of HOMER's *Odyssey:* Telemachia, Odyssey (The Wanderings of Ulysses), and Nostos (see *Letters,* I.145). Joyce also included chapter titles for each section. These helpful designations do not appear in the novel itself.

The *Ulysses* schema, however, goes beyond the outline sent to Quinn. It includes not just chapter titles but the more detailed chart that Joyce diagrammed to highlight the key ideas of each chapter. At least two versions of the schema exist, though the differences between them are relatively minor.

It is difficult to pinpoint when Joyce drew up the first, but in September 1920 he mailed a version, in Italian, to Carlo LINATI, the translator of *Exiles.* Joyce explained that he was sending "a sort of summary—key—skeleton—scheme (for home use only) . . . I have given only 'Schlagworte' [catchwords] in my scheme but I think you will understand it all the same. It is the epic of two races (Israel-Ireland) and at the same time the cycle of the human body as well as a little story of a day (life) . . . My intention is . . . to allow each adventure (that is, every hour, every organ, every art being interconnected and interrelated in the somatic scheme of the whole) to condition and even to create its own technique" (*SL* 271). The next year, Joyce lent it to Valéry LARBAUD, who used it in preparing the lecture on *Ulysses* that he gave at Adrienne MONNIER's Paris bookshop, La Maison des Amis des Livres. Throughout the 1920s a schema circulated among some of Joyce's closest friends, including Jacques Benoîst-Méchin, Sylvia BEACH, and Herbert GORMAN. In Gorman's chart, Joyce listed correspondences between characters and places in his novel and those found in *The Odyssey.* Stuart GILBERT published a slightly different version of the schema in his book *James Joyce's Ulysses: A Study* (1930). When Bennett CERF of RANDOM HOUSE was preparing to bring out the first authorized American edition of *Ulysses* (1934), he repeatedly tried to obtain Joyce's permission to publish some version of the schema as an appendix to the novel. Joyce, however, resisted, apparently because he did not wish to blur the lines between a critical tool and a work of art.

For a view of Joyce's attitude toward the use of the schema and a reproduction of the schema Joyce sent to Gorman, see H. K. Croessmann's "Joyce, Gorman, and the Schema of *Ulysses*: An Exchange of Letters—Paul L. Léon, Herbert Gorman, Bennett Cerf" in *A James Joyce Miscellany* (Second Series), edited by Marvin Magalaner. Holograph copies of Joyce's schema are held at the University Library of the State University of New York at Buffalo, the University of Texas Library, and the Southern Illinois University Library. Also see the appendix to *Ulysses on the Liffey,* where RICHARD ELLMANN reproduces the Linati schema with an English translation and compares it with the Gorman-Gilbert schema. For additional information, see the appendix on page 392, the *Ulysses* schema.

**Schmitz, Ettore** (1861–1928) He was a Trieste businessman and writer who was an English-language student of Joyce's at the Berlitz School there. Schmitz is best known by his pseudonym, Italo SVEVO. He and his wife Livia (whose appearance influenced Joyce's description of Anna Livia Plurabelle in *Finnegans Wake*) became close friends of the Joyces. Schmitz, who was Jewish, was one of Joyce's models for Leopold Bloom, and he was an important source of information regarding Jewish customs and tradition. Writing under his pen name, Schmitz had published a novel, *Senilità,* in 1898. (An English translation was published in 1932 under the title *As a Man Grows Older.*) After reading it, Joyce encouraged Schmitz's writing efforts, and in 1923 Schmitz published *La coscienza di Zeno* (published in an English translation in 1930 under the title *The Confessions of Zeno*). He died from injuries sustained in an automobile accident in 1928. Joyce wrote a brief public memorial to Schmitz, entitled "Letter on Svevo," published in the March–April 1929 issue of the Italian journal SOLARIA, which devoted a portion of that number to a tribute to Schmitz and his work.

**Scholasticism** This is a term used to designate a Christian philosophical methodology that evolved during the Middle Ages. Scholasticism sought to combine theological and rational approaches in the examination of complex religious and philosophical questions. Eminent Scholastics such as Albertus Magnus and his pupil St. Thomas AQUINAS endeavored in their writings to deploy reason to supplement faith within the structure of Christian theology. In this fashion they sought to delineate theology from a systematic rather than a mystical perspective.

Although most Scholastics drew heavily upon both the ideas and the formal structure of Aristotelian thought in their writings, they articulated them through a range of diverse, even disparate, opinions. Some, such as Duns Scotus, drew on Plato to develop a system of thought generally known as *Scotism.* Thus, one can find within the scope of Scholasticism many contrasting, but not necessarily opposing, views. The writings of Aquinas and Duns Scotus, for example, are on parallel tracks and not in opposition to one another. Nonetheless, the views of Aquinas eventually gained preeminence. His *Summa Theologica* became a standard theological text. Although Scholasticism suffered a decline in the 18th and 19th centuries, Pope Leo XIII stimulated a revival in 1879.

Scholasticism underlay the philosophy, the theology, and even the pedagogy of the Jesuit schools where Joyce received his formal education, and throughout his life Joyce acknowledged the value of the Scholastic approach to learning. In "The Holy Office," his satirical 1904 poem against the Dublin literati, Joyce very pointedly sets his Scholastic background against the facile learning of the men whom he lampoons: "So distantly I turn to view / The shamblings of that motley crew, / Those souls that hate the strength that mine has / Steeled in the school of old Aquinas."

**Senn, Fritz** (1928– ) He is a Swiss Joyce scholar, co-organizer of several international Joyce symposia (including the First International James Joyce Symposium, held in DUBLIN in June 1967), and founder and director of the ZURICH James Joyce Foundation. Senn has published numerous articles on a wide range of Joyce topics and has edited several volumes of Joyce criticism, including *New Light on Joyce from the Dublin Symposium* (1972), *A Conceptual Guide to Finnegans Wake* (coedited with Michael H. Begnal, 1974), and *Approaches to Ulysses* (with Thomas F. STALEY and Bernard BENSTOCK, 1970). In 1962 he cofounded *A Wake Newslitter.* Senn has also translated Joyce's *The Cat and the Devil* into German, published in 1966 by Rhein Verlag. In 1998, *A Collideorscape of Joyce: Festschrift for Fritz Senn,* edited by Ruth Frehner and Ursula Zeller, was published in celebration of Senn's 70th birthday.

**Shakespeare, William** (1564–1616) Allusions to Shakespeare appear throughout Joyce's work, but the most direct and sustained are found in *Ulysses,* and particularly in reference to Stephen Dedalus. In funereal clothes, with his dour demeanor, Stephen invites a comparison between himself and Hamlet. In the Scylla and Charybdis episode (chapter 9), Stephen delivers himself of a disquisition on Shakespeare in the NATIONAL LIBRARY OF IRELAND in which he offers an interpretation of Hamlet based on extended psychological speculation about Shakespeare and his family. Stephen's psychoanalytical approach includes numerous references to contemporary Shakespeare criticism, allusions to Shakespeare's life and work, and witty puns that integrate the Shakespearean ethos into Stephen's own discourse.

Joyce doubtless based many of Stephen's remarks on his own series of 12 lectures given from November 1912 through February 1913 in Trieste at the Università Popolare, offered under the general title "Amleto di G. Shakespeare" (Shakespeare's Hamlet). Although the lectures themselves are now lost, Joyce's notes have been preserved in the Joyce Collection at the Cornell University Library. In his Trieste library, Joyce had not only a volume of the complete works, but also 20 books of songs, sonnets, and individual plays (including two copies of *Hamlet*). Joyce also owned a number of books of Shakespearean criticism including works by several critics referred to directly or indirectly in the Scylla and Charybdis episode: Peter Alvor, Edwin Bormann, Georg Brandes, Maurice Clare (May Byron), Samuel Taylor Coleridge, Karl Elze, William Hazlitt, Anna Jameson, Ernest Jones, Ernest Law, Sidney Lee, Edward Naylor, Thomas Ordish, Walter Raleigh, and Oscar Wilde.

The Shakespearean references in *Finnegans Wake,* while every bit as complex as those in *Ulysses,* are far more diffuse. A good line-by-line explication of these allusions can be found in Vincent Cheng's *Shakespeare and Joyce: A Study of Finnegans Wake,* the format of which follows that of William Schutte's earlier study *Joyce and Shakespeare: A Study in the Meaning of Ulysses.*

**Shakespeare and Company** This is the PARIS English-language bookstore founded by American-born Sylvia BEACH in 1919. Located first in the rue Dupuytren, it moved about 18 months later to 12, rue de l'Odéon, across from Adrienne MONNIER's La Maison des Amis des Livres on the Left Bank.

In 1922, Shakespeare and Company published *Ulysses* when no conventional publishing house would do so, a gesture that brought Beach and her bookstore to the attention of writers and intellectuals. Within a short time the bookstore became a gathering place for literary expatriates, especially Americans. Shakespeare and Company also published Joyce's collection of verse, *Pomes Penyeach,* in July 1927, and OUR EXAGMINATION ROUND HIS FACTIFICATION FOR INCAMINATION OF WORK IN PROGRESS, a collection of critical articles on *Finnegans Wake,* in May 1929. In late 1941, Shakespeare and Company was forced to close shortly after Beach refused to sell her last personal copy of *Finnegans Wake* to a Nazi officer. It was symbolically "liberated" in 1944 by Ernest Hemingway, but in fact the bookstore never reopened, though in the 1950s Beach gave an American named Whitman permission to open a bookstore under that name. Indeed, Shakespeare and Company has acquired legendary status and has been copied by bookstores elsewhere. In New York City there are two, and in Paris, one. (For further information on the bookstore and its literary life, see Sylvia Beach's recollections in *Shakespeare and Company,* reprinted by the University of Nebraska Press, 1991.)

**"Shaun the Post"** This was Joyce's working name for Book III of *Finnegans Wake* (*FW* 403.1–590.30); he also called it "Shaun" or referred to it by the

James Joyce and Sylvia Beach at Shakespeare and Company with posters citing reviews of *Ulysses* on the walls *(Princeton University Library)*

siglum ∧ (see page 92). The name is that of a character in *Arrah-na-Pogue*, a play by Dion BOUCICAULT. An early version of most of "Shaun the Post" was serialized in *TRANSITION* magazine from the March 1928 issue to the November 1929 issue. Portions of it also appeared in book form in *Tales Told of Shem and Shaun* (1929), *transition stories: Twenty-three stories from "transition"* (1929), *Imagist Anthology 1930*, and *Haveth Childers Everywhere* (1930).

Book III encompasses a dream whose central character is Shaun, who emerges in various forms as the embodiment of Earwicker's aspirations and his hope for overcoming the failures that have dogged his own life. The dream records Shaun's flaws as well as his virtues, and it chronicles his defeats as well as his triumphs. While the dream reveals a desire for the future, an intrusive pragmatism insistently displaces any apparent optimism.

Book III is made up of four chapters. In the first, Shaun presents himself as a politician seeking election, and in this role he addresses the voters, disparaging his opponent, Shem. The second chapter has Shaun, now as Jaun (a variant of Don Juan), in the company of 28 schoolgirls and their princess, ISEULT, whom he lectures on the mysteries of life. In chapter 3, Jaun has metamorphosed into Yawn and in keeping with this name is stretched exhausted on a hill in the center of Ireland. The Four Old Men and their ass arrive to hold an inquest. Their inquiry anatomizes his faults, and Yawn finally disappears, reforming into H C E sleeping next to his wife, A L P. In the final chapter, the couple is awakened by the cries of one of the children, whom they attend to, and then return to their bedroom to engage in an ultimately unsatisfactory effort at sexual intercourse.

For details regarding the forces shaping the composition of this segment of the book, see *Letters*, III.90, 92–93, 110n.2, 131–132, 134, 138–146, 166, 178–179, 186, and 188.

**Sheehy-Skeffington, Francis** (1876–1916) Sheehy-Skeffington was an Irish social reformer who, as a student at UNIVERSITY COLLEGE, DUBLIN, was a friend of Joyce. His family name was originally Skeffington, but when he married Hannah Sheehy in June 1903, he incorporated her name into his own as a statement of his views on women's rights. While a student, he had made a name for himself by speaking out in favor of pacifism, women's rights, and vegetarianism and simultaneously denouncing smoking, drinking, and vivisection. With the exception of himself, Joyce considered Skeffington the cleverest man at University College, Dublin.

In 1901 when ST STEPHEN'S magazine refused to publish Joyce's "The Day of the Rabblement," Skeffington joined him in privately printing a pamphlet containing that essay and his own "A Forgotten Aspect of the University Question," which had also been rejected by St Stephen's. As an ardent pacifist, Sheehy-Skeffington opposed the violence of the Easter Rising in 1916. In a tragically ironic twist of fate, after venturing into the streets in an effort to stop Dubliners from looting shops during the Easter Week fighting, he was summarily executed at the order of a crazed British officer.

**Sinnett, A(lfred) P(ercy)** (1840–1921) Sinnett was an English journalist, writer, and Theosophist. After becoming involved in the Theosophical movement in 1879, he wrote *Esoteric Buddhism* (1883) and *The Growth of the Soul* (1896), two works that Joyce consulted when writing *Ulysses*.

(See also BLAVATSKY, HELENA PETROVNA; BESANT, ANNIE WOOD; GILBERT, STUART; and THEOSOPHY.)

**Skeffington, Francis** See SHEEHY-SKEFFINGTON, FRANCIS.

**Slingsby, G. V. L.** This is the pseudonym used by one of the two contributors of protest letters appearing in *OUR EXAGMINATION ROUND HIS FACTIFICATION FOR INCAMINATION OF WORK IN PROGRESS*. Slingsby complains that Joyce "invented his own words if you can dignify them by that name." Entitled "Writes a Common Reader," this carping letter presents its own interpretive challenge to the reader, mixing assertions of genuine admiration for Joyce's earlier writings with expressions of profound despair over the form of this final work. One can read the letter as honest criticism, included in the interest of balance, or as a parody of the complaints typically voiced by admirers of

Joyce's earlier work who felt that the effort he expended on *Work in Progress* simply wasted his talents. According to Sylvia BEACH, whose SHAKESPEARE AND COMPANY published *Our Exagmination,* Joyce wanted a disapproving article to appear with the collection of essays. When a customer at Shakespeare and Company criticized the new technique of *Work in Progress,* Beach seized the opportunity and asked the woman, who was a journalist, to contribute a piece. (The name G. V. L. Slingsby, as Beach points out in *Shakespeare and Company,* is taken from Edward Lear's "The Jumblies.")

**Slocum, John J.** (1914–1997) Slocum was an American Joyce scholar and early bibliographer. Although Slocum spent most of his adult life in U.S. government service, he was the first president of the JAMES JOYCE SOCIETY. Through his devotion to Joyce, Slocum made tremendous contributions to Joyce studies. Foremost among these achievements was the detailed bibliography of Joyce's work that he compiled in cooperation with Herbert CAHOON and published in 1953. His collection of Joyce material is now in the possession of Yale's Beinecke Rare Book and Manuscript Library.

**smugging** This is a term used late in chapter 1 of *Portrait of the Artist as a Young Man* by Athy, one of the CLONGOWES WOOD COLLEGE schoolboys, to describe an incident that has led the Jesuits to impose severe punishment on several older students. As an additional consequence, the incident has provoked a general tightening of discipline that the other students resent. The word is a Joycean fabrication intentionally presented without establishing its meaning. It is never defined, and, although Stephen Dedalus and his classmates act as if they understand Athy, the narrative development suggests otherwise. The word wonderfully illustrates the way Joyce employs the imaginative power of his audience to extend the creative limits of his discourse. In essence, the ambiguity of smugging allows it to mean as much or as little as the reader wishes it to mean and provides one of many opportunities to participate actively in the narrative dynamics of the work, a characteristic feature of the novel.

**Society of Jesus** This is the largest all-male religious order in the Roman Catholic Church. Its members are called Jesuits. The order was founded on August 15, 1534, by St. Ignatius de Loyola (1491–1556). Loyola and six university students in Paris, including St. Francis Xavier, committed themselves to lives dedicated to spiritual growth and governed by poverty, chastity, and obedience. In 1540 the Society of Jesus received the recognition of Pope Paul III, and St. Ignatius became its first superior general. The Jesuits soon became involved in the work of the Counter-Reformation and in missionary activity all over the world. The effectiveness of the society at instituting change within the church and at revitalizing its spiritual development can be judged to some degree by the frequency of attacks against it by entrenched elements within the church. These reached their peak in the efforts of Pope Clement XIV to abolish the order completely in 1773. Pope Pius VII restored the order in 1814, and the Jesuits committed themselves to ongoing missionary work and to education.

At CLONGOWES WOOD COLLEGE, BELVEDERE COLLEGE, and UNIVERSITY COLLEGE, DUBLIN, the Jesuits who taught the classes and administered the schools exerted profound influences on the spiritual and academic development of both Joyce and his fictional counterpart, Stephen Dedalus. Despite periods of intense anticlerical feelings, Joyce always retained a deep respect for the Jesuits and a high regard for the education he had received from them. Likewise, portrayals of individual Jesuits and of the Society of Jesus in his fiction, although by no means uniformly laudatory, always reflect a sophisticated appreciation for the complexity of the individuals and of the order. Thus, while Joyce's reference to "jesuit bark and bitter bite" (*FW* 182.36) seems to refer to the all-too-human flaws of some priests he had known, it also celebrates the commendable achievements both practical (in this case the discovery of the bitter bark of quinine that served as a treatment for malaria) and spiritual that members of the society had brought about.

***Solaria*** This was an Italian literary magazine founded in the early 1920s in Florence by students under the influence of FUTURISM. A portion of its

March–April 1929 issue was dedicated to commemorating Joyce's friend and fellow writer Italo Svevo (Ettore SCHMITZ), who had been killed in an automobile accident the previous year. The journal's editor asked Joyce to contribute a short piece to the "Omaggio a Svevo," and Joyce responded with a brief but evocative "Letter on Svevo."

***Speaker, The*** This was an English literary magazine published in London. With the help of W. B. YEATS, Joyce's review of a French translation of Henrik IBSEN'S play *Catilina* appeared in the March 21, 1903, issue of this journal. In addition, two of Joyce's poems—"Sweetheart, hear you" (*Chamber Music* XVIII) and "I would in that sweet bosom be" (*Chamber Music* VI)—were published respectively in the July and October 1904 issues.

**Spencer, Theodore** See Publication History, *Stephen Hero.*

**Staley, Thomas F.** (1935– ) Staley is an American Joyce scholar. In 1963, Staley founded the JAMES JOYCE QUARTERLY, a journal still publishing Joyce criticism, which he edited until 1989. In 1990 he founded and became the editor of the JOYCE STUDIES ANNUAL and professor of English and director of the Harry Ransom Humanities Research Center at the University of Texas at Austin. *Joyce Studies Annual* ceased publication in 2003. Besides editing and contributing to many works on Joyce, Staley published *An Annotated Critical Bibliography of James Joyce* in 1989.

**Stanislaus** See JOYCE, STANISLAUS.

**Stephens, James** (1882–1950) Stephens was an Irish poet, short-story writer, novelist, and contemporary of Joyce, who as a young man had viewed him as a rival and kept him at a distance. That attitude diminished with age and as Joyce became more successful and established. Stephens's fictional works include *The Crock of Gold* (1912), *The Charwoman's Daughter* (1912), *The Demi-Gods* (1914), *Deirdre* (1923), and *The Land of Youth* (1924). In 1926, he published his *Collected Poems.* Stephens also wrote a firsthand account of the Easter Rising, entitled *The Insurrection in Dublin* (1916). In 1927, when Joyce was in despair over criticisms that had already been raised over the early stages of *Finnegans Wake* (known then as WORK IN PROGRESS), Joyce toyed with the notion of asking Stephens to finish the work for him. (For further information, see Joyce's letter to Harriet Shaw WEAVER dated May 20, 1927, in *Letters,* I.253–254.) Precisely why Joyce would have chosen Stephens to complete the work is not certain, but it may have been because of the mixture of myth, fantasy, and realism found in Stephens's writings. Although nothing came of the idea, Stephens used the occasion to express his great admiration for *Finnegans Wake.* The two men became good friends (Joyce, at least, spurred on by a mistaken belief that both men were born in Dublin on February 2, 1882), and they remained close until Joyce's death. For further information, see Augustine Martin, *James Stephens: A Critical Study* (1977).

**stream of consciousness** This was a phrase coined by William James in his *Principles of Psychology* (1890) to describe the flow of ideas, perceptions, sensations, and recollections that characterize human thought. It has subsequently been adopted by literary critics and authors to describe the representation of this flow in writing.

Although it is very similar to and often confused with INTERIOR MONOLOGUE, stream of consciousness is characterized by markedly distinct technical features. The reason for the confusion is that, as in interior monologue, stream of consciousness jumps rapidly from topic to topic with little regard for logical progression or coherent transitions. However, unlike interior monologue, stream-of-consciousness writing is governed by basic rules of grammar and syntax. Although many critics associate Joyce with the stream-of-consciousness technique, it would be more accurate to identify Joyce's efforts as interior monologue, especially in *Ulysses* and, in particular, in the Penelope episode (chapter 18), which is given over entirely to the inner thoughts of Molly Bloom.

**Sullivan, John** (1877–1955) Sullivan, actually born O'Sullivan, was an Irish singer from Cork (home of Joyce's paternal ancestors) who emigrated to Rouen, France, at the age of 12. As his voice matured, Sullivan went on to establish an operatic career in France. In 1910 he began singing under the name Sullivan. He appeared with the Chicago opera company in 1919. In 1929 he was singing in Richard Wagner's *Tannhäuser* at the Paris Opera. At the urging of Stanislaus JOYCE, Sullivan made himself known to Joyce, who, after hearing the tenor sing, became his ardent champion. Joyce boasted that Sullivan was the only tenor of his day capable of singing the lead role in Rossini's *William Tell.* Joyce's desire to abet Sullivan's operatic success became a passion, and throughout the 1930s he expended a great deal of energy trying to secure for Sullivan the recognition that he felt he deserved. (According to Francois L. Nouvion, writing on the Tenorland website, http://tenorland.com/osullivan.html, Sullivan found this attention "ridiculous.")

**Svevo, Italo** This is the literary pseudonym used by Joyce's Trieste English-language student, friend, and fellow writer Ettore SCHMITZ, whose novels include *As a Man Grows Older, Confessions of Zeno,* and *The Nice Old Man and the Pretty Girl.* This pseudonym replaced his earlier nom de plume Ettore Samigli. According to his wife, Livia (on whom Joyce partially modeled Anna Livia Plurabelle), Svevo chose this name because (like his real name) it reflected "his German [Swabian] and Latin origins" (see Livia Veneziani Svevo, *Memoir of Italo Svevo,* p. 19; also see Richard Ellmann, *James Joyce,* p. 271).

**Swift, Jonathan** (1667–1745) Swift was a poet, essayist, and satirist, born in Dublin of English parents (his father, a lawyer, died before Swift was born). Although he spent an unhappy childhood in Ireland and as an adult sought preferment in England, after his ordination as a priest in the (Anglican) Church of Ireland he served as Dean of St. Patrick's Cathedral, DUBLIN, from 1713. While he had a real aversion to elements of the Irish Roman Catholic ethos, Swift nonetheless was a tireless advocate of social justice and an unremitting critic of English colonialism in *The Drapier's Letters* and in *A Modest Proposal.* As a consequence, even in Joyce's time he continued to enjoy a high reputation among the Irish.

One can find traces of Swift's influence throughout Joyce's canon, but in particular he was a stylistic and thematic inspiration for *Finnegans Wake.* In his *Journal to Stella,* a volume of letters, and accounts of his day-to-day life written to his close friend Esther Johnson—to whom, some critics claim, he was secretly married in 1706—Swift employed a private and highly idiosyncratic use of language, in which Joyce found a model for the neologisms and portmanteau words that characterize *Finnegans Wake.* Further, in Swift's troubled and ambivalent relationships with Johnson and with Esther Vanhomrigh, Joyce found inspiration for a variety of depictions of the characteristic emotional, sexual, spiritual, and psychological conflicts between men and women. In his notes for the play *Exiles,* Joyce offered the following observation on Swift: "The two greatest Irishmen of modern times—Swift and Parnell—broke their lives over women." Joyce's inclusion of Swift as one of the two greatest modern Irishmen underscores his high esteem for this writer. The comment indicates that Swift is in the forefront of Joyce's artistic consciousness. It anticipates the pervasive influence of Swift on *Finnegans Wake,* an influence that is evident from the second paragraph of the book (see *FW* 3.10–12) and that resonates especially in the motif of the letter and in the protean identities of H C E and his two sons, Shem and Shaun.

**Sykes, Claud W.** (1883–1964) Sykes, a professional actor, was a Zurich friend of the Joyce family with whom Joyce founded the ENGLISH PLAYERS, an amateur acting company. Sykes also helped Joyce by typing portions of the manuscript of *Ulysses.*

**symbolist movement** This is the designation of a literary movement that began in France around the middle of the 19th century. The date most often cited for its appearance is 1857, the year in which Baudelaire's *Les Fleurs du Mal* was published. Although the symbolist movement was slow to evolve, it eventually came to exert a pronounced effect upon many Irish and British writers—including Joyce—at around the turn of the century.

For the symbolist, personal emotion stands as the only proper topic for art, and its full expression is the only proper aim for art. Since human feelings are both highly subjective and frustratingly ephemeral, a complex system of symbols becomes the only way that they can be expressed. Forming and implementing such a system became the central concern of symbolist writers, and in some instances it led to a highly mechanical form of artistic creation. Nonetheless, like many others of his generation, as a young man Joyce was deeply affected by symbolism, especially after reading *The Symbolist Movement in Literature,* an influential book by Arthur SYMONS, published in 1899.

Joyce's use of symbolism throughout his works, from his early poems in *Chamber Music* to the highly charged words and motifs in *Finnegans Wake,* attests to the enduring influence that the symbolist movement had upon his creative imagination. Symbolism also provided Joyce with an aesthetic technique that he could use to balance and enrich the extraordinarily realistic features of his novels, thus elevating them beyond a merely mimetic art form.

John Millington Synge, a leading figure of the Irish Literary Revival *(Irish Tourist Board)*

**Symons, Arthur** (1865–1945) Symons was an early English advocate of the French SYMBOLIST MOVEMENT in literature. He established himself as a literary journalist in the 1890s, joined the Rhymers' Club (a group that met at the Cheshire Cheese pub on Fleet Street in London and included William Butler YEATS among its members), and became editor of the journal *Savoy.* In 1899, he published *The Symbolist Movement in Literature,* a work that Joyce read while a student at UNIVERSITY COLLEGE, DUBLIN, and one that had a strong influence on his writing.

En route to Paris in 1902, Joyce stopped in London, where Yeats introduced him to Symons. Several years later, Symons was instrumental in convincing Elkin MATHEWS to publish Joyce's first book of verse, CHAMBER MUSIC, and wrote the first review, a favorable assessment that was published in the June 1907 issue of the *Nation,* a London journal.

**Synge, John Millington** (1871–1909) Synge was a leading figure of the IRISH LITERARY REVIVAL, born in Rathfarnham, then a suburban district of DUBLIN. In the first decade of the 20th century Synge emerged as Ireland's foremost playwright with the appearance of *The Shadow of the Glen* (1903), which was followed in quick succession by RIDERS TO THE SEA (1904), *The Well of the Saints* (1905), *The Tinker's Wedding* (1907), and *The Playboy of the Western World* (1907). A final work, *Deirdre of the Sorrows,* premiered posthumously at the ABBEY THEATRE in 1910.

Although riots broke out at productions of *The Shadow of the Glen* and later at *The Playboy of the Western World*—some members of the Dublin audience were outraged by what they considered to be slanderous depictions of Irish women—there is no question that Synge's plays contributed enormously to the early success of the Abbey Theatre. The lyrical resonances of his peasant dialogue validated the claims made for the richness of Celtic rural tradition as a source for literary inspiration.

By the time that he came to write *Ulysses,* Joyce felt comfortable enough with Synge to include numerous references to him and to his works in the novel. In perhaps the most autobiographical allusion, Joyce has Buck Mulligan jokingly tell Stephen Dedalus that Synge is looking for him to avenge a supposed insult, one that Stephen claims is in fact Mulligan's responsibility (*U* 9.569–581). Adaline GLASHEEN has also found several references to Synge in *Finnegans Wake;* she delineates these in her *Third Census to Finnegans Wake.* With assistance from Nicoló Vidacovich, Joyce translated Synge's *Riders to the Sea* into Italian. Under the title *La Cavalcata al Mare,* the translation appeared in the September–October 1929 issue of the Italian magazine SOLARIA.

Joyce became acquainted with Synge when both men were living in PARIS in 1903. During that time Synge gave Joyce a manuscript version of *Riders to the Sea* to read, but the rivalry Joyce (then only at the beginning of his own literary career) must have felt toward Synge prevented him from finding any merit in it. Joyce later changed his opinion of Synge, and in the program notes for a production by the ENGLISH PLAYERS of *Riders to the Sea,* Joyce wrote, "Whether a brief tragedy be possible or not (a point on which Aristotle had some doubts) the ear and the heart mislead one gravely if this brief scene from 'poor Aran' be not the work of a tragic poet."

# T

**Tenebrae** In Joyce's time this was an informal ritual of the Holy Week liturgy of the Roman Catholic Church. The Tenebrae service in church involved the recitation of the matins and lauds of the following day, usually sung in the afternoon or the evening of Spy Wednesday (*spy* being a term used in Ireland, alluding to Judas), Holy Thursday, and Good Friday. During the Tenebrae celebration, the candles lit at the beginning of the service are extinguished one by one after each psalm, a sign of the darkness at the time of the Crucifixion. In *Stephen Hero* (*SH* 118), Cranly and Stephen Dedalus attend Tenebrae services on Spy Wednesday at the Pro-Cathedral.

Even after he had ceased the regular practice of his faith, Joyce retained his fascination with the church's liturgical elements, and he continued to attend Tenebrae services whenever the opportunity presented itself. In an April 4, 1903, letter to his mother, for example, Joyce asks that his brother Stanislaus send him a Holy Week Book in time for a Tenebrae service in Paris (see *Letters,* II.40). Also see *Letters,* II.10.

**Theology** See CATHOLICISM; SCHOLASTICISM; SOCIETY OF JESUS; TRANSACCIDENTATION; and TRANSUBSTANTIATION.

**Theosophy** This is a term identifying a body of religious doctrine strongly influenced by Buddhist mysticism. Modern Theosophy began in 1875 when the Theosophical Society was founded by Helena Petrovna BLAVATSKY and Henry Steel Olcott. They articulated a pattern of beliefs centering on the following tenets: an eternal, unchanging, and unknowable First Principle exists; within the universe, which is eternal, numerous smaller universes periodically appear and disappear; all souls are identified with an over-soul, which is itself identified with the First Principle; every soul goes through a series of rebirths as it continues its process of spiritual growth. In Joyce's work, the most concentrated references to Theosophy appear in the Scylla and Charybdis episode. Approximating the cynical attitude Stephen Dedalus has toward Theosophy and two of its leading proponents, William Butler YEATS and George RUSSELL (AE), the narrative voice alludes to Theosophical concepts and beliefs. For example, see *U* 9.61–71 and 279–286.

***This Quarter*** This was a literary magazine founded in Paris in 1925 by Ernest Walsh. Its contributors included Ezra POUND, Eugene JOLAS, Ernest Hemingway, and James Joyce. *This Quarter* published a selection from *Finnegans Wake,* the Shem the Penman episode (*FW* 169.1–195.6) in its Autumn–Winter 1925–26 issue under the title "Extract from Work in Progress." (For additional details about this publication, see *Letters,* III.116–117, 122, and 124–125.) In the same issue of *This Quarter* was an extract from George Antheil's unfinished opera *Mr. Bloom and the Cyclops,* based on the Cyclops episode (chapter 12) of *Ulysses.*

**Thomas Aquinas** (1225?–1274) Aquinas was a doctor of the church (a title that signifies his status as a revered theologian), a Dominican priest, and a Scholastic philosopher and theologian. He was born at Roccasecca, near Naples, early in the 13th century. Aquinas stands as a major figure in the medieval Roman Catholic Church, and continues to exert a powerful influence on theological thought. References to St. Thomas and to Thomistic philosophy occur frequently in Joyce's works. Aquinas studied in Paris under Albertus Magnus, went to the University of Cologne with Albertus in 1248, and developed a system of thought based on Aristotelian concepts. (See ARISTOTLE.) He taught in Paris and throughout the cities of Italy. He died on March 7, 1274, on his way to the Second Council of Lyons. In 1323, Aquinas was canonized by Pope John XXII, and in 1567 he was declared a doctor of the church by Pope Pius V. St. Thomas was made a patron of Roman Catholic schools by Pope Leo XIII in 1880. His Scholasticism forms the basis for the pedagogical approach followed by the Jesuit teachers of James Joyce and of Joyce's fictional character, Stephen Dedalus.

In his 1904 broadside, "The Holy Office," in which he attacks the Dublin writers of his day, Joyce metaphorically arms himself with the power of Aquinas:

> So distantly I turn to view
> The shamblings of that motley crew
> Those souls that hate the strength that mine
> has
> Steeled in the school of old Aquinas.

Thomistic ideas relating to the nature of the good and the beautiful form the basis of pivotal aesthetic principles critically important to Joyce's maturation as a young artist, as well as to the understanding of certain passages in Joyce's works, especially *Stephen Hero* and *A Portrait of the Artist as a Young Man.* While in POLA in late 1904, Joyce carefully wrote out his perception of the unique interplay between these two Thomistic notions of the good and the beautiful. See also THOMISTIC PHILOSOPHY.

**Thomistic Philosophy** Joyce demonstrates an original application of Thomistic principles. Joyce's reflections explicitly reappear in *Stephen Hero,* the novel he began at that time. At the beginning of chapter 19 the narrator comments that the aesthetic of Stephen Daedalus was essentially "applied Aquinas." Stephen's many discussions on the nature of art derive their philosophical underpinning from Aquinas. Joyce goes on to recast aesthetic ideas first articulated in *Stephen Hero* and derived from Thomistic categories to use in chapter 5 of *A Portrait of the Artist as a Young Man* as the basis for Stephen Dedalus's aesthetic theory. He explains to his schoolmate Vincent Lynch that the correspondence between artistic apprehension and the beautiful lies in the Thomistic concepts of *integritas, consonantia,* and *claritas,* terms that Stephen translates as wholeness, harmony, and radiance. In *Ulysses* the Thomistic philosophical framework provides Stephen with a formidable defense against any attack upon his own aesthetic system. In the Proteus episode (chapter 3) of *Ulysses,* Aquinas is referred to by Stephen as *frate porcospino,* "brother porcupine," implying a quality of mind difficult to assail. Later in the Scylla and Charybdis episode (chapter 9) of *Ulysses,* a more pragmatic aspect of Thomistic thought appears. In his discussion with the Dublin literati who have gathered in the National Library, Stephen finds his ideas increasingly assailed by hostile responses. He turns to the scholastic system, again incorporating Thomistic methods of thought and argument, to derive the form of his rebuttal. See also THOMAS AQUINAS.

**Thom's Official Directory** This is the title of an address directory of DUBLIN homes and businesses. It was first compiled by Peter Wilson in 1752 and was at that time known as *The Dublin Directory.* The *Directory* became the property of Alexander Thom in 1844, and from that date onward his name was included in its title. In Joyce's time *Thom's Official Directory* appeared annually, providing a street-by-street guide of Dublin households and commercial establishments. While writing *Ulysses,* Joyce used the 1904 edition extensively as a reference that allowed him to recapture the details and ambiance of Dublin as it had been then.

**Tindall, William York** (1903–1981) Tindall was one of the first American critics to study Joyce;

his writings have influenced critical opinion of Joyce for decades. Before his appointment at Columbia University, where he taught from 1931 to his retirement in 1971, Tindall was an instructor at New York University (1926–31), and was reputedly the first college teacher to make *Ulysses* required reading for his students, a bold assignment considering that the novel was banned in the United States at the time. His works on Joyce include *James Joyce: His Way of Interpreting the Modern World* (1950), an edition of *Chamber Music* (1954, for which he wrote an introduction and notes), *A Reader's Guide to James Joyce* (1959), *The Joyce Country* (1960; reprinted in 1972; a collection of invaluable photos relating to Joyce's life and works), and *A Reader's Guide to Finnegans Wake* (1969). He also contributed essays to many periodicals.

***Titbits*** This was the popular title of an Irish magazine, the full title of which is *Titbits from All the Most Interesting Books, Periodicals and Newspapers in the World.* It was a penny-weekly journal during Joyce's time that had begun publication in 1881. As the title suggests, *Titbits* presented a digest of weekly news items from the world press. Each number also had special features, timely articles, or selected pieces of fiction written especially for the magazine. At the close of the Calypso episode (chapter 4) of *Ulysses,* Leopold Bloom peruses one such piece in *Titbits,* Philip Beaufoy's short story "MATCHAM'S MASTERSTROKE," while sitting in the outhouse in the back of his garden.

**transaccidentation** As it appears in *Finnegans Wake,* Book I, chapter 7, it is a term employed by Shaun to describe the eucharistic doctrine of artistic creation, in which his brother Shem's appearance or "bodily getup" (his accidents) is transmuted into the accidents or appearance of ink and words, in which Shem's spiritual substance continues to reside. First used around 1300 by Duns Scotus, according to the *Oxford English Dictionary,* the term referred to a theological question concerning the accidents of bread and wine during the celebration of the eucharistic mystery. (In the Roman Catholic sacrament of the Eucharist, bread and wine are believed to be transubstantiated into the body and blood of Christ—see TRANSUBSTANTIATION.) Joyce, however, exploits the concept behind the term *transaccidentation* to express an extraordinary insight into the act of literary creation and into the artist's relation to art. The artist in producing words is "transaccidentated through the slow fires of consciousness into a dividual chaos, perilous, potent, common to allflesh, human only, mortal" (*FW* 186.3–6), and in them is present to all readers. The use of the eucharistic metaphor as a statement about art appears elsewhere in Joyce's writings; for instance, in the image of "a priest of eternal imagination, transmuting the daily bread of experience into the radiant body of everliving life" found in *A Portrait of the Artist as a Young Man* (*P* 221). But in *Finnegans Wake,* eucharistic imagery reaches a significantly higher plane with the use of the term *transaccidentation.* Paradoxically, the artist, who must deal with that which is intrinsically human, thus with that which is mortal, achieves an everlasting presence in the creation of art and invites all to share a radical freedom that transcends the limits of time. For a comprehensive discussion of Joyce's use of eucharistic imagery, see Robert BOYLE's *James Joyce's Pauline Vision: A Catholic Exposition* and "Miracle in Black Ink: A Glance at Joyce's Use of His Eucharistic Image" in *James Joyce Quarterly* 10 (Fall 1972): 47–60; also see Boyle's other related works mentioned in the bibliography.

***transatlantic review*** This is the title of a literary magazine founded in Paris, published in 12 monthly issues from January 1924 to January 1925. Its editor, Ford Madox FORD, guaranteed immediate acclaim for the *transatlantic review* by persuading Joyce, Ezra POUND, John QUINN, and Ernest Hemingway to serve as advisers. A selection by Joyce entitled "From Work in Progress" was published in the journal's fourth issue (April 1924). This passage eventually became the Mamalujo chapter of *Finnegans Wake* (*FW* 383.1–399.34).

***transition*** Subtitled *an international quarterly for creative experiment, transition* was a monthly avant-garde literary magazine founded in 1927 by Eugene JOLAS, Maria JOLAS, and Elliot PAUL. In 17 installments that appeared between April 1927 and May 1938, *transition* published the bulk of Joyce's WORK IN PROGRESS. These installments comprise pages 3–275, 282–331, 338–355, and 403–590 of *Finnegans Wake.* In addition to that of Joyce, *transition* also published work by such authors as Gertrude Stein, e. e. cummings, Franz Kafka, Dylan Thomas, and Marcel Duchamp as well as original art by Joan Miró, Alexander Calder, Ferdinand Leger, and others.

**translations** For a list of works translated by Joyce, see the appendix on page 381.

**transubstantiation** This is a Catholic theological term referring to the miraculous transformation of the substance, but not the accidents (or appearance), of bread and wine into the body and blood of Christ at the consecration of the Eucharist. Joyce utilized this religious doctrine for artistic ends in his writings. Along with other eucharistic imagery, Joyce employed the theological concept behind the doctrine of transubtantiation in formulating a profound aesthetic principle on the relationship between art and the artist. A process analogous to the transformation that occurs in the eucharistic mystery is articulated in the thoughts of Stephen Dedalus in chapter 5 of *A Portrait of the Artist as a Young Man,* where he likens the role of the artist to that of the priest consecrating ("transmuting") the eucharistic bread (p. 221). Additionally, in the Oxen of the Sun episode (chapter 14) of *Ulysses,* along with associated theological concepts, Stephen uses the derivative term "transubtantiality" (*U* 14.308), also within the context of artistic creativity. (In the Eumaeus episode [chapter 17] of *Ulysses,* the phrase "transubstantial heir" occurs, but is used by the narrator in a noneucharistic context to refer to Leopold Bloom [*U* 17.534]). Joyce further develops the theological and doctrinal concept of transubstantiation in *Finnegans Wake,* where he incorporates the related term TRANSACCIDENTATION to express the mystery of literary creativity.

**Trieste** This is a port city at the head of the Adriatic Sea. Trieste was part of the Austro-Hungarian Empire when Joyce first arrived there in 1905, but its citizens had strong ties to Italy, to which the city was ceded after World War I. Trieste is now located on the Italian side of the border with Slovenia. From 1905 until 1915 Joyce and his family resided in Trieste (with a brief hiatus in 1907, when they moved to ROME), where he earned a living as an English-language teacher. The Joyce family returned to Trieste after World War I, but they stayed only briefly (1919–20) before moving to PARIS. Joyce wrote most of *Dubliners,* all of *A Portrait of the Artist as a Young Man,* and significant portions of *Ulysses* while living in Trieste.

Although Joyce did not write much about Trieste itself, he does refer to the city several times in his works. In the Eumaeus episode (chapter 16) of *Ulysses,* the sailor D. B. Murphy refers to Trieste as a violent place, and during the LESSONS CHAPTER of *Finnegans Wake* the narrator exclaims "And trieste, ah trieste ate I my liver!" (*FW* 301.16). Judging from remarks made in his correspondence or recorded in the Richard ELLMANN biography, Joyce and his family seem to have had fond memories of their years in that city. Joyce's children grew up speaking the Triestine dialect of Italian, the language he and his family would use with one another even after they left Trieste. (See also *PICCOLO DELLA SERA, IL*; PREZIOSO, ROBERTO; and SCHMITZ, ETTORE. For more detailed information regarding Joyce's stay in Trieste, see Renzo S. Crivelli, *James Joyce: Triestine Itineraries,* and John McCourt, *The Years of Bloom: James Joyce in Trieste, 1904–1920.*)

**Trinity College** Trinity is the leading Irish university. It was founded as Dublin University in 1592 at the behest of Queen Elizabeth I to support efforts to foster Anglican faith and culture in Ireland. The foundation stone was laid by Lord Mayor Thomas Smith on land that had been confiscated by Henry VIII in 1538 from the Augustinian Order. The oldest building on the present campus dates from 1722. The rule restricting university admissions to Protestants was lifted in 1793, but until well into the 20th century, Trinity remained a bastion of the Protestant ascendancy. By the 1990s, however, fully 80 percent of the undergraduates were from Roman Catholic families. Although Joyce did not attend Trinity, a number of other notable Irish writers did, including Jonathan SWIFT, George BERKELEY, Edmund Burke, Oliver Goldsmith, Oscar WILDE, and Joyce's friend Samuel BECKETT. Trinity College has Dublin's oldest library, which contains, among its many treasures, the BOOK OF KELLS.

**Tristan and Isolde** They were the legendary heroic figures from medieval romance, sometimes rendered as Tristan and Iseult or Tristram and Isoud. One of Joyce's first sketches in early 1923, when he began composing *Finnegans Wake,* was a mock-heroic version of the Tristan and Isolde romance. In its final form it now comprises the whole of chapter 4 in Book II (*FW* 383–399).

Tristan is a knight of King Arthur's Round Table. Isolde is the daughter of the king of Ireland who nurses a wounded Tristan back to health. After his recovery, Tristan tells his uncle, King Mark of Cornwall, of the lovely young girl, and he is sent back to Ireland to fetch her to become King Mark's bride. On the way back to Cornwall, Tristan and Isolde unwittingly drink a love potion intended for her and King Mark, and become tragically enamored of each other. Eventually they make their way back to Cornwall, where Isolde against her will marries King Mark; when he discovers the love that Isolde still bears for Tristan, the nephew is forced to flee. Tristan's subsequent adventures vary from author to author, but most often these tales conclude with Tristan being slain by his still-jealous uncle King Mark or lying fatally wounded waiting in vain for Isolde to come again to cure him.

Although the most concentrated allusions to Tristan and Isolde appear in Book II chapter 4, Joyce drew upon these figures in fashioning the characters of Shem, Shaun, and Issy, and in developing the complex relationship among them. Various themes and motifs throughout *Finnegans Wake,* such as the cuckoldry of Humphrey Chimpden Earwicker (a King Mark figure) and Shaun's attempts at seducing Issy, relate directly to Tristan and Isolde. Isolde stands out as an avatar for Issy throughout the narrative of the *Wake,* and as with so many archetypes, the mythological Isolde provides both a straightforward model and an ironic counterpoint for characterizations of Issy. She combines a measure of innocence and sexuality (represented with wonderful ambiguity as unbridled desire produced by a magic potion) that allows her to embody the multifaceted and contradictory nature of young women.

Other important motifs relating to Earwicker's loss of authority, such as the forces usurping his parental status, are also based on Tristan and Isolde. In a June 1926 letter to Harriet Shaw WEAVER (*Letters,* I.241), Joyce referred to Joseph BÉDIER's *Tristan et Iseult,* a work with which he was very familiar and which he sent to Weaver to read. (See also CHAPELIZOD and PHOENIX PARK.)

# U

***Ulysses*** This is the title of a cinematic adaptation of Joyce's *Ulysses.* A British production directed by Joseph Strick, with a screenplay by Strick and Fred Haines, the film presents a greatly abridged and highly naturalistic version of the novel; critical judgment was generally unfavorable. Released in 1967, the 132-minute-long film stars Milo O'Shea as Leopold Bloom, Barbara Jefford as Molly Bloom, and Maurice Roeves as Stephen Dedalus, with T. P. McKenna as Buck Mulligan and Martin Dempsey as Simon Dedalus. An original soundtrack recording of the film was released by Caedmon. The movie was refused a certificate by Irish censors and the Film Appeals Board in 1967, apparently because of its sometimes vulgar language, effectively banning its screening in Ireland. In October 2000, Sheamus Smith, the current censor, lifted the ban by awarding the film a certificate restricting its showing to viewers at least 15 years old. See the appendix on page 381 for further information on productions.

***Ulysses* in concert** The novel has also inspired musical compositions by Matyas Seiber, George Antheil, Luigi Dallapiccola, Luciano Berio, and Anthony BURGESS. See the appendix on page 381 for further information on productions.

***Ulysses in Nighttown*** In 1958, the Circe episode of Joyce's novel was theatrically adapted by Marjorie Barkentin. See the appendix on page 381 for further information on productions.

***Ulysses* schema** See SCHEMA.

**Uncle Charles Principle** See FREE INDIRECT DISCOURSE.

**University College, Dublin (UCD)** This is the Dublin university that both Joyce and his fictional counterpart, Stephen Dedalus, attended from 1898 to 1902. It was founded by Cardinal NEWMAN in 1853 as a Catholic alternative to Protestant-aligned TRINITY COLLEGE, and was originally named the Catholic University of Ireland. It opened in November 1854. At the invitation of Archbishop Paul Cullen, Newman became its first rector. (As rector-elect, Cardinal Newman delivered the series of lectures that formed the basis for his book *The Idea of a University.*) The school was reorganized after the University Education Act of 1879, when its curriculum came under the jurisdiction of the Royal University. (The Royal University, precursor to the NATIONAL UNIVERSITY of Ireland, had no classroom facilities or faculty; it was essentially an oversight institution empowered to set broad academic criteria, examine degree candidates, and grant degrees in universities under its control in Dublin, Cork, Galway, and Belfast.) Catholic University's name was changed to University College, Dublin, in October 1882, and the university came under the administration of the SOCIETY OF JESUS in 1883, an arrangement that continued until 1909, one year after it became a college of the National University.

During Joyce's time, University College, Dublin, was located at Nos. 85 and 86 ST STEPHEN'S GREEN, adjacent buildings that were constructed as 18th-

The Newman House at the University College in Dublin *(Faith Steinberg)*

century Georgian mansions. No. 85 had been built for Captain Hugh Montgomery by Richard Castel, the architect who designed Leinster House and other notable Dublin buildings. It was subsequently acquired by Richard Chapel "Buck" Whaley in 1765, who wished to live in it during the construction of his home at No. 86 St Stephen's Green. Both buildings were purchased by the Catholic Church in the mid-19th century to house its new university.

In the four years that Joyce spent at University College, Dublin, the institution provided both the final elements of his formal education and the occasions for his rebellions against many features of Irish intellectual life. Early on the college numbered among its distinguished faculty Gerard Manley Hopkins, who served as professor of classics from 1884 until his death in 1889 and who had a room on the top floor of No. 86. Another well-known scholar, Thomas Arnold (brother of Matthew Arnold), was professor of English from 1882 to 1900, and was favorably impressed by a paper that Joyce wrote for him on *Macbeth.*

Despite his ambivalent feelings about the Catholic Church in general and individual Jesuits in particular, Joyce repeatedly affirmed his high regard for the education he had gotten at their hands. Rather than study classics, he took his degree in modern languages—one of the first the university awarded in that area. It prepared Joyce for the linguistic excursions that, beginning with *Dubliners* and continuing through *Finnegans Wake,* became an increasingly central feature of his writing. More prosaically, it gave him the means to support himself and his family as a language teacher during the first decade and a half of his self-imposed exile from Ireland.

During his time at University College, Joyce made a number of friends whose views shaped his own intellectual development and whose personalities became the models for those of a number of characters in his fiction. J. F. BYRNE, an older fellow student from Belvedere College, took on the role of Joyce's confidant and the whetstone for his imaginative development that Stanislaus had earlier occupied. As Cranly, Byrne appears throughout *Stephen Hero* and in chapter 5 of *A Portrait of the Artist as a Young Man,* and he is recalled in passing

Commemorative plaque at the entrance of the Newman House *(Faith Steinberg)*

in *Ulysses*. Vincent COSGRAVE, a coarse and self-indulgent student, provided the inspiration for Vincent LYNCH, a student with whom Stephen has a number of discussions in *Stephen Hero*, who listens to Stephen's aesthetic theory in chapter 5 of *A Portrait*, and who accompanies Stephen to the brothel owned by Bella Cohen in the Circe episode (chapter 15) of *Ulysses* and then deserts him when Stephen becomes involved in a brawl with two British soldiers. Francis SHEEHY-SKEFFINGTON, an iconoclastic intellectual, gave Joyce many of the details incorporated into the character MacCann who appears in *Stephen Hero* (where his name appears as Philip McCann) and in *A Portrait*. George Clancy inspired the character of the Irish nationalist called Madden in *Stephen Hero* and Davin in *A Portrait*. Another friend, Thomas Kettle, does not appear as a character in any of Joyce's works, but his intelligence, good humor, and strong character greatly impressed Joyce, who was deeply touched when he learned of Kettle's death in France in 1916 (see *Letters*, I.96).

James Joyce in his graduation picture from University College, 1902 *(Croessman Collection of James Joyce, Special Collections/Morris Library, Southern Illinois University)*

For much of the 20th century, UCD steadfastly ignored its connection with Joyce. In recent years, however, the work of scholars like Augustine Martin, Maurice Harmon, and Anne Fogarty has refocused attention on the rich literary tradition that began there with Joyce and his contemporaries. UCD now holds regular events relating to Joyce's work and life.

# V

**Valéry, (Ambrose) Paul** (1871–1945) He was a French poet and critic who, as a young man, was influenced by the SYMBOLIST MOVEMENT. Valéry was elected to the French Academy in 1925. He first met Joyce in Paris in the early 1920s and remained friends with him through the late 1930s, although their friendship was not particularly close. On June 27, 1929, Valéry was among the guests at the Déjeuner *Ulysse,* a luncheon organized by Adrienne MONNIER to celebrate the publication of the first French translation of Joyce's *Ulysses.* According to Joyce's biographer, Richard ELLMANN, Joyce especially liked the opening of Valéry's poem *Ébauches d'un serpent.*

**Vaughan, Rev. Bernard, SJ** (1847–1922) He was a English Jesuit priest and retreat-master renowned as an orator. Father Vaughan spent much of his adult life as a Jesuit doing pastoral work in the East End slums of London. (Five of his brothers were also priests.) Father Vaughan conducted retreats in DUBLIN, and, according to Joyce's brother Stanislaus, was extremely popular, though much disliked by Joyce himself (see *My Brother's Keeper,* p. 225). He became the model for Father Purdon, who near the end of the *Dubliners* story "Grace" conducts the businessmen's evening of recollection attended by Tom Kernan, Martin Cunningham, Jack Power, C. P. M'Coy, and others. Joyce also recalls the name of Father Vaughan in *Ulysses,* where his colloquial preaching style is noted both by Leopold Bloom (*U* 5.398) in the Lotus-Eaters episode and later by the Rev. John Conmee, SJ, (*U* 10.34) in the Wandering Rocks episode.

***Vice-Versa*** This is the title of an 1882 novel by F. ANSTEY (Thomas Anstey Guthrie) that was adapted for the stage by Edward Rose. The story is about the consequences of the metamorphosis of a father, Mr. Bultitude, into his schoolboy son, Dick, and Dick's change into Mr. Bultitude. The transformed father must take his son's place in Dr. Grimstone's school, with predictably farcical results. Joyce played the part of Dr. Grimstone in a performance of the play at BELVEDERE COLLEGE during Whitsuntide in 1898. It probably served as the model for the unnamed play in which Stephen acts in chapter 2 of *A Portrait of the Artist as a Young Man.*

**Vico, Giambattista** (1668–1744) He was an Italian philosopher of history, social thought, and jurisprudence, born in Naples. He was professor of Latin rhetoric at the University of Naples, where he wrote his most celebrated work, known in English as *The New Science* (*Principi di scienza nuova di Giambattista Vico d'intorno alla comune natura delle nazioni* is the posthumous title of the third edition of 1744).

In this highly original study of history, language, mythology, and society, Vico proposed a cyclical theory of history comprising three ages—those of gods, of heroes, and of humans—followed by a *ricorso* or brief transition into chaos, after which the process begins anew. Joyce had a pronounced interest in Vico's ideas. Vico's theories on recurring patterns of human development and his detailed study of language and mythology provide a foundation not only for understanding Joyce's use of myth and pattern-types in *Ulysses* but especially for penetrating the structure and dynamics of *Finnegans Wake,* a work that opens with an obvious allusion to Vico (*FW* 3.2; see *Letters,* III.117–118, 463, and 480).

**Viking Press, The** For many years, The Viking Press was the exclusive American publisher of *Chamber Music, Dubliners, A Portrait of the Artist as a Young Man, Exiles,* and *Finnegans Wake.* Joyce's links to The Viking Press stem directly from his longtime close association with the editor and publisher B. W. HUEBSCH. In 1914, Huebsch, at that time the head of his own firm, read and wished to publish *Dubliners.* Financial conditions prevented him from doing so until 1916. He subsequently published *A Portrait of the Artist as a Young Man* and *Exiles,* and from these initial contacts a friendship arose that continued for the rest of Joyce's life. Later, when Huebsch merged his publishing house with The Viking Press, he brought Joyce to that firm. Joyce's formal association with Viking began in 1931 when he signed a contract for the American edition of *Finnegans Wake.* Viking is now part of the Anglo-American publishing conglomerate Viking Penguin.

**villanelle** This is the designation of a complicated verse form consisting of five tercets and a quatrain all organized around two rhymes: aba aba aba aba aba abaa. In addition, the final lines of the first two stanzas are repeated alternately throughout the poem. The term *villanelle* originated in Italy (*villanella,* from *villano,* "peasant"), where it meant a rustic or folk song. It was in France in the late 16th century that it was used to designate this particular form, a short poem of popular character.

Although the form was not often employed in poetry written in English in the early 20th century, it has subsequently been taken up by poets like W. H. Auden, William Empson, Elizabeth Bishop, Dylan Thomas, and others. Joyce gives an example of the villanelle structure in the poem that Stephen Dedalus composes in chapter 5 of *A Portrait of the Artist as a Young Man.* (See "VILLANELLE OF THE TEMPTRESS.")

**"Villanelle of the Temptress"** This is the title of a rather mediocre poem that Stephen Dedalus jots down after he has awakened, probably from an erotic dream, in the middle of chapter 5. ("Are you not weary of ardent ways? / Tell no more of enchanted days"). Although the female subject of the poem remains unidentified, it is most likely Emma Clery, to whom Stephen's thoughts return repeatedly throughout the final chapter. According to Stanislaus JOYCE, "Villanelle of the Temptress" was based on a poem Joyce had written earlier, independent of *A Portrait.* Stephen composes a poem by the same name in the final chapter of *Stephen Hero.* (See *Shine and Dark* and *Stephen Hero.*)

**Villon, François** (1431–1463?) Villon was a French poet of the late Middle Ages. He was notorious as a brawler in the Latin Quarter in Paris. In 1462 Villon was sentenced to be hanged, but his punishment was commuted to banishment for 10 years. The poet dropped out of sight after that.

Villon's poetry—*Grand Testament* in particular—enjoyed a revival in the 19th century when his work became popular with the romantics and when he himself became a legendary rogue figure. His insouciant spirit informs the general rowdiness of Stephen Dedalus, Buck Mulligan, and the others at the Holles Street Maternity Hospital in the Oxen of the Sun episode (chapter 14) of *Ulysses.* In addition, Villon is alluded to even more directly in the Circe episode (chapter 15), when Stephen utters a phrase from Villon's *Ballade de la grosse Margot:* "Dans ce bordel où tenons nostre état" [In this brothel where we hold our court] (*U* 15.3536).

**Volta Cinema** This was Dublin's first motion picture theater, located at 45 Mary Street; it was opened at Joyce's initiative. In 1909 Joyce was able to interest four Triestine businessmen, who already owned several cinemas in other cities in Europe, in the idea of opening a theater in DUBLIN. In return for a share of the venture's profits, Joyce agreed to act as the local representative, and after much planning the theater opened on December 20, 1909. Subsequently, the Dublin City Corporation granted the theater a permanent license on January 19, 1910. Joyce, satisfied that the project was well under way, returned to TRIESTE on January 6, 1910. However, although the theater proved initially pop-

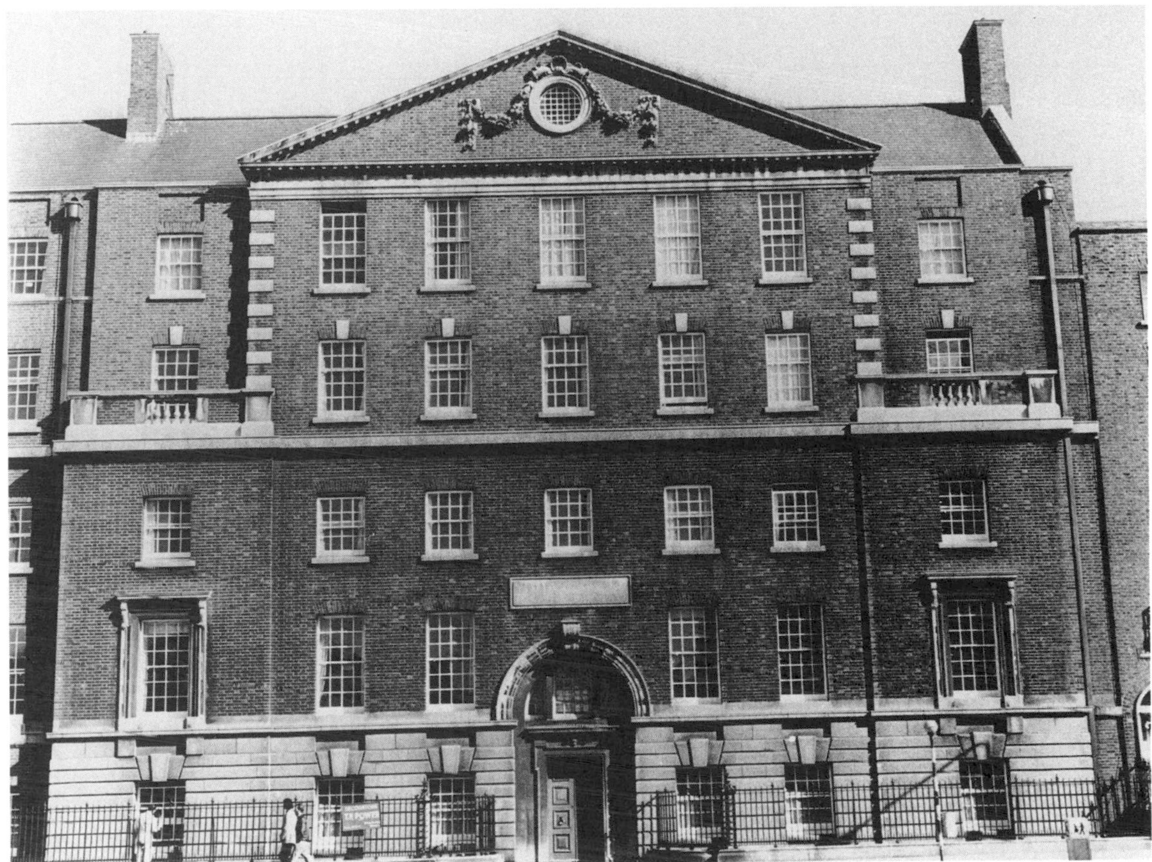

Holles Street Maternity Hospital, Dublin *(Irish Tourist Board)*

ular, it soon began to lose money. By the summer, the four partners decided that they could no longer sustain the investment, and they sold it at a loss.

Joyce's commercial interest in film virtually ended with this unsuccessful business venture, but his aesthetic interest continued throughout his life. According to Richard ELLMANN, in the mid-1920s Joyce expressed in conversation with Daniel Hummel the desire to have *Ulysses* made into a film. A film was made, but not until 1967, 26 years after Joyce's death. (See *ULYSSES*.)

***Vor Sonnenaufgang*** See *Before Sunrise* in "miscellaneous works."

# W

***Wake Newslitter, A*** This is the title of a journal devoted to printing notes and short essays that foster the study of *Finnegans Wake.* Founded by Fritz SENN and Clive HART, *A Wake Newslitter* was published on an irregular basis (numbers 1–18) from March 1962 to December 1963. At that point it began to appear on a bimonthly schedule, under the designation New Series, from volume 1 number 1, published in February 1964, to the final issue, volume 17 number 6, which appeared in December 1980. Over this same period it also published a number of monographs on diverse topics relating to *Finnegans Wake.*

**Weaver, Harriet Shaw** (1876–1961) She was a longtime patron and close friend of James Joyce and his family. Weaver grew up in an English village in Cheshire, the daughter of the district physician. Despite her conventional background, Weaver became an ardent feminist, and in 1936 joined the Communist Party. Weaver became acquainted with Joyce's work when she was principal editor of the London journal the EGOIST, and she oversaw the serialization of *A Portrait of the Artist as a Young Man* in that periodical from February 1914 to September 1915. Within a few years, drawing upon her relatively small private fortune, she became one of Joyce's most regular and generous benefactors, a relationship that continued for the remainder of Joyce's life. (One Joyce critic, Robert Adams Day, has estimated that today's value of what Harriet Shaw Weaver eventually gave Joyce would be the equivalent of $1,000,000.)

Weaver also took on various roles for the Joyce family, being often consulted as a literary critic, a personal confidante, and a financial adviser. Sometime in the mid-1930s, Joyce seems to have taken offense over some real or imagined act of Weaver's. Although she had no clear idea as to the source of Joyce's ensuing coolness and tried assiduously to repair the breach, a distance remained between them. After Joyce's death, Weaver was his literary executor; she continued to help members of the family whenever it was possible and was among the most devoted of those who worked to ensure the growth of Joyce's literary reputation.

**Wellington Monument** It is a 205-foot granite obelisk erected in PHOENIX PARK in 1817, the Wellington Monument is located just inside the park's main (eastern) entrance, on the site of the old Salute Battery. The four sides of the monument's base are decorated in bas-relief to commemorate various stages of the military career of the DUBLIN-born Arthur Wellesley (1769–1852), later duke of Wellington, the hero of the Battle of Waterloo and other engagements between England and France during the Napoleonic Wars. The monument is a popular Dublin landmark, and is referred to in *Finnegans Wake.* In chapter 1 of the *Wake,* it is combined with the Magazine in Phoenix Park and converted into the Willingdone Museyroom (*FW* 8.10), the setting of a humorous tour that plays on many levels of reality (*FW* 8.9–10.23).

The Wellington Monument in Phoenix Park, Dublin *(Irish Tourist Board)*

**Whiteboys** This is the name of a secret Irish agrarian society organized in Tipperary in 1761. The group, which took its name from the white shirts its members wore during their nighttime terrorist activities, lasted into the 19th century. The Whiteboys opposed tithing to the Church of Ireland and exorbitant land rents. The group was originally called Levelers, a name derived from the tactic of throwing down fences and leveling enclosures. Joyce's great-grandfather was a member of this organization, and in chapter 1 of *A Portrait of the Artist as a Young Man,* during the Christmas dinner scene, Simon Dedalus claims that his grandfather was a Whiteboy (*P* 38). (See also RIBBONMEN.)

**Wilde, Oscar** (1854–1900) Wilde was an Irish playwright, novelist, and essayist, born in DUBLIN on October 16, 1854. Wilde attended Portora Royal School, TRINITY COLLEGE, and graduated from Oxford with rare double first honors.

He moved to London in 1879, and though his writing was then undistinguished, he acquired a great reputation as a dandy, as a wit, and, influenced by Walter PATER and John RUSKIN, as the most dedicated practitioner of the art-for-art's-sake aesthetic in London. He married in 1884 and fathered two sons. In the mid-1880s his editorship of *The Woman's World* gave him an outlet for writing, but he did not fulfill the promise of his early years.

In the late 1880s, however, his literary production increased in volume and quality. He published collections of fairy tales and short stories and a series of important essays. In 1890 a version of *The Picture of Dorian Gray* appeared in *Lippincott's Magazine* and the full-length novel was published in book form a year later. In the early 1890s he wrote a series of witty comic plays, the greatest of which is *The Importance of Being Earnest* (1895).

That same year, however, he brought a libel suit against the marquess of Queensberry, who had accused him (correctly) of sexual involvement with Queensberry's son, Lord Alfred Douglas. Having lost the suit, he was charged with and convicted of "immoral acts" (that is, being a practicing homosexual) and sentenced to two years' hard labor. During his time in prison he wrote *De Profundis,* a rambling epistolary essay, and shortly after his release in 1897, "The Ballad of Reading Gaol." He never, however, recaptured the lightness, humor, and creative power that characterized his work before his incarceration. Because of the scandal of his trial and imprisonment, Mrs. Wilde had her and her sons' name legally changed; Wilde never saw his sons again. Deserted by former friends, Wilde went to live in France after leaving prison. For three years he led a restless, dissipated, and often indigent existence and died in Paris on November 30, 1900.

The perceived similarity of their relations to social and artistic convention predisposed Joyce to sympathy for Oscar Wilde—an Irish artist whose devotion to aesthetics and an unconventional morality threatened English sensibilities—and Joyce makes frequent reference to him and his work. Joyce used the occasion of a performance in TRIESTE of Richard Strauss's opera *Salomé* (which used Wilde's play *Salomé* as its libretto) to commemorate his countryman in "Oscar Wilde: The Poet of 'Salomé'," in the Trieste newspaper *Il* PICCOLO DELLA SERA of March 24, 1909. The Joyce scholar Don Gifford sees echoes of Wilde's poem "The Sphinx" in the opening lines of the villanelle that Stephen Dedalus writes in chapter 5 of *A Portrait of the Artist as a Young Man* ("Are you not weary of ardent ways"). In the Telemachus episode (chapter 1) of *Ulysses*, Stephen takes his image of the cracked looking-glass as the symbol of Irish art from Wilde's "The Decay of Lying," and other references to Wilde and his work occur throughout the novel. Likewise the figure of Wilde as exiled fallen artist recurs as an image throughout *Finnegans Wake*.

For further information, see Richard Ellmann, *Oscar Wilde* (1988).

Playwright Oscar Wilde, about whom Joyce wrote "Oscar Wilde: The Poet of 'Salomé'" *(Irish Tourist Board)*

**Wild Geese** Originally it was the name given to the Irish insurgents who went into exile after the defeat of the Catholic forces of the Stuart king James II deposed by the army of William III (to whom English Protestants had offered the crown in 1688) at the Battle of the BOYNE (1690) and the subsequent Treaty of Limerick (1691). Many of these men served as mercenary officers in the French, Spanish, and Austrian armies. Eventually, the term came to signify all Irish people who left their homeland as a political gesture against English rule. In the Proteus episode, Stephen Dedalus recalls his meeting in Paris with the Fenian Kevin Egan, a prototype of the 19th-century Wild Geese, and this recollection in turn evokes a series of references to such Irish political exiles. Joyce also plays on the word in *Finnegans Wake* (185.b).

**Williams, William Carlos** (1883–1963) He was an American poet, novelist, and man of letters, and for decades a practicing physician. In frequently anthologized works like "The Red Wheelbarrow," the unsentimental clarity of his imagery stands out. In his epic poem *Paterson* (5 vols., 1946–58), in novels—*White Mule* (1937), *In the Money* (1940), and *The Build-Up* (1952)—and in nonfiction works like *In the American Grain* ( 1925), Williams applies sharply analytical views of American life, culture, and the responsibilities of the poet. Williams was a highly original American modernist, practicing an aesthetic of plainness and directness, based on the rhythms and vocabulary of ordinary American speech. Though little honored in his lifetime, since his death (and the waning of the influence of T. S. ELIOT, his bête noir and literary rival) Williams's work has been extremely influential.

Williams knew Joyce in Paris in the 1920s and, like his friend Ezra POUND, was a great admirer of Joyce's work. He contributed to *OUR EXAGMINATION ROUND HIS FACTIFICATION FOR INCAMINATION OF WORK IN PROGRESS.*

Williams's essay in that collection, entitled "A Point for American Criticism," presents a direct response to a harsh critique of Joyce by the British author Rebecca West. After painstakingly summarizing the elements of West's argument and refuting various specific points, Williams turns to what he sees as the heart of the matter. He feels that West's conventional taste and literary expectations prevent her from understanding what Joyce is doing. To illustrate this point, Williams contrasts what he understands to be the British approach to literature, one that rigidly adheres to conventional expectations, with what he considers an American approach, more flexible and responsive, open to possibilities beyond charted boundaries. Williams advocates such an open, direct response to Joyce (and other innovative writing), that attempts not to confuse literary experience with extraliterary preconceptions. Rebecca West's reading, he says, approaches Joyce by way of nonliterary considerations as a way to avoid confronting difficult literature. She finds Joyce "strange," Williams concludes, because she "fails to fit" him into her expectations.

For further information, see Paul Mariani, *William Carlos Williams: A New World Naked.* (1990).

**Wilson, Edmund** (1895–1972) He was an American critic, essayist, and novelist whose essay "James Joyce," in his book *Axel's Castle: A Study of the Imaginative Literature of 1870–1930* (1931), was one of the earliest American efforts to offer a serious assessment of Joyce's *Ulysses.* In it, Wilson examines the European literary background of *Ulysses,* in particular the influence of French realism and symbolism. Wilson's essay on *Finnegans Wake,* entitled "The Dream of H. C. Earwicker" (based on his June and July 1939 reviews in the *New Republic* and collected in *The Wound and the Bow* [1947]), marked another important watershed in Joyce studies, for it laid before an American audience an approach to Joyce's work that combined an analysis of the work's intellectual rigor with a defense of the popular appeal the *Wake* had exerted on Europeans for over a decade. When Joyce read Wilson's *New Republic* reviews of *Finnegans Wake,* he commented in a July 1939 letter to Frank Budgen that "Wilson makes some curious blunders, e.g. that the 4th old man is Ulster" (*Letters,* I.405). (The revised version of Wilson's reviews published in *The Wound and the Bow* is also reprinted in *James Joyce: Two Decades of Criticism,* edited by Seon Givens; also see Criticism under *Finnegans Wake* above.)

**Woolsey, Hon. John M.** (1877–1945) Woolsey was the judge of the United States District Court, Southern District of New York, who on December 6, 1933, overturned the existing ban on the importation of *Ulysses* into the United States on grounds of obscenity. *Ulysses* had been banned since Margaret ANDERSON and Jane HEAP were convicted of obscenity when they published excerpts in their journal, the *LITTLE REVIEW,* in 1921. Bennett CERF OF RANDOM HOUSE in 1932 schemed to have the novel confiscated by a customs inspector and hired the New York attorney Morris Ernst to argue the case in court. Ernst maneuvered to set a court date at a time when the tolerant Judge Woolsey would be sitting (see Bennett Cerf, *At Random* [1977]). Woolsey presided without a jury and within two days ruled that "in spite of [the novel's] unusual frankness, I do not detect anywhere the leer of the sensualist. I hold, therefore, that it is not pornographic." A little over a month later, on January 25, 1934, Random House published the first authorized American edition. (For Judge Woolsey's complete statement, see the appendix on page 392. Also see *Letters,* III.314–315 for a reprint of the press releases from the *New York Herald.*) A brief biography of Woolsey, written by his son, appears in *James Joyce Quarterly* 37 (Spring/Summer 2000): 367–369.

***Work in Progress*** This was Joyce's provisional name for *Finnegans Wake* until it was published in book form in 1939. (The title, according to Richard ELLMANN, was suggested by Ford Madox FORD.) When sections of it appeared in various journals or were published separately in the 1920s and the 1930s, they were always identified as having come from *Work in Progress.* Until shortly before its publication, no one but Joyce's wife knew the work's actual title, and over the years Joyce took pleasure in encouraging various friends to try to guess it. To Joyce's dismay, one—Eugene JOLAS—did (see *Letters,* III.427).

**Yeats, William Butler** (1865–1939) Yeats was a Nobel Prize–winning Irish writer, cofounder of the Irish Literary Theatre, senator, and one of the most influential dramatists and poets of the 20th century, whose work dominated the Irish literary scene at the turn of the century. While Joyce admired Yeats's artistic achievements, their approaches to creating literature were very different. Yeats's involvement in the "Celtic Twilight"—that period of the IRISH LITERARY REVIVAL extending from the turn of the century to the beginning of World War I—his didactic and nationalist poetry, and his commitment to political activity all reflected personal and artistic positions to which Joyce was opposed. Some critics have speculated that Yeats's success as a poet influenced Joyce's decision to concentrate his energies on creating fiction. Yet despite occasional friction (like his attack on Yeats in "The Holy Office"), any rivalry that Joyce may have felt was ultimately neutralized by a deep admiration for Yeats's work.

In his book *Joyce Remembered*, Joyce's school friend Constantine Curran describes the esteem in which Joyce held Yeats's work and how, as a university student, Joyce had taken the trouble to commit to memory two of Yeats's stories, "The Tables of the Law" and "The Adoration of the Magi." Also during his student days, Joyce attended the premier of Yeats's *The Countess Cathleen* on May 8, 1899, and witnessed the uproar caused by fellow university students who thought the play anti-Irish. Joyce refused to sign their letter of protest, and staunchly defended the play. Later, he commemorated the uproar at the theater in a passage in chapter 5 of *A Portrait of the Artist as a Young Man.* (At the same time, the unease that he felt over the growing nationalistic sentiments of the Irish Literary Theatre, with which Yeats was involved, became evident in his essay "The Day of the Rabblement.")

Joyce first met Yeats in October 1902, introduced by a fellow Dubliner, the writer George RUSSELL. A few months later, when Joyce first left Ireland for the Continent, he stopped in London to visit Yeats, who generously spent the entire day with him, introducing him to editors at the offices of the *Academy* and the *SPEAKER* who might later offer him books to review, and taking him to meet the literary critic Arthur SYMONS.

When Joyce again passed through London in 1912, he and his son, George JOYCE, called on Yeats. Three years later, in 1915, Yeats and Ezra POUND worked together to secure from the British government a grant for Joyce of £75 from the Royal Literary Fund, and a year later Yeats again supported Pound's successful efforts to persuade the English government to grant Joyce £100 from the Civil List. Yeats became one of the first subscribers to *Ulysses* and, despite the mockery of him at several points in the book, praised the novel as a work of genius.

Yeats's influence on Joyce's artistic development cannot be denied, though its precise nature remains difficult to ascertain. Throughout his life, Joyce remained an admirer of Yeats's work and even, during his time in TRIESTE, tried unsuccessfully to arrange for an Italian translation of *The Countess Cathleen.* Joyce had about a dozen books

Irish dramatist and poet William Butler Yeats *(Irish Tourist Board)*

by Yeats in his Trieste and Paris libraries. And, in perhaps the most telling confirmation of the continuing presence of Yeats in Joyce's own creative consciousness, one finds numerous allusions to Yeats and his work throughout Joyce's work. Admittedly, even in his later works like *Ulysses,* Joyce could not resist the occasional sneer at Yeats's sometimes quirky personal traits, generally put in the mouth of Buck Mulligan (as in the Telemachus episode [chapter 1], and the Scylla and Charybdis episode [chapter 9]—"She gets you a job on the paper and then you go and slate her drivel to Jaysus. Couldn't you do the Yeats touch?" [*U* 9.1159–1161]). The friendship between Joyce and Yeats always seemed to be tempered by an element of reserve, but their mutual artistic respect never diminished. Yeats, like Joyce, was a unique artist whose work changed radically over the course of his career. He moved from symbolist poems in the 1890s, to nationalistic drama and poetry through the first two decades of the 20th century, and finally to modernist poems and postmodernist Noh drama in the last 20 years of his life. At the same time he sustained an active political career that encompassed Home Rule agitation, shock and dismay over the Rising and subsequent Civil War, service as a senator in the Irish parliament, and a late flirtation with fascism. In his last years he withdrew from public life, but his poetic power never diminished. Joyce always acknowledged Yeats's genius and paid tribute to him on the occasion of Yeats's death, sending a wreath to his grave at Roquebrune in southern France (see *Letters,* III.438n.1).

# Z

**Zola, Émile** (1840–1902) Zola was the best-known of a group of 19th-century French "naturalist" writers. Literary NATURALISM took as its subject the workings of broad social forces and their effects on the individual lives of ordinary people. Many naturalist works, and Zola's in particular, were quite popular. Zola provided an artistic model for Joyce early on as the latter strove to develop his own style. There is evidence of Zola's impact on Joyce as early as 1903 in his review of T. Baron Russell's *Borlase and Son* (reprinted in *The Critical Writings of James Joyce*), and in letters written in 1906 and 1907. Textual evidence in *Dubliners, Stephen Hero,* and *A Portrait of the Artist as a Young Man* strongly suggests that Joyce used Zola's writing (among others) as a guide for developing the technique of FREE INDIRECT DISCOURSE within his own narratives. See *Letters*, II.137, 202, and 211.

**Zurich** This is the Swiss city in which Joyce and Nora BARNACLE lived from 1915 to 1919 and briefly again from the end of 1940 until his death. Under the mistaken impression that a job teaching English for Berlitz awaited him in Zurich, Joyce and Nora first went there in 1904 en route, as it turned out, to POLA, where they lived for about five months before settling in TRIESTE. These cities, now in Croatia and Italy, respectively, were then part of the Austro-Hungarian Empire. In June 1915, because he held a passport issued by Great Britain, a country then at war with Austria-Hungary, Joyce was ordered by the authorities to leave Trieste. He decided to move his family to Zurich in neutral Switzerland. (His brother Stanislaus JOYCE, who also had a British passport but who was outspoken about his opinion that Trieste should be under Italian control, had been arrested and sent to a detention camp earlier in the year.)

A statue of James Joyce that sits by his gravesite in Zurich *(Lucretia Lyons)*

Joyce and his family lived in Zurich until 1919. He managed to support them all through private language lessons and a succession of financial gifts from both (British) government and private donors. He composed much of *Ulysses* during his time there, and made many enduring friendships, in particular with the artist and critic Frank BUDGEN and the actor Claud SYKES, with whom Joyce founded the acting company called the ENGLISH PLAYERS.

Although Joyce and his family left Zurich after the end of World War I, he and Nora regularly returned during the 1930s, often to consult doctors about his eye troubles or in an effort to find a mode of treatment that would halt the progressively deteriorating mental condition of his daughter, Lucia. In mid-December 1940 Joyce once again returned to Zurich as a refugee, this time fleeing the German occupation of France during World War II. Shortly after their arrival, he became ill and died on January 13, 1941. Joyce was buried in a plot in Fluntern Cemetery near the zoological gardens. When Nora died in April 1951, she too was buried in Fluntern, although in a different spot. In 1966, their remains were placed permanently next to one another in a third location in the cemetery. In 1981, Milton Hebald's sculpture of Joyce smoking a cigarette and sitting with legs crossed was erected at the gravesite.

**Zurich James Joyce Foundation** The Zurich James Joyce Foundation was set up in 1985 with Fritz Senn's collection of Joyceana as its nucleus. The former Union Bank of Switzerland, under Dr. Robert Holzach, its chairman, provided the funding for the first six years, and thanks to his foresight the foundation has since become independent.

The Zurich James Joyce Foundation is probably the most comprehensive working library on Joyce in Europe, a research center for scholars, students, and visitors. It holds regular weekly readings of *Ulysses and Finnegans Wake,* lectures by itinerant Joyceans, and, one week generally in early August, an international workshop on a given topic (like Song, Expectation, Dreaming, Naming, or Kitsch in Joyce). The foundation has also initiated some local Joyce exhibitions. In recent years the "Friends of the Zurich James Joyce Foundation" have offered scholarships that enable researchers to work on a Joycean project in the foundation for two months.

# PART IV

# *Appendices*

# CHRONOLOGICAL BIBLIOGRAPHY OF JOYCE'S WORKS AND ADAPTATIONS

## Joyce's Writings and Publications

*Dates are those of publication except for nonextant and posthumously published works, in which cases dates are the years (or approximate years) of composition.*

"Et Tu, Healy" (c. 1891; nonextant poem written sometime shortly after the death of Charles Stewart Parnell on October 6, 1891)

"Trust Not Appearances" (c. 1836; high school essay, published posthumously in *The Critical Writings of James Joyce* and in *James Joyce: Occasional, Critical, and Political Writing*)

*Silhouettes* (c. 1897; nonextant short stories)

*Moods* (c. 1897; nonextant collection of poems)

"Force" (1898; university essay, published posthumously in *The Critical Writings of James Joyce* and in *James Joyce: Occasional, Critical, and Political Writing*)

"The Study of Languages" (c. 1898–99; university essay, published posthumously in *The Critical Writings of James Joyce* and in *James Joyce: Occasional, Critical, and Political Writing*)

"Royal Hibernian Academy 'Ecce Homo' " (1899; college essay, published posthumously in *The Critical Writings of James Joyce* and in *James Joyce: Occasional, Critical, and Political Writing*)

"Drama and Life" (January 20, 1900; essay read to the Literary and Historical Society, University College, Dublin; published posthumously in *The Critical Writings of James Joyce* and in *James Joyce: Occasional, Critical, and Political Writing*)

"Ibsen's New Drama" (April 1, 1900; review, published posthumously in *The Critical Writings of James Joyce* and in *James Joyce: Occasional, Critical, and Political Writing*)

*A Brilliant Career* (Summer 1900; nonextant prose play)

*Dream Stuff* (Summer 1900; nonextant verse play)

*Shine and Dark* (c. 1900; nonextant poems, fragments of which exist and are published in Stanislaus Joyce's *My Brother's Keeper*, Faber and Faber, London, 1958, and in Richard Ellmann's *James Joyce*, Oxford University Press, New York, 1982)

"The Final Peace" (c. 1901; nonextant poem)

"The Passionate Poet" (c. 1901; nonextant poem)

"The Day of the Rabblement" (October–November 1901; essay, privately printed as a pamphlet in Dublin; reprinted in *The Critical Writings of James Joyce* and in *James Joyce: Occasional, Critical, and Political Writing*)

"James Clarence Mangan" (May 1902; address delivered on February 15, 1902, first published in St Stephen's, Dublin; reprinted in *The Critical Writings of James Joyce* and in *James Joyce: Occasional, Critical, and Political Writing*; also see "Giacomo Clarenzio Mangan," below)

"An Irish Poet" (December 11, 1902; review, first published in the *Daily Express*, Dublin; reprinted in *The Critical Writings of James Joyce* and in *James Joyce: Occasional, Critical, and Political Writing*)

"George Meredith" (December 11, 1902; review first published in the *Daily Express*, Dublin; reprinted in *The Critical Writings of James Joyce* and in *James Joyce: Occasional, Critical, and Political Writing*)

"To-day and To-morrow in Ireland" (January 29, 1903; review, first published in the *Daily Express*, Dublin; reprinted in *The Critical Writings of James Joyce* and in *James Joyce: Occasional, Critical, and Political Writing*)

"A Suave Philosophy" (February 6, 1903; review, first published in the *Daily Express*, Dublin; reprinted in *The Critical Writings of James Joyce* and in *James Joyce: Occasional, Critical, and Political Writing*)

"An Effort at Precision in Thinking" (February 6, 1903; review, first published in the *Daily Express,* Dublin; reprinted in *The Critical Writings of James Joyce* and in *James Joyce: Occasional, Critical, and Political Writing*)

"Colonial Verses" (February 6, 1903; review, first published in the *Daily Express,* Dublin; reprinted in *The Critical Writings of James Joyce* and in *James Joyce: Occasional, Critical, and Political Writing*)

Paris Notebook (February–March 1903; see "Aesthetics" below)

"The Soul of Ireland" (March 26, 1903; review, first published in the *Daily Express,* London; reprinted in *The Critical Writings of James Joyce* and in *James Joyce: Occasional, Critical, and Political Writing*)

"The Motor Derby" (April 7, 1903; interview, first published in the *Irish Times,* Dublin; reprinted in *The Critical Writings of James Joyce* and in *James Joyce: Occasional, Critical, and Political Writing*)

"Catilina" (May 21, 1903; review, first published in the *Speaker,* London; reprinted in *The Critical Writings of James Joyce* and in *James Joyce: Occasional, Critical, and Political Writing*)

"Empire Building" (c. September 1903; letter intended for an Irish newspaper; unpublished in Joyce's lifetime, published posthumously in *The Critical Writings of James Joyce* and in *James Joyce: Occasional, Critical, and Political Writing*)

"A Ne'er-do-Well" (September 3, 1903; review, first published in the *Daily Express,* Dublin; reprinted in *The Critical Writings of James Joyce* and in *James Joyce: Occasional, Critical, and Political Writing*)

"Aristotle on Education" (September 3, 1903; review, first published in the *Daily Express,* Dublin; reprinted in *The Critical Writings of James Joyce* and in *James Joyce: Occasional, Critical, and Political Writing*)

"A Peep into History" (September 17, 1903; review, first published in the *Daily Express,* Dublin; reprinted in *The Critical Writings of James Joyce* and in *James Joyce: Occasional, Critical, and Political Writing*)

"New Fiction" (September 17, 1903; review, first published in the *Daily Express,* Dublin; reprinted in *The Critical Writings of James Joyce* and in *James Joyce: Occasional, Critical, and Political Writing*)

"The Mettle of the Pasture" (September 17, 1903; review, first published in the *Daily Express,* Dublin; reprinted in *The Critical Writings of James Joyce* and in *James Joyce: Occasional, Critical, and Political Writing*)

"A French Religious Novel" (October 1, 1903; review, first published in the *Daily Express,* Dublin; reprinted in *The Critical Writings of James Joyce* and in *James Joyce: Occasional, Critical, and Political Writing*)

"Mr. Arnold Graves' New York" (October 1, 1903; review, first published in the *Daily Express,* Dublin; reprinted in *The Critical Writings of James Joyce* and in *James Joyce: Occasional, Critical, and Political Writing*)

"Unequal Verse" (October 1, 1903; review, first published in the *Daily Express,* Dublin; reprinted in *The Critical Writings of James Joyce* and in *James Joyce: Occasional, Critical, and Political Writing*)

"A Neglected Poet" (October 15, 1903; review, first published in the *Daily Express,* Dublin; reprinted in *The Critical Writings of James Joyce* and in *James Joyce: Occasional, Critical, and Political Writing*)

"Mr. Mason's Novels" (October 15, 1903; review, first published in the *Daily Express,* Dublin; reprinted in *The Critical Writings of James Joyce* and in *James Joyce: Occasional, Critical, and Political Writing*)

"The Bruno Philosophy" (October 30, 1903; review, first published in the *Daily Express,* Dublin; reprinted in *The Critical Writings of James Joyce* and in *James Joyce: Occasional, Critical, and Political Writing*)

"Humanism" (November 12, 1903; review, first published in the *Daily Express,* Dublin; reprinted in *The Critical Writings of James Joyce* and in *James Joyce: Occasional, Critical, and Political Writing*)

"Shakespeare Explained" (November 12, 1903; review, first published in the *Daily Express,* Dublin; reprinted in *The Critical Writings of James Joyce* and in *James Joyce: Occasional, Critical, and Political Writing*)

"Borlase and Son" (November 19, 1903; review, first published in the *Daily Express,* Dublin; reprinted in *The Critical Writings of James Joyce* and in *James Joyce: Occasional, Critical, and Political Writing*)

"Aesthetics: I. The Paris Notebook. II. The Pola Notebook" (February–March 1903 and November 1904, respectively; notes, first published in 1939 in Herbert Gorman's *James Joyce,* Farrar & Rinehart, Inc., New York; reprinted in *The Critical Writings of James Joyce* and in *James Joyce: Occasional, Critical, and Political Writing*)

*The Early Joyce: The Book Reviews, 1902–1903* (collection of book reviews, edited by Stanislaus Joyce and Ellsworth Mason; published in 1955 by Mamalujo Press, Colorado Springs; also published in *The Critical Writings of James Joyce* and in *James Joyce: Occasional, Critical, and Political Writing*)

"A Portrait of the Artist" (January 1904; prose sketch, edited by Richard M. Kain and Robert Scholes and first published in the *Yale Review,* Spring 1960; reprinted in *The Workshop of Daedalus,* collected and edited by Robert Scholes and Richard M. Kain, published by Northwestern University Press, Evanston, Ill., in 1965; again reprinted in *A Portrait of the Artist as a Young Man: Text, Criticism, and Notes,* edited by Chester G. Anderson, The Viking Critical Library, New York, 1968)

"Song" (May 14, 1904; poem [*Chamber Music* XXIV], first published in the *Saturday Review,* London)

"O Sweetheart" (July 30, 1904; poem [*Chamber Music* XVIII], first published in the *Speaker,* London)

"Song" (August 1904; poem [*Chamber Music* VII], first published in *Dana,* Dublin)

"The Sisters" (August 13, 1904; short story, first published under the name of Stephen Daedalus in the *Irish Homestead,* Dublin; significantly revised before it was republished in *Dubliners*)

"Eveline" (September 10, 1904; short story, first published under the name of Stephen Daedalus in the *Irish Homestead,* Dublin; somewhat revised before it was republished in *Dubliners*)

"A Wish" (October 8, 1904; poem [*Chamber Music* VI], first published in the *Speaker,* London)

"Christmas Eve" (autumn 1904; fragment of a short story, first published in 1962 and introduced by John J. Slocum and Herbert Cahoon in *A James Joyce Miscellany, Third Series,* edited by Marvin Magalaner, Southern Illinois University Press, Carbondale)

Pola Notebook (November 1904; see "Aesthetics" above)

"After the Race" (December 17, 1904; short story, first published under the name of Stephen Daedalus in the *Irish Homestead,* Dublin; republished in *Dubliners*)

*Epiphanies* (1898–1904; edited by O. A. Silverman, published in 1956 by the Lockwood Memorial Library, Buffalo)

*Stephen Hero* (1904–1905; novel, edited with an introduction by Theodore Spencer, first published by Jonathan Cape, London, and by New Directions, New York, in 1944)

"The Holy Office" (1904 or 1905; broadside poem, privately printed in Pola; reprinted in *The Critical Writings of James Joyce* and in *James Joyce: Poems and Short Writings*)

"Two Songs" (1905; poem [*Chamber Music* XII and XXVI], first published in *The Venture, an Annual of Art and Literature,* London)

"Il Fenianismo. L'Ultimo Feniano" (March 22, 1907; newspaper article, first published in *Il Piccolo della Sera,* Trieste; translated and published as "Fenianism: The Last Fenian" in *The Critical Writings of James Joyce* and in *James Joyce: Occasional, Critical, and Political Writing*)

"Ireland, Island of Saints and Sages" (see "Irlanda, Isola dei Santi e dei Savi")

"Irlanda, Isola dei Santi e dei Savi" (April 27, 1907; lecture in Italian delivered at the Università Popolare Triestina, Trieste; translated as "Ireland, Island of Saints and Sages" and published in *The Critical Writings of James Joyce* and in *James Joyce: Occasional, Critical, and Political Writing*)

"Giacomo Clarenzio Mangan" (c. May 1907; lecture in Italian delivered at the Università Popolare Triestina, Trieste; translated as "James Clarence Mangan" and published posthumously in *The Critical Writings of James Joyce* and in *James Joyce: Occasional, Critical, and Political Writing*)

*Chamber Music* (May 1907; suite of songs [a sequence of 36 poems], first published by Elkin Mathews in London; reprinted in *Collected Poems* in 1936, and elsewhere since)

"Home Rule Maggiorenne" (May 19, 1907; newspaper article, first published in *Il Piccolo della Sera,* Trieste; translated and published as "Home Rule Comes of Age" in *The Critical Writings of James Joyce* and in *James Joyce: Occasional, Critical, and Political Writing*)

"L'Irlanda alla Sbarra" (September 16, 1907; newspaper article, first published in *Il Piccolo della Sera,* Trieste; translated and published as "Ireland at the Bar" in *The Critical Writings of James Joyce* and in *James Joyce: Occasional, Critical, and Political Writing*)

"Oscar Wilde: Il Poeta di 'Salomé' " (March 24, 1909; newspaper article, first published in *Il Piccolo della Sera,* Trieste; translated and published as "Oscar Wilde: The Poet of Salomé' " in *The Critical Writings of James Joyce* and in *James Joyce: Occasional, Critical, and Political Writing*)

"La Battaglia fra Bernard Shaw e la Censura. 'Blanco Posnet Smascherato' " (September 5, 1909; newspaper article, first published in *Il Piccolo della Sera,* Trieste; translated and published as "Bernard Shaw's Battle with the Censor: *The Shewing-Up of Blanco Posnet*" in *The Critical Writings of James Joyce* and in *James Joyce: Occasional, Critical, and Political Writing*)

"Bid Adieu to Girlish Days" (November 1909; poem [*Chamber Music* XI], subsequently published in *The Dublin Book of Irish Verse, 1728–1909,* Dublin)

"Strings in the Earth and Air" (November 1909; poem [*Chamber Music* I], published in *The Dublin Book of Irish Verse*, 1728–1909, Dublin)

"What Counsel Has the Hooded Moon" (November 1909; poem [*Chamber Music* XII], published in *The Dublin Book of Irish Verse, 1728–1909,* Dublin)

"Song" (September 17, 1910; poem [*Chamber Music* I], published in the *Irish Homestead,* Dublin)

"La Cometa dell' 'Home Rule' " (December 22, 1910; newspaper article, first published in *Il Piccolo della Sera,* Trieste; translated and published as "The Home Rule Comet" in *The Critical Writings of James Joyce* and in *James Joyce: Occasional, Critical, and Political Writing*)

"Author and Publisher in Ireland" (August 26, 1911; letter, published in the *Northern Whig,* Belfast; controversial passages concerning *Dubliners* not included; became part of "A Curious History," 1914)

"Dubliners, To The Editor of *Sinn Féin*" (September 2, 1911; letter, published in *Sinn Féin,* Dublin; controversial passages concerning *Dubliners* included; became part of "A Curious History," 1914)

"Daniel Defoe" (March 1912; lecture in Italian delivered at the Università Popolare Triestina, Trieste; published posthumously in *Buffalo Studies,* vol. 1 [Winter 1964], Buffalo, and in *James Joyce: Occasional, Critical, and Political Writing*)

"William Blake" (March 1912; lecture in Italian delivered at the Università Popolare Triestina, Trieste; translated and published posthumously in *The Critical Writings of James Joyce* and in *James Joyce: Occasional, Critical, and Political Writing*)

"Verismo ed idealismo nella letteratura inglese (Daniele De Foe—William Blake)" (March 1912; lecture; see "Daniel Defoe" and "William Blake," above)

"L'Influenza Letteraria Universale del Rinascimento" (April 1912; essay, translated as "The Universal Literary Influence of the Renaissance" and published in *James Joyce in Padua;* see below)

"The Centenary of Charles Dickens" (April 1912; essay, published in *James Joyce in Padua;* see below)

"L'Ombra di Parnell" (May 16, 1912; newspaper article, first published in *Il Piccolo della Sera,* Trieste; translated and published as "The Shade of Parnell" in *The Critical Writings of James Joyce* and in *James Joyce: Occasional, Critical, and Political Writing*)

"La Città delle Tribù: Ricordi Italiani in un Porto Irlandese" (August 11, 1912; newspaper article, first published in *Il Piccolo della Sera,* Trieste; translated and published as "The City of the Tribes: Italian Echoes in an Irish Port" in *The Critical Writings of James Joyce* and in *James Joyce: Occasional, Critical, and Political Writing*)

"Il Miraggio del Pescatore di Aran. La Valvola dell'Inghilterra in Caso di Guerra" (September 5, 1912; newspaper article, first published in *Il Piccolo della Sera,* Trieste; translated and published as "The Mirage of the Fisherman of Aran. England's Safety Valve in Case of War" in *The Critical Writings of James Joyce* and in *James Joyce: Occasional, Critical, and Political Writing*)

"Politics and Cattle Disease" (September 10, 1912; subeditorial, first published in the *Freeman's Journal,* Dublin; reprinted in *The Critical Writings of James Joyce* and in *James Joyce: Occasional, Critical, and Political Writing*)

"Gas from a Burner" (c. September 1912; broadside poem, privately printed in Trieste; reprinted in *The Critical Writings of James Joyce,* in *James Joyce: Poems and Shorter Writings,* and in *Joycechoyce: The Poems in Verse and Prose of James Joyce*)

"At That Hour" (1913; poem [*Chamber Music* III]; published in *The Wild Harp. A Selection from Irish Poetry,* London, 1913)

"I Hear an Army" (1913; poem [*Chamber Music* XXXVI]; published in *The Wild Harp. A Selection from Irish Poetry,* London; reprinted in February 1914 in *Glebe,* New York, issue devoted to *Des Imagistes: An Anthology*)

"Strings in the Earth and Air" (1913; poem [*Chamber Music* I]; published in *The Wild Harp. A Selection from Irish Poetry,* London)

"Watching the Needleboats at San Sabba" (September 20, 1913; poem, first published in *Saturday Review,* London; reprinted in *Pomes Penyeach,* 1927)

"A Curious History" (January 15, 1914; letters with an introduction by Ezra Pound, published in the *Egoist,* London; reprinted as a broadside in May 1917 by B. W. Huebsch, New York, and in the *Evening Mail,* New York, on July 28, 1917; elsewhere since)

*Giacomo Joyce* (c. 1914; notebook begun perhaps in 1911, published in 1968 by The Viking Press, New York, with an introduction and notes by Richard Ellmann; also published in *James Joyce: Poems and Shorter Writings*)

*A Portrait of the Artist as a Young Man* (February 2, 1914, through September 1, 1915 [25 installments]; novel, first published serially in the *Egoist,* London; republished as a book, the first edition on December 29, 1916, by B. W. Huebsch, New York; first English edition, published on February 12,

1917 by The Egoist Ltd, London; elsewhere since; see below)

*Dubliners* (June 15, 1914; collection of 15 short stories, first published by Grant Richards Ltd, London; first American edition published by B. W. Huebsch in 1916; ["The Sisters," "Eveline" and "After the Race" were published earlier in 1904]; elsewhere since and individual stories anthologized)

"Dooleysprudence" (1916; poem, published in *The Critical Writings of James Joyce* and in *James Joyce: Poems and Shorter Writings*)

*A Portrait of the Artist as a Young Man* (December 29, 1916; see above)

"A Flower Given to My Daughter" (May 1917; poem, first published in *Poetry*, Chicago; reprinted in *Pomes Penyeach*, 1927, in *James Joyce: Poems and Shorter Writings* and in *Joycechoyce: The Poems in Verse and Prose of James Joyce*)

"Flood" (May 1917; poem, first published in *Poetry*, Chicago; reprinted in *Pomes Penyeach*, 1927, in *James Joyce: Poems and Shorter Writings* and in *Joycechoyce: The Poems in Verse and Prose of James Joyce*)

"Nightpiece" (May 1917; poem, first published in *Poetry*, Chicago; reprinted in *Pomes Penyeach*, 1927, in *James Joyce: Poems and Shorter Writings* and in *Joycechoyce: The Poems in Verse and Prose of James Joyce*)

"Simples" (May 1917; poem, first published in *Poetry*, Chicago; reprinted in *Pomes Penyeach*, 1927, in *James Joyce: Poems and Shorter Writings* and in *Joycechoyce: The Poems in Verse and Prose of James Joyce*)

"Tutto è Sciolto" (May 1917; poem, first published in *Poetry*, Chicago; revised and reprinted in *Pomes Penyeach*, 1927, in *James Joyce: Poems and Shorter Writings* and in *Joycechoyce: The Poems in Verse and Prose of James Joyce*)

"Alone" (November 1917; poem, first published in *Poetry*, Chicago; reprinted in *Pomes Penyeach*, 1927, in *James Joyce: Poems and Shorter Writings* and in *Joycechoyce: The Poems in Verse and Prose of James Joyce*)

"On the Beach at Fontana" (November 1917; poem, first published in *Poetry*, Chicago; reprinted in *Pomes Penyeach*, 1927, in *James Joyce: Poems and Shorter Writings* and in *Joycechoyce: The Poems in Verse and Prose of James Joyce*)

"She Weeps over Rahoon" (November 1917; poem, first published in *Poetry*, Chicago; reprinted, slightly revised, in *Pomes Penyeach*, 1927, in *James Joyce: Poems and Shorter Writings* and in *Joycechoyce: The Poems in Verse and Prose of James Joyce*)

*Ulysses* (March 1918 through December 1920; fragments of the novel [13 episodes and part of the 14th episode of 18 in toto] first published serially in 23 installments in the *Little Review*, New York, before the Society for the Suppression of Vice initiated action to cease publication; published as a book in 1922—see below)

IV.11 (incorrectly numbered V.11) (March 1918) 3–22 (*cf. U* chp. 1, Telemachus)
IV.12 (incorrectly numbered V.12) (April 1918) 32–45 (*cf. U* chp. 2, Nestor)
V.1 (May 1918) 31–45 (*cf. U* chp. 3, Proteus)
V.2 (incorrectly numbered IV.2) (June 1918) 39–52 (*cf. U* chp. 4, Calypso)
V.3 (July 1918) 37–49 (*cf. U* chp. 5, Lotus-Eaters)
V.5 (September 1918) 15–37 (*cf. U* chp. 6, Hades)
V.6 (October 1918) 26–51 (*cf. U* chp. 7, Aeolus)
V.9 (January 1919) 27–50 (*cf. U* chp. 8, Lestrygonians)
V.10–11 (February–March 1919) 58–62 (conclusion of *U* 8)
V.12 (incorrectly numbered V.11) (April 1919) 30–43 (*cf. U* chp. 9, Scylla and Charybdis)
VI.1 (May 1919) 17–35 (conclusion of *U* 9)
VI.2 (June 1919) 34–45 (*cf. U* chp. 10, Wandering Rocks)
VI.3 (July 1919) 28–47 (conclusion of *U* 10)
VI.4 (August 1919) 41–64 (*cf. U* chp. 11, Sirens)
VI.5 (September 1919) 46–55 (conclusion of *U* 11)
VI.7 (November 1919) 38–54 (*cf. U* chp. 12, Cyclops)
VI.8 (December 1919) 50–60 (continuation of *U* 12)
VI.9 (January 1920) 53–61 (continuation of *U* 12)
VI.10 (March 1920) 54–60 (conclusion of *U* 12)
VI.11 (April 1920) 43–50 (*cf. U* chp. 13, Nausikaa)
VII.1 (May–June 1920) 61–72 (continuation of *U* 13)
VII.2 (July–August 1920) 42–58 (conclusion of *U* 13)
VII.3 (September–December 1920) 81–92 (*cf.* beginning of *U* chp. 14, Oxen of the Sun)

*Exiles, A Play in Three Acts* (May 25, 1918; play, first published by Grant Richards, Ltd, London, and by B. W. Huebsch, New York; reprinted in *The Portable James Joyce*, edited by Harry Levin [New

York: The Viking Press, 1947], and separately, containing Joyce's notes and an introduction by Padraic Colum, *The Viking Press,* New York, 1951)

*Ulysses* (January–February, March–April, July, September, December 1919; fragments of the novel [a few episodes] serialized in the *Egoist,* London; see below)

VI.1 (January–February 1919) 11–14 (*cf. U* chp. 2, Nestor)
VI.2 (March–April 1919) 26–30 (*cf. U* chp.3, Proteus)
VI.3 (July 1919) 42–46 (*cf. U* chp. 6, Hades)
VI.4 (September 1919) 56–60 (conclusion of *U* 6)
VI.5 (December 1919) 74–78 (*cf.* beginning of *U* chp. 10, Wandering Rocks)

"Bahnhofstrasse" (August 15, 1919; poem, first published in *Anglo-French Review,* London; reprinted in *Pomes Penyeach,* 1927, in *James Joyce: Poems and Shorter Writings,* and in *Joycechoyce: The Poems in Verse and Prose of James Joyce*)

"A Memory of the Players in a Mirror at Midnight" (April 15, 1920; poem, first published in *Poesia,* Milan; also published in *Dial,* New York, July 1920; reprinted in *Pomes Penyeach,* 1927, in *James Joyce: Poems and Shorter Writings,* and in *Joycechoyce: The Poems in Verse and Prose of James Joyce*)

*Ulysses* (February 2, 1922; novel, first published by Shakespeare and Company, Paris; selected other editions: first British edition, by the Egoist Press, London, printed in France, October 12, 1922; reset second edition with Joyce's corrections published by Shakespeare and Company, Paris, May 1926; first American edition, unauthorized and pirated, 1929; published by The Odyssey Press, Hamburg, Paris, Bologna, December 1, 1932; first authorized American edition published by Random House, New York, on January 25, 1934; published by The Limited Editions Club, New York, 1935; first British edition printed in Britain, The Bodley Head, London, 1936; corrected reprint of the Random House 1934 edition published by Modern Library, New York, 1940; a reset of the 1934 Random House edition published by Random House, New York, 1961; critical-synoptic three-volume edition, prepared by Hans Walter Gabler, published by Garland Publishing, Inc., New York and London, 1984, and in one volume without the critical apparatus by Random House [and in paperback by Vintage], New York, 1986; facsimile of the original 1922 edition by Oxford University Press, 1993; a completely revised reader's edition edited by Danis Rose and published by Picador, London, 1997; facsimile of the first Shakespeare and Company 1922 edition published by The First Edition Library, Shelton, Conn., n.d.; facsimile of the first Shakespeare and Company 1922 edition published by Orchises, Washington, D.C., 1998; facsimile of the 1926 Shakespeare and Company reset edition with a preface by Stephen James Joyce, introduction by Jacques Aubert, and etchings by Mimmo Paladino, published by The Folio Society, London, 1998; and a reproduction of the 1922 Shakespeare and Company edition published by Dover, Mineola, N.Y., 2002)

"Poems" (Fall 1923; poems, republication of *Chamber Music* XII, XV, XXVI, XXIX, XXXVI in *Querschnitt,* Frankfurt)

"From Work in Progress" (April 1924; fragment of *Finnegans Wake* [*FW* 383–399], first published in *transatlantic review,* Paris)

"Letter on Pound" (Spring 1925; letter of tribute to Ezra Pound, published in *This Quarter,* Paris; reprinted in *The Critical Writings of James Joyce*)

"Fragment of an Unpublished Work" (July 1925; fragment of *Finnegans Wake* [*FW* 104–125], first published in the *Criterion,* London)

"From Work in Progress" (1925; fragment of *Finnegans Wake* [*FW* 30–34], first published in *Contact Collection of Contemporary Writers,* Paris)

"From Work in Progress" (October 1925; fragment of *Finnegans Wake* [*FW* 196–216], first published in *Navire d'Argent,* Paris)

"Extract from Work in Progress" (Autumn–Winter 1925–26; fragment of *Finnegans Wake* [*FW* 169–195], first published in *This Quarter,* Milan)

"Work in Progress" (September, December 1925, March, June, September 1926, five reprinted fragments of *Finnegans Wake* [*FW* 104–125, 30–34, 196–216, 169–195, 383–399]; reprinted by Samuel Roth from the *Criterion* [July 1925], *Contact Collection of Contemporary Writers* [1925], *Navire d'Argent* [October 1925], *This Quarter* [Autumn–Winter 1925–26], and *transatlantic review* [April 1924] in *Two Worlds,* New York) (see *Letters* III.139)

*Ulysses* (July 1926 through October 1927; 14 episodes of the novel in 12 installments; unauthorized, pirated publication in *Two Worlds Monthly,* New York, edited by Samuel Roth) (see *Letters* III.151–153)

I.1 (July 1926) 93–128 (*cf. U* chps. 1–3, Telemachus, Nestor, Proteus)

I.2 (August 1926) 205–252 (*cf. U* chps. 4–6, Calypso, Lotus-Eaters, Hades)
I.3 (September 1926) 353–376 (*cf. U* chp. 7, Aeolus)
I.4 (October 1926) 473–498 (*cf. U* chp. 8, Lestrygonians)
II.1 (December 1926) 93–118 (*cf. U* chp. 9, Scylla and Charybdis)
II.2 (January 1927) 213–239 (*cf. U* chp. 10, Wandering Rocks)
II.3 (February 1927) 311–357 (*cf. U* chp. 11, The Sirens, and beginning of chp. 12, Cyclops)
II.4 (March 1927) 425–476 (conclusion of *U* 12, and whole of *U* chp. 13, Nausikaa)
III.1 (April 1927) 101–116 (*cf. U* chp. 14, Oxen of the Sun)
III.2 (May–June 1927) 169–278 (continuation of *U* chp. 14)
III.3 (September 1927) 195–204 (continuation of *U* chp. 14)
III.4 (October 1927) 233–236 (conclusion of *U* chp. 14)

"Work in Progress" (April 1927 through April–May 1938; fragments of *Finnegans Wake* [*FW* 3–29, *FW* 30–47, *FW* 48–74, *FW* 75–103, *FW* 104–125, *FW* 126–168, *FW* 169–195, *FW* 196–216, *FW* 282–304, *FW* 403–428, *FW* 429–473, *FW* 474–554, *FW* 555–590, *FW* 219–259, *FW* 260–275 and 304–308, *FW* 309–331, *FW* 338–355] published [in 17 installments] in *transition*, Paris)

*Pomes Penyeach* (5 July 1927; collection of 13 poems [11 of which were published previously; see above]; collection first published by Shakespeare and Company, Paris; first American edition printed for copyright purposes by Princeton University Press for Sylvia Beach, May 2, 1931; privately printed in Cleveland, c. September 1931; first English edition, printed in France and published by The Obelisk Press, Paris, and Desmond Harmsworth, London, in October 1932, with letters designed and illuminated by Lucia Joyce; first English edition, printed in England, published by Faber and Faber, London, March 16, 1933)

*Work in Progress Volume I* (1928); extensive fragment of *Finnegans Wake* [*FW* 3–216], published by Donal Friede, New York)

"Letter on Hardy" (January–February 1928; note on Thomas Hardy published in *Revue Nouvelle*, Paris; reprinted in *The Critical Writings of James Joyce*)

*Anna Livia Plurabelle* (October 20, 1928; fragment of *Finnegans Wake* [*FW* 196–216], first edition published by Crosby Gaige, New York, preface by Padraic Colum; first English edition, published by Faber and Faber, London, 1930)

"Omaggio a Svevo" (see "Letter on Svevo," below)

"Letter on Svevo" (March–April 1929; note on Italo Svevo [Ettore Schmitz], published in *Solaria*, Florence; reprinted in *The Critical Writings of James Joyce*)

*Ulysse* (1929; French translation of *Ulysses* by Auguste Moral [assisted by Stuart Gilbert], published by Adrienne Monnier, Paris)

*Tales Told of Shem and Shaun* (August 9, 1929; three fragments from *Finnegans Wake* ["The Mookse and the Gripes," *FW* 152–159; "The Muddest Thick That Was Ever Heard Dump," *FW* 282–304; "The Ondt and the Gracehoper" *FW* 414–419]; first edition, published by The Black Sun Press, Paris; first English edition, published by Faber and Faber, London)

"A Muster from Work in Progress" (1929; seven excerpts from *Finnegans Wake* previously published in *transition* ["No Concern of the Guinnesses," *FW* 30–34; "A Mole," *FW* 76–78; "Peaches," *FW* 65; "Be Sage and Choose," *FW* 454–455; "On the Death of Mrs. Sanders (Pippip)," *FW* 413; "The River and the Mountain Converse," *FW* 23; "Vikingfather Sleeps," *FW* 74], published by Walter V. McKee, New York)

*James Clarence Mangan* (March 7, 1930; published by Ulysses Bookshop, London; a reprint of an address first published on May 6, 1902 in St Stephen's, Dublin; see above)

*Ibsen's New Drama* (March 11, 1930; published by Ulysses Bookshop, London; a reprint of an essay first published on April 1, 1900, in the *Fortnightly Review;* see above)

*Haveth Childers Everywhere* (June 1930; fragment from *Finnegans Wake* [*FW* 532–554], published by Henry Babou and Jack Kahane, Paris, and The Fountain Press, New York)

"Buy a Book in Brown Paper" (1930; poem on dust jacket for the *Anna Livia Plurabelle* fragment of *Finnegans Wake,* published by Faber and Faber, London; reprinted in Richard Ellmann's *James Joyce,* new and revised edition, Oxford University Press, New York, 1982)

"From Work in Progress" (Spring 1931; fragment from *Finnegans Wake* [*FW* 3–29], published in *New Experiment,* Cambridge, England)

"Anna Livia Plurabelle" (May 1, 1931; French translation of a fragment of *Finnegans Wake* [*FW* 196–201, 215–216], published in *La Nouvelle Revue Française,* Paris; Joyce collaborated)

"Humptydump Dublin Squeaks through His Norse" (1931; poem on dust jacket for *Haveth Childers Everywhere* fragment of *Finnegans Wake,* published by Faber and Faber, London; reprinted in Richard Ellmann's *James Joyce,* Oxford University Press, New York)

"Anna Livia Plurabelle" (October 1931; fragment of *Finnegans Wake* [*FW* 213–216], published in *Psyche,* London; Joyce collaborated)

"From a Banned Writer to a Banned Singer" (February 27, 1932; a tribute to the Irish tenor John Sullivan; published in the *New Statesman and Nation,* London; reprinted in *Turnstile One,* London, 1948, and again in *The Critical Writings of James Joyce* and in *James Joyce: Occasional, Critical, and Political Writing*)

"Ad-Writer" (May 22, 1932; humorous commentary on Stanislaus Joyce's preface to the English translation of Italo Svevo's *Senilità;* first published in *A James Joyce Yearbook,* edited by Maria Jolas, Transition Press, Paris, 1949; reprinted in *The Critical Writings of James Joyce*)

"Ecce Puer" (November 30, 1932; poem, first published in the *New Republic,* New York; reprinted in *Collected Poems, James Joyce: Poems and Shorter Writings,* and *Joycechoyce: The Poems in Verse and Prose of James Joyce*)

"From Work in Progress" (February 15, 1934; fragment from *Finnegans Wake* [*FW* 7–10], published in *Contempo,* Chapel Hill, N.C.)

"The Mime of Mick Nick and the Maggies" (February 23, 1934; fragment from *Finnegans Wake* [*FW* 258–259], published in *Les Amis de 1914, Bulletin Hebdomadaire de l'Académie de la Coupole,* Paris)

"Epilogue to Ibsen's Ghosts" (April 1934; poem written in Paris, published in Herbert Gorman's *James Joyce,* Farrar & Rinehart, Inc., New York, 1939; reprinted in *The Critical Writings of James Joyce*)

*The Mime of Mick Nick and the Maggies* (June 1934; fragment from *Finnegans Wake* [*FW* 219–259], published by The Servire Press, The Hague)

*The Cat and the Devil* (August 1936; children's story Joyce wrote in a letter to his grandson Stephen Joyce, dated August 10, 1936, first published without a title in 1957, in *Letters of James Joyce,* vol. I, 386–387; published with title, illustrated by Richard Erdoes, by Dodd, Mead & Company, Inc., New York, in 1964; published with illustrations by Roger Blachon, by Breakwater, St. John's, Newfoundland in 1990.)

*Collected Poems* (December 1936; poems [*Chamber Music, Pomes Penyeach,* and *Ecce Puer*]; published by The Black Sun Press, New York, and in 1937 by The Viking Press, New York)

"Communication de M. James Joyce sur le Droit Moral des . . . Écrivains" (June 1937; address delivered to the International P.E.N. Congress held in Paris; published in *The Critical Writings of James Joyce* and in *Joycechoyce: The Poems in Verse and Prose of James Joyce*)

*Storiella as She Is Syung* (October 1937; fragment from *Finnegans Wake* [*FW* 260–275, 304–308], published by Corvinus Press, London)

"A Phoenix Park Nocturne" (March–June 1938; fragment from *Finnegans Wake* [*FW* 244–246], published in *Verve,* Paris)

*Finnegans Wake* (May 4, 1939; fictional prose narrative, published by Faber and Faber, London, and The Viking Press, New York)

*Stephen Hero* (July 1944; a fragment of the original version of the novel that became *A Portrait of the Artist as a Young Man,* edited by Theodore Spencer and published by Jonathan Cape, London, and New Directions, New York)

*The Portable James Joyce* (January 1947 [and since]; selections, with an introduction and notes by Harry Levin, published by The Viking Press, New York)

*The Critical Writings of James Joyce* (various; edited by Ellsworth Mason and Richard Ellmann, published in 1959 by The Viking Press, New York, and Faber and Faber, London)

*James Joyce in Padua* (1977; two essays: "L'Influenza Letteraria Universale del Rinascimento" ["The Universal Literary Influence of the Renaissance" and "The Centenary of Charles Dickens"]; edited and translated by Louis Berrone, published by Random House, New York; see above)

*James Joyce: Poems and Shorter Writings* including *Epiphanies, Giacomo Joyce* and "A Portrait of the Artist" (various; edited by Richard Ellmann, A. Walton Litz and John Whittier-Ferguson, published in 1991 by Faber and Faber, London)

*Joycechoyce: The Poems in Verse and Prose of James Joyce* (various; edited by A. Norman Jeffares and Brendan Kennelly, published in 1992 by Kyle Cathie Limited, London)

*James Joyce: Occasional, Critical, and Political Writing* (various; edited by Kevin Barry and translations by

Conor Dean, published in 2000 by Oxford University Press, Oxford)

### *Works Translated by Joyce*

"O fons Bandusiae," Horace (c. 1896; translation of Ode III.13 into English; published in Gorman's *James Joyce*, pp. 45–46; in Richard Ellmann's *James Joyce*, pp. 50–51; and in *James Joyce: Poems and Shorter Writings*, edited by Richard Ellmann, A. Walton Litz, and John Whittier-Ferguson, p. 71)

"Les Sanglots longs," Paul Verlaine (c. 1900; verse, into English; published in Herbert Gorman's *James Joyce*, p. 59; in Richard Ellmann's *James Joyce*, p. 76; and in *James Joyce: Poems and Shorter Writings*, edited by Richard Ellmann, A. Walton Litz, and John Whittier-Ferguson, p. 74)

*Vor Sonnenaufgang*, Gerhart Hauptmann (summer 1901; play, into English [with the title: *Before Sunrise*]; published in *Joyce and Hauptmann* by Jill Perkins [Canoga Park, Calif.: PSP Graphics, 1978])

*Michael Kramer*, Gerhart Hauptmann (summer 1901; play, into English; nonextant)

*Riders to the Sea*, J. M. Synge (1908; play, into Italian, with Nicolò Vidacovich)

*The Countess Cathleen*, William Butler Yeats (1913; nonextant translation of play into Italian)

"Nun hab'ich gar die Rose aufgefressen," Gottfried Keller (1915; poem translated into English; whereabouts unknown)

"Un Romanzo di Gesuiti," Diego Angeli (1917; review of *A Portrait of the Artist as a Young Man* published in the Florentine journal *Il Marzocco* 22 [August 12, 1917], 2–3; Joyce's translation, "Extract from *Il Marzocco*," published in the *Egoist* 2 [February 1918], 30; Joyce translated the piece at the request of Harriet Shaw Weaver; also published in *James Joyce: The Critical Heritage*, vol. 1, edited by Robert H. Deming [New York: Barnes & Noble, 1970], "An Italian Comment of *A Portrait*," pp. 114–116)

"Des Weibes Klage," by Felix Béran (1918; poem, into English, as "Lament for the Yeoman"; published with the German text in Richard Ellmann's *James Joyce*, pp. 431–432; and without the German in *James Joyce: Poems and Short Writings*, edited by Richard Ellmann, A. Walton Litz, and John Whittier-Ferguson, p.116)

"Anna Livia Plurabelle" (May 1, 1931; Joyce collaborated in French translation of this fragment of *Finnegans Wake* [*FW* 196–201, 215–216], published in *La Nouvelle Revue Française*, Paris; also translated into Italian, with Nino Frank, and published in *Prospettive*, Rome [February and December 1940])

"Stephen's Green" by James Stephens (1933; poem translated into Italian, as "Il Vento" and published in *Sul Mare*, Trieste [May–June 1933]; also translated into French as "Les Verts de Jacques")

### *Letters*

*Letters of James Joyce*, vol. I (1957; edited by Stuart Gilbert, published by Faber and Faber, London, and The Viking Press, New York)

*Letters of James Joyce*, vols. II and III (1966; edited by Richard Ellmann, published by Faber and Faber, London, and The Viking Press, New York)

*Selected Letters of James Joyce* (1975; edited by Richard Ellmann, published by The Viking Press, New York)

## Musical, Theatrical, and Cinematic Adaptations of Joyce's Works Other Than *Chamber Music* and *Exiles*

*(A list of names of composers who musically arranged* Chamber Music *can be found below. For the television presentation of* Exiles, *see the entry on* Exiles. Also see the Current JJ Checklist regularly published in the *James Joyce Quarterly*.)

### Dubliners

Murray Boren, music, and Glen Nelson, libretto, *The Dead* (one-act opera), first staged New York, 1993

Dennis Courtney and Joseph Bierman, directors, *Araby* (film; Films for the Humanities and Sciences, Princeton, N.J.), 1999

John Huston, director, *The Dead* (film), 1987

Richard Nelson, lyrics, Shaun Davey, lyrics and music, *The Dead* (musical, Playwrights Horizons), 1999

Radio Telefis Éireann Production, *A Painful Case* (film; Films for the Humanities and Sciences, Princeton, N.J.)

### A Portrait of the Artist as a Young Man

*Luciano Berio (excerpt in)* Epifanie, for female voice and orchestra, 1959–61; revised in 1965

Luigi Dallapiccola, (excerpt in) *Requiescant*, for chorus and orchestra, 1957–58

Mátyás Seiber, *Three Fragments*, for speaker, chorus, ensemble, 1957

Joseph Strick, director, *A Portrait of the Artist as a Young Man* (film), 1977

### Ulysses

Marjorie Barkentin, *Ulysses in Nighttown* (play), first staged London, 1959

Luciano Berio, (excerpt in) *Thema (Omaggio a Joyce)*, two-track tape, 1958

George Antheil, (excerpt in) *Extract: Mr. Bloom and the Cyclops,* an unfinished opera, 1925–26

Enrico Frattaroli, *fluidofiumericorsi da Ulisse e ALP di James Joyce, 1998*

Mátyás Seiber, for tenor, chorus, and orchestra, 1946–47

Joseph Strick, director, *Ulysses* (film), 1967

Sean Walsh, director, *Bloom* (film), *2004*

### Pomes Penyeach

Herbert Hughes, ed., *The Joyce Book,* musical settings of *Pomes Penyeach,* published by The Sylvan Press in 1933

### Finnegans Wake

Stephen J. Albert, *To Wake the Dead,* song cycle, 1977–78; *Tree Stone,* song cycle, 1983–84; and *Riverrun,* a four-movement orchestral work, 1983–85

Mary Ellen Bute, *Passages from Finnegans Wake,* 1965; a film based on Mary Manning's play (see below)

John Cage, (excerpt in) *The Wonderful Widow of Eighteen Springs,* for mezzo-soprano, 1942

Jean Erdman, *The Coach With the Six Insides,* allegorical play (portraying the life cycle of Anna Livia Plurabelle), using elements from all performing arts, music by Teiji Ito, 1962

Enrico Frattaroli, *fluidofiumericorsi da Ulisse e ALP di James Joyce, 1998*

Ciceil L. Gross, *Nine Characters in Search of a Wake: A Panel Play Introducing the Themes in Finnegans Wake,* premier performance on February 2, 1997, at The Gotham Book Mart, New York City, in celebration of the 50th anniversary of The James Joyce Society

Michael Kvium and Christian Lemmerz, directors, *The Wake* (film), 2000

Mary Manning, *Passages from Finnegans Wake by James Joyce: A Free Adaptation for the Theatre,* 1955; made into a film by Mary Ellen Bute (see above)

Heather Ryan Kelley, artist, *This Way to the Museyroom: Studies after Finnegans Wake*

Harry Partch, (excerpt in) *Isobel and Annah the Allmaziful,* for two flutes and kithara, 1944

The Pilobolus Dance Theater, *Rejoyce: A Pilobolus Finnegans Wake,* 1993

Margaret Rogers, *A Babble of Earwigs, or Sinnegan with Finnegan,* a chorale, 1987

Humphrey Searle, (excerpts in) *The Riverrun,* for speakers and orchestra, 1951

Barbara Vann, director, *Finnegans Wake: Adapted from the Novel by James Joyce* (play), 2004

### *Other*

Sharon Fogarty, author and director, *Cara Lucia* (play), 2003

Patrick Horgan, reader, *Finnegans Wake* (sound recording produced by AFB), 1985

Rosemary House, director, *Bloomsday Cabaret* (film), 2004

Pat Murphy, director, *Nora* (film), 1999

Michael Pearce, director, *James Joyce's Women* (film), 1985

## Chamber Music Composers

*In* James Joyce's Chamber Music: The Lost Song Settings *(Bloomingdale: Indiana UP, 1993 [pp. 113–114]), Myra T. Russel has identified the following composers who have set to music one or more of the poems in* Chamber Music *(since the publication of Russel's book, the American composer Alfred Heller has set the entire suite to music):*

Adler, Samuel
Albert, Stephen
Avshalonov, Jacob
Barab, Seymour
Barber, Samuel
Barett, Syd
Bate, Stanley
Bauer, Marion
Becker, John
Beckett, Walter
Berio, Luciano
Betts, Lorne
Beveridge, Thomas
Billingsley, William
Bonner, Eugene
Boydell, Brian
Bridge, Frank
Brown, James
Burgess, Anthony
Caffrey, John G.
Calabro, Louis
Carr, Peter
Citkowitz, Israel
Clarke, Laurence
Cooper, [?]
Corbett, Sumsion
Coulthard, Jean
Creighton, Allen
Dallapiccola, Luigi
Davis, John Jeffrey
Del Tredici, David
Diamond, David
Dickinson, Peter
Dorati, Antal
Eads, Rob
Eaton, John
Ferris, Joann
Fetler, Paul
Field, Robin
Fine, Vivian
Finney, Ross Lee
Fox, Charlotte Milligan
Fox, J. Bertram
Freed, Arnold
Freeman, John
Genzmar, Harold
Ginsburg, Gerald
Goossens, Eugene
Grayson, Richard
Graziano, John

Greenburg, David
Griffis, Elliot
Harrison, Dorothy
Harrison, Sidney
Hart, Fritz
Hartzell, Eugene
Head, Michael
Healey, Derek
Holloway, Stanley
Hughes, Herbert
Jarrett, Jack
Kagan, Sergius
Kalmus, E.
Karlins, M. William
Karpienia, Joe
Karpman, Laura
Kauder, Hugo
Kelly, Denise
Keulen, Gerrt van
Kittleson, Carl
Klotzman, Dorothy
Koemmenich, Louis
Kunz, Alfred
La Fave, Kenneth
Le Fleming, Christopher
Linn, Robert
Lombardo, Robert
Luening, Otto
Lydiate, Frederick
Machover, Tod
McLennan, John Stewart
Mc Rae, Shirley
Mann, Adolph
Manneke, Daan
Martino, Donald
Meijering, Cord
Mengelberg, Rudolf
Mihaly, Andras
Moeran, E. J.
Nabokov, Nicholas
Naylor, Bernard
Nelson, Richard
Orr, C. W.
Palmer, G. Molyneux
Pattison, Lee
Pawle, Ivan
Pelligrini, Ernesto
Pendleton, Edmund
(melody by Joyce)
Perera, Ronald
Persichetti, Vincent
Pierce, Alexandra
Piket, Frederick
Pisk, Paul
Pitot, Genevieve
Planchart, Alejandro
Pope, Conrad
Powell, Mel
Ramsey, Gordon
Read, Gardner
Reutter, Hermann
Reynolds, W. B.
Richards, Howard
Ritchie, Tom
Roff, Joseph
Rogers, John E.
Rogers, Wayland
Rubinstein, David
Serly, Tibor
Smith, Russell
Smith, William
Spector, Irwin
Spencer, Williametta
Stainbrook, Lisa
Steele, Jan
Steiner, Gitta
Stephenson, Dorothy
Sterne, Colin
Stewart, Robert
Stocker, Clara
Strickland, William
Suits, Paul
Susa, Conrad
Sweeney, Eric
Szymanowski, Karol
Thomson, Waddy
Treacher, Graham
Victory, Gerard
Wagemans, Peter-Jan
Ward, Robert
Weigl, Vally
White, John
Wilcox, A. Gordon

# ULYSSES

## *Ulysses* Schema

"The Plan of Ulysses," from Hugh Kenner, *Dublin's Joyce,* Reproduced by Permission of Indiana University Press and Aitken, Stone & Wylie. Copyright © 1956 by Hugh Kenner.

| Title | Scene | Hour | Organ | Art | Colour | Symbol | Technic | Correspondences |
|---|---|---|---|---|---|---|---|---|
| 1. Telemachus | The Tower | 8 a.m. | | Theology | White, gold | Heir | Narrative (young) | *Stephen:* Telemachus, Hamlet.*Buck Mulligan:* Antinous. *Milkwoman:* Mentor. |
| 2. Nestor | The School | 10 a.m. | | History | Brown | Horse | Catechism (personal) | *Deasy:* Nestor *Sargent:* Pisistratus. *Mrs. O'Shea:* Helen. |
| 3. Proteus | The Strand | 11 a.m. | | Philology | Green | Tide | Monologue (male) | *Proteus:* Primal Matter. *Kevin Egan:* Menelaus. *Cocklepicker:* Megapenthus. |
| 4. Calypso | The House | 8 a.m. | Kidney | Economics | Orange | Nymph | Narrative (mature) | *Calypso:* The Nymph. *Dluglacz:* The Recall. *Zion:* Ithaca. |
| 5. Lotus-eaters | The Bath | 10 a.m. | Genitals | Botany, Chemistry | | Eucharist | Narcissism | *Lotus-eaters:* the Cab-horses. Communicants. Soldiers, Eunuchs, Bather, Watchers of Cricket. |
| 6. Hades | The Grave-yard | 11 a.m. | Heart | Religion | White, black | Caretaker | Incubism | *Dodder, Grand, and Royal Canals, Liffey:* the 4 Rivers. *Cunningham:* Sisyphus. *Father Coffey:* Cerherus. *Caretaker:* Hades. *Daniel O'Connell:* Hercules. *Dignam:* Elpenor. *Parnell:* Agarnemnon. Ajax. |
| 7. Aeolus | The News-paper | 12 noon | Lungs | Rhetoric | Red | Editor | Enthymemic | *Crawford:* Aeolus. *Incest:* Journalism. *Floating Island:* Press. |
| 8. Lestrygonians | The Lunch | 1 p.m. | Esophagus | Architecture | | Constables | Peristaltic | *Antiphates:* Hunger. *The Decoy:* Food. *Lestrygonians:* Teeth. |

*(continues)*

| Title | Scene | Hour | Organ | Art | Colour | Symbol | Technic | Correspondences |
|---|---|---|---|---|---|---|---|---|
| *(continued)* | | | | | | | | |
| 9. Scylla & Charybdis | The Library | 2 p.m. | Brain | Literature | | Stratford, London | Dialectic | *The Rock:* Aristotle, Dogma, Stratford. *The Whirlpool:* Plato, Mysticism, London. *Ulysses:* Socrates, Jesus, Shakespeare. |
| 10. Wandering Rocks | The Streets | 3 p.m. | Blood | Mechanics | | Citizens | Labyrinth | *Bosphorus:* Liffey. *European Bank:* Viceroy. *Asiatic Bank:* Conmee. *Symplegades:* Groups of Citizens. |
| 11. Sirens | The Concert Room | 4 p.m. | Ear | Music | | Barmaids | Fuga per canonem | *Sirens:* Barmaids. *Isle:* Bar. |
| 12. Cyclops | The Tavern | 5 p.m. | Muscle | Politics | | Fenian | Gigantism | *Noman:* I. *Stake:* Cigar. *Challenge:* Apotheosis. |
| 13. Nausikcaa | The Rocks | 8 p.m. | Eye, Nose | Painting | Grey, blue | Virgin | Tumescence, detumescence | *Phaeacia:* Star or the Sea. *Gerty:* Nausicaa. |
| 14. Oxen of the Sun | The Hospital | 10 p.m. | Womb | Medicine | White | Mothers | Embryonic development | *Hospital:* Trinacria. *Nurses:* Lampetie, Phaethusa, *Horn:* Helios. *Oxen:* Fertility. *Crime:* Fraud. |
| 15. Circe | The Brothel | 12 mid-night | Locomotor Apparatus | Magic | | Whore | Hallucination | *Circe:* Bella. |
| 16. Eumaeus | The Shelter | 1 a.m. | Nerves | Navigation | | Sailors | Narrative (old) | *Skin the Goat:* Eumaeus. *Sailor:* Ulysses Pseudangelos. *Corley:* Melanthius. |
| 17. Ithaca | The House | 2 a.m. | Skeleton | Science | | Comets | Catechism (impersonal) | *Eurymachus:* Boylan. *Suitors:* Scruples. *Bow:* Reason. |
| 18. Penelope | The Bed | | Flesh | | | Earth | Monologue (female) | *Penelope:* Earth. *Web:* Movement. |

## The Hon. John M. Woolsey's Decision to Lift the Ban on *Ulysses*

UNITED STATES DISTRICT COURT
SOUTHERN DISTRICT OF NEW YORK
United States of America,
*Libelant*
V. OPINION
One Book called "Ulysses" A. 110-59
Random House, Inc.,
*Claimant*

*On cross motions for a decree in a libel of confiscation, supplemented by a stipulation—hereinafter described—brought by the United States against the book "Ulysses" by James Joyce, under Section 305 of the Tariff Act of 1930, Title 19 United States Code, Section 1305, on the ground that the book is obscene within the meaning of that Section, and, hence, is not importable into the United States, but is subject to seizure, forfeiture and confiscation and destruction.*

United States Attorney—by Samuel C. Coleman, Esq., and Nicholas Atlas, Esq., of counsel—for the United States, in support of motion for a decree of forfeiture, and in opposition to motion for a decree dismissing the libel.

Messrs. Greenbaum, Wolff & Ernst,—by Morris L. Ernst, Esq., and Alexander Lindey, Esq., of counsel—attorneys for claimant Random House, Inc., in support of motion for a decree dismissing the libel, and in opposition to motion for a decree of forfeiture.

WOOLSEY, J.:

The motion for a decree dismissing the libel herein is granted, and, consequently, of course, the Government's motion for a decree of forfeiture and destruction is denied.

Accordingly a decree dismissing the libel without costs may be entered herein.

I. The practice followed in this case is in accordance with the suggestion made by me in the case of *United States v. One Book Entitled "Contraception"*, 51 F. (2d) 525, and is as follows:

After issue was joined by the filing of the claimant's answer to the libel for forfeiture against "Ulysses", a stipulation was made between the United States Attorney's office and the attorneys for the claimant providing:

1. That the book "Ulysses" should be deemed to have been annexed to and to have become part of the libel just as if it had been incorporated in its entirety therein.

2. That the parties waived their right to a trial by jury.

3. That each party agreed to move for decree in its favor.

4. That on such cross motions the Court might decide all the questions of law and fact involved and render a general finding thereon.

5. That on the decision of such motions the decree of the Court might be entered as if it were a decree after trial.

It seems to me that a procedure of this kind is highly appropriate in libels for the confiscation of books such as this. It is an especially advantageous procedure in the instant case because on account of the length of "Ulysses" and the difficulty of reading it, a jury trial would have been an extremely unsatisfactory, if not an almost impossible, method of dealing with it.

II. I have read "Ulysses" once in its entirety and I have read those passages of which the Government particularly complains several times. In fact, for many weeks, my spare time has been devoted to the consideration of the decision which my duty would require me to make in this matter.

"Ulysses" is not an easy book to read or to understand. But there has been much written about it, and in order properly to approach the consideration of it, it is advisable to read a number of other books which have now become its satellites. The study of "Ulysses" is, therefore, a heavy task.

III. The reputation of "Ulysses" in the literary world, however, warranted my taking such time as was necessary to enable me to satisfy myself as to the intent with which the book was written, for, of course, in any case where a book is claimed to be obscene it must first be determined, whether the intent with which it was written was what is called, according to the usual phrase, pornographic,—that is, written for the purpose of exploiting obscenity.

If the conclusion is that the book is pornographic that is the end of the inquiry and forfeiture must follow.

But in "Ulysses", in spite of its unusual frankness, I do not detect anywhere the leer of the sensualist. I hold, therefore, that it is not pornographic.

IV. In writing "Ulysses", Joyce sought to make a serious experiment in a new, if not wholly novel, literary genre. He takes persons of the lower middle class living in Dublin in 1904 and seeks not only to describe what they did on a certain day early in June of that year as they went about the City bent on their usual occupations, but also to tell what many of them thought about the while.

Joyce has attempted—it seems to me, with astonishing success—to show how the screen of consciousness with its ever-shifting kaleidoscopic impressions carries, as it were on a plastic palimpsest, not only what is in the focus of each man's observation of the actual things about him, but also in a penumbral zone residua of past impressions, some recent and some drawn up by association from the domain of the subconscious. He shows how each of these impressions affects the life and behavior of the character which he is describing.

What he seeks to get is not unlike the results of a double or, if that is possible, a multiple exposure on a cinema film which would give a clear foreground with a background visible but somewhat blurred and out of focus in varying degrees.

To convey by words an effect which obviously lends itself more appropriately to a graphic technique, accounts, it seems to me, for much of the obscurity which meets a reader of "Ulysses". And it also explains another aspect of the book, which I have further to consider, namely, Joyce's sincerity and his honest effort to show exactly how the minds of his characters operate.

If Joyce did not attempt to be honest in developing the technique which he has adopted in "Ulysses" the result would be psychologically misleading and thus unfaithful to his chosen technique. Such an attitude would be artistically inexcusable.

It is because Joyce has been loyal to his technique and has not funked its necessary implications, but has honestly attempted to tell fully what his characters think about, that he has been the subject of so many attacks and that his purpose has been so often misunderstood and misrepresented. For his attempt sincerely and honestly to realize his objective has required him incidentally to use certain words which are generally considered dirty words and has led at times to what many think is a too poignant preoccupation with sex in the thoughts of his characters.

The words which are criticized as dirty are old Saxon words known to almost all men and, I venture, to many women, and are such words as would be naturally and habitually used, I believe, by the types of folk whose life, physical and mental, Joyce is seeking to describe. In respect of the recurrent emergence of the theme of sex in the minds of his characters, it must always be remembered that his locale was Celtic and his season Spring.

Whether or not one enjoys such a technique as Joyce uses is a matter of taste on which disagreement or argument is futile, but to subject that technique to the standards of some other technique seems to me to be little short of absurd.

Accordingly, I hold that "Ulysses" is a sincere and honest book and I think that the criticisms of it are entirely disposed of by its rationale.

V. Furthermore, "Ulysses" is an amazing *tour de force* when one considers the success which has been in the main achieved with such a difficult objective as Joyce set for himself. As I have stated, "Ulysses" is not an easy book to read. It is brilliant and dull, intelligible and obscure by turns. In many places it seems to me to be disgusting, but although it contains, as I have mentioned above, many words usually considered dirty, I have not found anything that I consider to be dirt for dirt's sake. Each word of the book contributes like a bit of mosaic to the detail of the picture which Joyce is seeking to construct for his readers.

If one does not wish to associate with such folk as Joyce describes, that is one's own choice. In order to avoid indirect contact with them one may not wish to read "Ulysses"; that is quite understandable. But when such a real artist in words, as Joyce undoubtedly is, seeks to draw a true picture of the lower middle class in a European city, ought it to be impossible for the American public legally to see that picture?

To answer this question it is not sufficient merely to find, as I have found above, that Joyce did not write "Ulysses" with what is commonly called pornographic intent, I must endeavor to apply a more objective standard to his book in order to determine its effect in the result, irrespective of the intent with which it was written.

VI. The statute under which the libel is filed only denounces, in so far as we are here concerned, the importation into the United States from any foreign country of "any obscene book". Section 305 of the Tariff Act of 1930, Title 19 United States Code, Section 1305. It does not marshal against books the spectrum of condemnatory adjectives found, commonly, in laws dealing with matters of this kind. I am, therefore, only required to determine whether "Ulysses" is obscene within the legal definition of that word.

The meaning of the word "obscene" as legally defined by the Courts is: tending to stir the sex impulses or to lead to sexually impure and lustful thoughts. *Dunlop v. United States,* 165, U.S. 486, 501; *United States v. One Book Entitled "Married Love"*, 48 F. (2d) 821, 824; *United States v. One Book Entitled "Contraception"*, 51 F. (2d) 525, 528; and compare *Dysart v. United States,* 272 U.S. 655, 657; *Swearingen v. United States,* 161 U.S. 446, 450; *United States v. Dennett,* 39 F. (2d) 564, 568 (C.C.A. 2); *People v. Wendling,* 258 N.Y. 451, 453.

Whether a particular book would tend to excite such impulses and thoughts must be tested by the Court's opinion as to its effect on a person with average sex instincts—what the French would call *l'homme moyen sensuel*—who plays, in this branch of legal inquiry, the same role of hypothetical reagent as does the "reasonable man" in the law of torts and "the man learned in the art" on questions of invention in patent law.

The risk involved in the use of such a reagent arises from the inherent tendency of the trier of facts, however fair he may intend to be, to make his reagent too much subservient to his own idiosyncrasies. Here, I have attempted to avoid this, if possible, and to make my reagent herein more objective than he might otherwise be, by adopting the following course:

After I had made my decision in regard to the aspect of "Ulysses", now under consideration, I checked my impressions with two friends of mine who in my opinion answered to the above stated requirement for my reagent.

These literary assessors—as I might properly describe them—were called on separately, and neither knew that I was consulting the other. They are men whose opinion on literature and on life I value most highly. They had both read "Ulysses", and, of course, were wholly unconnected with this cause.

Without letting either of my assessors know what my decision was, I gave to each of them the legal definition of obscene and asked each whether in his opinion "Ulysses" was obscene within that definition.

I was interested to find that they both agreed with my opinion: that reading "Ulysses" in its entirety, as a book must be read on such a test as this, did not tend to excite sexual impulses or lustful thoughts but that its net effect on them was only that of a somewhat tragic and very powerful commentary on the inner lives of men and women.

It is only with the normal person that the law is concerned. Such a test as I have described, therefore, is the only proper test of obscenity in the case of a book like "Ulysses" which is a sincere and serious attempt to devise a new literary method for the observation and description of mankind.

I am quite aware that owing to some of its scenes "Ulysses" is a rather strong draught to ask some sensitive, though normal, persons to take. But my considered opinion, after long reflection, is that whilst in many places the effect of "Ulysses" on the reader undoubtedly is somewhat emetic, nowhere does it tend to be an aphrodisiac.

"Ulysses" may, therefore, be admitted into the United States.

JOHN M. WOOLSEY
UNITED STATES DISTRICT JUDGE
December 6, 1933

# FINNEGANS WAKE

### A Working Outline of *Finnegans Wake* from Bernard Benstock, *Joyce-Again's Wake,* 1965 (Used by Permission of the University of Washington Press)

**CHAPTER I** *([Book I, chap. 1,] pp. 3–29)*

3: Statement of themes
4: Battle in Heaven and introduction of Finnegan
5: Finnegan's fall and promise of resurrection
5–6: The City
6–7: The Wake
7–8: Landscape foreshadows H.C.E. and A.L.P.
8–10: Visit to Willingdon Museyroom
10: The Earwicker house
10–12: Biddy the hen finds the letter in the midden heap
12–13: Dublin language
132–152: Pre-history of Ireland—the invaders (including the birth of Shem and Shaun, p. 14)
15–18: Mutt and Jute recount the Battle of Clontarf
18–20: The development of the Alphabet and Numbers
21–23: The Tale of Jarl van Hoother and the Prankquean
23–24: The Fall
25: Finnegan's Wake revisited
25–29: Restless Finnegan is told about the present age
29: H.C.E. introduced

**CHAPTER 2** *([Book I, chap. 2,] pp. 30–47)*

30–32: The genesis and naming of Humphrey Chimpden Earwicker
32–33: Gaiety Theatre production of *A Royal Divorce*
33–35: Rumors about H.C.E.'s indiscretion
35–36: The Encounter with the Cad
36–38: The Cad dines and drinks
38–42: The Cad's story is spread
42–44: The making of the Ballad by Hosty
44–47: The Ballad of Persse O'Reilly

**CHAPTER 3** *([Book I, chap. 3,] pp. 48–74)*

48–50: The balladeer and all involved come to bad ends as Time Passes
50–52: Earwicker asked to tell the old story
52–55: Earwicker's "innocent" version is filmed, televised, and aired
55–58: A review of Earwicker's Fall
58: H.C.E.'s Wake
58–61: A reporter's interview with the populace concerning H.C.E.'s crime
61–62: A report of H.C.E.'s flight
62–63: A report of H.C.E.'s encounter with a masked assailant
63–64: The Banging on the Gate
64–65: Movie digression: Peaches and Daddy Browning
66–67: Inquiry concerning missing letters and stolen coffin
67: Lolly the Constable testifies on the arrest of drunken Earwicker
67–68: The demise of the two temptresses

69: The locked gate
69–71: A Midwesterner at the gate of the closed pub after hours reviles H.C.E.
71–72: The list of abusive names
72: H.C.E. remains silent
73: The braying ass retreats
74: Finn's resurrection foreshadowed as H.C.E. sleeps

## CHAPTER 4 (*[Book I, chap. 4,] pp. 75–103)*

75: The besieged Earwicker dreams
76–79: The burial in Lough Neagh (including the battle interlude, pp. 78–79)
79–81: Kate Strong recalls old times in the midden heap in Phoenix Park
81–85: Encounter between attacker and adversary repeats H.C.E.–Cad meeting
85–90: Festy King on trial for Park indiscretion
90–92: Pegger Festy denies any act of violence, wins Issy's love
92–93: King freed, reveals his deception and is vilified by the girls
93–94: The Letter
94–96: The Four Old Judges rehash the case and argue over the past
96–97: The Fox Hunt—in pursuit of H.C.E.
97–100: Rumors rampant regarding H.C.E.'s death or reappearance
101–103: The women usher in A.L.P.

## CHAPTER 5 (*[Book I, chap. 5,] pp. 104–125)*

104–107: Invocation and list of suggested names for A.L.P.'s untitled mamafesta
107–125: A scrutinization of the Document, including:
- Cautioning against impatience (108)
- Regarding the envelope (109)
- Citing the place where it was found (110)
- Regarding Biddy the finder (110–111)
- Contents of the letter (111)
- Condition of the letter (111–112)
- Various types of analyses of the letter: historical, textual, Freudian, Marxist, etc. (114–116)
- The Book of Kells (119–124)

## CHAPTER 6 (*[Book I, chap. 6,] pp. 126–168)*

126: Radio quiz program: Shaun answers Shem's questions
126–139: First question identifies the epic hero Finn MacCool
139: Second question regards Shaun's mother
139–140: Third question seeks a motto for the Earwicker establishment
140–141: Fourth question deals with the four capital cities of Ireland
141: Fifth question regards the Earwicker handyman
141–142: Sixth question regards Kate, the charwoman
142: Seventh question identifies the twelve citizens
142–143: Eighth question identifies the Maggies
143: Ninth question concerns the kaleidoscopic dream
143–148: Tenth question is a "pepette" letter of love
148–168: Eleventh question asks Shaun if he would aid Shem in saving his soul, includes:
- Professor Jones on the dime-cash problem (148–152)
- The Mookse and the Gripes (152–159)
- Barrus and Caseous (161–168)

168: Twelfth question identifies Shem as the accursed brother

## CHAPTER 7 (*[Book I, chap. 7,] 169–195)*

169–170: A portrait of Shem
170: The first riddle of the universe
170–175: On Shem's lowness
175: Football match song
175–176: The Games
176–177: Shem's cowardice during war and insurrection
177–178: Shem's boasting about his literary ability while drunk
178–179: Shem, venturing out after the war, finds himself facing a gun
179–180: Shem as a tenor
180–182: His career as a forger in various European capitals, booted out as foul
182–184: Shem's place of residence

184: Shem cooks eggs in his kitchen
185–186: Shem makes ink from his excrement in order to write his books
186–187: Shem arrested by Constable Sackerson in order to save him from the mob
187–193: Justius [Shaun] berates Shem
193–195: Mercius [Shem] defends himself

## CHAPTER 8 (*[Book I, chap. 8,] pp. 196–216*)

196–201: Two washerwomen on the banks of the Liffey gossip about A.L.P. and H.C.E.
201: Anna Livia Plurabelle's message
201–204: Gossip about the love life of the young Anna Livia
204–205: Washerwomen interrupt their gossip to wash Lily Kinsella's drawers
205–212: A.L.P. steals off to distribute presents to all her children
212–216: Darkness falls as the washerwomen turn into a tree and a rock

## CHAPTER 9 (*Book II, chap. I pp. 219–259*)

219: Program for the Mime of Mick, Nick and the Maggies
219–221: *Dramatis Personae* of the Mime
221–222: Credits for the Mime
222–224: The argument of the Mime
224–225: Glugg asked the first riddle—about jewels—loses
226–227: Seven rainbow girls dance and play, ignoring Glugg
227–233: Regarding Glugg's career as an exile and writer
233: Glugg asked the second riddle—on insects—loses again
233–239: Rainbow girls sing their paean of praise to their Sun-God, Chuff
239–240: Glugg feels the tortures of Hell
240–242: Review of H.C.E.'s resurrection
242–243: A.L.P. offers to forgive H.C.E.
244: Night falls and the children are called home
244–245: The Animals enter Noah's ark
245–246: The Earwicker Tavern
246–247: Glugg and Chuff fight, Glugg beaten
247–250: The rainbow girls laud Chuff with erotic praise
250: Glugg asked the third riddle—loses again
250–251: Defeated Glugg lusts after the Leap Year Girl
252–255: Father appears as if resurrected
255–256: Mother also appears and rounds up her children
256–257: Children at their lessons but Issy unhappy
257: Curtain falls—the Mime is over
257–259: Prayers before bed—then to sleep

## CHAPTER 10 (*Book II, chap. 2, pp. 260–308*)

260–266: Lessons begin with Shem writing left margin notes, Shaun right margin, and Issy the footnotes
266–270: Grammar
270–277: History
277–281: Letter writing
282–287: Mathematics
287–292: Interlude recounting political, religious, and amorous invasions of Ireland
293–299: Dolph explains to Kev the geometry of A.L.P.'s vagina (marginal notes reversed)
299–304: Kev finally comprehends the significance of the triangles during a letter-writing session—strikes Dolph
304–306: Dolph forgives Kev
306–308: Essay assignments on 52 famous men
308: The children's night-letter to the parents

## CHAPTER 11 (*Book II, chap. 3, pp. 309–382*)

309–310: The radio in Earwicker's pub
310–311: Earwicker at the beer pull
311–312: The Tale of Kersee the Tailor and the Norwegian Captain
332–334: Kate delivers Anna Livia's message that Earwicker should come to bed
335–337: H.C.E. begins his tale
337–355: Television skit by comics Butt and Taff of "How Buckley Shot the Russian General"
355–358: H.C.E. attempts an apology
358–361: Radio resumes with broadcast of nightingale's song
361–366: H.C.E. accused, speaks in his own defense
366–369: The Four Old Men harass H.C.E.
369–373: Constable Sackerson arrives at closing time while a new ballad is in the making

373–380: Earwicker, alone in the pub, hears the case against him reviewed during funeral games
380–382: Earwicker drinks up the dregs and passes out—as the ship passes out to sea

### CHAPTER 12 (*Book II, chap. 4, pp. 383–399*)

383–386: Four Old Men spy on the love ship of Tristram and Iseult
386–388: Johnny MacDougall comments on the sea adventure
388–390: Marcus Lyons comments
390–393: Luke Tarpey comments
393–395: Matt Gregory comments
395–396: The sexual union of the young lovers
396–398: The four old men reminisce over the voyage
398–399: The Hymn of Iseult la Belle

### CHAPTER 13 (*Book III, chap. 1 pp. 403–428*)

403: H.C.E. and A.L.P. in bed at midnight
403–405: The dreamer envisions a glorious sight of Shaun the Post
405–407: Shaun described at his gorgings
407–414: Shaun being interviewed
414–419: The Fable of the Ondt and the Gracehoper
419–421: Shaun denounces the Letter
421–425: Shaun vilifies Shem and claims equal ability as a man of letters
426–427: Shaun collapses into a barrel and rolls backward down the river
427–428: Issy bids Shaun a nostalgic farewell

### CHAPTER 14 (*Book III, chap. 2, pp. 429–473*)

429–431: Jaun rests along the road and meets the 29 girls from St. Bride's
431–432: Jaun's preamble addressed to his sister
432–439: Jaun delivers his moralizing sermon
439–441: Jaun singles out Issy for his sermon on sex
441–444: Jaun berates Shem the seducer
444–445: Jaun admonishes Issy with sadistic fury
445–446: Jaun's tirade turns into a sweet declaration of affection
446–448: Jaun campaigns for civic improvement
448–452: Jaun pays court to Issy with assurances of his success in business
452–454: Jaun ends his sermon
454–457: Jaun adds a gastronomic postscript
457–461: Issy replies in an amorous letter
461–468: The departing Jaun introduces her to his brother Dave
468–469: Jaun finally takes his leave
469–473: St. Bride's girls bid farewell to Haun, the ghost of Juan

### CHAPTER 15 (*Book III, chap. 3, pp. 474–554*)

474–477: The four old men find the exhausted Yawn on a midden heap
477–483: They interrogate Yawn
483–485: Yawn angrily reproaches his interrogators
485–491: Inquiry continues as Yawn explains his relationship to his brother
491–499: The voice of A.L.P. through Yawn discusses H.C.E.'s indiscretion
499–506: A ghost voice through Yawn discusses the Fall
506–510: Regarding Toucher "Thom"
510–520: Regarding the Wake
520–523: The interrogation takes a turn for the worse and tempers flare
523–526: Treacle Tom gives his version of the encounter in the park
526–528: Issy talks to her mirror image
528–530: Matt Gregory takes over the inquiry and recalls the constable
530–531: Kate is called upon to testify
532–539: H.C.E. himself is called to the stand and delivers his self-defense
539–546: H.C.E. boasts of the great city he has founded and rules
546–554: H.C.E. recounts the conquest of A.L.P.

### CHAPTER 16 (*Book III, chap. 4, pp. 555–590*)

555–559: Night in the Porter house—parents disturbed by Jerry's cry in his sleep
559–563: Matt's view of the parents in bed: First Position of Harmony

564–582: Mark's view: Second Position of Discordance (includes the court trials, pp. 572–576)
582–590: Luke's view: Third Position of Concord: unsuccessful union disturbed by the crowing of cock at dawn
590: John's view: Fourth Position of Solution

## CHAPTER 17 *(Book IV, pp. 593–628)*

593–601: Dawn of new era awakens the sleeping giant
601: 29 Girls celebrate Kevin
601–603: Morning newspaper carries the story of H.C.E.'s indiscretion
603–606: St. Kevin the hermit mediates in his bathtub-altar
606–609: The park scene of H.C.E.'s indiscretion revisited
609–613: Muta and Juva watch the encounter of St. Patrick and the Archdruid
613–615: Morning brings the cycle to its beginning
615–619: The Letter signed by A.L.P. is in the morning mail
619–628: Anna Livia's final soliloquy as she goes out to sea

## Translation of the Latin Passage on Page 185 of *Finnegans Wake*

*(The following translation has been rendered into English with the assistance of Sister Grace Florian McInerney, O.P.)*

First the artisan, the profound progenitor, approaching the fruitful and all-powerful earth, without shame or pardon, put on a raincloak and ungirded his pants, and with buttocks naked as they were on the day of birth, while weeping and groaning, defecated into his hand. Next, having relieved himself of the black living excrement, he—while striking the trumpet—placed his own excrement, which he called his scatterings (purgation), into a once honorable vessel (chalice) of sadness, and into the same place, under the invocation of the twin brothers Medardus and Godardus, he pissed joyfully and melodiously, continuously singing with a loud voice the psalm that begins: "My tongue is a scribe's quill writing swiftly." Finally, he mingled the odious excrement with the pleasantness of the divine Orion, and, from this mixture, which had been cooked and exposed to the cold, he made for himself indelible ink.

# FAMILY TREES

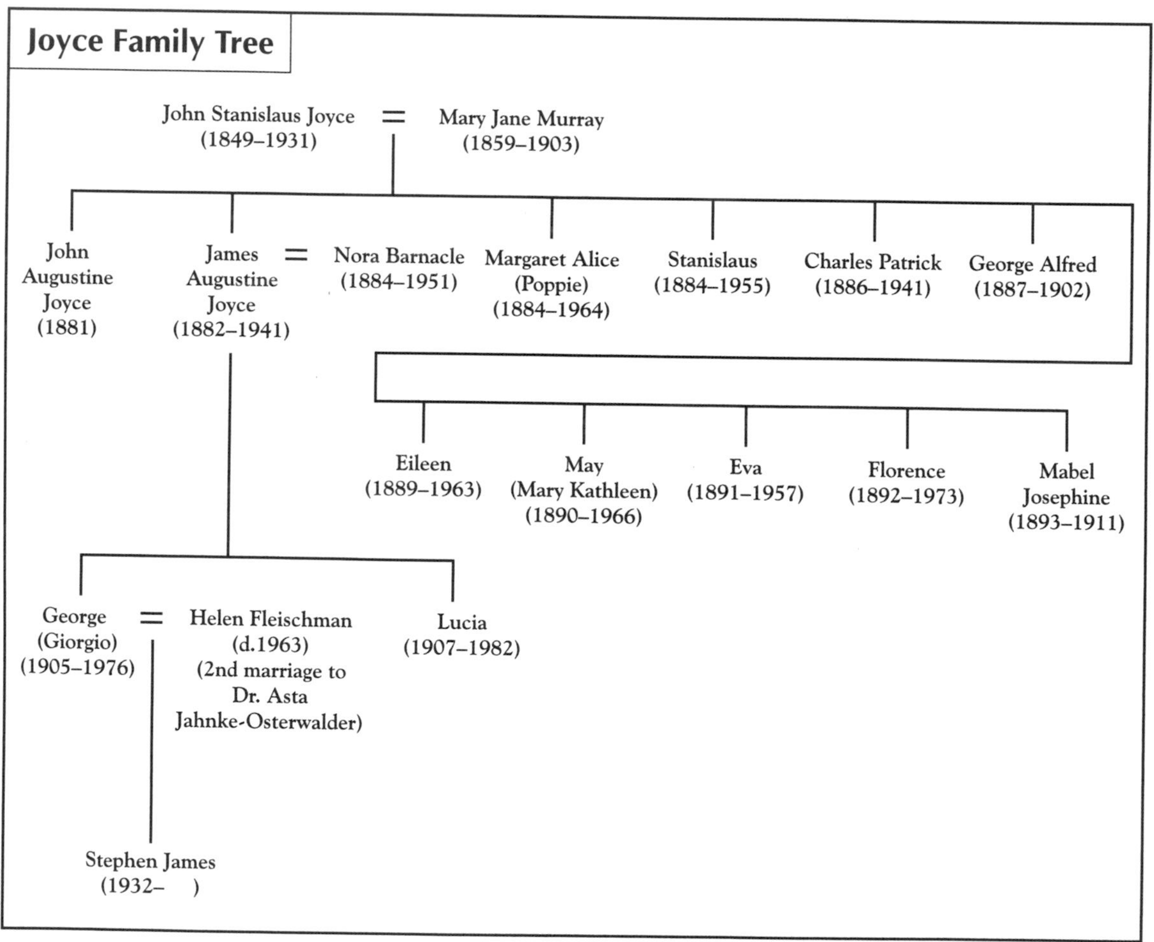

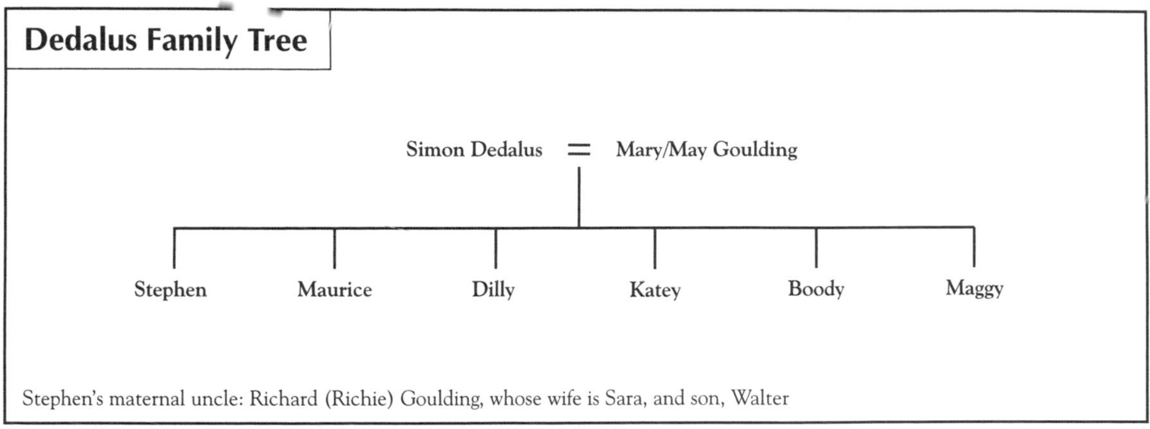
Dedalus Family Tree
Simon Dedalus = Mary/May Goulding
Stephen
Maurice
Dilly
Katey
Boody
Maggy
Stephen's maternal uncle: Richard (Richie) Goulding, whose wife is Sara, and son, Walter

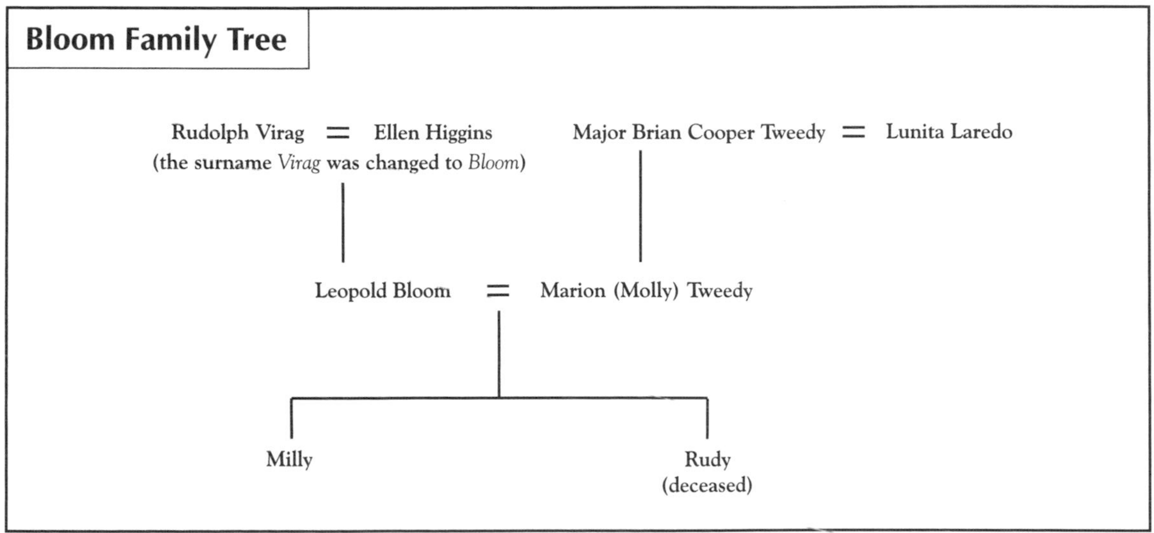
Bloom Family Tree
Rudolph Virag = Ellen Higgins
(the surname Virag was changed to Bloom)
Major Brian Cooper Tweedy = Lunita Laredo
Leopold Bloom = Marion (Molly) Tweedy
Milly
Rudy
(deceased)

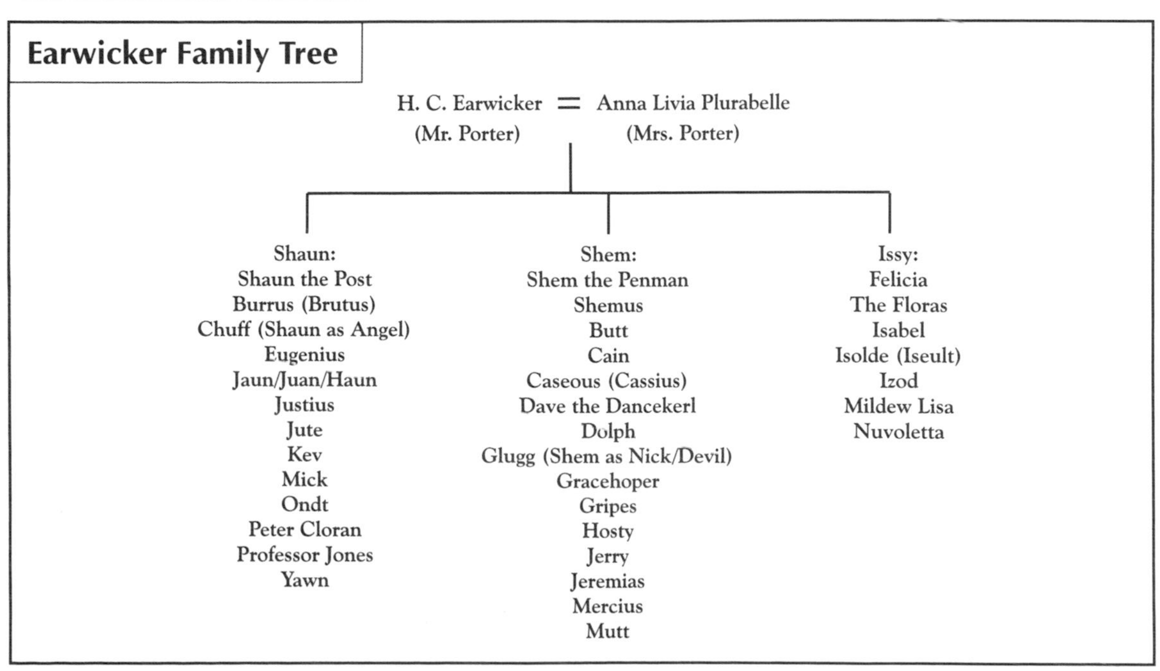
Earwicker Family Tree
H. C. Earwicker = Anna Livia Plurabelle
(Mr. Porter)
(Mrs. Porter)
Shaun:
Shaun the Post
Burrus (Brutus)
Chuff (Shaun as Angel)
Eugenius
Jaun/Juan/Haun
Justius
Jute
Kev
Mick
Ondt
Peter Cloran
Professor Jones
Yawn
Shem:
Shem the Penman
Shemus
Butt
Cain
Caseous (Cassius)
Dave the Dancekerl
Dolph
Glugg (Shem as Nick/Devil)
Gracehoper
Gripes
Hosty
Jerry
Jeremias
Mercius
Mutt
Issy:
Felicia
The Floras
Isabel
Isolde (Iseult)
Izod
Mildew Lisa
Nuvoletta

# Periodicals and Web Sites

*Abiko Quarterly (Literary Rag), The* (For additional information regarding this journal, which devotes considerable attention to Joyce, write to *The Abiko Quarterly (Literary Rag),* c/o Dr. Vince Broderick and D. C. Palter, Fiction Editors, 8-1-8 Namiki, Abikoshi, Chiba-ken 270-11, Japan.)

*James Joyce Broadsheet* (For additional information, write to the Editors, *James Joyce Broadsheet,* The School of English, University of Leeds, Leeds LS2 9JT, England.)

James Joyce Literary Supplement (For further information on submissions or subscriptions or for general inquiries, write to the Editor, James Joyce Literary Supplement, c/o Department of English, P.O. Box 248145, University of Miami, Coral Gables, Fla. 33124.)

*James Joyce Newestlatter* (For information write to the Editor, *James Joyce Newestlatter,* Department of English, Ohio State University Columbus, Ohio 43210.)

*James Joyce Quarterly* (For further information on subscriptions or for general inquiries, write to the Editor, *James Joyce Quarterly,* 600 S. College Avenue, University of Tulsa, Tulsa, Okla. 74104.)

*Joyce Studies Annual* (No longer being published; former address: *Joyce Studies Annual,* P.O. Box 7219, University Station, University of Texas, Austin, Tex. 78713.)

**American Friends of James Joyce** http://www.themodernword.com/afjj/

**FWAKE-L,** mailing list, subscribe to listserv@listserv.hea.ie with following message: subscribe FWAKE-L firstname lastname

**hypermedia joyce studies: electronic journal of joycean scholarship** http://www.geocities.com/hypermedia_joyce/

**International James Joyce Foundation** http://english.osu.edw/organizations/ijjf/

**The James Joyce Centre, Dublin** http://www.jamesjoyce.ie/home/

**The James Joyce Museum, Dublin** http://www.visitdublin.com/attractions/jamesjoyce.asp

**James Joyce Tower** http://www.dun-laoghaire.com/dir/jjtower.html

**The James Joyce Society** http://www.joycesociety.org

**J-JOYCE,** mailing list, subscribe to listproc@list.utah.edu with following message: subscribe j-joyce firstname lastname

**Joyce Museum Trieste** http://www.retecivica.trieste.it/joyce/default.asp?tabella_padre=sezioni&ids=2&tipo=blocchi_sezioni_2&pagina=-

# BIBLIOGRAPHIES

## Biographical Sources


Anderson, Chester G. *James Joyce and His World.* London: Thames & Hudson, Ltd., 1967.

Anderson, Margaret. *My Thirty Years War.* New York: Covici-Friede, 1930.

Bair, Deirdre. *Samuel Beckett: A Biography.* New York: Harcourt Brace Jovanovich, 1978.

Beach, Sylvia. *Shakespeare and Company.* New York: Harcourt Brace, 1959. Reprint, Lincoln: University of Nebraska Press, 1991.

Beja, Morris. *James Joyce: A Literary Life.* Columbus: Ohio State University Press, 1992.

Benco, Silvio. "James Joyce in Trieste." *The Bookman* 72 (December 1930): 375–380.

Berrone, Louis. *James Joyce in Padua.* New York: Random House, 1977.

Bradley, Bruce. *James Joyce's Schooldays.* Dublin: Gill and Macmillan, 1982; New York: St. Martin's, 1982.

Budgen, Frank. *Myselves When Young.* London: Oxford University Press, 1970.

Byrne, John Francis. *Silent Years: An Autobiography, With Memoirs of James Joyce and Our Ireland.* New York: Farrar, Strauss and Young, 1953.

Campbell, Sandy. "Mrs. Joyce in Zürich." *Harper's Bazaar,* October 1952.

Carpenter, Humphrey. *A Serious Character: The Life of Ezra Pound.* Boston: Houghton Mifflin, 1988.

Colum, Mary. *Life and the Dream.* New York: Doubleday, 1947.

———. "A Little Knowledge of Joyce." *Saturday Review of Literature* 33 (29 April 1950): 11–12.

———. "Portrait of James Joyce." *Dublin Magazine* 7 (April–June 1932): 40–48.

Colum, Mary, and Padraic Colum. *Our Friend James Joyce.* Garden City, N.Y.: Doubleday, 1958.

Connor, Stephen. *James Joyce.* Plymouth, England: Northcote House, with British Council, 1996.

Costello, Peter. *James Joyce: The Years of Growth 1882–1915.* New York: Pantheon Books, 1992.

———. *Leopold Bloom: A Biography.* Dublin: Gill and Macmillan, 1981.

Crivelli, Renzo S. *James Joyce: Triestine Itineraries.* Trieste: MGS Press, 1996.

Curran, Constantine. *James Joyce Remembered.* New York and London: Oxford University Press, 1968.

———. "When James Joyce Lived in Dublin." *Vogue* 109 (May 1947): 144–149.

Curtayne, Alice. "Portrait of the Artist as a Brother: an Interview with James Joyce's Sister." *Critic* 21 (1963): 43–47.

Davies, Stan Gébler. *James Joyce: A Portrait of the Artist.* London: Davis-Poynter, 1975.

Dawson, Hugh J. "Thomas MacGreevy and Joyce." *James Joyce Quarterly* 25 (Spring 1988): 305–321.

Edel, Leon. *James Joyce: The Last Journey.* New York: Gotham Book Mart, 1947.

Ellmann, Richard. *James Joyce.* New York: Oxford University Press, 1982.

———, ed. *Giacomo Joyce.* New York: Viking, 1968.

Epstein, Edmund L. "James Augustine Aloysius Joyce." *A Companion to Joyce Studies.* Edited by Zack Bowen and James F. Carens, 3–37. Westport, Conn.: Greenwood Press, 1984.

Fabricant, Nohan D. "The Ocular History of James Joyce." In *Thirteen Famous Patients.* Philadelphia: Chilton Books, 1960.

Faerber, Thomas, and Markus Luchsinger. *Joyce in Zurich.* Zurich: Unionsverlag, 1988.

Fitch, Noel Riley. *Sylvia Beach and the Lost Generation: Literary Paris in the Twenties and Thirties.* New York: W. W. Norton, 1983.

Francini Bruni, Alessandro. *Joyce intimo spogliato in piazza.* Trieste: La Editoriale Libraria, 1992. Translation in Potts (1979) (see below).

Frank, Nino. "Souvenirs sur James Joyce." *La Table Ronde* (23 November 1947): 1671–1693.

Freund, Giséle. *Trois Jours avec Joyce.* Paris: Denoël, 1982.

——— (with V. P. Carleton). *James Joyce in Paris: The Final Years.* New York: Harcourt, Brace, 1965; London: Cassell, 1965.

Giedon-Welcker, C[arola]. "James Joyce in Zurich." *The Golden Horizon.* Edited by Cyril Connolly, 383–387. New York: University Books, 1955.

———. *In Memoriam James Joyce.* Zurich, 1941.

Gillespie, Michael Patrick. "James Joyce." *Contemporary Authors* 126, 203–211. Detroit: Gale Press, 1989.

Gillet, Louis. *Claybook for James Joyce.* Translated by Georges Markow-Totevy. New York: Abelard-Schuman, 1958.

Gogarty, Oliver St. John. *As I Was Going Down Sackville Street.* London: Rich and Cowan, 1937.

———. *It Isn't This Time of Year at All: An Unpremeditated Autobiography.* Garden City: Doubleday, 1954.

———. "The Joyce I Knew" [Obituary of Joyce]. *Saturday Review of Literature* 23 (25 January 1941).

———. *Mourning Becomes Mrs. Spendlove and Other Portraits, Grave and Gay.* New York: Creative Age, 1948.

———. "They Think They Know Joyce." *Saturday Review of Literature* 33 (18 March 1950): 8–9, 35–37.

———. "The Tower: Fact and Fiction." *Irish Times* (Dublin), 16 June 1962, 11.

Gorman, Herbert S. *James Joyce: His First Forty Years.* London: Geoffrey Bles, 1926.

———. *James Joyce.* New York: Farrar & Rinehart. Revised edition, New York: Rinehart, 1948.

Hayman, David. "Shadow of His Mind: The Papers of Lucia Joyce." In *James Joyce: The Centennial Symposium.* Edited by Morris Beja et al. Urbana: University of Illinois Press, 1986.

Hoek, Kees van. "Mrs. James Joyce." *Irish Times* (Dublin), 12 November 1949.

Hyman, Louis. *The Jews of Ireland: From the Earliest Times to the Year 1910.* Shannon: Irish University Press, 1972.

Igoe, Vivien. *James Joyce's Dublin Houses & Nora Barnacle's Galway.* London: Mandarin, 1990.

Jolas, Maria, ed. *A James Joyce Yearbook.* Paris: Transition Press, 1949.

Joyce, Stanislaus. *The Dublin Diary of Stanislaus Joyce.* Edited by George H. Healy. London: Faber and Faber, 1962; Ithaca, N.Y.: Cornell University Press, 1962. Revised and published as *The Complete Dublin Diary of Stanislaus Joyce.* Ithaca, N.Y.: Cornell University Press, 1971.

———. "The Joyces." *The Listener* 41 (26 May 1949): 896.

———. *My Brother's Keeper: James Joyce's Early Years.* Edited with an introduction and notes by Richard Ellmann. Preface by T. S. Eliot. New York: Viking, 1958.

———. *Recollections of James Joyce.* Translated from the Italian by Ell[i]sworth Mason. New York: The James Joyce Society, 1950. First appeared under title of "Ricordi di James Joyce" in *Litterature* (Florence) 5.3 (July/September 1941): 25–35, and 5.4 (October/December 1941): 23–35.

Kain, Richard M. "An Interview with Carla Giedon-Welcker and Maria Jolas." *James Joyce Quarterly* 11 (Winter 1974): 94–112.

Lázaro, Alberto. *James Joyce in Spain: A Critical Bibliography (1972–2002).* La Coruña, Spain: Asociación Espanola James Joyce, with Universidade da Coruña, 2002.

Léon, Paul. "In Memory of Joyce." *Poésie* 5 (1942): 35.

Lidderdale, Jane. "Lucia Joyce at St. Andrew's." *James Joyce Broadsheet* 10 (February 1983): 3.

Lidderdale, Jane, and Mary Nicholson. *Dear Miss Weaver: Harriet Shaw Weaver, 1876–1961.* London: Faber and Faber, 1970.

MacDiarmid, Hugh. *In Memoriam James Joyce.* Glasgow: MacLellan, 1955.

Maddox, Brenda. *Nora: The Real Life of Molly Bloom.* Boston: Houghton Mifflin, 1988.

Magalaner, Marvin, and Richard M. Kain. *Joyce: The Man, The Work, The Reputation.* New York: New York University Press, 1956.

McAlmon, Robert. *Being Geniuses Together, 1920–1930.* Garden City: Doubleday, 1968.

McCourt, John. *The Years of Bloom: James Joyce in Trieste, 1904–1920.* Madison: University of Wisconsin Press, 2000.

McMillan, Dougald. *Transition: The History of a Literary Era, 1927–1938,* 179–231 and passim. New York: Braziller, 1976.

Mercanton, Jacques. "The Hours of James Joyce." Translated by Lloyd C. Parks. *Kenyon Review* 24 (1962): 700–730; 25 (1963): 93–118.

Meyers, Jeffrey. "James and Nora Joyce." In his *Married to Genius.* New York: Barnes and Noble, 1977.

Mikhail, E. H. *James Joyce: Interviews and Recollections.* Foreword by Frank Delaney. London: Macmillan, 1990.

Noel, Lucie. *James Joyce and Paul L. Léon: The Story of a Friendship*. New York: Gotham Book Mart, 1950.

O'Brien, Edna. *James Joyce*. New York: Viking, 1999.

O'Connor, Ulick, ed. *The Joyce We Knew: Memories by Eugene Sheehy, Will G. Fallon, Padraic Colum, Arthur Power.* Cork, Ireland: Mercier Press, 1967.

O'Laoi, Padraic. *Nora Barnacle Joyce*. Galway, Ireland: Kenny's Bookshop & Art Gallery, 1982.

Pierce, David. *James Joyce's Ireland*. New Haven, Conn.: Yale University Press, 1992.

Pinguentini, Gianni. *James Joyce in Italia*. Verona, Italy: Ghidini e Fiorini, 1966.

Pollack, Harry J. "The Girl Joyce Did Not Marry." *James Joyce Quarterly* 4 (Summer 1967): 255–257.

Potts, Willard, ed. *Portraits of the Artist in Exile: Recollections of James Joyce by Europeans*. Seattle: University of Washington Press, 1979; New York: Harcourt Brace, 1986.

Pound, Ezra. *Pound/Joyce: The Letters of Ezra Pound to James Joyce*. Edited by Forrest Read. London: Faber and Faber, 1967. Republished, New York: Directions, 1970.

Power, Arthur. *Conversations with James Joyce*. Edited by Clive Hart. New York: Barnes and Noble, 1974.

Reid, Benjamin L. *The Man from New York: John Quinn and His Friends*. New York: Oxford University Press, 1968.

Reynolds, Mary T. "Joyce and Nora: The Indispensable Countersign." *Sewanee Review* 72 (Winter 1964): 29–64.

———. "Joyce as a Letter Writer." In *A Companion to Joyce Studies*. Edited by Zack Bowen and James F. Carens, 39–70. Westport, Conn.: Greenwood Press, 1984.

Sheehy, Eugene. *May It Please the Court*. Dublin: Fallon, 1951.

Soupault, Philippe. *Souvenirs de James Joyce*. Paris: Charlot, 1945.

Shloss, Carol. *Lucia Joyce: To Dance in the Wake*. New York: Farrar, Straus and Giroux, 2003.

Staley, Thomas. "James Joyce in Trieste." *Georgia Review* 16 (October 1962): 446–449.

———. "Composition of Place: Joyce and Trieste." *Modern British Literature* 5 (1980): 3–9.

Staley, Thomas F., and Randolph Lewis, eds. *Reflections on James Joyce: Stuart Gilbert's Paris Journal*. Austin: University of Texas Press, 1993.

Sullivan, Kevin. *Joyce among the Jesuits*. New York: Columbia University Press, 1958.

Svevo, Italo (Ettore Schmitz). *James Joyce: A Lecture Delivered in Milan in 1927*. Translated by Stanislaus Joyce. New York: New Directions, 1950.

Svevo (Schmitz), Livia Veneziani. *Memoir of Italo Svevo*. Translated by Isabel Quigley. Preface by P. N. Furbank. Marlboro, Vt.: Marlboro Press, 1990.

Tindall, William York. *The Joyce Country*. Enlarged edition. New York: Schocken Books, 1966.

Walsh, Louis J. "With Joyce and Kettle at U.C.D." *Irish Digest* 12 (June 1942): 27–29.

## General

Adams, Robert M. *James Joyce: Common Sense and Beyond*. New York: Random House, 1966.

Armstrong, Alison. *The Joyce of Cooking: Food and Drink from James Joyce's Dublin*. Barrytown, N.Y.: Station Hill Press, 1986.

Attridge, Derek. *The Cambridge Companion to James Joyce*. Cambridge: Cambridge University Press, 1990.

———. *Joyce Effects: On Language, Theory, and History*. Cambridge: Cambridge University Press, 2000.

Attridge, Derek, and Daniel Ferrer, eds. *Post-structuralist Joyce*. Cambridge: Cambridge University Press, 1984.

Aubert, Jacques. *Introduction à l'esthétique de James Joyce*. Paris: Dedier, 1973.

Barta, Peter I. *Bely, Joyce, and Döblin: Peripatetics in the City Novel*. Gainesville: University Press of Florida, 1996.

Bauerle, Ruth, ed. *The James Joyce Songbook*. New York: Garland, 1982.

Beach, Sylvia. *Catalogue of a Collection Containing Manuscripts and Rare Editions of James Joyce, etc.* Paris: Shakespeare and Co., 1935.

Beebe, Maurice. "James Joyce: Barnacle Goose and Lapwing." *PMLA* 81 (June 1956): 302–320.

———. "Joyce and Stephen Dedalus: The Problem of Autobiography." In *A James Joyce Miscellany (Second series)*. Edited by Marvin Magalaner. Carbondale: Southern Illinois University Press, 1959.

Beja, Morris. *Epiphany in the Modern Novel*. Seattle: University of Washington Press, 1971.

Beja, Morris, and Shari Benstock. *Coping with Joyce: Essays from the Copenhagen Symposium*. Columbus: Ohio State University Press, 1989.

Benstock, Bernard. *James Joyce*. New York: Frederick Ungar, 1985.

———. *James Joyce: The Undiscovered Country*. New York: Barnes and Noble; Dublin: Gill and Macmillan, 1977.

———. *The Seventh of Joyce.* Bloomington: Indiana University Press; Sussex: Harvester Press, 1982.

———, ed. *Critical Essays on James Joyce.* Boston: G. K. Hall, 1985.

Benstock, Bernard, and Shari Benstock. *Who's He When He's At Home. A James Joyce Directory.* Urbana: University of Illinois Press, 1980.

Bérard, Victor. *Les Phéniciens dans l'Odyssée.* Paris: Armand Colin, 1902.

Bidwell, Bruce (with Linda Heffer). *The Joycean Way.* Dublin: Wolfhound Press, 1981.

Black, Martha Fodaski. *Shaw and Joyce: 'The Last Word in Stolentelling'.* Gainesville: University Press of Florida, 1995.

Boheemen-Saaf, Christine van. *Joyce, Derrida, Lacan, and the Trauma of History: Reading, Narrative and Postcolonialism.* Cambridge: Cambridge University Press, 1999.

Boldrini, Lucia, ed. *Medieval Joyce.* Amsterdam: Rodopi, 2002.

Bolt, Sydney. *A Preface to James Joyce.* London and New York: Longman, 1981.

Bowen, Zack. *Bloom's Old Sweet Song: Essays on Joyce and Music.* Gainesville: University Press of Florida, 1995.

Bowen, Zack, and James F. Carens, eds. *A Companion to Joyce Studies.* Westport, Conn.: Greenwood Press, 1984.

Boyd, Ernest A. *Ireland's Literary Renaissance.* Dublin: Maunsel and Co., 1916; New York: Alfred A. Knopf, 1922.

Brandabur, Edward. *A Scrupulous Meanness.* Chicago: University of Illinois Press, 1971.

Brannigan, John, Geoff Ward, and Julian Wolfreys, eds. *Re: Joyce: Text, Culture, Politics.* Basingstoke, England: Macmillan; New York: St. Martin's, 1998.

Brivic, Sheldon. *Joyce between Freud and Jung.* Port Washington, N.Y., and London: Kennikaat Press, 1980.

———. *Joyce the Creator.* Madison: University of Wisconsin Press, 1985.

———. *The Veil of Signs: Joyce, Lacan, and Perception.* Chicago and Urbana: University of Illinois Press, 1991.

Brown, Dennis. *Intertextual Dynamics within the Literary Group—Joyce, Lewis, Eliot, and Pound: The Men of 1914.* New York: St. Martin's Press, 1991.

Brown, Richard. *James Joyce and Sexuality.* Cambridge and New York: Cambridge University Press, 1985.

Burns, Christy L. *Gestural Politics: Stereotype and Parody in Joyce.* Albany: State University of New York Press, 2000.

Carey, Phyllis, and Ed Jewinski, eds. *Re: Joyce'N Beckett.* New York: Fordham University Press, 1992.

Carpenter, Martha C. *Ritual, Myth, and the Modernist Text: The Influence of Jane Ellen Harrison on Joyce, Eliot, and Woolf.* Amsterdam: Gordon and Breach, 1998.

Cheng, Vincent J. *Joyce, Race, and Empire.* Cambridge: Cambridge University Press, 1995.

Cixous, Hélène. *L'Exil de James Joyce.* Paris: Bernard Grasset, 1968. Translated as *The Exile of James Joyce.* New York: David Lewis, 1972.

———. *Readings: The Poetics of Blanchot, Joyce, Kafka, Kleist, Lispector, and Tsvetayeva.* Edited, translated, and introduced by Verena Andermatt Conley. Minneapolis: University of Minnesota Press, 1991.

Connolly, Thomas E., comp. *The Personal Library of James Joyce: Descriptive Bibliography.* 2d ed. Buffalo, N.Y.: University Bookstore, University of Buffalo, 1957.

Cope, Jackson I. *Joyce's Cities: Archaeologies of the Soul.* Baltimore and London: Johns Hopkins University Press, 1981.

Crise, Stelio. *Epiphanies & Phadographs: James Joyce e Trieste.* Milan: All'insegna del Pesce d'Oro, 1967.

Croce, Benedetto. *The Philosophy of Giambattista Vico.* Translated by R. G. Collingwood. London: Macmillan, 1913.

Cross, Richard K. *Flaubert and Joyce: The Rite of Fiction.* Princeton, N.J.: Princeton University Press, 1971.

Dasenbrock, Reed Way. *Imitating the Italians: Wyatt, Spenser, Synge, Pound, Joyce.* Baltimore: Johns Hopkins University Press, 1991.

Delaney, Frank. *James Joyce's Odyssey.* London: Hodder and Stoughton, 1982.

Deming, Robert H. *A Bibliography of James Joyce Studies.* 2d ed., revised and enlarged. Boston: G. K. Hall & Co., 1977.

———, ed. and comp. *James Joyce: The Critical Heritage.* 2 vols. London: Routledge & Kegan Paul, 1970.

Dettmar, Kevin J. H. *The Illicit Joyce of Postmodernism: Reading Against the Grain.* Madison: University of Wisconsin Press, 1996.

Diment, Galya. *The Autobiographical Novel of Co-Consciousness: Goncharov, Woolf, and Joyce.* Gainesville: University Press of Florida, 1994.

Dujardin, Edouard. *Les Lauriers sont coupés.* Paris: A. Messein, 1924.

———. *Le Monologue intérieur: son apparition, ses origines, sa place dans l'oeuvre de James Joyce.* Paris: n.p., 1931.

Dunleavy, Janet E., ed. *Reviewing Classics of Joyce Criticism.* Urbana and Chicago: University of Illinois Press, 1991.

Dunleavy, Janet E., Melvin J. Friedman, and Michael Patrick Gillespie, eds. *Joycean Occasions: Essays from the Milwaukee James Joyce Conference.* Newark: University of Delaware Press, 1991.

Eco, Umberto. *The Aesthetics of Chaosmos: The Middle Ages of James Joyce.* Translated by Ellen Esrock. Tulsa, Okla.: University of Tulsa Press, 1982.

Eide, Marian. *Ethical Joyce.* Cambridge: Cambridge University Press, 2002.

Ellmann, Richard. *The Consciousness of Joyce.* London: Faber and Faber, 1977.

———. *James Joyce's Tower.* Dun Laoghaire, Ireland: Eastern Regional Tourism Organisation, 1969.

Fahy, Catherine. *The James Joyce–Paul Léon Papers in the National Library of Ireland, A Catalogue.* Dublin: National Library of Ireland, 1992.

Fargnoli, A. Nicholas, ed. *James Joyce: A Literary Reference.* New York: Carroll & Graf, 2003.

———. "Oral History: B. W. Huebsch." *Dictionary of Literary Biography Yearbook: 1999,* 193–219. Detroit: The Gale Group, 2000.

Finneran, Richard, ed. *Anglo-Irish Literature: A Review of Research.* New York: Modern Language Association of America, 1976.

———. *Recent Research on Anglo-Irish Writers.* New York: Modern Language Association of America, 1983.

Fraser, Jennifer Margaret. *Rite of Passage in the Narratives of Dante and Joyce.* Gainesville: University Press of Florida, 2002.

Frehner, Ruth, and Ursula Zeller, eds. *A Collideorscape of Joyce: Festschrift for Fritz Senn.* Dublin: Lilliput, 1998.

Froula, Christine. *Modernism's Body: Sex, Culture and Joyce.* New York: Columbia University Press, 1996.

Garvin, John. *James Joyce's Disunited Kingdom.* New York: Barnes and Noble, 1977.

Gheerbrandt, Bernard. *James Joyce—sa vie, son oeuvre, son rayonnement.* Paris: Librairie la Hune, 1949.

Gibson, Andrew. *Joyce's Revenge: History, Politics, and Aesthetics in Ulysses.* New York: Oxford University Press, 2002.

Gilbert, Stuart. "The Latin Background of James Joyce's Art." *Horizon* 10.57 (London) (September 1944): 178–189.

Gillespie, Gerald. *Proust, Mann, Joyce in the Modernist Context.* Washington, D.C.: Catholic University of America Press, 2003.

Gillespie, Michael Patrick. *Inverted Volumes Improperly Arranged: James Joyce and His Trieste Library.* Ann Arbor, Mich.: UMI Research Press, 1983.

———. *James Joyce and the Fabrication of an Irish Identity.* Amsterdam: Rodopi, 2001.

——— (with Erick Bradford Stocker). *James Joyce's Trieste Library: A Catalogue of Materials.* Austin: Humanities Research Center/University of Texas, 1986.

———. *Reading the Book of Himself: Narrative Strategies in the Works of James Joyce.* Columbus: Ohio State University Press, 1989.

———, ed. *Joyce through the Ages: A Nonlinear View.* Gainesville: University Press of Florida, 1999.

Gillespie, Michael Patrick, and Paula Gillespie. *Recent Criticism of James Joyce's Ulysses: An Analytical Review.* Rochester, N.Y.: Camden House, 2000.

Gillet, Louis. *Claybook for James Joyce.* Translation and introduction by Georges Markow-Totevy. London and New York: Abelard-Schuman, 1958.

Givens, Seon, ed. *James Joyce: Two Decades of Criticism.* New York: Vanguard Press, 1948.

Golding, Louis. *James Joyce.* London: Thornton Butterworth, 1933.

Goldman, Arnold. *The Joyce Paradox.* London: Routledge & Kegan Paul, 1966.

Gordon, John. *James Joyce's Metamorphoses.* Dublin: Gill and Macmillan, 1981.

———. *Joyce and Reality: The Empirical Strikes Back.* Syracuse: Syracuse University Press, 2004.

Gottfried, Roy. *Joyce's Comic Portrait.* Gainesville: University Press of Florida, 2000.

Groden, Michael, ed. *The James Joyce Archive.* 63 vols. New York: Garland Publishing, 1977.

Gross, John. *James Joyce.* London: Collins/Fontana, 1971.

Harari, Roberto. *How James Joyce Made His Name: A Reading of the Final Lacan.* New York: Other Press, 2002.

Harper, Margaret Mills. *The Aristocracy of Art in Joyce and Wolfe.* Baton Rouge and London: Louisiana State University Press, 1990.

Hart, Clive, et al. *Images of Joyce.* Gerrards Cross, England: Smythe, 1998.

Hayman, David, and Sam Slote, eds. *Genetic Studies in Joyce.* Amsterdam: Rodopi, 1995.

Heller, Vivian. *Joyce, Decadence, and Emancipation.* Urbana: University of Illinois Press, 1995.

Henke, Suzette A. *James Joyce and the Politics of Desire.* New York and London: Routledge, 1990.

Henke, Suzette A., and Elaine Unkeless, eds. *Women in Joyce.* Urbana and Chicago: University of Illinois Press, 1982.

Herr, Cheryl. *Joyce's Anatomy of Culture.* Urbana and Chicago: University of Illinois Press, 1986.

Heymann, C. David. *Ezra Pound: The Last Rower, A Political Profile.* New York: Viking, 1976.

Herring, Phillip F. *Joyce's Uncertainty Principle.* Princeton, N.J.: Princeton University Press, 1987.

Hodgart, Matthew J. C. *James Joyce: A Student's Guide.* London: Routledge, 1978.

Hodgart, Matthew J. C., and Ruth Bauerle. *Joyce's Grand Operoar: Opera in Finnegans Wake.* Urbana: University of Illinois Press, 1996.

Hodgart, Matthew J. C., and Mabel P. Worthington. *Song in the Works of James Joyce.* New York: Columbia University Press, 1959.

Hogan, Patrick Colm. *Joyce, Milton and the Theory of Influence.* Gainesville: University Press of Florida, 1995.

Hulle, Dirk van, ed. *James Joyce: The Study of Languages.* Brussels: Peter Lang, 2002.

Hutchins, Patricia. *James Joyce's Dublin.* London: Grey Walls Press, 1950.

———. *James Joyce's World.* London: Methuen, 1957.

Jackson, Tony E. *The Subject of Modernism: Narrative Alterations in the Fiction of Eliot, Conrad, Woolf, and Joyce.* Ann Arbor: University of Michigan Press, 1994.

Jaurretche, Colleen. *The Sensual Philosophy: Joyce and the Aesthetics of Mysticism.* Madison: University of Wisconsin Press, 1997.

Johnsen, William A. *Violence and Modernism: Ibsen, Joyce and Woolf.* Gainesville: University Press of Florida, 2003.

Johnson-Roullier, Cyraina E. *Reading on the Edge: Exiles, Modernities, and Cultural Transformation in Proust, Joyce, and Baldwin.* Albany: State University of New York Press, 2000.

Jones, Ellen Carol, ed. *Modern Fiction Studies: Special Issue, Feminist Readings of Joyce* 35 (Fall 1989).

Jolas, Maria, ed. *A James Joyce Yearbook.* Paris: Transition Press, 1949.

Jung, Carl Gustav. *The Spirit in Man, Art, and Literature.* Vol. 15 of Bollingen Series 20: *The Collected Works of Jung.* Edited by Herbert Read, Michael Fordham, and Gerhard Adler. New York: Pantheon Books, 1966.

Kain, Richard M. *Dublin in the Age of William Butler Yeats and James Joyce.* Rev. ed. Newton Abbot, England: David and Charles, 1972.

Kelly, Joseph. *Our Joyce: From Outcast to Icon.* Austin: University of Texas Press, 1998.

Kenner, Hugh. *Dublin's Joyce.* London: Chatto and Windus, 1956.

———. *Joyce's Voices.* Berkeley, Los Angeles, and London: University of California Press, 1978.

———. *The Stoic Comedians: Flaubert, Joyce, and Beckett.* Berkeley, Los Angeles and London: University of California Press, 1974.

Kershner, R. B. *Joyce, Bakhtin, and Popular Literature: Chronicles of Disorder.* Chapel Hill and London: University of North Carolina Press, 1989.

Kimball, Jean. *Joyce and the Early Freudians: A Synchronic Dialogue of Texts.* Gainesville: University Press of Florida, 2003.

Knowles, Sebastian D. G., ed. *Bronze by Gold: The Music of Joyce.* New York: Garland, 1999.

Knowlton, Eloise. *Joyce, Joyceans, and the Rhetoric of Citation.* Gainesville: University Press of Florida, 1998.

Lamos, Colleen. *Deviant Modernism: Sexual and Textual Errancy in T. S. Eliot, James Joyce, and Marcel Proust.* Cambridge: Cambridge University Press, 1998.

Larbaud, Valéry. "James Joyce." *Nouvelle Revue Francaise* (April 1922): pp. 385–405.

———. "A Propos de James Joyce." *Nouvelle Revue Francaise* (January 1925): pp. 1–17.

Lawrence, Karen R., ed. *Transcultural Joyce.* Cambridge: Cambridge University Press, 1998.

Lernout, Geert. *The French Joyce.* Ann Arbor: University of Michigan Press, 1990.

Leavis, F. R. "James Joyce and the Revolution of the Word." *Scrutiny* 2 (1933): 193–201.

Leonard, Garry. *Advertising and Commodity Culture in Joyce.* Gainesville: University Press of Florida, 1998.

Levin, Harry. *James Joyce: A Critical Introduction.* London: Faber and Faber, 1944; rev. and origin. ed., New York: New Directions, 1960.

Levitt, Morton P., ed. *Joyce and the Joyceans.* Syracuse, N.Y.: Syracuse University Press, 2002.

Lewiecki-Wilson, Cynthia. *Writing against the Family: Gender in Lawrence and Joyce.* Carbondale: Southern Illinois University Press, 1994.

Lewis, Wyndham. "An Analysis of the Mind of James Joyce." In his *Time and Western Man.* New York: Harcourt, Brace, 1928.

Lilienfeld, Jane. *Reading Alcoholisms: Theorizing Character and Narrative in Selected Novels of Thomas Hardy, James Joyce, and Virginia Woolf.* New York: St. Martin's, 1999.

Litz, A. Walton. *James Joyce.* Boston: G. K. Hall, 1964.

Lobner, Corinna del Greco. *James Joyce's Italian Connection.* Iowa City: University of Iowa Press, 1989.

———. "James Joyce's Dublin." *Twentieth Century Studies* 4 (November 1970): 6–25.

Lund, Steven. *James Joyce: Letters, Manuscripts, and Photographs at Southern Illinois University.* Troy, N.Y.: Whitston, 1983.

Lyons, J. B. *James Joyce and Medicine.* Dublin: Dolmen Press, 1973.

MacCabe, Colin. *James Joyce and the Revolution of the Word.* New York: Barnes and Noble, 1979; Basingstoke, England: Palgrave Macmillan, 2003.

———, ed. *James Joyce: New Perspectives.* Brighton, England: Harvester Press, 1982.

Mackey, Peter Francis. *Chaos Theory and James Joyce's Everyman.* Gainesville: University Press of Florida, 1999.

McCourt, Frank. *yes I said yes I will Yes: A Celebration of James Joyce, Ulysses and 100 Years of Bloomsday.* New York: Vintage, 2004.

McLuhan, Herbert Marshall. "James Joyce: Trivial and Quadrivial." *Thought* 28 (108): 75–98 (1953).

———. "Joyce, Aquinas, and the Poetic Process." *Renascence* 4 (1951): 3–11.

Magalaner, Marvin. "James Mangan and Joyce's Dedalus Family." *Philosophical Quarterly* 31 (Oct. 1952): 363–371.

———. *Time of Apprenticeship: The Fiction of the Young James Joyce.* New York and Toronto: Abelard-Schumann, 1959.

Magalaner, Marvin, and Richard M. Kain. *Joyce: The Man, the Work, the Reputation.* New York: New York University Press, 1956; London: John Calder, 1957.

Mahaffey, Vicki. *Reauthorizing Joyce.* Cambridge: Cambridge University Press, 1988.

———. *States of Desire: Wilde, Yeats, Joyce and the Irish Experiment.* New York: Oxford University Press, 1998.

Manganiello, Dominic. *Joyce's Politics.* London: Routledge & Kegan Paul, 1980.

Martin, Timothy. *Joyce and Wagner: A Study of Influence.* Cambridge: Cambridge University Press, 1991.

Mayoux, Jean-Jacques. *James Joyce.* Paris: Gallimard, 1965.

Mays, J. C. C. *Poems and Exiles.* London: Penguin, 1992.

McCormack, W. J., and Alistair Stead. *James Joyce & Modern Literature.* London: Routledge & Kegan Paul, 1982.

Mercier, Vivian. *The Irish Comic Tradition.* Oxford: Clarendon Press, 1962.

Melchiori, Giorgio. *The Tightrope Walkers.* London: Routledge & Kegan Paul, 1956.

———, and Franca Ruggieri, eds. *Joyce's Feast of Languages: Seven Essays and Ten Notes.* Rome, Italy; Bulzoni, 1995.

Miller, Nicholas Andrew. *Modernism, Ireland and the Erotics of Memory.* Cambridge: Cambridge University Press, 2002.

Mizener, Arthur. *The Cornell Joyce Collection, given to Cornell University by William G. Mennen.* Ithaca, N.Y.: Cornell University Press, 1958.

Morse, J. Mitchell. *The Sympathetic Alien, James Joyce and Catholicism.* New York: New York University Press, 1959.

Mullin, Katherine. *James Joyce, Sexuality and Social Purity.* Cambridge: Cambridge University Press, 2003.

Murphy, Sean P. *James Joyce and Victims: Reading the Logic of Exclusion.* Madison, N.J.: Fairleigh Dickinson University Press; London: Associated University Press, 2003.

Nadel, Ira B. *Joyce and the Jews: Culture and Texts.* Iowa City: University of Iowa Press, 1989.

Noon, William T. *Joyce and Aquinas.* New Haven, Conn.: Yale University Press, 1957.

O'Brien, Darcy. *The Conscience of James Joyce.* Princeton, N.J.: Princeton University Press, 1968.

Oliphant, Dave, and Thomas Zigal, eds. *Joyce at Texas: Essays on the James Joyce Materials at the Humanities Research Center.* Austin: Humanities Research Center/University of Texas, 1983.

O'Nolan, Brian [Flann O'Brien], ed. *Envoy* (Dublin), James Joyce Special Number. 5.17 (April, 1951).

O'Shea, Michael. *James Joyce and Heraldry.* Albany: State University of New York Press, 1986.

Parker, Alan. *James Joyce: A Bibliography of His Writings, Critical Material, and Miscellanea.* Boston: F. W. Faxon, 1948.

Parrinder, Patrick. *James Joyce.* Cambridge: Cambridge University Press, 1984.

Peake, Charles. *James Joyce: The Citizen and the Artist.* Stanford, Calif.: Stanford University Press, 1977.

Pearle, Cyril. *Dublin in Bloomtime: The City James Joyce Knew.* New York: Viking Press, 1969.

Perelman, Bob. *The Trouble with Genius: Reading Pound, Joyce, Stein and Zukofsky.* Berkeley and Los Angeles: University of California Press, 1994.

Peterson, Richard F. *James Joyce Revisited.* New York: Twayne, 1992.

Peterson, Richard F., Alan M. Cohn, and Edmund L. Epstein, eds. *Work in Progress: Joyce Centenary*

*Essays.* Carbondale: Southern Illinois University Press, 1983.

Piette, Adam. *Remembering and the Sound of Words: Mallarmé, Proust, Joyce, Beckett.* Oxford: Clarendon, 1996.

Platt, Len. *Joyce and the Anglo-Irish: A Study of Joyce and the Literary Revival.* Amsterdam: Rodopi, 1998.

Potts, Willard. *Joyce and the Two Irelands.* Austin: University of Texas Press, 2000.

Rabaté, Jean-Michel. *Joyce upon the Void: The Genesis of Doubt.* New York: St. Martin's Press, 1991.

———. *Maurice Darantiere: les années vingt.* Dijon, France: Centre National des Lettres/Ulysse Fin de Siècle, n.d.

———. "'Thank Maurice': A Note about Maurice Darantiere." In *Joyce Studies Annual* 1991. Edited by Thomas F. Staley, 245–251. Austin: University of Texas Press, 1991.

———. *James Joyce and the Politics of Egoism.* Cambridge: Cambridge University Press, 2001.

Rainsford, Dominic. *Authorship, Ethics and the Reader: Blake, Dickens, Joyce.* London: Macmillan; New York: St. Martin's Press, 1997.

Reizbaum, Marilyn. *James Joyce's Judaic Other.* Stanford, Calif.: Stanford University Press, 1999.

Ress, Laura Jane. *Tender Consciousness: Sentimental Sensibility in the Emerging Artist—Sterne, Yeats, Joyce, and Proust.* New York: Peter Lang, 2002.

Reynolds, Mary T. *Joyce and Dante: The Shaping Imagination.* Princeton, N.J.: Princeton University Press, 1981.

———. "Joyce's Villanelle and D'Annunzio's Sonnet Sequence." *Journal of Modern Fiction* 5 (February 1976): 19–45.

Rice, Thomas Jackson. *James Joyce: A Guide to Research.* New York and London: Garland Publishing, 1982.

———. *Joyce, Chaos, and Complexity.* Urbana: University of Illinois Press, 1997.

Riquelme, John Paul. *Teller and Tale in Joyce's Fiction: Oscillating Perspectives.* Baltimore: Johns Hopkins University Press, 1983.

Roughley, Alan. *James Joyce and Critical Theory: An Introduction.* Ann Arbor: University of Michigan Press, 1991.

———. *Reading Derrida, Reading Joyce.* Gainesville: University Press of Florida, 1999.

Ruggieri, Franca, ed. *Classic Joyce.* Rome, Italy: Bulzoni, 1999.

Ryan, John, ed. *A Bash in the Tunnel: James Joyce by the Irish.* London and Brighton: Clifton Books, 1970.

Scholes, Robert E. *The Cornell Joyce Collection: A Catalogue.* Ithaca, N.Y.: Cornell University Press, 1961.

Scholes, Robert E., and Richard M. Kain. *The Workshop of Daedalus.* Evanston, Ill.: Northwestern University Press, 1965.

Schlossman, Beryl. *Joyce's Catholic Comedy of Language.* Madison: University of Wisconsin Press, 1985.

Schork, R. J. *Greek and Hellenic Culture in Joyce.* Gainesville: University Press of Florida, 1998.

———. *Joyce and Hagiography: Saints Above!* Gainesville: University Press of Florida, 2000.

———. *Latin and Roman Culture in Joyce.* Gainesville: University Press of Florida, 1997.

Schwarze, Tracey Teets. *Joyce and the Victorians.* Gainesville: University Press of Florida, 2002.

Scott, Bonnie Kime. *James Joyce.* Atlantic Highlands, N.J.: Humanities Press International, 1987.

———. *Joyce and Feminism.* Bloomington: Indiana University Press, 1984.

———. *New Alliances in Joyce Studies: "When It's Aped to Foul a Delfian."* Newark: University of Delaware Press; London and Toronto: Associated University Presses, 1988.

Senn, Fritz. *Joyce's Dislocutions: Essays on Reading as Translation.* Edited by John Paul Riquelme. Baltimore: Johns Hopkins University Press, 1984.

Senn, Fritz, and Christine O'Neill, eds. *Inductive Scrutinies: Focus on Joyce.* Baltimore: Johns Hopkins University Press, 1995.

Slocum, John J., and Herbert Cahoon. *A Bibliography of James Joyce, 1882–1941.* New Haven, Conn.: Yale University Press, 1953.

Slote, Sam. *The Silence in Progress of Dante, Mallarmé, and Joyce.* New York: Peter Lang, 1999.

Slote, Sam, and Wim Van Mierlo, eds. *Genitricksling Joyce.* Amsterdam: Rodopi, 1999.

Spielberg, Peter. *James Joyce's Manuscripts and Letters at the University of Buffalo.* Buffalo, N.Y.: University of Buffalo Press, 1962.

Spurr, David. *Joyce and the Scene of Modernity.* Gainesville: University Press of Florida, 2002.

Staley, Thomas, ed. *An Annotated Critical Bibliography of James Joyce.* Hemel Hempstead, England: Harvester Wheatsheaf, 1989.

———. *James Joyce Today: Essays on the Major Works.* Bloomington: Indiana University Press, 1966.

Strong, L. A. G. *The Sacred River. An Approach to Joyce.* London: Methuen, 1949.

Sultan, Stanley. *Eliot, Joyce & Company.* New York and Oxford: Oxford University Press, 1987.

———. *Joyce's Metamorphosis*. Gainesville: University Press of Florida, 2001.

Theall, Donald F. *Beyond the Word: Reconstructing Sense in the Joyce Era of Technology, Culture, and Communication*. Toronto: University of Toronto Press, 1995.

———. *James Joyce's Techno-Poetics*. Toronto: University of Toronto Press, 1997.

*Thom's Official Dublin Directory*. Dublin: Alex. Thom & Co. [annual], 1844–1966.

Thurston, Luke. *James Joyce and the Problem of Psychoanalysis*. Cambridge: Cambridge University Press, 2004.

Thwaites, Tony. *Joycean Temporalities: Debts, Promises, and Countersignatures*. Gainesville: University Press of Florida, 2001.

Tindall, William York. *James Joyce. His Way of Interpreting the Modern World*. New York: Scribner, 1950.

———. *A Reader's Guide to James Joyce*. New York: Octagon Books, 1959.

Tratner, Michael. *Modernism and Mass Politics: Joyce, Woolf, Eliot, Yeats*. Stanford, Calif.: Stanford University Press, 1995.

Troy, William. "Stephen Dedalus and James Joyce." *Nation* 138 (14 February 1934): 187–188.

Tysdahl, B. J. *Joyce and Ibsen: A Study in Literary Influence*. Oslo: Norwegian Universities Press; New York: Humanities Press, 1968.

Valente, Joseph. *James Joyce and the Problem of Justice: Negotiating Sexual and Colonial Difference*. Cambridge: Cambridge University Press, 1995.

———, ed. *Quare Joyce*. Ann Arbor: University of Michigan Press, 1998.

Verene, Donald Phillip, ed. *Vico and Joyce*. Albany: State University of New York Press, 1987.

Verstraete, Ginette. *Fragments of the Feminine Sublime in Friedrich Schlegel and James Joyce*. New York: State University of New York Press, 1998.

Wachtel, Albert. *The Cracked Lookingglass: James Joyce and the Nightmare of History*. Selinsgrove, Pa.: Susquehanna University Press, 1992.

Wales, Katie. *The Language of James Joyce*. New York: St. Martin's Press, 1992.

Wawrzycka, Jolanta W., and Marlena G. Corcoran, eds. *Gender in Joyce*. Gainesville: University Press of Florida, 1997.

Weaver, Jack W. *Joyce's Music and Noise: Theme and Variation in His Writings*. Gainesville: University Press of Florida, 1998.

Weir, David. *James Joyce and the Art of Meditation*. Ann Arbor: University of Michigan Press, 1996.

Wexler, Joyce Piell. *Who Paid for Modernism? Art, Money, and the Fiction of Conrad, Joyce, and Lawrence*. Fayetteville: University of Arkansas Press, 1997.

Whittier-Ferguson, John. *Framing Pieces: Designs of the Gloss in Joyce, Woolf, and Pound*. New York: Oxford University Press, 1996.

Williams, Trevor L. *Reading Joyce Politically*. Gainesville: University Press of Florida, 1997.

Wilson, Edmund. *Axel's Castle*. New York: Charles Scribner's Sons, 1931.

### *Dubliners*

Baker, James R. "Ibsen, Joyce and Living Dead: A Study of *Dubliners*." In *A James Joyce Miscellany*. Third Series. Edited by Marvin Magalaner, 18–32. Carbondale: Southern Illinois University Press, 1962.

Baker, James R., and Thomas F. Staley, eds. *James Joyce's Dubliners: A Critical Handbook*. Belmont, Calif.: Wadsworth, 1969.

Baker, Joseph E. "The Trinity in Joyce's 'Grace.'" *James Joyce Quarterly* 2 (Summer 1965): 299–303.

Barney, Rick, et al. "Analyzing 'Araby' as Story and Discourse: A Summary of the MURGE Project." *James Joyce Quarterly* 18 (Spring 1981): 237–255.

Beck, Warren. *Joyce's Dubliners: Substance, Vision, and Art*. Durham, N.C.: Duke University Press, 1969.

Beckson, Karl. "Moore's *The Untilled Field* and Joyce's *Dubliners*: The Short Story's Intricate Maze." *English Literature in Transition* 15 (1972): 291–304.

Beja, Morris, ed. *James Joyce, Dubliners and A Portrait of the Artist as a Young Man: A Selection of Critical Essays*. London: Macmillan, 1973.

Benstock, Bernard. "Arabesques: Third Position of Concord." *James Joyce Quarterly* 5 (Fall 1967): 30–39.

———. "Joyce's Rheumatics: The Holy Ghost in *Dubliners*." *Southern Review* 14 (January 1978): 1–15.

Blotner, Joseph L. "Ivy Day in the Committee Room." *Perspective* 9 (Summer 1957): 210–217.

Bollettieri Bosinelli, Rosa M., and Harold F. Mosher, Jr., eds. *ReJoycing: New Readings of Dubliners*. Lexington: University Press of Kentucky, 1998.

Bowen, Zack. "Hungarian Politics in 'After the Race.'" *James Joyce Quarterly* 7 (Winter 1969): 138–139.

———. "Joyce's Prophylactic Paralysis: Exposure in *Dubliners*." *James Joyce Quarterly* 19 (Spring 1982): 257–275.

Boyle, Robert. "Swiftian Allegory and Dantean Parody in Joyce's 'Grace.'" *James Joyce Quarterly* 7 (Fall 1969): 11–21.

———. "'Two Gallants' and 'Ivy Day in the Committee Room.'" *James Joyce Quarterly* 1 (Fall 1963): 3–9.

Brandabur, Edward. *A Scrupulous Meanness: A Study of Joyce's Early Work.* Urbana: University of Illinois Press, 1971.

Brodbar, Harold. "A Religious Allegory: Joyce's 'A Little Cloud.'" *Midwest Quarterly* 2 (Spring 1961): 221–227.

Brown, Terence. *Dubliners.* New York: Penguin, 1992.

Carpenter, Richard. "The Witch Maria." *James Joyce Review* 3, nos. 1–2 (February 1959): 3–7.

Carrier, Warren. "*Dubliners:* Joyce's Dantean Vision." *Renascence* 17 (1965): 211–215.

Chestnutt, Margaret. "Joyce's *Dubliners:* History, Ideology, and Social Reality." *Eire-Ireland* 14 (1979): 93–105.

Collins, Ben L. "Joyce's Use of Yeats and of Irish History: A Reading of 'A Mother.'" *Eire-Ireland* 5 (September 1970): 45–66.

Connolly, Thomas E. "Joyce's 'The Sisters': A Pennyworth of Snuff." *College English* 27 (December 1965): 189–195.

———. "Marriage Divination in Joyce's 'Clay.'" *Studies in Short Fiction* 3 (Spring 1966): 293–299.

Corrington, John William. "Isolation as Motif in 'A Painful Case.'" *James Joyce Quarterly* 3 (Spring 1966): 182–191.

Dadufalza, Concepcion D. "The Quest of the Chalice-Bearer in James Joyce's 'Araby.'" *The Diliman Review* 7 (July 1959): 317–325.

Davis, Joseph K. "The City as Radical Order: James Joyce's Dubliners." *Studies in the Literary Imagination* 3 (October 1970): 79–96.

Day, Robert Adams. "Joyce's Gnomons, Lenehan and the Persistence of an Image." *Novel: A Forum on Fiction* 14 (Fall 1980): 5–19.

Ellmann, Richard. "Backgrounds of 'The Dead.'" *Kenyon Review* 20 (Autumn 1958): 507–528.

Engel, Monroe. "*Dubliners* and Exotic Expectation." In *Twentieth-Century Literature in Retrospective.* Edited by Reuben A. Brower, 3–26. Cambridge, Mass.: Harvard University Press, 1971.

Epstein, Edmund L. "Hidden Imagery in James Joyce's 'Two Gallants.'" *James Joyce Quarterly* 7 (Summer 1970): 369–370.

Feshbach, Sidney. "Death in 'An Encounter.'" *James Joyce Quarterly* 2 (Winter 1965): 82–89.

Fischer, Therese. "From Reliable to Unreliable Narrator: Rhetorical Changes in Joyce's 'The Sisters.'" *James Joyce Quarterly* 9 (Fall 1971): 85–92.

Freimarck, John. "'Araby': A Quest for Meaning." *James Joyce Quarterly* 7 (Summer 1970): 366–368.

———. "Missing Pieces in Joyce's *Dubliners.*" *Twentieth-Century Literature* 24 (Winter 1978): 239–257.

French, Marilyn. "Missing Pieces in Joyce's *Dubliners.*" *Twentieth Century Literature* 24 (1978): 443–472.

Freyer, Grattan. "A Reader's Report on *Dubliners.*" *James Joyce Quarterly* 10 (Summer 1973): 445–457.

Friedrich, Gerhard. "Bret Harte as a Source for James Joyce's 'The Dead.'" *Philological Quarterly* 33 (October 1954): 442–444.

———. "The Perspective of Joyce's *Dubliners.*" *College English* 26 (1965): 421–426.

———. "The Gnomic Clue to James Joyce's *Dubliners.*" *Modern Language Notes* 72 (1957): 421–424.

Gabler, Hans Walker, "Preface." In *James Joyce's Dubliners: A Facsimile of Drafts and Manuscripts.* New York: Garland, 1978.

Garrett, Peter, ed. *Twentieth-Century Interpretations of Dubliners: A Collection of Critical Essays.* Englewood Cliffs, N.J.: Prentice Hall, 1968.

Ghiselin, Brewster. "The Unity of Joyce's *Dubliners.*" *Accent* 16 (Spring and Summer 1956): 75–88, 196–213.

Gifford, Don, and Robert J. Seidman. *Notes for Joyce: Dubliners and A Portrait of the Artist.* New York: E. P. Dutton, 1967.

Gillespie, Michael Patrick. "Aesthetic Evolution: The Shaping Forces behind *Dubliners.*" *Language and Style* 19 (Spring 1987): 149–163.

Groden, Michael. Preface to *Dubliners: A Facsimile of Proofs for the 1910 Edition.* New York: Garland, 1977.

Hagopian, John V. "Counterparts." In *Insight II: Analyses of Modern British Literature,* edited by John V. Hagopian, 201–206. Frankfurt: Hirschgraben Vlg., 1964.

Harmon, Maurice. "Little Chandler and Byron's 'First Poem.'" *Threshold* 17 (1962): 59–61.

Hart, Clive, ed. *James Joyce's Dubliners: Critical Essays.* New York: Viking, 1969.

Hart, John Raymond. "Moore on Joyce: The Influence of *The Untilled Field* on *Dubliners.*" *Dublin Magazine* 10 (Summer 1973): 61–76.

Ingersoll, Earl G. *Engendered Trope in Joyce's Dubliners.* Carbondale: Southern Illinois University Press, 1996.

Johnson, James D. "Joyce's 'Araby' and *Romans* VII and VIII." *American Notes & Queries* 13 (September 1974).

Joyce, Stanislaus. "The Background to *Dubliners.*" *The Listener* 51 (March 1954): 526–527.

Kefauer, Elaine M. "Swift's Clothing Philosophy in *A Tale of a Tub* and Joyce's 'Grace.'" *James Joyce Quarterly* 5 (Winter 1968): 162–165.

Kelleher, John V. "Irish History and Mythology in James Joyce's 'The Dead.'" *Review of Politics* 27 (July 1965): 414–433.

Kennedy, Sister Eileen. "Moore's *The Untilled Field* and Joyce's *Dubliners*." *Eire-Ireland* 5 (Autumn 1970): 81–89.

Knox, George. "Michael Furey: Symbol-Name in Joyce's 'The Dead.'" *The Western Humanities Review* 13 (Spring 1959): 221–222.

Lachtman, Howard. "The Magic Lantern Business: James Joyce's Ecclesiastical Satire in *Dubliners*." *James Joyce Quarterly* 7 (Winter 1969): 82–92.

Leonard, Garry M. *Reading* Dubliners *Again: A Lacanian Perspective*. Syracuse, N.Y.: Syracuse University Press, 1993.

Levin, Richard, and Charles Shattuck. "First Flight to Ithaca: A New Reading of Joyce's *Dubliners*." *Accent* 4 (Winter 1944): 75–99.

Loomis, C. C., Jr. "Structure and Sympathy in Joyce's 'The Dead.'" *PMLA* 75 (March 1960): 149–151.

Lyons, J. B. "Animadversions on Paralysis as a Symbol in 'The Sisters.'" *James Joyce Quarterly* 11 (Spring 1974): 257–265.

Lytle, Andrew. "A Reading of Joyce's 'The Dead.'" *Sewanee Review* 77 (Spring 1966): 193–216.

MacDonagh, Donagh. "Joyce and 'The Lass of Aughrim.'" *Hibernia* 31 (June 1967): 21.

———. "Joyce, Nietzsche, and Hauptmann in James Joyce's 'A Painful Case.'" *PMLA* 68 (March 1953): 95–102.

———. "'The Sisters' of James Joyce." *University of Kansas City Review* 18 (Summer 1952): 255–261.

Mandel, Jerome. "Medieval Romance and the Structure of 'Araby.'" *James Joyce Quarterly* 13 (Winter 1976): 234–237.

Moynihan, William T., ed. *Joyce's "The Dead."* Boston: Allyn and Bacon, 1965.

Newman, F. X. "The Land of Ooze: Joyce's 'Grace' and the *Book of Job*." *Studies in Short Fiction* 4 (Fall 1966): 70–79.

Niemeyer, Carl. "'Grace' and Joyce's Method of Parody." *College English* 27 (December 1965): 196–201.

Noon, William T. "Joyce's 'Clay': An Interpretation." *College English* 17 (November 1955): 93–95.

Norris, Margot. "Narration under a Blindfold: Reading Joyce's 'Clay.'" *PMLA* 102 (1987): 206–215.

———. *Suspicious Readings of Joyce's Dubliners*. Philadelphia: University of Pennsylvania Press, 2003.

O Hehir, Brendan P. "Structural Symbol in Joyce's 'The Dead.'" *Twentieth-Century Literature* 3 (April 1957): 3–13.

O'Neill, Michael J. "Joyce's Use of Memory in 'A Mother.'" *Modern Language Notes* 74 (March 1959): 226–230.

Ormsby, Frank, and John Cronin. "'A Very Fine Piece of Writing': 'Ivy Day in the Committee Room.'" *Eire-Ireland* 7 (Summer 1972): 84–94.

Owens, Cóilín. "'A Man with Two Establishments to Keep Up': Joyce's Farrington." *Irish Renaissance Annual* 4 (1983): 128–156.

Pecora, Vincent P. "'The Dead' and the Generosity of the Word." *PMLA* 101 (March 1986): 233–245.

Peters, Margot. "The Phonological Structure of James Joyce's 'Araby.'" *Language and Style* 6 (Spring 1973): 135–144.

Power, Mary. "The Naming of Kathleen Kearney." *Journal of Modern Literature* 5 (September 1976): 532–534.

Roberts, Robert P. "'Araby' and the Palimpsest of Criticism; or, Through a Glass Eye Darkly." *Antioch Review* 26 (Winter 1966/67): 469–489.

Rosenberg, Bruce A. "The Crucifixion in 'The Boarding House.'" *Studies in Short Fiction* 5 (Fall 1967): 44–53.

Ruoff, James. "'A Little Cloud': Joyce's Portrait of a Would-be Artist." *Research Studies of the State College of Washington* 25 (September 1957): 256–271.

San Juan, Epifano, Jr. *James Joyce and the Craft of Fiction: An Interpretation of Dubliners*. Rutherford, N.J.: Fairleigh Dickinson University Press, 1972.

Schmidt, Hugo. "Hauptmann's *Michael Kramer* and Joyce's 'The Dead.'" *PMLA* 80 (March 1965): 141–142.

Scholes, Robert. "A Commentary on 'Clay.'" In *Elements of Fiction*. New York: Oxford University Press, 1968, pp. 66–77.

———. "Further Observations on the Text of *Dubliners*." *Studies in Bibliography* 17 (1964): 107–122.

———. "Grant Richards to James Joyce." *Studies in Bibliography* 16 (1963): 139–160.

———. "Semiotic Approaches to a Fictional Text: Joyce's 'Eveline.'" *James Joyce Quarterly* 16 (Fall 1978/Winter 1979): 65–80.

———. "Some Observations on the Text of *Dubliners*: 'The Dead.'" *Studies in Bibliography* 15 (1962): 191–205.

Schwarz, Daniel R, ed. *James Joyce: The Dead.* Boston: Bedford, 1994.

Senn, Fritz. " 'He Was Too Scrupulous Always': Joyce's 'The Sisters.' " *James Joyce Quarterly* 2 (Winter 1965): 66–72.

———. "Not Too Scrupulous Always." *James Joyce Quarterly* 4 (Spring 1967): 244.

Short, Clarice. "Joyce's 'A Little Cloud.' " *Modern Language Notes* 72 (April 1957): 275–278.

Smith, Thomas F. "Color and Light in 'The Dead.' " *James Joyce Quarterly* 2 (Summer 1965): 304–313.

Sosnoski, James J. "*Story and Discourse* and the Practice of Literary Criticism: 'Araby,' A Test Case." *James Joyce Quarterly* 18 (Spring 1981): 255–267.

Staley, Thomas F. "Moral Responsibility in Joyce's 'Clay.' " *Renascence* 18 (Spring 1966): 124–128.

Steppe, Wolfhard. "The Merry Greeks (with a Farewell to *epicleti*)." *James Joyce Quarterly* 32 (Spring and Summer 1995): 597–617.

Stein, William B. "Joyce's 'Araby': Paradise Lost." *Perspective* 12 (Spring 1962): 215–222.

———. "Joyce's 'The Sisters.' " *Explicator* 21 (September 1962), item 2.

Stern, Frederick C. " 'Parnell Is Dead': 'Ivy Day in the Committee Room.' " *James Joyce Quarterly* 10 (Winter 1973): 228–239.

Torchiana, Donald T. *Backgrounds for Joyce's Dubliners.* Boston: Allen & Unwin, 1986.

———. "The Ending of 'The Dead': I Follow Saint Patrick." *James Joyce Quarterly* 18 (Winter 1981): 123–133.

———. "Joyce's 'After the Race,' The Race of Castlebar, and Dun Laoghaire." *Eire-Ireland* 6 (Fall 1971): 119–128.

———. "Joyce's 'Eveline' and the Blessed Margaret Mary Alacoque." *James Joyce Quarterly* 6 (Fall 1968): 22–28.

———. "Joyce's 'Two Gallants': A Walk through the Ascendancy." *James Joyce Quarterly* 6 (Winter 1968): 115–127.

———. "The Opening of *Dubliners:* A Reconsideration." *Irish University Review* 1 (Spring 1971): 149–160.

Trilling, Lionel. "Characterization in 'The Dead.' " In *The Experience of Literature,* compiled by Lionel Trilling, 228–231. New York: Holt Rinehart, and Winston, 1967.

Vesala-Varttala, Tanja. *Sympathy and Joyce's Dubliners: Ethical Probing of Reading, Narrative, and Textuality.* Tampere, Finland: Tampere University Press, 1999.

Voelker, Joseph C. " 'He Lumped the Emancipates Together': More Analogues for Joyce's Mr. Duffy." *James Joyce Quarterly* 18 (Fall 1980): 23–35.

Waisbren, Burton A., and Florence L. Walzl. "Paresis and the Priest: James Joyce's Symbolic Use of Syphilis in 'The Sisters.' " *Annals of Internal Medicine* 80 (June 1974): 758–762.

Walzl, Florence L. "A Date in Joyce's 'The Sisters.' " *Texas Studies in Literature and Language* 2 (Summer 1962): 183–187.

———. "*Dubliners:* Women in Irish Society." In *Women in Joyce,* edited by Suzette Henke and Elaine Unkeless, 31–56. Urbana: University of Illinois Press, 1982.

———. "Gabriel and Michael: The Conclusion of 'The Dead.' " *James Joyce Quarterly* 4 (Fall 1966): 17–31.

———. "Joyce's 'Clay.' " *Explicator* 20 (February 1962), item 46.

———. "Joyce's 'Clay': Fact and Fiction." *Renascence* 35 (Winter 1983): 119–137.

———. "Joyce's 'The Sisters': A Development." *James Joyce Quarterly* 10 (Summer 1973): 375–421.

———. "The Life Chronology of *Dubliners.*" *James Joyce Quarterly* 14 (Summer 1977): 408–415.

———. "The Liturgy of the Epiphany Seasons and the Epiphanies of Joyce." *PMLA* 80 (September 1965): 436–450.

———. "Patterns of Paralysis in Joyce's *Dubliners.*" *College English* 22 (1961): 519–520.

Ward, David F. "The Race before the Story: James Joyce and the Gordon Bennett Cup Automobile Race." *Eire-Ireland* 2 (Summer 1967): 27–35.

Wright, Charles D. "Melancholy Duffy and Sanguine Sinico: Humors in 'A Painful Case.' " *James Joyce Quarterly* 3 (Spring 1966): 171–180.

### *A Portrait of the Artist as a Young Man*

Anderson, Chester G. "The Sacrificial Butter." *Accent* 12 (1952): 3–13.

Anderson, Chester G., ed. *A Portrait of the Artist as a Young Man: Text, Criticism, and Notes.* New York: Viking, 1968.

Andreach, Robert J. "James Joyce." *Studies in Structure: The Stages of the Spiritual Life of Four Modern Authors,* 40–71. New York: Fordham University Press, 1964.

Atherton, James S. Introduction and notes for *A Portrait of the Artist as a Young Man,* ix–xxii; 239–258. London: Heinemann, 1964.

Beja, Morris, ed. *James Joyce: Dubliners and A Portrait of the Artist as a Young Man: a Casebook.* London: Macmillan, 1973.

Bidwell, Bruce, and Linda Heffer. *The Joycean Way. A Topographic Guide to Dubliners and A Portrait of the Artist as a Young Man.* Baltimore: Johns Hopkins University Press, 1982.

Brown, Homer Obed. *James Joyce's Early Fiction: The Biography of Form.* Cleveland, Ohio: Case Western Reserve University, 1972.

Burke, Kenneth. "Fact, Inference, and Proof in the Analysis of Literary Symbolism." In *Terms for Order,* edited by Stanley Edgar Hyman, 145–172. Bloomington: Indiana University Press, 1964.

Buttigieg, Joseph A. *A Portrait of the Artist in Different Perspective.* Athens: Ohio University Press, 1987.

Connolly, Thomas E., ed. *Joyce's Portrait: Criticism and Critiques.* New York: Appleton-Century-Crofts, 1962.

Deane, Seamus, ed. *A Portrait of the Artist as a Young Man.* New York: Penguin, 1992.

Doherty, James. "Joyce and *Hell Opened to Christians:* The Edition He Used for His Hell Sermons." *Modern Philology* 61 (1963): 110–119.

Epstein, Edmund L. *The Ordeal of Stephen Dedalus: The Conflict of the Generations in James Joyce's A Portrait of the Artist as a Young Man.* Carbondale: Southern Illinois University Press, 1971.

Feehan, Joseph, ed. *Dedalus on Crete: Essays on the Implications of Joyce's Portrait.* Los Angeles: St. Thomas More Guild, Immaculate Heart College 1957.

Fortuna, Diane. "The Labyrinth as Controlling Image in Joyce's *A Portrait of the Artist as a Young Man.*" *Bulletin of the New York Public Library* 76 (1972): 120–180.

Gabler, Hans Walter. "The Seven Lost Years of *A Portrait of the Artist as a Young Man.*" In *Approaches to Joyce's Portrait: Ten Essays,* edited by Thomas F. Staley and Bernard Benstock, 25–60. Pittsburgh, Pa.: University of Pittsburgh Press, 1976.

———. "The Christmas Dinner Scene, Parnell's Death, and the Genesis of *A Portrait of the Artist as a Young Man.*" *James Joyce Quarterly* 13 (1975): 27–38.

Gifford, Don, and Robert J. Seidman. *Joyce Annotated: Notes for Dubliners and A Portrait of the Artist As a Young Man.* 1967. 2d ed., Berkeley, Los Angeles, and London: University of California Press, 1982.

Gottfried, Roy. *Joyce's Comic Portrait.* Gainesville: University Press of Florida, 2000.

Halper, Nathan. *The Early James Joyce.* New York: Columbia University Press, 1973.

Hancock, Leslie. *Word Index to James Joyce's Portrait of the Artist.* Carbondale: Southern Illinois University Press, 1967.

Hardy, John Edward. "Joyce's *Portrait:* The Flight of the Serpent." In his *Man in the Modern Novel,* 67–81. Seattle: University of Washington Press, 1964.

Kenner, Hugh. "The *Portrait* in Perspective," In *James Joyce: Two Decades of Criticism,* edited by Seon Givens, 132–174. 1948; New York: Vanguard Press, 1963.

Kershner, R. B., ed. *A Portrait of the Artist as a Young Man: The Complete, Authoritative Text with Biographical and Historical Contexts, Critical History, and Essays from Five Contemporary Critical Perspectives.* New York: Bedford Books of St. Martin's Press, 1993.

Morris, William E., and Clifford A. Nault, eds. *Portraits of an Artist: A Casebook on James Joyce's A Portrait of the Artist as a Young Man.* New York: Odyssey, 1962.

"Portrait Issue." *James Joyce Quarterly* 4 (Summer 1967): 249–356.

Riquelme, John Paul. "Pretexts for Reading and for Writing: Title, Epigraph, and Journal in *A Portrait of the Artist as a Young Man.*" *James Joyce Quarterly* 18 (Spring 1981): 301–321.

Rossman, Charles. "Stephen Dedalus and the Spiritual-Heroic Refrigeration Apparatus: Art and Life in Joyce's *Portrait.*" In *Forms of Modern British Fiction,* edited by Alan W. Friedman, 101–131. Austin: University of Texas Press, 1975.

Ryf, Robert S. *A New Approach to Joyce: The Portrait of the Artist as a Guide Book.* Berkeley and Los Angeles: University of California Press, 1962.

Scholes, Robert. "Joyce and Epiphany: The Key to the Labyrinth." *Sewanee Review* 72 (Winter 1964): 65–77.

———. "Stephen Dedalus: Poet or Esthete?" *PMLA* 79 (1964): 484–489.

Scholes, Robert, and Richard M. Kain, eds. *The Workshop of Daedalus: James Joyce and the Raw Materials for A Portrait of the Artist as a Young Man.* Evanston, Ill.: Northwestern University Press, 1965.

Schorer, Mark. "Technique as Discovery." *Hudson Review* 1 (1948): 67–87.

Schutte, William M., ed. *Twentieth Century Interpretations of A Portrait of the Artist as a Young Man: A Collection of Critical Essays.* Englewood Cliffs, N J.: Prentice, Spectrum, 1968.

Smith, John Bristow. *Imagery and the Mind of Stephen Dedalus: A Computer-Assisted Study of Joyce's A Portrait of the Artist as a Young Man.* Lewisburg, Pa.: Bucknell University Press, 1980.

Staley, Thomas F., and Bernard Benstock, eds. *Approach to Joyce's Portrait: Ten Essays.* Pittsburgh, Pa.: University of Pittsburgh Press, 1976.

Sucksmith, Harvey P. *James Joyce: A Portrait of the Artist as a Young Man.* London: Arnold, 1973.

Swisher, Claire, ed. *Readings on A Portrait of the Artist as a Young Man.* San Diego, Calif.: Greenhaven, 2000.

Thornton, Weldon. *The Antimodernism of Joyce's Portrait of the Artist as a Young Man.* Syracuse, N.Y.: Syracuse University Press, 1994.

Thrane, James R. "Joyce's Sermon on Hell: Its Source and Its Background." *Modern Philology* 57 (1960): 172–198.

Van Laan, Thomas F. "The Meditative Structure of Joyce's *Portrait.*" *James Joyce Quarterly* 1 (Spring 1964): 3–13.

### *Exiles*

Adams, Robert M. "Light on Joyce's *Exiles?* A New MS, a Curious Analogue, and Some Speculations." *Studies in Bibliography* 17 (1964): 83–105.

———. "The Manuscript of James Joyce's Play." *Yale University Library Gazette* 39 (July 1964): 30–41.

Aitken, D. J. F. "Dramatic Archetypes in Joyce's *Exiles.*" *Modern Fiction Studies* 4 (1958): 26–37, 42–52.

Bandler, Bernard. "Joyce's *Exiles.*" *Hound and Horn* 6 (1933): 266–285.

Bauerle, Ruth. *A Word List to James Joyce's Exiles.* New York and London: Garland, 1981.

———. "Bertha's Role in *Exiles.*" In *Women in Joyce,* edited by Suzette Henke and Elaine Unkeless, 108–131. Urbana: University of Illinois Press, 1982.

Beausang, Michael. "In the Name of the Law: Marital Freedom and Justice in *Exiles.*" In *"Scribble" 1: Genèse des textes,* edited by Claude Jacquet, 39–55. Paris: Minard, 1988.

Benstock, Bernard. "*Exiles:* 'Paradox Lust' and 'Lost Paladays.' " *ELH* 36 (1969): 739–756.

———. "*Exiles,* Ibsen and the Play's Function in the Joyce Canon." *Forum* 11 (1970): 42–52.

Bowen, Zack. "*Exiles:* The Confessional Mode." *James Joyce Quarterly* 29 (Spring 1992): 581–586.

Brandabur, Edward. "Exiles." In his *A Scrupulous Meanness,* 127–158. Urbana: University of Illinois Press, 1971.

Brivic, Sheldon R. "Structure and Meaning in Joyce's *Exiles.*" *James Joyce Quarterly* 6 (1968): 29–52.

Browne, Carole, and Leo Knuth. "James Joyce's *Exiles:* The Ordeal of Richard Rowan." *James Joyce Quarterly* 17 (1979): 7–20.

Clark, Earl John. "James Joyce's *Exiles.*" *James Joyce Quarterly* 6 (1968): 69–78.

Clark, John M. "Writing *Jerusalem* Backwards: William Blake in *Exiles.*" *James Joyce Quarterly* 26 (Winter 1989): 183–197.

Colum, Padraic. Introduction to *Exiles,* 7–11. New York: Viking, 1951.

Cunningham, Frank R. "Joyce's *Exiles:* A Problem of Dramatic Stasis." *Modern Drama* 12 (1970): 399–407.

Dombrowski, Theo Q. "Joyce's *Exiles:* The Problem of Love." *James Joyce Quarterly* 15 (1978): 118–127.

Douglass, James W. "James Joyce's *Exiles:* A Portrait of the Artist." *Renascence* 15 (1963): 82–87.

Evans, Simon. *The Penetration of Exiles. A Wake Newslitter* Monograph no. 9. Colchester, Essex, England: A Wake Newslitter Press, 1984.

Farrell, James T. "*Exiles* and Ibsen." In *James Joyce: Two Decades of Criticism,* edited by Seon Givens, 95–131. New York: Vanguard Press, 1948.

Fergusson, Francis. "A Reading of *Exiles.*" In *Exiles,* by James Joyce, v–xviii. Norfolk, Conn.: New Directions, 1945.

———. "*Exiles* and Ibsen's Work." *Hound and Horn* 5 (1932): 345–53.

Ferris, William R. "Rebellion Matured: Joyce's *Exiles.*" *Eire-Ireland* 4 (1969): 73–81.

Golding, Louis. *James Joyce,* 69–82. London: Thornton Butterworth, 1933.

Grose, Kenneth. *James Joyce,* 36–41. London: Evans, 1975.

Harmon, Maurice. "Richard Rowan, His Own Scapegoat." *James Joyce Quarterly* 3 (1965): 34–40.

Keller, Dean H. "Linati's Translations of *Exiles:* An Unnoticed Appearance." *James Joyce Quarterly* 10 (Spring 1973): 265.

Kenner, Hugh. "Joyce's *Exiles.*" *Hudson Review* 5 (1952): 389–403.

Loss, Archie K. "Presences and Visions in *Exiles, A Portrait of the Artist,* and *Ulysses.*" *James Joyce Quarterly* 13 (Spring 1976): 148–162.

Loughman, Celeste. "Bertha, Victress, in Joyce's *Exiles.*" *James Joyce Quarterly* 19 (Fall 1981): 69–72.

Macleod, Vivienne Koch. "The Influence of Ibsen on Joyce." *PMLA* 60 (1945): 879–898.

———. "The Influence of Ibsen on Joyce: Addendum." *PMLA* 62 (1947): 573–580.

MacNicholas, John. *James Joyce's Exiles: A Textual Companion*. New York and London: Garland, 1979.

———. "The Stage History of *Exiles*." *James Joyce Quarterly* 19 (Fall 1981): 9–26.

———. "Joyce's *Exiles*: The Argument for Doubt." *James Joyce Quarterly* 11 (Fall 1973): 33–40.

Maher, R. A. "James Joyce's *Exiles*: The Comedy of Discontinuity." *James Joyce Quarterly* 9 (1972): 461–474.

Martin, Timothy P. "Wagner's *Tannhauser* in *Exiles*: A Further Source." *James Joyce Quarterly* 19 (Fall 1981): 73–76.

Metzger, Deena P. "Variations on a Theme: A Study of *Exiles* by James Joyce and *The Great God Brown* by Eugene O'Neill." *Modern Drama* 8 (1965): 174–184.

Moseley, Virginia. "Joyce's *Exiles* and the Prodigal Son." *Modern Drama* 1 (1959): 218–227.

———. "Aye to Aye." In her *Joyce and the Bible*, 45–56. Dekalb: Northern Illinois University Press, 1967.

Pearce, Sandra Manoogian. "'Like a stone': Joyce's Eucharistic Imagery in *Exiles*." *James Joyce Quarterly* 29 (Spring 1992): 587–591.

Pound, Ezra. "Mr. James Joyce and the Modern Stage." *Drama* 6 (1916): 122–132.

Reynolds, Mary T. "Dante in Joyce's *Exiles*." *James Joyce Quarterly* 18 (Fall 1980): 35–44.

Rodker, John, Israel Solon, Samuel A. Tannebaum, and Jane Heap. "*Exiles*: A Discussion of James Joyce's Plays." *Little Review* 5 (1919): 20–27.

Schaffer, Brian. "Kindred by Choice: Joyce's *Exiles* and Goethe's *Elective Affinities*." *James Joyce Quarterly* 26 (Winter 1989): 199–212.

Schwartzman, Myron. "A Successful *Exiles* in New York." *James Joyce Quarterly* 14 (Summer 1977): 361–362.

Simon, Elliott M. "James Joyce's *Exiles* and the Tradition of the Edwardian Problem Play." *Modern Drama* 20 (March 1977): 21–35.

Tindall, William York. *A Reader's Guide to James Joyce*, 104–122. New York: Noonday Press, 1959.

Tysdahl, Bjorn. "Joyce's *Exiles* and Ibsen." *Orbis Litterarum* 19 (1964): 176–186.

Voelker, Joseph. "The Beastly Incertitudes: Doubt, Difficulty, and Discomfiture in James Joyce's *Exiles*." *Journal of Modern Literature* 14 (1988): 499–516.

Watt, Stephen. *Joyce, O'Casey and the Irish Popular Theatre*. Syracuse, N.Y.: Syracuse University Press, 1991.

Weber, Roland von. "On and about Joyce's *Exiles*." In *James Joyce Yearbook*, edited by Maria Jolas, 47–67. Paris: Transition Press, 1949.

Williams, Raymond. "The *Exiles* of James Joyce." *Politics and Letters* 1 (1948): 13–21.

### *Ulysses*

Adams, Robert Martin. *Surface and Symbol: The Consistency of James Joyce's Ulysses*. New York: Oxford University Press, 1962.

Arnold, Bruce. *The Scandal of Ulysses*. London: Sinclair-Stevenson, 1991.

Barrow, Craig Wallace. *Montage in James Joyce's Ulysses*. Madrid and Potomac, Md.: Studia Humanitatis, 1980.

Beeretz, Sylvia. *'Tell Us in Plain Words': Narrative Strategies in James Joyce's Ulysses*. Frankfurt, Germany: Peter Lang, 1998.

Bell, Robert H. *Jocoserious Joyce: The Fate of Folly in Ulysses*. Gainesville: University Press of Florida, 1996.

Benstock, Bernard. *Narrative Con/Texts in Ulysses*. Urbana and Chicago: University of Illinois Press, 1991.

Blackmur, R. P. "The Jew in Search of a Son: Joyce's *Ulysses*" (1948). In his *Eleven Essays in the European Novel*, 27–47. New York: Harcourt, 1964.

Blamires, Harry. *The Bloomsday Book: A Guide through Joyce's Ulysses*. London: Methuen, 1966.

———. *The New Bloomsday Book*. Rev. ed. London: Routledge, 1988.

Bonnerot, Louis, ed. *Ulysses: Cinquante Ans Apres*. Paris: M. Didier, 1974.

Bowen, Zack. *Musical Allusions in the Works of James Joyce: Early Poetry through Ulysses*. Albany: State University of New York Press, 1974.

———. *Ulysses as a Comic Novel*. Syracuse, N.Y.: Syracuse University Press, 1989.

Budgen, Frank. *James Joyce and the Making of Ulysses*. Bloomington: Indiana University Press, 1960.

Card, James Van Dyck. *An Anatomy of "Penelope."* Rutherford, N.J.: Fairleigh Dickinson University Press, 1984; London and Toronto: Associated University Presses, 1984.

Caspel, Paul P. J. van. *Bloomers on the Liffey: Eisegetical Readings of James Joyce's Ulysses, Part II*. Groningen, Netherlands: Veenstra Visser, 1980; revised and enlarged edition, Baltimore: Johns Hopkins University Press, 1986.

de Almeida, Hermione. *Byron and Joyce through Homer: Don Juan and Ulysses*. New York: Columbia University Press, 1981.

Delaney, Frank. *James Joyce's Odyssey: A Guide to the Dublin of Ulysses.* London: Hodder and Stoughton, 1981; New York: Holt, Rinehart and Winston, 1981.

Dent, R. W. *Colloquial Language in Ulysses: A Reference Tool.* Newark: University of Delaware Press; London: Associated University Press, 1994.

Devlin, Kimberly J. *James Joyce's Fraudstuff.* Gainesville: University Press of Florida, 2002.

Devlin, Kimberly J., and Marilyn Reizbaum, eds. *Ulysses—En-Gendered Perspectives: Eighteen New Essays on the Episodes.* Columbia: University of South Carolina Press, 1999.

Driver, Clive, ed. *Ulysses: A Facsimile of the Manuscript,* 3 vols. New York: Octagon, 1975.

Duffy, Enda. *The Subaltern Ulysses.* Minneapolis: University of Minnesota Press, 1994.

Eliot, T. S. "*Ulysses,* Order, and Myth." *Dial* 75 (November 1923): 480–483.

Ellman, Richard. *Ulysses on the Liffey.* London: Faber and Faber, 1972; New York: Oxford University Press, 1972.

Empson, William. "The Theme of *Ulysses.*" *Kenyon Review* 18 (1956): 26–52.

Field, Saul, and Morton P. Levitt. *Bloomsday: An Interpretation of James Joyce's Ulysses.* Greenwich, Conn.: New York Graphic Society, 1972.

French, Marilyn. *The Book as World: James Joyce's Ulysses.* Cambridge, Mass.: Harvard University Press, 1976.

Friedman, Melvin J. "James Joyce: The Full Development of the Method." In his *Stream of Consciousness: A Study of Literary Method,* 210–243. New Haven, Conn.: Yale University Press, 1955.

Fuller, David. *James Joyce's Ulysses.* New York: St. Martin's Press, 1992.

Gabler, Hans Walter. "The Synchrony and Diachrony of Texts: Practice and Theory of the Critical Edition of James Joyce's *Ulysses.*" In *Text: Transactions of the Society of Textual Scholarship,* 305–326. New York: AMS Press, 1981.

Gifford, Don, with Robert J. Seidman. *Notes for Joyce: An Annotation of James Joyce's Ulysses.* New York: Dutton, 1974.

———. *Ulysses Annotated.* 2d ed. (of *Notes for Joyce*). Berkeley: University of California Press, 1988.

Gilbert, Stuart. *James Joyce's "Ulysses": A Study.* London: Faber and Faber, 1930; 2d ed. New York: Knopf, 1952.

Gillespie, Michael Patrick. "Why Does One Re-Read *Ulysses?*" In *Assessing the 1984 Ulysses,* edited by C. George Sandulescu and Clive Hart, 43–57. Gerrards Cross, Bucks, England: Colin Smythe; Totowa, N.J.: Barnes & Noble Books, 1986.

——— and A. Nicholas Fargnoli, eds. *Ulysses in Critical Perspective.* Gainesville: University Press of Florida, 2006.

Goldberg, S. L. *The Classical Temper: A Study of James Joyce's Ulysses.* London: Chatto and Windus, 1961.

Gose, Elliott B., Jr. *The Transformation Process in Joyce's Ulysses.* Toronto: University of Toronto Press, 1980.

Gottfried, Roy K. *The Art of Joyce's Syntax in Ulysses.* Athens: University of Georgia Press, 1980.

———. Joyce's *Iritis and the Irritated Text: The Dis-Lexic Ulysses.* Gainesville: University Press of Florida, 1995.

Groden, Michael. *Ulysses in Progress.* Princeton, N.J.: Princeton University Press, 1977.

Hanley, Miles. *Word Index to James Joyce's Ulysses.* New York: Random House, 1934. Reprint, Madison: University of Wisconsin Press, 1962.

Harkness, Marguerite. *The Aesthetics of Dedalus and Bloom.* Lewisburg: Bucknell University Press; London and Toronto: Associated University Presses, 1984.

Hart, Clive. *James Joyce's Ulysses.* Sydney, Australia: Sydney University Press, 1968.

Hart, Clive, and A. M. Leo Knuth. *A Topographical Guide to James Joyce's Ulysses.* 2 vols. Colchester, England: *Wake Newslitter* Press, 1975. For an expanded version, see Gunn, Ian, and Clive Hart. *James Joyce's Dublin: A Topographical Guide to the Dublin of* Ulysses. London: Thames and Hudson, 2004.

Hart, Clive, and David Hayman, eds. *James Joyce's Ulysses: Critical Essays.* Berkeley and Los Angeles: University of California Press, 1974.

Hayman, David. "Forms of Folly in Joyce: A Study of Clowning in *Ulysses.*" *ELH* 34 (1967): 260–283.

———. *Ulysses: The Mechanics of Meaning.* Englewood Cliffs, N.J.: Prentice Hall, 1970; rev. and expanded edition, Madison: University of Wisconsin Press, 1982.

Henke, Suzette. *Joyce's Moraculous Sindbook: A Study of Ulysses.* Columbus: Ohio State University Press, 1978.

Herring, Phillip F. "The Bedsteadfastness of Molly Bloom." *Modern Fiction Studies* 15 (1969): 49–61.

———. *Joyce's Notes and Early Drafts for Ulysses: Selections from the Buffalo Collections.* Charlottesville: University Press of Virginia, 1977.

———. *Joyce's Ulysses Notesheets in the British Museum.* Charlottesville: University Press of Virginia, 1972.

———. "Toward an Historical Molly Bloom." *ELH* 45 (1978): 501–521.

Houston, John Porter. *Joyce and Prose: An Exploration of the Language of Ulysses*. Lewisburg, Pa.: Bucknell University Press, 1989.

Hunter, Jefferson. *How to Read Ulysses, and Why*. New York: Peter Lang, 2002.

Hyman, Louis. "Some Aspects of the Jewish Background of *Ulysses*." In *The Jews of Ireland: From the Earliest Times to the Year 1910*, 167–192. Shannon: Irish University Press, 1972.

Janusko, Robert. *The Sources and Structures of James Joyce's "Oxen."* Ann Arbor, Mich.: UMI Research Press, 1983.

Jung, Carl Gustav. "*Ulysses*: A Monologue." Translated by W. Stanley Dell. Reprinted in *The Spirit in Man, Art, and Literature*. Vol. 15 of Bollingen Series 20: *The Collected Works of Jung*, edited by Herbert Read, Michael Fordham and Gerhard Adler, 109–134. New York: Pantheon Books, 1966.

Kain, Richard M. *Fabulous Voyager: James Joyce's Ulysses*. Chicago: University of Chicago Press, 1947; New York: Viking, 1959.

Kenner, Hugh. *Ulysses*. London: Allen & Unwin, 1980; rev. ed., Baltimore and London: Johns Hopkins University Press, 1987.

Kiberd, Declan, ed. *Ulysses*. New York: Penguin, 1992.

Killeen, Terence. *Ulysses Unbound: A Reader's Companion to James Joyce's Ulysses*. Bray, Ireland: Wordwell, 2004.

Kim, Chong-Keon. *James Joyce: Ulysses and Literary Modernism*. Seoul, Korea: Tamgu Dang, 1985.

Kimball, Jean. *Odyssey of the Psyche: Jungian Patterns in Joyce's Ulysses*. Carbondale: Southern Illinois University Press, 1997.

Knowles, Sebastian D. G. *The Dublin Helix: The Life of Language in Joyce's Ulysses*. Gainesville: University Press of Florida, 2001.

Larbaud, Valéry. "James Joyce." *Nouvelle Revue Française* 1 (April 1922): 385–409.

Lawrence, Karen. *The Odyssey of Style in Ulysses*. Princeton, N.J.: Princeton University Press, 1981.

Levine, Jennifer Schiffer. "Originality and Repetition in *Finnegans Wake* and *Ulysses*." *PMLA* 94 (1979): 106–120.

Litz, A. Walton. *The Art of James Joyce: Method and Design in Ulysses and Finnegans Wake*. London: Oxford University Press, 1961.

———. "The Genre of *Ulysses*." In *The Theory of the Novel*, edited by John Halperin, 109–120. New York: Oxford University Press, 1974.

Macaré, Helen H. *A Ulysses Phrasebook*. Portola Valley, Calif.: Woodside Priority, 1981.

McCarthy, Patrick A. *Ulysses: Portals of Discovery*. Boston: Twayne, 1990.

McGee, Patrick. *Paperspace: Style as Ideology in Joyce's Ulysses*. Lincoln and London: University of Nebraska Press, 1988.

McMichael, James. *Ulysses and Justice*. Princeton, N.J.: Princeton University Press, 1991.

Maddox, James H., Jr. *Joyce's Ulysses and the Assault upon Character*. New Brunswick, N.J.: Rutgers University Press, 1978.

Madtes, Richard E. *The "Ithaca" Chapter of Joyce's Ulysses*. Ann Arbor, Mich.: UMI Research Press, 1983.

Martin, Augustine. "Novelist and City: The Technical Challenge." In *The Irish Writer and the City*, edited by Maurice Harmon, 37–51. Gerrards Cross, Buckinghamshire: Smythe, 1984; Totowa, N.J.: Barnes and Noble.

Mason, Michael. *James Joyce: Ulysses*. London: Arnold, 1972.

———. "Why Is Leopold Bloom a Cuckold." *ELH* 44 (Spring 1977): 171–188.

Melchiori, Giorgio, *Joyce in Rome: The Genesis of Ulysses*. Rome: Bulzoni, 1984.

Newman, Robert A., and Weldon Thornton, eds. *Joyce's Ulysses: The Larger Perspective*. Newark: University of Delaware Press; London and Toronto: Associated University Presses, 1987.

Norris, Margot, ed. *A Companion to James Joyce's Ulysses*. Boston: Bedford, 1998.

O'Neill, Christine. *Too Fine a Point: A Stylistic Analysis of the Eumaeus Episode in James Joyce's Ulysses*. Trier, Germany: Wissenschaftlicher, 1996.

Osteen, Mark. *The Economy of Ulysses: Making Both Ends Meet*. Syracuse, N.Y.: Syracuse University Press, 1995.

Owen, R. W. *James Joyce and the Beginnings of Ulysses*. Ann Arbor, Mich.: UMI Research Press, 1983.

Pearce, Richard, ed. *Molly Blooms: A Polylogue on "Penelope" and Cultural Studies*. Madison: University of Wisconsin Press, 1994.

Pound, Ezra. "James Joyce et Pécuchet" (1992), translated by Fred Bornhauser, *Shenandoah* 3, no. 3 (1952): 9–20.

Power, Mary. "The Discovery of Ruby." *James Joyce Quarterly* 18 (Winter 1981): 115–121.

Praz, Mario. "James Joyce." In *James Joyce, Thomas Stearns Eliot: Due Maestri dei moderni*, 3–82. Turin, Italy: Edizioni Rai Radiotelevisione Italiana, 1967.

Raleigh, John Henry. *The Chronicle of Leopold and Molly Bloom: Ulysses as Narrative.* Berkeley and Los Angeles: University of California Press, 1977.

Rickard, John S. *Joyce's Book of Memory: The Mnemotechnic of Ulysses.* Durham, N.C.: Duke University Press, 1998.

Rossman, Charles, ed. *Studies in the Novel: A Special Issue on Editing Ulysses* 22 (Summer 1990): 113–269.

Sandulescu, C. George. *The Joycean Monologue: A Study of Character and Monologue in Joyce's Ulysses against the Background of Literary Tradition.* Cochester, England: *Wake Newslitter* Press, 1979.

Sandulescu, C. George, and Clive Hart, eds. *Assessing the 1984 Ulysses.* Gerrards Cross, Buckinghamshire: Colin Smythe; Totowa, N.J.: Barnes and Noble, 1986.

Schechner, Mark. *Joyce in Nighttown: A Psychoanalytic Inquiry into Ulysses.* Berkeley and Los Angeles: University of California Press, 1974.

Schutte, William. *Index of Recurrent Elements in James Joyce's Ulysses.* Carbondale: Southern Illinois University Press, 1982.

———. *Joyce and Shakespeare: A Study in the Meaning of Ulysses.* New Haven, Conn.: Yale University Press, 1957.

Schwaber, Paul. *The Cast of Characters: A Reading of Ulysses.* New Haven, Conn.: Yale University Press, 1999.

Seidel, Michael. *Epic Geography: James Joyce's Ulysses.* Princeton, N.J.: Princeton University Press, 1976.

Sherry, Vincent. *James Joyce/Ulysses.* Cambridge: Cambridge University Press, 1994.

Sicari, Stephen. *Joyce's Modernist Allegory: Ulysses and the History of the Novel.* Columbia: University of South Carolina Press, 2001.

Smith, Paul Jordan. *A Key to the "Ulysses" of James Joyce.* Chicago: Covici, 1927. Reprint, San Francisco: City Lights, 1970.

Staley, Thomas F., ed. *Ulysses: Fifty Years.* Bloomington: Indiana University Press, 1974.

Staley, Thomas F., and Bernard Benstock, eds. *Approaches to Ulysses: Ten Essays.* Pittsburgh, Pa.: University of Pittsburgh Press, 1970.

Stanford, William B. *The Ulysses Theme: A Study in the Adaptability of a Traditional Hero.* 1954; 2d ed. Oxford: Blackwell, 1963; New York: Barnes and Noble, 1964; 2d ed. rev., New York: Barnes and Noble, 1968.

Steinberg, Erwin R. *The Stream of Consciousness and Beyond in Ulysses.* Pittsburgh, Pa.: University of Pittsburgh Press, 1973.

Steppe, Wolfhard, with Hans Walter Gabler. *A Handlist to James Joyce's Ulysses.* New York and London: Garland Publishing, 1985.

Sultan, Stanley. *The Argument of Ulysses.* Columbus: Ohio State University Press, 1964.

———. *Ulysses, The Waste Land, and Modernism: A Jubilee Study.* Port Washington, N.Y.: Kennikat, 1977.

Thomas, Brook. *James Joyce's Ulysses: A Book of Many Happy Returns.* Baton Rouge: Louisiana State University Press, 1982.

Thompson, Lawrance R. *A Comic Principle in Sterne, Meredith, Joyce.* Oslo, Norway: University of Oslo British Institute, 1954; Norwood, Pa.: Norwood Editions, 1978.

Thornton, Weldon. *Allusions in Ulysses: An Annotated List.* Chapel Hill: University of North Carolina Press, 1968.

———. *Voices and Values in Joyce's Ulysses.* Gainesville: University Press of Florida, 2000.

Tucker, Lindsey. *Stephen and Bloom at Life's Feast: Alimentary Symbolism and the Creative Process in James Joyce's Ulysses.* Columbus: Ohio State University Press, 1984.

Ungar, Andras. *Joyce's Ulysses as National Epic: Epic Mimesis and the Political History of the Nation State.* Gainesville: University Press of Florida, 2002.

Van Caspel, Paul P. J. *Bloomers on the Liffey: Eisegetical Readings of James Joyce's Ulysses.* Baltimore: Johns Hopkins University Press, 1986.

Vanderham, Paul. *James Joyce and Censorship: The Trials of Ulysses.* New York: New York University Press, 1998.

Wicht, Wolfgang. *Utopianism in James Joyce's Ulysses.* Heidelberg, Germany: Carl Winter Universitätsverlag, 2000.

Wilson, Edmund. "James Joyce." In *Axel's Castle: A Study of the Imaginative Literature of 1870–1930,* 191–236. New York: Scribner, 1931.

Wright, David G. *Ironies in Ulysses.* Savage, Md.: Barnes & Noble Books, 1991.

### *Finnegans Wake*

Atherton, James S. *The Book at the Wake: A Study of Literary Allusions in James Joyce's Finnegans Wake.* New York: Viking Press, 1960.

Attridge, Derek. "Finnegans Awake: The Dream of Interpretation," *James Joyce Quarterly* 27 (Fall 1989): 11–29.

Beckett, Samuel, et al. *Our Exagmination round His Factification for Incamination of Work in Progress.*

Paris: Shakespeare and Co., 1929; 2d ed. New York: New Directions, 1972.

Begnal, Michael H., and Grace Eckley. *Narrator and Character in Finnegans Wake.* Lewisburg, Pa.: Bucknell University Press, 1975.

Begnal, Michael H., and Fritz Senn, eds. *A Conceptual Guide to Finnegans Wake.* University Park: Pennsylvania State University Press, 1974.

Benstock, Bernard. *Joyce-Again's Wake: An Analysis of Finnegans Wake.* Seattle: University of Washington Press, 1965.

Bishop, John. *Joyce's Book of the Dark: Finnegans Wake.* Madison: University of Wisconsin Press, 1986.

Boldereff, Frances Motz. *Hermes to His Son Thoth: Being Joyce's Use of Giordano Bruno in Finnegans Wake.* Woodward, Pa.: Classic Nonfiction Library, 1968.

———. *Reading Finnegans Wake.* Woodward, Pa.: Classic Nonfiction Library, 1959.

Boldrini, Lucia. *Joyce, Dante and the Poetics of Literary Relations: Language and Meaning in Finnegans Wake.* Cambridge: Cambridge University Press, 2001.

Bonheim, Helmut. *Joyce's Benefictions.* Berkeley: University of California Press, 1964.

———. *A Lexicon of the German in Finnegans Wake.* Berkeley: University of California Press, 1967.

Boyle, Robert, SJ. "*Finnegans Wake,* Page 185: An Explication." *James Joyce Quarterly* 4 (1966): 3–16.

———. *James Joyce's Pauline Vision: A Catholic Exposition.* Carbondale and Edwardsville: Southern Illinois University Press, 1978.

———. "Miracle in Black Ink: A Glance at Joyce's Use of His Eucharistic Image." *James Joyce Quarterly* 10 (1972): 47–60.

———. "Worshipper of the Word: James Joyce and the Trinity." In *A Starchamber Quiry: A James Joyce Centennial Volume, 1882–1982.* New York and London: Methuen, 1982.

Boyle, Robert H. " 'Flies Do Your Float': Fishing in Finnegans Wake." *The American Fly Fisher: Journal of the American Museum of Fly Fishing* 30 (Spring 2004): 13–29.

Brivic, Sheldon. *Joyce's Waking Women: An Introduction to Finnegans Wake.* Madison: University of Wisconsin Press, 1995.

Broes, Arthur T. "More People at the Wake (Contd.)." *A Wake Newslitter* 4 (1967): 25–30.

Brown, Norman O. *Life against Death: The Psychoanalytic Meaning of History.* Middletown, Conn.: Wesleyan University Press, 1959.

Burgess, Anthony. *Here Comes Everybody.* London: Faber and Faber, 1965. (Published in the United States in 1968 under the title *Re Joyce.*) Norton, 1968.

———. *A Shorter Finnegans Wake.* London: Faber and Faber, 1966.

———. *Joysprick.* London: Andre Deutsch, 1973.

Burrell, Harry. *Narrative Design in Finnegans Wake: The Wake Lock Picked.* Gainesville: University Press of Florida, 1996.

Campbell, Joseph, and Henry Morton Robinson. *A Skeleton Key to Finnegans Wake.* 1944. Reprint, New York: Viking Press, 1966.

Cheng, Vincent John. *Shakespeare and Joyce: A Study of Finnegans Wake.* University Park and London: Pennsylvania State University Press, 1984.

Christiani, Dounia Bunis. *Scandinavian Elements of Finnegans Wake.* Evanston, Ill.: Northwestern University Press, 1965.

Cixous, Hélène. *The Exile of James Joyce.* Translated by Sally A. J. Purcell. New York: David Lewis, 1972.

Connolly, Thomas E., ed. *James Joyce's Scribbledehobble: The Ur-Workbook for Finnegans Wake.* Evanston, Ill.: Northwestern University Press, 1961.

Dalton, Jack P., and Clive Hart, eds. *Twelve and a Tilly: Essays on the Occasion of the 25th Anniversary of Finnegans Wake.* London: Faber and Faber, 1966.

Deane, Seamus, ed. *Finnegans Wake.* New York: Penguin, 1992.

Deane, Vincent, ed. *The Finnegans Wake Notebooks at Buffalo, VI.B.1.* Turnhout, Belgium: Brepols, 2003.

———. *The Finnegans Wake Notebooks at Buffalo, VI.B.16.* Turnhout, Belgium: Brepols, 2003.

———. *The Finnegans Wake Notebooks at Buffalo, VI.B.33.* Turnhout, Belgium: Brepols, 2003.

Devlin, Kimberly J. *Wandering and Return in Finnegans Wake.* Princeton, N.J.: Princeton University Press, 1990.

DiBernard, Barbara. *Alchemy and Finnegans Wake.* Albany: State University of New York Press, 1980.

Eckley, Grace. *Children's Lore in Finnegans Wake.* Syracuse, N.Y.: Syracuse University Press, 1985.

Epstein, E. L. "Chance, Doubt, Coincidence and the Prankquean's Riddle." *A Wake Newslitter* 6 (February 1969): 3–7.

———. "Interpreting *Finnegans Wake:* A Half-Way House." *James Joyce Quarterly* 3 (Summer 1966): 252–271.

Fargnoli, A. Nicholas. "A-taufing in the *Wake:* Joyce's Baptismal Motif." *James Joyce Quarterly* 20 (Spring 1983): 293–305.

Glasheen, Adaline. *A Census of Finnegans Wake.* London: Faber and Faber, 1956.

———. *A Second Census of Finnegans Wake*. Evanston, Ill.: Northwestern University Press, 1963.

———. *A Third Census of Finnegans Wake: An Index of the Characters and Their Roles*. Berkeley: University of California Press, 1977.

Gordon, John. *Finnegans Wake: A Plot Summary*. Syracuse, N.Y.: Syracuse University Press, 1986.

Hart, Clive. *A Concordance to Finnegans Wake*. Minneapolis: University of Minnesota Press, 1963.

———. *Structure and Motif in Finnegans Wake*. London: Faber and Faber, 1962.

Hart, Clive, and Fritz Senn, eds. *A Wake Digest*. Sydney: Sydney University Press, 1968.

Hayman, David, ed. *A First-Draft Version of Finnegans Wake*. Austin: University of Texas Press, 1963.

———. *The "Wake" in Transit*. Ithaca and London: Cornell University Press, 1990.

Koch, Ronald J. "Giordano Bruno and *Finnegans Wake*." *James Joyce Quarterly* 9 (1971): 225–249.

Litz, A. Walton. *The Art of James Joyce: Method and Design in Ulysses and Finnegans Wake*. New York: Oxford University Press, 1961.

McCarthy, Patrick A. *The Riddles of Finnegans Wake*. Rutherford, Madison, and Teaneck, N.J.: Fairleigh Dickinson University Press; London and Toronto: Associated University Presses, 1980.

———, ed. *Critical Essays on James Joyce's Finnegans Wake*. New York: G. K. Hall & Co., 1992.

McGee, Patrick. *Joyce beyond Marx: History and Desire in Ulysses and Finnegans Wake*. Gainesville: University Press of Florida, 2001.

McHugh, Roland. *The Sigla of Finnegans Wake*. London: Edward Arnold, 1976.

———. *Annotations to Finnegans Wake*. Rev. ed. Baltimore and London: Johns Hopkins University Press, 1991.

———. *The Finnegans Wake Experience*. Dublin: Irish Academic Press, 1981.

McLuhan, Eric. *The Role of Thunder in Finnegans Wake*. Toronto: University of Toronto Press, 1997.

Mink, Louis O. *A Finnegans Wake Gazetteer*. Bloomington and London: Indiana University Press, 1978.

Norris, Margot. *The Decentered Universe of "Finnegans Wake": A Structuralist Analysis*. Baltimore: Johns Hopkins University Press, 1974.

O Hehir, Brendan. *A Gaelic Lexicon for Finnegans Wake*. Berkeley: University of California Press, 1967.

———, and John Dillon. *A Classical Lexicon for Finnegans Wake*. Berkeley: University of California Press, 1977.

Rose, Danis. *The Textual Diaries of James Joyce* Edinburgh: Split Pea Press, 1995.

Rose, Danis, and John O'Hanlon. *Understanding Finnegans Wake: A Guide to the Narrative of James Joyce's Masterpiece*. New York: Garland Publishing, 1982.

Sandulescu, C. George. *The Language of the Devil: Texture and Archetype in Finnegans Wake*. Gerrards Cross, England: Colin Smythe; Chester Springs, Pa.: Dufour Editions, 1987.

Solomon, Margaret C. *Eternal Geomater: The Sexual Universe of Finnegans Wake*. Carbondale and Edwardsville: Southern Illinois University Press, 1969.

———. "Sham Rocks: Shem's Answer to the First Riddle of the Universe." *A Wake Newslitter* 7 (1970): 67–72.

Tindall, William York. *A Reader's Guide to Finnegans Wake*. New York: Farrar, Straus & Giroux, 1969.

Troy, Mark L. *Mummeries of Resurrection: The Cycle of Osiris in Finnegans Wake*. Uppsala, Sweden: University of Uppsala, 1976.

Verene, Donald Phillip. *Knowledge of Things Human and Divine: Vico's New Science and Finnegans Wake*. New Haven, Conn.: Yale University Press, 2003.

Wilson, Edmund. "The Dream of H. C. Earwicker." In *The Wound and the Bow*. Boston: Houghton Mifflin, 1941.

# CHRONOLOGY

**1882**
Charles Stewart Parnell released from prison
Phoenix Park murders in Dublin
Gabriele D'Annunzio publishes *Canto Novo*
Henrik Ibsen publishes *An Enemy of the People*
Virginia Woolf born
Anthony Trollope dies
F. Anstey publishes *Vice-Versa*
Ralph Waldo Emerson dies
James Joyce born (2 February)

**1883**
Friedrich Nietzsche publishes *Also Sprach Zarathustra*
Karl Marx dies
Ivan Turgenev dies

**1884**
Mark Twain publishes *Huckleberry Finn*
Sean O'Casey born
First volume of *Oxford English Dictionary* published
"Love's Old Sweet Song" composed by James Lyman Molloy, lyrics by C. Clifton Bingham
Ibsen's *The Wild Duck*

**1885**
Ezra Pound born
George Meredith publishes *Diana of the Crossways*
William Dean Howells publishes *The Rise of Silas Lapham*
D. H. Lawrence born

**1886**
British prime minister William Ewart Gladstone introduces Irish Home Rule Bill; bill is defeated
Henry James publishes *The Princess Casamassima*
Paul O. Gottlieb Nipkov develops scanning device (first step in development of television)

**1887**
L. L. Zemenhof invents Esperanto

**1888**
Kaiser Wilhelm II (last German monarch) succeeds to throne
Matthew Arnold dies
T. S. Eliot born
Washington Monument completed
James publishes *The Aspern Papers*
Joyce enters Clongowes Wood College (September)

**1889**
Gerhart Hauptmann publishes *Vor Sonnenaufgang*
Gerard Manley Hopkins dies

**1890**
Ibsen publishes *Hedda Gabler*
First movies shown in New York City
Cardinal Newman dies
Volume 1 of James Frazer's *The Golden Bough* appears
William James publishes *The Principles of Psychology*

**1891**
Oscar Wilde publishes *The Picture of Dorian Gray*
Herman Melville dies
Arthur Bliss (composer) born
Joyce writes "Et Tu, Healy," poem on Parnell's betrayal (nonextant). For financial reasons, Joyce withdrawn from Clongowes Wood College

**1892**
Ibsen publishes *The Master Builder*

**1893**
Second Irish Home Rule Bill passed by the House of Commons but rejected by House of Lords
Cole Porter born
Henry Ford builds his first car
New Zealand adopts women's suffrage, first country to do so
D'Annunzio publishes *The Triumph of Death*
Joyce enters Belvedere College

**1895**
Wilde's *The Importance of Being Earnest* produced
Yeats publishes *Poems*
Marconi invents wireless radio
Röntgen discovers X-rays

**1897**
Havelock Ellis publishes *Studies in the Psychology of Sex*

**1898**
Spanish-American War
Bismarck dies
Gladstone dies
Lewis Carroll dies
Stéphane Mallarmé dies
Ernest Hemingway born
James publishes *Turn of the Screw*
Joyce graduates from Belvedere College, enrolls in University College, Dublin

**1899**
Boer War begins
Irish Literary Theatre founded
Ibsen publishes *When We Dead Awaken*

**1900**
Joseph Conrad publishes *Lord Jim*
Theodore Dreiser publishes *Sister Carrie*
Oscar Wilde dies
Thomas Wolfe is born
Nietzsche dies
Henri Bergson publishes *Le Rire*
Sigmund Freud publishes *Die Traumdeutung (The Interpretation of Dreams)*
John Ruskin dies
The first Gordon Bennett Cup motorcar race is held in France
*Daily Express* is founded by Cyril Arthur Pearson
D'Annunzio publishes *Il fuoco (The Flame of Life)*
Hauptmann publishes *Michael Kramer*
Joyce's first publication: "Ibsen's New Drama" in *Fortnightly Review* (April 1); Joyce writes *A Brilliant Career* (nonextant play)

**1901**
Queen Victoria dies
President McKinley assassinated
Giuseppe Verdi dies
First Nobel Prizes awarded
Joyce publishes "The Day of the Rabblement," essay attacking Irish Literary Theatre

**1902**
James publishes *The Wings of the Dove*
William James publishes *Varieties of Religious Experience*
*Times Literary Supplement* begins publication
Joyce graduates from University College, Dublin, with degree in modern languages; leaves for Paris, ostensibly to study medicine
Yeats produces *Cathleen ni Houlihan*
Enrico Caruso makes his first phonograph recordings
Emile Zola dies

**1903**
Wright brothers' first flight
James publishes *The Ambassadors*
Joyce's mother dies

**1904**
John Millington Synge publishes *Riders to the Sea*
Cy Young pitches first major league perfect game
Abbey Theatre founded
Freud publishes *Psychopathology of Everyday Life*
James publishes *The Golden Bowl*
Joyce meets Nora Barnacle (10 June); goes walking with her (16 June); they elope to Pola (October)

**1905**
Norway separates from Sweden
Sinn Féin founded
Albert Einstein publishes *Zur Elektrodynamik bewegter Körper (The Electrodynamics of Moving Bodies)*
Bloomsbury Group is founded
Joyce and Nora settle in Trieste; son, George, is born (July 27)

**1906**
Samuel Beckett born
Ibsen dies
Albert Schweitzer publishes *The Quest for the Historical Jesus*
Joyce, Nora, and George move to Rome

**1907**
Pablo Picasso paints *Les Demoiselles d'Avignon;* first exhibition of cubist paintings in Paris
Synge's *The Playboy of the Western World* performed at the Abbey Theatre; riot breaks out
Joyce, Nora, and George return to Trieste (March); *Chamber Music* published; daughter, Lucia, born (July 26)

**1908**
"Mutt and Jeff" begins to appear in the *San Francisco Examiner*

**1909**
U.S. Copyright Law passed
E. F. T. Marinetti publishes futurist manifesto, *Manifest du Futurisme*
Britain passes Cinematograph Licensing Act
Gertrude Stein publishes *Three Lives*
Joyce visits Ireland twice; second time, opens Volta cinema in Dublin

**1910**
King Edward VII dies, succeeded by George V
Mark Twain dies
Lev (Leo) Tolstoy dies
Volta cinema fails

**1911**
Pound publishes *Canzoni*
Ronald Reagan born

**1912**
*Titanic* sinks after hitting iceberg in North Atlantic
Pound publishes *Ripostes*
Hauptmann receives Nobel Prize in literature
C. G. Jung publishes *The Theory of Psychoanalysis*
*Poetry: A Magazine of Verse* founded in Chicago
George Bernard Shaw's *Pygmalion* produced
Enoch Powell born
Joyce visits Ireland with his family (Galway and Dublin), his last trip to his homeland; he writes "Gas from a Burner" after the *Dubliners* sheets are destroyed by the printer, John Falconer

**1913**
Balkan War
Richard Nixon born
D. H. Lawrence publishes *Sons and Lovers*
Edmund Husserl publishes *Phenomenology*
First Charlie Chaplin movies appear

**1914**
Pound and Wyndham Lewis found *Blast*
Panama Canal opens
World War I begins
*New Republic* begins publication
Robert Frost publishes *North of Boston*
*A Portrait of the Artist as a Young Man* serialized (through 1915) in the *Egoist; Dubliners* published; Joyce begins *Ulysses* and *Exiles*

**1915**
Franz Kafka publishes *Der Verwandlung (The Metamorphosis)*
Italy declares war on Austria-Hungary and Turkey
Germany sinks *Lusitania*
Joyce moves to Switzerland with his family; *Exiles* is completed

**1916**
Easter Rebellion in Ireland
Dada movement formed
Henry James dies
Einstein announces theory of relativity
Joyce publishes *A Portrait of the Artist as a Young Man*

**1917**

United States declares war on Germany
Russian Revolution (February and October)
Eliot publishes *Prufrock and Other Observations*
Guillaume Apollinaire coins term *surrealism*
C. G. Jung publishes *Psychology of the Unconscious*
Joyce undergoes first eye operation; publishes poems in *Poetry*

**1918**

World War I ends
Gerard Manley Hopkins's *Poems* published posthumously
Irish Home Rule measure abandoned by British government
*Ulysses* begins serialization in the *Little Review* (through 1920); *Exiles* published

**1919**

Irish War of Independence begins
Racehorse Man o' War suffers his only loss
Five installments of *Ulysses* serialized in the *Egoist;* first stage production of *Exiles,* in German at the Münchener Teater (September); Joyce, Nora, George, and Lucia return to Trieste (October)

**1920**

William Carlos Williams publishes *Kora in Hell*
Black-and-Tans reinforce British regulars against militant Irish nationalists; Government of Ireland Act passes in British Parliament, allowing Northern Ireland and southern Ireland to have separate Parliaments
New York Yankees acquire Babe Ruth
League of Nations formed in Paris; headquarters moved to Geneva
Britain's first public broadcasting company opens
Pound publishes *Hugh Selwyn Mauberly*
Joyce and family move to Paris (July); the *Little Review* ordered to cease publishing installments of *Ulysses*

**1921**

Anglo-Irish Treaty ends War of Independence
Luigi Pirandello's *Six Characters in Search of an Author* performed in Rome
Pound publishes *Poems 1918–1921*

**1922**

Ireland partitioned; Irish Free State proclaimed, given dominion status by Britain; Civil War begins
Eliot publishes *The Waste Land;* founds *The Criterion*
Wallace Stevens publishes *Harmonium*
P.E.N. Club founded
Benito Mussolini begins Fascist dictatorship in Italy
*Ulysses* published by Shakespeare and Company, Paris; United States Post Office destroys copies on arrival
Marcel Proust dies

**1923**

Yeats wins Nobel Prize in literature
Italo Svevo publishes *La coscienza di Zeno (Confessions of Zeno)*
Joyce begins *Finnegans Wake*

**1924**

Herbert Gorman publishes *James Joyce: His First Forty Years*
Lenin dies; Stalin begins his ascent
Ottoman Empire ends
André Breton publishes *Manifeste de surréalisme (Manifesto of Surrealism)*
First fragment of *Work in Progress* appears in *transatlantic review*

**1925**

Hitler publishes *Mein Kampf* (vol. 1) while in prison
Scopes "Monkey Trial" in Tennessee
Virginia Woolf publishes *Mrs. Dalloway*
Theodore Dreiser publishes *An American Tragedy*
F. Scott Fitzgerald publishes *The Great Gatsby*
Stein publishes *The Making of Americans*
*The Trial* by Franz Kafka is published posthumously
Pound publishes first *Cantos*
Fragments of *Work in Progress* continue to appear

**1926**

Stalin rises to power in the Soviet Union
John L. Baird successfully demonstrates television
Joyce's *Ulysses* pirated and published serially in *Two Worlds Monthly* (through 1927)

**1927**

Irish Civil War ends

Charles A. Lindbergh makes first solo transatlantic flight
Werner Heisenberg announces uncertainty principle
Joyce's *Work in Progress* begins to appear in regular installments in *transition,* 17 in all (through 1938); *Pomes Penyeach* published

### 1928
Lawrence publishes *Lady Chatterley's Lover*
12th volume of *Oxford English Dictionary* published
Joyce publishes *Work in Progress Volume I* (*FW* 3–216) in book form to protect copyrights

### 1929
Thomas Wolfe publishes *Look Homeward, Angel*
William Faulkner publishes *The Sound and the Fury*
Woolf publishes *A Room of One's Own*
Hemingway publishes *A Farewell to Arms*
*Ulysses* translated into French; *Our Exagmination Round His Factification for Incamination of Work in Progress* published by Shakespeare and Company; with Nicoló Vidacovich, Joyce translates Synge's *Riders to the Sea* into Italian

### 1930
Vannevar Bush builds first general-purpose analog computer
Stuart Gilbert publishes *James Joyce's Ulysses*
Joyce begins promotion of Irish tenor John Sullivan (until 1934)

### 1931
Max Planck publishes *Positivism and the Real Outside World*
James and Nora marry in London (July 4); Joyce's father dies (December)

### 1932
Eamon de Valera elected president of Ireland
Faulkner publishes *Light in August*
Franklin Delano Roosevelt elected president of the United States
Hitler becomes German citizen
Amelia Earhart first woman to make transatlantic solo flight
Joyce's grandson, Stephen James Joyce, born; Joyce writes "Ecce Puer"; Joyce's daughter, Lucia, has first mental breakdown

### 1933
Musical settings of *Pomes Penyeach* published under the title *The Joyce Book*
Hitler comes to power in Germany; first concentration camps built
Yeats publishes *Collected Poems*
Stein publishes *The Autobiography of Alice B. Toklas*
Judge John M. Woolsey of U.S. District Court at New York rules *Ulysses* not pornographic

### 1934
Williams publishes *Collected Poems*
Budgen publishes *James Joyce and the Making of Ulysses*
First American edition of *Ulysses* published by Random House

### 1936
Stevens publishes *Ideas of Order*
King Edward VIII abdicates
Margaret Mitchell publishes *Gone With the Wind*
J. M. Keynes publishes *The General Theory of Employment, Interest and Money*
First British edition of *Ulysses* published (The Bodley Head); *Collected Poems*

### 1937
Stevens publishes *The Man with the Blue Guitar*

### 1938
Kristallnacht

### 1939
Flann O'Brien (Brian O'Nolan) publishes *At Swim-Two-Birds*
World War II begins
Joyce publishes *Finnegans Wake*

### 1940
Herbert Gorman's biography *James Joyce* published
Joyce and Nora leave Saint-Gérand-le-Puy, where Lucia is hospitalized, for Zurich

### 1941
Joyce dies in Zurich (January 13); buried at Fluntern Cemetery (January 15)
Pearl Harbor attacked by Japanese (December 7); United States enters World War II

# Currency and Monetary Values

(For conversion to current U.S. values see http://eh.net/hmit)

**bob** This a slang term for a shilling; *bob* is used for both the singular and the plural: a bob, five bob.

**crown** A crown is worth 5s and abbreviated cr. (By definition, a crown could refer to any coin with an imprint of a crown stamped on it.)

**farthing** A farthing means a fourth of a unit. In British currency a farthing was a fourth of a penny. Two farthings equal a halfpenny (1/2d), four farthings a penny (1d). One farthing is written as 1/4d and the coin was last minted in 1956.

**florin** A florin is a gold coin worth 2 shillings. Its name is derived from the figure of a lily stamped on the original florin that was first issued in 1252 in Florence.

**groat** This coin has not circulated since the mid-17th century. It was worth four pence.

**guinea** Gold coin worth 21 shillings (1£ 1s). It ceased being minted in 1813, although the term continued to be used for the equivalent amount of money. The term was mainly reserved for expensive items. "The guinea," according to the OED, "is the ordinary unit for a professional fee and for a subscription to a society or institution; the prices obtained for works of art, racehorses, and sometimes landed property, are also stated in guineas."

**half crown** A coin worth 2 shillings sixpence (2s 6d); it ceased to be legal tender in 1970.

**halfpenny** A halfpenny (ha'penny) is equal to 2 farthings and written as 1/2d. Last minted in 1967, the coin was discontinued in 1984.

**half sovereign** A gold coin worth 10 shillings.

**£ s d** Symbols for pound, shilling, and penny.

**penny** The plural is pence. A penny consists of 4 farthings or 2 halfpence. The letter d (from the ancient Roman coin *denarius*) is used to designate the monetary value of a penny. Coins were minted as1d (1 penny), 3d (threepence), and 6d (sixpence).

**pound** Designated by the symbol £ from *libra,* the Latin word for pound (of silver), a pound is worth 20 shillings or 240 pence.

**quid** Slang for one pound sterling or a sovereign; quid is used for both the singular and the plural: one quid, three quid.

**shilling** A shilling is 12d. Its etymology is uncertain but may relate to the Latin *solidus.* The shilling is designated by the letter s or by the abbreviations sh., shil., or by /. The amount is normally immediately followed either by the s or a slash: 6/ or 6s (six shillings). The same amount may also be written as 6/-, indicating no pence. If the amount is followed by pence, it may be written as 6/4 or 6s 4d (read either as six shillings and four pence or six shillings four pence). (After decimalization in 1971, the coin stayed in circulation for a while but was no longer officially used.)

**sovereign** A gold coin worth 20 shillings (1 £).

# Index

Note: **Boldface** page numbers indicate main headings; *italic* page numbers indicate illustrations.

## C

## D

## J

## N